PHILOSOPHICAL
PROBLEMS
AND
ARGUMENTS:

AN
INTRODUCTION

PHILOSOPHICAL PROBLEMS AND ARGUMENTS:

AN INTRODUCTION

SECOND EDITION

James W. Cornman

University of Pennsylvania

Keith Lehrer

University of Arizona

Macmillan Publishing Co., Inc.

NEW YORK

Collier Macmillan Publishers

LONDON

Macmillan Publishing Co., Inc.
866 Third Avenue, New York, New York 10022

Collier-Macmillan Canada, Ltd.

Library of Congress Cataloging in Publication Data

Cornman, James W.
  Philosophical problems and arguments.

  Includes bibliographies.
  1. Philosophy—Introductions. I. Lehrer, Keith,
Joint author. II. Title.
BD21.C66 1974   100   73-5286
ISNB 0-02-325110-7

Printing: 4 5 6 7 8   Year: 5 6 7 8 9 0

TO BETTY AND ADRIENNE

PREFACE

To 2nd Edition

The authors, gratified by the enthusiastic response to our first edition, have undertaken a second. The changes were made to keep the book current and to correct some shortcomings. The first chapter is considerably expanded to amplify and clarify our conception of philosophy. There is a new section on induction and reasonable belief. The second chapter contains some new argumentation in defense of skepticism. The fourth chapter contains new material on materialism and the identity theory. In these chapters the conclusions that are reached differ from those in the original. The other chapters remain close to the original with some minor modification. The authors wish to thank Margery van Inwagen and Cheryl Noble for their assistance with the revision. We also wish to express our thanks to Miriam Gallaher for assisting us with the index, and to the Center for the Advanced Study of the Behavioral Sciences for providing her services.

J. W. C.
K. L.

PREFACE

To 1st Edition

Joseph Conrad said that his aim in writing was "before all, to make you *see*." Ours is, above all, to make you *think*. We want to make you think about the problems that philosophers have discussed. We also hope this introduction to philosophy will set you thinking about other problems. To achieve our aim, we have concentrated on five basic philosophical problems and tried to give a careful and thorough presentation and examination of the most plausible reasons for and against the solutions philosophers have proposed for these problems.

Each problem is discussed in a separate and virtually independent chapter. Each discussion, however, does rely on the material of the first chapter, where the nature of reasoning and argument is discussed and where certain basic philosophical terms are explained. Thus the first chapter is vital for a thorough grasp of the chapters that follow it, and it should be read before, or together with them. At the conclusion of each chapter we have presented a solution to the problem discussed. But because of the very nature of the problems, and because this is an introductory book, none of these solutions should be considered as final. They are, we claim, the most reasonable conclusions to reach on the basis of the material presented. But we have not, nor has anyone else, presented and examined all the material needed to solve these problems once and for all. To emphasize that you should think about these solutions rather than accept them, some of the exercises at the back of each chapter raise questions about points we have made. Others are designed to serve as review questions to test your grasp of the material. For those whose appetite is whetted for more reading on the various topics, we have provided an annotated bibliography after each chapter.

Committee efforts often produce compromise results. To avoid the pitfalls of such results, each of us has assumed complete responsibility for three chapters, Mr. Lehrer for the first three and Mr. Cornman for the last three. You will see differences in style, but we hope that you can also find an important common feature—the attempt to evaluate the subject matter dispassionately, fairly, and carefully.

Although we have divided responsibility, we are not divided in our thanks to many people who have read, criticized, and contributed to this book. Two we must especially thank are Lewis W. Beck and John D. Moore, both of whom carefully read and helpfully criticized the entire book. Others whose help in various ways deserves mention are Jean Hopson, Loretta Kopelman, Joel Levinson, Natalie Tarbet, and Peter van Inwagen.

J. W. C.
K. L.

CONTENTS

CHAPTER THREE
THE PROBLEM OF FREEDOM
AND DETERMINISM   151

CHAPTER FOUR
THE MIND–BODY PROBLEM   237

THE CONTENT AND METHODS OF PHILOSOPHY

CHAPTER ONE

WHAT IS PHILOSOPHY?

It is generally true of academic subjects, whether in the sciences or humanities, that the most satisfactory way to discover what the subject is about is to absorb oneself in the study of questions and problems characteristic of the field. General descriptions of a field are often either so abstract as to be uninformative or so idiosyncratic as to be misinformative. Nevertheless it is worthwhile to attempt some characterization of philosophy, if only a historical one, to give you a better understanding of the nature of philosophical inquiry. One principal reason for doing so is to explain the predominant role of disputation and argument in the study of philosophical problems.

To this end we shall, without pretending to offer a precise definition, present some information about philosophy as a discipline to provide a general orientation toward the field you are about to study.

First, a few words about the historical development of philosophy as a field. Not too long ago all scientific subjects were considered part of philosophy. *Philosophy of matter* encompassed what we now think of as physics and chemistry, *philosophy of mind* covered the subject of psychology and adjacent areas. In short, philosophy was once construed so broadly as to cover any field of theoretical inquiry. Any subject in which some general theory might be put forth to explain the content thereof would have been a branch of philosophy. However, once a field of study reached the point where some main theory dominated and with it developed standard methods of criticism and confirmation, then the field was cut off from the mother country of philosophy and became independent.

For example, philosophers once advanced a variety of theories to explain the nature of matter. One suggested that everything was made of water, another, somewhat closer to current conceptions, proposed that matter was composed of tiny, homogeneous, indivisible atoms. Once certain theories of matter, as well as experimental methods for testing such theories, became well established in the community of scholars, the philosophy of matter became the sciences of physics and chemistry. Another example of a philosophical problem that has been converted to a scientific one is the problem of the nature of life. At one time life was conjectured to be a spiritual entity that enters the body at birth and departs at death, and at another time a special vital force that activates the body. Currently the nature of life is explained in terms of biochemistry.

Thus it is a peculiarity of philosophy that once argument and disputation have brought us to some theory accompanied by a methodology adequate to cope successfully with some issue in philosophy, the theory and methodology become separated from philosophy and are considered part of another discipline. Certain subjects are currently in transition. One such example is the field of linguistics, and, more particularly, the subject of semantics within that field. Philosophers have articulated a variety of theories to explain how words can have meaning and what constitutes the meaning of words. The explanations were in terms of images, ideas, and other psychological phenomena. Currently philosophers and linguists explicate meaning in terms of the function of words in discourse and underlying semantic features which play a similar role in semantics to that played by the features of atomic particles in physics. In this field there is no sharp distinction between a philosopher and a linguist. Both apply newly developed methods of grammatical and semantic analysis to articulate laws and theories to explain the structure and content of language. It is characteristic of a field in transition that the question of whether an investigator is a philosopher or a scientist becomes moot. In philosophy the successful development of an area often leads to the independence and autonomy of the developed part. It is for this reason that any specification of philosophy in terms of subject matter is likely to be both controversial today and out of date tomorrow.

However, the preceding considerations explain one relatively constant feature of philosophy, to wit, the unsettled state of the art. The questions studied in philosophy are approached through dialectical methods of argument and counterargument. And a student can sometimes feel that after long and arduous inquiry, nothing has been settled. This impression is partly due to the fact that, at any given time, philosophy will be found to deal with those intellectual problems that have not yet been articulated in such a way that any single theory and methodology can be fastened upon to solve them. Where the human intellect is grappling with some complex intellectual problem and there is no standard and established experimental approach to the subject, one can expect to find the problem within the domain of philosophy. Once intellectual inquiry leads to the articulation of a standard theory together with an accepted method of experimental investigation, then, in all probability, the problem will no longer be considered part of philosophy. It will, instead, be attributed to some independent discipline. Thus philosophy loses some of its subject matter through its own success.

However, the preceding characterization should not lead you to think that *all* philosophical problems are potentially exportable through successful processing. Some questions and problems resist such exportation by virtue of their general and fundamental character. For example, in all fields of inquiry, men seek knowledge. But it is in philosophy that one asks what knowledge is and whether there is any such thing at all. Such questions belong in that branch of philosophy called *epistemology*. In some fields, economics and politics, for example, men study the causal consequences of various actions and policies. In philosophy one asks what general features make actions and policies right or wrong. Such questions belong to *ethics*. Again, critics, literary men, composers, and artists ask whether some object is a work of art. Philosophers are concerned with the more general question of what makes something a work of art. These are questions in *esthetics*. Other questions about the character of freedom, of mind, and of God appear to be the perennial subject matter of philosophy because they are both very basic and very general questions.

Moreover, successful treatment of a problem within one field can generate quite new problems. For example, explanation of physical phenomena in terms of laws and theories raises the question of whether the movement of human bodies, which are part of the physical universe, takes place in a purely mechanical way that makes a sham of our impression that we are free agents determining our own destiny by deliberation and decision. Similarly, the success of neurophysiology in explaining our behavior raises the question of whether thoughts and feelings are anything more than physical processes. We have no way of answering these questions by direct appeal to experiment or firmly established theory. Instead, we must rely on the methods of philosophical investigation—the careful examination of arguments offered in defense of divergent positions and the analysis of important terms contained therein.

There need be no fear of famine in philosophy. The subject matter of philosophy is only limited by the capacity of the human mind to ask new questions and to reformulate old ones in some novel way. By so doing additional content is provided to the one field that welcomes all those intellectual orphans rejected by other disciplines because of their unruly and difficult ways. Philosophy is the home of those intellectual problems with which others cannot cope. As a result, it is filled with the intellectual excitement of controversy and disputation taking place at the frontiers of rational inquiry.

FIVE PHILOSOPHICAL PROBLEMS

After an introduction to the methodology of argument, we shall turn to an examination of five philosophical problems. These problems have been the preoccupation of philosophers in the past, and are at the core of current philosophical controversy. Thus the ensuing chapters will provide paradigmatic examples of philosophical issues and arguments. Careful study of these chapters will reward you with a clear conception of current philosophical inquiry.

The first problem we will confront is the problem of knowledge and skepticism. Basically, we shall consider whether the claims to knowledge that most men commonly take for granted are really justified. For example, most men suppose that their senses provide a source of knowledge, that by looking, touching, and so forth they know of the existence of any number of familiar objects. But some philosophers have doubted that our senses can be the source of such information, and they have cogently defended the conclusion that we do not have knowledge of such matters. So the initial problem we shall face is that of investigating the merits of skepticism.

It is appropriate and useful to begin our study of philosophy by considering the problem of knowledge, because this subject is intertwined with all the others. We shall constantly be asking whether some belief is justified, no matter what issue we confront, and by considering the problem of knowledge and skepticism, we shall obtain a better understanding of how a belief may be justified or shown to be unjustified.

Secondly, we shall consider the problem of freedom and determinism. We ordinarily suppose that we do, at least now and then, act freely. This amounts to believing that we have genuine alternatives among which to choose and that whatever we actually choose to do, we could just as well have chosen and acted quite differently. However, we also suppose that there are causes for all that happens, including our own choices and actions. The difficulty is that this belief in universal causation appears quite inconsistent with the belief that we act freely, because the former belief has the consequence that all our actions are the inevitable results of causal processes. The problem is to determine whether we are justified in one rather than the other of these beliefs.

The third problem is closely connected to the second. It is the problem of the mental and physical. People differ from inanimate things in having thoughts, sensations and emotions, which are characteristic mental phenomena. It is reasonable to wonder in precisely what way these mental states are related to certain physical processes which occur within our bodies, for example, the neural processes that take place in the brain. Some maintain that there is some causal connection between our thoughts and what happens inside our heads. But philosophers have presented arguments to the contrary, and consequently they have defended an alternative theory about the relation of the mental and the physical. For example, some philosophers have held the thesis that thoughts simply *are* brain states, and therefore that the mental is identical with some aspect or part of the physical rather than being *causally* connected to it. The problem is to decide which of these conflicting theories is justified.

Next we shall discuss the problem of justifying belief in the existence of God. This problem requires little description. Most people, whether theists, atheists, or agnostics, must at some time wonder whether there is any way of rationally justifying belief in the existence of a supreme being. We shall study in detail the relevant arguments that have been offered by philosophers and theologians.

Finally, we shall turn to the field of ethics, and here we shall be concerned with the question of how a man can justify his ethical judgments concerning what is right and wrong. We shall attempt to find some moral rule or standard in terms of which we can reasonably judge the ethical merits of various courses of action. The search will proceed by a consideration of the arguments that have been offered both for and against various and conflicting ethical standards philosophers have proposed.

THE METHODS OF PHILOSOPHY

Before discussing the problems just outlined, it is essential to consider the methods and techniques of philosophy. Sometimes philosophy is said to be a dialectical discipline. This means that philosophy proceeds through a process of arguments and counterarguments. Of course, all disciplines depend on argument to some extent, but in philosophy logical reasoning plays an especially prominent role. The explanation for this is that philosophy strives to answer such fundamental questions that it is difficult to find any specific empirical facts to resolve the issues. When two people disagree about some philosophical matter, the only avenue of progress open to them is to consider and evaluate the arguments and objections on both sides. Therefore philosophical inquiry must be critical and logical if any gain is to result. To facilitate such inquiry, we must learn to ask critical questions about the arguments we encounter, and to examine the answers with logical acumen. These are questions of logic and semantics. We shall present a brief introduction to logic and semantics in order to approach the challenging problems of philosophy with those logical skills that are the requisite of intelligent and rigorous inquiry.

LOGIC

The field whose subject is *argument* is known as logic, or formal logic. The first question to answer in this field is: What is an argument? For our purposes, an argument is a group of statements in which one, the conclusion, is claimed to follow from the others. For example, consider the following argument: Everything is caused and, that being so, no one acts freely. This argument, the merits of which we shall consider in a later chapter, might be stated more formally as follows:

1. If everything is caused, then no one acts freely.
2. Everything is caused.
   Therefore
3. No one acts freely.

The word 'Therefore' above statement (3) indicates that what falls beneath it is the conclusion that is claimed to follow from the statements above. Statements (1) and (2) are the reasons given for concluding (3), and such statements are called premises. Thus every argument consists of a conclusion and one or more premises from which the conclusion is claimed to follow.

SOUNDNESS AND VALIDITY

There are, in general, two kinds of arguments, inductive and deductive. We shall consider inductive arguments subsequently, but first let us concentrate on deductive arguments, an example of which was just presented. A deductive argument is said to be *sound* when the premises of the argument are true and the argument is valid. Saying that an argument is valid is equivalent to saying that it is logically impossible that the premises of the argument are true and the conclusion false. A less precise but intuitively clear way of putting this is to say that in a valid argument *if* the premises are true, then the conclusion must be true. By this definition it is easy to see that the preceding argument is valid, and, if the premises are true, then it must be sound as well. For *if* the premises

1. If everything is caused, then no one acts freely.

and

2. Everything is caused.

are both true, then it must also be true that

3. No one acts freely.

As a simple matter of logic it is impossible that premises (1) and (2) should both be true and conclusion (3) be false. It is important to notice that the fact that this argument is valid does not prove the conclusion is true. Validity is a hypothetical or conditional characteristic; it assures us that the conclusion of the argument is true *if* the premises are.

The argument may also be said to be valid in virtue of its *form*. We can represent the form of the preceding argument by the following schema:

If *P,* then *Q*
P
Therefore
Q

The argument form is called *Modus ponens*. Every argument of this form is valid, and thus we may say that the argument form itself is valid. Consider the following argument:

If God is dead, then everything is permitted.
God is dead.
Therefore
Everything is permitted.

This argument, like the preceding one, is valid because it has the form of *Modus ponens*. We can obtain these arguments from *Modus ponens* by substituting the appropriate English sentences for the letters *P* and *Q* in the argument form. If we substitute the sentence 'God is dead' for the letter *P* and the sentence 'Everything is permitted' for the letter *Q* in the argument form, we will obtain the valid argument just cited. Whenever an argument form is valid, then we obtain a valid argument if we substitute in this way.

The following are other valid argument forms:

Modus Tollens	*Disjunctive Syllogism*
If *P*, then *Q*	Either *P* or *Q*
Not *Q*	Not *P*
Therefore	*Therefore*
Not *P*	*Q*
Hypothetical Syllogism	*Contraposition*
If *P*, then *Q*	If *P*, then *Q*
If *Q*, then *R*	*Therefore*
Therefore	If not *Q*, then not *P*
If *P*, then *R*	

This list of argument forms is not complete or definitive. However, by considering various arguments of these forms we can obtain an intuitive idea of what a valid argument is like. Many arguments can be shown to be valid by making the proper substitutions in the preceding argument forms. In some cases we will have to appeal to more than one argument form to show that an argument is valid. For example, consider the following argument:

If God does not exist, then everything is permitted.
If murder is not permitted, then not everything is permitted.
Murder is not permitted.
Therefore
It is not the case that God does not exist.

To show that this argument is valid, first notice that from

If murder is not permitted, then not everything is permitted.

and

Murder is not permitted.

we may conclude by *Modus ponens* that

Not everything is permitted.

We may now take this statement, which is a conclusion of this fore-going argument, and use it as a premise in another argument. From the premise

If God does not exist, then everything is permitted.

and the new premise

Not everything is permitted.

we may conclude by *Modus tollens* that

It is not the case that God does not exist.

This shows that from the original premises we could validly deduce the conclusion of that argument by appealing to the argument forms previously listed. A lesson to be learned from the argument just considered is that anything validly deduced from a set of premises, such as the statement

Not everything is permitted.

may be added to the original premises for the purpose of making further deductions.

EXERCISES

All the following arguments can be shown to be valid by appealing to the argument forms previously listed. Decide what argument form each of the following arguments has.

1. If the brain is needed for thought, then thought always occurs in the head.
If thought always occurs in the head, then no spirit without a body ever thinks.
Therefore
If the brain is needed for thought, then no spirit without a body ever thinks.

2. If reasons are the causes of actions, then all rational actions are caused.
Therefore
If not all rational actions are caused, then it is not the case that reasons are the causes of actions.

3. Either wars are avoided or the innocent suffer.
Wars are not avoided.
Therefore
The innocent suffer.

4. If all men could be mistaken in what they believe, then all men lack knowledge.
All men could be mistaken in what they believe.
Therefore
All men lack knowledge.

Show that each of the following arguments is valid by appealing to valid argument forms.

1. Either wars are avoided or the innocent suffer.
If wars are avoided, then all men love peace.
Not all men love peace.
Therefore
The innocent suffer.

2. If no actions are free, then no one is responsible for his actions.
If no one is responsible for his actions, then no one deserves to be punished.
No actions are free.
Therefore
No one deserves to be punished.

3. If the innocent suffer, then the world is not perfect.
If God exists, then the world is perfect.
Therefore
If the innocent suffer, then God does not exist.

OTHER VALID ARGUMENT FORMS

We obtain some valid arguments from argument forms by substituting into the forms expressions that are not sentences. To see why this is so, consider the following argument.

All right actions are actions that produce good consequences.
All right actions that produce good consequences are actions that maximize happiness and minimize pain.
Therefore
All right actions are actions that maximize happiness and minimize pain.

Brief reflection will convince you that if the premises of this argument are true, then the conclusion must also be true. This argument is not of the form of *Modus ponens,* or the other forms considered earlier. The argument is valid in virtue of being an argument of the following form:

All X are Y.
All Y are Z.
Therefore
All X are Z.

All arguments of this form are valid. We get an argument of this form by substituting expressions describing classes of things for the letters X, Y, and Z. If we substitute the expression 'right actions' for X, 'actions that produce good consequences' for Y, and 'actions that maximize happiness and minimize pain' for Z, then we will obtain the argument just considered. Other valid argument forms of this kind are

No X are Y.	All X are Y.	All X are Y.
All Z are X.	Some X are Z.	Some X are not Z.
Therefore	*Therefore*	*Therefore*
No Z are Y.	Some Y are Z.	Some Y are not Z.

Such arguments are known as categorical syllogisms.

VALIDITY AND TRUTH

Arguments of a valid form are valid even if they are completely absurd. For example, the following argument is valid:

All women are cats.
All cats are men.
Therefore
All women are men.

This argument has false premises (at least taken literally!) and a false conclusion. This brings out the hypothetical character of validity. What the validity of these arguments amounts to is that it assures us the conclusion must be true *if* the premises are true.

If an argument can be valid and yet have a preposterously false conclusion, what good is validity? Why should we be concerned with validity at all? The answer is that a valid argument is truth preserving. Truth in the premises of a valid argument is preserved in the conclusion. Of course, if the premises are not true to begin with, then even a valid argument cannot ensure that the conclusion is true. But *only* valid arguments are truth preserving. An analogy might help to clarify this point. Roughly, valid arguments preserve truth like good freezers preserve food. If the food you place in a freezer is spoiled to begin with, then even a good freezer cannot preserve it. But if the food placed in a good freezer is fresh, then the freezer will preserve it. Good freezers and valid arguments preserve food and truth, respectively. But just as the former cannot preserve food when the food is spoiled, so the latter cannot preserve truth when the premises are false. Nevertheless food freezers and valid arguments are worth having because they do preserve something good when one has it, and without them one may wind up with something rotten even when beginning with something impeccable. Thus validity is to be desired and invalidity is to be eschewed.

THE METHOD OF COUNTEREXAMPLE

We have considered several valid argument forms. However, these forms are only a few among many. For our purposes it is not necessary, even if it would be useful, to know all these valid argument forms. Instead we shall rely on a more intuitive test for validity. First we need a test for invalidity, that is, a method for showing that the conclusion of an argument does not follow validly from the premises. The technique we shall adopt is known as the method of counterexample.

The claim that an argument is valid may be refuted by finding an example of a situation in which the premises would be true and the conclusion false. Moreover, and this is crucial, the example need only be of something possible. It need not be an example of anything that has ever happened or of anything at all likely to happen. Just so long as the example clearly describes something possible, and clearly describes a state of affairs in which the conclusion is false and the premises true, the claim to validity is refuted.

To see how the method works, consider the following argument:

All communists are opposed to capitalism.
Jones is opposed to capitalism.
Therefore
Jones is a communist.

It is perfectly easy to describe a counterexample that shows the conclusion of this argument does not follow from the premises. Suppose that Jones is a man who believes that all wealth and property should be owned and controlled by his family and passed on by inheritance. Thus he rejects both capitalism and communism in favor of Jonesism, a heretofore unknown economic doctrine which states that everything should belong to the Joneses. What is described in this example is possible and, supposing that both the first and second premises are true, it is an example in which the premises are true and the conclusion false. This counterexample shows that even if the premises of the argument are true, it does not follow that the conclusion is true. The argument is invalid. Hence it will be pointless to defend the conclusion of the argument by maintaining that the premises are true. Some altogether different argument would be required to establish that conclusion.

We have shown an argument to be invalid by finding a counterexample. Sometimes it is easier to find such an example if you first consider the form of the argument. The preceding argument was of the following form:

All *C* are *O*.
J is *O*.
Therefore
J is *C*.

An argument of this form is invalid because the premises leave open the possibility that something that is *O* might not be *C*, and if this possibility is left open, then, obviously, it is possible for the premises to be true and the conclusion false.

Now if there are no counterexamples to an argument, that is, if there is no possible situation in which the conclusion would be false and the premises true, then the argument is valid. Of course, we have no way of proving that this is so without first studying the science of logic in some detail. However, let us adopt the following procedure. First, regard an argument as innocent until proved guilty. We may accept an argument as valid until we think of some counterexample to prove that it is invalid. Of course, this procedure must not be applied thoughtlessly or uncritically. We must ask ourselves if it is at all possible that this argument, or an argument of this form, is refutable by counterexample. If after careful reflection we conclude that there are no such examples to be found, we may tentatively accept the argument as valid. This is the procedure we will adopt.

EXERCISES

Find counterexamples to the following arguments. Remember that a valid argument may have false premises, so an example showing a premise to be false does *not* constitute a counterexample showing the argument to be invalid.

1. If Smith is the thief, then Jones was involved in the crime.
   Smith is not the thief.
   Therefore
   Jones was not involved in the crime.

2. All women hope to marry rich men.
   Jane is a woman who married the man she hoped to marry.
   Therefore
   Jane married a rich man.

3. Social change always produces violence.
   Violence is bad.
   Therefore
   Social change is bad.

4. If a man knows something, then he must have an idea of it.
   Therefore

All a man ever knows are his own ideas.

5. Scientists are constantly discovering that all sensations are caused by neurological processes.
Therefore
Sensations are nothing but physical processes.

6. I know for certain that I exist.
I do not know for certain that any physical thing exists.
Therefore
I am not a physical thing.

7. No argument has been found to prove that God exists.
Therefore
God does not exist.

QUESTION-BEGGING ARGUMENTS

There are other features of an argument, some of which have already been noted, which might lead us to reject an argument even though we consider it valid. For example, the premises of the argument might be known to be false. Another important reason for rejecting an argument is that we can see that the argument *begs the question*. An argument begs the question when a premise of the argument is simply a restatement of the conclusion.

Suppose a philosopher is arguing that no involuntary act should be punished. The following argument blatantly begs the question:

All acts that should be punished are voluntary.
Therefore
No involuntary act should be punished.

This argument is one in which the conclusion and the premise are different ways of saying the same thing. Thus, if the conclusion of the argument is what is at issue, then the argument begs the issue.

Sometimes the premise which restates the conclusion in a question-begging argument is better disguised. Consider the following argument:

1. An act without the volition of the agent should not be punished.

2. An involuntary act is an act without the volition of the agent.
Therefore
3. An involuntary act should not be punished.

This argument is discovered to be question-begging when we ask what it means to say an act is "without the volition of the agent," because once we reflect on that curious expression, it becomes obvious that it means no more or less than "involuntary." Thus, premise (1) of the argument, when we understand what it means, is revealed to assert precisely the same thing as the conclusion.

An example of an argument that is *not* question-begging and that has the same conclusion is the following:

1. No involuntary act is wrong.
2. An act should not be punished unless it is wrong.
Therefore
3. No involuntary act should be punished.

None of these premises is a disguised reformulation of the conclusion. To say that an act is voluntary is quite different from saying that it is wrong, because many voluntary acts are perfectly all right. The premises of this valid argument might be challenged. But that is the only way that a disputant could escape the conclusion.

FURTHER REMARKS ON TRUTH AND VALIDITY

We have already noted that a valid argument may have false premises and thereby fail to establish the truth of its conclusion. However, it is equally essential to notice that such an unsound argument, though it fails to establish the truth of its conclusion, may have a true conclusion nonetheless. Consequently, by showing that an argument is unsound because it has some false premise, one will not thereby have proved that the conclusion of the argument is false.

To illustrate these points let us consider two arguments, one a theistic argument and the other an atheistic argument, which, though valid, have contrary conclusions. The argument of the theist is the following:

1. The world exhibits conclusive evidence of design.
2. If the world exhibits conclusive evidence of design, then the world has a designer, who is God.
   Therefore
3. The world has a designer, who is God.

The second argument is one an atheist might put to use.

1*a*. If God exists, there is an all-powerful, all-knowing, and perfectly good being who created the world.
2*a*. If there is an all-powerful, all-knowing, and perfectly good being who created the world, then the world is free of evil.
3*a*. The world is not free of evil.
   Therefore
4*a*. God does not exist.

These two arguments have diametrically opposed conclusions. The conclusion of the first is inconsistent with the conclusion of the second; thus one of the arguments must have a false conclusion. Both arguments are perfectly valid. The conclusion of each must be true *if* the premises are true. Thus, one of the arguments, though valid, must be unsound. At least one of the premises of one of the arguments must be false.

Atheists who have attacked the first argument have contended that both premises of the first argument are false. They have denied that there is conclusive evidence of design and have also argued that even if there were such evidence it would fail to guarantee that God is creator or designer of the world. Theists have very rarely denied all the premises of the second argument but have instead attacked either the second or third premise. Some have asserted that an all-powerful, all-knowing, and perfectly good being might well create a world with evil—for example, the evil for which men and other free agents are responsible. Others have argued that, appearances to the contrary notwithstanding, there is no evil. What appears evil to men appears that way because of our limited ability to discern the true nature of the things we perceive.

We shall later consider the merits of such arguments. However, here it is important to notice that the critics of *both* arguments might be correct. Both arguments might contain some false premises, and in that case these valid arguments would both be unsound. This illustrates the fact that the unsound character of an argument does not show the conclusion of the argument to be false. Indeed it is possible that one of the arguments might have a true conclusion even though *both* the arguments are unsound. Therefore by attacking an argument, we can only establish that the argument is unsound. We cannot thereby show that the conclusion is false. On the other hand, by presenting an argument that is sound and not question-begging, we can establish that the conclusion of the argument is true. Hence constructing sound arguments, if more difficult than laying bare the fallacies of the arguments of others, is the task which yields the richer result.

POSSIBILITY, ANALYTICITY, AND CONSISTENCY

In defining the notion of validity, we often use the word 'impossible.' This term has many uses, but it is a single use of this term that has concerned us thus far. We have indicated this usage by speaking of *logical* impossibility. The intuitive idea of logical impossibility is as follows: there are some things that can be shown to be impossible by appealing to nothing more than logic and the meaning of terms. These things are logically impossible. That God both exists and does not exist is logically impossible, for it is a mere truth of logic that nothing both exists and does not exist. A statement describes something logically impossible just in case the statement is contradictory or inconsistent. Indeed, to say that a statement describes something logically impossible is equivalent to saying that the statement is contradictory or inconsistent. The following are examples of contradictory statements:

1. Jones will pass philosophy 100 and Jones will not pass philosophy 100.
2. All civil rights workers are liberals but some civil rights workers are not liberals.
3. A brother is a female.

Taken literally, none of these statements could possibly be true. But slightly different considerations are needed to show this in each case. The first statement is a perfectly explicit contradiction. The second conjunct of this conjunction denies with the word 'not' what the first conjunct asserts. The second statement, though obviously contradictory, differs from the first statement. In the second statement what is asserted in the first conjunct is not denied in the second conjunct simply by the use of the word 'not.' To show that the second statement is contradictory we need to consider the meaning of the words 'some' and 'all' as well as the word 'not.' These three words occur in the lexicon of the logician and are considered "logical words" because they appear in the valid argument forms of formal logic.

The third statement, though again contradictory, raises a somewhat different issue. To show that it is contradictory, one must, in addition to appealing to formal logic, also consider the meaning or definition of the term 'brother,' that is, one must know that a person to whom that term applies is by definition male and not female. Once this is clear it can be shown that the statement asserts that some person is and is not female. As a sheer matter of logic, this is impossible. However, the term 'brother' is not a term of formal logic; it is a descriptive term. Some philosophers deny that anything of philosophical importance turns on the distinction between terms of logic and descriptive terms because they maintain that, in the last analysis, the distinction turns out to be arbitrary and artificial. For our purposes it will suffice to notice that in order to show that certain statements are contradictory, such as the preceding statements (2) and (3), it is essential to consider the meaning or definition of key terms within the statement.

NECESSITY AND ANALYTICITY

Statements that describe something logically impossible are contradictory and hence may be shown to be false by appealing to nothing more than logic and the meaning of terms. There are also statements that may be shown to be *true* by appealing to nothing more than logic and the meaning of terms. Such statements describe something logically necessary and are often called analytic statements. The denial of any logically impossible statement is a logically necessary statement, and vice versa. For example, the statement

1a. It is not the case both that Jones will pass philosophy 100 and that Jones will not pass philosophy 100.

is the denial of statement (1) and it is logically necessary. Similarly, statements

2a. It is not the case that all civil rights workers are liberals and that some civil rights workers are not liberals.

and

3a. It is not the case that a brother is a female.

which are the denials of (2) and (3), respectively, are both logically necessary or analytic. The necessity of these statements can be made even more readily evident by reformulating them. For example, (1a) and (2a) are equivalent to

1b. Either Jones will pass philosophy 100 or Jones will not pass philosophy 100.

and

2b. Either all civil rights workers are liberals or some civil rights workers are not liberals.

respectively. It is fairly obvious that all these statements are logically necessary: the necessity of (2b) and (3a) could be made even more explicit by considering the definitions of the terms 'all,' 'some,' 'brother,' and 'female.' In order to understand precisely how this would be accomplished, we shall now consider the subject of definitions.

DEFINITION

There are many ways to explain the meaning of a word. Sometimes one can do it by example, or by telling a story, or in any number of other ways. But one very important way to express the meaning of a word is to give a definition of it. When a word is defined, certain other words are supplied which together have the same meaning as the word to be defined. For example, we might define the word 'brother' by using the words 'male sibling,' that is, the word 'brother' is equal by definition to the words 'male sibling.'

REPORTIVE DEFINITIONS

Such a definition is a report of an ordinary meaning of a word. We shall accordingly call such definitions *reportive*. If a reportive definition is accurate, then one may substitute the defining words for the word defined in most sentences without changing the meaning of the sentence. For example, consider the sentence

1. John's brother will inherit the money.

Because the word 'brother' may be defined as 'male sibling,' we may substitute the latter for the former in the foregoing sentence and obtain

1a. John's male sibling will inherit the money.

which is equivalent in meaning to (1). It is easy enough to see why such substitution should not alter the meaning of a sentence. If the only change we make in a sentence is to replace one word in the sentence with another having the same meaning, then we should not have altered the meaning of the sentence.

However, the foregoing remarks concerning substitution require one important restriction. Sometimes a word occurs in a sentence within quotation marks so that something is asserted about the word itself. For example, in the sentence

2. The word 'brother' has seven letters.

the word 'brother' occurs in quotation marks in order to assert something about the word 'brother' rather than about a brother. In cases where a word occurs in quotation marks, we may change the meaning of the sentence by substituting some other words for the word that occurs in quotation marks even if the words substituted are equal by definition to the original word. For example, if we substitute 'male sibling' for 'brother' in the preceding sentence (2), we get,

2a. The word 'male sibling' has seven letters.

which differs in meaning from the original.

Moreover, substitution of the sort just described must not be thought of as a method for testing definitions. The reason for this is that there will be sentences which contain both the defined term and the term to be defined, and such sentences will lead us in a circle if we attempt to employ substitution as a method for testing definitions. For example, suppose we are wondering whether 'triangle' is correctly defined as 'three-sided plane figure.' If substitution is to be used as a test, then we must decide whether the meaning of the sentence

3. Something is a triangle if and only if it is a three-sided plane figure.

will be changed if we substitute the words 'three-sided plane figure' for the word 'triangle' in that sentence. By so doing we obtain the sentence

3a. Something is a three-sided plane figure if and only if it is a three-sided plane figure.

However, it is apparent that (3a) has the same meaning as (3) only if the word 'triangle' is equal by definition to the words 'three-sided plane figure.' For the latter is logically necessary or analytic and therefore the former must also be analytic if the two sentences have the same meaning. So to determine whether the two sentences have the same meaning, we must first decide whether the definition is accurate. Because it is always possible to construct such a troublesome sentence, the method of substitution will always lead us in a circle if we attempt to use it as a test for definitions.

However, the problem we have just considered provides us with a clue to the proper test for reportive definitions. We have noted that the term 'triangle' is equal by definition to 'three-sided plane figure' just in case the sentence

Something is a triangle if and only if it is a three-sided plane figure.

is analytic or logically necessary. The latter sentence is analytic or logically necessary just in case it is logically necessary that the terms 'triangle' and 'three-sided plane figure' apply to exactly the same things, or, to put the same thing in other words, just in case it is logically impossible that one of the terms should apply to something to which the other term does not apply. We adopted a procedure for deciding whether certain things are logically impossible when discussing validity, namely, the method of counterexample. We can employ the same method for testing definitions.

We said earlier that we will tentatively consider it logically impossible that one statement is true and a second statement false if, after careful reflection, we can think of no possible example in which the first statement is true and the second false. Similarly, here we shall tentatively consider a definition satisfactory if, after careful reflection, we can think of no possible examples in which either the defined word truly applies to something but the defining words do not, or the defining words truly apply to something but the defined word does not. When we can think of such an example, then we have found a counterexample to the alleged definition showing that we do not have an accurate reportive definition. If we can find no counterexample to a definition, then we may regard it as innocent until a counterexample is found to prove otherwise.

An example or two should help to clarify this. To revert to one already considered, we shall not be able to find any possible example of a person who is a brother but not a male sibling, or vice versa. Consequently, we may define 'brother' as 'male sibling.' On the other hand, suppose someone foolishly alleges that we may define 'brother' simply as 'sibling.' It is quite easy to think of examples of people to whom it is true that the term 'sibling' applies but false that the term 'brother' applies, namely, all female siblings. Thus we have many counterexamples to this definition. When a definition is defective in that the defined term does not apply to something to which the defining terms do apply, as in the case just considered, then the definition is said to be too broad. On the other hand, if someone alleges that we may define 'brother' as 'married male sibling,' so that the defining terms would not apply to things to which the defined term does apply—namely, unmarried brothers—then the alleged definition is said to be too narrow.

A definition may have the unhappy defect of being both too broad and too narrow. For example, if someone suggests we define 'brother' as 'tenth oldest sibling,' then his definition would be at once too narrow and too broad. Obviously the definition is too narrow, because there are brothers who are not tenth oldest siblings. However, it is equally certain that the definition is too broad. For whatever the facts of life, it is at least possible there should be a tenth oldest sibling who is female and hence not a brother. Again it is essential to remember that to have a counterexample we need only find a logically possible example. The example need not be of anything actual or at all likely. Thus, to define 'brother' as 'tenth oldest sibling' is to present a definition that is both too broad and too narrow. An accurate reportive definition is one such that there is no possible example to show that it is either too broad or too narrow.

EXERCISES

Find counterexamples to the following reportive definitions.

1. 'Religion' equals by definition 'a system of basic values.'

2. 'Communism' equals by definition 'a system in which the government controls the economy.'

3. 'Science' equals by definition 'the search for truth.'

4. 'Good newspaper' equals by definition 'a newspaper that prints all the news that's fit to print.'

5. 'Good music' equals by definition 'music of which the critics approve.'

6. 'Desirable' equals by definition 'something that is desired.'

7. 'Father' equals by definition 'a parent who is never pregnant.'

8. 'Water' equals by definition 'H_2O.'

STIPULATIVE DEFINITIONS

So far we have attended to reportive definitions, definitions that are intended to be accurate reports of actual usage. But this is only one kind of definition that is of importance. There is a second kind of definition, not to be confused with the first, which plays a major role in philosophical writing. This kind of definition is not intended to be an accurate report of actual usage but is instead a stipulation of special or technical usage. Sometimes it is convenient and fruitful to use some word in a technical way for the purposes of precision or clarification. In such cases one may simply stipulate the special meaning assigned to the word. We shall call definitions of this kind *stipulative.*

Almost every book on a technical subject employs stipulative definitions. A book on chemistry defines 'mixture' and 'solution' in technical ways because it is useful to do so in chemistry. We have defined 'validity' in a technical way because it is useful to do so for our purposes. So long as stipulative definitions are not confused with reportive definitions, they are perfectly legitimate and useful conventions.

It is important to recognize that a stipulative definition cannot be rejected by producing a counterexample. When a man stipulates that he is going to define a term in a certain way, for example, if he stipulates that he is going to define 'straight line' as 'the path of light,' then that is what he means by the term and there is no arguing about it. It will not be true that the defined term in his usage applies to anything to which the defining term does not apply, because by stipulation they apply to exactly the same things. There are no counterexamples to stipulative definitions. Moreover, the one term may be substituted for the other in any sentence, and provided it does not occur in quotation marks, the original sentence and the sentence that results from the substitution will have precisely the same meaning. Thus, it is plain that stipulation is a convenient device.

However, there is a way of misemploying stipulative definitions in argument which is so common and fallacious that it deserves special consideration. The technique consists of making some controversial statement true, indeed, analytic, by stipulating a definition for some key term and then claiming to have shown the *original* statement to be true. When this happens, a stipulative definition is being masqueraded as a reportive one. We shall refer to this dubious procedure as the redefinist fallacy.

An example of the fallacy would be the following. Philosophers have debated the truth of the thesis that every event has a cause. Defenders of this thesis are known as *determinists.* Suppose that a determinist argues that every event has a cause by first defining the word 'event' as 'occurrence having a cause,' and then concluding that every event has a cause. This strategy would hardly fool anyone, for it is clear what has been done. The determinist has, by stipulating a special meaning for the word 'event,' changed the meaning of the controversial thesis. As he is using the word 'event,' the thesis reduces by substitution to the trivially true statement, every occurrence having a cause has a cause. This was hardly the subject of controversy. Because the determinist has appropriated the word 'event' for this special use, an opponent must either point out that this stipulative definition has changed the meaning of the statement under dispute, or he must formulate the statement in other words, or both. For example, he might reply,

It is true, given your idiosyncratic definition of the word 'event,' that every event has a cause. But this is quite irrelevant, for as the word 'event' is ordinarily used, it is not part of the definition of an 'event' that it is something caused. Perhaps the best way to clarify the issue in dispute, now that you have stipulated a special meaning for the word 'event,' is to reformulate the thesis. Let us now ask whether every *occurrence* has a cause. This question remains open, even if we accept your stipulated definition of 'event,' and is in fact the question that divides us.

This is the way to deal with the redefinist fallacy. The fallacy consists of redefining some word by stipulation in a significant thesis and thereby rendering it utterly trivial. This is a fallacy because the original statement has not been shown to be true as is claimed, but instead it has been supplanted by another statement that is not the subject of controversy at all. The antidote to this procedure is to show that by changing the meaning of the statement the discussion has simply been diverted from the thesis at issue to some trivial truth that is not the subject of controversy.

DEFINITION AND LOGIC

We are now in a position to see how definitions may be used to show that some statement is logically impossible or logically necessary. We have said that a statement that describes something logically impossible is a contradictory statement which can be shown to be false simply by appeal to logic and definition. There are some statements that can be shown to be false by appeal to logic and without appeal to definition. These are statements whose *form* alone is sufficient to guarantee that they are false. For example, a statement of the form

An X is not an X.

must be false no matter what X is. Again, a statement of the form

P and not P.

must be false no matter what P happens to be. We need not appeal to the definition of any term to know that statements of these forms are false. Such statements are said to be *formal* contradictions.

However, we noticed earlier that some contradictory statements are not formal contradictions. For example, the statement

A brother is a female.

is contradictory, but is not a formal contradiction. By appealing to definitions, and making the appropriate substitutions, it is possible to reduce this statement to a formal contradiction. We might define 'brother' as 'sibling that is male and not female.' This definition is a little redundant, but it is an accurate reportive definition. If we substitute as this definition permits us to, then the preceding statement becomes

A sibling that is male and not female is female.

This statement has the form

An X that is a Y and not a Z is a Z.

which is a formal contradiction. Any statement of this form is false no matter what X, Y, and Z are. Thus we began with a statement which was not a formal contradiction, and, substituting as we are permitted to by a definition, we reduce the original statement to one that is a formal contradiction. In this way definition may be employed to show some statements to be contradictory.

Similar remarks apply to analytic statements describing something logically necessary. These statements can be shown to be true simply by appealing to logic and definition, and some of them can be shown to be true by appealing to logic alone. The latter are statements whose form alone guarantees their truth. For example, statements of the form

An X is an X.

or

If P, then P.

or

Either P or not P.

must be true no matter what X or P might be. Such statements are *formal* truths.

Statements that are not formal truths may sometimes be reduced to formal truths by appealing to definitions. The analytic statement

A brother is a male.

which is not a formal truth may be reduced to one by appealing to the definition of 'brother' as 'sibling that is a male' and substituting to obtain the statement

A sibling that is a male is a male.

That statement, being of the form

An X that is a Y is a Y.

is a formal truth. This procedure may, upon superficial consideration, seem to resemble the redefinist fallacy mentioned earlier because in both cases a statement is shown to be trivially true by the use of definition. However, the crucial difference is that in the cases just considered the trivially true statement has the same meaning as the original statement. Thus the original statement is just as trivially true as the final one, even if that was not initially apparent. By contrast, in the case of the redefinist fallacy a definition is used to *change* the meaning of some word and hence of the entire statement. In itself this is not illegitimate, but if one goes on to claim to have shown the original statement to be true, then one has argued in an altogether fallacious way. This fallacy is avoided when, as was just the case, no change in meaning has taken place as a result of employing the definition. The fallacy may also be avoided, even when a change of meaning results from the employment of a stipulative definition, by simply refraining from drawing any conclusions about the truth or falsity of the statement when it has an ordinary rather than a technical meaning. It is perfectly acceptable to appeal to stipulative definitions to show that a statement is contradictory or analytic, just as we have appealed to reportive definitions, provided it is clear that the statement reduced to a formal contradiction or formal truth has a technical meaning. If this is clear, the reduction may be both fruitful and illuminating.

DEFINITION, REFERENCE, AND DENOTATION

So far we have considered one aspect of semantics, or theory of meaning, namely, definition. However, in addition to considering the definition of a word, it is often important to also consider its reference. Some philosophical questions turn on whether a term refers to something, even when the definition of the term is perfectly clear. Philosophers have, for example, disagreed about whether the expression 'physical process' can refer to the same thing to which the term 'thought process' refers. If these two terms cannot refer to the same thing, then the thought processes cannot possibly be physical processes. Were this so, thought could not possibly be any physical process that goes on in the brain or any other part of the body. Consequently, philosophers and psychologists who claim that thought processes are brain processes must also defend the view that the words 'thought process' and 'physical process' sometimes refer to the very same thing. However, they need *not* hold that these two expressions are defined in the same way. These expressions clearly mean something quite different even if they sometimes refer to the same thing.

The latter point may be clarified by considering a more common-place example. The expressions 'varsity football player' and 'member of Phi Beta Kappa' certainly have a quite different meaning. But they might refer or apply to the same person, for example, Billy Jones, who happens to be one of those rare individuals combining sufficient brain and brawn to distinguish himself both athletically and academically. These terms are defined in different ways, but both terms may refer to the same person.

In addition to speaking of those individual things to which a term refers, it is convenient to have some term to refer to the whole group or class of things to which the term refers. Following standard usage on this point, we shall call the group of things to which a term refers the *denotation* of a term. Thus John, Bill, Al, and so on, collectively compose the denotation of the word 'man.'

ENTAILMENT

It is essential at this juncture to introduce a term that occurs very frequently in philosophical writing. It is the term 'entails.' It is used in a technical sense in philosophy to describe a relation between statements, and may be defined in terms of the notion of validity. To say that one or more statements entail some conclusion is equivalent to saying that the conclusion follows validly from those statements. More precisely, '*P* entails *Q*' is equal by definition to '*Q* is validly deducible from *P*.' Thus, for example, the statements

If all men are wicked, then no man is to be trusted.

and

All men are wicked.

together entail the statement

No man is to be trusted.

because the latter is validly deducible from the former. On the other hand, the statement

All men are wicked.

does not entail

No man is to be trusted.

because the latter is not validly deducible from the former. It is at least logically possible that some wicked men are to be trusted.

The various terms that we have introduced are interrelated in a number of ways. We can explore some of these relations, while at the same time further elucidating the notion of entailment, by considering the various equivalent ways in which we might define the term 'entails.' By investigating these equivalent formulations we shall be able to summarize and perhaps clarify the discussion up to this point.

A second way of defining the term 'entails' is to say that one or more premises entail a conclusion if and only if it is logically impossible that the premises should be true and the conclusion false. The latter is equivalent to saying that a statement would be contradictory that asserted the premises to be true and the conclusion to be false. A third way of defining the term is to say that premises entail a conclusion just in case it is logically necessary that if the premises are true then the conclusion is also true. The latter is equivalent to saying a statement asserting that if the premises are true then the conclusion is true is analytic. Finally, to say that premises entail a conclusion is equivalent to saying that we can show by appealing simply to logic and definitions that if the premises are true then the conclusion is true rather than false. All four ways of defining the term 'entails' are equivalent given the way we have defined the terms 'logically impossible,' 'logically necessary,' 'contradictory,' and 'analytic.' It would be a useful exercise for the reader to explain precisely why this is so.

THE A PRIORI AND THE EMPIRICAL

Statements that are either analytic or contradictory are traditionally called *a priori* statements. An *a priori* statement is sometimes described as a statement whose truth or falsity may be known prior to any appeal to experience. However, this characterization is not intended to suggest that experience is irrelevant to discovering or learning what the statement means. Sometimes we need to know the definition of some key term in order to know that a statement is analytic or contradictory, and this knowledge depends on experience. But once the meaning of such a statement is understood, no evidence drawn from experience or observation is needed to justify the claim to know whether the statement is true or false. When we have learned enough to understand the meaning of such statements and the words contained therein, we can know whether they are true without any appeal to empirical evidence. Such statements are ones whose truth or falsity can be known *a priori*. The analytic and contradictory statements considered earlier are all examples of such statements.

In contrast to *a priori* statements are all those statements that can be known to be true or false only on the basis of evidence obtained from experience and observation. These are *a posteriori*, or empirical, statements. The following are examples of empirical statements:

1. I have a head.
2. The moon has craters.
3. Some mushrooms are poisonous.
4. All mules are sterile.

These statements are not only empirical but are also thought to be true. If you substitute the words 'tail,' 'vineyards,' 'apples,' and 'women' for the terms 'head,' 'craters,' 'mushrooms,' and 'mules,' respectively, in the preceding four statements, you will obtain four empirical statements that are considered false.

Philosophers have asked whether empirical statements, if true, are conclusively verifiable by observation in the sense that statements describing what a person could observe would entail that they are true. This amounts to the question of whether observation and deduction taken together are sufficient for discovering the truth of all empirical statements that are in fact true. Let us consider the four listed statements. Statement (1) is conclusively verifiable; it is easy enough for me to observe that I have a head. It would be more difficult to make observations which would entail that (2) and (3) are both true, but perhaps this could also be done. However, statement (4) is not conclusively verifiable by observation; there is nothing a person could observe which would entail that this statement is true. No matter how many mules we observe to be sterile, the premise that we had observed these things would never entail that *all* mules are sterile. For it will remain logically possible that some as yet unobserved mule will turn out not to be sterile.

To clarify these remarks let us consider the difference between an argument for the truth of the third statement which has premises gleaned from observation and an argument for the truth of the fourth statement having premises from the same source.

> I. We have observed people eating mushrooms who were observed to be poisoned as a result.
> *Therefore*
> Some mushrooms are poisonous.
> II. We have observed many mules, all of whom were observed to be sterile.
> *Therefore*
> All mules are sterile.

Using the term 'observe' in such a way that saying a person *observes* something to be the case entails that it really is the case, argument (I) is deductively valid. It is logically impossible that we should observe that people suffer poisoning as a result of eating mushrooms and that no mushrooms should be poisonous. However, it is equally clear that argument (II) is deductively invalid. For it is logically possible that all of the many mules we have observed should be sterile even though not all mules are.

The conclusion to be drawn from these considerations is that not all true *a posteriori* or empirical statements are conclusively verifiable by observation. Universal statements like 'all mules are sterile' are not. However, such statements, if false, are conclusively *falsifiable* by observation, that is, some observations that a person could make would entail that the statement is false. For example, suppose that I observe a mule which has an offspring. Then we could construct the following argument that would falsify statement (4):

> III. We have observed mules who have offspring.
> *Therefore*
> It is false that all mules are sterile.

On the other hand, statement (3), which we found to be conclusively verifiable, would not be conclusively falsifiable even if it were false. Consider the following argument:

IV. We have observed many people eating mushrooms and none were observed to suffer from poisoning as a result.
Therefore
It is false that some mushrooms are poisonous.

This argument is invalid; it is logically possible that we should observe people eating mushrooms that were not poisonous though there are other mushrooms that are poisonous.

Thus such universal statements as (4) are conclusively falsifiable but not conclusively verifiable by observation, and statements such as (3), which are called *particular* statements, are conclusively verifiable but not conclusively falsifiable by observation. There are other statements, such as statement (1), which are both conclusively falsifiable and verifiable by observation. To say this is not to say that statement (1) is both true and false; it is only to say that if it is false, then a person could observe this, and if it is true, then a person could observe this. Thus the *a posteriori* statements we have considered so far are conclusively verifiable or conclusively falsifiable by observation, or both.

May we conclude that all empirical statements are either conclusively verifiable or falsifiable by observation, or both? Unfortunately, this conclusion would be unjustified. There are statements which, if they can be known to be true at all, can be known to be true only on the basis of the evidence of experience but which are neither conclusively verifiable nor falsifiable by observation. One example is the statement 'Every physical substance has a solvent.' There is no way of knowing whether this is true apart from observing that certain substances, such as gold, dissolve in some solvent, such as aqua regia. So the statement is empirical and *a posteriori*. On the other hand, nothing we could observe would falsify or verify this statement. It is both universal (it is about *all* substances, and hence is not verifiable by observation) and particular (it is about *some* solvent, and hence not falsifiable by observation).

To see more clearly that this is so, let us ask how one might attempt to verify the statement. One might observe substance one, substance two, and so forth, through a million substances, finding a solvent for each substance. Having observed that a million substances have solvents, we cannot validly deduce from this premise the conclusion that *every* substance has a solvent. The premise does not entail that conclusion; it is logically possible that some substance that is not one of the million we have observed lacks a solvent. Thus the attempt to verify the hypothesis by observation will inevitably fail.

What about an attempt to falsify the hypothesis? Could it succeed? Suppose we observe the reaction between a certain substance and every *potential* solvent we can find with the result that none of these dissolves the substance. Having observed this, can we validly deduce from this premise the conclusion that it is false that every substance has some solvent? Again, the premise does not entail the conclusion; it is logically possible that there is some liquid, which we have not yet observed, that is a solvent for the substance in question.

INDUCTION

The preceding discussion shows that there are some *a posteriori* statements that are not conclusively falsifiable or verifiable by observation. Hence if it is reasonable to accept such statements on the basis of the evidence of observation, then it is reasonable to accept those statements as conclusions of arguments in which the premises fail to entail the conclusions. Such arguments are not valid deductive arguments and they are not necessarily truth preserving. These arguments are traditionally called *inductive* arguments.

Many of the conclusions or hypotheses we consider it reasonable to accept are supported by inductive argument alone. We have already considered some of the more unusual statements that, if they are supported at all, are supported inductively. There are many such statements. The theoretical statements of empirical science—for example, statements about unobserved submicroscopic particles—are neither empirically falsifiable nor empirically verifiable. Consider any statement of empirical science which concerns the behavior or properties of such particles as neutrinos. Nothing we could observe inside or outside the laboratory would entail that the neutrino has the properties ascribed to it. It is at least logically possible that the meter readings and other observable phenomena should occur and that there should not exist any neutrinos at all. It is logically possible, if scientifically implausible, to suppose that the correct explanation of the phenomena we observe inside the laboratory is one that does not depend on the hypothesis that neutrinos exist but rather on some as yet unconceived of and perhaps undreamt of theory which will be proposed many years hence. On the other hand, should the neutrino hypothesis come to be rejected in science, this will not result from our observing something that entails· the falsity of the neutrino hypothesis. It will remain at least logically possible that our present theory is correct, that the neutrino really does exist, no matter what we observe. The neutrino hypothesis is neither conclusively verifiable nor falsifiable by observation.

Of course, these remarks are not intended to suggest that the results of scientific inquiry are a mere chimera, mere guessing. On the contrary, the theories and hypotheses scientists accept are in many cases well supported and justified by the evidence of observation. But the point is that the evidence is inductive, as is the inference made from it. Furthermore, the *a posteriori* statements that are neither conclusively verifiable nor falsifiable are not the only class of statements we accept on the basis of inductive evidence. On the contrary, most statements that are conclusively verifiable or falsifiable by observation are also accepted on the basis of inductive evidence. The reason for this is quite simple. There are many statements that could be falsified or verified by observation but are such that we are not in a position to observe the things in question. Consider some statement about the past, for example, that a certain man was born on January 10, 1936. The fact that he was born on that date is something that could be observed, but, obviously, he is in no position to observe that hallowed event. If he accepts the statement, then his acceptance of it must be based on inductive evidence of the usual sort, his parents' word, the information on his birth certificate, and so forth. Indeed all statements about things that happen at other times and places are statements which, if we accept them at all, are accepted on the basis of evidence that does not entail their truth.

Universal statements, if accepted, must also be accepted on the basis of inductive evidence, because they are not conclusively verifiable by observation; and particular statements, if held to be false, must be so held on the basis of inductive evidence, because they are not conclusively falsifiable by observation. When we consider the vast number of things we believe, we will soon discover that induction is the warrant of most of them. It is rare to elicit premises from observation from which one can validly deduce the truth of those *a posteriori* statements one believes. The deduction almost always fails, but the powers of human reason refuse to be restrained by the limits of deductive reasoning. When a deductive argument is not forthcoming to defend our beliefs but the evidence seems strong nonetheless, then induction is called upon to meet our needs. Hence it is essential that we obtain some understanding of this variety of argumentation.

INDUCTIVE COGENCY

In an inductive argument the premises are *evidence* for the conclusion or *hypothesis*. Unlike a sound deductive argument in which the premises entail the conclusion, the evidence of sound inductive argument does not entail the hypothesis inferred from it. What, then, is a sound inductive argument? One condition of soundness is that the evidence must consist of true statements. This is a condition shared by deductive arguments. But if the evidence does not logically entail the hypothesis inferred from it, what is the condition for the soundness of inductive arguments corresponding to the condition of validity in the case of deductive ones?

It must be admitted right off that any answer to this question will be controversial in terms of current research in inductive logic. Inductive logic is one of those fields of inquiry in which there remain unsolved fundamental problems. Moreover, one of those problems is how to answer the question we now confront. Indeed some philosophers doubt that there is any satisfactory answer and, consequently, repudiate the idea of inductive logic altogether. However, having noted the controversy with which this subject is imbued, we shall, nevertheless, attempt to formulate a second condition of soundness for inductive argument. For to do otherwise would be to ignore the vast number of such arguments with which we are forced to deal in both practical affairs and philosophical inquiry.

Even if an inductive inference from evidence to hypothesis is not necessarily truth preserving, that is, even though it is logically possible that the evidence is true and the conclusion false, such inference is sound only if it is *reasonable* to think that the inference is truth preserving, that is, it is reasonable to think that the hypothesis is true if the evidence is. A sound deductive argument is one in which the premises are true and in which if the premises are true, the conclusion must be true. A sound inductive argument is one in which the statements of evidence are true, *and* in which if the premises are true, then it is reasonable to accept the hypothesis as true. So the second condition of soundness of an inductive argument, which we shall call *inductive cogency*, may be put as follows: If the evidence is true, it is reasonable to accept the hypothesis as true also.

TRUTH AND REASONABLE BELIEF

The term 'reasonable' is used here in a special sense as was the term 'possible' in our definition of the validity of deductive arguments. Whether it is reasonable to think that a statement is true depends on one's purposes. It may make someone happy to think it is true that God exists, and, if his purpose is to obtain happiness by thinking such things, perhaps for this end it is reasonable for him to think it true that God exists. But this has nothing whatever to do with inductive arguments or the kind of reasonableness required by them. Instead the kind of reasonableness required for inductive argument must have truth and the avoidance of error as the only ends. An inductive argument must be one in which if the statements of evidence are true, then it is reasonable to accept the inferred hypothesis as true for the purposes of accepting true hypotheses and avoiding the acceptance of false ones.[1]

It should, however, be noted that the ends of accepting true statements and avoiding the acceptance of false ones are somewhat at odds. For the simplest way to avoid accepting false statements is not to accept any statement. By so doing, one accepts nothing false. On the other hand, to accept what is true, the simplest way is to accept all statements, because by so doing one will accept every true statement. Of course, the trouble with accepting all statements,

---

[1] My account of induction diverges from but is indebted to Isaac Levi, *Gambling with Truth* (New York: Knopf, 1967).

even if one could do it, is that one would be accepting as many false statements as true ones. Similarly, the trouble with accepting no statements is that one thereby foregoes the chance of accepting true statements. The problem is to strike a balance between these two ends of accepting what is true and at the same time avoiding acceptance of what is false.

Inductive argument thus always runs the risk of failing to preserve truth, of leading from true statements of evidence to a false hypothesis. What makes the risk of error worth taking is the chance of accepting something true. The task of inductive logic is to formulate rules enabling us to determine when the risk is reasonable. However, as we have indicated, this issue is surrounded with controversy. We can both illustrate the issue and learn some inductive logic by considering some specific forms of inductive argumentation.

FORMS OF INDUCTIVE ARGUMENTS

One familiar variety of inductive argument is a statistical argument in which the evidence or the hypothesis is a statistical statement concerning the percentage of things of one sort that are another. One example of a statistical statement is the statement that 67 per cent of the cats of Dibar are rabid. This statement may be a hypothesis of an argument inferred from the evidence of observation. It may also be used as evidence for some conclusion about the health of a cat whose health is undetermined. Two forms of argument that could be employed are as follows:[2]

INDUCTION BY ENUMERATION

X per cent of the examined members of A are B.
Therefore
X per cent of the members of A are B.

STATISTICAL SYLLOGISM

X per cent of the members of A are B (X being greater than 50).
O is an unexamined member of A.

[2] The account of statistical argument forms discussed critically here is taken from Wesley C. Salmon, *Logic* (Englewood Cliffs, N.J.: Prentice-Hall, 1963), Chapter 3.

Therefore
O is a member of B.

The following two arguments instantiate these forms:

67 per cent of the examined cats of Dibar are rabid.
Therefore
67 per cent of the cats of Dibar are rabid.

and

67 per cent of the cats of Dibar are rabid.
The cat that bit me is an unexamined cat of Dibar.
Therefore
The cat that bit me is rabid.

These two arguments illustrate very familiar forms of inductive statistical argument. It is apparent that the hypotheses inferred from the evidence are not validly deducible from them. It is logically possible that what we have observed to be true of a certain percentage of cats in a sample is not characteristic of the same percentage of cats in the total population of Dibar, and it is logically possible that what is characteristic of a certain percentage of cats of Dibar is not characteristic of a particular unexamined cat. There is one exception that should be noted. If we have a statistical syllogism in which the evidence is that 100 per cent of the members of A are B, and O is a member of A (unexamined or not), then, of course, it follows deductively that O is a B. However, except for this extreme case, we must add other restrictions to render plausible the claim that arguments of these forms are inductively cogent.

The most important restriction on arguments having the form *induction by enumeration* is that the sample of examined members of A should be representative of things that are A, at least with respect to the question of whether such things are B. For example, imagine that our examined sample of cats consists entirely of cats that are captured after they have bitten someone. Now, most of us, on the basis of the evidence we have about rabid animals, would conclude that rabid cats bite people much more frequently than cats that are not rabid. If this is reasonably accepted as true, then the imagined sample of examined cats is not representative of the class of cats with respect to the issue of whether such cats are rabid. Though the precise definition of a representative sample is a matter of controversy, evidence concerning samples which we have reason to believe to be unrepresentative will not yield *cogent* induction by enumeration. It will not be reasonable to accept a hypothesis as true on the basis of such evidence.

The argument form of statistical syllogism requires further restriction as well. Again returning to our example concerning the cats of Dibar, suppose that our unexamined cat is known to have been inoculated against rabies while a very small percentage of the cat population of Dibar has been so inoculated. Then, even though the cat that has bit me has not been examined to determine whether it is rabid, the argument formulated above would not be cogent. It would not be reasonable to accept the hypothesis that the cat that bit me is rabid as true on the basis of the evidence. What is needed here is some requirement of total evidence, one to the effect that evidence includes all that is relevant to the hypothesis in question.

AN INCONSISTENCY

The two argument forms cited are among the most plausible candidates for forms of inductive argument which are such that if the statements of evidence are true, then it is reasonable to accept the hypotheses as true. But these argument forms, though they are the strongest candidates, fail to win the office. Moreover, further restrictions and qualifications will not rectify the matter. There is a fatal flaw.

To see what it is, let us return to the example of the cats of Dibar once more. Suppose that there are 100,000 cats in Dibar and we have examined a representative sample of 10,000 cats of which 67 per cent are rabid. Now suppose I spot a cat, one that is a total stranger to me, whom I name Cleo. By simple enumeration I conclude that 67 per cent of the cats of Dibar are rabid. Taking this conclusion now as evidence, I conclude by statistical syllogism that Cleo is rabid. Now suppose, starting from the same initial evidence that 67 per cent of the cats of Dibar are rabid, I construct a series of statistical syllogisms, 90,000 of them in fact, each of which has as the other statement of evidence that one of the unexamined cats is a cat of Dibar, and in each syllogism conclude that the unexamined cat is rabid. Thus, by statistical syllogism, I shall have drawn the conclusion that each of the 90,000 unexamined cats is rabid. This set of conclusions has the consequence, when taken together with our evidence concerning the sample of examined cats, that over 96 per cent, 96.70 per cent to be exact, of the cats of Dibar are rabid. This conclusion is, of course, logically inconsistent with a premise of our statistical syllogism, namely, that 67 per cent of the cats of Dibar are rabid. So from true evidence statements concerning a sample of examined cats we obtain by the argument forms of induction by enumeration and statistical syllogism a set of inconsistent conclusions. As a result of induction by enumeration we conclude that 67 per cent of the cats of Dibar are rabid. Then by statistical syllogism using that conclusion as evidence we infer a set of hypotheses about the unexamined cats entailing that 96.70 per cent of the cats of Dibar are rabid.

Inductive logicians, noting the problem, have made a variety of suggestions to deal with it. First, it has been suggested that inductive reasoning, unlike deductive reasoning, is *nonconjunctive*. If we have a series of valid deductive arguments having conclusions Q, R, and S, then we may deduce the conjunction of those three statements, that is, the statement *Q and R and S*, from a set of premises consisting of all the premises of the original arguments. But, it is claimed, the same is not true in the case of induction. We may have a series of cogent inductive arguments to hypotheses Q, R, and S, when there is no cogent inductive argument from the evidence statements of the original arguments to the conjunction of Q, R, and S. In terms of our example, it might be claimed, in the light of the principle of the nonconjunctivity of inductive argument, that though we can inductively infer that each of the unexamined cats, Cleo, Tom, and Tammy, and so forth, are rabid, we cannot inductively infer the conjunction of these hypotheses, that is, that Cleo and Tom and Tammy, and so forth, are all rabid. Consequently, we could not inductively infer that 96.70 per cent of the cats of Dibar are rabid.

The foregoing attempt to avoid paradox, though it has distinguished advocates, is ineffective. For even if we cannot inductively infer the statement that 96.70 per cent of the cats of Dibar are rabid, dire consequences follow. From our original evidence about the cats of Dibar, that there are 100,000 of them and in a representative sample of 10,000 cats, 6,700 were found to be rabid, we inductively infer by induction by enumeration, that 67 per cent of the cats of Dibar are rabid. Taking that conclusion as evidence we infer by a series of statistical syllogisms that each of 90,000 unexamined cats is rabid. But as a simple matter of arithmetic, the conclusions of these statistical syllogisms cannot possibly all be true if the evidence statements in those arguments are true. Thus this set of inductively inferred statements is logically inconsistent with the evidence from which they are inferred. This result confounds our objective of avoiding error. For a contradictory set of statements, whether or not we include a conjunction within it, must contain some error.

INDUCTION AND PROBABILITY: THE LOTTERY PARADOX

The foregoing argument illustrates a typical problem confronting the attempt to provide argument forms for inductive logic. There is an underlying difficulty that generates the problem. It is natural to assume that just as a valid deductive argument is one in which if the premises are true, then the conclusion must be true, so a cogent inductive argument is one in which, if the evidence statements are true, then the hypothesis is *probable*. The notion of probability is a complex one which we shall discuss subsequently. But it is essential to notice here that probability, even high probability, will not suffice for inductive cogency. In both induction by enumeration and statistical syllogism we may suppose that the inferred hypothesis is probable, even highly probable, on the basis of the evidence. Thus one is inclined toward the idea that the argument form is cogent. But this natural line of reasoning leads directly to inconsistency.

A more general argument is available to show that probability, even very high probability, of a hypothesis on the basis of evidence does *not* suffice for inductive cogency. It depends on considering fair lotteries which enable us to specify probabilities with precision. Suppose, for example, that we think any hypothesis having a probability of 99/100 or greater on the basis of evidence may be cogently inferred from the evidence by induction. Imagine we have a lottery containing 100 tickets numbered consecutively from 1 to 100. Imagine a ticket has been drawn and the lottery is fair. All this is our evidence. Now consider ticket number 100. The probability on the evidence that it was drawn is 1/100. There is one chance in a hundred that it was drawn. This means that the probability that some other ticket was drawn is 99/100. Assuming that this is a high enough probability for cogent inductive inference, we may cogently infer from the evidence that some ticket other than the 100 ticket was drawn. Beginning from the same evidence we could use an argument of the same form to infer that some ticket other than the 99 ticket was drawn, that some ticket other than the 98 ticket was drawn, and so forth. In each case the hypothesis would have a probability of 99/100 on the evidence. So for each ticket we could cogently infer that some other ticket was drawn. But then the set of conclusions would be inconsistent with our original evidence. For the set of conclusions would tell us, for each ticket, that it was not drawn, and this is inconsistent with our evidence which tells us that one ticket was drawn. In short, the set of hypotheses inductively inferred entails each of the tickets numbered from 1 to 100 is not drawn whereas our evidence tells us that one of them is.[3]

It is important to notice that this argument does not depend essentially on the number 99/100. If someone thinks that some higher probability will suffice for inductive cogency, so long as the number is less than 1, we can recast the paradox to refute him by simply considering a larger lottery. For example, if he thinks that a probability of 999,999/1,000,000 is large enough, we need only consider a lottery of 1,000,000 tickets and the hypothesis that the ticket number 1,000,000 is drawn. The probability that some other ticket is drawn is 999,999/1,000,000. And the probability that any other given ticket is not drawn is the same.

The preceding argument shows that inductive arguments of the following form are not cogent:

INDUCTION BY PROBABILITY

> It is highly probable that P.
> *Therefore*
> P.

They are not cogent because such argument forms lead from true evidence statements to inconsistent statements. We have said that

---

[3] This result is due to H. E. Kyburg, Jr., *Probability and the Logic of Rational Belief* (Middletown, Conn.: Wesleyan University Press, 1957), p. 197.

a cogent inductive argument is one in which, if the statements of evidence are true, then it is reasonable to accept the hypothesis as true for the purpose of accepting true hypotheses and avoiding error. By accepting an inconsistent set of statements we insure that some statement we accept is erroneous. Therefore, inductive argument forms are not cogent when they warrant the inference of an inconsistent set of statements from true evidence statements.

COGENCY AND COMPETITION

The preceding argument illustrates the difficulty of attempting to specify any form of argument that is inductively cogent. We may obtain an improved account of inductive cogency by noting the importance of the concept of *competition* among hypotheses as a feature of induction. Whether it is reasonable to accept a statement as true depends on what other statements it competes with as well as on the probability of the statement on the evidence. To understand this, consider once again the conclusion of the induction by enumeration concerning cats. The hypothesis inductively inferred was that 67 per cent of the cats of Dibar are rabid. Is it reasonable to accept that hypothesis on the basis of the evidence? The answer to the question depends on what statements you take that hypothesis to compete with. If the competition consists of other statements specifying the *exact* percentage of rabidity of the cats of Dibar, then it would be more reasonable to accept that hypothesis than any of the others because it is more probable than any others. On the other hand, if the competition includes not only hypotheses concerning exact percentages but also less exact hypotheses—for example, the statement that the percentage lies somewhere between 60 and 80 per cent—then the issue has been radically changed. For the hypothesis that the percentage lies within that interval is very much more probable than the more exact hypothesis specifying the percentage at a single point within that interval.

A PHILOSOPHICAL EXAMPLE:
THE EXISTENCE OF MAN

The same sort of problem arises in more directly philosophical contexts. Here too the concept of competition is central to an understanding of cogent inductive reasoning. Let us consider an example of inductive reasoning that once led philosophers and scientists to the conclusion that the universe was designed by some agent. To appreciate the inductive reasoning leading to this conclusion, it is important to recall that before the theory of evolution was conceived, there was a phenomenon that constituted a fundamental intellectual problem, the existence of man. Even if one had theories of matter adequate to account for many features of the physical universe, the existence of human beings remained puzzling. The existence of animals presented a striking contrast to inert matter, but, although some philosophers were willing to look upon animals as complex physical mechanisms, to draw the same conclusion concerning human beings was repugnant. Perhaps the principal reason for this aversion was the existence of conscious thought and rational cogitation. A philosopher who willingly rejected the idea that lower animals think and reason could not very well deny that he himself was thinking and reasoning while engaged in those very activities. So the existence of man, a thinking and reasoning being, constituted a problematic phenomenon indeed. Naturally, the question arose of how to explain it.

We can frame this question by asking what hypothesis it would be reasonable to accept as true by induction from the evidence. To some thinkers, there seemed to be only two competing hypotheses. One was that man came to exist as a sheer matter of cosmic chance or accident. The other was that man came to exist as a result of some design or plan. Hence, as these thinkers considered the matter, the following two hypotheses were the competitors for acceptance in this context:

1. Man came to exist by chance.
2. Man came to exist by design.

Given that these were the hypotheses from which to choose, it is not surprising that the second rather than the first was considered more probable on the evidence. It seemed extremely unlikely that anything so remarkably intricate and complex as a human being should come to exist by chance. Indeed the intricate and complex organization of men appeared strikingly analogous to the intricate and complex characteristics of objects designed by men. This argument by analogy, which we shall consider again later, was inductive, of course, but it was also based on a rather limited set of alternative hypotheses. With competition limited in this way it is not at all surprising that some of the most acute and critical thinkers of the past regarded hypothesis (2) as the one to be inductively inferred from the evidence.

Now the astute reader may have noticed that, strictly speaking, a person who considers hypotheses (1) and (2) should, to be completely judicious, consider one other hypothesis as well, namely, the hypothesis that neither (1) nor (2) was correct. Thus we could also consider the following negative hypothesis:

3. Man came to exist by something other than chance or design.

The omission of this hypothesis from the competition was justified because of its uninformative nature. It offers no explanation at all of the observed phenomena. Though it may well be true, if one is seeking a hypothesis to explain the existence of man, that hypothesis (3) does not compete for that role.

A much smaller proportion of philosophers and scientists would today consider cogent the inductive inference of hypothesis (2) from the evidence. But one reason for this is that today we do not consider these two hypotheses to be the *only* competing alternatives. There is of course the evolutionary hypothesis

4. Man came to exist by evolution.

Here it is most important not to confound the informative hypothesis (4) with the uninformative hypothesis (3). Hypothesis (3) is logically implied by (4), but the justification of (3) depends entirely on the cogency of inductive argument in favor of (4). Once the evolutionary hypothesis was conceived, then the competition included not only (1) and (2) but also (4). Since many scientists and philosophers, perhaps most, would consider hypothesis (4) to be the most probable of the competing three, they consider the induction of that hypothesis from the evidence to be cogent.

It is important to notice the difference between hypothesis (3) and hypothesis (4). The former is negative and does not explain the phenomenon in question, the existence of man. The latter, by contrast, offers a very sophisticated and comprehensive theory, the theory of evolution, as an explanation for that phenomenon. It is for that reason that a man who would not consider hypothesis (3) as a competitor would consider hypothesis (4) to be a competitor, and, indeed, a successful competitor.

The preceding arguments lead to a pair of final conclusions. First, the cogency of an inductive argument depends, in part, on what other statements the hypothesis of the argument competes with. Second, what statements a hypothesis competes with depends on what hypotheses have been conceived, and, in this way, on the context of inquiry. Considerations other than the *form* of an inductive argument determine its cogency. Representativeness of samples and relevance of evidence were mentioned earlier. These features vary from context to context. A sample that would be considered representative in one situation would not be so in another, for example, when we have additional evidence. Information that is not relevant in one context may be relevant in another. Finally, the hypotheses that any given hypothesis competes with is seen to depend on the situation in question. The argument from observed evidence to hypothesis (2) may have been cogent in a situation in which the only competing hypothesis was (1). But that does not mean that such an argument is cogent in a context in which (4) is also included in the competition.

INDUCTIVE COGENCY AS SUCCESSFUL COMPETITION

We conclude that inductive cogency depends in an essential way on the evidential and conceptual context of reasoning. We can give a definition of inductive cogency in terms of the notion of competition as follows: An inductive argument from evidence to hypothesis is inductively cogent if and only if the hypothesis is that hypothesis which, of all the competing hypotheses, has the greatest probability of being true on the basis of the evidence. Thus, whether it is reasonable to accept a hypothesis as true if the statements of evidence are true is determined by whether that hypothesis is the most probable on the evidence of those with which it competes.

The conclusion we have reached supplies us with a methodology for checking the cogency of an inductive argument. Confronted with an inductive argument, one should pose two critical questions:

1. What statements does the hypothesis of the argument compete with?

2. Is the hypothesis more probable than those hypotheses with which it competes?

Only if the answer to the second question is affirmative may we consider the argument cogent. Moreover, there is no automatic test or formal rule by which one provides an answer to either of these questions. To answer the first, we must make use of all the intellectual resources at our command. The failure to consider some competitor for a hypothesis may lead us to accept some hypothesis it is quite unreasonable to accept. However, if we have diligently searched for competitors and seriously considered the probability of each, then we may, tentatively, consider an argument inductively cogent when the conclusion is the most probable of all the competitors we can conceive.

The search for a more probable competitor to disprove inductive cogency is like the search for a counterexample to disprove deductive validity. The failure to find a counterexample does not prove there is none. Similarly, the failure to find a more probable competing hypothesis does not prove there is none. Moreover, these methods of refutation are no more effective than the person who employs them. In the end, when deciding on whether to accept an argument as deductively valid or inductively cogent, we shall depend not on any automatic procedure, but on our intelligence and integrity. This is not a defect. For all progress in science and the humanities depends ultimately on these elements. There is no methodology that transcends or overrides the human intellect.

EXERCISES

1. Of what does an argument consist? What is a valid argument? What is a valid argument form? How is a valid argument derived from a valid argument form? What is a sound argument?

2. Consider the following argument:

   Validity is of no importance. An argument can have false premises and still be valid. In fact, it can have false premises and a false conclusion, yet still be valid. Therefore, there is no connection between truth and validity. Thus is validity seen to be irrelevant to truth and therefore to philosophical inquiry.

How would you reply to this argument? Which statements of the argument are correct and which incorrect?

3. How does the method of counterexample serve as a test of invalidity? Why does a counterexample show an argument to be invalid? Why is an argument valid if there are no counterexamples to it? What procedure is proposed for deciding whether to accept an argument as valid? Do you think it is a sensible procedure? Why?

4. What is a question-begging argument? Why are they to be eschewed?

5. May an unsound argument have a true conclusion? Why? May an unsound but valid argument have a true conclusion? Why?

6. Consider the following argument:

Theists and theologians have offered any number of arguments to prove the existence of God. However, none of these is sound. Some have false premises and others are invalid, but all have one or the other of these defects. Therefore, we may validly conclude that God does not exist.

Is this argument sound? Why? Suppose that all the statements preceding the conclusion are true. Would the argument be sound, given that supposition? Why?

7. What is a logically impossible statement? What is a logically necessary statement? In what way are these two kinds of statements related? Which kind of statement is contradictory and which is analytic? How can a definition be used to show that a statement is logically necessary, or that it is logically impossible?

8. What is a reportive definition? What principal of substitution is warranted by a reportive definition? How must such a principle be qualified? Why cannot the principle of substitution be used as a test for definitions? What procedure may we adopt for testing definitions? When is a definition too broad and when is it too narrow? May a definition have both these defects? How?

9. What is a stipulative definition? Why cannot a stipulative definition be rejected by finding a counterexample? How may a stipulative definition be misemployed to produce the redefinist fallacy? What is that fallacy and how is it to be dealt with?

10. What is a *formal* contradiction? Why are not all contradictions formal contradictions? How is a definition employed to reduce a contradiction to a formal contradiction? Is a similar reduction possible in the case of analytic statements? How?

11. Consider the following argument:

> Some people contend that socialism is a system that helps the poor. However, the meaning of the word 'socialism' is quite different from the meaning of the words 'system that helps the poor.' Therefore, the former word does not refer to the same thing as the latter group of words. We may thus conclude that socialism is not a system that helps the poor.

What is the matter with this argument? Does the sentence beginning with the word 'therefore' follow from the sentence that precedes it? Why?

12. How is the word 'entails' defined? What alternative ways are there of defining this word? Why are all these definitions equivalent?

13. What is an *a priori* statement? What is an *a posteriori* statement? Are all *a posteriori* statements empirically verifiable or empirically falsifiable? Why? Be sure to give examples to support your contentions.

14. What is an inductive argument? How is induction distinguished from deduction? How is *inductive cogency* defined? How does it differ from validity?

15. What two forms of statistical inductive argument lead to inconsistent conclusions? How does the inconsistency arise? Does the principle of the nonconjunctivity of inductive argument enable one to avoid the inconsistency? Why?

16. What inconsistency is based on a consideration of lotteries? What does the inconsistency prove concerning the cogency of inductive argument forms?

17. What is the relevance of the concept of competition to inductive cogency? How does the problem of the explanation of the existence of man illustrate the importance of the concept of competition for inductive reasoning?

18. What method for testing the cogency of inductive argument is proposed? How are the concepts of competition and probability embodied in the method? How can inductive cogency be disproved?

19. Consider the following argument:

What matters in philosophy is that one obtains the truth. If your opinion is true and correct, then it matters little whether you can defend it with argument or reply to the arguments of others. On the other hand, if your opinion is false, then you will only be compounding your errors by defending your opinion with argument and attacking the arguments of more enlightened persons who have the truth. Thus argument is irrelevant to philosophical inquiry.

Discuss this argument.

BIBLIOGRAPHY

I. Textbooks

Textbooks on logic are numerous. Three quite elementary introductions to logic and semantics are Samuel Gorovitz and Ron G. Williams, *Philosophical Analysis* (New York: Random House, Inc., 1965); Wesley Salmon, *Logic* (Englewood Cliffs, N.J.: Prentice-Hall, Inc., 1963); and Irving Copi, *Introduction to Logic* (New York: Macmillan Publishing Co., Inc., 1961). There are many other useful introductory books on the subject. Among them are E. J. Lemmon, *Beginning Logic* (London: Nelson, 1965); R. Clark and P. Welsh, *Introduction to Logic* (New York: Van Nostrand Reinhold Company, 1962); Patrick Suppes, *Introduction to Logic* (New York: Van Nostrand Reinhold Company, 1960); A. Smullyan, *Fundamentals of Logic* (Englewood Cliffs, N.J.: Prentice-Hall, Inc., 1962); W. V. O. Quine, *Methods of Logic* (New York: Holt, Rinehart & Winston, Inc., 1959); Benson Mates, *Elementary Logic* (New York: Oxford University Press, 1965); and Max Black, *Critical Thinking* (Englewood Cliffs, N.J.: Prentice-Hall, Inc., 1962); W. V. O. Quine, *Philosophy of Logic* (Englewood Cliffs, N.J.: Prentice-Hall, Inc., 1970); R. J. Ackermann, *Modern Deductive Logic* (Garden City, N.Y.: Doubleday & Company, Inc., 1970); and Max Black, *The Labyrinth of Language* (New York: Praeger Publishers, Inc., 1968), an introductory survey of semantics. Three anthologies designed for the introductory level are Irving M. Copi and James A. Gould, *Readings on Logic* (New York: Macmillan Publishing Co., Inc., 1972); Robert Sleigh, *Necessary Truth* (Englewood Cliffs, N.J.: Prentice-Hall, Inc., 1970); and Adrienne and Keith Lehrer, *Theory of Meaning* (Englewood Cliffs, N.J.: Prentice-Hall, Inc., 1970).

II. Advanced Books and Articles

For the student who already has some understanding of logic, the following two books should be of interest: Rudolf Carnap, *Meaning and Necessity* (Chicago: Phoenix Books, 1956) and W. V. O. Quine, *From a Logical Point of View* (Cambridge, Mass.: Harvard University Press, 1961). In this book Quine raises some problems about the concept of analyticity that have attracted widespread attention. Two books discussing Carnap's position are Richard Butrick, Jr., *Carnap on Meaning and Analyticity* (The Hague: Mouton, 1970) and Paul Arthur Schilpp, ed., *The Philosophy of Rudolf Carnap* (La Salle, Ill.: Open Court Publishing Company, 1964). In Nicholas Rescher, *Topics in Philosophical Logic* (Dordrecht: D. Reidel, 1968), are many of the author's journal articles of the past decade and a bibliography of recent work in philosophical logic. The most important recent book on semantics is Jerrold J. Katz, *Semantic Theory* (New York: Harper & Row, Publishers, Inc., 1972). The following articles are recommended discussions of analyticity: P. Grice and P. Strawson, "In Defense of a Dogma," *Philosophical Review*, Vol. 65 (1956), pp. 141–58; Jonathan Bennett, "Analytic-Synthetic," *Proceedings of the Aristotelian Society*, Vol. 59 (1959), pp. 163–88; Alan Gewirth, "The Distinction Between Analytic and Synthetic Truths," *Journal of Philosophy*, Vol. 50 (1953), pp. 397–426; Nelson Goodman, "On Likeness of Meaning," *Analysis*, Vol. 10 (1949), pp. 1–7; Moreland Perkins and Irving Singer, "Analyticity," *Journal of Philosophy*, Vol. 48 (1951), pp. 485–97; Hilary Putnam, "The Analytic and the Synthetic," *Minnesota Studies in the Philosophy of Science* (Minneapolis: University of Minnesota Press, 1964), edited by H. Feigl and G. Maxwell; R. M. Martin, "On Analytic," *Philosophical Studies*, Vol. 3 (1952), pp. 42–47; John Kemeny, "Analyticity," *Synthese* (1963); Gustav Bergmann, "Two Cornerstones of Empiricism," in his *The Metaphysics of Logical Positivism* (New York: Longmans, Green & Company, 1954); Douglas Gasking, "The Analytic-Synthetic Controversy," *Australasian Journal of Philosophy*, Vol. 48 (1970), pp. 107–23; Bruce Aune, "On an Analytic-Synthetic Distinction," *American Philosophical Quarterly*, Vol. 8 (1971), pp. 235–42; Jerrold J. Katz, "Some Remarks on Quine on Analyticity," *Journal of Philosophy*, Vol. 63 (1967), pp. 36–52 (Quine's reply, same issue, pp. 52–54); N. L. Wilson, "Linguistical Butter and Philosophical Parsnips," *Journal of Philosophy*, Vol. 63 (1967) (a discussion of Katz above—see also Katz' reply, Vol. 64, pp. 29–45, to Quine and Wilson); Peter Hinman, Jaegwon Kim, and Stephen P. Stich, "Logical Truth Revisited," *Journal of Philosophy*, Vol. 66 (1969), pp. 495–500. Two anthologies containing articles on meaning, analyticity, and related issues from contemporary sources are Herbert Feigl and Wilfrid Sellars, *Readings in Philosophical Analysis* (New York: Appleton-Century-Crofts, Inc., 1949); and Herbert Feigl, Wilfrid Sellars and Keith Lehrer, *New Readings in Philosophical Analysis* (New York: Appleton-Century-Crofts, Inc., 1972).

In a recent book, *Word and Object* (Cambridge, Mass.: M.I.T. Press, 1960), Quine develops and defends his point of view. Another nontechnical book of interest is P. F. Strawson, *Introduction to Logical Theory* (London: Methuen and Co., 1960). For a historical and critical discussion of the concept of necessary truth, see Arthur Pap, *Semantics and Necessary Truth* (New Haven: Yale University Press, 1958). See also Alan Pasch, *Experience and the Analytic* (Chicago: University of Chicago Press, 1959).

III. Books and Articles on Probability

Henry E. Kyburg's *Probability and Inductive Logic* (New York: Macmillan Publishing Co., Inc., 1970) contains an excellent bibliography of work on probability and inductive logic up to 1970. Other important books and articles include L. Jonathan Cohen, *The Implications of Induction* (London: Methuen & Co., 1970); Jaakko Hintikka and Patrick Suppes, eds., *Aspects of Inductive Logic* (Amsterdam: North-Holland Publishing Company, 1966); Wesley C. Salmon, *The Foundations of Scientific Inference* (Pittsburgh: University of Pittsburgh Press, 1967), surveying current views on justification of induction and probability; Imre Lakatos, ed., *The Problem of Inductive Logic* (Amsterdam: North-Holland Publishing Company, 1968), discussing models of probability, justification of inductive rules of inference, probable knowledge, and including a history of the problem of inductive logic by Lakatos; Max Black, "The *Raison D'Etre* of Inductive Argument," *British Journal for the Philosophy of Science*, Vol. 17 (1966–67), pp. 177–204; Bredo C. Johnsen, "Black and the Justification of Induction," *Analysis*, Vol. 32 (1971), pp. 110–12; Brian Skyrms, *Choice and Chance: An Introduction to Inductive Logic* (Belmont, Calif.: Dickenson Publishing Company, 1966), an elementary book; Risto Hilpinen, *Rules of Acceptance and Inductive Logic, Acta Philosophica Fennica*, Vol. 22 (Amsterdam: North-Holland Publishing Company, 1968); Peter Rosenkrantz, "Induction and Probabilism," *Synthese*, Vol. 23 (1971), pp. 167–205; Henry E. Kyburg, Jr., "Epistemological Probability," *Synthese*, Vol. 23 (1971), pp. 309–26; George Schlesinger, "Induction and Parsimony," *American Philosophical Quarterly*, Vol. 8 (1971), pp. 179–85, a nontechnical examination of the problem of induction, tying it to description of events; J. R. Lucas, *The Concept of Probability* (Oxford: Clarendon Press, 1970), argues that only one correct analysis of the concept of probability is possible; Leonard J. Savage, "Implications of Personal Probability for Induction," *Journal of Philosophy*, Vol. 63 (1967), pp. 593–607; Wesley Salmon,

"Carnap's Inductive Logic," *Journal of Philosophy*, Vol. 63 (1967), pp. 725–39; C. D. Broad, *Induction, Probability and Causation* (New York: Humanities Press, 1968); Isaac Levi, *Gambling with Truth: An Essay on Induction and the Aims of Science* (New York: Alfred A. Knopf, Inc., and London: Routledge & Kegan Paul, Ltd., 1967); A. J. Ayer, *Probability and Evidence* (New York: Columbia University Press, 1972); and Richard C. Jeffrey, *The Logic of Decision* (New York: McGraw-Hill Book Company, 1965). Recent articles by the author include Keith Lehrer, "Induction: A Consistent Gamble," *Nous*, Vol. 3 (1969), pp. 285–97, discussion of points raised in Isaac Levi's *Gambling with Truth;* "Induction, Reason, and Consistency," *British Journal for the Philosophy of Science*, Vol. 21 (1970), pp. 103–14, proposes an inductive rule that avoids the paradox of the lottery; and "Induction and Conceptual Change," *Synthese*, Vol. 23 (1971), pp. 206–25.

THE PROBLEM
OF KNOWLEDGE
AND SKEPTICISM

CHAPTER TWO

There are many forms and varieties of skepticism. A philosopher is a skeptic with respect to a certain subject if he denies that men know what they ordinarily claim to know. For example, most men suppose that they have knowledge by means of the senses, more specifically, they suppose they see certain objects, a pen perhaps, and see the sensory qualities of these objects, the color and shape. Thus, a man who is not a skeptic would, if he were looking at my right hand now, aver that he knows by perception there is a blue pen held therein. But many philosophers have been skeptics in that they have denied that men know even such commonplace matters as this.

THE MOTIVES OF SKEPTICISM

You may well wonder what motive a philosopher might have for denying that we know what we think we do. The most direct motivation arises from theory and speculation. When philosophical inquiry leads a philosopher to conclusions that conflict with what men ordinarily claim to know, he will be inspired to undermine adverse claims to clear the way for his theory. Plato was a speculative philosopher who arrived at the conclusion that reality, the proper object of knowledge, consisted not of objects we apprehend with our senses, but of intelligible objects apprehended through the intellect.[1] These intelligible objects included the objects of mathematics, numbers, triangularity, and congruence; of morality, justice, goodness, and honor; and other equally abstract items. He argued that these intelligible objects were unchanging and eternal in contrast to the constantly changing and evanescent objects of sense experience. He repudiated the objects of sense experience as being but shadows of the reality of intelligible forms. Hence Plato was led to deny that we have knowledge of sensory objects such as tables, stars, or even specks of dirt. His skepticism was an ingredient in his speculative theory concerning the intelligible nature of reality.

Current forms of skepticism often emerge from scientific theory and speculation. For example, it takes a number of years for the light to reach us from a distant star. When we view the sky on a clear evening and think that we are seeing a star as it is at the moment of viewing, and, consequently, know at least something about how the star now looks, we are quite mistaken. The star might no longer exist at all, because what we see now is light that emanated from the star a number of years ago. Now, reflecting on this fact, Bertrand Russell noted that even nearby objects, say a chair a few feet in front of one, are also seen as a result of light waves striking the eye, and those light waves take some time to travel from the object to the surface of the eye. Hence, Russell argued, if we suppose that we are seeing the object just as it is and that we know something about how the object now looks, we may certainly be mistaken. For even in that very short time required

[1] Plato, *Republic*, pp. 476–79, 504–509, 509–11.

for the light emanating from the object to reach the eye, the object may undergo some change. Consequently, it may *now* not be the same as it looks to us. Russell concludes that we do not know that the objects are the way they look, that the chair is black, for example, or for that matter, that the objects we think we see now exist.[2] Just as an object can change in that short period of time it takes for the light waves to reach our eyes, so the object can be destroyed altogether in that time. In this case a scientific theory, one concerning light waves and the physiology of perceptual processes, provides the premises for skeptical argumentation.

Another instance of scientific theory leading to skeptical conclusions is to be found in the writings of Wilfrid Sellars. Sellars thinks that our common-sense convictions conflict with scientific conclusions concerning the color of objects. Suppose we have a transparent pink glass cube which, when carefully cut, appears to be pink through and through. We ordinarily would take the cube to be a homogeneous pink cube. Not so, according to Sellars. Science tells us the cube is made up of atoms, which are quite colorless, extended in space and time. There is no characteristic of the cube considered at the atomic level which the cube has homogeneously, through and through. Because of the explanatory power of science, Sellars concludes that we should accept atomic theory and reject the idea that the cube is homogeneously pink.[3] Thus Sellars would be led to reject the common-sense knowledge claim concerning the homogeneous color of objects.

Whether or not one agrees with these arguments, they illustrate a fundamental feature of most skeptical philosophy, namely, it receives its greatest support from speculation concerning other matters. We have mentioned philosophical and scientific theories that guided philosophers down the path to skepticism. But religious theories have evoked skeptical machinations as well. A fundamentalist, or anyone who believes in the revelation of truth from supernatural sources, may be lead to reject common-sense claims to knowledge. For example, if one believes from biblical interpretation that the earth has only existed for a few thousand years, one will

2 Bertrand Russell, *The Analysis of Mind* (London: Allen & Unwin, 1921), pp. 124–36.
3 W. F. Sellars, *Science, Perception, and Reality* (London: Routledge and Kegan Paul, 1963), pp. 25–29.

be led to reject for the sake of faith those assumptions, which most men suppose they know, sustaining the conclusion that the earth has existed for millions of years.

SKEPTICISM AND DOGMATISM

However, skepticism is worth considering quite apart from those theories that serve the ends of speculation, whether philosophical, scientific, or religious. For whether we are skeptics or not is likely to influence the manner in which we discourse and inquire after truth. If a man says that he *knows* the answer to some question or problem, and then tells us what he knows, his claim to know is intended to end discussion on the topic in question. If we are wondering whether all liquids expand when they freeze as water does or whether that is a special feature of water, and someone claims to know that this is a special feature of water and that other liquids do not behave in a similar manner, he is making a claim intended to terminate inquiry in this matter. Often we welcome such relief from epistemic uncertainty, but it is worth asking whether such relief from doubt is always philosophically salubrious. Once it is noted that a knowledge claim ordinarily is terminal in intent, we may reasonably become wary about acquiescing to such claims. In a subtle way such claims are dogmatic. It is not common to regard them as dogmatic, at least not in mundane matters, but once we raise fundamental issues, dogma and knowledge become inextricably intertwined. For example, most people when asked what they consider dogma will soon mention those religious teachings of the Middle Ages in which all questions of a general nature, and many that were more specific as well, were resolved by religious fiat. The basic principles, those concerning demons, demonic possession and related matters, for instance, were dogma. They were said to be known from revelation. Revelation was considered the ultimate source of knowledge. This illustrates a basic point. Our fundamental assumptions, those we take for granted automatically and without a moment of reflection, will influence what we think we know and how we think we know it. Our convictions concerning the source of knowledge, how we know, is a matter of dogma. At one time it was dogma that knowledge comes from revelation. A person accepting such dogma might think he knows that someone has become possessed by the devil by observing alterations in his personality and behavior which constitute demonic possession. Starting from different assumptions, we deny such people observed demonic possession. But it is important to notice how dogmatic our claims are. We begin with a different assumption, crudely put, that empirical science is the source of knowledge, and, having adopted that dogma, we reject those knowledge claims based on competing assumptions.

In short, every period in intellectual history has some dogma which is regarded at the time not as dogma, but merely as what is evident. Because men seek relief from unending reasoning and justification, they latch on to some first principle or basic dogma, claiming all along that it is something they know to be true. If religious revelation was the dogma of the past, scientific empiricism is the dogma of today. In an effort to understand the dogma that we automatically take for knowledge, we shall undertake a study of skepticism with regard to the senses. We suppose that by means of our senses we know of the existence and characteristics of the objects we perceive. That perception and perceptual belief are sources of knowledge is something the man in the street, the plain man of common sense, never doubts. But the plain man, we have suggested, is a dogmatist. He dogmatically assumes his perceptual beliefs, many of them at any rate, constitute knowledge. We shall consider how much or how little merit there is in his claims. Moreover, even if skepticism with regard to the senses wins the day, we need not find this disconcerting. Should it turn out that our customary claims to knowledge are unwarranted, that strictly speaking we do not know what we say and think we do, it does not by any means follow that most of our beliefs are mistaken. All that follows is that the dogmatic terminus of inquiry embodied in our knowledge claims was unwarranted. In that case, inquiry after truth must be considered an unending quest rather than a terminating investigation. There is, we suggest, nothing ignoble or discouraging in the idea that inquiry is always open ended. Such a conception is, as we have noted, already suggested by historical precedent.

AN ANALYSIS OF KNOWLEDGE

Before examining arguments for skepticism, and those concerning perceptual knowledge in particular, we must consider briefly what is meant by saying that a person knows something. In attempting to define this notion, we shall consider the matter from the standpoint of common sense, attempting to make our definition fit with our ordinary use of the word, and shall only subsequently raise the question of whether common-sense convictions on these matters are warranted. There is nothing dubious in this procedure. Our strategy is to begin by defining knowledge in line with the assumptions of the dogmatist. Starting with the conception of knowledge employed by the dogmatist, we shall turn to the claims of the skeptic. If a sound skeptical argument can be built on this conception of knowledge, then the skeptic will have defeated the dogmatist on his home territory. To do otherwise, the skeptic would run the risk of defining knowledge in a special way suited to his ends and thus would be subject to the charge of committing the redefinist fallacy.

What, then, does it mean to say that a man knows something? To answer this clearly, we must first specify more precisely what is being asked, for the word 'know' has a great variety of different uses and meanings. For example, a person might be said to know how to play golf, he might also be said to know Paris, and finally, he might be said to know that the University of San Marcos is the oldest university in the Western Hemisphere. The latter use of the word 'know' is the one most directly related to truth and is the familiar object of skeptical criticism. To say that a man knows the University of San Marcos is the oldest in the Western Hemisphere is equivalent to saying he knows it is *true* that San Marcos is the oldest in the Western Hemisphere. This sort of knowledge is also sometimes called theoretical or discursive. However, the distinguishing feature of such knowledge is that truth is its object: it is knowledge of the truth. Skepticism, as we shall study it, asserts that something, about which almost all men commonly assume we know the truth, is really something about which we do not know the truth. Such knowledge may be formulated either by saying a man knows that X or by saying he knows it is *true* that X. These two ways of stating such knowledge claims are equivalent. Thus, truth is a necessary condition of such knowledge; if a man knows that something is so, then it must be true that it is so.

Notice that a man may often *claim* to know something is so when it is not, but though he claims to know, he does not know. In fact, he is ignorant of the truth. For example, if a man claims to know that Harvard College is the oldest college in the United States, he would be mistaken, because this is not true. He does not know what he claims to know. When a man is mistaken and believes what is false, then he lacks knowledge. We have now seen that one necessary condition of a man knowing something is that it be true. Another necessary condition is that a man must at least believe the thing in question. Obviously, a man does not know that something is true if he does not even believe it is true. May we, then, simply equate knowledge with true belief? Absolutely not! To see why not, consider a man who has a hunch and thus believes that the final score of next year's Army–Navy football game will be a 21–21 tie. Moreover, suppose that the man is quite ignorant of the outcome of past contests and other relevant data. Finally, imagine, as a mere matter of luck, he happens to be right. That it is a mere matter of luck is illustrated by the fact that he often has such hunches about the final scores of football games and is almost always wrong. His true belief about the outcome of the Army–Navy game should not be counted as knowledge. It was a lucky guess and nothing more.

How is knowledge to be distinguished from mere true belief? Most philosophers, skeptics included, have argued that whether true belief is to be counted as knowledge depends on how well justified the man is in believing what he does. The man who has a true belief about the Army–Navy game is quite unjustified in believing what he does, for he really has no reason or justification for believing the score will be a 21–21 tie. On the other hand, a man watching the game who hears the final gun as a play ends is completely justified in such a belief and hence knows that the final score is twenty-one points apiece. Thus we may assume that a man lacks knowledge unless he is justified, and indeed, completely justified, in believing what he does. Moreover, ordinarily what will determine whether a man is well enough justified in his belief is the quality of the evidence that forms the basis for his belief. The evidence of the man in the stands watching the game is quite adequate, whereas the evidence of the man who guesses is exceedingly paltry.

There is a further qualification that is required. A man may be quite well justified in what he believes even though his justification is based on some false assumption.[4] For example, if a man parks

---

[4] Edmund Gettier, "Is Justified True Belief Knowledge?" *Analysis*, 1963, pp. 121–23.

his car in a public parking lot for a few hours, he is quite well justified, when he returns to his car and does not observe any alteration, in assuming that the engine of the car remains under the hood. Of course, if someone has stolen the engine while he was away, then his belief that there is an engine under the hood falls short of knowledge simply because it is untrue that the engine is there. However, imagine that after the engine was stolen a friend came along, and, noticing the engine had been removed, arranged to have it replaced with another before the owner returned so as to relieve the owner of the agony of finding his engine stolen. Then the owner will be quite correct in his belief that there is an engine under the hood of his car when he returns. Moreover, he is quite well justified in this belief as well. However, the owner's belief will be based on a false assumption, namely, that the engine that was under the hood of his car when he left remains there now. This false assumption leads him to the true conclusion there is an engine under his hood but the only justification he has for believing this is based on the false assumption. Therefore we may not say that the man *knows* that there is an engine under the hood of his car.

We must require not only that a man be well justified in what he believes, but also that his justification not depend essentially on any false assumption; otherwise, a man may not be said to know. This qualification may be articulated in a variety of ways. We shall require that a man be completely justified in believing something in order to know what he believes is true and also that his justification must be *undefeated* by any false assumption.

We conclude that a man knows something only when his belief is true, completely justified, and the justification is undefeated. A skeptic building his case on this analysis of knowledge may argue concerning those things men commonly assume they know either (1) that we do not even believe those things, (2) that they are not true, (3) that we are not completely justified in believing them, or (4) that our justification, though complete, is defeated by some false assumption on which it essentially depends. The most promising place for the skeptic to get a foothold is condition (3). A skeptic who wishes to defend some very extensive form of skepticism, for example, by contending we do not know that any of our perceptual beliefs are true, will do best to argue that condition (3) in the analysis is not satisfied by such beliefs. Of course, he may hold all such beliefs to be false, but if he concedes that we are completely justified in our perceptual beliefs, he will be hard pressed to convince his dogmatic detractors of the merits of his skepticism. To make tenable his position, it would be necessary, as a preliminary step, to argue that such beliefs are not completely justified.

SKEPTICISM WITH REGARD TO THE SENSES

We shall now turn to an examination of skeptical argument with respect to perceptual belief. By so doing we shall consider seriously and at length a challenge to one of the most fundamental and perhaps dogmatic assumptions of the current intellectual milieu, namely, that we obtain knowledge of the world by means of sense experience, by observation and perception. The initial stages of the argument may strike you as weird and disorienting. This is to be expected. When our fundamental assumptions and presuppositions are brought before the court of evidence and pronounced unfit, we feel abandoned in our uncertainty with nothing to sustain us. And then, however convincing the argument, we may repudiate the court as unjust. Such a response is both natural and unwarranted. A skeptic claiming our perceptual beliefs fall short of knowledge need not suggest that they be abandoned. As long as those beliefs remain more probable than those with which they compete, it is reasonable enough to maintain them. But if skepticism wins the day, then even those quite reasonable perceptual beliefs must be maintained with an open mind and be generously exposed to criticism and debate. To expose them to scrutiny and examination, though initially discomforting, like the exposure of one's flesh to the elements, soon becomes routine and, moreover, provides an invigorating sense of well-being. With these words of reassurance, we embark on our quest for skepticism with regard to the senses.

Our perceptual beliefs about what we hear, touch, and see are based on evidence. This might not at first seem obvious because such evidence is rarely formulated in words. We do not ordinarily justify our perceptual beliefs—for example, my belief that I see a red apple in my hand—by appealing to any other belief or statement. However, these beliefs are not without evidence. It is the unformulated evidence of our senses, the direct and immediate evidence of sensory stimulation, we assume justifies our beliefs. The question is whether this evidence provides complete justification for these beliefs.

A SKEPTICAL ARGUMENT

We shall begin our consideration of skepticism by turning to Plato. As we have said, Plato denied that we ever know that a pencil we see is yellow, or that any observable thing has or lacks any observable characteristic. One argument that Plato presented to defend his skepticism was an argument from the relativity of the observer.[5] Suppose something stimulates my sense organs and I see something red. It might happen that the object also stimulates the sense organs of someone else, who sees an object of a different color, for example, green. Imagine that the object is in fact white, that there is a transparent red plastic shield between the object and me, and a green plastic shield between the object and the other observer. If neither the other observer nor I know of the presence of these shields, then each of us might be entirely convinced that he sees the thing to be the color it really is. This rather contrived example has quite general implications. For if we pay close attention to what we see, it becomes plausible to claim that no two people see the same object in exactly the same way. For example, consider an ordinary copper penny. Pay very close attention to what you see when you look at this penny. If the penny remains stationary while you move about, or is moved while you remain stationary, what you see will constantly change. Thus when you see the penny from one angle you will see something almost perfectly round, but as you move away to one side and see the penny from a more oblique angle you will see something elliptical. Thus two people seeing the penny from different angles will not see the same thing. These are familiar facts of perceptual experience. How can they be used to serve the purposes of the skeptic?

This skeptical argument is exceedingly simple. If I see an object to be red and another sees it to be green, then the fact that I see an object a certain way does not prove that I know it is that way.

---

[5] Plato, *Phaedo*, 74; *Theaetetus*, 152–64.

If I know that an object is red, then it must indeed be red. But I might see an object as red when it is not red. Therefore I may see an object to be a certain color when it is not that color at all. Furthermore, exactly the same thing is true of shape and other characteristics we think we discern with our senses. We might see something to be red or elliptical when it is not true that the thing is red or elliptical at all and when, consequently, we do not know that it is red or elliptical. Let us call the characteristics we believe we discern with our senses *sensible qualities* or *sensible characteristics*. We may then conclude that it is perfectly possible to see something as having some sensible quality when it does not have that quality and, consequently, when we do not know it has that quality. We may also conclude, therefore, that seeing something as having some sensible quality does not constitute knowing that it has that quality.

Having reached the foregoing conclusion, it becomes possible to sustain the skeptical conclusion that we never know something has a sensible quality. Consider the way we think we know things have such qualities—for example, that the pencil before my eyes is yellow. Surely, if I know the thing is a yellow pencil, the only way I know this is by simply seeing that it is so. In this case, my knowing would have to consist of seeing the thing as a yellow pencil.

Of course, someone might tell me that something has a sensible quality and, consequently, I might know that it has, because he told me. But the reason I believe that his testimony gives me knowledge is that I assume someone, either this man or some other, has seen what quality the object has. If anyone knows what color the pencil is, or if anyone knows what sensible quality a thing has, then someone must know what color the pencil is, or what quality the object has, by having seen it to be that color or to have that quality.

Summary and Conclusion. The skeptical conclusion that no one ever knows what sensible quality a thing has can be derived from the preceding considerations. First from the premise

1. We sometimes see something as having some sensible characteristic when we do not know that it has that characteristic.

we derived the conclusion

2. Seeing something as having a sensible characteristic never constitutes knowing that it has that characteristic.

Using statement (2) as a premise together with the additional premise

3. We know something to have a sensible characteristic only if this knowledge sometimes consists of seeing the thing as having that quality.

we arrive at the skeptical conclusion

4. We never know that anything has any sensible characteristic.

If seeing that something has some sensible quality never constitutes knowledge, as premise (2) asserts, then it is false that knowing something has some sensible characteristic sometimes consists of seeing this is so. Thus, given premise (3) as well as (2), we may validly derive the conclusion that no one ever knows that anything has any sensible quality.

OBJECTION TO THE PRECEDING ARGUMENT
We might well object to the preceding remarks by noting that the skeptic appealed to exactly the kind of knowledge he is trying to prove we lack. Recall our earlier example where we imagined that one person saw an object to be red which another saw to be green. The object was really white. Thus the skeptical argument presupposes that we do know what color the object is. Similarly, when it was pointed out in defense of skepticism that a person sees a penny to be of different shapes as he moves about, the argument presupposed that we know that the object is a penny. In both examples the skeptic has presupposed that we know the very sort of thing he is trying to prove that we do not know. Therefore his argument is self-defeating.

REPLY OF THE SKEPTIC
There is a twofold reply to the preceding argument. In the first place, if a skeptic presents an argument starting from the assumption that we know certain things and shows that this leads by valid

reasoning to the conclusion that we do not know those things, then the argument, far from being self-defeating, would reduce the original assumption—that he knows the things in question—to absurdity. Indeed one typical way of refuting any contention is to show that if we assume that the contention is true, then we can show by argument that it is false. This kind of reasoning is often employed by master detectives in mystery thrillers. Someone thinks that the butler is the criminal, but this is shown to be false by the ingenious reasoning of the detective. The detective first asks us to assume, for the sake of argument, that the butler is the culprit and then he proceeds to show that this assumption is false because of the absurd consequences to which it leads. For example, it might lead to the conclusion that the butler traveled to the scene of the crime in five minutes from a city 100 miles away. Having shown that the assumption leads to absurdity, it is then rejected as false. Thus a skeptic may quite legitimately assume what he opposes is true in order to reduce this assumption to absurdity.

However, the skeptic need not assume that we know the things he is trying to prove that we do not know. To see that this is so, notice that the skeptic may, with perfect consistency, claim that he believes those things which he denies that anyone knows. For example, he might agree with us that the pencil before our eyes is yellow. He believes this is true, just as we do. But unlike those dogmatists who claim to know that the pencil is yellow, the skeptic roundly denies that he or anyone else knows this is true. In general, the skeptic may concede that he believes certain things have various sensible qualities, but he may simply deny that he knows this. The skeptic may believe the same things that we do, provided those beliefs do not concern what people do or do not know. He is a skeptic with respect to knowledge. Therefore the argument of the skeptic does not rest on the assumption that we know those things he is trying to prove we do not know. And even if his argument did start with such an assumption, this would in no way defeat his project. Skepticism can readily meet the foregoing objection.

A SECOND OBJECTION TO SKEPTICISM:
ON WHAT CONSTITUTES KNOWLEDGE

If there is nothing illicit in the procedure of the skeptic, then the only way of refuting him is to show either that his argument is invalid or that one of his premises is false. Where can we find such a weak link in his argument? The skeptic argues from the premise

1. We sometimes see a thing as having a sensible characteristic when we do not know it has that characteristic.

to the conclusion

2. Seeing a thing as having a sensible characteristic never constitutes knowing that it has that characteristic.

But this argument is invalid.

The skeptic has shown that it is not always the case that seeing something has some sensible quality constitutes knowing the thing has that quality. But this is a far cry from proving that such seeing never constitutes knowing. There may well be cases in which the two coincide—cases in which seeing does constitute knowing. There are counterexamples to the argument. When a person sees something that really is the case—for example, when a man sees a penny to be round—then surely sometimes he also knows the penny is round. Thus, in opposition to the skeptic we may maintain that his argument is invalid and that sometimes seeing something to be the case—*when it is in fact the case*—does constitute knowledge.

SKEPTICISM DEFENDED: THE POSSIBILITY OF ERROR

The argument of skepticism passes from the premise that we sometimes see something we do not know to the conclusion that seeing never constitutes knowing. But this inference can easily be bolstered by adding a perfectly true premise. For we may surely add that if a person knows something and is thus completely justified in believing it, he cannot possibly be mistaken in his belief. If a man says that he believes something but admits that he could be mistaken, then he has thereby admitted that he is not completely justified in his belief and does not know that what he believes is true. Similarly, if we say of another man that he could be mistaken, we have also asserted he lacks knowledge about the matter. Even when a man is not mistaken, if he could be mistaken, then he does not know that what he believes is true. Thus a person knows something only if he could not be mistaken in believing it.

The relevance of the preceding comments is easy to demonstrate. We argued that sometimes a person sees something to be the case when it is not the case and consequently he does not know it to be so. This shows that it is possible for a person to be mistaken in believing what he sees. Moreover, we are perfectly justified in arguing from the premise that people are sometimes mistaken when they believe what they see to the general conclusion that this is always logically possible. For either the premise that a person sees something to be a sensible quality entails that the thing is that quality or it does not entail this. Because we sometimes see something as having a sensible quality when it lacks that quality, obviously the entailment does not hold. If the entailment does not hold, then the premise that a person sees something to be the case does not entail that it is the case, and, therefore, it is always at least logically possible that a person should believe what he sees and yet be mistaken.

Having established the preceding points, we may now reconstruct the argument for skepticism. Whenever a person believes what he sees, it is possible that he is mistaken. If a person knows something, then it is not possible that he is mistaken. Therefore when a person believes something he sees, he does not know it. This conclusion is correctly derived from the premises antecedently defended.

Moreover, the argument employed to show that no one ever knows an object to have some sensible quality can be cogently generalized to show that no one even knows that any sensible object exists. For just as we sometimes see something as having some sensible *quality* when it does not have that quality, so we sometimes see some sensible *thing* when the thing does not even exist. Hallucinations are experiences of this sort. A man who has delirium tremens, or one who has taken a heavy dose of LSD, sometimes sees things—for example, pink rats—when there are no such things. Thus a person might believe what he sees exists and be completely mistaken in what he believes. Seeing an object does not constitute knowing that that object exists. A person who knows something cannot be mistaken.

Summary of the Argument. A key premise of the preceding argument is that perceptual beliefs, beliefs in what a person sees, allow for both qualitative and existential mistakes. By simplifying this premise, we may now formulate an argument for skepticism as follows:

1. We are sometimes mistaken in our perceptual beliefs.
2. If we are sometimes mistaken in our perceptual beliefs, then it is always logically possible that our perceptual beliefs are false.
3. If it is always logically possible that our perceptual beliefs are false, then we never know that any of our perceptual beliefs are true.
   Therefore
4. We never know that any of our perceptual beliefs are true.

This conclusion is validly deduced from the three premises which were just defended.

AN OBJECTION TO THE SECOND PREMISE
The skeptic has illicitly adopted the premise

2. If we are sometimes mistaken in our perceptual beliefs, then it is always logically possible that our perceptual beliefs are false.

In those cases in which our perceptual beliefs *are* false, it is obviously *possible* that they are false. But how does that prove it is *always* possible that our perceptual beliefs are false? It may be that there are some true perceptual beliefs which could not possibly be false. Until we have some reason for thinking otherwise, we are surely justified in asserting there are such true perceptual beliefs and, consequently, in rejecting premise (2) of the skeptical argument. We may also then reject the skeptical conclusion.

A SKEPTICAL REJOINDER: WHAT IS THE DIFFERENCE?
It is logically possible for any true perceptual belief to be mistaken. Often when a person has a true perceptual belief, he is in no better position to know that the belief is true than when his belief is false. Because a perceptual belief does not constitute knowledge when it is false, it does not constitute knowledge when it is true either.

To clarify this point suppose that two men are looking through different windows. The first man reports that there is a sphere on a table outside his window; he sees the sphere to be green. He sees this no matter from what vantage point he views things. Suppose further that the second man looking through his window sees and reports the very same thing. Each man has exactly the same justification for claiming to know that there is a green sphere outside his window. Each is in just as good a position to know this as the other, and neither is in any better position than the other. Surely, the only correct conclusion to reach is that either each man knows there is a green sphere outside his window or that neither of them knows this. It would be entirely arbitrary, and hence unreasonable, to say that one man knows this and the other does not.

However, it is perfectly possible that one of these men is mistaken and the other is not. Suppose the first man sees what he does because there is a green sphere outside his window. On the other hand, suppose the second sees what he does because he is being tricked with mirrors and drawings—there is no green sphere outside his window at all. Moreover, the deception is so excellent that from behind the windows no one could detect any difference in what is seen outside. The only reasonable conclusion is that neither man has knowledge. One man is mistaken and the other could have been.

What we have just imagined has perfectly general implications. We imagined two men who see the same thing even though what one of them sees really exists and what the other sees does not. In general, the experiences a man has when he sees somthing that really exists can be duplicated by the experiences of another man who is being deceived. Because the experiences in question provide the only evidence a man has for believing what he does, if one man fails to know what he believes, so must the other. If one is mistaken in believing something, then another man who has a similar belief based on similar experiences surely could have been mistaken—even if in fact he is not. Consider again the two men seeing a green sphere through their respective windows. The second man is mistaken in believing that there is a green sphere outside his window. This shows that the first man, who is in fact not mistaken, could have been mistaken. The second man was mistaken and the first man had no better evidence for what he believed than the first man did. Having the kind of evidence he has, the first man could have been mistaken. The proof is that the second man has just this kind of evidence and was mistaken. What was so in the one case could have been so in the other. The argument for skepticism requires no other assumption.

MODIFIED SKEPTICAL ARGUMENT

We may conclude then with a slightly modified formulation of the argument for skepticism. The first two premises of the argument, which differ from initial premises of the preceding skeptical argument, are as follows:

1. The experiences of a person who has a true perceptual belief may be exactly duplicated by the experiences of a person whose perceptual belief is exactly similar but false.
2. If the experiences of a person who has a true perceptual belief may be exactly duplicated by the experiences of a person whose perceptual belief is exactly similar but false, then it is always logically possible that our perceptual beliefs are false.

The next premise is the same as in the earlier argument.

3. If it is always logically possible that our perceptual beliefs are false, then no one ever knows that any of our perceptual beliefs are true.

From these three premises we can deduce the skeptical conclusion.

4. No one ever knows that any of our perceptual beliefs are true.

ANOTHER OBJECTION: A QUESTION
ABOUT GENERALIZATION

The preceding argument might be challenged, as were previous arguments of the skeptic, on the grounds that a general conclusion is drawn from a particular example. It is true that the two men looking through their respective windows might have almost exactly the same experiences even though one of them is mistaken and the other correct. Perhaps this shows that both of these men could have been mistaken and that neither of them knows what he believes. However, to concede this point is not to concede the more general conclusion that whenever anyone sees something which is in fact the case, his experiences may be exactly duplicated by the experiences of another person who sees the same thing, though in fact he is mistaken. For example, consider a man who is holding the object he sees directly in front of him. How could his experiences be duplicated by the experiences of someone who is not confronted with such an object? If they could not, then premise (1) of the preceding skeptical argument may be rejected.

FURTHER ARGUMENTS FOR SKEPTICISM: HALLUCINATION AND THE BRAINO

The sort of experiences a man has when he is really confronted with the object he sees may in general be duplicated by the experiences of a man who is not confronted with any such object. We noted in our experiment that both men view what they believe to be a green sphere from behind a window. But taking away the window, though it might help those two men to discover the trick that has been played on one of them, will not alter the primary force of the argument. For all of us view the world through the 'window' of our senses, and as a result, a man who sees something that does exist may in general have the same experience as one who sees something that does not exist.

THE ARGUMENT FROM HALLUCINATION

The clearest example of what we are trying to prove is supplied by Lady Macbeth. At one time, after the murder of Duncan, she sees blood on her hands. Moreover, she also feels the blood. Her hands are in fact covered with Duncan's blood. She goes mad. Part of her madness consists of seeing and feeling blood on her hands. Of course, this is an hallucination. Her hands are perfectly clean.

But the experiences she has when she is hallucinating might be exactly similar to the experiences she had when there really was blood on her hands. Because she could be mistaken at the later time in believing there is blood on her hands—indeed, she is mistaken—she could also be mistaken in believing the same thing at the earlier time. She had the same experiences to rely on in both cases. She was, from the standpoint of her own experiences, in no better position to know there was blood on her hands at the earlier time than at the later; the evidence of experience provided no better reason for believing this at the one time than the other. Consequently, it would be arbitrary, unreasonable, and epistemologically undemocratic to suppose that Lady Macbeth knows that she has blood on her hands at the earlier time but not at the later.

Hallucinations of this kind show that the experiences a person has when he sees something which exists may be duplicated by experiences when what he sees does not exist. Moreover, in addition to being misled by visual experience, the subject of hallucination may also be misled by tactual experience and the experience of the other senses as well. We may imagine that, when mad, Lady Macbeth not only sees but also feels and smells blood on her hand, though there is none there. Such an hallucination is complete and systematic with respect to all the senses. Unlike Macbeth's hallucination of seeing a dagger he cannot touch or feel, which is a partial and unsystematic hallucination affecting only one of his senses, Lady Macbeth's hallucination extends to all the senses and is, therefore, complete and systematic.

The example that we have just considered involves both existential and qualitative error. Lady Macbeth mistakenly believes there is blood on her hand when no blood exists—an existential error—and she believes that her hands are red and smell from blood when they are not red and do not smell from blood—a qualitative error. These perceptual beliefs involve both existential and qualitative errors and therefore do not constitute knowledge.

However, even when Lady Macbeth's perceptual beliefs are correct (immediately after the slaying of Duncan), they are based on sense experiences that are later duplicated when she is hallucinating and her perceptual beliefs are erroneous. Thus our defense of the premise

    1. The experiences of a person who has a true perceptual belief

may be duplicated by the experiences of a person whose perceptual belief is exactly similar but false.

is that such duplication of experiences may always result from hallucination. Erroneous perceptual beliefs based on hallucinatory experience obviously do not constitute knowledge, and correct perceptual beliefs are no better corroborated by experience. Therefore perceptual beliefs in general, whether true or in error, never constitute knowledge.

Again, it is important to guard against misunderstanding. By distinguishing between those cases which involve hallucination and those which do not, the skeptic is not contradicting himself by supposing that we know which cases are which. All the skeptic need suppose is that some beliefs about such matters are true and others false. The skeptic would deny that Lady Macbeth knows she has blood on her hands immediately after the slaying of Duncan, but he could consistently concede that she believed this and that her belief was true. We may, with perfect consistency, both agree that there is a distinction between hallucination which evokes false perceptual belief and ordinary experience which evokes true perceptual belief, and deny that we know the former is false and the latter true. That is the position adopted here by the skeptic.

A COMMON-SENSE OBJECTION: IS HALLUCINATION ALWAYS POSSIBLE?

Our objection to the preceding argument of the skeptic is exactly analogous to our objection to his argument based on the example of the man who sees a nonexistent green sphere. In that case we objected that the skeptic was arguing from a single example to a perfectly general conclusion. We pointed out that this is an entirely illegitimate procedure. Though we conceded that the experiences of the man who sees the existent green sphere might be exactly duplicated by the experiences of the man who sees a nonexistent green sphere, we denied that the experiences of a man who sees something that really exists can always be duplicated by the experiences of a man who sees something that does not exist. We conceded what was said about the particular example but denied the general conclusion derived from it.

Again we are faced with a similar case. The skeptic produces an example, Lady Macbeth with and without bloody hands. The experiences she has when she sees something that exists are duplicated in hallucination when she sees something that does not exist. It is concluded that when a person sees something that exists, his experiences may well be exactly duplicated in hallucination when he sees something that does not exist. But how does this general conclusion follow from that one example? By what means does the skeptic prove that it is always possible to duplicate in hallucination the sense experiences we have when our perceptual beliefs are true? How does he demonstrate that hallucination is always possible no matter what our experiences are like? So far no such demonstration has been given; therefore we have no reason to accept the skeptic's conclusion.

SKEPTICISM DEFENDED: THE ONE AND THE MANY

There is a question here of where the burden of proof lies. If one concedes that a hallucination like Lady Macbeth's is possible, what reason is there for denying that hallucination is possible no matter what? When we believe we see something in our own hands, that is the kind of belief that we ordinarily accept with the greatest confidence and equanimity. When we believe we see something at a distance or when our vision is obscured in some other way, we may have some doubt. But when we see something in our very own hands and feel it and smell it as well, then we have no doubt. Instead we feel certain that the thing exists. If experiences of this kind may be produced by hallucination, and the resultant perceptual beliefs be in error, then how can we reasonably deny that any experiences can be produced by hallucination and consequently be accompanied by mistaken perceptual beliefs? Surely we cannot deny this. The range of experiences that hallucination might possibly produce is without limit. And the argument for skepticism is perfectly sound.

A DEFENSE OF COMMON SENSE: COHERENCE
AND THE TESTIMONY OF OTHERS

The argument for skepticism just stated assumes that complete and systematic hallucination is always possible. This is the premise we shall now refute. Sometimes hallucinations occur and mislead us concerning what exists in our very hands. But we are not entirely at the epistemological mercy of such hallucinations, for we do have ways of discovering when our experiences are hallucinatory. Indeed, unless there were some way of telling that we do have hallucinations, even when these hallucinations are very systematic and complete, we would not now be in any position to assert that such hallucinations are possible. But if we do have some way of telling whether or not we are suffering an hallucination, then there must be some perceptual beliefs that are accompanied by experiences that rule out the possibility of hallucination. In this case the experiences on which our belief is based could not be hallucinatory.

Moreover, it is not difficult to explain what kind of experiences rule out the possibility of hallucination. It is only necessary to ask ourselves how we in fact discover that we are suffering a hallucination. One way such a discovery is made is through the testimony of other people who know that our experiences are hallucinatory. Many people were in a position to tell Lady Macbeth that her experiences were hallucinatory, and although in her madness she would not accept such information, it was entirely available to her. Because we are not primarily concerned with madness but rather with normality, it is quite relevant that a normal man may discover that some of his experiences are hallucinatory through the help of others. Moreover, when one is in the company of others and all agree concerning what they see, it is altogether reasonable to assume that no hallucination is taking place. Nonetheless, one qualification is necessary. Sometimes, in unusual circumstances, we know that a whole group of people is susceptible to hallucination. For example, suppose a whole group of people have taken a drug known to produce hallucinations or suppose they have suffered some acute physical hardship like being deprived of drink or sleep. Such conditions might produce group hallucinations. However, if people and circumstances are altogether ordinary, as they usually are, then agreement in perceptual belief rules out the possibility of hallucination.

There is another way in which hallucination is detected which does not require the testimony of others. It concerns the coherence among our experiences. A person who suffers the hallucination of drinking water when none is available to him may see, feel, and even taste water which, because of his hallucination, he mistakenly believes exists. However, if he has been long deprived of water, he will soon notice that his thirst is not at all abated. Men have, in fact, concluded from such experiences that they were suffering a hallucination. They were subsequently no longer misled. Thus in this case there is a failure of experiential coherence. By drinking water one expects to quench his thirst, and when one has the experience of seeing, feeling, and drinking water but one's thirst is not quenched, then the experiences seem incoherent and incomprehensible. Incoherence is therefore a sign of hallucination, and coherence is, on the other hand, a sign of reality. Indeed experiences that are sufficiently coherent exclude the possibility of hallucination.

Finally, these criteria of nonhallucination, or of veridical experience, may be satisfied together and may thereby mutually reinforce each other. Often our experiences are entirely coherent and our perceptual beliefs completely agree with the beliefs of others in our company.

SKEPTICISM DEFENDED: ON HOW NOT TO BEG QUESTIONS

The appeal of the foregoing argument to the testimony of others as a safeguard against being misled by hallucination begs the question. For to know what the testimony of another is, we must first know that we are confronted by another and know what he is saying. But to know these things is to know something by seeing or otherwise perceiving that they are so. The argument rests squarely on the assumption that perceiving such things constitutes knowledge. Of course, it is precisely this assumption that the arguments for skepticism are intended to refute. Moreover, it is quite possible to extend these arguments so that they apply to the present case. Suppose Lady Macbeth, in addition to having the hallucination of seeing, feeling, and smelling blood on her hands, also has the hallucination of hearing others tell her that there is blood on her hands. The experience of hearing such testimony of agreement from others may be duplicated in hallucinatory experiences just as well as other experiences of seeing, feeling, smelling, and tasting.

Moreover, the second argument based on experiential coherence has the same weakness. Some hallucinations do make themselves manifest to their victim by some kind of incoherence, but such a hallucination is partial or incomplete. Some expected experiential feature does not turn up, and the experience shows itself to be hallucinatory by being a bit too surprising. But why must we assume that hallucinations always expose themselves in this way? What proof is there that coherent and systematic experiences cannot possibly result from hallucination? There is no reason to suppose that such hallucinations are impossible. Therefore, we are again justified in concluding that the experiences that a man has when his perceptual beliefs are true may be exactly repeated in hallucination when his perceptual beliefs are false. Consequently, such beliefs never constitute knowledge.

THE BRAINO ARGUMENT

However, we must pause long enough over the argument of our critic to ensure that we are not again accused of passing too quickly from the particular example to a general conclusion. To rid ourselves of this recurring objection, let us indulge in a bit of science fiction and by so doing prove once and for all that skepticism is the tenable and correct position. Imagine that a superscientist invents a machine, we shall call it a "braino," which enables him to produce hallucinations in certain subjects. The machine operates by influencing the brain of a subject who wears a special cap, called a "braino cap." When the braino cap is placed on the head of a subject, then the operator of the braino can affect the brain of the subject in such a way as to produce any hallucination in the subject that the operator of the braino wishes. The braino is a superhallucination-producing machine. The hallucinations produced by it may be as complete, systematic, and coherent as the operator of the braino desires to make them.

It is to be admitted that there are no such machines. However, such a machine is certainly a possibility. There is no contradiction whatsoever involved in the idea of such a machine, and, for all we know, someone may actually invent such a machine in the future. What does the possibility of such a machine prove? It proves the experiences a person has when his perceptual beliefs are true could be duplicated in hallucination when the same perceptual beliefs are false. This shows that there is no mark or sign in experience by which we may distinguish true perceptual beliefs from those false perceptual beliefs which are confusions resulting from hallucination.

An analogy helps to illustrate the importance of the preceding considerations. Suppose that you are confronted with a barrel full of apples some of which are rotten and others of which are not. Usually there will be some sign or mark by which you can tell the rotten apples from the good ones. The rotten apples will be brown or soft, or they will have some other visible defect by which you can detect their condition. On the other hand, the good apples will be firm, red, and otherwise appear desirable. Thus we can tell the difference between a good apple and a rotten one because we have signs to guide us.

However, suppose we are confronted with a barrel of apples that are quite indistinguishable in appearance, though some of the apples are rotten at the core. There is, we may imagine, no external sign by which we can tell whether the apples are rotten. We are now presented with an apple from this barrel and prohibited from cutting it open. In this predicament if someone should ask us whether the apple is rotten or good, the only thing to reply is, "I don't know." We might add, "There is no way to tell."

Similarly, because there is no mark or sign in experience by which we can distinguish true perceptual beliefs of ordinary experience from false perceptual beliefs arising in hallucination, if someone should ask us whether a perceptual belief of ours is true or false, the only thing to reply is, "I don't know." We might add, "There is no way to tell." Just as there is no way to tell whether the apples in the second barrel are rotten because we have no experiential signs to guide us, so there is no way to tell whether our perceptual beliefs are true because we have no experiential signs to guide us.

There is no way to tell by experience whether our perceptual beliefs are true, and with only experience to guide us, we have no way to rule out the possibility of error. Even when our perceptual beliefs happen to be true, we could just as well have been mistaken. Indeed, when a perceptual belief is true this is more a matter of good luck than good sense. Of course, no belief that turns out to be true as a matter of luck can reasonably be counted as knowledge.

AN OBJECTION: POSSIBILITY AND ACTUALITY

In the first arguments we examined the skeptic argued from a single example of hallucination to a general conclusion, which is surely a fallacy, but having now avoided this fallacy, he argues from possibility to actuality, which is no less of a fallacy. The present argument starts from the premise that the braino is a logical possibility, and consequently that it is a logical possibility that there should be hallucinations that are coherent, complete, and systematic in every way. From this premise of logical possibility he arrives at the conclusion that we *in fact* have no way of telling whether or not we are hallucinating. By what line of reasoning may such a factual conclusion be got from a premise concerning mere possibility? Even if it is logically possible that hallucinations should be coherent, complete, and systematic, hallucinations are not in fact so hard to detect. Therefore experience does *in fact* enable us to tell whether our perceptual beliefs are true or false.

A SKEPTICAL REPLY: HOW TO PASS FROM POSSIBILITY TO ACTUALITY

The contention that "hallucinations are not in fact so hard to detect" is the very heart of the issue. If the braino is a logical possibility, then how can we tell that hallucinations are not in fact so hard to detect? Perhaps, on the contrary, we constantly suffer hallucinations that we cannot detect. If it is logically possible that hallucinations should be coherent, complete, and systematic in every way, then there is no way of detecting at any moment that we are not suffering an hallucination. Our critic supposes there are in fact many hallucinations we can detect, but this is beside the basic point. The problem is to explain how it is possible to tell that we are *not* hallucinating. Our braino argument was intended to establish that we can never tell this, even if we can sometimes tell that we are hallucinating.

That the argument does establish this can be seen by reflecting again on our barrels of apples. Suppose it is easy to detect some rotten apples. They have brown spots, are squishy, and so on. But suppose it is difficult to tell that other apples are rotten, and if we are limited to external examination, this is quite impossible. There is no external sign of the rottenness of some rotten apples. It would be quite ridiculous in this case to claim that we can tell when an apple is not rotten because we can sometimes detect that apples are rotten.

An exactly analogous argument applies to the case of hallucination. We can sometimes detect that our experience is hallucinatory.

But it would be ridiculous to conclude from this that we can always tell when an experience is not hallucinatory. Sometimes we can tell that we are hallucinating, but we have no way of telling that we are not.

Our argument to support this claim is best put in the form of a challenge. Consider some perceptual belief that you would maintain does not result from hallucination. What experience or experiences guarantee this? Indeed, what experiences provide you with any *evidence* of it? Notice that whatever experience you indicate, the braino argument will be quite sufficient to prove that such an experience is no guarantee that you are not hallucinating. All we need do is imagine that you have, unknown to yourself, a braino cap on your head. The operator of the braino is producing hallucinatory experiences which are the very experiences you claim guarantee that you are not hallucinating!

The passage from the possibility of hallucination to the conclusion that there is in fact no way of telling that one is not hallucinating is legitimate because the former possibility may be used to reject any experience that is so impertinent as to present itself as a sure sign of reality. Any such experience can be shown to be unequal to this task on the grounds that it is perfectly possible for such an experience to be produced in hallucination.

THE EVIL-OPERATOR ARGUMENT

The preceding argument may be reinforced if we let our examples become even more fanciful than we have heretofore. Descartes imagined a very powerful evil genius who is bent on constantly deceiving us. We have supplied Descartes with the technical means for this imaginary experiment. Imagine that all men are controlled by the braino and that the machine is run by some evil being, Dr. O, who plots to keep us completely in error through hallucination. Dr. O does not wish to be detected, so he supplies hallucinations that are coherent, complete, and systematic. Indeed, the hallucinations he produces in us are a perfect counterfeit of reality. Our experiences fulfill our expectations and contain no more surprises than we would expect from reality. But it is not reality we experience; our perceptual beliefs about the world are quite mistaken, for the source of our experiences is a mere machine, the braino, which creates hallucinations. In such a predicament we might have just the sort of perceptual beliefs we now have, based on exactly similar experiences to those we now have. But our perceptual beliefs would be altogether false.

The imagined situation does not differ from ours with respect to the reasons or evidence we would have for our perceptual beliefs. Experience is virtually the same in both cases. Consequently, if we lack knowledge in one situation, we must surely lack it in the other. Obviously we lack knowledge when we are controlled by the braino, for our perceptual beliefs are false then. Hence, we also lack knowledge in our present situation. More precisely, our perceptual beliefs fail to constitute knowledge in either case.

We are not suggesting that the braino exists or that we are controlled by it. The preceding argument does not depend on believing anything so strange as that; it depends only on the premise that a certain situation is imaginable, and hence, logically possible. This possibility shows that the experiences on which we base our perceptual beliefs might lead as easily to error as to truth. If the imagined situation really existed, then we would be led to error. We believe we are not controlled by such a machine, and if we are fortunate in this belief, then no doubt many of our perceptual beliefs are true. But it is good fortune and not good evidence that we should thank for the correctness of these beliefs. We are just lucky if there is no Dr. O controlling us with a braino. Our perceptual beliefs, when true, are so merely as a matter of good luck. Based on virtually the same experiences, those beliefs are false if we are not lucky. If a belief is true as a result of luck, then it is a lucky guess—not knowledge. In short, we are fortunate if there is no evil being controlling us with a braino, and from that good fortune may result the further good fortune that most of our perceptual beliefs are true. But it is just a matter of luck, nothing epistemologically more glorious than that.

SUMMARY OF THE SKEPTICAL POSITION

Earlier we defended skepticism by employing an argument the first premise of which was

1. The experiences of a person who has a true perceptual belief may be exactly duplicated by the experiences of a person whose perceptual belief is exactly similar but false.

From this premise and the following two premises

2. If the experiences of a person who has a true perceptual belief may be exactly duplicated by the experiences of a person whose perceptual belief is exactly similar but false, then it is always logically possible that any of our perceptual beliefs are false.

and

3. If it is always logically possible that any of our perceptual beliefs are false, then no one ever knows that any of our perceptual beliefs are true.

we deduced the skeptical conclusion

4. No one ever knows that any perceptual belief is true.

Premise (1) of the argument was called into question by the opponents of skepticism, and we have now derived this premise from the following premises:

5. The braino hypothesis is logically possible.
6. If the braino hypothesis is logically possible, then any experience may be duplicated in hallucination.
7. If any experience may be duplicated in hallucination, then the experiences of a person who has a true perceptual belief may be exactly duplicated by the experiences of a person whose perceptual belief is exactly similar but false.

From these true premises, premise (1) may be validly deduced.

AN OBJECTION: THE DEGRADATION OF DR. O

Let us examine the situation we are imagining, namely, one in which we are all deceived by the evil genius Dr. O, who is busy supplying hallucinations to us with his braino. Is this situation really possible? Consider it in very concrete terms. Imagine Dr. O contriving to deceive us. Moreover, let us concentrate on the experience of one man, whose name is Tom, as Dr. O goes about deceiving him. Eventually we shall consider how Dr. O might deceive Tom with the braino, but first let us consider a somewhat different technique Dr. O has for deceiving Tom. The point of doing so will become clear later.

Suppose Dr. O is that evil genius of whom Descartes writes:

I shall then suppose, not that God who is supremely good and the fountain of truth, but some evil genius not less powerful than deceitful, has employed his whole energies in deceiving me; I shall consider that the heavens, the earth, the colors, figures, sound, and all other external things are nought but illusions and dreams of which this evil genius has availed himself, in order to lay traps for my credulity. . . .[6]

Let us now imagine our evil genius about to deceive Tom. Our imagination will be guided by the witty hand of O. K. Bouwsma, who writes:

He took no delight in common lies, everyday fibs, little ones, old ones. He wanted something new and something big. He scratched his genius; he uncovered an idea. And he scribbled on the inside of his tattered halo, "Tomorrow, I will change everything, everything, everything. I will change flowers, human beings, trees, hills, sky, the sun, and everything else into paper. Paper alone I will not change. There will be paper flowers, paper human beings, paper trees. And human beings will be deceived. They will think that there are flowers, human beings, and trees, and there will be nothing but paper. It will be gigantic. And it ought to work. After all men have been deceived with much less trouble. There was a sailor, a Baptist I believe, who said that all was water. And there was no more water than there is now. And there was a pool-hall keeper who said that all was billiard balls. That's a long time ago of course, a long time before they opened one, and listening, heard that it was full of the sound of a trumpet. My prospects are good. I'll try it."

[6] René Descartes, *Philosophical Works of Descartes,* trans. by E. S. Haldane and G. R. T. Ross, two vols. (Cambridge: Cambridge University Press, 1912), Vol. I, p. 147.

And the evil genius followed his own directions and did according to his words. And this is what happened.

Imagine a young man, Tom, bright today as he was yesterday, approaching a table where yesterday he had seen a bowl of flowers. Today it suddenly strikes him that they are not flowers. He stares at them troubled, looks away, and looks again. Are they flowers? He shakes his head. He chuckles to himself. "Huh: that's funny. Is this a trick? Yesterday there certainly were flowers in that bowl." He sniffs suspiciously, hopefully, but smells nothing. His nose gives no assurance. He thinks of the birds that flew down to peck at the grapes in the picture and of the mare that whinnied at the likeness of Alexander's horse. Illusions! The picture oozed no juice, and the likeness was still. He walked slowly to the bowl of flowers. He looked, and he sniffed, and he raised his hand. He stroked a petal lightly, lover of flowers, and he drew back. He could scarcely believe his fingers. They were not flowers. They were paper.

As he stands, perplexed, Milly, friend and dear, enters the room. Seeing him occupied with the flowers, she is about to take up the bowl and offer them to him, when once again he is overcome with feelings of strangeness. She looks just like a great big doll. He looks more closely, closely as he dares, seeing this may be Milly after all. Milly, are you Milly?—that wouldn't do. Her mouth clicks as she opens it, speaking, and it shuts precisely. Her forehead shines, and he shudders at the thought of Mme. Tussaud's. Her hair is plaited, evenly, perfectly, like Milly's but as she raises one hand to guard its order, touching it, preening, it whispers like a newspaper. Her teeth are white as a genteel monthly. Her gums are pink, and there is a clapper in her mouth. He thinks of mamma dolls, and of the rubber doll he used to pinch; it has a misplaced navel right in the pit of the back, that whistled. Galatea in paper! Illusions!

He noted all these details, flash by flash by flash. He reaches for a chair to steady himself and just in time. She approaches with the bowl of flowers, and, as the bowl is extended toward him, her arms jerk. The suppleness, the smoothness, the roundness of life is gone. Twitches of a smile mislight up her face. He extends his hand to take up the bowl and his own arms jerk as hers did before. He takes the bowl, and as he does so sees his hand. It is pale, fresh, snowy. Trembling, he drops the bowl, but it does not break, and the water does not run. What a mockery!

He rushes to the window, hoping to see the real world. The scene is like a theatre-set. Even the pane in the window is drawn very thin, like cellophane. In the distance are the forms of men walking about and tossing trees and houses and boulders and hills upon the thin cross section of a truck that echoes only echoes of chugs as it moves. He looks into the sky upward, and it is low. There is a patch straight above him, and one seam is loose. The sun shines out of the blue like a drop of German silver. He reaches out with his pale hand, crackling the cellophane, and his hand touches the sky. The sky shakes and tiny bits of it fall, flaking his white hand with confetti. Make-believe![7]

The lesson to be learned from this story is not that evil always fails, but that deception always presupposes the possibility of detection. To discover that he is being deceived, all Tom needs to do is notice that what he takes to be flowers, Milly, and so on, are really paper. So the fraud is exposed to him.

However, the skeptic has asked us to imagine that Dr. O is not relying on anything so flimsy and dubious as paper, instead the evil genius will supply our experiences by using the braino. Thus he does not need to bother using one thing to make us think it is something else. Indeed we might well imagine that he carries out his mischief when we are confronted with nothing whatever. Because it is the braino that produces hallucinations, we need not suppose that there are any of the usual things around in the world at all when Dr. O deceives his victims. Therefore let us suppose that all those things are destroyed. We may thus imagine that Tom stands alone on a barren world, a braino cap firmly attached to his skull. He is, of course, quite oblivious to his predicament, for Dr. O, true to his plan, is supplying Tom with hallucinations that exactly duplicate the experiences of his usual existence. Were Tom to write in his diary (which, alas, no longer exists), he might write as Bouwsma imagines:

[7] O. K. Bouwsma, "Descartes' Evil Genius," *The Philosophical Review*, Vol. 58 (1949), pp. 141–42.

"Today, as usual, I came into the room and there was the bowl of flowers on the table. I went up to them, caressed them, and smelled over them. I thank God for flowers! There's nothing so real to me as flowers. Here the genuine essence of the world's substance, at its gayest and most hilarious speaks to me. It seems unworthy even to think of them as erect, and waving on pillars of sap. Sap! Sap!"

There was more in the same vein, which we need not bother to record. I might say that the evil genius was a bit amused, snickered in fact, as he read the words "so real," "essence," "substance," etc., but later he frowned and seemed puzzled. Tom went on to describe how Milly came into the room, and how glad he was to see her. They talked about the flowers. Later he walked to the window and watched the gardener clearing a space a short distance away. The sun was shining, but there were a few heavy clouds. He raised the window, extended his hand and four large drops of rain wetted his hand. He returned to the room and quoted to Milly a song from *The Tempest*. He got all the words right, and was well pleased with himself. There was more he wrote, but this is enough to show how quite normal everything seems. And, too, how successful the evil genius is.[8]

The success of the evil genius is quite complete. What he has destroyed he deceives Tom into believing exists by causing Tom to hallucinate. Tom's hallucinating experiences exactly duplicate the experiences he would have if the things destroyed still existed. It is an extraordinarily clever deception, but in spite of this apparent success Dr. O has more nearly succeeded in fooling himself than Tom. Why is this so? Let us return to the supposedly barren scene of the drama.

Imagine that Dr. O, having deceived Tom, grows weary of his unacknowledged success and wishes, while continuing the deception, to have Tom acknowledge this accomplishment. The next day when Tom is having the experience of entering the room where the flowers stand, the evil genius tactfully suggests to Tom that

8 Ibid., pp. 146–47.

there are no flowers. Tom then has the experience of raising the flowers to his nose, smelling them, and touching them. Tom is reassured. He denies there is deception. After all, having looked, sniffed, felt, with satisfying results, what could the evil genius possibly mean by saying he is deceived? To this the evil genius replies, "Your flowers are nothing but a hallucination." But Tom is unpersuaded. His flowers are perfect. A hallucination? Never!

At this point in the drama Dr. O is sorely tempted just to throw the switch on the braino and expose the fraud to Tom. But to do so is to give up the deception, which he does not want to do because of all his labors. So the evil genius, not feeling so ingenious now, is faced with a dilemma. Either he can maintain the deception—in which case Tom, refusing to acknowledge the deception, will deny that it exists—or he can alter his plan—in which case Tom, detecting that he has been fooled, will convert a perfect deception into a perfect farce. Either way Dr. O will fail to attain his goal. For if the deception continues, how is Dr. O to make any sense of the idea to Tom?

From Tom's standpoint the perfect deception is no deception at all. Once all the usual experiences are made to occur, the suggestion that Tom is suffering a hallucination is made senseless. Tom can make no sense of it. It is just as senseless if we suppose such a deception is being played on us. When a man is hallucinating there must be ways to detect that this is so, even if the victim, like Lady Macbeth, fails to detect the hallucination in these ways. Once all the appropriate tests are made in order to ensure one is not hallucinating, the suggestion that one might still be hallucinating is meaningless. What we mean by saying that a person is hallucinating is that some such tests will fail. The perfect hallucination is a bubble of semantic incongruity that disappears under the pressure of semantic scrutiny.

The skeptic argues that there is no sure way of detecting a perfect hallucination, that is, a perfectly coherent, complete, systematic hallucination. He concludes that the belief that we are not hallucinating is, if true, nothing more than a lucky guess. The defect in his argument is that he assumes a perfect hallucination is possible. Imagination, when it works overtime, might convince one this is so, but it cannot be. For something to be possible it must be meaningful. However, imagination is not restricted by bonds of meaningfulness. There is little difficulty in imagining something when the very idea of it is completely meaningless. We can imagine a cat in a tree with the parts of the cat disappearing one by one, first the tail, then the paw, then the body, until finally all that is left of the cat in the tree is a feline grin. We can imagine this, but the idea of the grin without a head is perfectly meaningless. The remarkable scope of the human imagination is a joy in life, but it is a trap for philosophical reflection. This is true precisely because it is so easy to suppose that whatever is imaginable is possible, which is a treacherous and mistaken supposition.

The worldless hallucination of a world is precisely like the catless grin of a cat. We can imagine both but neither is literally meaningful.

Thus our reply to skepticism is a semantic one. The evil genius argument of the skeptic proceeds from the premise that a perfect hallucination is possible. But the idea of a perfect hallucination is meaningless, and hence such a hallucination is not possible. Because the argument of the skeptic proceeds from a false premise it must be rejected.

SKEPTICISM DEFENDED: A CAUSAL THEORY OF PERCEPTION

The preceding argument rests on a thesis about what we mean when we say we see the flowers, blood, cats, and so forth. However, the meaning of such statements, when properly analyzed, favors skepticism instead of refuting it. Suppose I say or believe there really is an object—for example, a pink rose—which I see. What does this statement mean? It means that my experience of seeing a pink rose is caused in a very direct way by a pink rose—not a braino or any other source of hallucinatory experience. Thus, perceptual beliefs are causal beliefs, beliefs about the cause of our sensory experiences.

If this is a correct analysis of perceptual belief, the argument to prove that the idea of a perfect hallucination is meaningless must itself be rejected. For if a perceptual belief amounts to the belief that the experiences one is having, the seeing and feeling, are caused by the object one sees, then it is surely possible such beliefs are mistaken, because those experiences may be caused by the braino instead. To return to the saga of Tom and Dr. O, if Tom believes that the experiences of seeing, smelling, and touching a flower are caused by a pink rose, then it is meaningful, even if false, to suppose those experiences are caused not by flowers, but by a braino in the hands of Dr. O.

To switch from flowers to apples, let us consider again the rotten apples that are externally indistinguishable from the good ones. When we assert that an apple is rotten at the core even though it appears to be good, we are asserting that our experiences are not a reliable guide to the internal condition of the apple. Once we get past appearances we will find a rotten core. But suppose we have no way of telling whether the apple is rotten except by considering its external appearance. In this case rotten apples that are completely pleasing in appearance would go undetected. Under these conditions it must be admitted that some rotten apples are undetectable, and therefore we do not know whether the apples before us are rotten or good.

However, suppose that we are now confronted with someone who roundly declares that the idea of undetectable rotten apples is meaningless. He might continue, "Part of what is meant by saying that an apple is rotten is that there are *external* ways of detecting this even if the apple grader, being careless, fails to detect rottenness in these ways. Once you have made all the appropriate external tests to insure that the apple is not rotten, the suggestion that, after all, you might still have a rotten apple, is meaningless." It is perfectly apparent that this argument is utterly mistaken. Even after all the appropriate external tests have been made to ensure that the apple is not rotten, it might be rotten anyway. So much the worse for our tests! There is nothing meaningless about the idea that rotten apples might be indistinguishable from good ones, as far as external appearances go.

There is an obvious analogy between the rotten apples that are externally indistinguishable from good ones and the perfect hallucination that is indistinguishable from reality. The perfect hallucination is similar in a crucial respect to the rotten apple. The belief that the experience of seeing a pink rose is caused by a rose is like the belief that the appearance of a healthy apple is caused by the apple being healthy. The former belief will be mistaken when seeing a rose is caused not by a rose, but by the braino, just as the latter belief will be mistaken when the appearance of a good apple is caused not by a healthy apple, but by a rotten one. The beliefs are alike in that they are beliefs about the causes of our experiences.

Ordinarily we think that our experiences are good guides to their causes, but it is not meaningless to suppose otherwise. It is altogether meaningful to suppose that there are apples that look perfectly good even though they are rotten, and it is just as meaningful to suppose that there are experiences that look perfectly good even though they are hallucinations.

There is one more point concerning this analogy that is illuminating to explore. In the case of the apples, it is possible, so we believe, to penetrate beyond the external appearances and get directly at the core. Then we shall be able to tell in the most direct and immediate way whether the apple is rotten. However, suppose that there was no possible way of doing this. Then we would have no way whatever of telling what the apple was like beneath the skin other than by observing the skin itself. If we had no way of telling what the apple was like beneath the skin, we would have no opportunity to observe that apples with a certain appearance are almost never rotten. Of course, apples rotten at the surface are easily detected. But what of all those apples that are not rotten at the surface? We would have no way of discovering them at all. It is only by observing a correlation between the external appearance of apples and their internal condition that we can discover that certain outer appearances are the sign of a rotten apple. If we could never observe the inner state, we could never establish such a correlation. Any apple that was not rotten at the surface would be an apple about whose inner state we would have to confess we were entirely ignorant. We would have absolutely no way of knowing what it was like at the core.

Our belief that reality is the cause of our experiences is exactly like the belief that the apple is good when we have no way of observing the inner state of any apple. We can no more "penetrate the skin" of our experiences to observe the cause than we could, in the case imagined, penetrate the skin of the apple to see what is beneath. We have nothing to go on but our experiences in deciding what reality is like. So our situation with respect to knowing reality is just like the situation in which we have no way of telling whether an apple is good but by observing its external appearance. We concluded with respect to the apples that we would have no way of knowing that they were good if we never had anything to go on except our experiences.

Assuming that our perceptual beliefs are beliefs about the causes of our sensory experiences, we have no way of knowing whether these perceptual beliefs are true. If we believe a pink rose caused us to see a pink rose, we have no way of knowing that this is true. We are never able to observe a correlation between the experience of seeing a rose and the cause of that experience, because we have nothing to go on except those experiences themselves. We have no way of observing things beyond our experience. But if we have nothing to go on but our experiences, then it is quite meaningful, even if false, to suppose that anything whatever is the cause of our most coherent, complete, and systematic experiences. For example, it is meaningful to suppose that they are hallucinations caused by a braino. If our experiences are caused by the things we believe they are, then we are lucky enough to have true beliefs. But, once again, whether such beliefs happen to be true will be a matter of sheer luck; consequently, such beliefs cannot constitute knowledge.

DOGMATISM DEFENDED: THE MEANING OF PERCEPTUAL BELIEFS

The apple argument, as it may fittingly be called, rests on the assumption that our perceptual beliefs are beliefs about the causes of our sensory experiences. Assuming this to be so, the skeptic concludes that we might be deceived by hallucination concerning the true nature of such causes, and he concludes that the idea of a perfect hallucination is meaningful and possible. The whole argument depends on the first assumption, namely, that perceptual beliefs are about causes. Can we show this assumption to be false?

If we reflect on our earlier experiment with Tom and extend the experiment to include ourselves, we shall discover that our perceptual beliefs are about what we do or would experience and about nothing else. They are not beliefs about something that lies beneath the "skin" of experience and is the forever unobservable cause of experience. To see that this is so, imagine the following. Dr. O is using his braino to deceive all of us—or better yet, suppose he has found an even better means to induce hallucinations without using any apparatus at all. Now imagine that he wants to deceive us all as he has deceived Tom. The first thing he does is to destroy all the animals, vegetables, and things of the physical world. He leaves intact only a barren earth and as much of us as he requires to practice his deception. We leave it to the reader to imagine precisely how much of us he leaves. Descartes thought bodyless minds would be enough to make the deception work, but if you hold some view according to which we need a body or some part of a body to have hallucinations, we can allow you that. There is no need to stretch your imagination beyond its capacity.

We now have only a barren earth and people (or some part of them) undergoing hallucinations. Dr. O, our evil genius, wishes to deceive us perfectly, so hallucinatory experiences go on as usual. When I awake in the morning I have these familiar experiences of feeling drowsy, rising slowly, seeing the knubby green curtains protecting me from the pain of day, stretching sleep-stiffened muscles, and so on. The day goes on as usual, with its customary pleasures and annoyances, and is ordinary in every respect. The experience of other days will, happily, be different, and so it will go until I die and experience no more. But if all the usual experiences occur, what sense is there in saying that I am suffering a hallucination? The deception fails because it is meaningless.

We have been through this argument before. The difference lies in applying it to your own case. What sense would it make to *you* if you were told that your whole life to date was a hallucination, and one, moreover, that would continue until death do you and Dr. O part? How would you prove that what you had been told was false? Surely the only thing you could point out in reply is that the word 'hallucination' was being used in an odd way. For, what we mean by 'reality' as opposed to 'hallucination,' is that certain sorts of experiences rather than others are to be had, and, indeed, have been had. What we call experiences of reality, as opposed to hallucinatory experiences are just the sort of experiences we are now having. These experiences, which we are supposing to be supplied by Dr. O, are just the sort of experiences we refer to when we speak of reality. They are, in effect, a paradigm of nonhallucinatory experiences; consequently, the idea that such experiences are hallucinatory is meaningless.

Therefore Dr. O has unwittingly reproduced the reality he meant to destroy. From his point of view, if we imagine him to have peculiar powers of perception that we lack, there might be something missing. But from our standpoint nothing at all is missing. Reality is spread out before us in all its variety.

This argument shows that our perceptual beliefs are *not* beliefs about the causes of our experiences but are instead beliefs about what experiences we are having and about what experiences we would have if conditions were altered. The proof is that there is no other explanation for why Dr. O must fail, that is, for the fact that in attempting to destroy reality and replace it with a hallucination he has unwittingly reproduced that very reality. Surely the explanation for his lack of success is that talk about reality, and the things of which it is made—roses, erasers, pretty girls, specks of dust, and so on—should be construed as statements about what we do or would experience and nothing else.

Moreover, this is entirely plausible when considered in concrete terms. Consider an eraser. When we speak and think about an eraser we see, certainly we are not saying anything about some esoteric, never-to-be-observed cause of our experiences. What we have in mind is nothing so peculiar as that. Rather, what we are saying concerns only experiences we have and those we expect to have. The meaning of the statement 'There is an eraser' is contained in all those statements that describe our present eraser experiences—seeing an eraser, feeling an eraser, and so on—together with all those statements describing certain expected experiences, that is, seeing pencil marks disappear if the eraser is rubbed over them, seeing the eraser bounce if dropped, and so on. Statements about physical things are nothing more than statements about what we experience and what we would experience if. . . . Thus such statements and the perceptual beliefs they are used to express are hypothetical or conditional.

Summary of the Dogmatist's Strategy. Before proceeding to elucidate the theory of meaning mentioned earlier, let us consider in what way that theory would undermine the skeptical argument. As we have seen (page 86), to establish the premise

  1. The experiences of a person who has a true perceptual belief may be exactly duplicated by the experiences of a person whose perceptual belief is exactly similar but false.

the skeptic appealed to the premise

  5. The braino hypothesis is logically possible.

We have argued, against the skeptic, that premise (5) is false because the braino hypothesis is meaningless. For a hypothesis to be either possible or impossible it must at least be meaningful. Premise (5) would be shown to be meaningless by proving a perfect hallucination to be a meaningless hypothesis. We shall now attempt to establish the meaninglessness of this hypothesis by defending a theory concerning the meaning of statements expressing our perceptual beliefs.

PHENOMENALISM:
FORMULATION AND DEFENSE

The theory just described in brief outline is known as phenomenalism. It will be useful for the purpose of defeating skepticism to formulate the theory in a somewhat more precise way. We have said that according to this theory statements about physical reality are nothing more than statements about what we do and would experience. Let us call statements of the former kind "physical-object statements" and statements of the latter kind "sense-data statements." This terminology requires some explanation. When we have some sense experience, such as seeing a tomato, we thereby sense something. What we sense might not have any physical reality, it might be some sort of illusion or hallucination, but we do sense something. One way to describe what we experience is to say that we experience an appearance of, for example, a tomato. So what we always experience, when we believe we see some physical thing, is an appearance of the thing in question. In that case, if our experience is hallucinatory, then we are experiencing the appearance of a tomato even though there is no tomato. Thus we might call those statements that describe sensory experience appearance statements rather than sense-data statements.

However, there are certain facts about both language and experience that makes the introduction of a technical term useful. First, sometimes what we experience is not the appearance of anything. For example, we experience images of various sorts, such as afterimages, and these images are not appearances of anything. If I shine a red light in my eyes and subsequently close them and experience a green afterimage, I am not experiencing the appearance of anything. Images as well as appearances are among the things we experience. Second, talking of the appearance of something, a tomato, for example, suggests it is the sort of appearance that is caused by a tomato, and the doctrine of phenomenalism is aimed precisely at extricating the intellect from such bewildering and confusing suggestions. Third, there are various kinds of illusions that are neither appearances nor images. A rainbow in the sky is just such a thing. We know that those colored bands that arc across the sky are not solid, as we might have thought in childhood days. Alas, no one can slide down a rainbow to a pot of gold—vain, sweet illusion. A rainbow is thus like a hallucination; it is neither an appearance nor an image. It is just a rainbow and nothing else.

In view of such considerations as these, it is useful to have a common term to describe these various objects of experience. We choose, for the sake of tradition, the term 'sense-data.' Images and appearances are data of sense experience, and consequently, are fittingly called sense-data. Sense-data statements are, of course, nothing else but the statements that describe sense-data.

We can now state the theory of phenomenalism in a way that is quite precise. It is the theory that physical-object statements, for example, 'There is a tomato before me'—assert nothing over and above what could be formulated in terms of categorical sense-data statements, for example, 'I am sensing a red and bulgy sense-datum,' and hypothetical sense-datum statements, for example, 'If I have the sense-data characteristic of striking what is before me, then I will sense a red, drippy, seedy sense-datum.' These sense-data statements will thus constitute the meaning, the whole meaning, of the statement about the tomato.

The preceding formulation of phenomenalism requires some modification to forestall an obvious objection. When we consider the hypothetical statements that would be required to express the entire meaning of even such a simple statement as, 'There is a tomato before me,' in terms of sense-data statements, we quickly discover that the project is not feasible. The resources of our language are not adequate to formulate all the sense-data statements that would be needed to exhaust the meaning of a physical-object statement. The reason for this is that our language is not well suited to describing the sense-data we experience. Simply try, if you will, to describe in exact detail all the sense-data you would expect to experience if you suppose that there is a tomato before you. If that is the only supposition we entertain, it is clear that our expectations must immediately take on a completely hypothetical character. They would be expressed by some such hypothetical statement as the one mentioned previously, namely, 'If I have the sense-data characteristic of striking what is before me, then I will sense a drippy, seedy, reddish sense-datum.' That is the sort of hypothetical statement that would come to mind. But on careful consideration it will become clear that this statement is unsatisfactory in any number of ways. Let us explore them in detail.

First, the consequent of our hypothetical statement does not really do justice to what we would expect to experience if we were to strike a tomato before us. It is true that we expect to sense a drippy, seedy, reddish sense-datum, but that is not a very precise description of all that we expect. To see that this is so, take one nice ripe tomato, place it on a table before you, and smash it with your fist. Notice all that takes place and you will see how hopeless it would be to attempt to describe that extraordinary experience in all its messy glory. It would be quite impossible because of the paucity of our language for describing such matters. There is no terminology fully adequate to describe that sight of the tomato squishing or the feeling of splattering it. Moreover, having seen that the consequent of our hypothetical statement is not an adequate description of the sense-data we would expect to receive after striking a tomato, we must also notice that the antecedent is not an adequate sense-data description to ensure that the tomato is struck. For suppose I have the sense-data characteristic of striking what is before me. I might nevertheless fail to strike anything, or I might strike something other than the tomato.

Second, in either of these events, although the antecedent of our hypothetical statement would be true, the consequent would be false. As a result, the hypothetical statement would be false even though there is a tomato before me. This shows that as it stands the statement 'There is a tomato before me' does not entail the hypothetical statement we have been considering. Thus, our attempt to formulate the meaning of the statement 'There is a tomato before me' in terms of hypothetical sense-data statements will require serious emendation in two ways: the consequent must be modified to express all that I should expect to experience if I were to smash the tomato, which, as we have noted, cannot be done; and, the antecedent must be modified to express in sense-data terminology some condition that guarantees that I have smashed the tomato. To accomplish the second task we would have to formulate in sense-data terminology the statement 'I have smashed the tomato before me,' which will present exactly the same problems all over again that we have already encountered in attempting to formulate the statement 'There is a tomato before me' in such terms.

Third, we have already noted that the consequent of the statement 'If I have the sense-data characteristic of striking what is before me, then I will sense reddish, drippy, seedy sense-data' does not specify precisely all that we would expect to sense if we were to strike a tomato, and in this way it is too indefinite. But we must now admit that the consequent is also too definite. There are many things that might happen if I were to strike a tomato before me, depending not only on how I strike it, but on what sort of condition the tomato is in. A tomato that is rotten inside will produce quite different results from one that is hard and green. Just as the antecedent of the proposed hypothetical statement would have to be altered to guarantee that certain physical conditions obtain, so the consequent must also be altered to allow for a variety of different physical conditions.

However, these considerations do not constitute a proof that physical-object statements cannot be reformulated in terms of categorical and hypothetical sense-data statements. It might nonetheless be possible to translate the statement 'There is a tomato before me' into some statement that refers only to sense-data and to the persons who do or would have them. It is not at all clear that this is true, and indeed the preceding considerations might reasonably be held to undermine the case for thinking so.

All of this was mentioned to forestall an objection. We have said that phenomenalism is the theory that physical-object statements assert nothing beyond what could be formulated in terms of categorical and hypothetical statements about sense-data. One might well object to it on the grounds that any attempt to formulate physical-object statements in terms of such statements about sense-data will fail. We have not said that such failure is certain, but our preceding remarks seem to render failure more likely than success. Suppose physical-object statements cannot be formulated or reformulated in terms of sense-data statements. Must we reject phenomenalism?

The answer to this question is negative. But phenomenalism requires a more cautious statement. Let us define phenomenalism as the doctrine that physical-object statements mean nothing more than what could in principle be formulated in terms of categorical and hypothetical sense-data statements. The words 'in principle' are crucial here, for it may well be the case that *in fact* no such re-formulation of physical object statements can be made. Neverthe-less, what cannot be done may still be possible in principle. What is the point of saying this is possible *in principle*? It is to contend that what stands in the way of such translations is only the character and limitations of language, which is not designed for performing such tasks, and perhaps the limitations of the people who attempt to carry out such translations. To say the problem of translation is soluble in principle, if not in fact, is to say that it is not the meaning or content of physical-object statements that makes it impossible for us to carry out the translation. What makes translation difficult are linguistic peculiarities entirely extraneous to the question of what physical-object statements do or do not mean.

The situation is quite analogous to the one that would arise if some sentence in English were such that we could not *in fact* translate it into Russian. The proper words in Russian might simply not exist. This would only show that the English sentence was not in fact translatable into Russian, but it would be in principle possi-ble to do so. It is more or less an accident that such translations could not be made. All that would need to happen to make the translation possible is for Russian to be enriched. Similarly, though in fact it might be impossible to translate physical-object statements into the sense-data language, all that would need to happen to make that translation possible in fact, as well as in principle, is for sense-data language to be enriched. For many reasons it might not be practically feasible to do this, but what bars the way are accidents of fact, not matters of principle.[9]

Thus, phenomenalism remains a tenable doctrine when construed as the thesis that physical-object statements are translatable in prin-ciple into the sense-data language.

Phenomenalism serves to undermine skepticism, for skepticism arises when we think of reality as something forever concealed from us in sense experience, a kind of inner core beneath the "skin" of sense experience. When we think of any physical thing as an in-accessible cause of sense experience, we shall inevitably conclude that physical objects are things, we know not what, that produce experiences in us in some way, we know not how. Then it will turn

[9] Cf. A. J. Ayer, "Phenomenalism," in *Philosophical Essays* (London: Mac-millan, 1954), esp. pp. 138–43.

out that we have no more reason to think that a physical object, the pencil we see, is the source of our sense experience than we have to think that a braino is. However, once we notice that statements about reality tell us not about some hidden cause of our experiences, but rather about what we do or would experience, then the braino hypothesis evaporates. Our experiences themselves can guarantee that we see reality, that our perceptual beliefs are true, because those beliefs about reality, about pencils, people, and planets, are beliefs about experience and nothing else. Experience can ensure the truth of such statements and give us perceptual knowledge. Our perceptual beliefs are converted into knowledge by the experimental evidence of our senses.

PHENOMENALISM REJECTED BY THE SKEPTIC

The theory of phenomenalism has more serious defects than are evident at the outset. Indeed, despite a certain plausibility in it, we shall argue (1) that the theory is false, and (2) that even if the theory were true it would not provide a refutation of skepticism.

To show that the theory is false, we must construct an argument to the effect that no matter how much our sense-data language were enriched it would still be impossible to reformulate physical-object statements in terms of sense-data statements. We must prove, moreover, that this difficulty is one of logical principle and not factual coincidence. We shall show that no physical-object statement entails any possible sense-data statement we can imagine. If we prove this, then we will have proved that any sense-data statement can be false when any given physical-object statement is true. Because the two statements can differ in truth value, it is clear that one is not the translation of the other.

How can we prove that no physical-object statement entails any sense-data statement? First, let us consider a very simple physical-object statement, not one about something so impermanent as a tomato, which is quickly eaten and forgotten, but something solid and lasting. Consider a brass doorknob on a door in front of you, and correspondingly the statement 'There is a doorknob in front of me.' Now let us consider what sort of sense-data statement this statement might entail. According to the preceding formulation of phenomenalism, the statement will entail either categorical or hypothetical sense-data statements or both. What about categorical sense-data statements? Does the doorknob statement entail any of these? A categorical sense-data statement is one that asserts that some person is sensing a certain sense-datum. The doorknob statement might be thought to entail some such categorical statement, for example, that I am sensing sense-data characteristic of doorknobs. However, brief reflection shows this to be false, because I could be entirely unaware of the doorknob before me. Imagine that my eyes are closed, that I am not touching the doorknob, and so on. Thus, it is clear that from the mere statement 'There is a doorknob before me' nothing categorical follows about what I, or anyone else, am now sensing. What we sense depends in part on *us*. Consequently, by imagining the appropriate alteration in ourselves we can see that any specific categorical sense-data statement could well be false when the doorknob statement is true.

Thus it is quite clear that if the doorknob statement entails any sense-data statement, it must be a hypothetical one. However, the same sort of argument that was used to prove that the doorknob statement did not entail any categorical sense-data statement can also be marshalled to prove it does not entail any hypothetical sense-data statement. Let us consider a specific attempt to provide a hypothetical sense-data statement entailed by the doorknob statement: 'If I were to have the sense-data characteristic of reaching out to touch what is before me, then I would sense cold, metallic-feeling sense-data.' It is quite clear that this statement could be false even though the doorknob statement is true. Imagine that my hands are anesthetized and that I consequently feel no sensation in them. There would then be a doorknob before me even though I would not sense the tactile sense-data characteristic of brass doorknobs. In this case the hypothetical statement would be false. What we sense depends, again, not only on external circumstances but on the condition of the observer as well. Consequently, we can prove that it is possible that any physical-object statement is true while any sense-data statement is false by imagining an observer who is peculiar in a way that guarantees that he will not have the sense-data we would ordinarily expect him to have in the presence of such a physical object.[10]

One might object to what we have just argued by saying that

---

[10] Cf. R. M. Chisholm, *Perceiving* (Ithaca, N.Y.: Cornell University Press, 1957), pp. 189–97.

though the hypothetical statement in question is not entailed by the doorknob statement, the latter nevertheless does entail some other hypothetical sense-datum statement. Indeed, the objection might continue, you yourself have explained how the hypothetical statement would have to be modified. It would have to be modified in such a way that the antecedent of the hypothetical statement ensures that the person in question is normal.

In line with this objection, consider how the hypothetical would have to be reformulated. Suppose we try the following: 'If I were to have the sense-data characteristic of reaching out to touch what is before me and if I were normal, then I would have cold, metallic-feeling sense-data.' Leaving aside considerations of the possibility that I might reach out to touch what is before me and miss, or that I might have the sense-data characteristic of doing this when I am not doing it at all, the hypothetical statement as amended has a fatal defect. The defect is that it is no longer a sense-data statement. For what does it mean to say that I, or anyone else, am *normal*? It might mean that my body is in a perfectly normal state, that I am not drugged, exhausted, and so on. In this case it is perfectly clear that the statement 'I am normal' is a physical-object statement. For my body is as much a physical object as a doorknob is, and statements about its condition, like statements about the condition of the doorknob, are physical-object statements.

Moreover, it is logically possible that I should be normal in this sense and that the hypothetical statement should be false despite the fact that the doorknob is before me. Even if my body is in normal condition, it is at least logically possible that my hand might go numb for a moment. Even normal bodies fail to operate perfectly now and then. I might, consequently, be reaching for the doorknob and not feel anything.

To remedy the defect we must take more drastic measures. Indeed, what must be meant by the word 'normal' in this context is simply that I am in a state such that I sense things the way they are and not otherwise. If I reach out for the doorknob and I am in a state in which I sense things the way they are, then what I sense will be cold and metallic. But when we mean this by the word 'normal,' then it is absolutely clear that the original hypothetical statement is no longer exclusively a sense-data statement. It is *in part* a physical-object statement asserting what sense-data a man will have when confronted with physical objects of a certain sort.

The conclusion to draw from this is clear and simple. Either the hypothetical candidates for sense-data statements entailed by physical-object statements involve a reference to normality and are really not exclusively sense-data statements at all or they do not contain any such reference. In the latter case, if we suppose an observer not to be normal, it is easily proved that the physical-object statement can be true when the hypothetical statements are false and that, consequently, the former does not entail the latter. Therefore either the hypothetical statement is not a sense-data statement or it is not entailed by the physical-object statement. Thus phenomenalism collapses over the problem of the normality of the observer.

To summarize, according to the phenomenalist it is possible, at least in principle, to reformulate physical-object statements in terms of categorical and hypothetical sense-data statements. Were this true, then the physical-object statements would entail those sense-data statements that constitute the reformulation. But we have argued that one particular physical-object statement that is a paradigm candidate for phenomenalistic reformulation does not entail any categorical or hypothetical sense-data statement. Consequently, the physical-object statement in question, the doorknob statement, cannot be reformulated in terms of categorical and hypothetical sense-data statements. If this statement cannot be reformulated in the required way, there is no reason to think that any physical-object statement can be; and indeed there is very good reason to think it cannot.

In fairness to the phenomenalist, it must be conceded that we have not proved that the term 'normal,' as it is required in the translation, could not be analyzed in the language of sense-data. That is, a phenomenalist might object to what we have said and argue that what it means to say that a person is 'normal' is specifiable without reference to how things are. But there is no reason to think this can be done. Moreover, the need to introduce such a notion sheds doubt on the whole enterprise of phenomenalism. For phenomenalism holds that we can describe the way things are in terms of how we sense. But in the process of such formulation some term has to be introduced to ensure that we sense things the way they are. This circle has every appearance of being the precise noose that will hang the theory.

However, having shown that phenomenalism is a doubtful doctrine, we shall now argue that it is also useless. It is useless in that, even if true, it would not be a bulwark against skepticism. To prove this let us imagine that phenomenalism, rather than being doubtful, is in fact true. In that case, a perceptual belief to the effect that one sees some physical thing would in principle be formulatable in terms of categorical and hypothetical sense-data statements. For example, suppose I believe there is a yellow pencil in front of me, which I see. Obviously, a large number of hypothetical statements would be required to formulate the content of this belief, for as I move to different places, still looking at the pencil, I should have different sense-data. Thus we would need some hypothetical statement to express the idea that if I were to move 12 inches to the right, I would have such and such sense-data, another to express the idea that if I were to move 12 inches closer to the pencil I would have such and such sense-data, and so on.

Considerations of this kind have led some philosophers to say that the number of hypothetical statements required to formulate a single physical-object statement in sense-data terminology is infinite. One reason for holding this view is that there are an infinity of different places from which one can view an object, and it has been thought that a phenomenalistic formulation of a statement about such an object would have to describe what sense-data a person would have when viewing the object from each of these places. Of course, if this doctrine were correct, then it would not even be possible in principle to formulate a physical-object statement in the terminology of sense-data, because it is in principle impossible for a person to formulate an infinity of statements. However, we need not suppose that the number of such hypothetical statements is really infinite in number. For even if it is theoretically correct to say that there are an infinite number of places from which to view an object, this fact is quite irrelevant, because there is only a finite number of places that a person can discriminate. Between 1 inch and 2 inches there are, theoretically speaking, an infinite number of lengths, but a human being can only discriminate a finite number of such lengths. Eventually, lengths and places get so close together that there is no noticeable difference between them. For the purpose of formulating physical-object statements in the terminology of sense-data, all that matters to us are noticeably different places, and these are finite in number.

Therefore we have reached the conclusion that the number of hypothetical statements required for the reformulation we are imagining is very large but finite. This conclusion, though it is quite compatible with the truth of phenomenalism, is sufficient to prove that the truth of the doctrine is no defense against skepticism. Why not? Because no one will be in a position to verify all the hypothetical statements that would constitute the reformulation, and hence the meaning, of a physical-object statement. A person will be forced to act in one way rather than another and, consequently, to verify one sense-data statement rather than another. If I move 12 inches to the right to view the pencil, and indeed have just the sense-data which a hypothetical sense-data statement asserts that I would sense were I to move in that way, then I forego the opportunity to verify a hypothetical statement which asserts that I would have such and such other sense-data if I had moved 12 inches to the left instead. In short, I have to choose between verifying one hypothetical statement and another, and once this choice is made the unchecked hypothetical statement becomes a contrary-to-fact statement about what would have happened if I had chosen a different action and made some other test. Moreover, the situation is worse than it might seem. When I act in such a way as to verify one of the hypothetical statements in question, I forego the opportunity to verify a whole multitude of others. There will always be a great number of alternative actions, which I neglect to perform as a result of choosing the action I do choose, and each one might lead to my sensing different sense-data. If any of the neglected hypothetical sense-data statements is false, then so is the physical-object statement it formulates. When that statement is false I would be mistaken in believing it is true. This proves that even if phenomenalism is true it is perfectly possible for any perceptual belief to be false because the physical-object statement expressing the belief entails some unverified hypothetical sense-data statement which, in fact, happens to be false.

The conclusion is that phenomenalism will not rescue common sense from skepticism. We argued that, on the basis of the evidence of experience, it is entirely a matter of luck whether our perceptual beliefs turn out to be true. We have now seen that the truth of phenomenalism would not undermine skepticism, but instead would provide a basis for establishing it. If phenomenalism were true it would explain exactly why our perceptual beliefs sometimes turn out to be true and sometimes false—when based on exactly the same experiential evidence. The explanation is that no matter what the evidence of sense experience, the physical-object hypothesis we believe will have all sorts of consequences that we have not tested. More precisely, no matter how many of the hypothetical sense-data statements—used to formulate a physical-object hypothesis—are verified by sense experience, there will be many other such hypothetical statements—also part of the meaning of the physical-object hypothesis—which must remain untested. They are contrary-to-fact hypothetical statements about what sense-data we would have sensed if we had acted differently. Because these other hypothetical statements will remain untested, good luck rather than good evidence will be fully responsible for the truth of our perceptual beliefs. For the hypothetical content of such beliefs, expressed in the terminology of sense-data, far exceeds our ability to test for truth. Consequently, we have arrived back at our skeptical conclusion. Perceptual beliefs, when true, are true as a matter of luck; hence such beliefs do not constitute knowledge.

The phenomenalistic account of our perceptual beliefs is no better defense against skepticism than the causal account considered earlier. According to the causal theory, our belief that we see a physical object, a rose, for example, amounts to the belief that our experience of seeing a rose is caused in a direct way by a rose and not another thing. This account was rejected by the dogmatist because it implies that the braino hypothesis is meaningful. If our perceptual beliefs were beliefs about the causes of our experience, whose existence we could never verify in sense experience, then we would have to admit that it is at least meaningful, even if false, to suppose that we are constantly experiencing the perfect hallucination caused by Dr. O. The perfect hallucination was said to be meaningless, and the explanation offered for the meaninglessness of the hypothesis was that our perceptual beliefs are beliefs about what we do or would experience. Phenomenalism was intended to show in precisely what way our perceptual beliefs about physical objects may be construed as being about what we do or would experience and nothing more.

However, we can now see that even if we do suppose that phenomenalism is true and that our perceptual beliefs are about what we do or would experience, the perfect-hallucination hypothesis remains meaningful. In fact, the two accounts of our perceptual beliefs have exactly analogous epistemological consequences. According to the causal theory of perceptual beliefs, such beliefs entail that our sense experiences are caused by something outside sense experience. We are never in a position to verify such a hypothesis in sense experience; consequently, we have no way of telling whether it, or the belief that entails it, is true. Therefore our perceptual beliefs never constitute knowledge. Similarly, the phenomenalistic theory of perceptual beliefs has the consequence that such beliefs entail contrary-to-fact hypothetical statements asserting that we would have had certain experiences if certain other conditions had prevailed. We are never in a position to verify such hypothetical statements in sense experience, and consequently, we have no way of telling whether they, or the beliefs that entail them, are true. Therefore, assuming the phenomenalistic theory of our perceptual beliefs, such beliefs never constitute knowledge. The perfect-hallucination hypothesis is not only meaningful but irrefutable on both theories, because on both it is logically possible for any perceptual belief to turn out to be false no matter what the experience is like, and hence logically possible for any experience to be hallucinatory.

We conclude, first, that the theory of phenomenalism is dubious, and, second, that even if true, phenomenalism fails to protect the prejudices of common sense from the critique of skepticism. Phenomenalism provides as good a basis for defending skepticism as does the alternative theory of perceptual beliefs.

MEANINGLESSNESS EXPLAINED

Having reached these conclusions it might be useful to undermine completely the argument of the other side by explaining why that argument seemed plausible. The strongest argument in favor of phenomenalism is based on the premise that the perfect-hallucination hypothesis is meaningless. It seems absurd to propose that all our experiences to date have been hallucinatory experiences resulting from the evil machinations of Dr. O. One way to explain the absurdity of just this hypothesis is to appeal to the doctrine that our perceptual beliefs are about what we do or would experience, nothing more. But we have now seen that the perfect hallucination will turn out to be meaningful even if that doctrine is true.

Why does it seem so plausible to contend that the perfect-hallucination hypothesis is meaningless? The explanation of the apparent meaninglessness of this doctrine stems from an ambiguity in such terms as 'nonsense' and 'meaningless.' All these terms are used in both a semantic and an epistemic sense. A sentence is nonsense, or meaningless, in the semantic sense of the term only if the sentence asserts nothing, and consequently is neither true nor false. A perfect example of such a sentence is 'Pirots carulize elactically.' That sentence asserts nothing; it is neither true nor false. It is not made up of meaningful words. An example of a sentence that is meaningless in the semantic sense but that is made up of meaningful words is 'Verb at do fog Joe.' The defect of this sentence is that it is ungrammatical. We can even have a sentence that is grammatical and composed of meaningful words but that is nevertheless meaningless in the semantic sense. An example is 'Worms integrate the moon by $C^{\#}$ homogeneously when moralizing to rescind apples.' This sentence, like the preceding ones, asserts nothing.

All the sentences we have considered are nonsense and meaningless in that they are either semantically or grammatically defective in such a way that a person who uttered them would, in ordinary circumstances, be asserting nothing. In contrast to this semantic sense of the terms 'nonsense' and 'meaningless' there is an epistemic sense. Sometimes we say that a sentence is meaningless because, though it asserts something, what is asserted is preposterous. If a man says, "Everyone has died," we might reply, "Nonsense," or alternatively, "What do you mean?" or possibly even, "That is meaningless." It is not that the sentence asserts nothing; on the contrary, it is because the sentence asserts something patently false that we reply as we do. The sentence uttered is perfectly meaningful; what is nonsensical and meaningless is the fact that the man has uttered it. To put the matter another way, we can make sense of the sentence; we know what it asserts. But we cannot make sense of the man uttering it; we do not understand why he would utter it. Thus when we use terms like 'nonsense' and 'meaningless' in the epistemic sense, the correct use of them requires only that what is uttered seem absurdly false. Of course, to seem preposterously false, the sentence must assert something, and thus be either true or false.

These remarks are directly relevant to the perfect-hallucination hypothesis. The perfect-hallucination hypothesis is "nonsense" and "meaningless" in the epistemic sense of these terms and in that sense only. It is correct to apply such terms to the perfect-hallucination hypothesis because it seems preposterously false. And even the skeptic may concede, it should be remembered, that the hypothesis seems false. However, for the hypothesis to seem false it must be meaningful; it must assert something in order to seem false.

If the perfect-hallucination hypothesis is meaningful in the semantic sense—that is, if it asserts something—then the fact that it is not meaningful in the epistemic sense is irrelevant to the contentions of skepticism. As we pointed out earlier, the skeptic may with perfect consistency concede that the perfect-hallucination hypothesis seems false. He may even believe that it is false. All men, whether skeptics or not, presumably believe this. But though we all believe the hypothesis is false, the skeptic argues that no one knows it is false. He concludes that because no one knows it is false, no one knows that any of his perceptual beliefs are true. Therefore, such beliefs do not constitute knowledge.

ATTACKING ANOTHER SKEPTICAL
PREMISE: PROBABILITY, NOT LUCK

Suppose we dogmatists concede, for the sake of avoiding an impasse, that the perfect-hallucination hypothesis does assert something, that it is either true or false. Moreover, let us attempt to meet the argument of skepticism without assuming any particular analysis of the content of our perceptual beliefs. Henceforth we shall, therefore, assume neither the truth nor the falsity of phenomenalism. Further, we shall concede that the evidence we have from sense experience is always such that it is logically possible that our perceptual beliefs based on this evidence are false.

If we make all these concessions, must we also concede the day to skepticism? To see that we need not, let us examine in some detail the logical structure of the argument for skepticism.
The argument is as follows:

1. The experiences of a person who has a true perceptual belief may be exactly duplicated by the experiences of a person whose perceptual belief is exactly similar but false.
2. If the experiences of a person who has a true perceptual belief may be exactly duplicated by the experiences of a person whose perceptual belief is exactly similar but false, then it is always logically possible that any of our perceptual beliefs are false.
3. If it is always logically possible that any of our perceptual

beliefs are false, then no one ever knows that any of our perceptual beliefs are true.

Therefore

4. No one ever knows that any of our perceptual beliefs are true.

By defending the possibility of a perfect hallucination and refuting the doctrine of phenomenalism, the skeptic has substantiated premise (1). Moreover, let us concede the truth of premise (2) as well. To extricate ourselves from the consequences of skepticism we shall now direct our attack against premise (3).

The skeptic's defense of premise (3) can be found in his statement of the evil-operator argument (page 85), where he tries to attribute the truth of perceptual beliefs to luck. This enables him to derive premise (3) from

8. If it is logically possible that any of our perceptual beliefs are false, then a perceptual belief that turns out to be true is nothing more than a lucky guess.

and

9. If any perceptual belief that turns out to be true is nothing more than a lucky guess, then no one ever knows that any of our perceptual beliefs are true.

Although the deduction of premise (3) from (8) and (9) is valid, premise (8) should be rejected. In this way we can avoid accepting premise (3).

In premise (8) the skeptic has assumed that if it is logically possible for a belief to be false, then when the belief turns out to be true this is nothing more than a lucky guess, and hence not something we know. For convenience let us label as corrigible any belief of such a kind that it is logically possible for any belief of that kind to be false. Thus in premise (3) the skeptic is implying that no one ever knows any corrigible belief to be true. This assumption must be decisively refuted, because it has broad and pernicious implications.

Almost all our beliefs about subjects outside logic and mathematics are corrigible. Our beliefs about the past, the future, other persons and distant places, to take just a few examples, are all corrigible. It is easy enough to imagine how the braino could be used to deceive us in such matters. Moreover, all beliefs that depend on inductive argument, where the evidence we have does *not* entail the hypothesis we believe, are corrigible beliefs. If the evidence we have does not entail the hypothesis we believe is true, then it is logically possible that we are mistaken. Therefore if we accept the skeptical assumption that no one knows any corrigible belief to be true, then we will be forced to deny that there is any such thing as inductive knowledge. Thus let us now turn to the task of showing premise (8), and with it premise (3), to be as doubtful as they are damaging.

The skeptical contention that corrigible belief leaves us entirely at the mercy of luck—as premise (8) asserts—is not difficult to refute soundly. Evidence which does not exclude the logical possibility of error may greatly reduce the probability of error. Moreover, when the probability of error is reduced by our evidence to a point where it is negligible, it is preposterous to say that escaping from error is nothing but luck. To believe what is extremely probable and to disbelieve what is immensely improbable is completely reasonable. When a man believes something that is rendered exceedingly probable by the evidence on which he bases his belief, then it is no mere matter of luck if he is right and his belief is true.

Consider probabilities in a game of chance. If I bet on an alternative in such a game and the odds in favor of that alternative are ten to one, my calculated bet is no mere guess. Moreover, when the odds are a million to one, there is hardly a point to "spinning the wheel of fortune" at all. When the probability is sufficiently strong, there is no need to guess, and indeed there is no need for luck. Beliefs that are sufficiently probable, even if corrigible, should be considered knowledge whenever they are true.

A REJOINDER OF THE SKEPTIC:
POSSIBILITY, PROBABILITY, AND FREQUENCY

Every attempt to escape skepticism knocks, sooner or later, on the door of probability. But there is no help behind that door. Indeed once we pass through it we shall find ourselves securely locked in the very den of skepticism. Let us consider how to bolt the door.

If the appeal to probability is to succeed, the opponent of skepticism must claim not merely that our corrigible beliefs are based on evidence that renders them highly probable, he must also establish that we *know* such beliefs are highly probable. It is not enough that a belief be highly probable, the one who has the belief must know this to be so, or the belief will again, if true, be so merely as a matter of luck. To see this let us return to the example of the gaming table. Imagine that a man is invited to play a game of "Millee," which is played as follows. There is a machine with a window which, when a button is pushed, closes and subsequently opens to display either a red or a green square. Moreover, part of the definition of the game involves the following rule concerning the behavior of the machine: it must be set so that the green square appears only once in a million plays. Thus the odds are one in a million that the red square will fail to appear when the window opens.

Imagine that a man is invited to play Millee but is not told the odds. He might choose to bet that the red square will appear when the window opens, and of course he is correct. In spite of the odds in his favor, he would be entirely justified in saying that his belief that red would appear was, from his point of view, a lucky guess. The reason is that he does not know that the odds are a million to one in his favor. Indeed for all he knows the odds might be anything at all. In the absence of such knowledge, his being right is nothing more than luck.

Now suppose that a man believes that there really is a tomato in front of him and that this belief is based on the evidence of sense experience or any other inductive evidence you please. The odds might be a million to one that the hypothesis will turn out to be true when based on such evidence. But if the man does not know that these are the odds, and if, moreover, for all he knows the odds may be anything at all, then were he right, this would be nothing more than luck. In both this case and the case of the man at the gaming table, being right is a matter of luck even though the odds are fantastically in favor of both men being right. It is a matter of luck because both men are *ignorant* of the odds.

Of course, both the gambler and the perceptual believer would be in an entirely different position if they knew the odds. If both men knew the odds, then neither one would correctly be described as being right merely through luck. The question to be answered by the skeptic is the following: Need we suppose that the perceptual believer is ignorant of the odds in favor of his belief? Could not a man who based his belief on evidence that rendered his belief highly probable also know how probable his belief is? To establish the case for skepticism we must prove that the perceptual believer is inescapably ignorant of such probabilities.

As a first step, let us consider briefly how we ever know anything about probabilities. The term 'probability' is interpreted in a number of different ways, but the idea that seems most relevant in this context is concerned with truth frequency. If a man is to convert his perceptual beliefs to epistemic gold by his knowledge of probability, he must know that his belief, based on the evidence he has, is the kind of belief that is more frequently—indeed, exceedingly more frequently—true than false when based on the evidence he has. The perceptual believer must know that perceptual beliefs based on the usual evidence of sense experience are much more frequently true than false.

But he cannot know any such thing, for consider how a man knows that a frequency statement is true. The kind of frequency involved is relative frequency, the frequency with which one kind of thing occurs relative to the occurrence of things of another kind. For example, suppose we wish to know how probable it is that a person without a college degree will earn $40,000 a year. To establish this probability a person must find out how frequently it happens that a person without a college degree earns $40,000. The way to find this out is to find a representative sample of men without college degrees. Suppose, for simplicity, that your sample contains 1,000 men who lack college degrees and that exactly eleven of these men are earning $40,000 a year. You might then conclude that, on the basis of your finding, it is reasonable to expect the relative frequency mentioned to be 11/1,000. The same figure is the approximate probability of a man without a college degree earning the specified sum.

In summary, to find out the frequency with which things of a kind A turn out to be things of a kind B as well, we must find a sample of things that are A and determine how many of these are B. Consider therefore the problem a man faces who wishes to establish that perceptual beliefs based on the evidence of sense experience are much more frequently true than false. To find this out he would have to find a sample of beliefs of the specified kind and determine how many of them were true. The information about such a sample would be absolutely essential to his finding out that beliefs of this kind are much more frequently true than false. But how is he to acquire this information? To obtain such knowledge he must be able to determine how many of the beliefs in his sample are true. To determine how many of these beliefs are true he must know which of them constitute knowledge and which do not.

However, this requirement is calamitous, because we have already shown that a perceptual belief can constitute knowledge only if the man knows that beliefs of this kind are much more often true than false. We have now concluded that in order to know that beliefs of this kind are more frequently true than false, we must first know which of these beliefs are true and which false. Therefore before we can know that *any* perceptual belief is true, we must *first* know that certain perceptual beliefs are true. This is an altogether pernicious epistemic situation. Moreover, the only alternative is skepticism. In short, either we know that certain perceptual beliefs are true before we know *any* perceptual beliefs are true, which is absurd, or we do not know that any perceptual beliefs are true. It is obvious the latter alternative must be accepted.

Let us review the argument briefly. In order to escape skepticism concerning corrigible beliefs, it must be shown that such beliefs are based on evidence which renders them highly probable, and also that we *know* those beliefs are highly probable. To know the latter, we must know that such beliefs, when based on evidence of a specified sort, are much more frequently true than false. However, to find out that such beliefs are much more frequently true than false, we must consider a sample of such beliefs and determine what percentage of the beliefs in the sample is true. To determine what percentage of the beliefs is true, we must know which of a certain sample are true.

Therefore before a person can know that any corrigible belief based on inductive evidence is true, he must know that a certain probability statement is true. But he cannot know such a statement is true unless he already knows certain corrigible beliefs based on inductive evidence are true. Therefore no one can know any corrigible belief based on inductive evidence is true. The escape route *via* probability is, in fact, an expressway to skepticism.

THE DOGMATIST RETURNS:
FREQUENCY, ADEQUACY, AND PROBABILITY

The basic reply to this formidable argument is that probability is not all frequency. The preceding argument assumes that the thesis, corrigible beliefs based on inductive evidence are highly probable, amounts to the claim that such beliefs are much more frequently true than false. It is this premise of the argument that takes us down the path to skepticism; it is the one we shall reject.

Indeed, because probability often suggests frequency, it is better to express *our* thesis without using the term 'probability' at all. Our thesis is as follows: Though it is logically possible for any corrigible belief to be false, when such beliefs are *true* this is not always a matter of luck, because sometimes the beliefs are completely justified. In short, if a belief is completely justified, then, if correct, this is a matter of knowledge, not luck. Moreover, we can know our corrigible beliefs are completely justified *without* first knowing how frequently such beliefs are true. Epistemological questions of whether certain evidence justifies believing something are analogous to ethical questions of whether certain conditions justify doing something. Both questions are resolved by appealing to some standard, or criterion. The standards, or criteria, to which we appeal need not be established by determining frequencies. A short excursion into ethics should help to clarify this contention.

Imagine that a man has promised his friend and benefactor to drive his friend's wife to another city and to see that no harm comes to her en route. Moreover, suppose that while driving this charming lady to her destination the sexual passions of the man are aroused and, because he knows she is faithful beyond the possibility of seduction, he decides to assault her. Was the man justified in doing what he did? No reasonable man, even if he be quite a lusty soul, could deny that the man was a rogue and that his action was as unjustified as it was uncouth. To reach this conclusion one need not know anything about the frequency with which events of this sort, or any other sort, occur. All he need do is consult his standards of conduct. One would not need to know that the consequences of such assaults are more frequently bad than good. Indeed whatever the consequences of doing such a thing, it is unjustifiable because of the very kind of action it is. An action that is a combination of ingratitude, infidelity, insult, and injury is one whose very character stamps it as ethically abhorrent and unjustifiable.

Similarly, some beliefs are ones whose very character stamps them as epistemically abhorrent and unjustifiable. A contradictory belief is one example, and a belief that flies completely in the face of overwhelming evidence is another. A man who refuses, on an ordinary occasion of life, to believe what his senses would lead him to believe, and who, moreover, believes quite the opposite instead, is a man who is as epistemically unreasonable as the previously considered man is ethically unreasonable. On the other hand, a man who believes precisely what the evidence of his senses leads him to believe is epistemically justified.

Thus just as an action might be completely justified even though the agent does not know that actions of this kind more frequently lead to good consequences than bad, so a belief might be completely justified even though the believer does not know that beliefs of this kind are more frequently true than false. A belief might, therefore, be completely justified by the evidence we have for it, even though we have no way of establishing that such beliefs are more frequently true than false.[11]

It is worth noticing that there is a kind of artificiality in the argument of the skeptic, which may now be completely exposed. It was argued by the skeptic that before we can know that any corrigible belief is true, we must first determine that beliefs of this kind are more frequently true than false. In fact, it is quite easy to determine such things, for example, to determine that if a man believes he has a head, then more frequently than not this belief is true. It is always true. Suppose the skeptic replies, "To determine the latter one must first determine in a sample the proportion of cases in which this belief was true. Consequently, to show that any such belief is true we must first know that such beliefs are more frequently true than false." Surely this reply is absurdly artificial. How ridiculous and irrelevant it is to argue that before we can know that a man has a head we need to consider a sample of cases in which a man believes that he has a head and determine what proportion of such beliefs are true. Obviously, we need do no such thing to know that a man is completely justified in believing he has a head. Our knowledge that we are completely justified in believing such things does not depend on any antecedent knowledge of frequencies. Quite the contrary, because we are completely justified in believing certain things, we can know when such beliefs are true and subsequently decide how frequently corrigible beliefs of a certain kind are true.

Thus a skeptic, to win the day, must prove that there is something

[11] Ibid., pp. 31–39.

wrong with the epistemic standards we accept. That we have no way of knowing whether our corrigible beliefs are more frequently true than false before we know whether any of them are true is utterly irrelevant. Given our epistemic standards, we are completely justified in many of our inductive beliefs (for example, perceptual beliefs) before we become embroiled, and even if we never become embroiled, in statistical investigations concerning the truth frequency of our inductive beliefs. Of course, such investigations are quite relevant to establishing that certain beliefs are completely justified, but there are other beliefs, the majority of the more familiar ones, whose justification does not depend on the outcome of any statistical investigation. Having accepted standards of evidence that permit us to conclude that some corrigible beliefs (for example, perceptual beliefs) are completely justified, we leave open the question of whether *other* beliefs are completely justified. This might be settled by determining frequencies. But the idea that all beliefs must be based on the determination of frequencies and that none are justified unless they are so based leads to skepticism. However, we may escape skepticism by repudiating the absurd idea that no belief is completely justified unless it is based on a statistical investigation.

In summary, our standards of evidence ensure that at least some of our corrigible beliefs are completely justified. Thus though such beliefs are corrigible, it is no mere matter of luck when they turn out to be true. It is knowledge. To show that these claims are false, the skeptic must offer some reason for rejecting our standards of evidence, and so far no such argument has been presented.

SKEPTICISM DEFENDED: JUSTIFICATION AND TRUTH

The preceding argument does not altogether succeed in defeating the frequency argument presented earlier. For there is an obvious connection between how well justified a belief is when based on specific evidence and how frequently beliefs of this kind are true when based on evidence of that sort. Indeed if a belief is completely justified on the basis of certain evidence, then surely beliefs of that kind must be more often true than false when based on that sort of evidence. If the evidence a man has for his belief is such that it is more likely he will be mistaken than correct, surely he is not completely justified in his belief. However, once this point is conceded, the foregoing reply to skepticism is undermined. It follows that if a man knows he is completely justified in believing something on the basis of his evidence, then he must also know that beliefs of this kind are more frequently true than false when based on such evidence. Therefore to know that a belief is completely justified, one must (yes, *must*) first know that some high-relative-frequency statement is true. Knowing the latter, of course, poses exactly the insoluble problem we presented earlier.

The appeal to epistemic standards fails precisely because the correctness of those standards depends on certain frequencies. The very reason we think certain corrigible beliefs are completely justified is that we assume such beliefs are more frequently true than false. To know that any such belief is true we must know that we are completely justified in our belief. But to know that we are completely justified in our belief we must know that beliefs of that kind are more frequently true than false when based on evidence of the sort we have. To know this we must first determine that in a sample of beliefs of this kind, based on evidence of that sort, more of our beliefs are true than false, and to know this already requires that we know some of our corrigible beliefs are true. Again knowledge of such beliefs is impossible because to have such knowledge we would have to know that some of our corrigible beliefs are true before we know that any of them are true.

Summary of Preceding Skeptical Argument. To see the strength of the preceding argument it is useful to present it somewhat more formally. The argument is as follows:

1. If we know that any corrigible belief is true, then we must know that we are completely justified in our belief.
2. If we know that we are completely justified in our belief, then we must know that corrigible beliefs of this kind are more frequently true than false.
3. If we know that corrigible beliefs of a given kind are more frequently true than false, then we must antecedently determine in a sample of beliefs of this kind that more of the beliefs are true than false.

4. We cannot antecedently determine in a sample of beliefs of this kind that more of the beliefs are true than false.
Therefore
5. We do not know that any corrigible belief is true.

A DOGMATIST REPLY: AN ETHICAL ANALOGY

The proper reply to the preceding argument centers on the second premise—if we know that we are completely justified in our (corrigible) belief, then we must know that corrigible beliefs of this kind are more frequently true than false. This conditional statement, hereafter to be referred to as the "frequency condition," is the most important premise of the skeptic's argument. However, there is also another important premise, which we have not yet challenged. The third premise tells us that the only way to establish general frequencies is by determining frequencies in a sample. We shall argue that even if the frequency condition is true, the third premise might well be false. This is one reason for rejecting the frequency condition, and we shall present another independent argument to that end.

Suppose the frequency condition is true. Now let us return to my belief that the pencil I see in my hand really does exist, a belief based on the most overwhelming and compelling evidence of sense experience. Our epistemic standards, like our ethical standards, sometimes enable us to conclude with absolute certainty that something is justified or unjustified. Surely our epistemic standards enable me to conclude with certainty that I am completely justified in believing there is really a pencil in my hand. Nothing could possibly be more evident to me than this. Consequently, if we suppose that the frequency condition is true, we could establish, in a direct way and without appealing to any statistical sample, that beliefs of this kind are more frequently true than false. We could simply argue that we know the belief is completely justified, that being certain given our epistemic standards, and, assuming the frequency condition, we can conclude without appealing to samples that beliefs of this kind are more frequently true than false. Thus premise (3) would be shown to be false.

The preceding argument is sure to appear entirely specious to a skeptic, because he wishes to argue in exactly the opposite way, namely, we do not know such beliefs are more frequently true than false, and assuming the frequency condition, we can conclude that we do not know such beliefs are completely justified. In fact both of the preceding arguments, the skeptic's *and* ours, are unsound. But our argument is no worse than the skeptic's. The skeptic starts with a perfectly evident premise, namely, that the only way to establish frequencies is by determining frequencies in a sample. We started with an equally evident premise, namely, that a certain kind of belief is completely justified. Starting with these two perfectly good premises we reach contradictory conclusions. Something is wrong, but what? Not those two premises. There remains only that additional premise we both appeal to—the frequency condition. The fault must lie with it. We have, consequently, an excellent reason for rejecting that premise. By doing so we leave ourselves free to accept both evident premises, ours and the skeptic's.

Another way of seeing that the frequency condition should be rejected is to draw another ethical analogy. Imagine that a man is walking along the shore of a lake and sees a small child in the lake crying for help. The man jumps in the water and rescues the child. Surely such an action is a fine and justified one. However, suppose the child grows up to be a vicious dictator, like Adolf Hitler, who destroys millions of completely innocent people. By saving the child, a perfectly justified act, the man has done something which will have quite disastrous consequences. Actions of this kind, saving such infant dictators from drowning, will almost always lead to evil results. But this does not show that the man was unjustified. He was perfectly justified, especially because *he had no way of knowing* the child would grow up to be a monster.

Now compare this case to that of a man who sees a pencil in front of him. He sees a long, thin, yellow object that tapers at one end. It is tan at the beginning of the taper and black at the point. The object has six equal sides that run from the tapered end of the object to the other end, where first it becomes round with green and yellow stripes, and then pink at the end. Naturally, he believes that there really is a pencil which he sees, and this belief, based on the evidence of sense experience described previously, is completely justified. However, imagine that the man is the victim of a very clever optical trick designed precisely to make him believe that there is a pencil before him when none is there. The belief is thus quite false. Moreover, beliefs of just this kind, beliefs that something really is before one when one is the victim of such an optical trick, will almost always turn out to be false. But this does not show that the man was unjustified in his belief. He was perfectly justified, especially if we suppose he had no way of knowing a trick was being played on him. Indeed, the more perfect the deception, the more completely justified the man is in his belief.

The last point is worth some elaboration. We noted earlier that there was something peculiar about the skeptical assumption of the possibility of a perfect hallucination, for example, one induced by the evil genius Dr. O. The source of that peculiarity can now be exposed. A man can discover most hallucinations, that is, the situation differs in some discernible way from ordinary cases of sense perception. This admits of degrees; some hallucinations are more nearly perfect than others. However, it is fallacious to argue that as an hallucination becomes more perfect the victim of the hallucination becomes less justified in what he believes. Exactly the opposite is true. The more perfect we imagine the hallucination to be, the more justified the man is in his beliefs. In the first place, the more perfect the hallucination, the more closely the evidence of hallucination will approximate ordinary sense experience. Consequently, the evidence of hallucinatory experience might be just the sort of evidence that completely justifies the belief. Second, the more perfect the hallucination, the more difficult it would be for the person to discover that he is suffering a hallucination. But the result of this is that the man is all the more justified in believing what he does. Once the hallucination becomes perfect, the victim is completely justified in his perceptual beliefs. The evidence is all in favor of his beliefs and he cannot discover any evidence to the contrary.

The conclusion to draw from these remarks is that the frequency condition is false. A belief of a kind that almost always turns out to be false may nonetheless be completely justified. What is more, we have seen that a belief based on a perfect hallucination is more justified than one based on a less perfect hallucination. The frequency with which a belief of a certain kind turns out to be true does not determine whether it is justified. On the contrary, we know that beliefs of certain kinds, those based on hallucinations or other sensory tricks that are extremely difficult to detect, are completely justified beliefs, even though they are more often false than true.

The preceding reflections constitute a refutation of the skeptic's argument, which is premised on the frequency condition. The frequency condition—that if a person is completely justified in believing something on the basis of his evidence, then beliefs of that kind are more frequently true than false—must be rejected as incorrect and fatuous. With the demise of this condition the skeptic's argument is shown to be fallacious. A person may be completely justified in what he believes, and indeed know that he is completely justified, by simply appealing to his epistemic standards of justification and without knowing how frequently such beliefs turn out to be true.

THE SKEPTIC REJOINS: OUR STANDARDS CHALLENGED

The speculations of the dogmatist have rested on an ethical analogy and an appeal to epistemic standards. Such appeals are the common refuge of all who seek to escape from the pains of inquiry and criticism. It is time to expose this form of reasoning as the intellectual protectorate of the status quo. Having once exposed it, we can then elaborate a skeptical alternative to the dogmatic conservation of accepted opinion.

Let us lay out the dogmatist's argument with some greater care than he has been wont to do. It is as follows:

1. Some of our beliefs are completely justified in terms of our epistemic standards of epistemic evaluation.
2. If any of our beliefs are completely justified in terms of our standards of epistemic evaluation, then those beliefs are completely justified even if beliefs of that kind almost always turn out to be false.
   Therefore
3. Some of our beliefs are completely justified even if beliefs of that kind almost always turn out to be false.

That is the argument, and surely it only needs to be stated this baldly to be rendered ineffective for the purposes of refuting skepticism. The dogmatist in presenting the argument has very cleverly attracted our attention to premise (1), which may well be sustained by the ethical analogy he presses. But this strategy is doomed by the inadequacy of premise (2), which is needed to bring us to the dogmatist conclusion.

The problem for the dogmatist is that it does not at all follow from the fact that something is completely justified *in terms of our standards* of evaluation that it is completely justified. This is especially clear when the kind of belief in question almost always turns out to be false. For, after all, what does it mean to say that some belief is completely justified in terms of our standards of evaluation? What it means, surely, is that we *accept* a principle according to which beliefs of that kind are completely justified. But the fact that some principle is accepted in no way shows that it is true. Hence when such a principle tells us that a belief is completely justified, we still may reasonably ask whether what the principle tells us is correct. If what it tells us is not, then those beliefs it certifies as completely justified may be absolutely counterfeit; that is, they may not be completely justified at all.

The preceding comments are best illustrated by consideration of a practical example. Suppose a man avers that sexual relations between people not joined by holy wedlock are unnatural. Imagine, when challenged he simply retorts that such actions are unnatural by his standards of moral evaluation. Now this is plain dogmatism. A detractor will surely reply, so much the worse for your standards of moral evaluation. In moral disputation, a man cannot even pretend to support his moral judgments by simply laying it down that his moral standards are the ones we must accept. On the contrary, if he chooses to reason with us, it becomes incumbent upon him to offer us some argument on behalf of his opinions and his standards. The refusal to do so—and simply asserting that one's judgment is completely justified because one's moral standards say so is just such a refusal—is a repudiation of reason and inquiry.

In this example we have chosen an issue where many people would disagree with our dogmatic moralist and therefore be sensitive to the inadequacy of his appeal. However, when almost all men agree, and we agree with them, then we are likely to mistake our common agreement for a sanctified first principle. When we agree, we are inclined to assume our agreement is based on some standard of evaluation that is beyond the possibility of error or of criticism. But the standards of the many are no different from the standards of the few. To conclude that some action or belief is completely justified because it is so justified in terms of some standard of evaluation we accept is to offer an argument without any merit whatever. For it simply does not follow in any way that we are completely justified in some action or belief merely because that action or belief conforms to some standard of evaluation. The standard itself may be totally defective.

The point may be further illustrated, and usefully so, by considering a controversial epistemological claim. Imagine that some person is entirely convinced that he has some extrasensory powers, and, more specifically, that he can tell what cards are drawn from a deck, even though he does not see the cards, by concentrating in a special way. He then repeatedly claims to know what card is drawn from the deck. When we challenge his claim to know, he says his claim is completely justified in terms of his epistemic standards. We then note that he is much more often incorrect than correct in such claims; indeed, we might even note that he is no more often correct in what he says than one would expect by chance. He then regards us with disdainful credulity and remarks that apparently we have not understood. His beliefs in such matters are completely justified in terms of his standards of epistemic evaluation, and hence are completely justified, even if beliefs of that kind are almost always false. Those are his standards and there is an end to it.

No one would accept that argument as having any credibility whatever. It obviously does not follow from the fact that a belief is completely justified in terms of his standards that such a belief is completely justified. This point remains cogent when generalized. No matter what the belief or standard might be, it does not follow from the fact that the belief is completely justified according to some standard, that the belief is actually so justified. It might not be justified at all. As we noted, this point is likely to be overlooked when the standards in question are ones we accept. But the argument of the dogmatist is no better than the argument of our self-acclaimed master of extrasensory powers. The dogmatic appeal to common epistemic standards is but one more evasive movement to avoid the noose of skepticism. The dogmatist must show, without surreptitious appeal to *his* standards of evidence, that perceptual beliefs are more frequently true than false or candidly concede defeat.

A DOGMATIST REMARK: INNOCENT JUSTIFICATION

It may be conceded that our appeal to epistemic standards is ineffective if some argument is required to show that such standards are correct. But is any such argument needed? The skeptic continually supposes that we have to know that certain frequencies obtain or that certain frequencies do not obtain if we are to know that our corrigible beliefs are true. But he has put the shoe on the wrong epistemic foot. Certain corrigible beliefs—for example, our perceptual beliefs and memory beliefs—are not ones that we need to corroborate by antecedently establishing that beliefs of this kind are more frequently true than false. On the contrary, unless there is some reason to believe that such beliefs are more frequently false than true, we are completely justified in such beliefs. One way of putting the matter is to say that such beliefs are epistemically innocent until proved guilty. They are justified unless they are shown to be unjustified.[12]

Moreover, often our perceptual beliefs are so completely justified that it would be epistemically pointless, and indeed unreasonable, to attempt to justify them by arguing that such beliefs are more frequently true than false. For example, if I see my wedding ring on my finger and feel it there as well, my belief that there really is such a ring on my finger is not one that could reasonably be defended by such an argument. This belief is so completely justified that any such argument mustered in defense of it would surely proceed from premises less evident, or at least no more evident, than the conclusion they support. Such an argument would be epistemically useless. For to *justify* a conclusion, some of the premises of the argument must be more evident than the conclusion, and none of the premises may be any less evident. Only such an argument can add epistemic weight to the conclusion. Unless some of the premises are initially more evident than the conclusion, there would be no more reason for accepting the premises than there was for accepting the conclusion. Thus for an argument to justify the conclusion deduced from the premises, at least some of the premises must be more evident, more reasonable to accept, than the conclusion.

However, the belief about the wedding ring is so completely justified that there is no belief that is more reasonable or evident. When I see something that I also touch and feel, in absence of evidence to the contrary the belief that such a thing exists is so evi-

12 Ibid., p. 9.

dent, so reasonable, that it would be pointless to seek a frequency argument to justify the belief. To what premises could I appeal? Surely, any premise to which I might appeal would be less evident, or at least no more evident, than the very belief I was attempting to justify. The belief is so completely justified that no such argument to justify it could reasonably be given.

A SKEPTICAL QUERY: A QUESTION OF INNOCENCE

The primary defect of this defense of dogmatism is the manner in which all equity and fairness in disputation are set neatly aside for the convenience of dogmatism. We begin by questioning whether perceptual beliefs are completely justified. And what is the response to our query? It is the bold assertion that these beliefs are so evident and completely justified in themselves that no argument can even be offered to sustain them. But this reply constitutes a most immediate and obvious begging of the question against skepticism. The dogmatist has simply laid it down that what *seems* most evident and completely justified to him must be conceded to be completely justified without argument or debate. We agree that the beliefs in question may *seem* completely justified to the dogmatist, indeed, so completely justified that no argument would serve to render those beliefs any more evident to *him*. What we deny is that those beliefs are completely justified, and what we require is some argument to convince *us* that those beliefs are so justified. We, it seems, are destined to remain unsatisfied.

If matters remain at the level of denial and simple assertion, we have arrived at an impasse, and defeat must not be marked against either party to the dispute. It is essential that we move beyond this level of argumentation if we are to claim a victory for skepticism. We may do so very easily because the preceding considerations readily supply a needed skeptical premise. If a dispute is to proceed in a fair and equitable manner, then neither side should be assumed to have the right on its side at the outset. Neither should the conclusions advanced by one disputant be assumed at the outset to be justified and those advocated by the other unjustified.

The dogmatist says he sees there is a pencil in his hand and is completely justified in believing he sees this. We then advance some skeptical hypothesis, such as the braino hypothesis, and note that if this hypothesis is true then he does not see that there is a pencil in his hand, and, hence he is not completely justified in this belief. He replies by merely asserting that his belief in this matter is so completely justified that he can offer no argument to support his position. But this means his dogmatic perceptual claim, denied by the skeptical hypothesis, is unsupported by argument. We do not assume that our skeptical hypothesis is justified. To do so would be to beg the question in our favor. Correspondingly, the dogmatist should not assume that his perceptual claim is justified, because to do so equally begs the question on his side. A principle of impartiality requires that until some justificatory argument is offered, we shall not assume that the claims of either party are justified or unjustified.

However, and here is the crux, this principle of impartiality curiously favors the skeptic. If the claims of neither the dogmatist nor the skeptic are assumed to be completely justified, then the perceptual beliefs of the dogmatist must not be assumed to be completely justified. If they are not assumed to be completely justified, then they must not be assumed to constitute knowledge either. In this way does simple fairness and impartiality in discourse and disputation sustain the case for skepticism. The dogmatist claim that certain beliefs may be assumed to be completely justified until some argument to the contrary is mustered controverts the truth. Rules of equitable debate require that we assume *no* beliefs in dispute to be completely justified unless some justificatory argument is brought forth to support them. So we must assume at the outset that the beliefs in question, including those perceptual beliefs cited by the dogmatist, are not completely justified until some argument is presented to justify them. If skepticism is treated fairly before the bar of evidence, it must be acknowledged that the burden of proof rests entirely with the dogmatist.

THE IMPLAUSIBILITY OF SKEPTICAL HYPOTHESES: A PLUS FOR DOGMATISM

The foregoing argument may be squarely met. First, note that the skeptic must not construe the burden of proof so that a dogmatist is required to demonstrate his perceptual beliefs are completely justified by proceeding from some completely justified premises, because, whatever premises he calls forth, the justification of those premises can be challenged in cross examination. Since it is the complete justification of belief that is in question, the dogmatist can only be expected to show that his claims are more reasonable than those of his opponent. As we noted in the first chapter, a belief or conclusion may be considered reasonable if it is more probable than those with which it competes for acceptance. With this principle of reasonable acceptance in mind, let us consider very briefly the matter at issue.

I claim to see that there is a yellow pencil in my hand. It is admitted that all the sensory evidence corroborates this belief. That is our claim. Now consider the skeptic. He propounds a skeptical hypothesis that I do not see any such thing but rather that these sensory experiences are provided by a braino operated by Dr. O. These two claims are inconsistent with each other and compete for acceptance. But truly the competition is a farce. Even allowing that the skeptical hypothesis meaningfully describes a logical possibility, it is so improbable in comparison to the simple perceptual belief we put forth, that any man of sense agrees it is reasonable to accept that belief instead of the preposterously improbable hypothesis advanced by the skeptic. If the skeptic does not concede the perceptual belief is any more probable than the braino hypothesis he lays before us, there is no way to enlighten him.

SKEPTICISM AND THE LOTTERY PARADOX

Again, we could demur at these bold unsupported claims of the dogmatist and demand of him some argument to convince us that his belief is more probable than our hypothesis. Why, after all, should we agree that his claim is the more probable? What is there to sustain this claim except the dogmatic conviction of the vulgar? However, such questions appear destined to suffer neglect, and they are better put aside. Indeed let us be philosophically magnanimous and concede, for the sake of argument, that what he says is more probable is genuinely so. We may even yet refute the dogmatist.

We base our final refutation of skepticism on the lottery paradox mentioned in the preceding chapter. We shall argue that a man is not completely justified in what he believes unless there is no chance whatever that he is mistaken. If there is some chance that he is mistaken, however small, then he is not completely justified in his belief, and, therefore, he lacks knowledge. This thesis is highly contentious. Men often say that they know, when there is obviously some chance that they are in error. So ordinary speech suggests that we should not require that all chance of error be excluded before a man may be said to know. However, as we shall prove by appeal to the lottery paradox, a contradiction results from assuming a belief may be completely justified without all chance of error being excluded. Hence we shall conclude that this assumption must be rejected to save our conception of knowledge from inconsistency.

Suppose, for the sake of argument, that a belief could be completely justified without all chance of error being excluded. How great a chance of error is to be allowed? One chance in ten? One chance in a million? It won't matter. If there is one chance in n, whatever number n may be, we shall be led into contradiction. Imagine we say one chance in a million is acceptable. Now suppose we set up a fair lottery with a million tickets numbered consecutively from 1 and a ticket has been drawn but not inspected. Of course, there is only one chance in a million that the number 1 ticket has been drawn. So, by the current proposal, we would be completely justified in believing that the number 1 ticket was not picked. There is only one chance in a million of error. Hence we would be completely justified in claiming to know that the number 1 ticket was not picked.

Moreover, people really do speak this way about lotteries; they do say they know that the ticket they hold was not drawn because there is so little chance of it. However, a similar claim can be made concerning the number 2 ticket, for there is equally little chance that it was picked. So we can say that we know that the number 2 ticket was not picked. But then the same reasoning applies to each ticket in the lottery. Of each ticket in the lottery, we would be completely justified in believing, and, hence, in claiming to know that the ticket was not drawn in this fair lottery in which the winning ticket has been drawn. But the set of things we would thus claim to know is inconsistent. It is contradictory to claim that each of the tickets in a fair lottery with one winning ticket is not the winner. For if each is not the winner, then the lottery with one winning ticket has no winning ticket. Of course, requiring the chance of error be less than one in a million will not help. For however small the chance, we can find a large enough lottery to create the paradox. Since the assumption that a belief may be completely justified though there is some chance of error leads to contradiction, we must reject it. To analyze knowledge in terms of complete justification that allows for some chance of error is to render knowledge logically inconsistent.

We now have established a critical premise in our final argument for skepticism, namely, that if a man is completely justified in what he believes, then his justification must exclude all chance of error. Note, in passing, that this assumption eliminates the need for a fourth condition in the analysis of knowledge. We said earlier that for a man to know he must not only be completely justified but justified in such a way that his justification does not depend essentially on any false assumption, that is, his justification must be undefeated. If we require a completely justified belief to be such that the justification excludes all chance of error, we have thereby insured that the justification does not depend essentially on any false assumption. For one way in which the chance of error may creep into justification is through dependence on some false assumption. If the justification is so complete as to exclude all chance of error, it also excludes dependence on error. Hence the fourth condition collapses into the third.

With these remarks we drive ahead easily to our skeptical conclusion. The braino hypothesis, and other hypotheses of the same skeptical cut, show that there is some chance that our perceptual beliefs are false. There is some chance that the braino hypothesis is true, however slight, and therefore some chance that our ordinary perceptual beliefs are in error. Since there is some chance that those beliefs are in error, they are not completely justified. Because they are not completely justified, we do not know that they are true.

SUMMARY OF THE ARGUMENT
The argument just advanced may be laid out as follows:

1. If anyone knows that any perceptual belief of his is true, then he is completely justified in his perceptual belief.
2. If anyone is completely justified in his perceptual belief, then his justification for his perceptual belief excludes all chance of error.

From these two premises we conclude

> *Therefore*
> 3. If anyone knows that any perceptual belief of his is true, then his justification for his perceptual belief excludes all chance of error.

Having reached this conclusion, we appeal to material from an earlier argument to reach our skeptical conclusion.

> 4. If there is some chance that the braino hypothesis is true, then the justification anyone has for his perceptual belief does not exclude all chance of error.
> 5. There is some chance that the braino hypothesis is true.
> *Therefore*
> 6. The justification anyone has for his perceptual belief does not exclude all chance of error.

From conclusions (3) and (6) we obtain our further skeptical conclusion

> 7. No one knows that any perceptual belief of his is true.

We here rest our case for skepticism.

NO CHANCE FOR THE BRAINO HYPOTHESIS: THE DOGMATIST REJOINS

We may concede most of this argument without conceding the conclusion. For we may deny there is some chance the braino hypothesis is true. We have conceded that the braino hypothesis is logically possible. But the logical possibility of truth does not show there is any chance whatever that the hypothesis is true. To argue that a belief is not completely justified because some conflicting hypothesis is logically possible is to argue fallaciously. We have shown this earlier. So if the skeptic attempts to argue from the logical possibility of the braino hypothesis to the conclusion that there is some chance that it is true, his argument will be ill founded. There is no chance that the braino hypothesis is true; it is simply preposterous.

A MORE REALISTIC CHANCE OF ERROR:
THE SKEPTIC AND THE GOOGOLS

We do not by any means concede that there is no chance that the braino hypothesis is true. After all, how do you know that it is false? Note that any alleged evidence of the falsity of the hypothesis could be explained in terms of the attempts of Dr. O to mislead us so that we would not hypothesize his existence. However, again for the sake of argument, it will be useful to present a skeptical hypothesis that is more apt to obtain agreement from an impartial consideration. So we shall construct, ultimately, a hypothesis which obviously has some chance of being correct.

To accomplish this we shall first invent a story that is perhaps even more incredible than the story of Dr. O. We shall then make use of this hypothesis in constructing a skeptical hypothesis that is, we allege, one that must be conceded to have some chance of being true.

Imagine that the earth has been observed by members of a very advanced civilization on another planet. Imagine that these beings are many times more intelligent than we are, roughly 10^{100} as intelligent. Since that number has been named Googol, we shall refer to these beings as Googols. Now one of the Googols, Henry by name, has made earthmen his special study. With the aid of his remarkable computer he arrived at a shocking conclusion. It was that the earthmen were very adept scientifically but very equally inept morally and politically. In fact, his computer gave him a projection, with a very high degree of probability, that the earthmen would destroy themselves in less than a hundred years because they would prove incompetent to handle the scientific information and technological skills they were sure to develop. Henry became very disheartened to learn of this, as he had grown very fond of this somewhat amusing if egregiously aggressive civilization. He could think of no satisfactory remedy. So he ran an ad in the Googol press offering a prize for the best workable strategy to save the earthmen. The prize was won by a Googol named Mary.

Mary noted that the earthmen had a brain containing a certain area, a pleasure center, which when stimulated gave intense pleasure to the person in question. She then explained how this pleasure center could be stimulated electrically by a power source near the earth controlled by a Googol computer. The plan she proposed was as follows. She argued, having mastered the psychology of earthmen in a matter of hours, that earthmen could be conditioned to have certain beliefs by stimulating their pleasure centers when they entertained such beliefs and withholding such pleasurable stimulation otherwise. She concluded that if the pleasure centers of men are stimulated when their perceptual beliefs are slightly erroneous and not otherwise, over a relatively short period of time they will come to have almost entirely erroneous beliefs, provided the error is not so great as to lead to an immediately painful experience. If men are thus conditioned to have slightly erroneous perceptual beliefs in this way, they will never arrive at those scientific theories or develop those technological skills that would lead to their demise. They will, to be sure, conceive many scientific theories and devise many technological skills, but there will always be sufficient confusion and incoherence within their scientific conception of the world resulting from their defective perceptual beliefs so they will fail to hit on those scientific truths that would destroy them.

Now some earth philosopher or scientist will note that even perceptual beliefs may sometimes have to be rejected for the sake of theory. The reason that such beliefs will have to be rejected is that they will be erroneous in such a way that no theory could fit them all. To arrive at their rudimentary science and technology they will repudiate some of their perceptual beliefs. But they will retain a commitment to empiricism which will lead them to check their theories again and again in terms of perceptual beliefs which will always remain erroneous. Of course, Mary explained with a smile of scientific satisfaction, these perceptual errors are necessary for their continued existence.

And that is how Mary won the prize and saved the earthmen.

Perhaps you might be willing to believe that this story, or one somewhat like it, is true. If you concede there is some chance it is true, then there is some chance, not excluded by the justification we have for our perceptual beliefs, that our perceptual beliefs are erroneous because the Googols have conditioned us to believe erroneously. On the other hand, if the story seems like idle fantasy without any chance in the world of being true, that does not matter. The object of telling the tale, other than for what amusement it might afford, is to call to your attention the fact that our survival may depend on our ignorance. There is at least some chance that if our perceptual beliefs were not slightly wide of the mark, slightly incorrect, then we would indeed destroy ourselves as a result of scientific discovery and mishandled technology based upon it. Thus, we propose there is at least some chance that erroneous beliefs have survival value, and, moreover, that the erroneousness of our perceptual beliefs has saved us from destroying ourselves long ago. There is some chance, however small, that the erroneousness of our perceptual beliefs has survival value.

Suppose, to illustrate, that there is some particular theory that is especially dangerous to mankind. Imagine that some discovery in physics—perhaps one enabling us to formulate a wholly deterministic theory at the subatomic level, thus vindicating Einstein, who advocated such a theory—would enable us to understand how to release vast amounts of energy in a simple way with common materials. If we imagine, moreover, that such devices may have the power of thermonuclear bombs and any man could easily learn how to construct them from materials to which we all have access, then we can see that such devices would place us all at the mercy of demented and desperate men willing to destroy themselves to destroy others. And then the holocaust would result from the madness of the few.

The foregoing is but one way in which the discovery of some principle might serve to destroy us. There are countless others that one might imagine. If the discovery of such a principle would obliterate life, then the failure to discover it would be necessary for our continued existence. Now one way in which we might be prevented from discovering such a principle is by virtue of perceptual error. If we are misled at the perceptual level, our attempts to check those theories that might lead to the fatal one will be subverted at the level of observation. We shall, by dint of our defective observation, be encouraged to accept some slightly incorrect theories that are more probable in terms of our slightly erroneous perceptual beliefs than those correct but fatal theories we reject. In short, theory is based, either directly or indirectly, on observation, and, therefore, faulty observation, erroneous perceptual beliefs, can prevent us from arriving at correct theories. We propose that there is some chance, however small you might think it is, that our very survival at this moment depends on our failure to accept some correct theory because of our erroneous perceptual beliefs. In this way, then, there is some chance that our perceptual beliefs are erroneous, and, indeed, that our survival has depended on it. If you ask how it could be that the error has gone undetected, the answer is that had it been detected there would be no one here now to report the result.

The foregoing argument can be abbreviated as a challenge. If someone claims to know that our perceptual beliefs are not erroneous and that such error does not have survival value, let him answer a critical question. How do you know that error in our perceptual beliefs does not have survival value? We skeptics contend that no one has a satisfactory answer to that question. Indeed, no matter what class of beliefs we pick out, if we ask a dogmatist with respect to such beliefs how he knows that error among such beliefs does not have survival value, we may expect only silence as a retort. But if the dogmatist cannot explain how he knows these things, then he must admit that there is some chance of error here, and that he does not know what he dogmatically says he does.

SUMMARY OF THE FINAL SKEPTICAL ARGUMENT

We now present a summary of the preceding argument. In our summary we refer to the hypothesis that the erroneousness of our perceptual beliefs has survival value as the *survival hypothesis*. The argument then is as follows:

1. If anyone knows that any perceptual belief of his is true, then his perceptual belief is completely justified.
2. If anyone is completely justified in his perceptual belief, then his justification for his perceptual belief excludes all chance of error.
   Therefore
3. If anyone knows that any perceptual belief of his is true, then his justification for his perceptual belief excludes all chance of error.

We continue our argument:

4. If no one knows that the survival hypothesis is false, then no one's justification for his perceptual belief excludes all chance of error.
5. No one knows that the survival hypothesis is false.
   Therefore

6. No one's justification for his perceptual belief excludes all chance of error.

Finally, from statements (3) and (6) we conclude

7. No one knows that any perceptual belief of his is true.

We have, by this argument, formulated our argument for skepticism. We shall rest the matter here. However, it is important to understand the implications of the doctrine. Standards of evidence and epistemic evaluation telling us that some beliefs are completely justified beyond all risk and chance of error must be laid aside in favor of a more skeptical and flexible theory of reasonable belief. We are not repudiating reason; instead, we are claiming that nothing is beyond its reach. There is nothing so secure or sacrosanct as to be beyond rational criticism. Hence we may always ask whether it is reasonable to accept some statement as a hypothesis, or even whether it is reasonable to accept some statement as evidence for a hypothesis. The question is not resolved by appeal to some infallible beliefs beyond all chance of error. It is settled instead, tentatively and subject to subsequent reconsideration, by appeal to the probabilities, to the very genuine risk of error we admit. The statement that is more probable than those with which it competes for the status of hypothesis or evidence is reasonable to accept. In this way, and by induction, we may proceed to reason in terms of evidence and hypothesis without dogmatism or pseudocertainties of knowledge.

In conclusion, it is important to point out that we are not disputing here over the mere use of the word 'know.' Our objection to the dogmatic contention that men know certain of their beliefs to be true is the roadblock to inquiry indigenous to such claims. If a man says he knows that something is true, then he intends his listener to take what he says as true on his authority. It is not a matter to be questioned. The word 'know' functions this way in ordinary discourse, and we consider this a defect of such discourse. We affirm the right and the need to submit any statement or belief to criticism and requisite justification. None are allowed exemption from this ordeal of reason. We concede, of course, that a person might succeed in using the word 'know' without such dogmatic implications.

And if someone uses the word in some weaker sense, allowing for the fallibility, the chance of error, and the appropriateness of criticism, then we wish him well. We only warn that such a frame of mind is congenial to that dogmatic epistemic lexeme.

EXERCISES

1. What is skepticism? Why have speculators also sometimes been skeptics? Are you a skeptic, a speculator, or both? Why?

2. Consider the following claim:

   We may define "knowing" as "having the right answer." When a person knows the answer, then he has the right answer, and when he has the right answer, then he knows the answer. Thus, the definition given is exactly right.

   What is the matter with this definition?

3. Consider the following argument:

   No unjustified belief can be counted as a case of knowledge. On the other hand, every case of knowledge involves a justified belief. Thus, there is no difference between knowledge and justified belief.

   What is the matter with this argument?

4. It is sometimes said that knowledge and truth are one and the same. Would you agree to this? Explain and justify your answer.

5. Consider the following argument:

   When a man sees something, he does not have any evidence for believing what he sees. Therefore, perceptual beliefs are those for which we have no evidence.

   Is this contention correct? Why?

6. What is the skeptical argument to show that seeing something to have a sensible characteristic does not constitute knowing it has that quality? What additional premise is needed to arrive at the skeptical

conclusion that we never know that anything has any sensible characteristic? Which argument is said to be invalid by the dogmatist?

7. The skeptic contends that if we are sometimes mistaken in our perceptual beliefs, then it is always logically possible that our perceptual beliefs are false. How does he employ this premise to support the skeptical conclusion that we never know that any of our perceptual beliefs are true? How is the premise challenged by the dogmatist? Is the challenge successful?

8. In reply to a dogmatist objection, the skeptical argument is modified. A major premise of the modified argument is one assuming that the experiences of a person who has a true perceptual belief may be exactly duplicated by the experiences of a person whose perceptual belief is exactly similar but false. How does the skeptic defend this premise? How does the dogmatist question it? What other premises are needed for the deduction of the skeptical conclusion? Were any of these premises used in an earlier argument?

9. What skeptical premise is defended by appeal to hallucination? How does the skeptic attempt to prove that hallucination is always possible? How does the skeptic reply to the dogmatist objection that hallucinations can be detected by applying the tests of experiential coherence and the testimony of others?

10. Consider the following dogmatist argument:

The appeal to hallucination in defense of skepticism is entirely illegitimate. In describing some experiences as hallucinatory, the skeptic is tacitly assuming that we can tell the difference between experiences that are hallucinatory and those that are not. But if we can tell the difference, then skepticism is false. The skeptical use of hallucination is thus self-defeating.

What is the skeptical reply to this argument? Who is right? Why?

11. The braino argument is brought in by the skeptic to defend a premise of his argument and to meet an objection of the dogmatist. What is the premise and what was the dogmatist objection to it? What objection, involving the distinction between possibility and actuality, is raised by the dogmatist against the braino argument? How does the skeptic think that we may legitimately pass from possibility to actuality?

12. Consider the following dogmatist argument:

The idea that such a machine as the braino exists is nothing more than idle fantasy. It need not be taken any more seriously than tales of Santa Claus. Thus, the idea that we are controlled by the braino, which the skeptic puts forth as a serious hypothesis, may be rejected without further argument. Rejecting the idea allows us to reject the conclusions of skepticism as well.

What would the skeptic reply to these remarks?

13. The story of Tom and Dr. O is intended to refute a premise of the skeptic's argument. What is the premise? Why is the perfect deception said to be no deception at all? Why is the perfect hallucination said to be meaningless? Is what the dogmatist says correct? Does it refute skepticism?

14. Consider the following skeptical argument:

No one can imagine what anything contradictory would be like. For example, no one can imagine what a round square would be like. Therefore, if we can imagine something, then it is logically possible and not contradictory. So the mere fact that we can imagine what a perfect hallucination would be like, as we did in the story of Tom and Dr. O, shows that such a hallucination is possible.

How might a dogmatist reply to this argument? Would the reply be successful? Why?

15. What theory of the meaning of perceptual beliefs is employed by the skeptic in order to prove the possibility and meaningfulness of a perfect hallucination? How does he argue from the theory to his conclusion? Is the argument cogent?

16. In reply to the skeptic, the dogmatist defends a theory, phenomenalism, concerning the meaning of perceptual beliefs. What is the theory? How does this theory enable the dogmatist to rebut skepticism? What premises used by the skeptic will be undermined, according to the dogmatist, if phenomenalism is a correct theory? Does the dogmatist succeed in his formulation and defense of phenomenalism?

17. How does the skeptic attempt to show that phenomenalism is an incorrect theory? How does the question of the normality of the observer come into his argument? What argument does the skeptic present to show that even if phenomenalism were true it would not serve to support dogmatism? Can phenomenalism be salvaged in any way? Is it worth salvaging for the purpose of dogmatism?

18. The skeptic draws a distinction between the semantic and epistemic sense of such terms as 'nonsense' and 'meaningless.' What assumption of skepticism is defended by appeal to this distinction?

19. To defeat skepticism the dogmatist contends that evidence which does not exclude the possibility of error may nonetheless greatly reduce the probability of error. What premise of the skeptic does the dogmatist hope to refute by contending this? Why is it especially important, from the standpoint of dogmatism, to defeat that premise of skepticism? Does the dogmatist succeed?

20. What argument does the skeptic employ to show that the dogmatist's appeal to probability will lead to skepticism? How does the question of establishing frequencies in a sample enter into the argument? How does the dogmatist use an ethical analogy to attack this argument of the skeptic? What premise of the argument is the analogy intended to refute? Is any other premise of the skeptical argument vulnerable to attack?

21. The dogmatist claims that some beliefs may be assumed to be completely justified until some argument to the contrary is offered. What is the skeptic's reply to this contention? What is the role of the principle of impartiality in the reply? Is the reply effective?

22. How does a contradiction result from the assumption that a belief may be completely justified without all chance of error being excluded? How does this support skepticism? What argument is offered to show that all chance of error cannot be excluded?

23. Consider the following argument:

> The skeptic argues that all chance of error must be excluded before we are completely justified in a belief. This leads to the conclusion that we never are so justified and hence that we know nothing. But surely that conclusion is absurd. Consequently, it is most reasonable to reject the premise on which it was based. While we must admit that high probability will not suffice for complete justification, it is possible that high probability plus some other factor may suffice and also permit us to elude the lottery paradox. The only problem is to say what that other factor is.

What do you think of this argument? Is it plausible? Can you propose the missing factor?

BIBLIOGRAPHY

CLASSICAL SOURCES

Two of Plato's dialogues, *The Theaetetus* and *The Republic,* are recommended. There are many editions and translations, most of which are of some value, but the translations by F. M. Cornford are especially recommended. A less famous but very important writer is Sextus Empiricus. For an interesting formulation of skepticism, see his *Outlines of Pyrrhonism* in Vol. 1 of *Sextus Empiricus* (London: Loeb Classical Library, 1933). The *Discourse on Method* and the *Meditations* of René Descartes are enjoyable reading; although Descartes ultimately reaches conclusions that are far from skeptical, his initial arguments in both books constitute a foundation for the defense of skepticism. Almost any of the editions of these works will prove adequate. George Berkeley often denied that his doctrines led to skepticism, but there are many arguments in his *Three Dialogues Between Hylas and Philonous* to please a skeptic. A more explicit defender of skepticism is David Hume in his *Treatise of Human Nature* and *Inquiry into the Human Understanding.* In both books see sections entitled, "Of Scepticism with Regard to the Senses."

CONTEMPORARY SOURCES

I. Books by a Single Author
The following books on the theory of knowledge are written expressly for the beginning student: A. J. Ayer, *The Problem of Knowledge* (Baltimore: Penguin Books, 1956); R. M. Chisholm, *Theory of Knowledge* (Englewood Cliffs, N.J.: Prentice-Hall, Inc., 1966); A. D. Woozley, *Theory of Knowledge* (London: Hutchinson's University Library, 1949); David Pears, *What Is Knowledge?* (New York: Harper & Row, Publishers, Inc., 1971); D. W. Hamlyn, *The Theory of Knowledge* (Garden City, N.Y.: Doubleday & Company, Inc., 1971); Bruce Aune, *Knowledge, Mind, and Nature: An Introduction to the Theory of Knowledge and the Philosophy of Mind* (New York: Random House, Inc., 1967); Elizabeth Ramsden Eames, *Bertrand Russell's Theory of Knowledge* (London: George Allen & Unwin, Ltd., 1969).

After these there are a large number of books that are intended primarily for a professional audience but that prove intelligible to the serious student. Works with a particular emphasis on the subject of skepticism are numerous, but few are sympathetic to the skeptic's point of view. For a very readable defense of skepticism, see Bertrand Russell's *The Problems of Philosophy* (London: Oxford University Press, 1912). Arne Naess, in *Scepticism* (London: Routledge & Kegan Paul, 1969), is sympathetic to the skepticism of Sextus Empiricus. Books written from the opposite point of view are Michael A. Slote, *Reason and Scepticism* (New York: Humanities Press, 1970); Ludwig Wittgenstein, *On Certainty*, German and English text, edited by G. E. M. Anscombe and G. H. von Wright; translated by Denis Paul and G. E. M. Anscombe (Oxford: Basil Blackwell, 1969); and S. Coval, *Skepticism and the First Person* (London: Methuen & Co., Ltd., 1967).

On the topic of perception, see C. D. Broad's *Mind and Its Place in Nature* (London: Kegan Paul, Trench, Trubner and Company, 1925). Chapter IV contains a discussion of various theories of sense perception. This account is examined by Martin Lean in *Sense-Perception and Matter* (London: Routledge and Kegan Paul, 1953). A. J. Ayer defends phenomenalism in *The Foundations of Empirical Knowledge* (New York: Macmillan Publishing Co., Inc., 1940). Some other analyses of perception are to be found in the following books: D. M. Armstrong, *Perception and the Physical World* (London: Routledge and Kegan Paul, 1961); R. M. Chisholm, *Perceiving: A Philosophical Study* (Ithaca, N.Y.: Cornell University Press, 1957); D. W. Hamlyn, *Sensation and Perception* (London: Routledge and Kegan Paul, 1961); R. J. Hirst, *The Problems of Perception* (London: George Allen & Unwin, Ltd., 1959); G. E. Moore, *Some Main Problems of Philosophy* (London: George Allen & Unwin, Ltd., 1953); Maurice Mandelbaum, *Philosophy, Science and Sense-Perception* (Baltimore: Johns Hopkins Press, 1964); G. Ryle, *The Concept of Mind* (London: Hutchinson and Company, 1949), especially Chapter VIII; H. H. Price, *Perception* (London: Methuen & Co., Ltd., 1932); C. I. Lewis, *Mind and the World Order* (New York: Charles Scribner's Sons, 1929); W. F. Sellars, *Science, Perception and Reality* (London: Routledge and Kegan Paul, 1963); W. T. Stace, *Knowledge and Existence* (London: Oxford University Press, 1932); Colin Murray Turbayne, *The Myth of Metaphor* (New Haven: Yale University Press, 1962); C. J. Ducasse, *Nature, Mind and Death* (La Salle, Ill.: Open Court Publishing Company, 1951); Norman Malcolm, *Knowledge and Certainty* (Englewood Cliffs, N.J.: Prentice-Hall, Inc., 1963); Don Locke, *Perception and Our Knowledge of the External World* (New York: Humanities Press, 1967), especially the second part; David Armstrong, *A Materialist Theory of the Mind* (London: Routledge and Kegan Paul, 1968); Fred I. Dretske, *Seeing and Knowing* (London: Routledge and Kegan Paul, 1969); J. W. Cornman, *Materialism and Sensations* (New Haven: Yale University Press, 1971), especially Part III; George Pitcher,

A Theory of Perception (Princeton, N.J.: Princeton University Press, 1971), especially Chapters I and II; Wilfrid Sellars, *Science and Metaphysics: Variations on Kantian Themes* (New York: Humanities Press, 1968), Chapters 1 and 2. Two philosophical books on perception written from a somewhat different point of view are J. R. Smythie's *Analysis of Perception* (London: Routledge and Kegan Paul, 1956), approaching the subject from neurophysiology, and M. Merleau-Ponty's *The Phenomenology of Perception*, translated by Colin Smith (London: Routledge and Kegan Paul, 1962), approaching the subject from the philosophy of phenomenology.

More general books on theory of knowledge are Jacob Joshua Ross, *The Appeal to the Given* (London: George Allen & Unwin, Ltd.; New York: Humanities Press, 1970); Panayot Butchvarov, *The Concept of Knowledge* (Evanston, Ill.: Northwestern University Press, 1970); Robert J. Fogelin, *Evidence and Meaning* (London: Routledge and Kegan Paul, 1967); H. H. Price, *Belief* (London: George Allen & Unwin, Ltd., 1969); Arthur C. Danto, *Analytical Philosophy of Knowledge* (London: Cambridge University Press, 1968); R. I. Aaron, *Knowing and the Function of Reason* (New York: Oxford University Press, 1970); and A. J. Ayer, *Russell and Moore: The Analytical Heritage* (London: Macmillan & Company, Ltd., 1971).

II. Anthologies and Textbooks

There are a number of useful anthologies of published articles. Any serious student would find it worthwhile to obtain Robert J. Swartz's anthology, *Perceiving, Sensing, and Knowing* (Garden City, N.Y.: Doubleday & Company, Inc., 1965), which contains articles by contemporary authors. It also has a very complete bibliography of important articles and books. See also J. W. Yolton's *Theory of Knowledge* (New York: Macmillan Publishing Co., Inc., 1965). Anthologies with a good chapter on the theory of knowledge include Joel Feinberg's *Reason and Responsibility* (Belmont, Calif.: Dickenson Publishing Company, 1965); Paul Edwards and Arthur Pap, *A Modern Introduction to Philosophy: Revised Edition* (New York: The Free Press, 1965); and Mandelbaum, Gramlich, and Anderson, *Philosophical Problems* (New York: Macmillan Publishing Co., Inc., 1957). A more difficult anthology but one worth examining is H. Feigl and W. Sellars, *Readings in Philosophical Analysis* (New York: Appleton-Century-Crofts, Inc., 1949). Chapters 2, 3, and 6 in John Hospers' textbook *Introduction to Philosophical Analysis* (Englewood Cliffs, N.J.: Prentice-Hall, Inc., 1953) are worth study. George Nakhnikian's *An Introduction to Philosophy* (New York: Alfred A. Knopf, Inc., 1967), Part Two, discusses Descartes' "evil demon" hypothesis. Selections from Descartes to the present are contained in

Douglas G. Arner, *Perception, Reason, and Knowledge: An Introduction to Epistemology* (Glenview, Ill.: Scott, Foresman and Company, 1972). Finally, four anthologies of contemporary sources are Lawrence Foster and J. W. Swanson, editors, *Theory and Experience* (Amherst: University of Massachusetts Press, 1970); Robert R. Ammerman and Marcus G. Singer, editors, *Belief, Knowledge and Truth: Readings in the Theory of Knowledge* (New York: Charles Scribner's Sons, 1970); and Avrum Stroll, editor, *Epistemology: New Essays in the Theory of Knowledge* (New York: Harper & Row, Publishers, Inc., 1967); and Michael D. Roth and Leon Galis, editors, *Knowing* (New York: Random House, 1970).

III. Articles in Books and Journals

A very large number of the most important articles written on the theory of knowledge are contained in the anthology by Robert J. Swartz mentioned in Section II. The following are additional articles not contained in any of the anthologies listed. The following are articles on perception: W. N. F. Barnes, "On Seeing and Hearing," *Contemporary British Philosophy, Third Series*, edited by H. D. Lewis (London: George Allen & Unwin, Ltd., 1956); C. A. Baylis, "Professor Chisholm on Perceiving," *Journal of Philosophy*, Vol. 56 (1959), pp. 773–91; John Dewey, "The Naturalistic Theory of Perception by the Senses," *Journal of Philosophy*, Vol. 22 (1925), pp. 596–605; T. Duggan and R. Taylor, "On Seeing Double," *Philosophical Quarterly*, Vol. 8 (1958), pp. 171–74; Noel Fleming, "Recognizing and Seeing As," *Philosophical Review*, Vol. 66 (1957), pp. 161–79; Roderick Firth, "Phenomenalism," in *Proceedings of the American Philosophical Association, Eastern Division*, Vol. 1 (1952), pp. 1–20, and "Chisholm and the Ethics of Belief," *Philosophical Review* (1959), pp. 493–506; Gustav Bergmann, "Sense Data, Linguistic Conventions, and Existence," *Philosophy of Science*, Vol. 14 (1947); Paul Marhenke, "Phenomenalism," *Philosophical Analysis* (Ithaca, N.Y.: Cornell University Press, 1950), edited by Max Black; Max Black, "The Language of Sense-Data," in *Problems of Analysis* (Ithaca, N.Y.: Cornell University Press, 1946); Stuart Hampshire, "Perception and Identification," *Aristotelian Society Proceedings*, Supplementary Volume XXXV (1961), pp. 81–96; J. J. C. Smart, "Colours," *Philosophy*, Vol. 36 (1961), pp. 121–42; P. F. Strawson, "Perception and Identification," *Aristotelian Society Proceedings*, Supplementary Volume XXXV (1961), pp. 97–120; A. R. White, "The Causal Theory of Perception," in *ibid.*, pp. 153–68; and P. G. Winch, "The Notion of Suggestion in Thomas Reid's Theory of Perception," *Philosophical Quarterly*, Vol. III (1953), pp. 327–41. See also a symposium by C. I. Lewis, Nelson Goodman, and Hans Reichenbach, "The Experiential Element in Knowledge," *The Philosophical Review*, Vol. 61 (1952), pp. 147–75.

PHILOSOPHICAL PROBLEMS AND ARGUMENTS

IV. Very Recent Articles
In case the student is curious about the nature of very recent writing in the theory of knowledge, a list of articles written since 1963 is included here.

The following articles deal with problems in the theory of perception: Clement Dore, "Ayer on the Causal Theory of Perception," *Mind*, Vol. 73 (1964), pp. 287–90; Fred I. Dretske, "Observational Terms," *The Philosophical Review*, Vol. 74 (1965), pp. 25–42; R. N. Bronaugh, "The Argument from the Elliptical Penny," *Philosophical Quarterly*, Vol. 14 (1964), pp. 151–57; David K. Lewis, "Percepts and Color Mosaics in Visual Experience," *Philosophical Review*, Vol. 75 (1966), pp. 357–68; G. E. Myers, "Perception and the Sentience Hypothesis," *Mind*, Vol. 72 (1963), pp. 111–20; John O. Nelson, "An Examination of D. M. Armstrong's Theory of Perception," *American Philosophical Quarterly*, Vol. 1 (1964), pp. 154–60; Katherine Pyne Parsons, "Mistaking Sensation," *Philosophical Review*, Vol. 79 (1970), pp. 201–13; John Pollock, "Perceptual Knowledge," *Philosophical Review*, Vol. 80 (1971), pp. 287–319; Maurice Mandelbaum, "Definiteness and Coherence in Sense-Perception," *Nous*, Vol. 1 (1967), pp. 123–38; David M. Johnson, "A Formulation Model of Perceptual Knowledge," *American Philosophical Quarterly*, Vol. 8 (1971), pp. 54–62.

A great deal has been written recently on the nature of knowledge and on what constitutes good reason for belief. Some articles in this area of investigation are Edmund Gettier, "Is Justified True Belief Knowledge?" *Analysis*, Vol. 23 (1963), pp. 121–23; L. Jonathan Cohen, "More About Knowing and Feeling Sure," *Analysis*, Vol. 27 (1966), pp. 1–11; Keith Lehrer and Thomas Paxson, Jr., "Knowledge: Undefeated Justified True Belief," *Journal of Philosophy*, Vol. 66 (1969), pp. 225–37 [this article is discussed by J. R. Kress in "Lehrer and Paxson on Nonbasic Knowledge," *Journal of Philosophy*, Vol. 68 (1971), pp. 78–82; Ernest Sosa has also commented in "Two Conceptions of Knowledge," *Journal of Philosophy*, Vol. 67 (1970), pp. 59–66]; James W. Lamb, "Knowledge and Justified Presumption," *Journal of Philosophy*, Vol. 69 (1972), pp. 123–27; Marshall Swain, "Knowledge, Causality, and Justification," *Journal of Philosophy*, Vol. 69 (1972), pp. 291–300; Charles Pailthorp, "Is Immediate Knowledge Reason Based?" *Mind*, Vol. 78 (1969), pp. 550–66; Charles Pailthorp, "Knowledge as Justified True Belief," *Review of Metaphysics*, Vol. 23 (1969), pp. 25–47 [see also Lehrer's response to this article, "The Fourth Condition of Knowledge: A Defense," *Review of Metaphysics*, Vol. 25 (1970), pp. 122–28 and Pailthorp's reply to Lehrer in that same issue, pp. 129–33]; John Turk Saunders, "Does Knowledge Require Grounds," *Philosophical Studies*. Vol. 27 (1966), pp. 7–13; Fred Dretske, "Conclusive Reasons," *Australasian Journal of Phi-*

losophy, Vol. 49 (1971), pp. 1–22; Fred Dretske, "Reasons and Consequences," *Analysis*, Vol. 28 (1968), pp. 166–68 [there is a discussion by David Finn, "Dretske on Reasons and Justification," *Analysis*, Vol. 29 (1969), pp. 101–102]; John L. Pollock, "The Structure of Epistemic Justification," *American Philosophical Quarterly Monograph Series*, edited by Nicholas Rescher, Number 4 (Oxford: Basil Blackwell, 1970), pp. 62–78. Articles by one of the authors include Keith Lehrer, "Knowledge and Probability," *Journal of Philosophy*, Vol. 61 (1964), pp. 368–72; "Knowledge, Truth and Evidence," *Analysis*, Vol. 25 (1965), pp. 168–75; "Belief and Knowledge," *Philosophical Review*, Vol. 77 (1968), pp. 491–99.

Gilbert Harman, "The Inference to the Best Explanation," *Philosophical Review*, Vol. 74 (1966), pp. 88–95; R. C. Sleigh, Jr., "A Note on Some Epistemic Principles of Chisholm and Martin," *Journal of Philosophy*, Vol. 61 (1964), pp. 216–18; Colin Radford, "Knowledge—By Examples," *Analysis*, Vol. 27 (1966), pp. 1–13; Peter Unger, "Experience and Factual Knowledge," *Journal of Philosophy*, Vol. 64 (1967), pp. 152–73 [see Gilbert Harman's remarks, "Unger on Knowledge," *Journal of Philosophy*, Vol. 64 (1967), pp. 390–95]; Peter Unger, "An Analysis of Factual Knowledge," *Journal of Philosophy*, Vol. 65 (1968), pp. 157–70; Alvin I. Goldman, "A Causal Theory of Knowing," *Journal of Philosophy*, Vol. 64 (1967), pp. 357–72; Brian Skyrms, "The Explication of 'X knows that P'," *Journal of Philosophy*, Vol. 64 (1967), pp. 373–89 [see Marshall Swain's discussion, "Skyrms on Nonderivative Knowledge," *Nous*, Vol. 3 (1969), pp. 227–31]; Ronald De Sousa, "Knowledge, Consistent Belief, and Self-consciousness," *Journal of Philosophy*, Vol. 67 (1970), pp. 66–73; Gilbert Harman, "Knowledge, Inference, and Explanation," *American Philosophical Quarterly*, Vol. 5 (1968), pp. 164–73; Manley Thompson, "Who Knows?" *Journal of Philosophy*, Vol. 67 (1970), pp. 856–68; Bernard Rosen, "Chisholm on Knowledge and Principles," *Mind*, Vol. 77 (1968), pp. 411–16; James E. Broyles, "Knowledge and Mistake," *Mind*, Vol. 78 (1969), pp. 198–211; Richard Robinson, "The Concept of Knowledge," *Mind*, Vol. 80 (1971), pp. 17–28; John Pollock, "Chisholm's Definition of Knowledge," *Philosophical Studies*, Vol. 17 (1966), pp. 72–76; John Pollock, "What Is an Epistemological Problem?" *American Philosophical Quarterly*, Vol. 5 (1968), pp. 183–90; Ernest Sosa, "Propositional Knowledge," *Philosophical Studies*, Vol. 20 (1969), pp. 33–42; Ernest Sosa, "On the Nature and Objects of Knowledge," *Philosophical Review*, Vol. 81 (1972), pp. 364–71; Herbert Heidelberger, "Chisholm's Epistemic Principles, *Nous*, Vol. 3 (1969), pp. 73–82; David Annis, "A Note on Lehrer's Proof That Knowledge Entails Belief," *Analysis*, Vol. 29 (1969), pp. 207–208; W. R. Abbott, "What Knowledge Is Not," *Analysis*, Vol. 31 (1971), pp. 143–44; James Cargile,

"On Near Knowledge," *Analysis*, Vol. 31 (1971), pp. 145–52; Carolyn Black, "Knowledge Without Belief," *Analysis*, Vol. 31 (1971), pp. 152–58.

The following articles deal with the problem of skepticism:

Paul Olscamp, "Wittgenstein's Refutation of Skepticism," *Philosophy and Phenomenological Research*, Vol. 26 (1965–66), pp. 239–47; Keith Lehrer, "Why Not Skepticism?" *Philosophical Forum*, Vol. III (1971), pp. 283–98; Peter Unger, "A Defense of Skepticism," *Philosophical Review*, Vol. 80 (1971), pp. 198–219; Julian Wolfe, "Dreaming and Skepticism," *Mind*, Vol. 80 (1971), pp. 605–606; Joseph Agassi, "The Standard Misinterpretation of Skepticism," *Philosophical Studies*, Vol. 22 (1971), pp. 49–50; John Kekes, "Skepticism and External Questions," *Philosophy and Phenomenological Research*, Vol. 31 (1971), pp. 325–40; Richard Purtill, "Epistemological Scepticism Again," *The Philosophical Forum*, Vol. 3 (1971), pp. 138–44 (reply to Lehrer above); Thompson Clarke, "The Legacy of Skepticism," *Journal of Philosophy*, Vol. 69 (1972), pp. 754–69.

Finally, articles on a variety of relevant topics:

W. Donald Oliver, "A Sober Look at Solipsism," *American Philosophical Quarterly Monograph Series*, edited by Nicholas Rescher, Number 4 (Oxford: Basil Blackwell, 1970), pp. 30–39; Peter Unger, "Our Knowledge of the Material World," *American Philosophical Quarterly Monograph Series*, edited by Nicholas Rescher, Number 4 (Oxford: Basil Blackwell, 1970), pp. 40–61; Barry Stroud, "Transcendental Arguments," *Journal of Philosophy*, Vol. 65 (1968), pp. 241–56; Richard Rorty, "Incorrigibility as the Mark of the Mental," *Journal of Philosophy*, Vol. 67 (1970), pp. 399–424; Richard Rorty, "Verificationism and Transcendental Arguments," *Nous*, Vol. 4 (1970), pp. 3–14; Joseph Margolis, "Indubitability, Self-intimating States, and Logically Privileged Access," *Journal of Philosophy*, Vol. 67 (1970), pp. 918–31; R. K. Scheer, "Knowledge of the Future," *Mind*, Vol. 80 (1971), pp. 212–26; W. H. Walsh, "Knowledge in Its Social Setting," *Mind*, Vol. 80 (1971), pp. 321–36.

THE PROBLEM
OF FREEDOM
AND DETERMINISM

CHAPTER THREE

The problem of freedom and determinism is basically a paradox. A paradox arises when two equally evident assumptions lead to apparently inconsistent results. A paradox is, therefore, rationally intolerable. No rational man can accept inconsistent results; consequently, no rational man can tolerate a paradox.

What paradox is connected with the problem of freedom and determinism? Basically, it is this. Determinism is the thesis of universal causation, the thesis that everything is caused. On the other hand, the doctrine of freedom maintains that some of our actions are free. Both these things seem true. We believe both that everything is caused and that some of our actions are free. However, these two beliefs lead to results that are apparently inconsistent. To see that this is so, consider the case for determinism.

151

AN ARGUMENT FOR DETERMINISM:
SOMETHING WE ALL BELIEVE

The first thing to notice about the thesis of determinism is that we all do believe it is true. All of us believe, or at least are disposed to believe, that everything that happens has a cause. To see that you do believe this, consider what your reaction would be to the following situation. One morning you wake up and go out to start your new automobile. You put the key in the ignition, step on the gas pedal, push the starter, and nothing happens. Your automobile will not start. So you lift up the hood, look underneath, check the spark plugs, the carburetor, the battery, and so on; but everything seems to be in perfect order. Still the fact remains; the car will not start. Somewhat disgruntled over this state of affairs, you call the local mechanic, who arrives on the scene teeming with confidence. He will fix the car so that it will start. He carefully looks it over, checks it with the thoroughness of an expert, but he too fails to find anything out of order.

Because the car is quite new, you become rather impatient at this point and call the factory representative. Shortly thereafter he arrives with a clean white shirt, characteristic of his vocation, and begins to check your car. When he has finished a very thorough investigation and his shirt is no longer white, you ask him, "What is the matter?" His reply is, "Nothing." Because your car still does not start, you decide to pursue the issue in different terms. "Well, what is the cause of the trouble?" you ask. At this point the factory representative straightens his tie and replies in an official voice, "There is no cause. There is nothing the matter with the car. It simply does not start." He continues, "This is one of those curious situations in which some problem arises which really has no cause whatever. There is no cause for the failure of your car to start. It just won't start, and that is all there is to be said."

His report is preposterous. You would remain convinced that there must be some cause. From the fact that the factory representative has failed to find the cause of the trouble, it does not follow that there is no cause. There must be some cause which the man has been unable to discover. The reason you find the report unacceptable is that you are convinced that things have causes. You, like all men of good sense, believe that determinism is true.

To reinforce the point, let us consider just one more example.

Suppose that a scientist has been employed by The National Health Association to find the cause of a disease called "recnac." After many years of research, the scientist files the following report on his research:

> For many years we have been searching for the cause of recnac. We have discovered that animals as well as human beings are sometimes stricken with this disease. It is a disease that is rarely fatal either in animals or men, but it has a very disagreeable group of symptoms that are well known. Having studied the biological and environmental conditions of the diseased—the state of the blood, the vital organs, the respiratory system, the nervous system, and the genes, as well as all the external influences we could isolate—we have arrived at the inescapable conclusion that the disease is uncaused. We realize that after investing several million dollars to study recnac it might seem unfortunate to have arrived at this result. But it should have been recognized from the outset that this was one possible outcome of the research. Ordinarily when we study a disease we find, sooner or later, that it has some cause, that there is some germ or virus or other causative agent which produces the disease. But this disease recnac is not an ordinary one. It occurs now and then, but it has no cause. It just exists. We are sorry to have to present a report which many sufferers of the disease will, because of their subjective bias, regard as discouraging. However, we make no apology for our conclusion; it was arrived at objectively and scientifically by the most careful and painstaking experimental research.

This report would be rejected as so much pretentious nonsense. The failure of the scientists to find the cause of recnac would fail to establish that the disease has no cause. On the contrary, we would all suppose that it *must* have some cause, that it could not possibly lack one.

Of course, in both cases under consideration we would be willing to accept the conclusion that the most skilled investigators could not *find* the cause. Causes may be difficult to find, but to say that a cause is difficult to find is not to say that the cause does not exist. Thus we are all convinced that both the failure of the car to start and the disease have some cause. These are just two examples of things that we believe are caused, but the same argument could be extended to show that we believe all other things are caused too. Anything on which you focus your attention, anything about which you wonder, is a thing for which you might seek the cause. "Why did that happen?" you ask, and you expect a causal explanation. No matter what happens, you may always ask, "Why did it happen?" Or alternatively, "What was the cause of that?" All of us believe that such questions must have an answer. This shows that we are all convinced that whatever happens is caused, even those of us who have not considered the matter in such general terms.

We accept as a matter of common sense that things are caused. Like other beliefs of common sense, it may be false. However, this belief—unlike some common-sense beliefs—cannot be refuted by our failure to discover the cause of something. Determinism is a thesis we all believe to be true, and it is not refutable by the failure to find the causes we seek. Let us suppose then that everything does have a cause. Why should this generate a paradox? What problem arises from this common-sense conviction?

THE PROBLEM

Suppose that a man has a hereditary disease and that the disease is the result of causal factors over which he has no control. Nothing he could have done would have prevented him from catching the disease. It is not something that he has of his own free will; it is the inevitable outcome of events and processes that were beyond his influence. Consequently, he could not reasonably be held responsible for having it. Another way of putting the matter is this. Having a disease is not something a man does; it is not his *action*. It is something that happens to him. In this respect the man is basically passive.

What is the relevance of this example to the thesis of determinism? Common sense says everything that happens is caused. It follows that everything I do must be caused, for among the things that happen in the universe are the actions that I perform. Imagine that I move my trigger finger. This must be caused. Moreover, whatever caused this movement must itself be caused by some antecedent, earlier, conditions and factors. Those conditions and factors must be caused by still earlier factors, and so on. This series of causal factors must extend backward indefinitely into the past.

Thus the movement of my finger is caused ultimately by factors that existed in the remote past before I was born—consequently, by factors over which I have no control.

If, however, it is a consequence of the thesis of determinism that a person's actions are the inevitable outcome of casual processes that began before he was born and over which he had no control, then no matter what a person does, he could not have done otherwise. He could not have prevented his actions from occurring, nor could he have performed any other action instead. His action and inaction alike are the inevitable outcome of events and processes beyond his influence. He had no choice when he acted. Consequently, no person may reasonably be held responsible for any of his actions.

To see that this conclusion is inescapable, let us compare the case of the man who has a hereditary disease with that of a man who has just shot and murdered another human being. We said earlier that a man who has a hereditary disease may not reasonably be held responsible for having it, because it is not something he has of his own free will. But why not? The answer, of course, is that his having the disease is the inevitable outcome of causal factors over which he has no control. However, exactly the same thing must be conceded with respect to the murderer when we suppose that determinism is true. For his act of pulling the trigger on the murder weapon was as inevitable as his contracting a hereditary disease. He could no more have prevented himself from moving the trigger than the diseased man could have prevented himself from having the disease. Moving the trigger and contracting the disease are both the inevitable outcome of causal processes extending back in time before the birth of either man. The men are thus equally powerless. The murderer, like the diseased man, is really more passive than active. He has no choice, no free will, no real option. He is, in effect, more the one who is moved than the one who moves. Consequently, the murderer is no more responsible for pulling the trigger than the sick man is for contracting the disease.

At this point a certain objection must be dealt with. It may seem that there is an important difference between the two cases we have just considered in that the murderer must have done many things to place himself in the position to shoot his victim. He had to obtain a gun, confront his victim, take careful aim, and so on. It might be said that the murderer could quite easily have avoided committing murder by simply having omitted any one of these preparatory actions. But this is sheer delusion. Each of these preparatory actions was itself the inevitable causal consequence of antecedent conditions that existed before the man was born and that, consequently, were entirely outside the scope of his control. By the same argument that we used to show that his pulling the trigger was something he was powerless to prevent, we could show that he was equally powerless to prevent any of the actions that led up to the climactic one. None of his actions are free. They are determined by things entirely beyond his control.

One further qualification is in order. We have spoken of the man as not having any choice about what he does. This should not be taken to suggest that the man does not choose or decide to do the things he does. If this looks peculiar at first, it should be remembered that it is perfectly possible for a person to choose to do something when, in fact, he has no choice. He can think he has options that actually do not exist. A classic case of this, derived from John Locke, is the following.[1] Suppose that a man is brought into a room while asleep and that the door to the room, being the only way of escape, is locked from the outside. But the man does not know or even suspect that the door is locked. He awakens, finds himself in the room, and notices that he has very agreeable company. Not knowing that he is locked in, the man might consider leaving but choose to remain instead. Of course, the man really has no choice, he cannot leave, but he does truly choose. Occasionally, we choose to do something when we really have no choice.

This point is of importance to the determinist position. Spinoza was a determinist, and he put the point in the following manner: We think that we are free because we are ignorant of the causes of our actions.[2] Like the prisoner, if we were but enlightened concerning the true nature of our situation, we would see that we are not free. Human conduct is determined in the same way as that of a projectile. If the projectile were conscious, it might say to itself as it flew through the air, "I am free to swerve to the left or right but

---

[1] John Locke, *Essay Concerning Human Understanding*, Book II, Chapter XXI, paragraph 10.

[2] Benedict De Spinoza, *Ethic,* Part One, Appendix, paragraph two, and Part Two, Prop. XXXV, Schol.

I choose to continue to travel in this path." Of course, this is just so much nonsense. The projectile has no choice. The path it takes is causally determined; it cannot swerve either to the left or to the right. Were the projectile conscious and ignorant of the causal determination of its flight, it might well fancy itself free. According to Spinoza, such a projectile would be no more foolish than most men are, for the motions that men make are no more free than the motions of a projectile. We are no more free to swerve from the paths we take than the projectile is free to swerve from its path. Because we are conscious, and ignorant of the causal determination of our actions, we think that we are free to swerve to the left or right, but we choose not to swerve at all. Hence, the delusion that we are free. We choose only because we fail to realize that we are not free. Choosing when one has no choice—when one is not free— is founded on ignorance.

Of course, if we are ignorant and choose when we really have no choice, all this is determined too. If it is foolishness to choose when one has no choice, at least we may have the comfort of the assurance that we cannot help it. We are powerless to prevent this state of affairs. Consequently, though it may appear foolish, it is not folly. Foolishness that one cannot help is not folly but misfortune, and that is the only correct way to describe what appears to be folly or wickedness. The man who murders another man is powerless to prevent the action he performs. Like a projectile, he is more passive than active, his movements are the causal consequences of processes and forces that render them as inevitable as the movement of a projectile.

It is now clear that the thesis of determinism does have paradoxical consequences indeed. For if we accept that thesis, as we are all disposed to do, then we must accept the consequences that no human action is free and, therefore, that no one is responsible for the actions he performs. We are no more responsible for our actions than is a diseased man for having a hereditary disease or a projectile for following the path it does.

This line of thought greatly influenced the novelist Samuel Butler. It seemed to him that it was no more reasonable to punish criminals than it would be to punish the sick, for criminals have no more control over their behavior than the diseased have over the state of their health. Both are the result of causal processes that the afflicted are incapable of controlling. To drive this point home,

Butler wrote a satirical novel, *Erewhon,* about a country in which
the penal system was interestingly different from ours. In Erewhon
people who perform criminal acts, such as defrauding insurance
companies, committing murder, and so forth, are treated as we
treat the ill. They are sent off to hospitals to be treated for moral
ailment. There is no stigma attached to being cared for in this way.
On the other hand, people who are sick are prosecuted in the courts
and punished as we punish criminals. The following is a description
of a trial in Erewhon:

> The prisoner was placed in the dock and the jurors were sworn
> in much as in Europe; almost all of our modes of procedure
> were reproduced even to requiring the prisoner to plead guilty
> or not guilty. He pleaded not guilty, and the case proceeded.
> The evidence of the prosecution was very strong, but I must do
> the court the justice to observe that the trial was absolutely im-
> partial. Counsel for the prisoner was allowed to urge everything
> that could be said in his defense. The line taken was that the
> prisoner was simulating consumption in order to defraud an
> insurance company from which he was about to buy an annuity
> and that he hoped thus to obtain it on more advantageous
> terms. If this could have been found to be so, he would have
> escaped criminal prosecution and been sent to a hospital as for
> a moral ailment. This view, however, was one which could not
> be reasonably sustained. In spite of all the ingenuity and
> eloquence of one of the most celebrated advocates of the coun-
> try, the case was only too clear. For the prisoner was almost
> at the point of death and it was astonishing that he had not
> been tried and convicted long previously. His coughing was
> incessant during the whole trial and it was all that the two
> jailors in charge of him could do to keep him on his legs until
> it was over.[3]

The summing up of the judge was admirable. He dwelt upon
every point that could be construed in favor of the prisoner,
but as he proceeded it became clear that the evidence was too
convincing to admit of doubt and there was but one opinion

---

[3] Samuel Butler, *Erewhon* (London: A. C. Fifield, 1919), pp. 112–13.

in the court as to the impending verdict when the jury retired
from the box. They were absent for about ten minutes and on
their return the foreman pronounced the prisoner guilty. There
was a faint murmur of applause that was instantly repressed.
The judge then proceeded to pronounce sentence in words
which I can never forget and which I copied out into a note-
book. . . . The sentence was as follows: "Prisoner at the bar,
you have been accused of a great crime of laboring under
pulmonary consumption and after an impartial trial before a
jury of your countrymen you have been found guilty. Against
the justice of the verdict I can say nothing. The evidence
against you is conclusive and it only remains for me to pass
such a sentence upon you as will satisfy the ends of the law.
That sentence must be a very severe one. It pains me much to
see one who is yet so young and whose prospects in life were
otherwise so excellent brought to this distressing condition by
a constitution which I can only regard as radically vicious; but
yours is no case for compassion. This is not your first offense.
You have led a career of crime and have only profitted by the
leniency shown you upon past occasions to offend yet more
seriously against the laws and institutions of your country. You
were convicted of aggravated bronchitis last year and I find
that though you are now only twenty-three years old you have
been in prison on no less than fourteen occasions for illnesses
of a more or less hateful character; in fact, it is not too much
to say that you have spent the greater part of your life in jail.[4]

"It is all very well for you to say that you came of unhealthy
parents and had a severe accident in your childhood which
permanently undermined your constitution; excuses such as
these are the ordinary refuge of the criminal; but they cannot
for one moment be listened to by the ear of justice. I am not
here to enter upon curious metaphysical questions as to the
origin of this or that—questions to which there would be no
end were their introduction tolerated and which would result
in throwing the only guilt upon the tissues of the primordial
cell or upon the elementary gasses. There is no question of
how you came to be wicked but only this—namely, are you

[4] Ibid., pp. 113–14.

wicked or not? This has been decided in the affirmative, neither can I hesitate for a single moment to say that it has been decided justly. You are a bad and dangerous person and stand branded in the eyes of your fellow countrymen with one of the most heinous known offenses. . . . You may say that it is not your fault. The answer is ready enough at hand and it amounts to this—that if you had been born of healthy and well-to-do parents and been well taken care of when you were a child you would never have offended against the laws of your country nor found yourself in your present position. If you tell me that you had no hand in your parentage and that it was therefore unjust to lay these things to your charge, I answer that whether your being in a consumption is your fault or no, it is a fault in you and it is my duty to see that against such faults as this the commonwealth shall be protected. You may say that it is your misfortune to be criminal; I answer that it is your crime to be unfortunate."[5]

The refusal of the judge to enter into a consideration of "curious metaphysical questions" amounts to a refusal to see the incongruity of his position. Obviously, he accepts the thesis of determinism; consequently, he should admit that it is not the prisoner's fault that he is ill. It is not the prisoner's fault because his condition is the inevitable causal consequence of factors beyond his control. Thus, it is absolutely unreasonable to hold the prisoner responsible for his state of health or to sentence him to be punished.

If, however, Butler is correct, our penal system is as unreasonable as the penal system of Erewhon, for our judges sentence people to be punished for criminal actions when, determinism being true, what a person does is no more his fault than having consumption was the fault of the prisoner in Erewhon. Both the criminal action in our society and the criminal illness in Erewhon are the outcome of causal processes that the criminal is powerless to prevent. It is not up to a person whether those processes occur. Consequently, neither can he be said to be responsible.

This line of thought has led some men to a very humanitarian outlook. For example, Clarence Darrow, a famous lawyer, often de-

---

[5] Ibid., pp. 114–15, 117.

fended people who were being tried for a crime punishable by execution by appealing to the thesis of determinism.[6] His appeal was based on the common ground that we share with the criminal. For if the behavior of the criminal is the outcome of such causal factors as hereditary and babyhood environment, so is the behavior of the man who sits in the jury box. Good deeds and misdeeds alike are causal consequences of things that happened in the remote past and were beyond the influence of the doer of the deed. We are the fortunate or unfortunate result of a causal chain of events that began before any of us existed. As such, we are not responsible for our deeds. It would be wrong to execute a man for a deed he has committed. Juries were often persuaded by Darrow's appeal. As we can see, he did not hesitate to raise curious metaphysical questions to save the life of his client.

SUMMARY

The argument we have considered, that of the determinist, has seemed persuasive to many philosophers. It will be useful at this point to summarize the premises and assumptions of the argument. Obviously, one premise is

1. The thesis of determinism is true.

This amounts to the assertion of universal causation, that is, to the claim that everything is causally determined. A second premise is

2. If the thesis of determinism is true, then there are no free actions.

These two premises yield the conclusion

3. There are no free actions.

This conclusion taken together with the further premise

---

[6] For Darrow's views see Clarence Darrow's speeches collected in *Attorney for the Damned* (New York: Simon and Schuster, 1957), ed. by Arthur Weinberg.

4. If there are no free actions, then no one is responsible for his actions.

yields the further conclusion

5. No one is responsible for his actions.

It is important to notice that premise (2) is quite independent of premise (1). Either premise might be true while the other is false. Thus, a person who wished to deny conclusion (3), that is, to affirm that some actions are free, might deny either premise. Premise (2) does not assert that determinism is true. It is merely a hypothetical statement about what would be the case *if* determinism were true. In this respect, premise (2) is like the statement 'If it rains, we will get wet!' A person who makes this statement has not asserted that it will rain or that we will get wet; his statement is merely a hypothetical one about what will happen *if* it rains. So premise (1) might be true and premise (2) false. It might be that, although the thesis of determinism is true, there are some free actions. Similarly, premise (2) might be true and premise (1) false. It might be the case that although the thesis of determinism is not true, if it were true, then there would be no free actions.

Premise (2) asserts the incompatibility of free action with universal causation. Thus the position we have been considering so far rests not only on the premise that determinism is true, but also on the premise that determinism and free action are incompatible. Certain philosophers who have rejected statements (3) and (5) have been led to reject premise (1) and accept premise (2), and others have rejected premise (2) and accepted premise (1). The only position we have considered so far, that of the determinist, is one that is committed to both premises (1) and (2). To furnish ourselves with some labels for alternative views, let us call a person who rejects premise (2) (and consequently, who affirms the compatibility of free action and universal determinism) a compatiblist. Then one who accepts premise (2) we can call an incompatiblist. Therefore a determinist, as we are using the term, is an incompatiblist who accepts the thesis of determinism. Finally, let us call a person who rejects premise (1) a libertarian. Contrary to the argument we have considered so far, the libertarian affirms that there is free action, but because he accepts premise (2), he denies the truth of determinism. The libertarian position is the one we shall next consider.

THE LIBERTARIAN POSITION

We have examined the arguments advanced by the determinists to show that there is no free action. What is there to be said for the libertarian view? The libertarian holds that people do have free will, that there is free action, and that, consequently, the thesis of determinism is false. So the libertarian denies that all human actions are caused. We have already noted that it seems to be a plain matter of common sense to accept the thesis of determinism. We all do seem to believe that everything is causally determined. If this is a simple matter of common sense, then how can one reasonably hold, without flying in the face of common sense, that there are free actions? The answer advanced by certain libertarians—for example, Thomas Reid and C. A. Campbell—is quite compelling. According to both Campbell and Reid, it is every bit as much a matter of common-sense conviction to believe that we act freely as it is to believe that the thesis of universal determinism is true.

A LIBERTARIAN ARGUMENT: DELIBERATION AND THE BELIEF THAT WE ARE FREE

In order to see why these and other philosophers have thought that it was a plain matter of common sense to believe that people perform free actions, it will be useful to examine with some care the notion of a free action. We remarked earlier that according to the determinist we are all powerless to act other than we do. Thus according to the determinist, whenever we act, it is not in our power not to act, and whenever we do not act, it is not in our power to act. The libertarian holds two different views. He maintains that sometimes when we act, it is in our power not to act; and sometimes when we do not act, it is in our power to act. In short, it is sometimes within our power to act other than we do. Another way of putting it is to say that sometimes it is up to us whether or not we perform the actions we do perform. When this is true, then our actions are free actions. Thus to say that an action is free is to say that we could have done otherwise, that we were free to do otherwise, or that it was in our power to do otherwise. According to the libertarian, we all believe that we perform free actions; consequently, the belief that we perform free actions is as much a matter of common sense as the belief that the thesis of determinism is true. How can the libertarian show that we do all believe this?

One way is to reflect upon the nature of deliberation. At some time or other each of us does deliberate. Some of us may deliberate for only a very short time; others of us may deliberate at great length. Sometimes our deliberations may be foolish and sometimes wise, but it is a familiar fact that deliberation does indeed occur. None of us completely avoids the task of deliberating about whether or not to perform certain actions. Moreover, each of us can tell by simple introspection that he does in fact deliberate. How does this fact—that we all do deliberate—show that we believe that we have free will? The argument is quite simple. Part of what is involved in deliberation is the belief that we are free. If I deliberate about whether or not to perform some act, I must believe that it is in my power to perform the action and that it is also in my power not to perform it. If I believed that I was powerless with respect to performing or not performing the action, it would be absurd for me to deliberate about whether or not to perform it. Indeed if I really did believe that I was powerless in this respect, then I do not think that it would even make sense to say that I was deliberating about whether or not to perform the action. I might be deliberating about whether or not I would perform the action *if* it were in my power to perform it and in my power not to perform it. But to deliberate about what one would do if one were not powerless is not the same thing as to deliberate about what to do.

To clarify the relation between deliberation and the belief that we are free, consider a concrete example. Suppose a man is deliberating about whether or not to pay his rent. He weighs the considerations on both sides. For example, he remembers that the landlord did not turn on the heat until rather late in the evening; he remembers that the landlord did not fix the leak in his bathroom; he remembers that the landlord did not shovel the walk after the last snowstorm; and so forth. On the other side, he remembers that the landlord was rather patient when, because of a long illness, he was unable to pay his rent last winter and that the landlord himself has not been in very good health recently. After weighing the pros and cons, he finally reaches a decision. He decides that, all things considered, he ought to pay his rent. If he is a conscientious man, he will then, of course, pay his rent if he is able to, for that is what duty requires. This is a perfectly ordinary example of deliberation. Moreover, all that we have imagined might well have taken place even though the man was not able to pay his rent. Imagine that his bank account was depleted, although he did not know it, and that he would be unable to get hold of enough money to pay his rent. In this case, though he might deliberate about whether or not to pay his rent, it is not up to him whether or not it is paid. It is perfectly possible that a man should deliberate about whether or not to do something, like paying his rent, even though one of the alternatives is not within his power.

However, it is important to notice that a man must not know or believe that he is unable to pay his rent if he is to be properly described as deliberating about the matter. If we modify the example and imagine that the man knows that his bank account is depleted and that he cannot get any money, then we could not correctly describe him as deliberating about whether or not to pay his rent. He might be deliberating about whether he would pay his rent if it were in his power to pay it. But that is quite a different thing from deliberating about whether or not to pay one's rent. It would be absurd, indeed nonsensical, to describe this man as deliberating about whether or not to pay his rent when he knows perfectly well that he does not have the money to do so. For the man to be correctly described as deliberating about whether or not to pay his rent he must at least believe that he can pay it, and, of course, he must believe that he could leave the rent unpaid. He must believe that it is up to him whether or not the rent is paid. This case of deliberation is typical of all cases of deliberation in this one respect. A person who deliberates about whether to do A or B must believe that it is in his power to do A and in his power to do B. If he believes that one of these things is not in his power, then he is not deliberating about whether to do A or B. Therefore, deliberation implies the belief that we are free. All men who deliberate must believe at the time of deliberation that they perform free actions.

Because all men deliberate at some time, it is a conviction of common sense that we perform free actions. Thus, the libertarian argues that by merely introspecting we can discern that we often believe that we perform free actions. Sometimes we feel this in prospect, when we are considering some future action, and sometimes we feel it in retrospect, when we consider some past action.

OBJECTIONS TO THE PRECEDING ARGUMENT: ACTING FROM THE STRONGEST MOTIVE

Some determinists have challenged this purported data of introspection. That is, some determinists have denied that we really do find upon introspection that we believe we could have done otherwise. For example, Adolf Grunbaum, a determinist, argues as follows:

> Let us carefully examine the content of the feeling that on a certain occasion we could have acted other than the way we did in fact act. What do we find? Does the feeling we have inform us that we could have acted *otherwise under exactly the same external and internal motivational conditions?* No, says the determinist, this feeling simply discloses that we were able to act in accord with our strongest desire at that time, and that we could indeed have acted otherwise if a different motive had prevailed at that time.[7]

The point of this argument is clear enough. It is that whenever we reflect on a past action we do not discover that we believe that we could have acted differently than we did in fact act, but rather that we always act from our strongest desire. C. A. Campbell has replied that there are some cases in which we can discover by introspection that we do not act from our strongest desire, namely, when we "rise to duty" through moral effort. Campbell maintains that when he is in a situation where doing his duty, X, conflicts with satisfying his strongest desire, Y,

[7] Adolf Grunbaum, "Causality and the Science of Human Behavior," reprinted in part in *Philosophic Problems* (New York: Macmillan, 1957), ed. by Maurice Mandelbaum et al., p. 336.

I find that I cannot help believing that I *can* rise to duty and choose X; the "rising to duty" being effected by what is commonly called "effort of will." And I further find, if I ask myself just what it is I am believing when I believe that I "can" rise to duty, that I cannot help believing that it lies with me here and now, quite absolutely, which of two genuinely open possibilities I adopt; whether, that is I make the effort of will and choose X or, on the other hand, let my desiring nature, my character so far formed "have its way," and choose Y, the course "in the line of least resistance."[8]

Campbell's reply is typical of the libertarian rejoinder to the sort of contention that Grunbaum has made. When we are faced with a situation of moral conflict, according to the libertarian we must be convinced that no matter how we choose we could have chosen to act differently in exactly that situation, that is, under exactly the same external and internal motivational conditions. In such situations we must be convinced that both actions are in our power and that the action we perform is up to us. Thus, the libertarian argues, introspection shows that we are sometimes convinced we are not acting from our strongest desire and moreover, that we believe our action is free.

It is important to notice at this point that the claim that we always act from our strongest desire may be construed in such a way that it is simply true by definition. Suppose that by the words 'strongest desire' we simply mean that desire from which a person acts. In that case it will be true by definition that a man always acts from his strongest desire, provided that he acts from a desire at all. However, if it is true by definition, or rather if it is made true by definition, that one always acts from one's strongest desire, then that contention will be irrelevant to the question of the truth or falsity of determinism. In fact, we shall be faced with the redefinist fallacy. The reason is not difficult to see. It is surely not true by definition that everything is caused or that every human action is caused, or even that any given particular human action

[8] C. A. Campbell, "Is the Problem of Free Will a Pseudo-Problem?" reprinted in *A Modern Introduction to Philosophy*, revised edition (New York: The Free Press, 1965), ed. by Paul Edwards and Arthur Pap, p. 73.

is caused. Now suppose that someone does something when he desires to do it. It by no means follows from the fact that he desired to do it that his desiring to do it was the cause of his doing it. It might or might not have been the cause. For example, suppose I desire to smoke a cigarette and walk across the street to the tobacco shop. The action of walking across the street might be caused by my desire to smoke, but it might also be caused by any one of a myriad of other things. Perhaps it was not this particular desire that caused the action, but the desire to buy a magazine or to chat with the friendly tobacconist. Indeed, the action may even be the result of habit—I always go to the tobacco store after dinner—rather than any desire. At any rate, if desire or habit is the cause, it is not true by definition that such a desire or habit produces this behavior. It is a matter of contingent empirical fact and nothing more.

So the question of whether or not a particular desire caused him to perform the action that he did perform is a question of contingent fact. It is not true by definition that the desire caused him to perform that action. But it could be made true by definition that he acted from his strongest desire. Then it would be true by definition that he acted from his strongest desire, but it is not true by definition that any one of his desires caused him to act as he did. In short, it is not true by definition that a man's desires or anything else *cause* the action that he performs, and no amount of juggling of the definition of the phrase 'strongest desire' will alter this fact in any way.

Thus we may conclude that it is in fact a datum of introspection that each of us does believe at some time that we have free will and that some of our actions are free. Indeed, Campbell's emphasis upon situations of moral conflict is needless. It is not only in cases of moral conflict that we find that we believe that there are genuine alternatives before us and that it is up to us which of two actions we perform. We believe it in all serious deliberation. Sometimes we deliberate concerning a pair of alternatives, when no serious moral question is involved. It may be a situation where our decision will affect (and in a morally insignificant way) only ourselves, but the situation nonetheless seems to merit serious deliberation. Thus even in such situations where no question of duty versus desire arises, we find that there is deliberation and, consequently, the belief that we are free.

SUMMARY

Let us take stock of our results. The determinist claims that it is a plain matter of common sense to believe that the thesis of determinism is true. We have now discovered from examining the libertarian position that it seems to be every bit as much a matter of common sense to believe that we are free. Where does this leave us?

It leaves us with our original paradox. For it seems to be a matter of common sense to believe both that the thesis of determinism is true and that people do perform free actions. But according to both the determinist position and the libertarian position, this cannot be. Let us return briefly to the argument we considered earlier. It consisted of two premises; the first premise was

1. The thesis of determinism is true.

and the second premise was

2. If the thesis of determinism is true, then there are no free actions.

Both the libertarian and the determinist accept the second premise of this argument, but whereas the determinist accepts the first premise and, consequently, the conclusion that there are no free actions, the libertarian holds that there are free actions and, consequently, rejects the first premise. We have now seen that common sense adjudicates in favor of neither side. Are there any considerations to show that it is more reasonable to accept the thesis of determinism or that it is more reasonable to accept the belief that we perform free actions? So far we have noted that it is as much a matter of common sense to believe that there are free actions as it is to believe that the thesis of determinism is true and vice versa. But now we must consider seriously the question we have just asked. Leaving aside the question of what we do in fact believe, we must turn to the question of what is reasonable to believe when logical consistency forces us to sacrifice one of our beliefs. Let us first see what sort of considerations may be urged to show that it is reasonable to sacrifice our belief in determinism and to retain our belief that we perform free actions.

A LIBERTARIAN DEFENSE: REASON AND CONSISTENCY

There are two ways to show that one belief is more reasonable than another. The first way is to show that we have stronger evidence for one belief than we do for another, that is, to point to something we know that supports the one belief more strongly than the other. But there is also a second way of defending the reasonableness of one belief against another. The second way is to show that we can avoid logical inconsistency by following one path but not the other. It may be that of two alternative beliefs we can consistently accept the first and reject the second, but we cannot consistently accept the second and reject the first.

One libertarian argument to show that it is reasonable to believe that there are free actions is an argument of just this second sort. The argument is this. It often happens that though we believe something is caused—that the thesis of determinism holds with respect to that particular case—we are nevertheless perfectly able to reject this belief. I might, for example, believe that my bodily movements are causally determined and that what causes them is itself causally determined as part of a causal chain extending indefinitely into the past. I might be completely tempted to be a determinist. However, I could adjust to not believing these things. One might with practice get used to relinquishing such a conviction, at least with respect to certain things that happen—that is, with respect to certain human actions. One is in the habit of thinking that determinism is true, of thinking that there is always a cause to be found; but this habit, like other habits, is no doubt one that could be broken with time and discipline.

However, the libertarian argues against this with respect to the belief that we perform free actions. He argues that we cannot help believing that we are free. If the libertarian can establish his position that, although we could learn to relinquish our belief in determinism, we could not help believing that we perform free actions, then it would seem only reasonable, for the sake of consistency, to reject our belief in determinism and retain the belief that we perform free actions. If we cannot consistently believe both that determinism is true and that we perform free actions, and the belief that we perform free actions is inescapable, then it is reasonable to reject determinism. By doing so we avoid inconsistency.

The libertarian argument to prove we cannot escape the belief that our actions are free appeals to certain considerations that have already been raised. We have already noted that deliberation implies the deliberator believes that he is free, that it is up to him which of two alternatives he chooses. This being the case, all the libertarian need establish to prove this belief is inescapable is simply that deliberation is inescapable. It is certainly doubtful that anyone ever completely escapes from deliberation. It is quite clear that all of us do for some interval, however short, deliberate about whether to perform one action or another. But perhaps this is all a matter of habit that could be unlearned. Deliberation is, after all, a process in which one weighs alternatives, in which one thinks before one acts. Perhaps with enough practice we could learn to act without thinking. Many of us in fact manage to accomplish this effortlessly a great deal of the time.

However, the suggestion that we should all give up thinking before we act, in order to salvage the thesis of determinism, is not one we would expect to meet with universal acclaim. Reflective action is, after all, the hallmark of a wise man, and reflection and deliberation are very near cousins. The question we must now put to the determinist is the following: Is it possible to drive a wedge between reflective action and deliberative action? If not, then it must be conceded that the libertarian has won the day.

A DETERMINIST REJOINDER:
DELIBERATION AND ELIBERATION

The determinist's reply to the foregoing argument is based upon an aspect of deliberation we noticed earlier, namely, that one can deliberate about what he would do if he were free, even when one knows perfectly well that he is not. For instance, suppose one were a determinist. In this case one might well recognize that his behavior is causally determined and that, consequently, he never acts freely. Thus it would be absurd for such a person to deliberate about whether to do A or B. He would believe that it is not up to him whether he does A or B, because what he will do is causally determined by factors beyond his control. However, he might, nevertheless, reflect upon what he would do if it were within his power to do A and also in his power to do B; that is, he might reflect about what he would do if he were free. Such reflection, though it is to be distinguished from deliberation, is nevertheless the basis for reflective behavior. As a result of such reflection he might choose one alternative rather than the other. To distinguish this kind of reflection from deliberation we might call it "eliberation." Therefore a determinist might claim that to be consistent one must never deliberate, but one may eliberate instead and lose nothing of importance. For eliberation is the basis for reflective action, indeed, action that is every bit as reflective as that performed by a man subsequent to deliberation. Practical sagacity may be founded on eliberation quite as well as upon deliberation.

A LIBERTARIAN REPLY: DELIBERATION AND CHOICE

This verbal sleight of hand will not alter the basic issue, for it is important to notice that the result of eliberation as well as of deliberation is, we hope, decision or choice. But choice and decision by themselves imply a belief that we are free. If a man chooses to do A rather than B, he must believe it in his power to adopt the other alternative. The same thing is true of decision. If I decide to study philosophy, I must believe that it is in my power not to study it. The prisoner who knows he is locked in a cell which he cannot leave is not someone who can choose or decide to remain in the cell. The man who knows he has no money is not a person who can choose or decide to pay his rent. In short, when one believes he has no alternative, then he has no choice and no decision. So if eliberation is supposed to result in decision or choice, then the determinist position is again dubious; that is, the position again becomes inconsistent. A determinist believes there is no free action, but, at the same time, he is a person who chooses and decides what course of action to pursue and, therefore, believes that he is free. We cannot help believing that we are free because we cannot help choosing and deciding what course of action to pursue. Consequently, it is only reasonable to accept the view that we perform free actions, and reject the thesis of determinism.

A SECOND DETERMINIST REJOINDER:
A QUESTION OF EVIDENCE

Suppose we concede for the sake of argument that decision and choice are as inescapable as the libertarian contends. Does this force us to accept his conclusion that it is reasonable to reject the thesis of determinism in favor of the belief that we are free? To see it most certainly does not, we need only notice a special assumption on which the entire libertarian argument rests. The libertarian has assumed all along that if we can consistently accept one of a pair of alternative beliefs but cannot consistently accept the second, then to be reasonable the first must be accepted and the second rejected. But this assumption is false. This assumption, rather than determinism, must be rejected for the sake of reason. For what we can and cannot help believing fails to determine what it is reasonable to believe. What determines the latter is the evidence we have for a belief. If we have adequate evidence to justify a belief, then the belief is reasonable, whereas if we have adequate evidence to justify the contrary, then the belief is unreasonable. If it should happen that we cannot help believing something even though we have adequate evidence to justify the contrary, then it is unreasonable to accept the belief.

The preceding remarks may be clarified by an example. Suppose there is a man whose personality is such that he cannot help believing his mother loves him. He needs above all else to believe this and so it happens he can entertain no contrary belief. Does this prove that it is reasonable for him to believe his mother loves him and to reject any contrary belief? If you are at all tempted to think so, imagine the mother to be a ballerina who loathes her bastard son because his birth besmirched her reputation and ended her career. Moreover, imagine she is nasty and sadistic in all her actions toward her son. She constantly offers him every conceivable sort of evidence of her loathing and he, the fundamentalist son, continues to believe in her maternal love. Is he reasonable? Surely he is completely unreasonable, and he is so precisely because he cannot help believing one thing when reason requires that he believe something else instead.

The moral of this story is that it may be unreasonable to believe something you cannot help believing. It all depends on the evidence. That we cannot help believing we perform free actions fails to prove it is reasonable for us to believe this, even if we can easily disbelieve determinism, just as the fact that the son cannot help believing his mother loves him fails to prove it is reasonable for him to believe this, even though he can easily disbelieve the opposite. To show one belief to be more reasonable than another, it must be shown that the evidence for the one is stronger than the evidence for the other. Therefore, to establish the libertarian position, the libertarian must prove the evidence for the belief in free action to be stronger than the evidence for determinism. No proof of this has yet been offered.

THE SECOND LIBERTARIAN ARGUMENT:
INTROSPECTIVE EVIDENCE FOR FREEDOM

We have already noted that there are two kinds of arguments the libertarian could employ to prove his position more reasonable than the determinist's. We have investigated an argument that does not raise the question of the evidence for the libertarian position, but instead appeals to the question of what one can consistently believe. However, this argument seems to have failed. The only route now open to the libertarian is to show the evidence for his position to be stronger than the evidence for determinism. How can the libertarian establish this? To answer this question it will be useful to clarify to some extent the libertarian's position. We have spoken of the conviction that we are free, that we perform free actions, that we are free to do otherwise, and so forth. For the sake of economy as well as clarity, let us fix our attention upon some one locution that we can use to express the idea that people perform free actions. Perhaps the word best suited to accomplish this task is the little word 'can.' All the other ideas that the libertarian seeks to express may be expressed by using this word in its various tenses. For example, the libertarian sometimes formulates his views by saying that if a person is free with respect to some action A, then it is in his power to do A and it is also in his power not to do A. This idea can easily enough be expressed by saying that the person can do A and also that he can, if he wishes, not do A. Another way of putting the libertarian position is to say that when a person is free, when his action is free, then it is up to him whether or not he performs that action. Again this idea can be expressed by saying that the person can perform the action and also that he can, if he wishes, not perform it. Still another way of expressing the libertarian idea is to say that a person is free when he has a choice. Now if a person really has a choice, it must be that whatever he chooses to do he could have done otherwise. Thus we may express the idea that a man has performed a free action by saying that although he did the action, and, obviously could do it, it's also true that he could have done something else instead. Thus, a man performs a free action if and only if he could have done something else instead.

Whether we have evidence that people are free, outweighing the evidence we have for the thesis of determinism, depends on how strong our evidence is for the hypothesis that a person could have done something other than what he did do on some occasion. How strong is this evidence?

THE DATA OF INTROSPECTION

We noted earlier that a convinced determinist might, while eliberating, escape the belief that he is free. But this should not overshadow the libertarian contention that we do all in fact believe that we are free. That is, we do in fact all deliberate, not just eliberate, and this means that all of us do at some time or other believe that we could have done otherwise. Thus it must be taken as an undeniable fact of introspection that we do believe that we could have done otherwise. The question we must now consider is this. Does our believing this constitute evidence that it is true? We often believe things that are false and our believing that they are true does not constitute any evidence that they are true. However, sometimes the reverse is true. Occasionally the mere fact that a person believes something does constitute some evidence for the truth of what he believes. For example, if I am the eye witness to a killing, and I believe that it is Little Brentano who is the killer, then my belief would constitute evidence, indeed, perhaps very strong evidence, that Little Brentano is in fact the killer. In this case my believing something is so provides adequate evidence for concluding that it is so. Does our belief that we are free constitute adequate evidence that we are in fact free?

Some determinists have argued that this feeling or belief that we are free constitutes no evidence whatsoever for believing that we are free or that determinism is false. For example, Carl Hempel argues as follows:

As for the first objection to determinism which refers to a stubborn feeling of freedom of choice, . . . it cannot count as evidence against determinism, for this kind of feeling can surely be deceptive. Indeed I think that the feeling is irrelevant to the question of causal determination. For in order to decide whether a given kind of choice is causally determined, we have to judge whether there is an antecedent event with which the choice is *connected by a general law* of simple form. And surely the data obtainable by introspection, especially the stubborn feeling of freedom, have no bearing on this question. The timid man in a hypnotist's audience, for example, who gets up to make a speech, may truthfully protest a feeling of complete freedom in choosing to do so: this is quite compatible with the possibility that his choice was causally determined (via general laws concerning the effects of hypnosis) by the instructions he received earlier under hypnosis.[9]

It is important to notice that Hempel is not questioning what we find by introspecting. He concedes that upon introspecting we do discover that we believe or have the feeling that we are free, but he questions the relevance of this introspective data to the issue of whether our actions are causally determined. He concedes that we may discover by introspecting that we have this belief that we are free, but he denies that this belief constitutes any evidence for the claim that we are free. Therefore the libertarian conviction that we sometimes could have done otherwise is, Hempel contends, not at all supported by the fact that we do believe this is so. His basic argument is that such a belief can be deceptive; the datum of introspection is not adequate evidence for the claim that we could have done otherwise, because we can be deceived by introspection. For this reason he contends that the datum of introspection has no bearing on the question of whether our actions or choices are causally determined by some antecedent event.

In spite of the persuasiveness of Hempel's argument, the libertarian might well reject it. In the first place, it does not follow from the fact that a person can be deceived by accepting an hypothesis on the basis of some experience, that his having that experience

[9] Carl G. Hempel, "Some Reflections on 'The case for Determinism,' " in *Determinism and Freedom* (New York: New York University Press, 1958), ed. by Sidney Hook, p. 161.

fails to give him adequate evidence for accepting the hypothesis. The experiences that give us adequate evidence for accepting hypotheses about any number of things are experiences that can be deceptive. For example, suppose that I see a chair in front of me. The experiences that I am having would provide me with adequate evidence for believing that a chair is there. No one would deny that those experiences I have do constitute adequate evidence for that hypothesis. But, nevertheless, as we noted in the last chapter, this experience might be deceptive. For instance, a hypnotist might generate in me experiences of just this sort when there is no chair in front of me. Thus just as the hypnotist deceives a man into believing that he is free when he is not, so the hypnotist might deceive him into believing that there is a chair in front of him when there is not. Yet both experiences might constitute adequate evidence for the hypotheses the man accepts.

The argument we have just considered may be generalized. The experiences which give us adequate evidence for accepting a hypothesis about some physical object, such as that there is a chair before us, about some other person, such as that he is speaking to us, or about some past event, such as that we were married yesterday, are all experiences that can be deceptive. They are experiences that a hypnotist can use to deceive us. Just as the hypnotist deceives a man into believing that he is free when he is not, so the hypnotist deceives him into believing that there is a chair in front of him when there is not, that he is talking to another person when he is not, and that he was married yesterday when he was not. Yet the experiences the man is having do give him adequate evidence for accepting the hypotheses which he accepts, even though the hypotheses are false.

The reason that such experiences give a person adequate evidence for his beliefs is that those experiences are not different in character from the experiences that we have when we see a chair in front of us, talk to another person, or remember that we were married yesterday.

As we have seen in the preceding chapter, there is some chance that we are in error when we believe almost anything. And this may be considered grounds for denying that we *know*, when knowledge is construed as requiring that all chance of error be excluded. But even if we conclude that the evidence we have in all these cases does not give us knowledge, as the skeptic avers, we may still fairly maintain that the evidence makes it reasonable for us to accept the hypotheses in question. Hypotheses *may* be false in spite of our evidence, but some are reasonable nonetheless. From the fact that the evidence may deceive us, it by no means follows that the evidence is inadequate to make our beliefs reasonable. The argument that the evidence may be deceptive does not prove, in the case of physical objects, other minds, past events, or free action, that our experiences have no bearing or relevance to the question of whether it is reasonable to believe such things. To argue that because an experience may be deceptive it does not provide adequate evidence for accepting a hypothesis is to commit oneself to a nihilistic position according to which almost nothing would be reasonable.

Moreover, it will not be legitimate for the determinist to reply to the foregoing argument that the case of free will is different from the other cases in that we have good evidence that some human actions and choices are connected to preceding events by a law of nature, that is, are causally determined. For this reply employs the same logic as the preceding argument. That some of our actions are causally determined by preceding events fails to prove that our introspective datum is not adequate evidence for believing that we sometimes could have done otherwise. Similarly, that people sometimes suffer hallucinations fails to prove that our senses do not give us adequate evidence for believing in the existence of material objects. Finally, that we are sometimes mistaken about past events fails to prove that memory does not give us adequate evidence for believing in the existence of past events. From the premise that in particular cases we are not free, we cannot validly argue to the general conclusion that introspection does not give us adequate evidence that we are free, any more than, from the premise that in particular cases we are misled by our senses and memory may we validly argue to the general conclusion that our senses and our memory do not give us adequate evidence for the beliefs they lead us to accept.

Our beliefs in the existence of physical things, other persons, past events, and free action provide their own justification; indeed, their very existence is their justification. Having such beliefs provides us with adequate evidence that what we believe is true. The preceding line of argument stems from the libertarian Thomas Reid. Of the belief that we are free, Reid said:

It resembles, in this respect, our belief of the existence of the material world, our belief that those we converse with are living and intelligent beings; our belief that those things did really happen which we distinctly remember; and our belief that we continue the same identical persons.

We find difficulty in accounting for our belief of these things; and some philosophers think they have discovered good reasons for throwing it off. But it sticks fast, and the greatest skeptic finds that he must yield to it in his practice, while he wages war with it in speculation. . . .

This natural conviction of our acting freely, which is acknowledged by many who hold the doctrine of necessity, ought to throw the whole burden of proof upon that side; for by this the side of liberty has . . . a right of ancient possession, which ought to stand good 'til it be overturned. If it cannot be proved that we always act from necessity, there is no need to arguments on the other side to convince us that we are free agents.[10]

We have argued that our conviction that we are free is like our convictions that there is an external world, that there are other minds, and that there is a past because none of these convictions need justification. Since we all hold such convictions, no one can seriously doubt that they are justified, that is, that we have adequate evidence for their truth. The burden of proof is entirely on those who deny that we have adequate evidence for such convictions.

THE DETERMINIST REJOINDER:
THE NEED FOR INDEPENDENT EVIDENCE

The determinist can be expected to regard the kind of evidence that beliefs supply for themselves as a rather Pickwickian sort of evidence. In other words, to say that a certain belief is adequate evidence for its own truth is not, in the most usual sense, to supply any evidence whatever for that belief. It is simply a way of saying that the belief is one which needs no evidence, that it is a belief

---

[10] Thomas Reid, *The Philosophical Works of Thomas Reid* (London: James Thin Publisher), ed. by Sir William Hamilton, p. 617.

which is evident but for which we need no evidence. The determinist is likely to regard this simply as begging the question. For it is precisely the determinist's view that such beliefs are not justified, and the libertarian argument shows only that we all have such beliefs. However, that we have such beliefs does not show that we are justified in having them. And that is precisely the question at issue.

Well, then, is there any independent evidence that we are free? By independent evidence we mean evidence for the belief other than the belief itself, that is, some evidence in the form of things that we know to be true and which support that belief. Only if the libertarian can supply such independent evidence is he justified in claiming that we have strong evidence for that belief in the sense of evidence relevant to the question at issue.

A THIRD LIBERTARIAN ARGUMENT: EMPIRICAL EVIDENCE THAT WE COULD HAVE DONE OTHERWISE

The libertarian might well argue that we do in fact have such independent evidence. It is quite clear that we sometimes have sufficient evidence for the hypothesis that a person can do something, for we often see a person do something, and when we see him do it, then, of course, we assume that he can do it. Indeed, that a person does something entails that he can do it. The crucial question is whether we can have adequate independent evidence for the hypothesis that a person can do something, when we do not see him do it and, moreover, when he does not do it. First let us examine the question of whether we can have independent evidence that a person can do something when we do not see him do it. How are we to get such evidence?

To see a man do something at some other time is one way to get evidence that he can do it when we do not actually see him do it. That is, if a person does something today, and if he did it yesterday and the day before, and if his capacity to do this has not been altered negatively, then when tomorrow rolls around we may infer that he can still do it, even if we do not see him do it then. Of course, having seen a person do something is not the only relevant consideration, but it is a very significant one. What we must now ask is: What are the other relevant considerations?

There are four other conditions of great importance. They are the conditions of temporal propinquity, circumstantial variety, agent similarity, and simple frequency.

Temporal Propinquity. The amount of time which has elapsed between our seeing a person perform an action and the time at which it is claimed that he can perform the action is of considerable importance. For example, if we saw a man perform forty push-ups twenty years ago and have not seen him do it since, we would hardly be justified in claiming to know that he can do it now. On the other hand, if we saw him do it yesterday, our claim would have much greater merit. The less time elapsing between the time at which we see a person perform an action and the time at which we claim to know that he can perform it, the more justified our claim. This condition requires one qualification. Certain actions— for example, running a four-minute mile—require unusual endurance, and, consequently, if we have just seen a person do such a thing, it is a good guess that, being tired, he cannot do it now. The condition is relevant even in the case of such actions, but we must add the qualification that sufficient time has elapsed between the time at which we saw the person perform the action and the time at which it is claimed that he can perform the action to ensure that the agent will not be hindered.

Circumstantial Variety. The greater the variety of circumstances under which we have seen a person perform an action, the more justified we are in claiming that he can perform it. A qualification is also needed here. Sometimes, although we have not seen a person perform an action in a very great variety of circumstances, we have seen him perform the action under circumstances very similar to the ones he is in when it is claimed that he can perform it. In this case the greater the similarity of the circumstances, the better the evidence.

Agent Similarity. If the condition of the agent changes radically from the time at which we have seen him perform an action to the time at which it is claimed that he can perform it, then our evidence that he can perform the action may be greatly weakened. For example, if we have seen a man lift a 200-pound weight, and he subsequently breaks his arm, our having seen him lift the weight is surely not very good evidence that he can do it now that his arm is broken. Thus the greater the similarity of the agent's condition when we have seen him perform the action to his condition at the time at which we claim he can perform it, the greater the justification for our claim. To some extent this condition, like the preceding one, may be formulated as a condition of variety, rather than as a condition of similarity. However, with respect to the circumstances, variety is more important, whereas with respect to the condition of the agent, similarity is more important. The reason for this is that great changes of circumstances are often unimportant, whereas small changes in the condition of the agent are often crucial.

Simple Frequency. Other conditions aside, the more frequently we have seen a person perform an action, the more justified we are in claiming to know that he can perform the action when we do not see him perform it.

These four conditions are related in various ways. For example, temporal propinquity produces agent similarity, because generally people change less in a shorter time than in a longer time. Of course, circumstantial variety contributes to simple frequency and vice versa. Thus these conditions, which are simple canons of inductive evidence for a certain sort of hypothesis, are inductively interrelated.

Moreover, the importance of the various conditions depends to a considerable extent upon the kind of action involved. With respect to actions that one usually retains the ability to perform for a long time, such as wiggling one's ears, temporal propinquity is less important, whereas with respect to actions one quickly loses the ability to perform, such as running a four-minute mile, the condition of temporal propinquity is much more important. Now if all these conditions are well satisfied, we possess empirical evidence sufficient to support the hypothesis that a person can perform an action when we do not see him perform it, and in the absence of any evidence to the contrary, we are certainly quite justified in claiming that the hypothesis is true. These conditions are so typical of the usual canons of inductive evidence that if they are satisfied, then by the usual canons of inductive evidence our evidence is excellent.

The question that we must now investigate is the following: Are these conditions, these canons of evidence, ever satisfied? In other words, do we by satisfying all these conditions ever acquire evidence sufficient to support the hypothesis that a person could have done otherwise? There are many actions that we rarely see a person perform and almost never see the same person perform more than once. With respect to unusual or generally private actions the conditions that we have mentioned will not be very well satisfied. We will not see a person perform the action often, so the condition of simple frequency will not be satisfied. We will not see the agent perform the action under a great variety of circumstances, so the condition of circumstantial variety will not be satisfied.

However, there are actions that people perform many times, and it is also true that these familiar actions are often the constituents of less familiar and more unusual actions. For example, consider walking across a room, raising an arm, moving a finger, or other commonplace actions. These are actions which do satisfy the four canons of evidence. We see people perform them frequently under a variety of conditions, and often we have seen a person, who has changed little, perform such an action a moment earlier. We can easily imagine a situation that would satisfy all these conditions in a paradigmatic way.

Let us imagine that we are trying to set up an experiment to prove that a man can do otherwise at a certain time. Moreover, let us take some very simple action, the lifting of an arm, so as to avoid any irrelevant complications. Now we are to set up an experiment to show that at a certain time the man could do otherwise. We find a subject that is normal in every way and investigate when our subject can and cannot perform the very simple action involved. For example, we might first instruct him to lift his arm whenever we tell him to, and then observe that he does it. We might then instruct him to lift his arm whenever we tell him not to, observing that he does this. We might then tell him to heed or not to heed our instructions as he wishes and see that he sometimes lifts his arm when we tell him to, and sometimes does not. We might then run this same experiment under a variety of circumstances, indoors and outdoors, under stress and under relaxed conditions, with a weight attached to his arm, without impediment, and so on. Moreover, we might keep careful records on the condition of the subject throughout our experiments; finally, we might vary the condition of the subject by use of drugs, hypnotism, and so forth.

Now suppose we instruct our subject to heed or not to heed our directions as he wishes, and ensure that the condition of the subject as well as the situation in which he is placed are those that we have found to be most propitious for arm lifting. Moreover, suppose we watch him lift his arm, and then we avert our eyes for a moment and, subsequently, see him lift his arm again. In this case the conditions of temporal propinquity, circumstantial variety, agent similarity, and simple frequency would certainly be satisfied.

Consequently, we would then have sufficient empirical evidence to support the hypothesis that the agent could have lifted his arm during that brief period when we did not see him lift it. We would be quite justified in claiming that the hypothesis is true. Therefore it is perfectly possible for us to acquire evidence, perfectly sound empirical evidence, for the hypothesis that a person could have done otherwise. This experiment has probably never been carried out, but it might well be. By so doing we would obtain adequate empirical evidence that determinism is false, because we would have strong empirical evidence that a person could have done otherwise.

Reflecting upon this imagined experiment should show us that many actions—both familiar and unfamiliar, simple and complex—are such that, when a person performs them, we have adequate evidence to support the claim that he could have done otherwise. For most unfamiliar and complex actions contain as essential parts familiar and simple actions. For example, let us return to the murderer. Suppose that the weapon that he uses is a gun, that he aims carefully at his victim and then squeezes the trigger. The deed is then done, his victim has been shot. Notice that one crucial element or constituent of his action is his pulling the trigger. If he could have held that finger still, he could also have avoided shooting his victim and thereby committing murder. Thus if he could have done otherwise with respect to the action of moving his finger, the act of murder could have been avoided. Of course, the act of moving a finger is very simple and familiar, one that we have often seen performed under a great variety of circumstances and conditions. It might well be argued that those complex actions that we judge the agent could have avoided performing each contains as an element some simple and familiar action that we know on the basis of empirical evidence the agent could have avoided performing. Thus our judgments that a person could have done otherwise may all ultimately rest upon the empirical evidence that we have for the hypothesis that familiar and simple actions could have been avoided, that though the agent performed them, he could have desisted. Therefore our belief—a belief that all men of common sense accept—that we often could have done otherwise is a belief strongly supported by empirical evidence.

SUMMARY OF THE ARGUMENT

To see the force of this libertarian argument let us consider how the conclusion is derived from the premises we have defended.

First, we have argued

1. We sometimes have adequate empirical evidence that we could have done otherwise.

Secondly, because we have said that when a person could have done otherwise, then his action is free, we may add the premise

2. If we sometimes have adequate empirical evidence that we could have done otherwise, then we also sometimes have adequate empirical evidence that we perform free actions.

Moreover, because we have also said that if we perform free actions, then the thesis of determinism is false, we may also accept the premise

3. If we sometimes have adequate empirical evidence that we perform free actions, then we have adequate empirical evidence that the thesis of determinism is false.

From these three premises we may validly deduce the conclusion

4. We have adequate empirical evidence that the thesis of determinism is false.

Of course, from the first two premises alone it follows that we sometimes have adequate empirical evidence that we perform free actions.

THE DETERMINIST REJOINDER:
EMPIRICAL EVIDENCE THAT INANIMATE
THINGS COULD HAVE DONE OTHERWISE

The determinist may well be unpersuaded by this argument, and he will attack the first premise in one of two ways. The first way is to deny that it is possible for us to have empirical evidence that a person could have done otherwise. To substantiate this claim he would have to find some defect in the conditions the libertarian has offered as sufficient to give us evidence that a person could have done otherwise. That is, the determinist would have to maintain that, although the four conditions might well be satisfied, their satisfaction does not guarantee us adequate evidence that a person could have done otherwise. The second way of defeating the libertarian's contentions would be to concede that the conditions are adequate (if the conditions are ever satisfied, then we have adequate empirical evidence that a person could have done otherwise), but to deny that the conditions are in fact ever satisfied.

Is there any reason to argue that the conditions are not adequate? There is one rather interesting line of argument to show they may not be. We often say that something could have happened, even that something could have been done, when we do not mean to deny that the thing in question was determined causally. For example, suppose that your automobile is sitting out in front of the house. Suppose, moreover, that someone is wondering whether he could have used your automobile to transport himself to some distant place a short time ago. You might, knowing the condition of your automobile, assert that it could have started. But to say that it could have started is not to say that the automobile was free, that it was free to start. The behavior of the automobile is completely determined in a thoroughly mechanical fashion. However, the sort of evidence given in support of the hypothesis that a man could have lifted his arm when he did not is exactly similar to the sort of evidence showing that the automobile could have started when it did not. If conditions like circumstantial variety, temporal propinquity, agent similarity, and simple frequency were all well satisfied with respect to the automobile, then we would have adequate or sufficient evidence that the automobile could have started by virtue of the satisfaction of these conditions. If their satisfaction shows only that a person could have lifted his arm in the way in which the automobile could have started, then the fact that such evidence shows that the man could have lifted his arm does not prove that he was free, any more than the fact that such evidence shows that the automobile could have started proves that it was free. Therefore the satisfaction of the four conditions mentioned previously does not show that a person could have done otherwise in that sense relevant to free action. The argument fails to show that we can have empirical evidence that a man has performed a free action.

A LIBERTARIAN REPLY: AGENTS AND THINGS

The reply of the libertarian to the preceding objection is that it ignores a fundamental difference between those things which are agents and those which are not. An agent does something; it acts. That which is not an agent does nothing; it is acted upon. Thus we speak of the car starting, but it would be more precise to say that the car was started. The car does not start itself; it does not initiate that change. It is started by someone else who initiates the change. So the car is not an agent; it does not do anything.

When we say that the car could have started, we do not thereby assert that it was within the car's power to start. We do not imply that it was up to the car whether or not it started. On the other hand, when we say of a man that he could have lifted his arm, we do assert that it is within his power to lift it. We do imply that it was up to him whether or not his arm moved. But this difference rests solely upon the fact that the car is not an agent and the man is. When the car starts, that is not something the car does, because it is not an action that the car performs. But when the man moves his arm, that is something he does; it is an action that he performs. Thus the determinist's argument fails.

There is, however, an important lesson to be learned from the determinist's objection. It is that there is some evidence that we have in the case of a man, but lack in the case of an inanimate object, to show that a man could have done something which he did not do. The evidence consists of our knowing whether a man tried to do something. The question of whether or not a man could have done otherwise may rest entirely upon whether or not he tried to. To see that this is so, let us return to our imaginary experiment. Suppose that our experimental subject does not raise his arm when we tell him to after he has been injected with a special drug. We then wonder whether he could have raised his arm or not. The best way to find out is to ask him whether or not he tried to do so. If he says he made no attempt to move his arm, then the mere fact that his arm did not move provides no evidence that he could not have moved it. So if a man does not try to do something, then his not doing it fails to provide evidence that he could not do it. On the other hand, if he says that he tried as hard as he could to move his arm and failed nonetheless, that is exceedingly strong evidence that he could not have moved it.

The analogy with the automobile is again illuminating. The automobile cannot try to start itself. There is nothing that the car can do to get itself moving—that is why it is not an agent. Therefore one kind of evidence that we can accumulate to show that an agent could have done something, which we cannot get from an object, is the agent's testimony. For if the agent testifies that when his arm did not move it was not the case that he tried and failed, his not moving it provides no evidence that he could not have moved it. Moreover, this evidence is crucial. We might have evidence that a man could do something because the conditions of evidence mentioned earlier might all be well satisfied, but we nevertheless might fail to have adequate empirical evidence that he could have done otherwise. For we might also have overwhelming evidence that he could not have done it, evidence that the man tried as hard as he could and failed nevertheless. This is good evidence that he could not have done what he tried to do. However, when the four conditions are all well satisfied, and when in addition we have no evidence that the agent could not have done the thing in question (that is, we have his testimony that he did not try and subsequently fail to do it), then surely we have impressive empirical evidence that he could have done what he did not do.

A SECOND DETERMINIST OBJECTION: EVIDENCE AND CAUSATION

A second objection that the determinist might raise against the preceding argument is that the evidence mentioned by the libertarian is not adequate to establish the hypothesis in question. Let us reconsider the imaginary experiment in some detail. What evidence do we gain from the experiment? The evidence consisted of watching a man raise his arm under a wide variety of circumstances. We varied both the external circumstances and the internal condition of the agent. We then asked whether he could have raised his arm at some time when he did not raise his arm, and we noted that the evidence previously gained supported the hypothesis that he could have raised his arm. But is this evidence adequate to establish the hypothesis? Surely it is not. For, in the first place, notice that the evidence is perfectly compatible with the hypothesis that his behavior was causally determined. Moreover, it is quite easy to tell in precisely what way it was determined because we know a good deal about the mechanical operation of the arm. We know that certain muscles remaining still and unflexed while other muscles remain flexed would be quite sufficient for his arm to remain still.

Thus we could have quite easily established that at the time that his arm did not move, the state of his muscles was sufficient for his arm to remain motionless. We might have the evidence from the experiment and also know that the state of his arm was causally determined to remain still; it was quite impossible for it to move. Because his arm could not have moved, he could not have moved it. Therefore the evidence from the experiment fails to show that the subject could have moved his arm when it remained still.

THE LIBERTARIAN REJOINDER: CONTROLLING CAUSAL CONDITIONS

To this argument the libertarian is bound to reply promptly that it begs the very question at issue. He can willingly concede that the behavior of the subject's arm was causally determined by the state of his muscles, but claim that it fails to follow from this that the subject could not have moved his arm. Though the state of his arm was causally determined, it might well be that the agent could have altered the conditions determining that his arm would remain still. The state of his muscles was causally sufficient to determine that his arm would remain still, but that state of his muscles was something well within his control. He could have moved certain muscles, and if he had, his arm would not have remained still; it would have moved instead.

The evidence of the experiment shows that the subject could have moved his arm, and from this we must conclude that the evidence equally shows that any condition that causally determined his arm to remain still was a condition the agent could have altered.

Any necessary condition for moving his arm must have been a condition that he could have brought about, because, in fact, he could have moved his arm. Anything a man could have done is such that he could obviously also have done anything which was a necessary means to doing it. Therefore the evidence that we often have for the hypothesis that a man could have done otherwise indeed survives as adequate and sufficient to sustain that conclusion.

SECOND THRUST BY THE DETERMINIST: ANCESTRAL DETERMINATION

Suppose the determinist concedes the preceding point. What is he then likely to reply? Recall that determinism entails not only that a given event is causally determined, that is, that there are earlier conditions which determine the event, but also that these conditions are themselves causally determined by earlier events, that those conditions are in turn determined by still earlier events, and so forth into the indefinite past. A person's behavior is, therefore, not merely causally determined but also, let us say, *ancestrally* determined by a chain of events stemming from the indefinite past. So the determinist rejoinder is going to hinge upon the fact that determinism implies not only that behavior is causally determined, but that it is ancestrally determined as well.

The argument is simply this. One might have the sort of evidence that we imagined in our experiment to support the hypothesis that a person could have raised his arm when, in fact, his behavior is not only causally determined, but ancestrally determined. The state of a man's arm is determined by the state of certain muscles within his body. We assume that the state of those muscles is determined by certain physical processes that go on in the body, and these physical processes are no doubt causally determined by earlier physical processes, and those by yet earlier ones, and so on into the indefinite past. Consequently, if the motion of his arm is not only causally determined, but ancestrally determined as well, then it is determined by conditions that existed before he was born and over which he had no control. Therefore whether he moves his arm must be determined by conditions that he could not control.

The preceding remarks are predicated on the assumption that determinism is true. But the crucial point is that the evidence we have from the libertarian's experiment is perfectly consistent with the motion of the subject's arm being ancestrally determined. It is perfectly consistent with the truth of determinism. If the evidence for the hypothesis that a person could have done otherwise is consistent with the ancestral determination of the man's behavior, then obviously the evidence is not adequate to establish the hypothesis that the man could have done otherwise. For if the evidence from our experiment is consistent with the hypothesis that the motionless state of the subject's arm was ancestrally determined, then it is also consistent with the hypothesis that he could not have done otherwise. Because the evidence fails to show that his behavior was not ancestrally determined, it also fails to show that he could have done otherwise. Therefore the evidence of our experiment is inadequate to support the libertarian position.

SUMMARY OF THE PRECEDING ARGUMENTS

To appreciate the preceding dialectic, and hence to appreciate the strength of the determinist position, it is well to consider the preceding arguments in a more precise form. Originally, we defended determinism against the evidence for free actions by arguing

1. The alleged evidence for free action is consistent with something being causally determined and thus is insufficient evidence that the action is not causally determined.

because we often assume that a movement is caused, by the state of the muscles and so forth, when we also have the evidence alleged to show free action. To this premise we mistakenly added the premise

2. If the alleged evidence for free action is insufficient evidence that the action is not causally determined, then the alleged evidence for free action is insufficient evidence for the falsity of determinism.

Finally, adding the premise

3. If the alleged evidence for free action is insufficient evidence for the falsity of determinism, then the alleged evidence for free action is insufficient evidence for such action.

we validly concluded from the preceding premises

> 4. The alleged evidence for free action is insufficient evidence for such action.

However, this argument proved faulty. Premise (2) rests on the mistaken assumption that if the evidence for an action being free is sufficient to refute determinism, then the evidence must be sufficient to show that the action was not causally determined. The reply of the libertarian to the foregoing argument helped clarify the nature of our error. Evidence for an action being free which is insufficient to show the action was not causally determined is nevertheless sufficient to refute determinism, if it is sufficient to show the action was not ancestrally determined. The reason is that determinism implies every action is ancestrally determined. However, we can now easily modify our argument to make it sound.

First, in place of premise (1) we put the equally sound premise

> 1a. The alleged evidence for free action is consistent with ancestral determination and thus is insufficient evidence that the action is not ancestrally determined.

and in place of the false premise (2) we put the true premise

> 2a. If the alleged evidence for free action is insufficient evidence that the action is not ancestrally determined, then the alleged evidence for free action is insufficient evidence for the falsity of determinism.

From these two new premises and premise (3) in the preceding argument, we deduce conclusion (4). That is the case against the evidence for free action.

A LIBERTARIAN REJOINDER: JUSTIFICATION WITHOUT DEDUCTION

The libertarian reply to this argument resembles the reply to the determinist objection against the evidence of introspection. The determinist's objection to the claim that we have introspective evidence adequate to establish that a person could have done otherwise was that all such evidence is logically consistent with the claim that the person in question could not have done otherwise. The determinist concluded that the evidence had no bearing on or relevance to the hypothesis that the person could have done otherwise.

The libertarian rejoinder—which is a rejection of premise (1a)—is that this argument has the form of many irrational arguments and, as such, suffers the defect of being a kind of argument that if generalized would lead to almost total irrationalism. All the determinist's argument establishes is that the evidence we have for the hypothesis that a person could have moved his arm, when in fact he did not, does not logically entail that conclusion. To escape from irrationalism, however, the determinist must concede that evidence not logically entailing a hypothesis is nevertheless often sufficient inductive evidence to believe it reasonably.

Again it is important to notice that the determinist argues in a way that would be rejected as unacceptable in other contexts. Because the determinist's only complaint against the evidence cited by the libertarian is that it is logically consistent with the denial of the hypothesis it is meant to establish, the determinist's objection embodies the view that no amount of evidence is sufficient to justify a claim or belief that a person could have done something if the evidence does not entail that conclusion. This would seem to commit him to the quite untenable general thesis that no amount of inductive evidence, evidence that does not entail its conclusion, is adequate or sufficient to sustain any conclusion. This is surely absurd. All the hypotheses we accept about the future and the past are based on inductive evidence for those hypotheses. The evidence that we have about the past (for example, that a person was married yesterday) or about the future (for example, that there will be an eclipse of the sun at some specific time) are hypotheses that are only inductively supported. The evidence for these hypotheses surely does not entail that they are true. Nevertheless, inductive evidence may be perfectly adequate and sufficient to sustain these things.

Moreover, we can see that the determinist's objection is mistaken by reflecting upon a case in which a person performs an action, thus proving that he could perform it, where we have only inductive evidence to show that he did so. For example, if we see a man standing with his finger on the only button attached to a bell, and though we do not see him push the button, we hear the bell ring, then we have adequate evidence for the hypothesis that he did and hence could push the button. The evidence that we have does not entail that conclusion, but it might well be adequate nonetheless. In short, the determinist's objection to the acceptance of the evidence in question as adequate for the hypothesis that a person could have done otherwise rests upon the slender support of the premise that the evidence does not entail the hypothesis. That support is much too weak. The evidence might well be sufficient to sustain that hypothesis inductively even if it is perfectly consistent with the denial of the hypothesis, that is, even though it does not entail that the hypothesis is true. To deny this is to head pell-mell down the road of irrationalism.

THE DETERMINIST REPLY: DETERMINISM WITHOUT IRRATIONALISM

We must not buy a refutation of libertarianism at the cost of purchasing irrationalism along with it. But the determinist has more to say; he need not embrace irrationalism in order to refute the libertarian contention that we have adequate evidence that a person could have done otherwise. Notice that in many cases, though our evidence does not entail the hypothesis, it is nevertheless at least possible to obtain evidence which entails it. That is, in most cases where our evidence is adequate inductive evidence for a hypothesis, it is at least logically possible to obtain some further evidence that would entail that the hypothesis is true. In such cases we may surely accept the evidence as sufficient and adequate. Consider the example just mentioned, where we have very strong inductive evidence that a man could have pushed the bell; though our evidence does not entail that conclusion, this is a case in which it is at least logically possible to obtain some further evidence which would entail that conclusion. For we are no doubt supposing that the man did push the button. If he did push the button, then it was logically possible to observe that he pushed it and thereby to obtain evidence which would entail that he could push it. In general, whenever a person actually performs an action, it is at least logically possible to obtain evidence entailing that he did and could perform the action. But, on the other hand, in those cases in which a person does not perform an action, it is impossible to obtain such evidence. It is logically impossible to see that a man does something when he is not doing it. Therefore in any case when a man does not perform an action it is logically impossible to obtain evidence which entails that he does perform it. We may conclude that in such cases it is impossible to obtain adequate or sufficient evidence to show that the person could have performed the action in question. That is all that is required for the determinist position. For the only question at issue is whether we may ever obtain adequate inductive evidence for the hypothesis that a person could have done something that he did not do.

THE LIBERTARIAN REPLY: TRUTH, FALSITY, AND INDUCTION

To defend the libertarian argument it is only necessary to perceive how arbitrary the determinist's contention is. No special reason has been given for rejecting the particular kind of evidence we have cited as being adequate evidence for the hypothesis in question. Moreover, it would be peculiar and arbitrary to maintain that the evidence mentioned (the evidence one might obtain by performing our experiment) is adequate for the hypothesis that a man could have lifted his arm when he does lift it, and yet deny that the evidence is adequate when he did not lift it. The hypothesis that he could have lifted his arm is either adequately supported by that evidence or it is not, and the mere fact that he does or does not lift his arm at the time in question is quite irrelevant to the question of the adequacy of that evidence.

An analogy should be helpful here. Suppose we have very strong evidence that there is a cat in the living room closet. This evidence consists of having heard a meow, a scratchy noise, or some other feline give-away. Is this evidence adequate to support the hypothesis that there is a cat in the closet? It would surely be peculiar to maintain that it is adequate evidence that there is a cat in the closet if there is one there, but not adequate evidence if there is none there. The evidence for the hypothesis is just as strong when there is no cat in the closet as when there is. The question of how strongly the evidence supports the hypothesis that a cat is in the closet must be answered independently of the question of whether or not a cat is in the closet. If the evidence is good when the cat is present, then the same evidence must also be good even when the cat is absent. Similarly, if the evidence for the hypothesis that a man could have raised his arms is good evidence for that hypothesis when in fact the man raises his arm, then it must also be good evidence that he could have raised his arm when in fact he does not raise his arm. In short, whether or not evidence supports a hypothesis, that is, supports it inductively, does not depend upon any further consideration of the truth or falsity of the hypothesis.

THE IRREFUTABILITY OF THE THESIS OF DETERMINISM: A DETERMINIST ARGUMENT

We have not yet examined with care the strongest argument that the determinist has to offer against all the preceding remarks. For the strongest argument against all the libertarian claims that we have adequate evidence that a person could have done otherwise —and hence, for the falsity of determinism—is one based on the idea that the thesis of determinism cannot be refuted by any empirical test. Let us consider an argument by G. J. Warnock in defense of this conclusion. Warnock defines the thesis of determinism as the thesis "for every event E, there is some set of antecedent conditions such that, whenever these conditions obtain, an event of kind E occurs." Warnock refers to this thesis as S. He argues as follows:

> Suppose then that we now raise the question what would have to occur in order to establish that S is false? . . . It is easy enough to imagine an event E, conditions sufficient for the occurrence of which have always been supposed to be ABC; and that some day that these conditions may obtain and yet the event E does not occur. But clearly this has no tendency to falsify S. For it was said in S only that there are *some* conditions sufficient for the occurrence of any event; it was not specified what these conditions are in any instance nor was it implied that anyone necessarily knows in any instance whether the conditions are sufficient. To say that there are some laws of nature does not imply that anyone knows, or indeed ever will know exactly what they are. And thus the operation of S is compatible with the rejection of every particular statement

of law, and every causal statement, that is or ever has been or will be asserted. If I say 'Someone now in this house has green hair,' it can be shown what I say is untrue: for everyone now in this house can be paraded and none observed to have green hair. But if I say 'There once was or is or will be, somewhere in the universe, a person who has green hair,' I need never admit that I am wrong. For it could never be said that every part of the universe at every possible date had been inspected and found to contain no green-haired person. Similarly, if I were to say, 'Some set of the conditions ABCDF is sufficient for the occurrence of E,' you could be shown that I am mistaken. For all of the finite number of combinations of numbers could be tried and none found to be sufficient for the occurrence of E. But if I merely affirm that there are *some* conditions, and do not delimit the area of search for them at all, I need never admit that I am mistaken. For it could never be said that every conceivable factor and set of factors that might be conditions of E had been tried and rejected; so it could always be said that the right combination of conditions had not yet been found.[11]

From this Warnock concludes:

> . . . there could never occur any event which it would be necessary, or even natural, to describe as an un-caused event. It could never be said that among its complex and indefinitely numerous antecedents none could be said to be sufficient for its occurrence. And this is to say that nothing could occur which would require us to hold that S is false. . . .
>
> It calls for no supporting empirical evidence, for none could count against it. It cannot be empirically tested, for no test could fail—or rather, nothing could be made to count as a test.[12]

It is not difficult to see how Warnock's remarks may be used in a reply to the libertarian argument we have been considering. Sup-

[11] G. J. Warnock, "Every Event Has a Cause," reprinted in *Logic and Language*, Second Series (Oxford: Basil Blackwell, 1959), ed. by Anthony Flew, p. 106.

[12] Ibid., pp. 106–107.

pose that Warnock is correct and that the thesis of determinism cannot be refuted by empirical test; suppose that no empirical evidence
would ever be sufficient to refute it. According to the libertarian
there is some empirical evidence which would be sufficient to establish that a person could have done otherwise. Any evidence that is
sufficient to establish the truth of a hypothesis is also sufficient to
establish the falsity of any hypothesis incompatible with it. Thus,
for example, if I have sufficient empirical evidence to establish that
one person in the universe has green hair, I have sufficient evidence
to establish the falsity of any hypothesis incompatible with it, say,
the hypothesis that everybody in the universe has either brown,
yellow, red, or gray hair. Now if the hypothesis that a person could
have done otherwise is incompatible with the hypothesis that his
behavior was ancestrally determined (and, therefore, incompatible
with the thesis of determinism) and if I have sufficient empirical evidence to establish the truth of the hypothesis that a person could
have done otherwise, that evidence will also be sufficient to establish the falsity of determinism. However, if the thesis of determinism is not refutable by any empirical evidence, then there is no
empirical evidence that would establish its falsity. Therefore since
the thesis of determinism is not refutable by any empirical evidence,
the empirical evidence mustered by the libertarian in support of the
hypothesis that a person could have done otherwise cannot be adequate evidence to establish that hypothesis. As a result, the libertarian is mistaken in contending that the empirical evidence which
he has, and which we could all have, to support the hypothesis that
a person could have done otherwise is adequate evidence to support that hypothesis. It cannot be adequate because it is not adequate to show determinism is false.

THE LIBERTARIAN REPLY: THE POSSIBILITY OF
INDUCTIVE EVIDENCE

It is true that no matter how long we search for and fail to find a
person with green hair, and no matter how long we search for and
fail to find the cause of some event, the logical possibility always
remains that there is a person with green hair and that the event
has a cause. So Warnock is right when he says that it would never
be necessary to describe an event as uncaused. But it hardly follows
from this that no empirical evidence can count against the hypothe-

sis that an event is uncaused. Nor does it follow from what he says that no empirical evidence can count against the hypothesis that there is someone with green hair.

To see that this is so, let us reflect on the hypothesis "there once was, or is, or will be, somewhere in the universe a person who has green hair." It is of course true that no amount of evidence that we could ever gain by observation and research would ever entail that this hypothesis is false. That is, no matter how much inductive evidence we might gather for the falsity of this hypothesis it would still be logically possible, even given that evidence, that the hypothesis should be true. However, it hardly follows from this that we could not ever have adequate inductive evidence for its falsity. Indeed, we might very well claim at the present time to have such evidence. The mere fact that no amount of looking, searching, and investigating would ever provide us with evidence from which we could deduce that the hypothesis is false proves very little. The same thing is true with respect to the thesis of determinism. No amount of looking, searching, and investigating would provide evidence that entails that the thesis was false. No matter how much evidence we got, it would still be logically possible, even given that evidence, that the thesis should be true. No amount of such empirical evidence would ever allow us to deduce the falsity of determinism validly. But it may well be that we can have empirical evidence sufficient to establish inductively the falsity of the "green hair" hypothesis and other evidence sufficient to sustain the falsity of determinism.

It is perfectly possible that some empirical evidence should inductively sustain that there is no one with green hair or that some event is uncaused even though the evidence leaves open the logical possibility that there is a person with green hair and that the event has a cause. Once again, the crux of the matter is quite simple. It is that induction, and the inductive proof for any hypothesis, begins where deduction ends. When deductive proof is not available, we are on precisely the proper ground for inductive investigation and proof. So the mere fact that no empirical evidence is deductively sufficient to establish the falsity of determinism does not imply or in any way show that no amount of empirical evidence is sufficient to establish inductively the falsity of determinism. But if the falsity of determinism may be established by empirical test, the thesis of determinism, contrary to what Warnock has argued, is open to empirical refutation. Moreover, from our imaginary investigation of arm lifting it is perfectly clear that it is not only possible to obtain empirical evidence sufficient to refute the thesis of determinism, but it is also true that such evidence is available to us.

THE DETERMINIST REPLY: THE EXACT CHARACTER OF THE EVIDENCE

Perhaps there is no conclusive general consideration that can be brought to bear to show that the evidence from your imaginary experiment is insufficient to refute the thesis of determinism. It is not by any means certain that this is so, but let us suppose that it is correct. Nevertheless, if you simply reflect on the exact character of that evidence it is perfectly absurd to suppose that it should be sufficient to refute the thesis of determinism. After all, what does it amount to? The evidence consisted of observing a person under a variety of conditions and circumstances performing the simple action of raising his arm. Now watching a person raise his arm, or not raise it, on a great number of occasions under very carefully controlled circumstances and conditions is simply not the sort of evidence that could refute the thesis of determinism. How could it? This evidence is perfectly consistent with the causal determination and, indeed, with the ancestral determination of everything that we observe. In fact, the evidence appears to be simply irrelevant to determination of either sort. The behavior might be causally determined or ancestrally determined, and the evidence in question would shed no light on whether either of these things is so.

To conclude, even if a determinist must concede that there is no absurdity involved (no logical absurdity, at any rate) in the idea that there should be empirical evidence sufficient to test or refute the thesis of determinism, it is absurd to suppose that the kind of evidence obtainable from the experiment imagined earlier should be sufficient to refute the thesis of determinism. There might be some kind of evidence that could refute that thesis, but the evidence from the experiment is surely not it.

A LIBERTARIAN REPLY: A FINAL WORD

The reply of the libertarian to this criticism consists in reiterating his original claim. He originally held that this evidence was adequate to support the thesis that a person could have done otherwise. What the determinist has argued is that this evidence does not seem to be the kind that could refute the thesis of determinism. The libertarian replies that the reason this evidence does not seem to refute the thesis of determinism is that the hypothesis that a person could have done otherwise is not obviously incompatible with the thesis of determinism. The evidence showing that a person could have done otherwise also shows that any hypothesis incompatible with this one must be false. However, it might well be the case that some hypothesis is actually incompatible with the hypothesis that a person could have done otherwise, but does not appear to be incompatible with it. In that case, the evidence for the hypothesis that a person could have done otherwise, which is sufficient evidence for that hypothesis, might not appear to be conclusive evidence to refute the other hypothesis. However, though it might not appear to be conclusive, it is conclusive, nonetheless.

An analogy should help to clarify this point. A person might see a die resting on his desk and thus have conclusive evidence that there is a die on his desk. Now a die is by definition a cube, and a cube is something that has twelve edges. That is, from the fact that something is a cube we may validly deduce that it has twelve edges. However, suppose that the man who observes the die on his desk and knows that it is a cube does not realize that from the fact that something is a cube it follows that it has twelve edges. Though it would be apparent to this person that he has adequate evidence that there is a cube on his desk, it might not be apparent to him that he has adequate evidence that something on his desk has twelve edges. But the evidence that he has is adequate for the latter, nonetheless. His seeing a die on his desk gives him evidence sufficient to establish that the thing on his desk has twelve edges. The fact that it would not seem to him that the evidence of seeing a die is sufficient to establish that there is a thing on his desk that has twelve edges is beside the point. The evidence is sufficient to support that hypothesis whether or not he realizes that this is so. Similarly, if the statement that a person could have done otherwise is such that we can validly deduce from it that the person's behavior was not ancestrally determined and, therefore, that the thesis of determinism is false, then the evidence that we have to support the hypothesis that a person could have done otherwise is also evidence supporting the hypothesis that determinism is false.

A person who does not realize that one may validly deduce the falsity of determinism from the statement that a person could have done otherwise is one to whom evidence for the truth of the latter statement would not seem to be evidence for the falsity of determinism. But it would be evidence, and sufficient evidence, for the latter, and therefore for the falsity of determinism. So the evidence that we have obtained from our imaginary experiment and the evidence available to us from the uncontrolled but abundant resources of everyday life is sufficient to show that a person could have done otherwise and, therefore, that the thesis of determinism is false.

That such evidence might not seem to be the sort sufficient to refute the thesis of determinism stems from the fact that it might seem that one cannot validly deduce the falsity of determinism from the statement that a person could have done otherwise. However, that deduction is valid, and the refutation of the thesis of determinism is conclusive.

THE COMPATIBLIST POSITION

One could contend that there is some merit to the final remarks of both the libertarian and the determinist. The determinist claims with some plausibility that the evidence that a person could have done otherwise is not adequate to refute the thesis of determinism. Indeed, this seems to be true. On the other hand, we must surely agree with the libertarian that there is very strong evidence for the hypothesis that a person could have done otherwise. But if that hypothesis entails the falsity of determinism, then we should agree with the libertarian that we have sufficient and adequate evidence for the falsity of determinism. The merit in both positions has led some to search for an alternative view.

The determinist and libertarian views are not the only ones available. In order to see this, we need only to review the arguments considered earlier. The determinist argument might be stated as follows:

1. If the thesis of determinism is true, then there are no free actions.

2. The thesis of determinism is true.
Therefore
3. There are no free actions.

On the other hand, the libertarian argument would run as follows:

1. If the thesis of determinism is true, then there are no free actions.
2. There are free actions.
Therefore
3. The thesis of determinism is not true.

The libertarian and the determinist share a common premise: if determinism is true then there is no free action, or, if there is free action then determinism is not true. In other words, determinism and free action are incompatible. Consequently, we can easily see that someone might equally reject both the determinist's and the libertarian's position by denying their common premise. Philosophers who do so we shall refer to as compatiblists, in contrast to determinists and libertarians, to whom we shall refer jointly as incompatiblists.

It is perfectly clear that the position of a compatiblist is philosophically tempting. We said earlier that the problem of freedom and determinism presents a paradox, because the thesis of determinism, as well as the hypothesis that people sometimes act freely, are both things a man of common sense accepts as evident. That two beliefs which are perfectly evident from the standpoint of common sense should turn out to be inconsistent is a paradox indeed. The compatiblist position is an attempt to dispel the appearance of inconsistency and thereby to dissolve the paradox by showing that what appears to be inconsistent really is not. The alleged inconsistency, according to the compatiblist, is only apparent and not real.

How is the compatiblist position defended? It does seem implausible to suggest that a person could have done otherwise, even though his behavior was determined causally by conditions existing before he was born and over which he had no control. Nevertheless, this is precisely the view that compatiblists defend. Their line of defense has taken two directions. In the first place, some compatiblists have tried, by analyzing the notion of causal determination, to show that the thesis of causal determinism implies nothing that is incompatible with free action. The most famous defender of this idea is perhaps John Stuart Mill, but many philosophers have followed this line of thought. Secondly, some compatiblists have tried to show that the idea of free action, that is, the idea that a person could have done otherwise, does not imply anything incompatible with determinism. These two approaches are really two sides of the same coin. For, of course, if the idea of free action implies nothing incompatible with the thesis of causal determinism, it will also be true that the thesis of causal determinism implies nothing incompatible with free action. However, from a methodological point of view, one might start by analyzing either notion in an effort to establish this compatibility. Finally, one might attempt to prove the compatibility of free action and determinism without offering an analysis of either. That may appear to be the least promising route, but it is one we must also investigate.

A COMPATIBLIST ARGUMENT: CAUSATION AS A CONSTITUENT OF ACTION

Certain arguments advanced to prove the compatibility of free action and determinism are unique because they try to prove compatibility by showing that determinism is indispensable to free action. This view has taken a number of forms. One is an argument that the distinction between action and mere passivity has itself to do with causation. Earlier, when we were examining the determinist case, we noticed that according to the determinist the truth of determinism implies that people are more passive than active. If human action is the inevitable outcome of causal forces beyond the person's control, it would seem he is more acted upon than actor. The man who pulls the trigger on the murder weapon appears active, appears to be performing an action. But, according to some determinists, he is not really active; instead, he is passively responding to causal forces that lie entirely outside of his influence. According to certain compatiblists, this is a complete inversion of the truth. For as they see it, the difference between passive response and action must itself be delineated in causal terms.

What is the difference between a simple action (such as raising one's arm) and a mere movement of the body (one's arm going up), which is not an action? One compatiblist answer to this question is that in the case in which I raise my arm, something happening within me causes my arm to go up. My performing the simple action of raising my arm involves my arm going up in response, causal response, to something which takes place within me. Compatiblists have described this thing which goes on within me in various ways. For example, it has sometimes been referred to as a volition, the idea being that my raising my arm consists of my arm going up as a causal consequence of a volition occurring within me. The volition might well be described as "arm-going-up volition" or something of the sort. However, the state as so described is one whose very existence might be, and indeed has been, doubted. It is by no means evident that there is any such thing as a volition to have one's arm go up that occurs within a man whenever he raises his arm. A volition would have to be some kind of occurrence, some episode that occurs within the person but is not identifiable through introspection. For it is not at all clear that when a man raises his arm he can ever detect by introspection such a volition occurring.

The theory of volition may, however, be put forward in a form impervious to problems of this sort. It might be that the volition consists of some well-known and familiar kind of psychological state. For example, it may be argued that when my arm goes up because I want it to go up, I have raised my arm. My doing something thus consists of a certain event taking place because I want it to. This view requires that there be some connection between my wanting to perform the action and its occurrence. The obvious connection, suggests the compatiblist, is a causal one. The wanting causally produces the doing. If this view or any variation of it is correct, then my doing something requires its being caused by some psychological state which occurs within me. Consequently, action, and therefore free action, must be compatible with causal determination since it involves causal determination as a constituent.

AN INCOMPATIBLIST REJOINDER: WHAT CONTROLS THE CAUSE?

This point of view has a number of defects. In the first place, it is by no means obvious from introspection that whenever a person performs an action his action is accompanied by some antecedent want, wish, desire, or any other specific psychological state. Actions occur under a variety of circumstances and subsequent to any number of different kinds of psychological states. Thus it is initially implausible to suggest there is any one introspectable kind of psychological state that is a constituent of every human action.

However, even if we accept a notion of volition that is not an introspectable state, and allow for the possibility that every human action might have as a necessary constituent some such ingredient of which none of us is aware, the compatiblist will still not have won the day.

To see this let us suppose that every action does have as a necessary constituent some state which causes the action to occur. It is by no means clear that what we are here supposing is at all intelligible. The idea has certain internal defects. For example, if the state in question is said to be a volition, then we must be inclined to ask what the volition is a volition of. Suppose I raise my arm. Is the volition which is a constituent of this action a volition that my arm go up? If it is a volition that my arm go up, then is that volition itself an action? And if that volition is itself an action, then must there be a volition which in turn is a necessary constituent of that action? In that case, when I raise my arm there would have to be a volition that my arm go up and, that volition itself being an action, would have to have as a necessary ingredient a volition, and so on. This regress might be avoided by denying that volitions are actions or that all actions have volitions as a constituent. But either of these alternatives leaves open the reply that we might just as well end the matter with the action of raising my arm as with the volition to raise it.

Be that as it may, even if we grant the supposition that actions do have some causal ingredient as a necessary constituent, the view has an overwhelming difficulty inherent in it. Let us consider an action caused by another action. Suppose that I lift a bar by pulling on it. In this case I perform one action (lifting the bar) by performing some antecedent action (pulling on the bar). It is my pulling on the bar that causes it to rise off the ground and therefore brings about the occurrence of my action, lifting the bar. Indeed, in this case my pulling on the bar is a necessary constituent of my lifting the bar. This is a perfectly clear case, then, of an action which does have as an ingredient a causal constituent. Were it not for the causal relationship between pulling on the bar and the bar moving, the action would not have taken place.

However, this simple fact is perfectly compatible with the idea that neither the action of pulling on the bar nor the action of lifting the bar was a free action. For suppose my pulling on the bar was the outcome, the inevitable outcome, of events over which I had no control. In that case, I could not have done otherwise. Because my lifting the bar inevitably resulted from my pulling on it as I did, it follows that just as I could not have done anything but pull on the bar, so I could not have done anything but lift it. Therefore, though my action of lifting the bar has an element of causal determination in it, and indeed requires causal determination for its occurrence, it is perfectly possible that the action was not free. Moreover, and this is the crucial point, it might well be the case that even though causal determination was an essential ingredient in the action, it is the truth of determinism that yielded the result that the action was not free.

To clarify this point we should recall that it follows from the truth of determinism that whatever I do is causally determined by conditions existing before I was born and over which I had no control. It is a further contention of the incompatiblist that it follows from this that I could not have done anything but what I did do, that I could not have done otherwise. Thus it might well be the case that even though causal determination was necessary to performing the action of lifting the bar, the truth of universal causal determinism implied that the action was not free. From the supposition that causal determination is a necessary constitutent of an action, it does not follow that the action must be free, or that determinism is compatible with that action's being free. Even if human action has as a constituent some causal relation, it may still be that free action is inconsistent with determinism.

The crux of this argument depends upon the distinction between causal determination and ancestral determination. An action may be causally determined by certain factors and yet free, provided that the agent himself controlled those factors which brought it about. If my pulling on the bar was itself something within my control, something that was a free action of mine, then some of the causal consequences of that action would also be free actions of mine. If pulling on the bar is a free action and it causes the bar to rise, then my lifting the bar is also a free action. In general, if my performing some action X causally results in my also performing some action Y, then the action Y, though it is causally determined, may still be free provided that action X was free. The causal determination of an action is compatible with the action being free. However, if an action is causally determined by some antecedent action, and the antecedent action it not itself free, then the action resulting from it is not free either. Moreover, the thesis of determinism entails more than that an action is causally determined: it also entails that action is ancestrally determined. If an action is ancestrally determined, then it is causally determined by things that happened before the agent was born and over which he had no control. Consequently, the agent could not have done otherwise; his action was not a free action. Therefore the thesis of determinism cannot be shown to be compatible with free action by showing that action, and therefore free action, always involves as a constituent the causal determination of action by some psychological state.

THE COMPATIBLIST REPLY: REASONS AND CAUSES

The preceding incompatiblist argument hinges on the idea that one action may be the cause of another action. Suppose we concede that if one action is the cause of another action, the first action must be shown to be free if the second action is, and, therefore, to show actions to be caused by actions would not prove that free action and determinism are compatible. However, that does not settle the matter. For the compatiblist contention is not only that actions are caused, but that they are caused by something not itself an action.

Perhaps the paradigm of action, and of free action in particular, is rational action. A rational action is one for which the agent has reasons. Now suppose that a man not only performs an action, but has reasons for performing it. These reasons explain why he did it. Thus if a man is asked why he raised his hand and he replies that he wished to answer the question asked, then he has performed an action for which he has a reason. The reason—that he wished to answer the question—explains the act. Reasons often imply a cause, but this is not to say that every reason is a cause. If somebody presents an argument, then he gives reasons for the conclusions of the argument, but in so doing he obviously has not caused the conclusion. However, there must be some connection between the content of a reason and the action for which it is a reason, or the reason would have absolutely nothing to do with the action. The reason is manifestly connected with the action in some way.

The most plausible way of explaining the connection between action and reason is to say it is a causal relation. It might be quite difficult to explain in just what way a man's reason is connected causally with his action. For example, it seems somewhat implausible to suggest that when a man raised his hand because he wished to answer a question, there occurred within him a wish to raise his hand which in turn caused his arm to go up. Surely that would be a very inadequate causal account of why his arm went up. An adequate account of the way in which the wish was causally related to this action might contain a reference to a very complex set of conditions, other than those immediately apparent, which existed at the time. A helpful analogy is that of striking a match to light it. No one doubts that striking a match is causally connected with its lighting, but to say that the striking of the match caused its lighting is to give a very inadequate causal account. We know very well that striking matches is not sufficient to make them light. All sorts of additional conditions must prevail: there must be adequate oxygen, the pressure on the match must be heavy enough, the match must be dry, and so forth. Nevertheless, to say that the match lighted because it was struck is only intelligible because there is some, perhaps indirect, causal connection between striking a match and its lighting. Similarly, to say that a man raised his hand because he wished to answer a question is intelligible only because there is some, perhaps indirect, causal connection between his wishing to answer the question and the raising of his arm.

All this taken together provides the basis for a proof of the compatibility of rational action and determinism that escapes the preceding argument of the incompatiblist. The argument is this. The reasons that a man has for performing a certain action are not themselves actions. Having certain reasons for performing an action is not also something performed. Indeed, it is nonsense to speak of performing reasons. Moreover, a man may not have any control over whether or not certain reasons occur to him. For example, a man might see something happen which provides him with a reason for some action, when his having that reason is beyond his control. If we see something happen which provides a reason for action, then we cannot help having that reason for doing what we do. However, this fails to show the resultant action to be unfree. It might be perfectly free, although the reasons for which it was performed are reasons the man could not help having. Suppose I see that a beam is about to fall on a man's head and I warn him. My reason for acting was that I saw the beam was about to hit the man on the head. Although I could not help having that reason, the action is nevertheless free. Therefore an action may result from having a reason which one could not help having, that is, a reason that one was not free not to have, and the action might nevertheless be free. This shows that a free action may causally result from some condition the agent was powerless to prevent.

This, however, means the collapse of the argument for the incompatibility of free action and determinism. That argument depends upon the assumption that if an action is causally determined by some condition beyond the control of the agent, then the agent could not help doing what he did. It depends upon the premise that if a man's action is ancestrally determined it is not a free action. But the way to refute this premise is now clear. If an action is causally determined by some reason that a man could not help having, then he is performing an action causally determined by conditions beyond his control. But such an action may nevertheless be free. My warning a man that a beam is about to strike his head is an example of a free action of just this sort. Therefore the rejoinder to the incompatiblist is simply that an action may be free even if it is ancestrally determined, and therefore causally determined by conditions over which the agent has no control. Because the thesis of determinism implies nothing except that an action is ancestrally determined which even appears to be incompatible with the idea that the action is free, we may conclude that free action and determinism are indeed compatible.

SUMMARY OF PRECEDING ARGUMENTS

To pinpoint the weakness in the incompatiblist argument, let us restate the premises from which he derives his conclusion. First he says, quite correctly,

1. If determinism is true, then some of the conditions that

causally determine actions are beyond the control of the agent.

but then he contends,

2. If some of the conditions that causally determine actions are beyond the control of the agent, then there are no free actions.

from which premises he validly deduces the incompatiblist conclusion

3. If determinism is true, then there are no free actions.

But we have now shown premise (2) of the argument is equivalent to the false claim that if an action is free, then all conditions causally determining the action must be within the control of the agent. In fact, as we have seen, there are free actions that are determined by conditions some of which are beyond the agent's control.

AN INCOMPATIBLIST REJOINDER: CHOOSING OUR REASONS

The best reply to the preceding argument comes from Jean-Paul Sartre. It depends on noticing that whether a man finds something a reason to act might depend entirely on choice. Indeed, according to Sartre, such things always depend completely upon choice.[13] However, let us consider the more modest claim that when a man performs a free action, then something was a reason for performing it only because he chose to make it a reason. Consider the man who acts to prevent a beam from crashing down on someone's head. There are certain aspects of this situation over which the man may have no control whatsoever. For example, he might not be able to help believing that the beam is about to fall on the other

---

[13] Jean-Paul Sartre, *Existentialism and Humanism* (London: Methuen, 1948), pp. 34, 36–38, 54. Also compare relevant sections in *Being and Nothingness* (New York: Philosophical Library, 1956).

man's head were he not to prevent this from occurring. The question still remains, however, whether the observer will find this belief to be a reason for action. He cannot help perceiving the situation, but he is free to find it uninteresting. For something to be a reason for him depends upon his choice. He is free to recognize some information without choosing to regard it as a reason for action. Were he an entirely crass, misanthropic character, he might well regard with indifference the falling beam and its likely consequences. In this case, although the information should be a reason for action, in fact it is not.

We are now in a position to see that the compatiblist's argument is totally ineffective. It is plausible to say both that a person could not help having the reasons he has and that he nevertheless acts freely, but only because a crucial distinction is blurred. It is true that sometimes a person cannot help having a certain belief. Moreover, it is also true that in such a situation the person might act freely, with that belief as his reason for acting. But whether the person acts freely depends entirely on whether he could have refrained from acting in spite of the belief. Another way of putting the matter is to say that the man acted freely only if he could have rendered his belief ineffective. We make beliefs into reasons by letting them influence our behavior. It is in this sense that we choose to let a belief be a reason. Suppose that a man has a belief and that as a result of having that belief he cannot help but perform some action. In this case, supposing that he also cannot help but have the belief in question, the man surely is not acting freely. Lady Macbeth, when she has gone mad, is a perfect example of a person of just this sort. She believes that her hands are stained with blood, and having this belief, she cannot help but wash her hands. Her behavior is compulsive and not at all free. She must respond in a certain way to a belief she cannot help having.

Now it is an immediate consequence of determinism that if a person believes something, then he cannot help having that belief, because his having the belief is determined by conditions over which he has no control. Moreover, the fact that he acts as a result of that belief is also something he cannot help, because his actions are also determined by conditions beyond his control. Therefore if determinism is true, then though we may act for reasons, we shall never be acting freely.

At this point take note that the argument we have just formulated will effectively undermine the entire line of thought the compatiblist has pursued so far. The compatiblist has argued that free action is compatible with determinism because actions, either all actions or actions of specified kinds (for example, rational actions) must be analyzed in causal terms. The suggestion is that the actions in question have two constituents, C and E, where the latter is at least the indirect causal consequence of the former. Now either C is an action or it is not. If C is an action, then a person has performed action E freely only if he has performed C freely. Thus despite its being true that a person can perform an action freely even though it is caused by another action, this does not prove the compatibility of free action and determinism. The caused action is free only if the action that caused it was free, and to prove compatibility the latter must be shown to be compatible with determinism.

Moreover, on pain of regress, it seems as though some actions must be basic in the sense that they are not caused by any other action of the agent. That is, although some actions that an agent performs might be caused by other actions he performs, some actions must be such that they are not caused by others. Of course, these basic actions might well be caused by something else. But the question that then comes up demanding an answer is this: Is it consistent to say that there are free basic actions and that determinism is true? To this question our answer is negative, and the argument of the compatiblist that some actions are the causes of other actions is irrelevant.[14]

On the other hand, if the compatiblist contends that basic actions are caused by something that is not itself an action, and this is perfectly possible, then another argument is perfectly conclusive against the compatiblist. For whatever is supposed to cause the action, the compatiblist must answer two questions concerning the thing C which caused the action E. First, could the person have prevented C? Second, could the person have not done E once C had occurred? It seems clear that if we suppose that determinism is true, then the answer to both these questions is negative, and in that case, as we illustrated with the case of Lady Macbeth, the person must perform E. Hence, the person was not free. That both

[14] Cf. Arthur Danto, "Freedom and Forebearance," in *Freedom and Determinism* (New York: Random House, 1966), ed. by Keith Lehrer, pp. 47–50.

questions are to be answered in the negative is due to the fact that both the occurrence of C and of the person doing E as a result of C are things that, if determinism is true, were determined by conditions over which the person had no control.

Summary of the Argument. The crux of the preceding argument is that if determinism is true, then *each and every* condition which determines an action is ancestrally determined by conditions beyond the control of the agent; consequently, no such condition is within the agent's control. Thus our argument is as follows: from the premises

1. If determinism is true, then *all* the conditions that determine actions are ancestrally determined by conditions beyond the control of the agent.

and

2. If *all* the conditions that determine actions are ancestrally determined by conditions beyond the control of the agent, then there are no free actions.

we deduce the incompatiblist conclusion

3. If determinism is true, then there are no free actions.

The second premise of this argument differs from the second premise of the argument previously ascribed to the incompatiblist, namely,

If *some* of the conditions that causally determine actions are beyond the control of the agent, then there are no free actions.

The latter implies that all conditions causally determining a free action must be within the agent's control. Some of the conditions do not have to be within the agent's control, as the compatiblist's examples show. However, premise (2) of the present argument implies only the weaker claim that *at least some* of the conditions that determine a free action must be within the agent's control. This assumption is surely cautious enough to be immune from doubt.

A SECOND COMPATIBLIST ARGUMENT:
WHAT WILL HAPPEN, NOT WHAT MUST HAPPEN

The primary defect in the incompatiblist's previous reply is the assumption that if determinism is true, then a person cannot help doing what he does even when he has a reason for doing it. A person who acts as a result of having a reason could, if he is unlike Lady Macbeth, refrain from acting even with the same reason. And to say this is perfectly consistent with the truth of determinism. However, apparently no argument will establish this position unless we show that it is logically consistent to say both that determinism is true and that it is also true that people sometimes could have acted otherwise.

There are two equally good methods of establishing this. One is to consider what is involved in saying that something is caused; the other is to consider what is involved in saying that someone could have done otherwise. Let us take causation first. There are many obscurities surrounding the concept of causation, because causal talk has many uses, and consequently, the word 'cause' has many senses. There is, however, no reason to think with the vulgar, even if we are often forced to speak with them, and so there is no reason to investigate the various and sundry uses and abuses of this term. Instead let us consider a concept of causation that is closely related to science, and more specifically, to scientific explanation.

The most common model of scientific explanation is the deductive model. Suppose we want to explain some phenomenon, say that a piece of iron sinks in water. We then seek to find some antecedent condition and some law of nature such that, from the premise that the condition in question exists and a premise stating the law, we can deduce the thing to be explained. In the case of the iron sinking in water, the antecedent condition is that the given volume of iron weighs more than the comparable volume of water, that is, the specific gravity of iron is greater than that of water. The law is that whenever a solid object is placed in a liquid and the specific gravity of the solid is greater than the specific gravity of the liquid, the solid object sinks below the surface of the liquid.

Another way of putting this would be to say that the condition of the solid object having a greater specific gravity than the liquid is a sufficient condition for the solid object's sinking when placed in the liquid. Thus, if E is explained by virtue of the fact that there are certain conditions C and a law of nature L such that E is deducible from C in conjunction with L, then we shall say that C is causally sufficient for E. Thus, the thesis of determinism means that there are antecedent conditions sufficient for everything that happens.

When we describe determinism in this way, it becomes clear that there is no inconsistency in saying that a person could have done otherwise on certain occasions even though determinism is true. Consider what is involved in determinism: does determinism help us decide what could or could not happen? It does not. As John Stuart Mill long ago pointed out, the most we can decide with the aid of determinism is that given knowledge of certain antecedent conditions, there is some law from which we may deduce what *will* happen at some subsequent time.[15] But to deduce that something will happen is not to say that it must happen or that nothing else could happen instead.

Moreover, it is quite clear that such prediction is altogether compatible with free action. Some people have been inclined to think that if we can predict what a person will do, then it follows that he could have done nothing else. But this is rank confusion. In a prescientific way we often predict accurately what people will do, but this fails to prove that their actions are not free. Indeed, we often predict that people will do things and, furthermore, do them freely. For example, suppose that I know a dear friend of mine is going to receive a scholarship he has greatly desired and worked hard to win. I can certainly predict that, when the scholarship is offered to him, he will accept it. Moreover, I can also predict that he will accept it freely. No one will force him to take it. Nothing would prevent him from refusing, were that his wish. He acts freely, because he could have done otherwise. But he also acts predictably, because we easily predicted what he did. This is the crux of the matter, for it might well be the case that there are scientific laws stating that when a person is in a specified set of conditions he will subsequently perform some action freely. The antecedent conditions not only might be sufficient for the person performing the action, but they might also be sufficient to ensure that

[15] John Stuart Mill, *A System of Logic* (London: Longmans, Green, 1936), p. 549.

he could have done otherwise. In short, there is no contradiction of any sort involved in the idea of predicting that a person will perform an action even though he could have performed another.

AN INCOMPATIBLIST REJOINDER: WHAT MUST HAPPEN TO A BRICK

Suppose we accept the compatiblist's formulation of determinism and his contention that prediction of an action is consistent with the action being free. That is still not conclusive. The reason is that, given this formulation of determinism, it implies more than simply that everything may be predicted. Prediction in terms of laws does warrant our saying, in some sense, that nothing else could have happened. Imagine that a brick dropped off a tall building with nothing to prevent it from falling to the ground. On the basis of these conditions and some familiar laws, we can predict that the brick will fall. But surely it is not only the case that the brick will fall, but that it must fall; it could not possibly remain suspended in midair. Thus from the fact that some set of antecedent conditions is sufficient for the occurrence of an event, we may conclude not only that the occurrence of that event was predictable, but also that nothing could have happened instead. Thus from the fact that there are sufficient conditions for what happens we may conclude that nothing else could have happened.

A COMPATIBLIST REJOINDER: WHAT COULD NOT, COULD?

Suppose we grant that if there is a set of conditions sufficient for the occurrence of some event, then nothing else could have happened instead. We might as well concede this point, because one could easily enough define such a sense of 'could.' However, even if we concede that if determinism is true, then in some sense of 'could' nothing else could have happened, a crucial question remains. Is the sense of 'could' involved when we say, "There being antecedent sufficient conditions for something, nothing else could have happened," the same sense that is involved when we say, "A man being free, he could have done otherwise"? If these two senses of 'could' are not the same, then the former statement might very well be compatible with the latter statement. If they are compatible, the statement that a man could have done otherwise would be compatible with the thesis of determinism. Indeed, the appearance of incompatibility would rest on nothing more than simple equivocation on the word 'could.' It would be like the case in which you say that there is a car in an open lot and I deny it; our remarks appear incompatible. Suppose that there is a train car in the lot. If by 'car' you mean train cars as well as automobiles, and by 'car' I mean simply automobiles, then our remarks would be entirely compatible, appearances to the contrary notwithstanding.

So let us ask whether the sense of 'could' related to causal sufficiency is the same sense of 'could' as the one related to freedom. If they are different, then the argument of the incompatiblist rests on an equivocation on 'could.' There is a very simple argument to show that this is so. Earlier we conceded that one action—say, pulling on a dumbbell—might cause another action—say, lifting a dumbbell. Moreover, both actions might be free; the agent could have done otherwise. Finally, because the latter action is caused by the former action, there is some set of antecedent conditions sufficient for the latter action. Thus there are antecedent sufficient conditions for the man lifting the bar; hence, in the sense of 'could' related to causal sufficiency, nothing else could have happened. Therefore here we have a case in which a man could have done otherwise, in the sense of 'could' related to freedom, even though nothing else could have happened, in the sense of 'could' related to causal sufficiency. Therefore the two senses of 'could' are different, and the appearance of incompatibility between determinism and freedom vanishes in a puff of semantic clarification.

AN INCOMPATIBLIST REPLY:
THE AMBIGUITY OF 'COULD'

We have come full circle to a point raised earlier. True, it does *not* follow from the fact that a person's action is caused by some antecedent action or by some other antecedent condition that he could not have done otherwise or that his action was unfree. There is an ambiguity in the word 'could,' and the statement that a person could have done otherwise, in the sense of 'could' related to freedom, is compatible with the statement that nothing else could have happened, in the sense of 'could' related to causal sufficiency.

However, this point is entirely indecisive. Formerly, we noticed that determinism implies not only causal determination but ancestral determination as well. This point bears reformulation and reiteration in terms of the more precise conceptions of determinism we have been considering.

According to the present formulation of determinism, it amounts to the thesis that there are antecedent sufficient conditions for everything that happens. Suppose that the thesis is true and that some event E occurs. We may conclude that there is some antecedent set of conditions D that is sufficient for E. But we may also conclude that there is some set of antecedent conditions C sufficient for D, and so on. However, the important thing to notice is that if C is antecedent to and sufficient for D, and D is antecedent to and sufficient for E, then C is antecedent to and sufficient for E. This is evident from our definition of 'sufficient.' To say that X is sufficient for Y is to say that Y is deducible from X together with a premise stating the appropriate laws. Thus, if we can deduce E from D together with one or more laws of nature L_1, and we can deduce D from C together with one or more laws of nature L_2, then we can deduce E from C together with one or more laws of nature. All we need to do is to take C together with L_1 and deduce D, then take D with L_2 and deduce E. Thus when we take L_1 and L_2 together with C, we can obviously deduce E.

What does all this fancy logic show? It shows that if determinism is true and I perform an action A, then there is a set of antecedent conditions that is sufficient for my performing A, and there is a set of antecedent conditions sufficient for those conditions, and so on, back in time to conditions that existed before I was born. Actions that are determined in this way, we said earlier, are not only causally determined, they are ancestrally determined. In the light of the preceding reasoning, we may conclude that any of those sufficient conditions, in the chain of sufficient conditions that resulted in my performing action A, is itself sufficient for my performing A. Because some of those conditions existed before I was born, we may conclude that if determinism is true, then there are antecedent conditions sufficient for my performing A which existed before I was born and over which I had no control. Thus if determinism is true, and I perform action A, then not only is it true that nothing else could have happened, it is also true that nothing else could have happened because of conditions over which I had no control. That is the crucial point.

For it is correct to say that a person could have done otherwise when there are antecedent conditions sufficient for his performing the action he did *only if* he had control over some part of the conditions themselves. We believe that at least some part of the conditions sufficient for my lifting the bar, such as my pulling on the bar, were things within my control. That is why it seems reasonable to believe that, although there were sufficient conditions for my lifting the bar, I could have done otherwise. We believe I could have prevented some of these conditions from occurring. However, no one can prevent anything from happening before he was born. Consequently, if determinism is true, and my actions are ancestrally determined, then there will always be conditions, sufficient for my performing the action, which existed before I was born and over which I had no control. But if when I perform an action it is true that nothing else could have happened because of antecedent conditions *over which I have no control*, then obviously I could not have done otherwise. All the means for having done otherwise were rendered unavailable to me by conditions that preceded my birth.

Therefore, though the statement that a person could have done otherwise (in the sense of 'could' related to freedom) is compatible with the statement that nothing else could have happened (in the sense of 'could' related to causal sufficiency) this fails to prove that the statement that a person could have done otherwise is compatible with the truth of determinism. The truth of determinism has a stronger implication, to wit, that nothing else could have happened as a causal consequence of conditions I could not have prevented (in the sense of 'could' related to freedom). I had no control over those things that occurred before I drew my first breath.

A COMPATIBLIST REJOINDER:
FURTHER REFLECTIONS ON 'COULD'

The question at the heart of the dispute is the following: Is the statement that a person could have done otherwise compatible with the statement that there are sufficient conditions for his action over which he has no control? To simplify the discussion let us use the word 'could' only in the sense related to freedom. Now let us consider how we might analyze the meaning of the statement that a person could have done otherwise. By analyzing this statement, we will be able to prove that the answer to our question is affirmative.

The statement that a person could have done otherwise may be analyzed hypothetically. To say that a person could have done otherwise means no more or less than that he would have done otherwise if some specific condition had existed. For example, suppose I say that a person could have lifted a dumbbell. What does that mean? Surely what it means is that he would have succeeded in lifting the dumbbell if he had tried to lift it. Now consider the latter statement. The statement that a person would have succeeded in performing an action if he had tried to perform it is perfectly compatible with the statement that, determinism being true, his behaving in some contrary way was determined by conditions that existed before he was born. For the former statement asserts that, had antecedent conditions been different (that is, had his trying to perform the action been among the antecedent conditions), then the total result would have been different. This is perfectly compatible with the statement that antecedent conditions being what they actually were, it was determined that he not perform the action. Thus, determinism is again shown to be compatible with free action.

One qualification is needed. Sometimes we say that a person could have performed an action when it would not make much sense to say that the person tried to perform the action. For example, if we say of a normal man that he could have moved his trigger finger, it would be peculiar to analyze this statement as meaning that he would have succeeded in moving his trigger finger if he had tried, for it seems strange to speak of a normal man as trying to move his finger. Usually we move our fingers without trying. Such a statement might better be analyzed in terms of a different hypothetical statement—for example, as meaning that the man would have moved his finger if he had chosen to do so. We need not commit ourselves to one kind of hypothetical analysis for all statements about what a person could have done. But whenever there is a statement of the form 'S could have done A' this statement may always be analyzed in terms of some hypothetical statement of the form 'S would have done A if C.' The condition C might vary from context to context. All we need to assert is that *some* such hypothetical analysis is always possible, because given such analyses it is easy to prove that free action and determinism are perfectly consistent.

AN INCOMPATIBLIST REPLY: IFS, CANS, AND CHAINS

If we were to accept the kind of analysis proposed, we could prove the compatibility of free action and determinism. But the analyses are unsatisfactory. Statements of the form 'S could have done A' are not analyzable as statements of the form 'S would have done A if C.' Moreover, statements of the latter form do not even imply the former. Suppose that a man is chained to a wall but would like very much to move. Suppose now that someone argues that the man could have moved and that he supports his argument with the contention that the man would have moved if he were not chained. Surely this would be an absurd argument. The reason that it is absurd is that though the statement

The man would move if he were not chained.

is true, it certainly does not imply the statement

The man could have moved.

which is false. The man could not have moved precisely because he was chained. Moreover, the reason that he could not have moved is that he cannot get unchained. The conditions that prevent his movement are entirely beyond his control.

So far we have only considered one hypothetical analysis of one statement about what a person could have done, and though the hypothetical statement in question does not imply that statement, there is still the possibility of analyzing the statement about what a person could have done in terms of some *other* hypothetical statement.

However, the argument can be generalized. For whether you say of a man that he would have moved if he was not chained, if he tried to, if he chose to, if he wanted to, or if anything else of the sort, what you say will still not imply that he could have moved. Why not? Because it remains possible that there are conditions entirely beyond the man's control that prevent him from trying, choosing, or wanting to do the thing in question. For example, if a man is prevented from trying to do something by conditions beyond his control, then the fact that he would have done the thing if he had tried to do it fails to prove that the man could have done it.

Moreover, if determinism is true, then there are antecedent conditions sufficient for whatever happens; consequently, there are conditions sufficient to prevent whatever did not happen. Furthermore, those conditions extend indefinitely backward into the past. Therefore, if a man does not try to do something, then, if determinism is true, there were antecedent conditions sufficient to prevent his trying, and those antecedent conditions, because they existed before the man was born, are entirely beyond his control.

Thus no statement of the form 'S could have done A' is implied by a statement of the form 'S would have done A if C,' because it is perfectly possible that there should be conditions that prevent C from occurring and that these conditions are entirely beyond the control of S. Consequently, it is possible that a statement of the latter form is true but the former is false. Moreover, if determinism is true, then this will always be the case when C does not occur, because there will be antecedent conditions sufficient to prevent it from occurring which are entirely beyond the control of S. In short, if determinism is true, then no matter what a person would have done had conditions been different, he could not have done the thing in question because the conditions could not have been different because of circumstances over which the person had no control. Thus, once again, if determinism is true, then a person could never have done otherwise. Consequently, determinism is incompatible with free action.

ANOTHER COMPATIBLIST ARGUMENT: FINALE

The preceding argument begs the question. Obviously, if there are conditions sufficient to prevent a person from doing something, then he cannot do it. But not all conditions that are sufficient for a person to perform one action *prevent* him from doing something else. Thus even though there are antecedent sufficient conditions for a person performing a given action and even though those conditions existed before the man was born, it is sometimes true

that he could have done otherwise. If he could have done otherwise, it must also be true that there was nothing to prevent him
from doing otherwise. Thus there are conditions, over which a
person has no control and sufficient for his performing a specific
action, that do not prevent him from performing some other action
instead. In short, not all conditions that are sufficient for something
are conditions that prevent other things from happening.

An example should help to illustrate this point. We previously
considered a man who is locked in a room but does not know it.
Compare him with a man who is in a room but not locked in. In
this example, because both men believe they can leave, both might
deliberate about whether to leave but decide to remain. Now the
man who is locked in is prevented from leaving, but the other man
is not. Moreover, the example will not be altered in any important
respect if we suppose that the behavior of each is such that there
are conditions sufficient for its occurrence, even conditions that
existed long before they were born. Not all sufficient conditions are
preventive, only some are, such as being locked in a room.

However, we must not leave the argument at this level, because
the incompatiblist will reply that if determinism is true, then neither
man could have done otherwise and both were prevented from
doing so by conditions in the remote past if not by a lock on the
door. Rather than leave the argument in this unsatisfactory state, let
us consider one final argument to prove the compatibility of determinism and free action. We will let everything ride on its merits.

To see what the argument is, let us return to an argument employed earlier by the libertarian. It was argued by the libertarian
that we have perfectly adequate empirical evidence to show that a
person could have done otherwise, evidence that passes muster
before the canons of scientific method. We imagined a carefully
controlled experiment to investigate when a man could and when
he could not lift his arm. We not only checked his capacities under
a great variety of internal and external conditions, we also took
note of his own reports of what he did or did not try to accomplish.
We then supposed that he was exposed to conditions that are ideal
for arm lifting, as far as our subject is concerned. Then we argued
that if he does not lift his arm at such a time and if we know from
his report that he did not try to do so and he is certain that he would
have succeeded had he tried, then we have adequate evidence that

he could have lifted his arm. Thus we have adequate evidence that a person could have done otherwise. To this argument of the libertarian, the determinist replied that such evidence is not adequate evidence to prove the thesis of determinism false. For, argues the determinist, how could such evidence prove that anything is uncaused or that there are not sufficient conditions for something that occurred? Obviously, it could not prove any such thing.

Now the compatiblist maintains that what both parties to the dispute have said is perfectly correct. The libertarian is correct in arguing that the evidence is adequate to show that the person could have done otherwise, and the determinist is correct in arguing that the evidence is not adequate to refute the thesis of determinism. Both positions are eminently reasonable, and we may enjoy the luxury of accepting both arguments for the small price of conceding the compatibility of determinism and free action.

If the truth of determinism is compatible with the truth of the statement that a person could have done otherwise, then evidence that is adequate for the truth of the latter need not be adequate for the falsity of the former. Indeed, there is no reason why the evidence for the truth of the latter should be relevant to either the truth or the falsity of determinism. The statement that I am a philosopher is compatible with the statement that I am a male, but there is evidence for the former statement that is quite irrelevant to the question of whether or not I am a male. On the other hand, if the truth of determinism is incompatible with the truth of the statement that a person could have done otherwise, then evidence adequate for the truth of the latter will be evidence adequate for the falsity of determinism. The statement that the object on my desk is a ball is incompatible with the statement that the object is a cube. Whatever evidence shows the object to be a cube must also show it not to be a ball. Thus there is only one way of accepting the position that there is evidence adequate to show that people perform free action but not adequate to show that determinism is false, namely, by holding that the thesis that people perform free actions is compatible with the thesis of determinism. For that reason the position of the compatiblist should be accepted. Free action and causal determinism are not incompatible, as they might appear; they are perfectly compatible. Because this is so, problem and paradox are dissolved in the light of logical clarity.

EXERCISES

1. What argument does the determinist offer to show that we all believe the thesis of determinism? Does the argument justify accepting
   determinism? Why?

2. What problem or paradox arises if we accept the thesis of determinism? How did Butler and Darrow manage to reason from the truth
   of determinism to the conclusion that criminals are not responsible
   for their deeds?

3. Consider the following argument:

   > Some philosophers and lawyers have argued that men are not
   > responsible for their deeds because all human actions are
   > causally determined by things in the remote past. This argu-
   > ment is easily refuted. The law tells us when people are re-
   > sponsible for their misdeeds; the law defines responsibility. It
   > does not matter what the causal history of an act happens to
   > be. If the action is one of a kind specified by the law—as, for
   > example, murder—then the agent is responsible for that deed
   > and deserves the specified punishment regardless of how the
   > murderous act came to be committed. Therefore, it is useless
   > to argue that people are exempt from responsibility because of
   > the causal history of their crimes. A deed that is a crime under
   > the law is one for which a man is responsible and liable to be
   > punished.

   What do you think Butler or Darrow might reply to this argument?
   Is the argument sound?

4. What argument is given by libertarians, for example, Reid and
   Campbell, to support the conclusion that our belief that we are free
   is a belief of common sense? How does the matter of deliberation
   enter the argument? In what way does Grunbaum object to this
   libertarian argument? Is Campbell's reply to Grunbaum adequate?
   Why?

5. Consider the following determinist argument:

   > It is easy to prove that every human action is caused. In the
   > first place, every action must have a motive of some sort. Even
   > the most seemingly fortuitous and inadvertent actions can be

shown to have a motive if one is not put off by appearances and investigates the matter in depth. Psychologists—Sigmund Freud, for example—discover motives behind such apparently accidental acts as a slip of the tongue. So every act has a motive. Now if we go on to ask whether an act is caused, the obvious answer is that it is caused by a motive which motivated the act. Which motive? Clearly the strongest one. Indeed, the very proof that a motive is the strongest is that it prevailed; it, rather than another motive, caused the action. Thus are all actions seen to be caused by the strongest motive.

What might a libertarian reply to this argument? Who is right?

6. What argument does the libertarian present to show that we can only escape logical inconsistency by rejecting determinism in favor of the doctrine of free action? How does he define free action? Is the definition sensible? How is the argument bolstered by appealing to the phenomena of decision and choice? What is the most important objection raised against this libertarian argument by the determinist? Is the objection decisive? Why?

7. Consider the following argument:

> At one point the libertarian appeals to the notion of *logical consistency* to defend his conclusion. This is his basic error. Consistency is of little or no importance. It is the hobgoblin of small minds. However, the whole problem of freedom and determinism results from the alleged inconsistency of the two doctrines. But what if they are inconsistent? Why let that concern us? Let us boldly admit the inconsistency and say we shall accept *both* doctrines nonetheless. Thus is the problem of freedom and determinism laid to rest.

What is the matter with this bold suggestion? Does the determinist's rejection of the libertarian argument from logical consistency (mentioned in the preceding question) commit him to the view that logical consistency is unimportant? Why?

8. What argument, based on the data of introspection, is offered by the libertarian to show we have adequate evidence for free action? What objection does Hempel raise against this argument? Is the libertarian reply to this objection cogent? Why?

9. What argument does the libertarian put forth to prove that we have independent evidence to justify the belief that we perform free actions? Why is this argument required in addition to the argument based on the data of introspection to prove the libertarian conclu-

sion that we have adequate evidence for free action? What objections are raised by the determinist against the libertarian argument for independent evidence of free action? What premise in the determinist's argument against the alleged evidence required reformulation? Why? Is the reformulated argument decisive?

10. Consider the following libertarian argument:

> The determinist argues that we should accept the doctrine of determinism and reject the doctrine of freedom. But in so doing, he reveals that even he does not believe the thesis he defends. For suppose we are not free but are determined so that we cannot help doing what we do. In that case, it would be pointless to argue that we should accept one doctrine rather than another, for we cannot help accepting the doctrine we do accept, whatever that might be. Thus if the determinist is serious in his attempt to persuade us to accept determinism, then he must believe that we *could* accept that doctrine even if, in fact, we do not. So he must believe that we are free, although he argues that we are not. Thus the determinist's belief refutes his words.

What might a determinist reply to this argument? Is the argument sound? Why?

11. What argument does the determinist obtain from Warnock against the libertarian claim that we have adequate evidence that a person could have done otherwise? What is the libertarian reply? Is the final word of the determinist decisive? Why?

12. What premise accepted by libertarians and determinists alike is rejected by the compatiblist? If the compatiblist accepts *both* the doctrine of determinism and the doctrine of freedom, does this mean that he is committed to an inconsistent position? Why would the compatiblist deny that he is committed to an inconsistency?

13. The compatiblist defends his position by contending that causation is a constituent of action. How does the theory of volitions enter into his argument? In what way does the determinist object to this argument? How does the compatiblist's claim that actions are caused by something which is not itself an action help meet the objection raised by the determinist? What is the final determinist argument against this libertarian argument? Is it immune from doubt?

14. Consider the following incompatiblist argument:

> The idea that volitions are causes is absurd. A cause, if it be genuine, must be described independently of its effects. Thus,

for example, it will not do to say that the sleep-inducing capacity of a pill causes people to sleep, because the capacity, if it is a genuine cause, must be described independently of its alleged effect. Now suppose that a violition to raise my arm occurs within me. Such a volition cannot be a genuine cause of my raising my arm, because the volition is *not* described independently of its alleged effect, of my raising my arm. Thus, the volition to raise my arm, like the sleep-inducing capacity of the pill, is not a genuine cause; it is merely a pseudocause. Neither the pill nor the volition is described independently of the effect it is falsely alleged to produce.

Does this argument favor the libertarian or the determinist? Is the argument correct? Why?

15. What compatiblist argument is derived from an analysis of the concept of causation in terms of scientific explanation? How does the compatiblist think this analysis demonstrates the compatibility of freedom and determinism? Why, according to the incompatiblist, does the consistency of prediction and freedom fail to prove the compatibility of determinism and freedom? What question remains even if we suppose that determinism implies that in some sense of 'could' nothing could have happened except what did happen? How does the compatiblist answer this question? How does the distinction between causal determination and ancestral determination form the basis of an incompatiblist rejoinder? Is the rejoinder decisive?

16. Consider the following incompatiblist argument:

The compatiblist argues that determinism involves nothing more than universal predictability based on scientific laws. However, this notion of determinism is sufficient to prove the incompatibility of freedom and determinism. Let us first concede that free actions must at least sometimes result from decision. So decision is essential to freedom. One feature of decision is that no one can possibly know what his own decision is going to be before he makes it. Once a man knows what his decision is going to be, he has already decided. However, 'determinism' defined as 'universal predictability based on scientific laws' has the consequence that it is possible for anyone to predict anything. All one needs to know to make a prediction is the antecedent conditions and appropriate laws, and it is at least possible for a person to know this even if in fact we do not. Thus, if determinism is true, it is possible for a person to predict what his own decision is going to be before he makes it. But if there are any decisions, as freedom requires there should be, it is impossible for a person to know what his decision is going to be before he makes it. Therefore if determinism as defined is true, there are no free actions.

How might a compatiblist reply to this argument? How might he reply if he concedes that decision is essential to free action? Is the argument sound? Cf. article by Carl Ginet in bibliography.

17. How does the compatiblist argue from the hypothetical analysis of 'could' to the compatibility of freedom and determinism? What example does the incompatiblist present in reply? How does he generalize from this example?

18. Consider the following compatiblist argument:

The compatibility of freedom and determinism is easily proved. Determinism tells us that everything is causally, and indeed, ancestrally, determined. But it does not tell us which things are thus determined and which are not. Therefore, suppose that I lift my arm and that, as freedom requires, I could have done otherwise. I could have left it at my side. What conclusion about this supposition can we draw from the thesis of determinism? All that we may conclude is (i) that I lift my arm is causally and ancestrally determined and (ii) that I could have done otherwise is causally and ancestrally determined. However, the fact that both these things are so determined is perfectly compatible with their happening. Therefore what follows from determinism concerning free action is that the action *and* its being free are causally and ancestrally determined. This proves that free action and determinism are entirely compatible.

What might an incompatiblist reply to this argument? What would you say about it?

19. What is the final argument of the compatiblist? Do you consider it sound? What might the compatiblist reply to the following objection:

The reply to the argument is one given earlier by the libertarian. Sometimes evidence which actually supports a hypothesis appears irrelevant to it because one is ignorant of the logical implications of the hypothesis. That is precisely the case here. The reason that some people think the evidence from the imaginary arm-lifting experiment is not adequate to show the falsity of determinism is that they are ignorant of one logical implication of determinism, to wit, that it entails no one could have done anything but what he did. Once this entailment is recognized, it becomes apparent not only that freedom and determinism are incompatible, but that the evidence from the experiment supports the hypothesis that determinism is false.

BIBLIOGRAPHY

CLASSICAL SOURCES
A formulation of determinism is to be found in Benedict Spinoza's *Ethics*, especially Part III, and in Baron D'Holbach's *System of Nature*. Libertarian sources of importance include Thomas Reid's chapter on liberty and necessity in his *Essays on the Powers of the Human Mind* and Schopenhauer's *Essay on the Freedom of the Will* (1841), translated by Kolenda (1960). Also see William James's famous essay "The Dilemma of Determinism," in his *The Will to Believe*. There are many classical defenses of compatiblism. Among them are Thomas Hobbes's *Leviathan* (1951), Chapter 21; John Locke's *Essay Concerning Human Understanding*, Book II, Chapter 21; David Hume's *Treatise of Human Nature*, Book II, Part iii, sections 1–3, and *Enquiry Concerning Human Understanding*, section viii, and John Stuart Mill's *System of Logic*, Book IV, Chapter 2. A difficult but important source is Immanuel Kant, *Critique of Practical Reason*, Book I, Chapter 3.

CONTEMPORARY SOURCES

I. Anthologies, Collections, and Textbooks
A number of excellent anthologies and collections of articles from symposia entirely devoted to the topic of freedom and determinism have recently appeared. Two anthologies, one edited by Sidney Morgenbesser and James Walsh, *Free Will* (Englewood Cliffs, N.J.: Prentice-Hall, Inc., 1962) and the other edited by Bernard Berofsky, *Free Will and Determinism* (New York: Harper & Row, Publishers, Inc., 1966), contain the works of both classical and contemporary writers. Three collections of articles from recent symposia are *Determinism and Freedom in the Age of Modern Science* (New York: New York University Press, 1958), edited by Sidney Hook; *Freedom and Determinism* (New York: Random House, Inc., 1966), edited by Keith Lehrer; and *Freedom and the Will* (London: Macmillan & Company, Ltd., 1963), edited by D. F. Pears.

The latter contains some material taken from radio broadcasts intended for a general audience.

Three general anthologies containing valuable material on the subject of freedom and determinism are *Philosophic Problems* (New York: Macmillan Publishing Co., Inc., 1957), edited by Mandelbaum, Gramlich, and Anderson; *A Modern Introduction to Philosophy*, Revised Edition (New York: The Free Press, 1965), edited by Paul Edwards and Arthur Pap; and *Reason and Responsibility* (Belmont, Calif.: Dickenson, 1965), edited by Joel Feinberg. See also *Royal Institute of Philosophy Lectures*, Vol. I (1966–1967): *The Human Agent* (New York: St. Martin's Press, 1968); *Knowledge and Necessity, Royal Institute of Philosophy Lectures*, Vol. 3 (1968–1969), foreword by G. N. A. Vesey (London: Macmillan & Company, Ltd., 1970), containing essays on the questions of determinism and knowledge; Robert W. Binkley, Richard N. Bronaugh, and Ausonio Marras, eds., *Agent, Action, and Reason* (Toronto: University of Toronto Press, 1971), a selection from the works of contemporary philosophers. Two anthologies on a more technical level which contain readable articles on this subject are *Readings in Philosophical Analysis* (New York: Appleton-Century-Crofts, Inc., 1949), edited by Herbert Feigl and Wilfrid Sellars, and *Readings in Ethical Theory* (New York: Appleton-Century-Crofts, Inc., 1949), edited by Wilfrid Sellars and John Hospers.

The following textbooks contain useful chapters on the topic: John Hospers, *Human Conduct* (New York: Harcourt Brace Jovanovich, Inc., 1961), Chapters 9 and 10; Richard Taylor, *Metaphysics* (Englewood Cliffs, N.J.: Prentice-Hall, Inc., 1963), Chapter 4; R. B. Brandt, *Ethical Theory* (Englewood Cliffs, N.J.: Prentice-Hall, Inc., 1959), Chapter 20; Stephan Körner, *What Is Philosophy? One Philosopher's Answer* (London: Allen Lane, The Penguin Press, 1969), Part Four being devoted to the problem of freedom; and F. A. Westphal, *The Activity of Philosophy: A Concise Introduction* (Englewood Cliffs, N.J.: Prentice-Hall, Inc., 1969), an introductory text containing a chapter on free will and determinism.

II. Books by a Single Author

The following books, though not exclusively devoted to the subject of freedom and determinism, contain interesting chapters on the subject. G. E. Moore, *Ethics* (London: Oxford University Press, 1912), Chapter 6; C. L. Stevenson, *Ethics and Language* (New York: Yale University Press, 1944), Chapter 14; C. A. Campbell, *On Selfhood and Godhood* (New York: Macmillan Publishing Co., Inc., 1957), Lecture 9; A. J. Ayer, *Philosophical Essays* (New York: Macmillan Publishing Co., Inc., 1954), Chapter 12; G. Ryle, *The Concept of Mind* (New York: Barnes &

Noble, Inc., 1949), Chapter 3; C. D. Broad, *Ethics and the History of Philosophy* (London: Routledge & Kegan Paul, 1952), Section III; J. L. Austin, *Philosophical Papers* (Oxford, England: The Clarendon Press, 1961), Chapter 7; and S. Zink, *The Concepts of Ethics* (New York: St. Martin's Press, 1962), Chapters 6 and 7.

The following books are primarily devoted to the subject of freedom and determinism. G. H. Palmer, *The Problem of Freedom* (Boston: Houghton Mifflin Company, 1911); M. Davidson, *The Free Will Controversy* (London: C. S. Watts Company, 1942); J. Laird, *On Human Freedom* (London: George Allen & Unwin, Ltd., 1947); A. Farrer, *The Freedom of the Will* (London: A. & C. Black, Ltd., 1958); A. I. Melden, *Free Action* (New York: Humanities Press, 1961); K. W. Rankin, *Choice and Chance* (Oxford: Basil Blackwell & Mott, Ltd., 1961); H. Ofstad, *An Inquiry into the Freedom of Decision* (New York: Humanities Press, 1962); F. Vivian, *Human Freedom and Responsibility* (New York: Harper & Row, Publishers, Inc., 1964); S. Hampshire, *Freedom of the Individual* (New York: Harper & Row, Publishers, Inc., 1965); C. A. Campbell, *In Defense of Free Will, with Other Philosophical Essays* (New York: Humanities Press, 1967); Edward D'Angelo, *The Problem of Freedom and Determinism* (Columbia: University of Missouri Press, 1968), an introductory work on the problem, emphasizing hard vs. soft determinism. M. R. Ayers, *The Refutation of Determinism: An Essay in Philosophical Logic* (London: Methuen & Co., Ltd., 1968); R. L. Franklin, *Free Will and Determinism: A Study in Rival Concepts of Man* (New York: Humanities Press, 1968), making a case for libertarianism; and Bernard Berofsky, *Determinism* (Princeton, N.J.: Princeton University Press, 1972).

The following books are somewhat broader in scope. Henri Bergson, *Time and Free Will* (New York: Macmillan Publishing Co., Inc., 1921); Isaiah Berlin, *Historical Inevitability* (London: Oxford University Press, 1954); Paul Weiss, *Man's Freedom* (New Haven: Yale University Press, 1950); S. Hampshire, *Thought and Action* (New York: The Viking Press, Inc., 1960); Jean-Paul Sartre, *Being and Nothingness* (New York: Philosophical Library, Inc., 1946); and R. Taylor, *Action and Purpose* (Englewood Cliffs, N.J.: Prentice-Hall, Inc., 1966). For an encyclopedic treatment of the subject of freedom see *The Great Ideas* (Chicago: Encyclopedia Britannica, 1952), edited by M. J. Adler, Vol. I, Chapter 47, *Liberty*.

III. Contemporary Articles
The anthologies listed previously contain many of the most important articles on the subject of freedom and determinism. The following are a

sample of the most recent articles. George Pitcher, "Necessitarianism," *Philosophical Quarterly* (1961), pp. 201–12; Carl Ginet, "Can the Will Be Caused?" *Philosophical Review* (1962), pp. 49–55; R. L. Franklin, "Moral Libertarianism," *Philosophical Quarterly* (1962); pp. 24–35; J. Wheatley, "Hampshire on Human Freedom," *Philosophical Quarterly* (1962), pp. 248–60; D. Gallop, "On Being Determined," *Mind* (1962), pp. 181–96; J. V. Canfield, "The Compatibility of Free Will and Determinism," *Philosophical Review* (1962), pp. 352–68; B. Aune, "Abilities, Modalities, and Free Will," *Philosophy and Phenomenological Research* (1963–1964), pp. 397–413; R. C. Skinner, "Freedom and Choice," *Mind* (1963), pp. 463–80; Kurt Baier, "Could and Would," *Analysis Supplement* (1963), pp. 20–29; R. N. Bronaugh, "Freedom as the Absence of an Excuse," *Ethics* (1963–64), pp. 161–73; Clement Dore, "On the Meaning of 'could have,' " *Analysis* (1962), pp. 41–43; L. Kenner, "Causality, Determinism and Freedom of the Will," *Philosophy* (1964), pp. 233–48; R. M. Chisholm, *Human Freedom and the Self*, Lindley Lecture (Lawrence: University of Kansas Press, 1964); S. Körner, "Science and Moral Responsibility," *Mind* (1964), pp. 161–72; A. M. Honoré, "Can and Can't," *Mind* (1964), pp. 463–79; K. T. Gallagher, "On Choosing to Choose," *Mind* (1964), pp. 480–95; Nelson Pike, "Divine Omniscience and Voluntary Action," *Philosophical Review* (1965), pp. 27–46; C. H. Whiteley, "Can," *Analysis* (1962), pp. 91–93; R. G. Henson, "Responsibility for Character and Responsibility for Conduct," *Australasian Journal of Philosophy*, Vol. 43 (1965), pp. 311–20; M. F. Cohen, "Motives, Causal Necessity, and Moral Accountability," *Australasian Journal of Philosophy*, Vol. 42 (1964), pp. 322–34; D. F. Gustafson, "Voluntary and Involuntary," *Philosophy and Phenomenological Research*, Vol. 24 (1964), pp. 493–501; Daniel Kading, "Moral Action, Ignorance of Fact, and Inability," *Philosophy and Phenomenological Research*, Vol. 25 (1965), pp. 333–55; Daniel Bennett, "Action, Reason, and Purpose," *Journal of Philosophy*, Vol. 62, (1965), pp. 85–96; T. F. Daveney, "Choosing," *Mind* (1964), pp. 515–26; W. Wick, "Truth's Debt to Freedom," *Mind* (1964), pp. 527–37; Raziel Abelson, "Because I Want To," *Mind* (1964), pp. 540–53; A. C. Danto, "Basic Actions," *American Philosophical Quarterly* (1965), pp. 141–48; Arnold Kaufman, "Ability," *Journal of Philosophy* (1963), pp. 537–51; Lewis White Beck, "Conscious and Unconscious Motives," *Mind* (1966), pp. 155–79; David Gauthier, "How Decisions Are Caused," *Journal of Philosophy*, Vol. 63 (1967), pp. 147–51; Nani L. Ranken, "The 'Unmoved' Agent and the Ground of Responsibility," *Journal of Philosophy*, Vol. 64 (1967), pp. 403–408; Henry Margenau, "Quantum Mechanics, Free Will, and Determinism," *Journal of Philosophy*, Vol. 64 (1967), pp. 714–25; Frederick Stoutland, "Basic Actions and Causality," *Journal of Philosophy*, Vol. 65

(1968), pp. 467–75; Joseph Margolis, "Puzzles Regarding Explanation by Reasons and Explanation by Causes," *Journal of Philosophy*, Vol. 67 (1970), pp. 187–95; Myles Brand, "Causes of Acting," *Journal of Philosophy*, Vol. 67 (1970), pp. 932–47; Harry G. Frankfurt, "Freedom of the Will and the Concept of a Person," *Journal of Philosophy*, Vol. 68 (1971), pp. 5–20; R. E. Ewin, "Actions, Brain-Processes, and Determinism," *Mind*, Vol. 77 (1968), pp. 417–19; S. I. Benn and W. L. Weinstein, "Being Free to Act, and Being a Free Man," *Mind*, Vol. 80 (1971), pp. 194–211; Michael Stocker, "Knowledge, Causation, and Decision," *Nous*, Vol. 2 (1968), pp. 65–73; Gerald Dworkin, "Acting Freely," *Nous*, Vol. 4 (1970), pp. 367–83; Stuart Hampshire, "Spinoza's Theory of Human Freedom," *Monist*, Vol. 55 (1971), pp. 554–66; Pamela Huby, "The First Discovery of the Freewill Problem," *Philosophy*, Vol. 42 (1967), pp. 353–62; Bernard Mayo, "The Incoherence of Determinism," *Philosophy*, Vol. 44 (1969), pp. 89–100; Marie Louise Friquegnon, "The Paradoxes of Determinism," *Philosophy and Phenomenological Research*, Vol. 33 (1972), pp. 112–16; James N. Jordan, "Determinism's Dilemma," *Review of Metaphysics*, Vol. 23 (1969), pp. 48–66; Bruce Aune, "Hypotheticals and 'Can': Another Look," *Analysis*, Vol. 27 (1967), pp. 191–95; J. L. Cowan, "Deliberation and Determinism," *American Philosophical Quarterly*, Vol. 6 (1969), pp. 53–61; Adolf Grünbaum, "Free Will and Laws of Human Behavior," *American Philosophical Quarterly*, Vol. 8 (1971), pp. 299–317; A. Aaron Snyder, "The Paradox of Determinism," *American Philosophical Quarterly*, Vol. 9 (1972), pp. 353–56; D. F. Pears, "Ifs and Cans-II," *Canadian Journal of Philosophy*, Vol. I (1972), pp. 369–91.

Many of the preceding articles have been discussed in subsequent articles. The article by Ginet is discussed by I. Thalberg, "Foreknowledge and Decisions in Advance," *Analysis*, Vol. 24 (1964), pp. 49–54; Andrew Oldenquist, "Causes, Predictions, and Decisions," *Analysis*, Vol. 24 (1964), pp. 55–58; Peter Swiggart, "Doing and Deciding to Do," *Analysis* (1962), pp. 17–19; and Keith Lehrer, "Decisions and Causes," *Philosophical Review* (1963), pp. 224–27. The article by Dore is discussed by David S. Scarrow, "On the Analysis of 'could have,'" *Analysis*, Vol. 24 (1963), pp. 118–20. The book by A. I. Melden listed previously is discussed by Bruce Goldberg, "Can a Desire Be a Cause?" *Analysis*, Vol. 25 (1964–1965), pp. 70–72. Keith Lehrer, "Cans Without Ifs," *Analysis*, Vol. 29 (1965), pp. 29–32, is a reply to Aune, "Hypotheticals & 'Can': Another Look." Bernard Mayo, "On the Lehrer-Taylor Analyses of 'Can'-Statements," *Mind*, Vol. 77 (1968), pp. 271–78, is a discussion of Lehrer and Taylor, "Time, Truth, and Modalities, *Mind*, Vol. 74 (1965). Bruce Aune, "Freewill, 'Can' and Ethics: A Reply to Lehrer," *Analysis*, Vol. 30 (1970), pp. 77–83, is on Lehrer's "Cans Without Ifs." Clement

Dore, "On a Recent Discussion of If's and Can's," *Philosophical Studies*, Vol. 21 (1970), pp. 33–37, is on Aune (above) and Lehrer. David Blumenfeld, "Lehrer's Proof of the Consistency Thesis," *Philosophical Studies*, Vol. 22 (1971), pp. 26–30, is on Lehrer's "An Empirical Disproof of Determinism?" *Freedom and Determinism*, pp. 175–202. J. F. M. Hunter, "Aune and Others on Ifs and Cans," *Analysis*, Vol. 28 (1968), pp. 107–109, is on Chisholm, Lehrer, Aune.

A bibliography on free will by R. Hall, *Philosophical Quarterly* (1965), pp. 179–81, contains many valuable references.

THE MIND–BODY PROBLEM

CHAPTER FOUR

What is a person? For one thing a person is a complex being that can do many things. Unlike many other beings he can move himself; he can crawl, walk, and swim. These are clearly bodily activities. A person, then, surely seems to have a body, in which many processes and events take place, such as the beating of the heart, the functioning of the kidneys, and the complex functioning of the brain. Such bodily processes are essential for keeping a person alive and healthy. Indeed, we describe the state of a person's body by stating the condition of such vital bodily processes.

There are, however, many other things a person can do which do not seem to be bodily activities. A person, unlike many other beings that can move themselves, can think about things; decide on courses of action; hope for, desire, and dream about many different things. These seem to be mental activities, quite different from bodily activities and processes. They seem, therefore, to involve a mind rather than a body, a mind with states quite different from bodily states. We describe a man's mental state when we call him happy or sad, gay or depressed, in love or full of hate, nervous or calm, bold or afraid. A person, thus, seems to be not merely a complex body, but an entity with a mind distinct and quite different from his body.

We do not merely describe a person in this way; we also try to explain his bodily behavior and understand the workings of his mind. In doing this we usually become involved in claims about relationships, between his mind and his body. We explain, for example, Mrs. Jones' uncharacteristic screaming at her children by referring to her splitting headache. We claim that the reason Smith will not climb mountains is because he is deathly afraid of heights, or that Mr. Brown has stopped smoking because he has decided the risk of cancer is too great. We also explain the abnormal behavior of persons as being caused by guilt feelings, repressed desires, or neurotic fixations. On the other hand, we explain someone's pain by isolating its cause as some bodily injury; we use certain injections in his body to make him unconscious, and sometimes we perform brain operations in order to change the whole mental state, the whole personality of a person. It seems, then, that certain mental phenomena can affect the body and that certain bodily phenomena can affect the mind.

We have described a person as a complex entity with a mind and a body: an entity involving both bodily events and states, and mental events and states, an entity in which certain bodily events causally affect the mind and certain mental events affect the body. Furthermore, because it seems that the realm of the mental is quite distinct and different from the realm of the material, this description seems to lead to the theory known as *dualistic interactionism.* According to this theory a person consists of two quite radically different parts, a mind and a body, each of which can causally act upon the other.

Dualistic interactionism is accepted by many people. Most of us, in our own cases at least, distinguish sharply between those mental phenomena of which we are aware, such as our own sensations, and our body with all its complex physical processes. Furthermore, a mind–body dualism seems to be essential to most religions. The body will disintegrate after death but, according to the doctrines of many religions, the soul, that immaterial part of us which is quite distinct and different from the body, will live on eternally. However, although it may be easy to explain the widespread acceptance of dualistic interactionism, such an explanation is not a philosophical concern. The primary philosophical problem is to find out whether dualistic interactionism or some other position is the most plausible view about the nature of a person. Obviously, there are many possible alternatives. There are several monistic views: reductive materialism, which claims that there are no minds but only bodies; idealism, which claims that there are no bodies, only minds; and a neutral theory, which claims that a person is neither mind nor body, but something quite different from either. There are also dualistic theories that deny all or part of the claim of causal interaction between minds and bodies. Epiphenomenalism denies that the mind can causally affect the body because the mind is merely a kind of by-product of certain complex physical processes. Parallelism claims that there is no causal interaction of any kind between minds and bodies. Each proceeds in its own way, parallel to but independent of the other.

Some of these views are plausible; others are not. All face problems but some problems are more damaging than others; and because no view is obviously correct, each requires a reasoned defense if we are to justify it. It will be our task to evaluate critically the leading alternative positions with the hope that we will be able to choose from among them one that can be shown to be more plausible than any other. We shall start with dualistic interactionism.

DEFINITIONS OF KEY TERMS

Before beginning the discussion proper we must first indicate how certain key expressions, containing the terms 'material' and 'mental,' shall be used. We have already discussed bodies (material objects) and minds (mental objects). We have also discussed events and states, both mental and material. Let us construe these two different kinds of objects, events, and states in the following ways.

Material object: An object (such as a stone) that has size, shape, mass, and spatial and temporal position, and that can exist independently of any conscious being.

Mental object: An immaterial object that is either a conscious being, that is, a being aware of things (such as a mind), or a being that cannot exist independently of some conscious being (such as a thought or sensation).

Material event: Something (such as the movement of an arm) that occurs over a period of time and consists of only material objects.

Mental event: Something (such as a dream) that occurs over a period of time and consists of only mental objects.

Material state: A condition or situation (such as an infection) of some material object.

Mental state: A condition or situation (such as a psychosis) of some mental object.

It is important to notice that, as characterized previously, the mental and the material are radically different. Whatever is mental depends essentially on consciousness or awareness, but what is material does not. Furthermore it certainly seems that nothing mental has size, shape, mass, or spatial location; such qualities seem only to characterize the material. The only characteristic that the mental and the physical seem to have in common is that both *can* have temporal positions. We say "can have" here because although all material objects and all human minds have temporal positions, it may be that there are minds that do not exist in time, for example, the mind of God. It should also be noted that the word 'material,' rather than 'physical,' has been used throughout. This is because by 'physical' we shall mean 'part of the subject matter of the physical sciences,' and it may well be that not all physical objects are material objects. An object which is a *person* is, if the dualists are correct, neither a mental object nor a material object; rather, it is a composite of both kinds of objects. However, such a being falls within the subject matter of physics. We are not, then, interested so much in the physical as in the mental and the material, although the physical is relevant because part of the debate surrounding the mind-body problem concerns whether physics, which supposedly can explain the behavior of all material objects, can explain all human behavior.

DUALISTIC INTERACTIONISM

The classical exposition of dualistic interactionism is that given by René Descartes. According to Descartes we can clearly distinguish three different kinds of substances: one the eternal substance God, and the other two, substances created by God. He says: "We may thus easily have two clear and distinct notions or ideas, the one of created substance which thinks, the other of corporeal substance, provided we carefully separate all the attributes of thought from those of extension."[1]

However, although there are these two radically different created substances, one which is extended and does not think (body) and one which thinks but is not extended (mind), Descartes claims that he, and therefore other men, are essentially thinking substances. Yet he finds that he is not only a mind, for as he says, "I have a body which is adversely affected when I feel pain, which has need of food or drink when I experience the feelings of hunger and thirst, and so on. . . ."[2] But it is not that men are merely minds that happen to have bodies, according to Descartes. It would be better to call them embodied minds, for he claims to have found

> that I am not only lodged in my body as a pilot in a ship, but that I am very closely united to it, and so to speak so inter-mingled with it that I seem to compose with it one whole. For if that were not the case, when my body hurt, I, who am merely a thinking thing, should perceive this wound by the under-standing only, just as the sailor perceives by sight when something is damaged in his vessel. . . .[3]

These two kinds of substances which make up each person inter-mingle in such a way that they causally act upon each other. Although it might be that a mind interacts with each part of its body separately, Descartes' view is that mind interacts only with the brain. This agrees with findings of science that various brain proc-

[1] René Descartes, *The Philosophical Works of Descartes* (New York: Dover, 1955), p. 241.
[2] Ibid., p. 192.
[3] Ibid.

esses bring about certain bodily movements and that certain bodily events causally affect the brain. The usual view, then, is a mind–brain interaction theory. It is usually held, for example, that a material event that causally stimulates one of our five senses—for example, light waves hitting the retina of the eye—results in a chain of physical causation which leads to a certain brain process from which a certain sensation results. It is also held that because certain bodily behavior has been brought about by affecting the brain in certain ways, mental events act on the body by affecting the brain. Descartes thought he could pinpoint mind–brain interaction more precisely than this. He claimed that there is just one point of immediate "contact" or interaction between mind and body. Through this point of contact the causal effects of the mind are carried to all parts of the body and the causal effects of all parts of the body are transmitted to the mind. As Descartes says, "the part of the body in which the soul exercises its functions immediately is in nowise the heart, nor the whole of the brain, but merely the most inward of all its parts, to wit, a certain very small gland which is situated in the middle of its substance. . . ."[4] Again he adds that,

the small gland which is the main seat of the soul is so suspended between the cavities which contain the spirits that it can be moved by them in as many ways as there are sensible diversites in the object, but that it may also be moved in diverse ways by the soul, whose nature is such that it receives in itself as many diverse impressions, that is to say, that it possesses as many diverse perceptions, as there are diverse movements in this gland. Reciprocally, likewise, the machine of the body is so formed that from the simple fact that this gland is diversely moved by the soul, or by such other cause, whatever it is, it thrusts the spirits which surround it towards the pores of the brain, which conduct them by the nerves into muscles, by which means it causes them to move the limbs.[5]

This gland that Descartes thought to be the "seat" of the mind or soul is the pineal gland. It functions, according to him, as the inter-

[4] Ibid., p. 345.
[5] Ibid., p. 347.

mediary that transmits the effects of the mind to the brain and the effects of the brain to the mind. He was wrong about this, however, because there is reason to think the gland is not affected by all brain processes that affect the mind nor by all mental phenomena that affect the body. Consequently, although we shall agree with Descartes in construing dualistic interactionism as a mind–brain theory, we shall disagree with him about the role of the pineal gland in this interaction. We shall also disagree with him on another point. As more recent dualists have claimed, it is, strictly speaking, wrong to speak of minds and brains interacting, because it is *events* that are causally related, not *substances*. Thus, although we shall sometimes talk of minds and brains interacting, and also of mental events and brain events interacting, these statements should always be construed to mean either that some brain event is causing a mental event or that some mental event is causing some brain event.

Although accepted by many people, dualistic interactionism is by no means immune to powerful objections, objections that many philosophers have found so damaging that they have rejected the position. In general, there have been two kinds of objections, those based on the requirement of science and those based on philosophical grounds. We shall consider the three strongest objections of each kind.

THREE PHILOSOPHICAL OBJECTIONS TO DUALISTIC INTERACTIONISM

FIRST PHILOSOPHICAL OBJECTION: WHERE DOES INTERACTION OCCUR?

According to dualistic interactionism certain mental phenomena, such as fear, cause certain bodily behavior, and certain bodily events, such as spraining an ankle, causally bring about mental events. Supposedly, this point of interaction between mind and body is in the brain, because mental events directly affect brain processes. But, goes the objection, no mental event has a spatial location; no mental event occurs at some place. How then can it be said that the mental events that causally affect brain events are located *in* the brain? To be in the brain is to have a spatial location.

Thus because they have no spatial location, mental events are not in anything. They are therefore not in the brain and thus do not interact with events that are in the brain.

This objection emphasizes something important about mental phenomena—they have no spatial locations. Where are your thoughts, your desires, your dreams, your sensations and emotions? Surely not several inches behind your eyes, somewhere in your brain. No one examining your brain, no matter how thorough the examination, would ever find them there. Being mental, they have no spatial location. It will not help to talk about some place as the seat of the mind, as Descartes did, because a seat is a place where something is spatially located, and the mind has no spatial location. We can conclude, then, that there is no place at which mental events causally interact with brain events, because mental events do not occur anywhere. We can, consequently, reject the question, "Where do minds and brains interact?" as senseless. There is no such place.

But how does this affect the claim of the interactionist? The objection asserts that the interactionist is committed to claiming that the interaction takes place in the brain, because he claims that what mental events directly interact with are brain events that are in the brain. The core of the objection, then, is that if one thing interacts with another, the first must be located where the second one is. This seems quite reasonable regarding material events, especially when based on the doctrine that there is no action at a distance. But there is no reason to think that this is at all relevant to mind–brain causal action. Mental events are neither close to nor at a distance from brain events, because they have no location. The interactionist, then, can rebut this objection by denying that he is committed to locating mental events in the brain. All he claims is that mental events interact with certain bodily events that are in the brain, but it does not follow from this that the mental events must also be in the brain.

The first objection is not fatal to interactionism, but it does bring to light the puzzling nature of the so-called interaction. It might bring someone to argue that there can be no mind–body interaction because brain events can interact only with something located at some place and mental events cannot be located at a place. This objection, however, begs the question at issue because it assumes that brain events can interact only with bodily events, and this is the very question at issue. We can, then, dismiss the first objection, although we should remember that there are some puzzling factors involved in such an interaction. It is these factors that give rise to the second objection.

SECOND PHILOSOPHICAL OBJECTION:
HOW CAN INTERACTION OCCUR?

The main point emphasized by the first objection is that mental events and bodily events are radically different. Consequently, it would seem that these two different kinds of events would have radically different kinds of causal abilities. Consider how material phenomena are causally affected. Material bodies and events are causally affected by something exerting physical force upon them in some way. To move or change a material body or to begin or change some bodily process it seems that some physical force must be exerted upon some material object. But because physical force is a product of mass and acceleration, whatever can exert physical force must have mass and must be capable of acceleration, that is, change of rate of motion through space. But nothing mental has mass; nothing mental can accelerate, because nothing mental can travel from place to place. Therefore, states the objection, nothing mental can exert physical force; thus, nothing material can be causally affected by anything mental. Consider also how one body causally affects something else. As brought out earlier the causal efficacy of a body is the result of its physical force. But how can physical force be exerted upon that which has no mass, no size, no spatial location? There is neither action of mind on body nor action of body on mind.

This objection has been considered by C. D. Broad, one of the leading contemporary defenders of dualistic interactionism. He has summarized the objection as follows:

Now the common philosophical argument is that minds and mental states are so extremely unlike bodies and bodily states that it is inconceivable that the two should be causally connected. It is certainly true that, if minds and mental events are just what they seem to be to introspection and nothing more, and if bodies and bodily events are just what enlightened common sense thinks them to be and nothing more, the two *are* extremely unlike. And this fact is supposed to show that, however closely correlated certain pairs of events in mind and body respectively may be, they cannot be causally connected.[6]

Broad goes on to refute this argument as follows:

> One would like to know just how unlike two events may be before it becomes impossible to admit the existence of a causal relation between them. No one hesitates to hold that draughts and colds in the head are causally connected, although the two are extremely unlike each other. If the unlikeness of draughts and colds in the head does not prevent one from admitting a causal connection between the two, why should the unlikeness of volitions and voluntary movements prevent one from holding that they are causally connected?[7]

Broad, then, is willing to admit that mental events, such as making decisions, are quite different from those things to which they are supposed to be causally relevant, namely, certain voluntary bodily movements. But because many causes are radically different from their effects, there is no reason to think mental events and brain events cannot causally interact merely because they are so different.

There are two replies that someone might make to Broad. First, he could point out that Broad is correct if the objection is construed to assert that mind–body interaction is logically impossible, but the objection should not be taken this way. It is meant to assert that the denial of mind–body interaction is completely justified. Surely it is possible that things which are extremely dissimilar causally interact, but when they are so dissimilar that the only characteristic they have in common is temporal position, then it seems most unreasonable to claim that they do interact. It is logically possible that a single ant will move the Washington Monument, but we are surely justified in saying, nevertheless, that it will not. And an ant is more like a monument than a mental event is like a bodily event.

The second reply to Broad is that the original argument, before

---

[6] C. D. Broad, *The Mind and Its Place in Nature* (London: Routledge and Kegan Paul, 1962), p. 97.

[7] Ibid., p. 98.

he reformulated it, is not based merely upon the absence of like characteristics, but ultimately upon the absence of characteristics relevant to causal interaction. Although a draught and a cold are quite different, both are still material. A cold is a condition of certain parts of a person's body, and we can understand how a draught, which is a movement of air molecules, could have some sort of effect on something bodily. We can see certain effects of air on bodies time and time again. A flow of air occurs at a place, has a certain temperature, a certain moisture and pollen count, and a certain amount of physical force. Such characteristics are quite relevant to having causal affects upon material objects. The point of emphasizing the great dissimilarity between mental events and bodily events is not to justify the claim that dissimilarity rules out causation, but to emphasize that of all the usual characteristics relevant to causal interaction with material objects, the only one found in mental events is temporal position, which by itself is surely not sufficient for causal action.

What can Broad say to these replies to his claim? Both replies state, essentially, that there is good reason to conclude that minds and bodies do not causally interact either because they have only one property in common or because whatever other properties each has, they are not causally relevant to the other. His best retort would be to rely on the reply of another contemporary interactionist, C. J. Ducasse. He says,

> The causality relation does not presuppose at all that its cause-term and its effect-term both belong to the same ontological category, but only that both of them be *events*.
>
> Moreover, the objection that we cannot understand how a psychical event could cause a physical one (or vice versa) has no basis other than blindness to the fact that the "how" of causation is capable at all of being either mysterious or understood only in cases of *remote* causation, never in cases of *proximate* causation. For the question as to the "how" of causation of a given event by a given other event never has any other sense than *through what intermediary causal steps* does one cause the other.[8]

[8] C. J. Ducasse, "In Defense of Dualism," in S. Hook, ed., *Dimensions of Mind* (New York: Collier Books, 1961), p. 88.

There are two relevant claims here. The first is that the matter of determining what things are causally related is completely empirical; the only restriction is that it be events that are causally related. Thus before we have examined specific situations we can impose no restrictions upon what kinds of events can causally interact. We must observe actual situations and do actual experiments to decide the issue. Thus we must find out by observation and experiment whether minds and bodies interact rather than proclaim that they cannot or do not because they are so different. Nor should we proclaim what characteristics are relevant to causation. We must also find this out by observation and experimentation. The second relevant claim made by Ducasse is that when we come to proximate, or immediate, causes we must accept them as brute facts. There is no way to explain them because we can explain how one event causes another only when the cause is remote rather than proximate, that is, only if the cause brings about the effect by means of some other intervening events. We can, for example, explain why heating a gas causes the pressure of the gas on its container to increase by saying that increasing the temperature of a gas causes the molecules of the gas to move more rapidly and thus hit the walls of the container with more force. But if an increase of temperature is an immediate or proximate cause of an increase of molecular speed, we cannot explain how this causal action works. Explanation comes to an end with proximate causes and we must merely accept that such causes have the effects they do. Consequently, although we can explain how a desire for a cigarette causes us to reach for a pack by explaining that the desire causally affects the brain, which by means of the nerves causally affects the arm, we cannot explain how a desire affects the brain because this is a case of proximate causation. We should, then, as with all cases of proximate causation, accept it as a brute fact, a fact no more and no less mysterious than any brute fact.

Ducasse's reply seems to be satisfactory *if* it is indeed true that observation and experimentation provide grounds for claiming that minds and brains have a causal relationship that is proximate rather than remote. Ducasse is correct in warning us not to approach any situation with a preconceived view of what the relevant causal factors are. But unless he can provide some evidence based upon observation of minds and bodies that they do causally interact, then we have a right to use the results of other observations to help us decide. Consequently, because in all other observed cases of causal interaction involving material events we find that both cause and effect involve objects with mass and spatial position, we have some evidence, meager though it may be, against the claim that minds and bodies interact. If there is no evidence for the claim to counteract this contrary evidence, then, in spite of the claims of Broad and Ducasse, we should follow the evidence and conclude that minds and bodies do not interact.

The crucial question before us now is whether or not the data we gather from experience provide any evidence in favor of the claim that minds and bodies interact. Broad thinks that it does, because he thinks that "in voluntary action, and there only, we are immediately acquainted with an instance of causal connexion. If this be true the controversy is of course settled at once in favour of the Interactionist."[9] His reason for this is,

> It is perfectly plain that, in the case of volition and voluntary movement, there *is* a connexion between the cause and the effect which is not present in the other cases of causation, and which does make it plausible to hold that in this one case the nature of the effect can be foreseen by merely reflecting on the nature of the cause. The peculiarity of a volition as a causal-factor is that it involves as an essential part of it the idea of the effect. To say that a person has a volition to move his arm involves saying that he has an idea of his arm (and not of his leg or his liver) and an idea of the position in which he wants his arm to be. It is simply silly in view of this fact to say that there is no closer connexion between the desire to move my arm and the movement of my arm than there is between this desire and the movement of my leg or my liver. We cannot detect any analogous connexion between cause and effect in causal transactions which we view wholly from the outside, such as the movement of a billiard-ball by a cue. It is therefore by no means unreasonable to suggest that, in the one case of our own voluntary movements, we can see without waiting for the

[9] Broad, op. cit., pp. 100–101.

result that such and such a volition is a necessary condition of such and such a bodily movement.[10]

In this passage Broad is claiming not only that in the case of voluntary bodily movements we have evidence that minds and bodies are causally connected, but also that in such a case we have perhaps the best evidence available that there are causal connections. We can, I think, agree with Broad on his first, more modest, claim that there are times when we decide to move one of our arms and its subsequent movement clearly seems to have resulted from our decision. That we seem to experience causal connections between some decisions and some bodily movements is surely some evidence that there are causal connections between minds and bodies. However, Broad thinks that we can support a stronger claim, namely, that we have adequate (indeed, even fully sufficient) evidence for such a causal connection because of one unique feature of decisions. A decision unlike any other causal factor involves the idea of the effect. This unique connection between cause and effect provides, according to Broad, the grounds for this stronger claim. However, at this point Broad seems to be arguing contrary to the lesson we learned from Ducasse in his defense of mind–body interaction. That is, the only factors we should count as causally relevant are those we find to be so through experience. The idea a person has of, for example, his arm's movement should be declared causally relevant to the movement of the arm only if there is evidence that mental phenomena such as ideas are causally relevant to bodily phenomena. To proclaim that they are relevant is no better justified than to proclaim that they are not. Thus Broad cannot justify his defense of interactionism by reliance upon a claim that having an idea of an event under certain conditions (for example, when deciding) is relevant to the causation of the event.

We should reject Broad's stronger claim. But because his weaker claim is acceptable we can say that there is some evidence in favor of mind–body causal interaction. Here, then, is some evidence to counteract the evidence against interaction. This means that we have not yet found grounds sufficient for rejecting dualistic interactionism, but neither have we found grounds sufficient for accept-

[10] Ibid., pp. 102–103.

ing it. What we seem to experience cannot be counted as sufficient evidence. Consequently, the acceptability of dualistic interactionism depends upon the seriousness of the remaining objections to it.

THIRD PHILOSOPHICAL OBJECTION:
THE PROBLEM OF OTHER MINDS

The third objection is based upon what is called the problem of other minds. Each of us thinks that he knows that there are other persons, beings with minds as well as bodies, beings who perform mental as well as physical acts and who are in both mental and physical states. But if, as dualistic interactionism claims, the mind is completely distinct and different from the body, there is no way to justify the belief that there are other beings with minds; hence there is no way of knowing whether there are other persons. All I perceive when I see or hear another entity is bodily behavior—movements and sounds. But bodily behavior is surely not mental. Thus I never perceive another being's mind. Furthermore, there is no way I can check to discover whether, as in my own case, some of this bodily behavior is accompanied by anything mental. It may be, but I have no way to find out. Other beings whom I believe to be persons may be only automata. Dualistic interactionism, by construing minds as radically different from bodies, has forced us to a conclusion contrary to what we all believe. Surely, states this objection, a theory that can avoid this consequence is to be preferred to dualistic interactionism.

The core of this argument can be restated as follows: If the mind–body dualist is correct, then no statements about bodily behavior entail any statements about minds. Therefore no deductive argument based on what I perceive can be used to justify any of my beliefs that there are other minds, because no premises about what I perceive entail conclusions about other minds. Furthermore, if the dualist is correct then the only case in which I know that mental activity accompanies bodily activity is my own. But no inductive argument based upon such scant evidence is sufficient to justify my belief that there are other minds. I can justify this belief in only three ways: by deductive inference, by inductive inference, and noninferentially, by perception. Therefore if the dualist is correct I cannot justify my belief that there are other minds.

We can agree with this third objection that all else being equal any theory which contradicts what we think is true should be discarded in favor of a theory that accords with our beliefs. Thus we must remember this objection when we begin to compare the various mind–body alternatives. However, there are two things about this objection that we should note before we move on. The first is that not everyone who considers the problem of other minds thinks that it is insoluble for a mind-body dualist. Although a discussion of this point belongs more properly in Chapter 2, we can indicate here one attempt to handle this problem. If we agree with the person who is skeptical about our knowledge of other minds that our canons of evidence allow a belief to be justified only by perception, deduction, or induction based on a variety of observations, then we must also agree that if the dualist is correct there is no knowledge of other minds. A. J. Ayer, in an attempt to resolve this problem, and also the problem of our knowledge of the past, says:

> If it is required of an inductive argument that the generalization to which it leads should be based on a wide variety of experienced instances, both candidates fail the test. One has only a limited experience of the connection of "inner" states with their outer manifestations; and one has no experience at all of the connection of a present with a past event. But these are not ordinary limitations; what is suspect about them is that they are logically necessary. As we have several times remarked, it is by insisting on an impossible standard of perfection that the skeptic makes himself secure.[11]

Ayer's point here is that the skeptic is demanding that we use canons of evidence so restrictive that it is logically impossible to meet their requirements in these cases. Why should we use those canons the skeptic requires? Why not those that can account for our usual claims to knowledge? Although we do not think that Ayer's quick treatment effectively refutes the skeptic, he has at least suggested the beginnings of a way that may save the dualist from the skeptic.

[11] A. J. Ayer, *The Problem of Knowledge* (Baltimore: Penguin Books, 1965), p. 222.

The second point to note is that this is a telling objection to dualism only if the skeptic is wrong. Perhaps the correct conclusion is that we really do not have knowledge of other minds, perhaps Ayer and others who try to refute the skeptic are the ones who are wrong. Although it is true that all else being equal, we should accept the nonskeptical position, it may be that, as is usually the case, all else is not equal. Possibly we should sacrifice the knowledge claim rather than some other. In other words, the knowledge claim is only one among many other factors that we must weigh in our evaluation of the various mind–body positions. It has no privileged status.

THREE SCIENTIFIC OBJECTIONS TO DUALISTIC INTERACTIONISM

We have examined three philosophical objections to dualistic interactionism, two against interaction and one against dualism. We have found that none of them inflicts irreparable damage, although together they cast some doubt upon the position. Let us now turn to three objections based on certain scientific claims.

FIRST SCIENTIFIC OBJECTION: INTERACTION VIOLATES CONSERVATION OF ENERGY PRINCIPLE

The first scientific objection is based upon the principle of the conservation of energy, which states that the amount of energy in a closed physical system remains constant. According to this objection, however, if there is causal interaction between mental events and bodily events, then the principle is violated. When some bodily event causes a mental event, then the physical energy involved in the bodily event is expended in such a way that it is not transferred to anything else; energy is lost. When some mental event causes a bodily event, then the energy gained or lost by the resultant bodily event has not been transferred from or to anything physical so that the total amount of energy is changed. According to this objection, because both minds acting on bodies and bodies acting on minds would violate the principle of the conservation of energy, we have good reasons for concluding that there is no such interaction.

The following example will illustrate this objection. Surely King Canute was absurd in thinking that he could stop the tide merely by willing that it stop; similarly, anyone who tried to start or stop a billiard ball by an act of will would be frustrated. Starting a billiard ball by an act of will would cause the ball to gain kinetic energy, which (because it was not transferred from anything else) would constitute an overall gain in energy. Stopping a billiard ball by an act of will would cause the ball to lose kinetic energy, which (because it was not turned into heat or potential energy, nor transferred to anything else) would constitute an overall loss of energy. According to the first scientific objection, because the only relevant difference between starting or stopping a billiard ball in motion and starting or stopping a brain process is the amount of energy involved, if doing the one violates the principle of the conservation of energy, and is thus physically impossible, then so is doing the other. A converse example illustrates the converse problem. If a rolling billiard ball suddenly stops only because it brought about a mental event, then because the kinetic energy of the ball was neither turned into heat nor into potential energy nor transferred to anything else, physical energy is lost and the principle violated again. This is surely physically impossible. Therefore, according to this objection, because the only relevant difference between a rolling ball causing a mental event and a brain process causing a mental event is the amount of energy lost, if one violates the principle then so does the other.

Both Broad and Ducasse have replied to this objection. Ducasse states his reasons for rejecting it as follows:

(A) One reason is that the conservation which that principle asserts is not something known to be true without exception, but is, as M. T. Keeton has pointed out, only a defining-postulate of the notion of a *wholly closed* physical world, so that the question whether psycho-physical or physico-psychical causation ever occurs is (but in different words) the question whether the physical world *is* wholly closed. And that question is not answered by dignifying as a "principle" the assumption that the physical world is wholly closed.

(B) Anyway, as C. D. Broad has pointed out, it might be the

case that whenever a given amount of energy vanishes from, or emerges in, the physical world at one place, then an equal amount of energy respectively emerges in, or vanishes from, that world at another place.

(C) And thirdly, if "energy" is meant to designate something experimentally measurable, then "energy" is defined in terms of causality, *not* "causality" in terms of transfer of energy. That is, it is not known that *all* causation or, in particular, causation as between psychical and physical events, involves transfer of energy.[12]

We can, I think, quickly show that the first two reasons have little force, but the third is considerably more powerful. It is surely true that in a certain sense the conservation principle is not an empirical scientific law, because it is not a generalization derived from careful observations and experiments. It is, then, unlike Boyle's law, Hooke's law, and others, which is why it is more properly called a scientific *principle*. Nevertheless no one has ever found reason to reject it, and because it is an essential ingredient in many scientific theories which have great explanatory and predictive power, these theories and thereby the principle are surely justified. Consequently, if as previously claimed, the theory of dualistic interactionism involves a violation of a principle that has been justified, the theory is doubtful and there is reason to reject it. Ducasse's second reason can also be rejected because, like the first reason, it does no more than show it is possible that something is true, which by itself provides no grounds for claiming that it is true. Just as there is no reason to think that the conservation principle does not hold for the physical universe, so there is no reason to think that by chance or even design the amount of energy of the physical world is kept constant by counterbalancing losses and additions. This may be what happens but it is highly unlikely that the many, many gains and losses of energy that supposedly result from millions of mind–body interactions all balance out evenly. Such an improbable hypothesis cannot carry much weight. Consequently, we can rely only on the third of Ducasse's reasons to save interactionism from the first scientific objection.

---

[12] Ducasse, op. cit., pp. 88–89.

Ducasse's third reason is based on an important truth, namely, nothing in the definition of 'causation' entails that all cases of causation involve a transfer of physical energy. It is therefore at least logically possible that some mental events cause bodily events and that some bodily events cause mental events without in any way affecting the amount of energy involved in the bodily events. But can we accept either of these logical possibilities, or is there some reason sufficient for rejecting them? We must consider each one separately because each faces special problems. Is there any reason to reject the claim that a bodily event can cause a mental event without expending energy which is lost to the physical world? If, as envisioned in the billiard-ball analogy, bodily causes must always behave like a rolling ball which loses energy, then we must reject this claim. But physical energy need not be required to bring about a mental event, because mental phenomena involve no physical energy. Thus no energy is transferred from bodily causes to mental effects and thus there is, accordingly, no reason to think that bodily causes of mental events should behave like a ball stopping. Such bodily causes could maintain their total amount of energy or perhaps transfer it to some other bodily event, thereby being the cause of a bodily event *and* a mental event at the same time. If someone objects that such a dual causation is most mysterious, we can answer by reminding him about the brute, unexplainable nature of immediate causations. We must take them as we find them. We can, then, accept as a plausible position the hypothesis that bodily causation of mental events involves no loss of energy. Thus there is no reason to think that physicopsychical causation involves a violation of the conservation principle.

Can we accept or should we reject the claim that mental causation of bodily events does not affect the amount of energy involved in the bodily event? If, once again, we accept the billiard-ball analogy, then we must reject the claim. To start something moving is to give it kinetic energy, and if that is how mental causes affect the body, then mental causation of bodily events violates the conservation principle. Broad, in reply to this objection, counters the billiard-ball analogy with one of his own. He says,

Take the case of a weight swinging at the end of a string hung from a fixed point. The total energy of the weight is the same at all positions in its course. It is thus a conservative system.

But at every moment the direction and velocity of the weight's motion are different, and the proportion between its kinetic and its potential energy is constantly changing. These changes are caused by the pull of the string, which acts in a different direction at each different moment. The string makes no difference to the total energy of the weight; but it makes all the difference in the world to the particular way in which the energy is distributed between the potential and the kinetic forms. . . .

Here, then, we have a clear case even in the physical realm where a system is conservative but is continually acted on by something which affects its movement and the distribution of its total energy. Why should not the mind act on the body in this way?[13]

Broad's analogy brings out the point that there are two quite different ways in which one thing can causally affect the movement of another. Either it can cause it to change its speed, as in the billiard-ball example, or it can causally affect the direction in which the object moves, as in the pendulum example. The first kind of cause changes the total amount of energy involved; the second need not. If Broad's analogy is apt, then various mental events can be said to affect brain processes, not by starting or stopping them, but rather by affecting the course they take. Thus if we assume for purposes of discussion that in each brain only one process occurs at one time and that it is started and stopped by other bodily events, then such a brain process is like a string pendulum which is started and stopped by the expenditure of physical energy. But after something hits the weight and begins its movement, where it goes depends upon the length of the string attached to it. Thus attaching strings of different length to the weight changes the course of the weight but in no way affects the overall amount of energy of the weight. According to this analogy we are to take the causal role of different mental events to be like the causal role of different lengths of string. There would, consequently, be different results in the brain, which would in turn have different bodily results, so that the body would be affected in many different ways given the

13 Broad, op. cit., pp. 107–108.

same input of energy. But while the string analogy solves one problem it raises another. To change the direction of motion without a physical cause is no less a violation of scientific principles than to violate the conservation principle. If mental causes must act like strings to change the direction of motion, then Broad's reply to the first objection is not enough. We must, therefore, examine in more detail the way in which, according to Broad, mental events affect brain processes. To do this we must turn to his examination of the second scientific objection.

SECOND SCIENTIFIC OBJECTION:
NO PLACE FOR MENTAL CAUSES IN
THE EXPLANATION OF HUMAN BEHAVIOR

Broad states this objection, which he calls the "argument from the structure of the nervous system," as follows:

> It is admitted that the mind has nothing to do with causation of purely reflex actions. But the nervous structure and the nervous processes involved in deliberate action do not differ in kind from those involved in reflex action; they differ only in degree of complexity. The variability which characterizes deliberate action is fully explained by the variety of alternative paths and the variable resistances of the synapses. So it is unreasonable to suppose that the mind has any more to do with causing deliberate actions than it has to do with causing reflex actions.[14]

This argument is based on physiological facts. All human bodily behavior is brought about by neural processes; which behavior occurs depends causally on which nerve fibers are affected and how they are affected. These neural responses in turn depend upon the level of resistances of the various synapses connecting the neurons, or nerve cells, because the path that a nerve impulse will take depends upon the relative resistances of certain synapses. It is also true that the kind of neural processes involved in reflex actions (that is, actions clearly having no mental causes) is no different from that involved in other kinds of human behavior. It is, consequently,

[14] Ibid., p. 110.

reasonable to suppose that there is no place for mental causes in any kind of human behavior.

There are two possible interpretations of this objection. The first depends upon interpreting 'no place for mental causes' to mean that there is no place *within the causal chain* for mental causes, and the second depends upon interpreting it to mean that there is no place *in the explanation* for mental causes. Broad claims that the interactionist is committed to a gap in the explanations of certain human actions if we do not consider mental causes, but he is not committed to a gap within causal chains if mental causes are omitted. Thus, Broad thinks that the interactionist need not worry about the first interpretation just so long as he is careful to specify correctly the way mental causes affect the body. He goes on to suggest what this way is.

[The facts considered in the second objection] suggest that what the mind does to the body in voluntary action, if it does anything, is to lower the resistance of certain synapses and to raise that of others. The result is that the nervous current follows such a course as to produce the particular movement which the mind judges to be appropriate at the time.[15]

In this passage Broad shows how it can be that there is no gap within the neural causal chain that constitutes a nerve process which must be filled by a mental event. Mental events, according to Broad, would not be parts of such causal chains as M is in Figure 1. They would rather work upon the chains by affecting the distribution of resistance among certain synapses as in Figure 2. Thus interactionism is not committed to what there is reason to think is false, namely, that there is a gap between some neural events and others, a gap no neural event fills. In such a manner Broad tells us how the first interpretation can be avoided, and also more carefully specifies the nature of the immediate causal action of mind on body.

We are still left, however, with the second interpretation. In this case the interactionist seems to be committed to a gap, a gap in the explanation of certain human behavior if no mental events are in-

15 Ibid., p. 113.

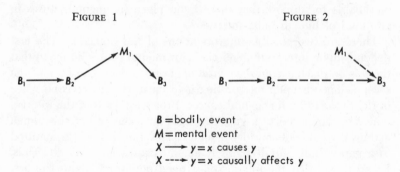

FIGURE 1   FIGURE 2

B = bodily event
M = mental event
X ⟶ y = x causes y
X ---⟶ y = x causally affects y

cluded in the explanation, because, if he is right, it would seem we cannot fully explain why certain synapses have the resistance they do without reference to mental causes. If, therefore, the interactionist is right, then mental causes are essential to explanations of human behavior. This brings us to a crucial point. Are there reasons for accepting or for rejecting the claim that facts about mental phenomena are essential to any full explanation of human action? Broad tries to provide reasons for accepting the need for such mental factors by arguing that,

> In deliberate action, the response is varied *appropriately* to meet the special circumstances which are supposed to exist at the time, or are expected to arise later; whilst reflex action is not varied in this way, but is blind and almost mechanical. The complexity of the nervous system explains the *possibility* of variation; it does not in the least explain why the alternative which actually takes place should as a rule be appropriate and not merely haphazard. And so again it seems as if some factor were in operation in deliberate action which is not present in reflex action; and it is reasonable to suppose that this factor is the volition in the mind.[16]

Broad bases his argument on the following two premises: (1) With so many responses possible because of the great complexity of the nervous system, we must explain why so often only the appropriate responses occur; and (2) it is reasonable to explain this appropriate-

[16] Ibid., p. 112.

ness by the effect of mental causes upon the appropriate nerve synapses.

Although we think that this may be the best argument for accepting Broad's claim, there are several reasons for rejecting it. Many human actions are not merely reflex actions and do not seem to involve mental causes, but are usually appropriate. During our waking hours much of what we do, such as our habitual responses and absent-minded behavior, seems to be done without thought or decision or volition or any other mental cause. Yet these actions are not reflex actions. Very often they are appropriate to the situation, and this appropriateness requires an explanation. But it certainly seems no matter how we explain the appropriateness of these actions, we shall not include a mental factor. And if we can explain these actions without reference to mental causes, there is no reason to think that a mental factor is needed to help explain fully any other human actions, even those we would call deliberative actions.

Broad would probably reply at this point that habitual actions are those in which the synapses have acquired regular resistances as the result of continuous causal action by the mind, but there is no reason to think such habitual acquiring of synapse-response requires previous mental causation. The best illustration that mental factors are not needed either for "learning" or for the one appropriate response out of many possible responses is afforded by the complex computers we find operating today. Not only do some of these machines have a huge number of possible responses available from which they usually "choose" the appropriate one, but they also are capable of improving in their responses. They can "learn" in playing chess and thus improve their game. All this requires explanation, but surely no part of the explanation of machine behavior requires a mental causal factor. Consequently, there seems to be no reason to think that mental causal factors are needed to explain certain human actions. There seems to be no place in the explanation of human actions that requires mental factors. And, because it seems that dualistic interactionism requires that there be such a gap, we have found a strong objection to dualistic interactionism, an objection that may tip the scale of evidence in favor of some other position.

Broad has not avoided the second scientific objection. How has he fared with the first? We have seen that he can give an explanation of how mental events can affect neural processes without violating the conservation principle, but we have not investigated how he might answer the change-of-direction objection. The answer is that, strictly speaking, mental events do not cause changes in the direction of neural currents, because what they immediately bring about are changes in the distribution of resistances rather than changes in the direction nerve currents take. It is the relative levels of resistances that cause the current to take a certain direction. This is surely understandable. If you ask, however, how mental events can affect the relative distribution of resistances, the answer is that once again we have a case of immediate, and therefore unexplainable, causation. This, we find, is the best reply a dualistic interactionist can give to the objection. It is surely not completely satisfactory and does not fully dispel the mystery of how mental events can affect the body. Yet it does at least neutralize the damage of this objection to a great extent. Nevertheless, it may well be that some other theory will be able to handle this problem more easily.

THIRD SCIENTIFIC OBJECTION: WHAT EVOLVES FROM MATERIAL PHENOMENA IS MATERIAL

The third objection based upon scientific premises derives from the theory of evolution. It begins by noting that according to the accepted doctrine of evolution man has evolved over a long period of time from other less complex forms of life; that is, man's ancestry can be traced back through his primitive ancestors, to apes, to certain forms of sea life, and finally to single-cell living beings which themselves resulted from certain material forces operating at certain places in the universe. Man, then, is a complex being who has evolved from primitive forms of life. And these primitive forms of life in turn resulted from physical and chemical reactions among nonliving things. Man ultimately, then, has evolved from nonliving, completely material things. One possible theory is that everything in this universe can trace its ancestry back to simple hydrogen atoms which under different conditions of temperature and pressure resulted in heavier and more complex atoms and molecules, some of which became the basis for life on this planet. Man, then, has evolved from simple material particles by means of a continuing process of increasing complexity. Consequently, according to this objection, man is no different in kind from any other material objects. He may be more complex than most material objects and be made up of unique kinds of molecules, but he evolved from the same basic particles as did the trees, flowers, flies, amoebas, and viruses. We should conclude, therefore, that just as these other things are merely material objects and do not have minds, so also man is merely a material object with no mind.

This objection to dualism has two forms. The first states that because humans have evolved from primitive particles which were material only and had no minds, humans themselves have no minds. The second form of the objection states that because humans have evolved from the same primitive particles as all material objects that do not have minds, humans themselves have no minds. Neither form is cogent. The first is based on the premise that only material objects can evolve from material objects. That is, material processes can causally bring about only other material processes. But as we have already seen when we examined the second philosophical objection, there is no reason to think that certain material processes cannot causally bring about mental events as well as material events. As Ducasse pointed out, we must always examine a particular event to see just what causal results it produces. There is no reason to think that the causal results of certain material events are never mental events. Thus it may well be that somewhere along the path of evolution something material evolved which had mental events among its causal results. Consequently, the fact that man evolved from matter casts no doubt on a mind–body dualism.

The second form of this objection can be rebutted in a similar way. It is not at all strange that everything that evolved from primitive matter except sentient beings is itself merely matter. Sentient beings are quite different from other material objects. It is true that if all we knew about man were that he evolved from the same things that all objects without minds evolved from, then we would have some reason to think that man is merely material. But all of us have other knowledge of man, especially about his abilities and, at least in our own cases, about events and states that seem quite different from material phenomena. Thus the second form of the third scientific objection, like the first form, provides little reason to reject a mind–body dualism. Man with a mind as well as a body might well have evolved in his own unique way from matter. The theory that describes the path of evolution does not cast any doubt on mind evolving from matter.

We have examined six objections to dualistic interactionism, four against interaction, and two against dualism. Neither of the objections to dualism, the problem of other minds or the objection from evolution, is strong enough to overcome what seems to be true, that is, people have both minds and bodies. Two of the objections against interactionism—the objection that questions where interactions take place and the objection from the principle of the conservation of energy—have been either dismissed or neutralized to some degree. The other two objections to interaction, however—the philosophical objection from the lack of factors in both mental and material phenomena relevant to the one causally affecting the other, and the scientific objection from the lack of a gap in the physiological explanation of human behavior—cast some doubt upon dualistic interactionism. We are not, then, justified in accepting this position until we have examined alternative positions to find out whether any are less doubtful than dualistic interactionism. And because two of the strongest objections are directed at the causal interaction between minds and bodies, one obvious candidate for a less doubtful theory is a dualism that avoids interaction. This, in essence, is the position of parallelism.

PARALLELISM

Parallelism is one form of mind–body dualism. Like interactionism it claims that a person has both a mind and a body, that he consists of mental and bodily events and processes, and that mental and material phenomena are radically different. It differs from interactionism, however, in that it denies that there is any causal interaction between minds and bodies. Mental events proceed over a temporal period, some causing others, but none causally affecting any material events. Similarly, material events occur at different places and times, some causing others, but none causally affecting any mental events. The two different kinds of events proceed completely independently of each other. In the case of an individual person it is granted that certain bodily events, such as breaking an arm, regularly precede certain mental events, such as having a pain, and that certain mental events, such as deciding, regularly precede certain bodily behavior, such as moving the pawn instead of the bishop. But it is claimed that in such cases there is no causal interaction at all. Having an arm broken does not cause pain, and deciding to move a pawn does not cause someone to move it. Such events merely parallel each other, in the sense that certain mental events are accompanied by certain bodily events and certain bodily events are accompanied by certain mental events. Parallelism, therefore, escapes the two objections which we found cast doubt on dualistic interactionism. Can we therefore conclude from this that we should choose parallelism over interactionism? Not yet at least, because there is an objection to parallelism which does not face interactionism. If it is damaging, then we may have to reject parallelism as inferior to interactionism.

AN OBJECTION TO PARALLELISM: CANNOT EXPLAIN OBSERVED REGULARITIES

If parallelism is correct and mental events and material events proceed completely independently of each other, then there is no reason why there are regular relationships between certain of them. There is no reason why what follows the breaking of an arm should not be pain one time and joy another time. We can understand why the breaking of an arm should be followed by pain if bone breaks cause pain, but such regularity where there is no causal relationship calls for some kind of explanation. It seems unlikely that such regularities of parallel mental and bodily occurrences would happen merely by chance. Consequently, such regularities must be explained, but how can parallelism explain them? It cannot rely on the usual kind of causal explanation, the kind that interactionism uses, and no other kind of explanation seems available. This objection, then, is that parallelism, unlike interactionism, cannot adequately explain what requires explanation and, consequently, it should be rejected in favor of some other theory, such as interactionism, which can provide the relevant explanations.

Parallelists have answered this objection in the past in two different ways. It will be our task to see if either answer is adequate. Historically, the two different kinds of explanations of mind–body regularities offered by parallelists have been based either on the theory of occasionalism or on the pre-established harmony theory. Let us consider each.

ONE REPLY: OCCASIONALISM

Occasionalism, propounded by the Catholic philosopher Male-branche, is the theory that on the occasion that certain bodily events occur, God, who can do all things possible, causes certain mental events, and on the occasion that certain mental events occur God causes certain bodily events. Thus although there is no causal action between minds and bodies, we can explain the regularity among certain mental and physical events by stating that God, who has a most orderly and powerful mind, constantly causes the same kind of mental event each time a certain kind of bodily event occurs, and the same kind of bodily event each time a certain kind of mental event occurs.

A SECOND REPLY:
THE PRE-ESTABLISHED HARMONY THEORY

The pre-established harmony theory, as proposed by Leibniz, claims that the procession of bodily events and the procession of mental events both proceed according to a pre-established plan, presumably God's. Thus which material event follows a certain material event is predetermined, and which mental event follows a certain mental event is predetermined. In addition, there is a predetermined harmony between these two independent series of events. That is, the two independent series are so arranged that certain events in the material series are always accompanied by certain events in the mental series, and vice versa. This situation has been likened to two clocks, one of which has a face and hands but no bells to toll the hours, and one of which has bells but no face or hands. If someone were to observe that each time the hands on the one clock were in one position the other clock struck once, and when the hands were in a different position the second clock struck twice, and so on, he might conclude that there is some causal connection between the two clocks, that is, one causes something to happen in the other. But if he examined the situation more carefully he would realize that there is no causal connection between the two clocks at all. It is just that some being regulated each one and then set them running in such a way that whenever the hands of one were in a certain position the other happened to strike its bell a certain number of times. These two clocks run parallel to each other and exhibit a joint regularity or harmony which results not from the causal effects of one clock on the other at certain times and not from the continual intervention of some outside causal force, but rather from the causal effect of some being who at some previous time set each clock independently so that each would run in a certain way. Now, says Leibniz,

> put the soul and body in the place of these two timepieces. Then their agreement or sympathy will also come about in one of these three ways. The *way of influence* [interactionism] is that of the common philosophy. But since it is impossible to conceive of material particles or of species or immaterial qualities which can pass from one of these substances into the other, this view must be rejected. The *way of assistance* [occasionalism] is that of the system of occasional causes. But I hold that God should help only in the way in which he concurs in all other natural things. Thus there remains only my hypothesis, that is, the *way of preestablished harmony*, according to which God has made each of the two substances from the beginning in such a way that, though each follows only its own laws which it has received with its being, each agrees throughout with the other, entirely as if they were mutually influenced or as if God were always putting forth his hand, beyond his general concurrence.[17]

The two parallelist positions have one thing in common: They both postulate the existence of some unobservable entity—which they call God—in order to explain certain observed mind–body regularities. Such an entity is called a *theoretical entity* because it is an unobservable entity postulated as part of a theory designed to explain certain observed phenomena. Leibniz justifies his particular postulation in two steps. First, he claims that it is necessary to postulate something or other because mind–body regularities cannot be explained as the result of mind–body causal interaction, and where postulation is necessary for explanation it surely is justified. Second, he justifies his own particular postulation as preferable to that of Malebranche's on the grounds that Malebranche's hypothesis re-

[17] G. W. von Leibniz, *Philosophical Papers and Letters*, edited by L. E. Loemker (Chicago: University of Chicago Press, 1965), p. 751.

quires more action by the postulated entity than is necessary. Surely we should postulate nothing more than is necessary to explain what is observed. And because mind–body regularities can be explained by postulating God but not postulating his continual intervention at each instance of mind–body regularity, Leibniz is justified in rejecting Malebranche's theory as inferior to his own.

OBJECTION TO BOTH THEORIES:
THEY POSTULATE A *Deus ex Machina*

The principle used to reject occasionalism is that if an explanation can be given without postulating something, then the postulation should not be made. How does this principle apply to Leibniz' own version of parallelism? If, as he claims, it is impossible that minds and bodies interact, then some postulation is necessary for explanation and therefore is justified. But although we have seen that mind–body interaction may be quite mysterious and even unlikely, we have found no reason to think it impossible. Thus it is not necessary to postulate the causal action of an unobservable entity to explain mind–body regularities, and Leibniz' reasoning against interactionism and for a postulated cause fails.

Can we now reject Leibniz' theory—and with it occasionalism and, therefore, parallelism—or is there some other way to justify postulating a theoretical entity which might apply in this case? There is one. If it can be shown that by a particular postulation we can not only explain the phenomena requiring explanation, but can also correctly predict facts that otherwise would have gone undiscovered, then we can justify accepting the postulation on the grounds of its fruitfulness in increasing knowledge. Such predictive power is important in another way because it enables the hypothesis postulating the theoretical entity to be tested by observation and experimentation, and thereby confirmed or disconfirmed. Such testability is essential for a hypothesis to be scientific. But when a hypothesis lacks testability and predictive power and is not needed to explain anything, then it clearly should be rejected. It would be merely an *ad hoc* hypothesis, and any entity it postulates to explain something would be what Leibniz calls a *deus ex machina*, that is, a theoretical entity the sole use of which is to enable its theory to explain what the theory otherwise could not explain.

Is Leibniz' hypothesis of pre-established harmony *ad hoc* and therefore can his claim that occasionalism requires a *deus ex machina* be turned against his own theory? Leibniz' hypothesis about God as the cause of mind–body regularities would have predictive power only if we could read God's mind and discover which of the kinds of mind–body regularities not yet observed he will bring about in the future. But such mind reading is beyond our ability. Consequently, the hypothesis has no predictive power and therefore is not testable by observation and experimentation. It is indeed an *ad hoc* hypothesis, and its postulated entity is a *deus ex machina*. It should be rejected in favor of interactionism, although this theory faces problems of its own. This is especially true where, in spite of the difficulties, it does seem to be the case that mental events and bodily events do causally interact. We should not reject a theory that is in accordance with the way things seem for a second competing theory having in its favor only that it can avoid certain difficulties that face the first theory. Consequently, we can reject parallelism, whether based on the pre-established harmony theory or on occasionalism, as a candidate to replace dualistic interactionism as the most plausible mind–body theory. Parallelism as an attempt to avoid the difficulties of interactionism goes too far in claiming that mind and body are completely independent.

EPIPHENOMENALISM

If we review the objections to dualistic interactionism we can recall that one of the most forceful objections to mind–body causal interaction is the one based on the lack of a gap in the physiological explanation of behavior. We found that although this objection casts some doubt on the existence of psychophysical causation, that is, the causation of a material event by a mental event, it has no force when applied to physicopsychic causation. Thus we have found no reason to doubt that certain material events can cause mental events, and we have rebutted the objection from evolution on these grounds. Consequently, this objection to mind–body interaction can be avoided without going to the extreme of parallelism. All that we need to deny is that mental events causally affect bodily events.

This leads us to epiphenomenalism, a view stated by Thomas Huxley, who claims,

> All states of consciousness in us, as in [brutes], are immediately caused by molecular changes of the brain-substance. It seems to me that in men, as in brutes, there is no proof that any state of consciousness is the cause of change in the motion of the matter of the organism. If these positions are well based, it follows that our mental conditions are simply the symbols in consciousness of the changes which take place automatically in the organism; and that, to take an extreme illustration, the feeling we call volition is not the cause of a voluntary act, but the symbol of that state of the brain which is the immediate cause of that act. We are conscious automata. . . .[18]

We can see from this quotation that epiphenomenalism, like interactionism and parallelism, is a mind–body dualism. Humans (and according to Huxley, even some brute animals) are conscious beings. That is, certain mental events occur to humans. In addition, of course, men have bodies. Where epiphenomenalism differs from the other two dualistic theories is in its view of the relationship between mind and body. According to the epiphenomenalist a mental event is merely an epiphenomenon, or in other words a by-product of certain material processes. When these material processes occur, they both cause other material processes and produce by-products, which themselves have no effect on anything else at all. Santayana has likened the relationship between bodily events and mental events to the relationship between a mountain stream running over and around rocks and into pools, and the babbling sound produced by the flowing water. The babbling sound is caused as a by-product of the water flowing around the rocks. It does not affect the course of the water, which speeds on its way affected only by the rocks and other objects in its path. Neither does the babbling by-product at any one moment affect the sound which results at any later moment. Each moment's sound is caused by the action of rocks and water, only to die out without a single effect of its own. Similarly, each mental event is the causal by-product of some material event in the

[18] T. H. Huxley, *Method and Results* (New York: Appleton-Century-Crofts, 1893), p. 244.

uninterrupted series of material events. Each mental event is produced, occurs, and ends without causally affecting anything at all.

Epiphenomenalism is attractive for several reasons. One reason, which is probably what attracted Huxley, is that it fits nicely with the theory of evolution. As more and more complicated physical processes evolve it is not hard to conceive of consciousness evolving as a by-product which does not causally affect the basic evolving material processes. Second, because it claims that only material events are causally efficacious, epiphenomenalism avoids the problem of a gap in the physiological explanation of human behavior which faces interactionism. Third, epiphenomenalism is also attractive to many people who greatly value scientific controllability. If epiphenomenalism is correct, we do not need to know anything about mental events to be able to explain, predict, and control human behavior, because mental events would play no role in causally determining behavior. As a consequence of this no hidden mental factors are necessary for accurate predictions. A fourth reason is that, unlike parallelism, epiphenomenalism requires no *deus ex machina* to explain mind–body regularities because it claims that each mental event is the causal by-product of a certain material event. Epiphenomenalism, therefore, avoids the most crucial objections to its two rival dualistic theories. It does, however, share one objection with both of these theories (that is, the objection to dualistic theories which derives from the problem of other minds) and one with interactionism alone (that is, the objection derived from the apparent lack of factors in material phenomena relevant to causing mental events). However, because we found neither of these objections to be very damaging, it may well be that we should accept epiphenomenalism unless it faces crucial objections that we have not yet examined. Let us, hence, turn to an examination of the three strongest objections that have been raised against epiphenomenalism.

FIRST OBJECTION TO EPIPHENOMENALISM: REJECTS THE EFFECTS OF MEN'S MINDS ON THE COURSE OF EVENTS

If epiphenomenalism is true, then no mental phenomena have any causal effect upon the history of mankind. Thus none of man's hopes, desires, dreams, joys, sorrows have in any way affected the course of human events. Nor is it correct to talk of psychosomatic illnesses, or to claim that any psychological disturbances affect human behavior. We should not explain someone's behavior by referring to his neurosis or psychosis. Indeed, according to this objection, if epiphenomenalism is true, the entire course of human history would have been exactly the same if human beings felt no joys or sorrows, had no hopes or fears, and sought no goals. But surely this is an absurd conclusion. Human hopes, fears, aspirations, and the like are intimately connected to the course of human events. Epiphenomenalism should, therefore, be rejected.

There are actually two different attacks on epiphenomenalism embodied in this one objection, one with some force and one quite mistaken. The first claims that it surely seems that the mental side of man has played a causal role in the lives of men. This, as we have seen, lies behind much of the initial plausibility of interactionism, and also counts against parallelism. We should, therefore, also count it against epiphenomenalism, although we should also remember that there may be overriding reasons for accepting epiphenomenalism. The second attack goes beyond the first and claims that if epiphenomenalism is true then the mental side of men is irrelevant to the course of human events. Although such a charge might be leveled at a parallelist who rejected both pre-established harmony and occasionalism, it is quite off the mark when applied to epiphenomenalism. The mistake in this claim is that from the fact that A does not cause B it is inferred that A is in no way relevant to whether or not B occurs. But this is a fallacious inference because if B is the cause of A, then B occurs only if A occurs. Therefore if A were not to occur, then B would not occur and the whole course of things could be changed. For example, assume that a certain brain process causes someone to pull the trigger of a gun and also has the causal by-product of a desire to kill someone. Thus, if the assassin of President Kennedy had not had that desire, then neither the brain process which caused it, nor the pulling of the trigger which also resulted from the brain process would have occurred. In such ways the mental side of man's nature is related to what happens even if epiphenomenalism is true. Thus we can reject the second prong of the first objection to epiphenomenalism while remembering the first.

SECOND OBJECTION TO EPIPHENOMENALISM:
THEORY MAKES ITS OWN JUSTIFICATION IMPOSSIBLE

The second objection has been stated by J. B. Pratt, who says,

To say that a thought is even in a minute degree a co-cause of the following thought would be to wreck [epiphenomenalism]. In the process known as reasoning, therefore, it is a mistake to suppose that consciousness of logical relations has anything whatever to do with the result. . . . We may happen to think logically; but if we do, this is not because logic had anything to do with our conclusion, but because the brain molecules shake down, so to speak, in a lucky fashion. It is plain, therefore, that no conclusion that we men can reach can ever claim to be based on logic. It is forever impossible to demonstrate that any thesis is logically necessary.[19]

From this Pratt further concludes the epiphenomenalist is in a hopeless position because he wants to assert that he can prove his own theory, but his own theory implies that proofs are impossible.

This is quite a popular objection which is usually raised against the determinist rather than the epiphenomenalist. However, because epiphenomenalism is committed to the claim that all mental phenomena have causes, the objection applies equally well or, more accurately, equally badly, to it, for this is a totally misguided objection to both views. Let us grant for the purposes of the discussion that every event, whether material or mental, is causally determined. Thus, each time I come to some conclusion I have been caused to do so by certain preceding events. Does it follow from this, first, that my conclusion has not been proved and, second, that I have not proved it? First, a conclusion is proved deductively, for example, when it is shown to follow deductively from true premises. It does not matter how it is shown or by whom or under what conditions. A computing machine can be used to derive certain conclusions, but this does not show that the conclusion has not been proved. A justification or proof of a claim depends on logical relations among statements, not on psychological and causal relations among thoughts or molecules. Thus, because epiphenomenalism makes claims about causal rather than logical relations, it does not imply that conclusions cannot be proved.

Second, epiphenomenalism does not imply that humans cannot prove conclusions even if we assume that to prove a conclusion is to

[19] J. B. Pratt, *Matter and Spirit* (New York: Macmillan, 1922).

proceed through certain steps of one's own free will, because epiphenomenalism does not deny either that humans are able to proceed through such steps or that they have free will. Epiphenomenalism does imply that I am caused to proceed through the steps of a proof, but this does not imply that I do not do it of my own free will. It is true that if causal determinism and free will are incompatible and if I am caused to do something, then I do not do it freely. However, although epiphenomenalism implies mental determinism, it does not imply that this is incompatible with free will. Furthermore, as we have seen previously in Chapter 3, there is reason to deny the thesis of incompatibility. We can, therefore, reject Pratt's objection to epiphenomenalism. The theory does not imply that no theory can be proved, so the epiphenomenalist can consistently claim that his theory is provable and that he can prove it. Whether he has proved it, however, is yet to be decided.

THIRD OBJECTION TO EPIPHENOMENALISM: REQUIRES NOMOLOGICAL DANGLERS

Herbert Feigl has stated the third objection to epiphenomenalism. He attempts to evaluate competing mind–body theories by giving them a comparative ranking much as we are doing. Feigl first ranks epiphenomenalism over interactionism, but then he rejects it for still another theory. He justifies his rejection of interactionism by claiming that it is inconsistent with a basic goal of science. According to Feigl, science should strive to reach the point where all behavior, human and nonhuman, can be explained and predicted by the physical sciences and the relevant publicly observable behavior. Consequently, he thinks that epiphenomenalism is preferable to interactionism, which requires private, that is, unobservable causes, and thus is incompatible with this goal of science.

Feigl rejects epiphenomenalism because he thinks it requires us to interpret certain scientific laws in a very peculiar way. He says,

> It accepts two fundamentally different sorts of laws—the usual causal laws and laws of psychophysiological correspondence. The physical (causal) laws connect the events in the physical world in the manner of a complex network, while the correspondence laws involve relations of physical events with purely mental "danglers." These correspondence laws are peculiar in

that they may be said to postulate "effects" (mental states as dependent variables) which by themselves do not function, or at least do not seem to be needed, as "causes" (independent variables) for any observable behavior.[20]

Feigl's objection to epiphenomenalism is that it requires that there be two quite different kinds of causal laws. Usually causal laws are laws expressing causal connections between events each of which is part of the continuing series of causes and effects that causally determines what occurs at each moment. Thus the usual causal laws relate events which, although caused, are themselves causal factors determining what occurs after them. However, if epiphenomenalism were true, then psychophysical laws—that is, laws relating mental and physical events—would be quite different. They would be laws expressing a causal relationship between physical events in causal chains and mental events that are neither part of a causal chain nor causally affect some chain. These mental events would be what Feigl has called "nomological danglers,"—that is, factors which, although integral components of certain laws, dangle uselessly because they are unnecessary for the explanation and prediction of human behavior. Feigl thinks that any theory that requires laws involving nomological danglers is inferior to a theory that requires only the usual kind of law. Consequently, although he thinks that epiphenomenalism is preferable to interactionism, which requires nonobservable *causes*, he also thinks that a theory that also does not require nonobservable *effects* would, in turn, be preferred to epiphenomenalism. As we shall see when we examine the double-language theory, Feigl thinks that he has found such a theory.

There are two things we can say about Feigl's argument. First, he rejects interactionism for reasons similar to those expressed in the second scientific objection. We saw that Broad does admit that interactionism leaves a gap in the physiological explanation of human behavior, but we have not yet decided how damaging this problem is. Second, although we can agree that if there were no other grounds available for choosing between two theories—if all else were equal—then we should accept the one that does not require nomological danglers, Feigl's objection by itself does not seem

---

[20] H. Feigl, "Mind-Body, *Not* a Pseudoproblem," in Hook, op. cit., p. 37.

particularly forceful. Although it shows that psychophysical laws would be unique if epiphenomenalism were true, it does not show that epiphenomenalism requires anything different of any scientific procedures of observation and experimentation. It has consequences only for how we interpret the laws based on what is observed. Such an objection then is surely not fatal and not even terribly damaging.

COMPARISON OF INTERACTIONISM AND EPIPHENOMENALISM

How do interactionism and epiphenomenalism compare when we weigh the various objections to each? We have found that both share two objections:

1. The objection from the problem of other minds.
2. The objection from the apparent lack of characteristics relevant to causal interaction.

We have also found that epiphenomenalism faces two objections which interactionism avoids:

3. The objection that epiphenomenalism denies what seems to be true, that mental events have causal efficacy.
4. The objection that epiphenomenalism requires nomological danglers.

And we have found two objections to interactionism avoided by epiphenomenalism:

5. The objection that interactionism requires something contrary to empirical evidence, namely, that there is a gap in a purely physiological explanation of human behavior.
6. The objection that interactionism requires that mental events causally affect the body in a way that either is inexplicably mysterious or violates a scientific principle.

How are we to evaluate the relative strength of these objections, and consequently how are we to decide between the two theories?

It surely appears that objection (5) is the most serious because it ac-
cuses interactionism of requiring something that conflicts with
empirical evidence. It would seem, then, that the seriousness of (5)
outweighs that of (4), and perhaps we should discount the seeming
efficacy of mental events and choose epiphenomenalism over interactionism. However, before making this decision let us look once
again at objection (5), because it has become crucial.

We have been accepting that what Broad says about the place of
mental events in the explanation of human behavior correctly states
what is required by interactionism. We have been assuming that
one of the most likely ways that mental events affect the body is by
varying the resistance of certain nerve synapses in the brain and
thereby changing the paths of certain nerve impulses. It seems
obvious, then, that we must include something like the effect of the
mental events on the resistance of synapses if we are to explain
certain human behavior. Thus objection (5) seems cogent. Nevertheless it may be that interactionism can avoid it. It is true that if
mental events do causally affect the brain, then a *complete* explanation must include mental causes. But it is not clear that an explanation adequate for all the needs of the physiologist must be a
complete explanation.

Let us assume that every event, whether material or mental, has
a cause. Given this, it is possible that a certain kind of brain event,
call it *B*, is always followed by a certain kind of nerve impulse, call
it *N*, and also a certain kind of mental event, *M*. Assume also that
the paths of nerve impulses depend on the relative resistances of
synapses and that mental events can causally affect these resistances.
Given all this, then we can see how *M* could be caused by *B* and
how *M* could, in turn, causally affect the path of *N* by causally
affecting the resistance of certain synapses, as in Figure 3. The
consequence of this is that, given the occurrence of *B*, *N* always is
caused to take a certain path because of the effect of *B* on *M* and *M*
on the synapses. From what the neurophysiologist could observe,
however, there would seem to be no need of a mental cause in his
explanation of the neural events. It would seem that *B* alone caused
N to take a certain path, as in Figure 4. A neurophysiologist might
even take this to be a case of proximate causation and thus consider
it to be a brute fact not itself explainable. At any rate he could explain
and predict all human behavior to which *B*, *N*, and *M* are causally
relevant without any need of a mental cause. Thus his explanation

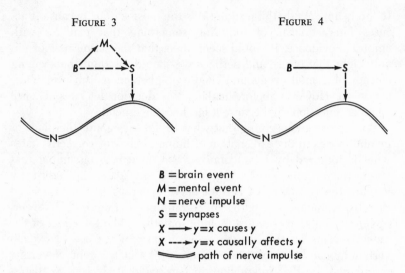

Figure 3

Figure 4

B = brain event
M = mental event
N = nerve impulse
S = synapses
X ⟶ y = x causes y
X ---→ y = x causally affects y
⟿ path of nerve impulse

is both purely physiological and scientifically adequate. But in an important sense it is not complete because it omits one causal factor, mental event M. Consequently, dualistic interactionism is, contrary to objection (5), consistent with the observed evidence that no mental causes are needed for explanations of human behavior that meet all the requirements of the physiologist.

Interactionism, then, is consistent with there being no gap in physiological explanations, and it is also consistent with there being gaps that require mental causes. This distinguishes it from many competing theories. Therefore instead of the lack of an observed gap counting against interactionism, the possibility of mental causes would count in favor of interactionism if further examination gives evidence of a gap requiring mental causes. Where people who raise objection (5) may have gone wrong is in thinking that interactionism implies that causal determinism does not apply to mental events, so that there would be no way of establishing how M would affect synapses. Thus, given only B and N, there would be no way of knowing which path N would take. But interactionism is consistent with complete causal determinism.

Let us return to our comparative evaluation of interactionism and epiphenomenalism now that we have rejected objection (5) to interactionism. Although interactionism, unlike epiphenomenalism, requires no nomological danglers and can accommodate the plausible belief that mental events causally affect the body, it avoids these problems only by requiring an inexplicable kind of effect of the mental on the physical. Neither theory, then, is completely satisfactory. But is one more reasonable than the other? We have agreed that the interactionist can at least neutralize the damage of objection (6) by claiming what is inexplicable is the immediate effect of mental events on the brain, and no cases of immediate causation are explicable. On the basis of this we can conclude that interactionism faces less serious objections than epiphenomenalism, and so interactionism is the more reasonable of the two. We can further conclude that interactionism is the most plausible dualism, because we have previously rejected both versions of parallelism. Nevertheless, it still faces objections which some different theory may be able to avoid. If we are to find such a theory, we must turn to monistic theories, the most well known of which is reductive materialism.

MATERIALISM

Materialism is generally considered to be the chief opponent of dualistic interactionism. It is the theory that whatever exists is material and that what is taken to be mental, and thus immaterial, either does not exist or is really identical with something material. The classical exposition of this theory occurs in the philosophy of Hobbes, although Hobbes, like many other materialists as we shall see, has trouble being completely consistent. At the center of Hobbes' materialism is his conception of sense, which he claims is the source of all man's thoughts, imaginings, dreams, and remembrances, "for there is no conception in a man's mind, which hath not at first, totally or by parts, been begotten upon the organs of sense. The rest are derived from that original."[21] His materialism becomes clear when he says that sense is "some internal motion in the sentient, generated by some internal motion, of the parts of the object,

[21] Hobbes, *Hobbes Selections,* edited by F. J. E. Woodbridge (New York: Scribner's, 1930), p. 139.

and propagated through all the media to the innermost part of the organ."[22] Thus for Hobbes all that exists is either a material object or some physical event consisting of some material objects in motion. Certain of these physical motions are what constitute sense and, consequently, the whole realm of the mental. Hobbes, then, does not deny the existence of mental phenomena. Rather, he appears to be reducing them to motion and thus to material phenomena.

Because of his reduction of the mental to physical motion, Hobbes can go beyond his claim of materialism to an assertion of mechanism. In his introduction to the *Leviathan* he says,

> For seeing life is but a motion of limbs, the beginning whereof is in some principle part within; why may we not say, that all *automata* (engines that move themselves by springs and wheels as doth a watch) have an artificial life? For what is the *heart,* but a *spring;* and the *nerves* but so many *strings,* and the *joints* but so many *wheels,* giving motion to the whole body such as was intended by the artificer?[23]

On this view living things, including man, are no different from nonliving things. They are in principle just like a machine such as a watch, although much more complicated. We can explain and predict all the motions of machines and their parts by applying the laws of mechanics to our knowledge of the spatial locations and masses of the relevant material objects and the forces acting upon them. By similar uses of these laws we can, according to Hobbes, explain all the behavior of living things. According to Hobbes, then, everything is some kind of material object, and the science of mechanics is sufficient to explain and predict the behavior of everything, living and nonliving. Hobbes, then, is not only a materialist but also a mechanist. However, Hobbes' mechanism is not essential to his materialism, because materialism does not imply mechanism. It is possible that everything is material and some events happen by chance and, consequently, are neither explainable nor predictable

[22] Ibid., p. 107.
[23] Ibid., p. 136.

by the science of mechanics. Because we are here interested only in materialism we need not consider mechanism further.

It follows from Hobbes' materialistic solution to the mind–body problem that the science of psychology is reducible to or replaceable by physics although the converse is not true—that is, if psychology is reducible to physics, it does not follow that living things are no different in principle from nonliving things. What follows is only that the data of psychology are no different from the data of physics. For example, if it is claimed that the data of psychology are only behavior, that is, overt motions and sounds of human bodies, then psychology might well be reducible to physics, in the sense that we could explain and predict with physical laws all the behavior that we could explain and predict with psychological laws.

One view clearly consistent with this view of psychology as behavioristic but inconsistent with materialism is epiphenomenalism, which, as we have just seen, states that whereas certain material processes cause and indeed give rise to mental states and events, these states and events have no effect on any material processes or even on other mental processes. Consequently, if epiphenomenalism is true, then a behavioristic psychology is sufficient to explain and predict all human behavior, but materialism is false. Other vews consistent with a behavioristic psychology but not with materialism are a neutral identity theory, which will be discussed later, and parallelism, which, although dualistic, denies mind–body interaction and thereby is compatible with a completely physicalistic explanation of human behavior.

Nevertheless, although there are good reasons to class Hobbes as a materialist, there are passages in his writings where he sounds more like a dualist of the epiphenomenalist variety. This is apparent when he says that "sense, in all cases, is nothing else but original fancy, caused, as I have said, by the pressure, that is by the motion, of external things upon our eyes, ears, and other organs there unto ordained."[24] Sense, then, is fancy, and fancy is, according to Hobbes, the appearance of motion rather than motion itself, contrary to Hobbes' previous characterization of sense as motion. But if sense is appearance, then it would seem that there are not only material objects in motion or at rest, but also appearances that are quite

[24] Ibid., p. 140.

different. Hobbes is thus faced with the central problem for materialists: how to incorporate into their theory that which seems to be completely alien to it, that is, appearances such as hallucinations, dreams, and mental images, and such other phenomena as sensations, emotions, and thoughts.

At the beginning of the discussion it was stated that a materialist could try to handle mental phenomena in either of two ways. He might admit, as did Hobbes, that there are mental phenomena, such as sensations, but claim that they are really reducible to something material. If he were to do this, he would be what we shall call a "reductive" materialist. However, he might deny there are any mental entities at all. If he were to do this, he would be what we shall call an "eliminative" materialist. On the face of it, neither attempt looks very promising. The first attempt seems to be self-contradictory, for in saying that all mental phenomena are really material, the materialist seems to be saying that all nonmaterial phenomena are really material. Another way to see this is to point out that saying that all mental events are really material events seems to be equivalent to saying that all events involving only objects with no size, shape, mass, and so on, are really events involving only objects with size, shape, mass, and so on. This again is self-contradictory. Consequently, it seems that the materialist cannot handle mental phenomena in this way. The second way seems to be little better, however, because if he denies that there are mental phenomena he seems clearly to be denying that there are thoughts, feelings, desires, hopes, dreams, and even pains. But surely any theory that denies the existence of such phenomena is false, because if there is anything each of us can be certain about it is that we are aware of feelings, desires, pains and the like. Furthermore, because just being aware or conscious is a mental state, we would have to deny that anyone is conscious or aware of things. But as Descartes pointed out, although each of us can doubt the existence of almost everything including other minds, he cannot doubt that he is doubting, and if he is doubting, he is conscious. Thus that at least one being is in the mental state of consciousness seems to be an undeniable fact. If a theory implies the contrary, then we have good reason for rejecting the theory. Consequently, the second way the materialist could try to handle mental phenomena seems to be no more helpful than the first.

Can we, as a consequence of the preceding discussion, reject materialism without further discussion? It seems not, because there have been several quite recent attempts to rescue materialism from the preceding predicament. Let us first consider two theories proposed as ways to save eliminative materialism. The first, known as analytical or logical behaviorism, attempts to avoid the problem facing eliminative materialism by analyzing the meaning of psychological expressions of language in terms of purely physicalistic expressions. This elimination of the need for psychological terms is thought to justify a corresponding elimination of psychological entities. A second theory concentrates on the reference or denotation of psychological terms, instead of their meaning, in order to eliminate psychological entities. This attempt utilizes what is called the "double-language theory" because it claims that there are two quite different sorts of ways to refer to certain physical entities. Psychological terms and certain physicalistic terms refer to, or denote, or name the very same entities, namely, certain physical processes in human bodies. As can be seen, both theories approach a substantive philosophical issue by an explicit examination of certain features of language. In this respect they exemplify the recent trend in Great Britain and the United States to take a linguistic approach to philosophy. It is the vew of many of these linguistic philosophers that language holds the key to the final termination of the problems and puzzles that have perplexed philosophers for centuries.

ANALYTICAL BEHAVIORISM AND ELIMINATIVE MATERIALISM

Analytical behaviorism is the theory that all sentences using psychological or mentalistic terms are transformable by analyses of what they mean into sentences using no psychological terms, but using only terms that refer to some kind of bodily behavior. This theory, then, claims that although there are many true sentences using psychological terms, we do not have to infer from this that these terms refer to mental objects, events, and states, because we can reformulate every one of these sentences in such a way that we use only terms that refer to material objects, events, and states. Consequently, the analytical behaviorist admits that sentences such as 'I like you,' 'Smith believes that it is raining,' and 'Jones suffers from inferiority feelings' are in many cases true. Therefore he is not committed to defending the implausible sentence 'There are no mental phenomena such as beliefs and feelings.' But having made this admission, he claims that he can still consistently be a materialist because to admit that a sentence is true is not to commit oneself to what it refers to. The analytical behaviorist says psychological sentences really refer to human bodily behavior, and he attempts to show this by the way he analyzes their meanings. It seems, then, that by considering language, by "operating on a semantical plane," the materialist may be able to avoid the predicament just described.

Before we move on to evaluate critically analytical behaviorism, there are two other things we should do. The first is to distinguish analytical behaviorism from methodological behaviorism, a distinction often ignored, and the second is to explain the concept of analysis relevant to analytical behaviorism. In discussing Hobbes' position we claimed that a behavioristic psychology is consistent with epiphenomenalism and also parallelism. It is also consistent with the deterministic version of interactionism developed when we discussed the objection to interactionism based upon an allegedly required gap in physiological explanation. Thus a behavioristic psychology is consistent with all the mind–body dualisms we have discussed. This is because a behavioristic psychology, as we saw, takes the only subject matter of psychology to be human bodily behavior, but it need not decree that there are no mental phenomena. The theory that proposes this kind of psychology has been called behaviorism. But because it is a theory only about the methodology of the science of psychology, it would be better to call it "methodological behaviorism." We can see, then, that methodological behaviorism, the behaviorism relevant to the science of psychology, is consistent with a mind–body dualism as well as with materialism. Thus it differs markedly from analytical behaviorism. Analytical behaviorism, as interpreted here, entails materialism, but methodological behaviorism does not, because it is consistent with dualism. It is true that many methodological behaviorists, especially such early ones as Watson, seem to have thought that materialism is implied by methodological behaviorism, but this is because they did

not distinguish sufficiently between statements about the methodological requirements of science and statements that assert metaphysical positions.

In discussing analytical behaviorism we are interested in analyzing what certain linguistic expressions mean, and therefore we are
interested in what is called meaning analysis. This can be defined
as the linguistic method that analyzes the meaning of a linguistic
expression (the analysandum) in either of two ways. The first is by
providing another linguistic expression (the analysans) synonymous
with the analysandum. The second way is by providing expressions
such that (1) each is synonymous with certain key expressions containing the analysandum, and (2) none contains any expression
synonymous with the analysandum. The first kind of meaning
analysis is explicit definition and the second is contextual definition.
The distinction between these two is important because only the
latter is relevant to analytical behaviorism, as some examples will
show. We can give an explicit definition of 'human' by saying that
'human' equals by definition 'rational animal,' or, as we shall state it:

'human' = $_{df.}$ 'rational animal'

We would explicitly define 'bachelor' as follows:

'bachelor' = $_{df.}$ 'unmarried male'

On the other hand, we could begin to give a contextual definition
of the term 'existent' by seeing that a sentence such as, 'Many
strange things are existent,' can be analyzed as:

'Many strange things are existent' = $_{df.}$ 'There are many strange
things.'

Here in the analysans there is no word or phrase synonymous with
'existent.'

Let us now see why only contextual definitions are relevant to
analytical behaviorism. Consider the following sentence:

The average American family has 1.3 cars.

Let us assume that it is true, that we convince someone it is true, and that he then exclaims that he had never before realized that there was in the United States a family with a fraction of a car. We would of course try to explain to him that he had misunderstood what we meant. We were not talking about—referring to—a real family. Although the sentence is true, there really is no such family. This might leave our friend completely puzzled. How can that sentence be true and there not be such a family? What we would have to do is show him that average families are in an important way eliminable unlike ordinary families. The problem in eliminating this average-family is like that of the eliminative materialist. We cannot identify this average family with some ordinary family, for that would seem to imply that somewhere there really is a family with 1.3 cars. What would we do to eliminate this average-family? We would try to restate the whole sentence in such a way that no expression in it seems to refer to an average family, but only to ordinary families. For this purpose an explicit definition will not help. Suppose in the preceding sentence we replace 'the average American family,' with the following analysans:

the American family which has the average number of cars.

Here we have attempted to provide an explicit definition. Will it help our mistaken friend? Not at all, because the analysans of 'the average American family' we have provided is an expression that seems to refer to that same strange family. We can help our friend, however, if we contextually define 'the average American family' by providing a sentence synonymous with the puzzling sentence but containing no phrase synonymous with 'the average American family.' Consider the following:

The number of family-run cars in the United States divided by the number of American families equals 1.3.

Here we do not have 'the average American family' or any expression synonymous with it. We only have expressions that refer to ordinary families and cars, and no one need wonder about the strange family with its fractional car. We have "analyzed away" a very strange kind of entity by a contextual definition because we have shown that no expression that seems to refer to such an entity needs to be used. We need only use expressions that refer to ordinary entities. Thus if we are to analyze away certain entities, we cannot use explicit definitions. Only contextual definitions can help. Let us see if they can help the analytical behaviorist.

AN ATTEMPT TO JUSTIFY ANALYTICAL BEHAVIORISM: VERIFIABILITY CRITERION OF MEANING

Many people would doubt that sentences involving psychological terms could be contextually defined in terms of sentences containing only behavioral terms. There are others, however, who say that no matter how difficult it may be to find adequate contextual definitions of this kind, it can nevertheless be done. This confidence in analytical behaviorism was expressed by Carl Hempel, who at one time claimed:

All psychological statements which are meaningful, that is to say, which are in principle verifiable, are translatable into propositions which do not involve psychological concepts, but only the concepts of physics. The propositions of psychology are consequently physicalistic propositions. Psychology is an integral part of physics.[25]

An example of a psychological sentence which Hempel claims to be verifiable, thus meaningful and translatable into a physicalistic sentence, is a statement "that Mr. Jones suffers from intense inferiority feelings of such and such kinds. . . ."[26] Because this sentence can only be confirmed or falsified by observing Jones' behavior, the sentence "means only this: such and such happenings take place in Mr. Jones' body in such and such circumstances."[27]

It is important to note that although a statement such as 'Jones suffers from inferiority feelings *a*, *b*, and *c*,' which we can call sentence *J*, does not seem to mean or to be translatable into any kind of physicalistic sentence, there is nothing else such a sentence can mean, given Hempel's criterion of meaning, if it is to be considered

[25] C. Hempel, "The Logical Analysis of Psychology," in H. Feigl and W. Sellars, eds., *Readings in Philosophical Analysis* (New York: Appleton-Century-Crofts, 1949), p. 378.
[26] Ibid.
[27] Ibid.

a meaningful sentence. We can put Hempel's point into a deductive argument as follows:

i. The conditions of the verification of *J* are Jones' behavior under such and such conditions.
ii. The meanings of sentences are the conditions of their verification.
Therefore
iii. The meaning of *J* is Jones' behavior under such and such conditions.

Because *J* is no different from other psychological sentences, this argument can be generalized to conclude that the meaning of any psychological sentence is the behavior of some person or persons under certain conditions. Consequently, given the preceding argument, it follows that for each psychological sentence we can find a physicalistic sentence having the same meaning. And because the relevant physicalistic sentences are about certain bodily events and states, we can conclude that all psychological sentences can be analyzed into sentences using only behavioral terms—that is, analytical behaviorism is true. But, of course, the crucial question is whether Hempel's argument is sound. It surely seems acceptable if there is good reason to accept premise (ii), because all we need do to justify premise (i) for any particular psychological sentence is to find out the particular way we actually verify it when we observe human behavior. But premise (ii) is by no means obvious.

If we look at premise (ii) it can be seen that it embodies a specific theory about the meaning of sentences. This is the kind of theory that any linguistic approach on the semantic level must consider. The particular theory offered by Hempel is the one proposed over the last forty years by those philosophers known as logical positivists or logical empiricists.[28] It is the position of these philosophers that there are only two different kinds of sentences which are literally either true or false. All other sentences lack truth-value. Everyone agrees that there are kinds of sentences which lack truth-

[28] For the classical statement of logical positivism, see A. J. Ayer, *Language, Truth and Logic* (New York: Dover, 1952).

value, that is, are neither true nor false, but the logical positivist rejects more sentences than most others. We would all agree that sentences which express commands (such as 'Shut the door!'), sentences which are used to ask questions (such as 'Where are you going?'), sentences which express feelings (such as 'Hurrah for the home team!'), and several other kinds of sentences are neither true nor false. But most of us think that sentences such as 'God created heaven and earth and all things,' 'We ought to help others,' 'This is a beautiful picture,' and 'The mind is distinct from the body' are either true or false. That is, we think that religious, ethical, aesthetic, and metaphysical utterances are, by and large, either true or false. But here the logical positivist disagrees, because he thinks that the only kinds of sentences that have truth-values are those that are empirically verifiable and those that are analytically true or false. The positivist, then, holds the view that if a sentence is not analytically true or false and there is no possible way to verify it by observation, then we should conclude that the sentence is neither true nor false, but rather plays some different role in language. Such a theory has been called the *verifiability criterion of meaning.* Thus many ethical, aesthetic, religious, and metaphysical utterances are not analytically true or false and are not verifiable by observation, and hence positivists have claimed that they function to express certain feelings or desires or hopes of speakers rather than to assert something either true or false.

Hempel has claimed in his second premise that the meanings of sentences are the conditions of their verification so that if there is no possible way to verify a sentence, then it has no truth-value and is what we can call cognitively meaningless. Thus premise (ii) implies the verifiability criterion of meaning, because if the meaning of sentences are the conditions of their verification, then all cognitively meaningful sentences are verifiable. Consequently, if there is reason to reject the verifiability criterion, then there is reason to reject Hempel's premise. Incidentally, it should be noted that the verifiability criterion does not imply Hempel's premise, because it might be true that sentences are empirically verifiable and thereby cognitively *meaningful*, but false that the meaning of sentences are the conditions of their verification. Consequently, even if the verifiability criterion is acceptable, Hempel's premise is still confronted with the additional problem of justifying its claim about what the meaning of a sentence is. However, because we shall find enough reasons to cast doubt on the verifiability criterion we need not examine the additional problem here.

There is one problem for the verifiability criterion of meaning that we shall not examine even though it is critical. It is this. The criterion is supposed to separate certain sentences from others on the basis of empirical verifiability, and although it seems intuitively evident where the division should be made, no one has yet provided a definition of verifiability that is at all adequate for the job. Each attempt at an adequate definition has either been so broad it allows obvious nonsense to count as meaningful, or it has been so narrow that it has excluded many sentences vital to empirical sciences. Thus the criterion is of no use in deciding whether or not a particular sentence is meaningful. But because it has not yet been shown that there can be no adequate definition we should not rest the case against the criterion on this problem.[29]

The most serious problem for the verifiability criterion of meaning is that it seems to be self-defeating. It claims that the only true sentences are analytic sentences and empirically verifiable sentences. Consequently, the criterion itself, if it is true, must be either analytic or empirically verifiable. But it is not analytic, because there is nothing self-contradictory about the claim that some nonanalytic, nonverifiable sentences are true. Indeed it would seem that most people untutored in theories of meaning would reject the criterion as false because they think many religious and ethical utterances, among others, are true. Consequently, it does not seem to be a generalization based upon empirical observation of the actual ways in which people use and respond to sentences. It seems, then, to be neither analytic nor empirically verifiable. Some positivists, recognizing this problem, have claimed that this is merely a proposal about what we should consider meaningful and have backed up their proposal by saying that it is surely necessary for a meaningful language of empirical science. But although it may well be that the language of science should meet an adequate verifiability cri-

---

[29] For detailed but difficult discussions of this problem, see I. Scheffler, *The Anatomy of Inquiry* (New York: Knopf, 1963), pp. 150–54; D. Makinson, "Nidditch's Definition of Verifiability," *Mind* (April, 1965); and J. W. Cornman, "Indirectly Verifiable: Everything or Nothing," *Philosophical Studies* (June, 1967).

terion of meaning, this provides no reason to think that any other meaningful area of language must meet similar requirements.

In short, we have found good reason to reject the verifiability criterion. It is acceptable only if there is reason to think that it is true of the way things are or that it is a sound proposal about the way things should be. But we have found no reason to accept it as a proposal and good reason to reject its truth, because it is not either analytic or empirically verifiable, as the criterion itself requires of all true sentences. Consequently, because Hempel's premise (ii) implies the verifiability criterion, we should reject the premise as well as the criterion.

We must give up the short road to analytical behaviorism and try the longer, more difficult route. That is, we must see whether analytical behaviorism is justified by trying to provide some specific contextual definitions of particular psychological sentences. If we meet with some success, then there is reason to accept analytical behaviorism; if we have no success, then we should reject it.

AN OBJECTION TO ANALYTICAL BEHAVIORISM: CANNOT ANALYZE BELIEF SENTENCES

One philosopher who claims that the program of analytical behaviorism will not be accomplished is Roderick Chisholm. He has been willing to rest his whole case against the analysis of psychological sentences in terms of behavioral sentences upon the inability of anyone to analyze satisfactorily sentences containing 'believe.' In various articles he has shown that all the attempts made so far have failed to provide adequate analyses of belief sentences. The consequence of this, of course, is that because 'believe' is a psychological term, analytical behaviorism must be rejected. To see Chisholm's reasoning we must turn to examples of how he criticizes certain specific analyses. In each case he shows either that the analysans is not synonymous with the belief sentence or that it has been made synonymous only by using some technical term that is not needed to describe merely bodily phenomena. The second prong of Chisholm's attack is as important as the first because many people have tried to avoid psychological language not by translating it into behavioral language, but by coining scientific-sounding terms which seem to have only one function, namely, to avoid psychological terms. For example, some psychologists, instead of saying,

The subject of the experiment expects food.

say,

The subject of the experiment has an F-expectancy.

As Chisholm points out, such ploys cannot be considered as providing behavioral analyses of psychological sentences because "In all probability . . . the psychologist has only one means of conveying what such expressions as 'F-expectancy' or even 'food-expectancy' might mean; namely, he can tell us that an animal may be said to have food-expectancy if and only if the animal expects food."[30] Thus if certain technical terms require the use of certain usual psychological terms to explain their meanings, then analyses of psychological sentences containing such technical terms should not be used as cases supporting analytical behaviorism.

Let us examine the four main kinds of behavioral analysis Chisholm has considered, for in doing so we shall begin to see that behavioral analyses of belief sentences seem doomed to failure.[31] He considers in turn what he calls the "specific response" analysis, the "appropriate behavior" analysis, the "satisfaction" analysis, and the "verbal response" analysis. In each case we shall consider an analysis of the belief sentence:

Jones believes that there is a fire nearby.

According to the specific-response analysis we might try to analyze this sentence as:

Jones exhibits fire-responses to his immediate environment.

But we have a technical term, 'fire-responses,' in this analysis. How are we to explain what it means? An analytical behaviorist might say that:

---

[30] R. M. Chisholm, "Intentionality and the Theory of Signs," *Philosophical Studies* (1952).

[31] For Chisholm's discussion of these kinds of analysis, see *Perceiving* (Ithaca, N.Y.: Cornell University Press, 1957), pp. 168–73.

> Jones exhibits fire-responses.

means:

> Jones is exhibiting that behavior which he exhibits when and only when there is a fire.

But this will not do, because it entails that Jones believes that there is a fire when and only when there really is a fire. Jones, however, like all the rest of us, often believes things that are false. And, of course, it will do no good to patch up the analysis by saying 'when and only when *he thinks* that there is a fire' because 'thinks' is a psychological term. In this way, Chisholm refutes the specific-response analysis.

The appropriate-behavior analysis fares no better. This kind of analysis would analyze:

> Jones believes that there is a fire nearby.

as:

> Under circumstances relevant to there being a fire nearby, Jones would behave in a way appropriate to there being a fire nearby.

Here we have a purely behavioristic analysis which includes no special technical terms. Thus, unless there is reason to think that it is possible that one of the sentences is true and the other false, we can accept this analysis. What we need to do, then, is see whether we can think of a situation in which one sentence would be true and the other false. This is not hard to do. We can conceive of a case where Jones is involved in a fire drill and behaves just the way he would in a real fire. His behavior is certainly appropriate to there being a fire nearby. Let us also take this to be a case in which, unknown to anyone, a fire has broken out in the building just before the scheduled drill. Surely, then, Jones is behaving in circumstances relevant to there being a fire nearby. Thus the analysans is true. But Jones, knowing that this was merely the scheduled drill, believes that there is no fire nearby. Thus the analysandum is false and the analysis fails. In such a way Chisholm refutes the appropriate-behavior analysis.

The satisfaction analysis proposes to analyze:

> Jones believes that there is a fire nearby.

as:

> Jones is in a bodily state which would be satisfied if and only if a fire were to occur nearby.

Here again, although we have a purely behavioral analysis, we can conceive of numerous counterexamples to the claim that the two sentences are synonymous. We can conceive of a situation in which Jones has an uncontrollable urge to toast marshmallows over an open fire. He has the marshmallows on a stick and needs only a fire. Thus Jones is in a bodily state that would be satisfied if a fire were to occur nearby and that would be satisfied only if a fire were to occur nearby. But let us construct the situation in such a way that Jones has no means to start a fire and has searched everywhere for a fire but found none. He consequently believes that there is no fire nearby. Here the analysandum is false and the analysans true, so that once again an attempt at a behavioral analysis of a psychological sentence fails.

The last attempt we shall consider is the verbal-response analysis, which is favored by many linguistic philosophers, such as Rudolf Carnap. Carnap has analyzed such sentences as:

> Jones believes that there is a fire nearby.

as:

> Jones has relation B to 'There is a fire nearby' as a sentence in English.

The immediate reaction to this analysis is to point out that it uses a technical term, 'relation B,' which is needed only for analyzing away psychological terms. In reply to this attack on the analysis, however, it has been pointed out that people have relationships of various kinds to different verbal utterances and that it is part of the job of natural science to study them. Thus the preceding analysis, because it uses an expression which describes a relationship between people and language, is using an expression required whether or not it is used in an analysis of psychological sentences. Nevertheless, although this first objection may have been refuted, there remains the problem of explaining the meaning of 'relation *B*' without having to rely on psychological terms. This has not been done. Furthermore, because it is not necessary that someone understand English if he is to believe that there is a fire nearby, the explanation of what 'relation *B*' means cannot imply that Jones knows English. Thus an equally good analysans should be:

> Jones has relation *B* to 'Il y a un feu près d'ici' as a sentence in French.

We might try to explain the analysans by claiming that it means:

> Jones has *B*-responses to a sentence in his language synonymous with the English sentence, "There is a fire nearby."

However, not only does this sentence take us right back to the specific-response analysis, with its problems, but it would seem that the phrase 'in his language' means 'in the language he understands,' and 'understands' is surely a psychological term. Perhaps 'understands' can be avoided and '*B*-response' elucidated without relying on psychological terms, but so far no such attempts have succeeded. The verbal-response analysis, then, appears also headed for failure even though there are philosophers who still seek to perfect it.

We have examined four of the most plausible attempts to provide a behavioral analysis of belief sentences and have found reasons to reject the analysis offered in each case. With Chisholm we can conclude that it seems highly unlikely that any other behavioral analyses will fare better. Thus although we have not examined, and cannot examine, all possible behavioral analyses of psychological sentences, we have examined a sufficiently good sample to conclude that we should reject analytical behaviorism because it claims that belief sentences and all other psychological sentences can be given behavioral analyses. Consequently, if eliminative materialism is to be saved as a viable alternative to dualistic interactionism, we must depend upon the double-language theory.

THE DOUBLE-LANGUAGE THEORY AND ELIMINATIVE MATERIALISM

The double-language theory has been summarized as follows by Feigl, who has been its chief proponent:

> Certain neurophysiological terms denote (refer to) the very same events that are also denoted (referred to) by certain phenomenal terms. The identification of the objects of this twofold reference is of course logically contingent, although it constitutes a very fundamental feature of our world as we have come to conceive it in the modern scientific outlook. [We can say] that neurophysiological terms and the corresponding phenomenal terms, though widely differing in [meaning], and hence in the modes of confirmation of statements containing them, do have identical *referents*. I take these referents to be the immediately experienced qualities, or their configurations in various phenomenal fields.[32]

J. J. C. Smart maintains a thesis much the same as Feigl's but he states it specifically in terms of sensations and brain processes. He says that

> insofar as "after-image" or "ache" is a report of a process it is a report of a process that *happens to be* a brain process. It follows that the thesis does not claim that sensation statements can be *translated* into statements about brain processes. Nor does it claim that the logic of a sensation statement is the same as that of a brain-process statement. All it claims is that insofar as a sensation statement is a report of something, that something is in fact a brain process. Sensations are nothing over and above brain processes.[33]

There are three important features of the theories of these two men which we should carefully note.

---

[32] Feigl, op. cit., p. 38.

[33] J. J. C. Smart, "Sensations and Brain Processes," *The Philosophical Review*, 68 (1959), pp. 144–45.

First, both Feigl and Smart discuss certain expressions of language and what these expressions refer to or are used to talk about. Thus both men are taking a linguistic approach to the mind–body problem. But this should not be taken to mean that they are concerned only with language, because what the expressions refer to are not other linguistic expressions but some kinds of nonlinguistic phenomena. Thus both men are interested in getting from certain facts about language to certain conclusions about nonlinguistic reality.

Second, both men stress that the psychological expressions and the physiological expressions they are considering differ widely in meaning, so that the psychological sentences are not analyzable or translatable into physiological sentences. They claim only that these two different kinds of terms have the same *referents,* not that they have the same *meanings.* They claim, for example, that the expression 'brain process' has the same referents as the expression 'sensation,' but the two are clearly different in meaning. Consequently, although they are like analytical behaviorists in being linguistic philosophers, they are not analytical behaviorists, because they deny that psychological sentences are synonymous with behavioral sentences.

Third, although both Feigl and Smart are double-language theorists, there is one important point on which they disagree. As brought out in the preceding quotations, they have very different views about the common referents of psychological and certain physiological terms. Feigl claims that the common referents are immediately felt qualities, that is, feelings in their uninterpreted or raw state. Smart, on the other hand, claims that sensation terms refer to entities that are nothing but brain processes. These surely are not uninterpreted feelings. This is a most important difference for our purposes, because Smart's thesis, if generalized to include all psychological terms, becomes the theory of materialism, but Feigl's thesis is inconsistent with materialism, because on his view the referents are mental entities. Because we are here discussing materialism we shall concentrate primarily on Smart's materialistic version of the theory, which we can now see consists of two claims. The first is that psychological and certain physiological expressions have common referents, and the second is that this common referent is in every case material.

Any double-language theorist who holds the two preceding claims is a materialist, but this is not enough to determine whether he is an eliminative materialist or a reductive materialist. An example will help distinguish between these two kinds of double-language materialists. Consider a materialist who claims that, first, the psychological term 'experience of pain' denotes, or refers to, the very same things as the neurophysiological term 'firing of C-fibers,' and, second, these common referents are nothing but firings of C-fibers, that is, certain neural processes in brains that consist entirely of certain nerve cells being triggered to fire. Such a materialist is a double-language theorist. If he further claims that there really are no experiences of pains or other sensations, he is an eliminative materialist. If, however, he claims instead that the reason the two terms have common referents is because each experience of pain is identical with a firing of C-fibers, then he is not an eliminative materialist, because if experiences of pains are identical with actual brain processes, then there are experiences of pain. He is instead a reductive materialist. Smart, for example, is a reductive materialist. He claims not only that 'sensation' and 'brain process' have common referents, but also that sensations are nothing over and above brain processes, that is, sensations are really reducible to, and thereby identical with—the same thing as—certain brain processes. We shall examine this thesis later, but let us first consider the double-language theorist who is also an eliminative materialist.

The chief objection to an eliminative materialist is that he must claim that whenever anyone says, even with complete sincerity and conviction, "I have a sharp, throbbing, aching pain," what he is reporting, or actually referring to, is never a pain which is aching, throbbing, or sharp, but rather something extremely different from a pain, namely, a purely physiological neural process. But this is initially extremely implausible, indeed, even quite absurd. Could there possibly be a way to defend such an initially implausible thesis?

A DEFENSE OF ELIMINATIVE MATERIALISM: AN ANALOGY BETWEEN DEMONS AND PAINS

Richard Rorty, who is an eliminative materialist, provides a defense by drawing an analogy between the use of strange demons by a primitive tribe to explain illnesses and our own present use of pains and other sensations to explain certain human behavior. He first describes this imaginary tribe:

A certain primitive tribe holds the view that illnesses are caused by demons—a different demon for each sort of illness. When asked what more is known about these demons than that they cause illness, they reply that certain members of the tribe—the witch-doctors—can see, after a meal of sacred mushrooms, various (intangible) humanoid forms on or near the bodies of patients. The witch-doctors have noted, for example, that a blue demon with a long nose accompanies epileptics, a fat red one accompanies sufferers from pneumonia, etc. They know such further facts as that the fat red demon dislikes a certain sort of mold which the witch-doctors give people who have pneumonia. If we encountered such a tribe, we would be inclined to tell them that there are no demons. We would tell them that diseases were caused by germs, viruses, and the like. We would add that the witch-doctors were not seeing demons, but merely having hallucinations.[34]

He then uses the analogy to dispel the initial absurdity of claiming that no one has pains:

The absurdity of saying "Nobody has ever felt a pain" is no greater than that of saying "Nobody has ever seen a demon," if we have a suitable answer to the question "what was I reporting when I said I felt a pain?" To this question, the science of the future may reply "You were reporting the occurrence of a certain brain-process, and it would make life simpler for us if you would, in the future, say 'My C-fibers are firing' instead of saying 'I'm in pain.'" In so saying, he has as good a *prima facie* case as the scientist who answers the witch-doctors' question "What was I reporting when I reported a demon?" by saying "You were reporting the content of your hallucina-

[34] R. Rorty, "Mind-Body Identity, Privacy, and Categories," *Review of Metaphysics* (1965–1966), pp. 28–29.

tion, and it would make life simpler if, in the future, you would describe your experiences in those terms."[35]

On this view, then, it will be reasonable to eliminate sensations in the future if, as is likely, the somewhat primitive, explanatory function of sensation terms is replaced by the more advanced terms of physiology. At that point, we will be justified in casting sensations away as we already have done with demons.

If Rorty's analogy with demons succeeds, then he has a rebuttal to the strong objection to rejecting his theory; if it does not succeed, then we shall have reason to reject this theory. Rorty realizes that there is an important disanalogy between the two cases, but he fails to see it destroys his defense. He has provided the eliminative materialist with an answer to the question of what I report when I say I have a pain, but, unlike the demon case, he has not provided any plausible way to explain why there is such a widespread mistake of believing and reporting that there are pains. And he must provide such an explanation instead of merely an answer if he is to rebut the charge that his theory implies an absurdity. Scientists explain why the witch doctors believe they see demons by stating that eating sacred mushrooms causes them to have hallucinations of demons, and these hallucinations fool the witch doctors who believe they are actual demons. An eliminative materialist, however, cannot use hallucinations to explain why we mistakenly believe we experience pains, because even if it made sense to talk of an hallucination of a pain, these hallucinations would be mental objects rather than neural states, and some mental entities would not be eliminated. Furthermore, there seems to be nothing else a materialist could use to explain our common mistake of believing and reporting certain occurrences, which are merely neural processes, to be sharp, throbbing, and aching pains. Thus the absurdity remains, and this attempt to defend eliminative materialism fails.

With the failure of this last attempt, we can conclude that eliminative materialism should be rejected. There seems to be no way to make plausible the complete elimination of sensations. Nevertheless, materialism is not thereby refuted, because reductive materialism remains unscathed. By claiming that sensations are nothing

[35] Ibid., pp. 30–31.

but, and therefore are identical with brain processes, it rejects the claim that no one has pains, and thus avoids the objection that is fatal to the eliminative version.

THE IDENTITY THEORY AND
REDUCTIVE MATERIALISM

The crucial claim of a reductive materialist is that mental entities, such as sensations, are nothing over and above certain physical entities, such as brain processes. This reductive claim states *more* than that each sensation is the same thing as some brain process, because the use of the phrase 'nothing over and above' also implies that sensations have *only* the physiological properties of certain brain processes. Thus they are said to have no psychological properties, in spite of the way it may seem. This is clearly essential to a reductive materialist, because he claims that sensations are really material entities.

Notice that someone can hold the identity theory without also being a reductionist. We have seen that Feigl is not a materialist. There is also the seventeenth-century philosopher, Spinoza, who sounds much like a reductive materialist when he says, "the mind and the body are one and the same thing conceived at one time under the attribute of thought [that is, when understood as mental], and at another under the attribute of extension [that is, when understood as physical]."[36] But Spinoza disagrees with materialists when he goes on to claim that what is conceived in these two different ways is neither mental nor material because it has both physical properties and mental properties. Let us call this version of the identity theory the "neutral theory" because it proposes entities that are neither mental nor material. Spinoza, then, is an identity theorist, but not a materialist.

A materialist requires a reductive version of the identity theory, and this raises the crucial objection to his theory. Unlike Spinoza,

---

[36] B. Spinoza, *Spinoza Selections*, edited by John Wild (New York: Scribner's, 1930), p. 209.

he must claim that whenever anyone says, even with complete sincerity and conviction, "I have a sharp, throbbing, aching pain," what he is reporting is never a pain which is sharp, throbbing, and aching, but rather a pain which has the purely material properties of the neural brain phenomenon with which it is identical. Thus although, unlike an eliminative materialist, he can agree that we often report pains, he must deny that we ever report something which has the psychological properties of being sharp, throbbing and aching, because pains never have those nonmaterial properties. But this is initially extremely implausible, indeed, even quite absurd. Could there possibly be a way to defend such an initially implausible thesis?

A DEFENSE: CENTRAL STATE MATERIALISM

The only remotely plausible defense of the claim that there are sensations but they lack all psychological properties, is one that construes sensations as entities postulated to explain certain sorts of bodily behavior. For example, when we see someone injured, writhing, and screaming, we postulate that the injury has caused him to experience pain, and we explain the writhing and screaming as caused by this experience. On this view, such experiences are essentially understood in terms of the roles they have in these causal explanations of behavior. As one materialist says, "The definitive characteristic of any experience as such is its causal role."[37] Given the additional plausible premise that all bodily behavior is in principle explainable in terms of the physiological processes and states of a person's central nervous system, this materialist goes on to conclude that these central physiological states have the definitive causal explanatory roles of experiences. Consequently, he argues, each experience is nothing over and above a materialistic state of a central nervous system. This is central-state materialism.

There are three objections to this argument. First, although we generally do assign causal explanatory roles to sensations and experiences, we certainly do believe that in our own cases we immediately experience certain properties of sensations which they have

[37] D. Lewis, "An Argument for the Identity Theory," *The Journal of Philosophy*, LXIII (1966), p. 19.

whether or not they have any causal relationships to any of our bodily behavior. To think that all the properties that pains actually have are to be discovered or postulated by science is to treat one's own sensations as if they belonged to someone else. Surely each person is directly aware of some properties of his own sensations and experiences.

But, second, even if we assume that each psychological state has certain definitive causal relationships and that physiology is in principle adequate to explain all human behavior, we need not conclude that these psychological states are identical with central states. We have seen how a dualistic interactionist can accept the explanatory adequacy of physiology if he postulates a certain sort of causal role for mental entities. Each one would be caused by some brain event and would in turn causally affect another brain event in a way that leaves no gap in the adequacy of physiological explanations of behavior.

Furthermore, third, even if we reject dualism and agree that each psychological state is identical with a state of a person's central nervous system, it does not follow from this that these states are material states. They would have certain physiological properties because of their causal role in physiological explanations, but they also could have those psychological properties that each person so intimately experiences them to have in his own case. For these three reasons, then, this argument in defense of reductive material-ism fails. It does not succeed in dispelling the initial absurdity in the thesis of a reductive materialist about pains and other sensations.

With the failure of this, the most plausible attempt to defend reductive materialism, we can conclude that materialism, whether eliminative or reductive, should be rejected. There seems to be no way to make plausible either the complete elimination of sensations with their psychological properties or the stripping of all psycho-logical properties from sensations. Nevertheless, although this one monistic theory is refuted, neither the double-language theory nor mind–body monism has been refuted, because a neutral or nonre-ductive version of the identity theory remains unscathed. By agree-ing that psychological states are brain states having both psycho-logical and physiological properties, this neutral theory avoids the defeating objections to the three materialistic theories we examined. By relying on the double-language theory, it does not require a behavioral analysis of psychological sentences. Thus it avoids what

refutes analytical behaviorism. And by retaining sensations and
their psychological properties, it avoids the objections to Rorty's
version of eliminative materialism and to central-state materialism.
Furthermore, as we shall see, it also avoids all but one of the objections to the various dualistic theories. This neutral monistic theory
is, then, most appealing.

THE NEUTRAL VERSION OF THE IDENTITY THEORY

Let us see how easily the neutral identity theory avoids the objections that have plagued the various forms of mind–body dualism.
This will clearly show the advantages of the theory.

1. *Epiphenomenalism.* The neutral identity theory avoids both of
the objections that we have seen uniquely face epiphenomenalism.
First, epiphenomenalism denies what seems to be true, that mental
events causally affect the body. The identity theory, however, by
identifying sensations and the like with brain phenomena, asserts
that mental events do causally affect the body because brain processes obviously affect the body. Second, as Feigl points out, epiphenomenalism requires causal laws involving danglers, which
makes such laws uniquely different from all other scientific laws.
That is, such laws involve mental effects which do not causally
affect anything at all. The identity theory, however, requires no
nomological danglers because, as Feigl stresses, the sentences that
express relationships between mental and physical phenomena, such
as 'Sensation S_1 occurs if and only if brain process B_1 occurs,' are
not causal laws. Causal laws express causal relationships between
different events. They state that certain events are the causes of
other different events. But if the identity theory is correct, those
sentences relating mental and physical events do not relate *different*
events which are causally related. They express *identity*, which, of
course, is not a relationship between different events. Thus, such
psychophysical sentences are not causal laws and will not involve
danglers if the identity theory is correct. We can see how the
identity theory avoids danglers in another way. A dangler is an
effect which is not part of some continuing causal process. But

brain processes surely are parts of causal processes and if, as the identity theory claims, mental events are identical with brain processes, then mental events are parts of causal processes.

2. *Parallelism.* The crushing objection to parallelism is that it requires a *deus ex machina* to explain mind–body regularities. Furthermore, by denying mind–body interaction, it goes contrary to what seems to be true. The identity theory easily avoids these two objections. Because mental events are identical with brain processes and because brain processes causally interact with other parts of the body, it follows that mental events causally interact with parts of the body. And obviously no *deus ex machina* is needed to explain mind–body regularities, because they are completely explained by pointing out that underlying the regularities are identities. Where there is identity there must be regularity.

3. *Dualistic Interactionism.* Dualistic interactionism is the theory we have found to be preferable to those we have so far compared with it. We saw six objections leveled at the theory, although most of them turned out to be of little consequence after we carefully refined what the theory required. The only three objections left that seem to have any force are the objection from the problem of other minds, the objection from the apparent lack of characteristics relevant to causal interaction, and the objection concerning the inexplicability of how the mental affects the body. We shall examine how the neutral theory fares with these three objections, but let us first briefly indicate how easily it avoids the other three. The problem of deciding where mind–body interaction takes place is solved by discovering where those brain processes that are identical with mental events occur. This poses no insurmountable problem. The problem of a gap in physiological explanations and causal chains is quite obviously avoided, because if mental events are identical with certain brain events, then nothing nonphysiological is required either for full explanations or continuous causal chains. In this regard, a neutral theorist could even agree with our central-state materialist that certain causal roles are *definitive* of experiences. But, of course, he could also claim that they have these roles merely as a matter of fact.

The objections stemming from evolution are countered by saying that although no new nonphysical entities evolve through time as the dualist claims, certain bodies have evolved in such a way that they come to have properties of a new kind, namely, psychological properties. Such properties are often called "emergent" properties, because they emerge only when certain sorts of complex physical systems have evolved from simpler material stuff. So far, then, the identity theory easily dispenses with problems that have bothered other mind–body theories. Let us turn to the three more serious problems facing dualistic interactionism.

The objection from an apparent lack of characteristics relevant to causal interaction between mental and physical events is no more troublesome for the identity theory than any of those objections discussed previously. The identity theory need only point out that if it can be granted that brain events have characteristics relevant to causally interacting with other bodily events—something we all grant—then there should be no worry about mental events because they are identical with brain processes. This same point, furthermore, dispels the mystery of how the mental affects the body without violating any scientific principles. Each mental event affects a brain event in just the way any physiological event affects another. We have, then, two important points at which the neutral version of the identity theory is clearly superior to dualistic interactionism. If it can avoid the problem of other minds and faces no objections uniquely its own, it is clearly the theory we should accept.

At first glance it may seem that the identity theory can dispense with the objection from other minds as easily as it has with all the others directed at dualistic interactionism. It will be remembered that this problem arises for dualism because if dualism is true, then no one perceives other minds, nor can he deductively or inductively infer that there are other minds from premises decribing what he perceives. And because the belief in other minds can be justified only in one of these three ways, it follows that the belief cannot be justified. Now it seems that if the identity theory is correct, we can perceive mental events because we can perceive, or at least detect by perception, those brain processes that are identical with mental events. Thus, it seems, each of us can justify his belief that there are mental events other than his own, and consequently, that there are other minds. Although we may not be able to justify the belief by a sound inference, we do not need one, because if the identity theory is true, we can justify it noninferentially by perceiving mental events.

However, before the identity theorists claim victory, they should look more carefully at this way out of the problem of other minds. It is true that if mental events are identical with certain brain processes, then we perceive mental events when we perceive brain processes. But this is more like seeing a conglomeration of H_2O molecules when we see water, than it is like seeing a white sheet of paper when we see the page of a book. We both see a white sheet and *see that* there is a white sheet. But although we may see H_2O molecules we do not *see that* there are H_2O molecules here. We must infer this from what we see. Similarly, we may be seeing a mental event occur when we observe a brain process, but we do not see that a mental event is occurring. We must *infer that* a mental event is occurring, and this is obviously not noninferential perceiving. Thus, we can *conclude that* someone else has mental phenomena by using a statement of the identity theorist as a premise:

1. Brain process B_1 is occurring in Jones (because I perceive that it occurs).
2. Sensation S_1 is identical with brain process B_1.
   Therefore
3. Jones is having sensation S_1.

We can, however, reach the same conclusion by using a statement of the interactionist instead of premise (2):

2a. Sensation S_1 *is caused by* brain process B_1.

But, of course, premises such as (2) and (2a) are just the key ones a skeptic about other minds attacks, and neither theory is able to handle his attack better than the other. Consequently, we cannot use the problem of other minds to help choose between the two theories.

Incidentally, of all the positions we have examined, only analytical behaviorism avoids this problem. If that position is true, then psychological sentences are entailed by behavioral sentences and so conclusions about other minds can be deduced from premises describing certain behavior that we observe. But although this is an attractive feature of analytical behaviorism, it is of little help in salvaging the theory because it seems that no such entailments hold.

Although we have not found that either the most plausible dualism or what surely seems to be the most plausible monistic theory avoids the problem of other minds, we have found that the neutral identity theory does handle quite easily two objections that interactionism is unable to rebut in a completely satisfactory way. Does this clear advantage, then, allow us to proclaim the neutral theory as the most plausible mind–body theory? This would be, unfortunately, premature because there is one important objection to the neutral version of the identity theory we have not yet considered.

AN OBJECTION TO THE IDENTITY THEORY:
THE NONIDENTITY OF DISCERNIBLES

The crucial objection to the identity theory has already been mentioned. It surely is wrong to claim that mental phenomena, such as sensations or thoughts, are identical with certain physical phenomena, such as brain processes, because we cannot say of mental phenomena many of the things we say of physical phenomena, and vice versa. This objection can be made more specific by using the principle of the identity of indiscernibles. According to this principle, objects that may seem to be different from each other are really identical if "both" have all the same properties, and if they are identical, then both have all the same properties. For example, the forty-ninth state of the United States is identical with Alaska. Both the forty-ninth state and Alaska have all the same properties, such as the properties of being the most northerly state, the largest state, and the state nearest Russia. However, the fiftieth state is not identical with Alaska, because the fiftieth state has the property of being an island, which Alaska does not have. The two are discernible and so nonidentical.

Let us now apply the principle to what the mind–body identity theory claims are identical.[38] On one side of the identity claim, we have things such as sensations, pains, afterimages, beliefs, and desires. On the other side are certain physical entities, especially brain processes and constituents of brains such as nerve fibers. We ascribe properties to all these things. For example, we describe pains as intense, sharp, throbbing, aching, and unbearable; and we

---

[38] This point is discussed in some detail in J. R. Stevenson, "Sensations and Brain Processes: A reply to J. J. C. Smart," *The Philosophical Review*, 69 (1960), pp. 505–10.

describe nerve fibers as located in the brain, publicly observable, conducting neural impulses, and constituted of molecules. Consequently, if the neutral identity theory is correct about the identity of pains with firing C-fibers, then by applying the principle of the identity of indiscernibles, we can conclude that sensations such as pains are located in the brain, are publicly observable, conduct nerve impulses, and are constituted of molecules. And we can also conclude that certain nerve fibers are intense, sharp, throbbing, aching, and unbearable. But surely these conclusions are not true. Therefore, according to this objection the neutral theory is incorrect.

It must be admitted that the two preceding conclusions are extremely odd, perhaps even a misuse of language. Indeed, the sentences 'My pain conducts nerve impulses' and 'My nerve fibers are aching unbearably' seem to be like the sentence 'My birthday is asleep in bed.' This third sentence seems to be clearly meaningless, and therefore neither true nor false, because it makes no sense to say such a thing about the day of someone's birth. The sentence, it is claimed, involves what is called a "category mistake." That is, in this sentence the predicate 'is asleep in bed,' which is in one linguistic category, is ascribed to the term 'birthday,' which belongs in a different category. Whenever this occurs the resulting sentence is meaningless.[39]

If the sentences about pains and nerve fibers involve category mistakes, then they are meaningless and are, therefore, not true. It would seem, then, that this objection would be quite damaging. If, however, the neutral theory can avoid these odd-sounding and seemingly meaningless sentences, it can rebut this objection. Let us assume here that the sentences are meaningless, and see how a neutral theorist could handle the objection on that assumption. Consider the following sentence he might use to express his view: 'The very same entity that is aching and throbbing unbearably is conducting nerve impulses and is constituted of molecules.' This may be an unusual sentence but it is not particularly odd and certainly

---

[39] See G. Ryle, "Categories," in A. Flew, ed., *Logic and Language,* 2nd series (Oxford: Basil Blackwell, 1955), pp. 65–81 for a discussion of category mistakes; and for a more extensive and detailed study, see J. Cornman, "Types, Categories, and Nonsense," *American Philosophical Quarterly, Monograph Series* 2 (1968), pp. 73–97.

not meaningless. Furthermore, this theorist might even devise a new term to refer to such entities, for example, 'fibain.' He would then claim that there are fibains, that is, entities with those properties usually associated with pains, and also with the properties usually associated with firing C-fibers. He can, then, avoid category mistakes by saying that what are thought to be pains and what are thought to be firing C-fibers are really fibains. And a double-language theorist could say what 'pain' denotes is what 'firing C-fibers' denotes, namely, fibains.

The neutral theorist has a way to refute the preceding objection with the help of a new technical term, 'fibain.' However, it is at least possible that the neutral theory will become widely accepted in the future, and also that, as a result of this, the terms 'pain' and 'firing C-fiber' will change in meaning so they become synonymous with 'fibain.' If that should happen, 'fibain' would no longer be needed, and even the initial plausibility of the objection would be lost. One moral of this is that to base an argument about a non-linguistic theory on linguistic considerations is often to rely on something that is precariously inconstant.

CONCLUSION ABOUT THE MIND–BODY PROBLEM

With the rejection of the one objection we found to the neutral version of the identity theory, it is easy to see that it is the most plausible of the many proposed solutions to the mind–body problem. It avoids the problems unique to each of the alternative theories and faces none uniquely its own. We have, then, reason to reject the theory that our description of a person at the beginning of the chapter seemed to support, namely, dualistic interactionism. Nevertheless that theory is correct about there being interaction, although it is wrong about the entities that interact. It is also correct about there being a dualism, although it is wrong about the two sorts of entities involved. There are entities with only physical properties, such as stones and certain human organs, and there are also "neutral" entities, such as "fibains," which have both physical and psychological properties. It is these neutral entities, rather than mental entities, that interact with bodily processes. Human beings, then, are different from material objects, but not because they have minds or spirits in addition to their bodies.

This difference between persons and material objects is important. It is important for deciding the basic ethical question of how we ought to treat other persons, because it seems that beings with thoughts, sensations, feelings, and emotions should not be treated merely as an unfeeling, nonthinking material object such as a rock. This difference also has religious significance. If immortality, or life after death, requires a mind or spirit that is distinct from a body so that it survives when the body decays after death, then on the neutral theory there is no life after death. The mental activity of a person ceases when the brain activity with which it is identical ceases. However discomforting this may be, it is nevertheless reassuring that with no firings of C-fibers after death there will be no pain or suffering then either.

EXERCISES

1. Do you think that the characterizations of mental and material phenomena on page 240 are satisfactory? Using these characterizations, classify the following terms. (Note that some of these are neither mental nor material and thus do not belong in any of the classes.) Give reasons for your choices.

a loud sound	the number 3
the color blue	democracy
bodily pleasure	mirror images
intellectual pleasure	afterimages
desires	fire
lightning	dizziness
rainbows	dying

2. On page 240 it is claimed that mental objects are not located in space, yet we talk of mental pictures or images "in one's head," and we speak of pains, which are supposedly mental, as being located at different places in our bodies. Can these "locations" of what seems to be mental be reconciled with the claim on page 240, or must we revise the claim?

3. In the passage quoted on page 260, C. D. Broad states that one of the causal factors involved in voluntary movements of our bodies is a mental phenomenon called a "volition." Do you think that when someone moves his arm intentionally he has a volition and thereby "an idea of his arm (and not his leg or liver) and an idea of the position which he wants his arm to be"? Does this happen when, for example, you type a paper or ride a bike or swim? How do you think Broad could best answer these questions?

4. Broad claims that mental causes act on neural causal chains by varying the resistances of certain synapses to nerve currents. He concludes from this that there is no gap in physiological causal chains. But if we think of a synapse as like an electrical circuit with a variable resistor, must not energy be expended in "turning the knob" that changes the resistance? That is, how can the "knob be turned" by something such as a mental event that has no energy to expend? How could Broad best reply to this?

5. Reread the quotation from Broad on page 260. Consider that the behavior of ants, oysters, protozoa, and certain internal-guidance missiles is "varied appropriately to meet special circumstances." Must Broad conclude that all of these have minds? Surely he should not conclude that missiles have minds? Is there a reply Broad can make?

6. Can you think of any kind of human behavior that seems to be explicable only on the hypothesis that humans have minds? Consider falling in love, getting angry, telling a joke, writing poetry, dreaming, seeing a mirage. State whether you think that these or any other human activities require explanations in terms of mental phenomena, or whether you think no such explanation of any human behavior is needed. Give reasons for your answer.

7. Suppose that someone invents a computing machine that expresses itself in verbal utterances which sound much like a person talking. Suppose also that it can learn from past mistakes and improve its ability to arrive at answers to questions of many different kinds. Suppose, furthermore, that we ask it whether it thinks about the questions it is asked and whether it has feelings and desires of its own; its answer is "yes." Should we conclude that it has a mind? If not, should we conclude that humans also lack minds? Justify your answer.

8. There is an objection to the existence of minds that we have not considered. We have seen that it is possible that the mental has evolved from the material, but according to the theory of evolution

there is reason to think that it has not. According to this theory all our physical organs exist because they have contributed to our ability to survive as individuals or as a species. A mind, however, is clearly not at all necessary to enhance these abilities. Consequently, we should conclude that nothing mental has evolved from the original material primordial mass. How could an interactionist reply to this? An epiphenomenalist? What is your reply?

9. Interactionists claim that certain material events are causally related to certain mental events, either as causes or as effects. Parallelists claim that no material events are causally related to mental events. Rather, some material events are constantly accompanied by mental events. Is there some way to decide by observation and experimentation whether there are mind–body causal relations or merely constant correlations? Is there any way to decide between the two theories on the basis of experimental evidence? Can epiphenomenalism be experimentally distinguished from these other two dualistic theories? If not, what do you think are the consequences for the mind–body problem?

10. If the reply to objection 5 on pages 277–78 is true, then it might be claimed that there would be no way to explain scientifically how brain events cause nerve impulses to take certain paths, because such causation would have to be regarded by scientists as cases of proximate causation. But, it can be objected, all physical causation is ultimately to be explained in terms of atomic and subatomic occurrences. Consequently, scientists should not conclude that neurological causation is proximate; thus, it should be concluded that the reply to objection 5 is false. Is this objection sound? Explain your answer.

11. Distinguish between materialism and mechanism, and explain how one may be a materialist but not a mechanist. Can one be a mechanist but not a materialist? Explain.

12. Distinguish between methodological behaviorism and analytical behaviorism, and explain how one can be a methodological behaviorist but not an analytic behaviorist. Can one be an analytic behaviorist but not a methodological behaviorist? Explain.

13. Explain in your own words the difference between an explicit and a contextual definition. Give an example of each not given in the text.

14. Evaluate the following argument:

Analytical behaviorism is merely a thesis about the contextual definitions of psychological terms. Consequently, it is not a metaphysical position, nor does it entail any, because such a position is about what there is, not about the definitions of words. Therefore, the text is wrong when it asserts that analytical behaviorism entails materialism.

15. According to the verifiability criterion of meaning which of the following sentences are cognitively meaningful? Explain your answers.

The planet Pluto is made of green cheese.
Everything in the universe is twice the size it was yesterday.
John is certainly a good son.
Either God exists or He does not exist.
Please drive carefully.
There is life after death.
There is no life after death.

16. Some people claim that the verifiability criterion of meaning is a metaphysical thesis. If this were so what would the consequences be for the criterion itself?

17. On page 295 it was concluded that it is reasonable to reject analytical behaviorism on the grounds that those attempted analyses of psychological sentences examined in the text all failed. Do you agree that this is sufficient reason to reject analytical behaviorism? Explain. Do you think a scientifically more "penetrating" analysis might succeed? If you do, suggest how one might proceed.

18. Consider the following argument from W. V. O. Quine, *Word and Object* (New York: John Wiley & Sons, 1960).

If there is a case for mental events and mental states, it must be just that the positing of them, like the positing of molecules, has some indirect systematic efficacy in the development of theory. But if a certain organization of theory is achieved by thus positing distinctive mental states and events behind physical behavior, surely as much organization could be achieved by positing merely certain correlative physiological states and events instead. . . . The bodily states exist anyway; why add the others?

Is Quine's view compatible with the identity theory? Explain. Evaluate his argument utilizing the discussion in the text about sensations as entities postulated to explain behavior.

19. Evaluate the following objection to the identity theory.
No one can see that I am in pain by looking at my pain and therefore no one can see my pain. But neurosurgeons can see

brain processes, so none of my or anyone else's pains are identical with brain processes. The identity theory is false.

20. Consider the following objection to the identity theory from R. Abelson, "A Refutation of Mind—Body Identity," *Philosophical Studies*, 21 (1970), 85–89. It is possible that human beings can think of any particular number. But there are infinitely many numbers. Thus it is possible for there to be infinitely many different human thoughts. But there is only a finite number of human beings throughout time, and there is only a finite number of discrete brain states for each person. Thus there are only a finite number of different human brain states. From this Abelson concludes that there are more mental states possible than there are brain states available. Thus someone might be in a mental state with which no discrete brain state is uniquely correlated. But then that mental state would not be identical with any brain state, and so the identity theory would be false.

21. The conclusion reached in this chapter is that on the basis of the data discussed in the chapter the neutral version of the identity theory is the most reasonable position. Are there any data overlooked? Do you think some other position is more reasonable—perhaps because of something overlooked here? If you do, give a short defense, of your claim.

BIBLIOGRAPHY

HISTORICAL SOURCES

I. Original Works
For the views of Plato on the soul see especially the *Phaedo*. Aristotle's position can be found in the *De Anima*. Among the ancients a materialistic position is found in *The Nature of the Universe* by the Roman poet Lucretius. The Aristotelian position as adapted to Christian theology can be seen in *Summa Theologica* by St. Thomas Aquinas. The classical statement of dualistic interactionism occurs in the *Meditations* and *On the Passions of the Soul* by René Descartes. Thomas Hobbes in *De Corpore* stated mechanistic materialism, which is also defended by Julien Lamettrie in *Man a Machine*.

Parallelism is stated in its occasionalistic version by Nicolas Male-branche in *Dialogue on Metaphysics and Religion,* and in its pre-established harmony version by Gottfried Leibniz in *Exposition and Defense of the New System.* Benedict Spinoza presents the classical statement of the double-aspect, or neutral theory, in his *Ethics,* whereas Thomas Huxley is the best-known proponent of epiphenomenalism, in his *Animal Automatism* and *Collected Essays.*

II. Collections Containing Excerpts from Historical Works

Three anthologies devoted exclusively to the philosophy of mind are *Body, Mind, and Death* (New York: Crowell-Collier, 1964), edited by A. Flew; *Body and Mind in Western Thought* (Baltimore: Penguin, 1958), edited by J. W. Reeves; and *Body and Mind* (London: George Allen & Unwin, Ltd., 1964), edited by G. N. A. Vesey. The following more general anthologies contain sections on the philosophy of mind: *A Modern Introduction to Philosophy,* revised edition (New York: The Free Press, 1965), edited by P. Edwards and A. Pap; *Philosophic Problems* (New York: Macmillan Publishing Co., Inc., 1957), edited by M. Mandelbaum, F. Gramlich, and A. R. Anderson; and *Reason and Responsibility* (Belmont, Calif.: Dickenson, 1965), edited by J. Feinberg.

RECENT AND CONTEMPORARY SOURCES

I. Original Works

The mind–body problem has received an increasing amount of attention from philosophers as this century has progressed. Earlier works include J. B. Pratt, *Matter and Spirit* (New York: Macmillan Publishing Co., Inc., 1926); G. F. Stout, *Mind and Matter* (Cambridge, England: The University Press, 1931); C. J. Ducasse, *Nature, Mind and Death* (La Salle, Ill.: Open Court Publishing Company, 1951); J. Wisdom, *Problems of Mind and Matter* (Cambridge, England: The University Press, 1934); C. D. Broad, *Mind and Its Place in Nature* (New York: Macmillan Publishing Co., Inc., 1925); B. Russell, *The Analysis of Mind* (London: George Allen & Unwin, Ltd., 1921); E. Schrodinger, *Mind and Matter* (Cambridge, England: The University Press, 1958). Both Pratt and Ducasse defend dualistic interactionism. Broad's book contains a careful analysis of many different mind–body positions and the problems that confront each. Russell argues in his book for his doctrine of neutral monism, according to which mental and material things are both logical constructions out of a third, neutral stuff. An examination and comparison of traditional and contemporary approaches to the mind–body problem occurs in Part I of J. Cornman, *Metaphysics, Reference, and Language* (New Haven: Yale University Press, 1966).

Among contemporary authors, D. M. Armstrong has written extensively on the mind–body problem. His books include *Perception and the Physical World* and *Bodily Sensations* (both London: Routledge & Kegan Paul, 1961 and 1962). These two books deal particularly with the status of sensations, one sort of seemingly mental entity. J. Cornman's *Materialism and Sensations* (New Haven: Yale University Press, 1971) also focuses on this problem, giving extensive consideration to the various ways in which a materialist might try to deal with sensations, through their reduction or elimination. Armstrong has also written *A Materialist Theory of the Mind* (London: Routledge & Kegan Paul, 1968), in which he argues for one version of reductive materialism, a form of the identity theory in which mental states are identified with states of the central nervous system. D. C. Dennett, in his *Content and Consciousness* (London: Routledge & Kegan Paul, 1969), considers this central state theory in detail, focusing on the way in which the intentionality of consciousness might be accommodated.

Two specific problems that have received book-length attention are *the problem of other minds* and the question of *modeling mentality in machines*. Among works on the former problem are J. Wisdom, *Other Minds* (Oxford: Basil Blackwell, 1952); S. Coval, *Skepticism and the First Person* (London: Methuen & Co., Ltd., 1966); D. Locke, *Myself and Others* (Oxford: Oxford University Press, 1968). Among works on the latter problem are K. Sayre, *Consciousness: A Philosophical Study of Minds and Machines* (New York: Random House, Inc., 1969); K. Gunderson, *Mentality and Machines* (Garden City, N.Y.: Doubleday & Company, Inc., 1971).

Other recent books which contain discussions of various aspects of the mind–body problem are B. Aune, *Knowledge, Mind and Nature* (New York: Random House, Inc., 1967); G. N. Vesey, *Embodied Mind* (New York: Humanities Press, 1965); J. Yolton, *Metaphysical Analysis* (Toronto: University of Toronto Press, 1967); J. Beloff, *The Existence of Mind* (London: MacGibbon & Kee, 1962); S. Hampshire, *Freedom of Mind* (Princeton, N.J.: Princeton University Press, 1971); H. D. Lewis, *The Elusive Mind* (New York: Humanities Press, 1969); J. Fodor, *Psychological Explanation* (New York: Random House, Inc., 1968).

One of the most influential recent books in the philosophy of mind is G. Ryle, *The Concept of Mind* (New York: Barnes and Noble, 1949), in which Ryle tries to show that the Cartesian conception of a person as an embodied mind, what Ryle calls the "myth of the ghost in the machine," is radically mistaken, as a careful understanding of the logic of psychological discourse will show. Another influential work is P. F. Strawson's "Persons," which is included as Chapter 3 of his book *Individuals* (London: Methuen & Co., Ltd., 1959). Strawson, like Ryle, claims that there really is no traditional mind–body problem, because a person is an ontologically basic entity and therefore is not in any way reducible to a mind and/or a body; again like Ryle, he tries to establish his thesis by considering certain features of language. Both these works have received extensive comment in the philosophical journals. See the following for a sampling of relevant articles.

Both Ryle and Strawson are among the many philosophers influenced by the later work of L. Wittgenstein. Most of the discussion of private language and many other novel ways of approaching the philosophy of mind stem from Wittgenstein's influence. His most influential works are *Philosophical Investigations* (London: Blackwell, 1953) and *The Blue and Brown Books* (London: Blackwell, 1958). Other books relevant to the philosophy of mind and influenced by Wittgenstein are G. Anscombe, *Intention* (London: Blackwell, 1957); P. Geach, *Mental Acts* (London: Routledge and Kegan Paul, 1957); S. Hampshire, *Thought and Action* (London: Chatto and Windus, 1959); N. Malcolm, *Dreaming* (London: Routledge and Kegan Paul, 1959).

II. Collections of Articles and Textbooks

Each of the following collections contains contemporary articles devoted to the philosophy of mind, many of which are directly relevant to the problems discussed in this chapter: *Dimensions of Mind* (New York: Collier Books, 1961), edited by S. Hook; *Essays in Philosophical Psychology* (Garden City, N.Y.: Doubleday & Company, Inc., 1964), edited by D. F. Gustafson; *Minds and Machines* (Englewood Cliffs, N.J.: Prentice-Hall, Inc., 1964), edited by A. R. Anderson; *Philosophy of Mind* (New York: Harper & Row, Publishers, Inc., 1966), edited by S. Hampshire; *The Philosophy of Mind* (Englewood Cliffs, N.J.: Prentice-Hall, Inc., 1962), edited by V. Chappell; *Mind and Brain* (New York: Humanities Press, 1965), edited by J. R. Smythies; *Behaviorism and Phenomenology* (Chicago: University of Chicago Press, 1966), edited by T. W. Wann; *Modern Materialism: Readings on Mind-Body Identity* (New York: Harcourt Brace Jovanovich, Inc., 1969), edited by J. O'Connor; *The Mind-Brain Identity Theory* (London: Macmillan & Company, Ltd., 1970), edited by C. Borst; *Materialism and the Mind-Body Problem* (Englewood Cliffs, N.J.: Prentice Hall, Inc., 1971), edited by D. M. Rosenthal. *Mind, Matter and Method* (Minneapolis: University of Minnesota Press, 1966), edited by P. K. Feyerabend and G. Maxwell; *Theories of the Mind* (New York: The Free Press, 1962), edited by J. Sher; *Philosophy of the Body: Rejection of Cartesian Dualism* (Chicago: Quadrangle Books, 1970), edited by S. Spicker; *Intentionality, Minds and Perception* (Detroit: Wayne State University Press, 1967), edited by H. Castañeda; *The Physical Basis of Mind* (Oxford: Basil Blackwell, 1950), edited by P. Laslett; *The Identity Theory of Mind* (St. Lucia, Queensland: University of Queensland Press, 1967), edited by C. F. Presley; *The Modeling of Mind* (Notre Dame, Ind.: University of Notre Dame Press, 1963), edited by K. Sayre and F. Crosson; *The Encyclopedia of Philosophy* (New York: Collier-Macmillan, 1967), edited by P. Edwards, also contains many excellent articles on the mind–body problem.

Three recent introductory textbooks are devoted entirely to the mind–body problem: J. Shaffer, *Philosophy of Mind* (Englewood Cliffs, N. J.: Prentice-Hall, Inc., 1968); K. Campbell, *Body and Mind* (Garden City, N.Y.: Doubleday & Company, Inc., 1970); and A. R. White, *The Philosophy of Mind* (New York: Random House, Inc., 1966). Several other textbooks have sections devoted to the mind–body problem, including the following: E. Beardsley and M. Beardsley, *Philosophical Thinking* (New York: Harcourt Brace Jovanovich, Inc., 1965); J. Hospers, *An Introduction to Philosophical Analysis* (Englewood Cliffs, N.J.: Prentice-Hall, Inc., 1953); M. Scriven, *Primary Philosophy* (New York: McGraw-Hill Book Company, 1966); R. Taylor, *Metaphysics* (Englewood Cliffs, N.J.: Prentice-Hall, Inc., 1963).

III. Contemporary Articles

The preceding collections contain many of the most important articles on the mind–body problem. What follows is a sampling of these and other interesting recent articles.

The mind–body position most widely discussed at present is the *identity theory.* Here the work of H. Feigl, U. T. Place, and J. J. C. Smart have had wide influence. Feigl's views are expressed in "The Mind-Body Problem in the Development of Logical Empiricism," *Revue Internationale de Philosophie* (1950), "The 'Mental' and the 'Physical,'" *Minnesota Studies in the Philosophy of Science*, Vol. II (Minneapolis: University of Minnesota Press, 1958), "Mind-Body, Not a Pseudoproblem," *Dimensions of Mind*, and "Some Crucial Issues of Mind-Body Monism," *Synthese* (1971). Feigl's views are discussed in several of the articles included in *Mind, Matter and Method*, edited by Feyerabend and Maxwell, listed above. Place's contribution is "Is Consciousness a Brain Process?" which is reprinted in *The Philosophy of Mind*, edited by Chappell. S. Munsat discusses Place's article in "Could Sensations Be Processes?" *Mind* (1969); Place responds to Munsat in "Sensations and Processes—A Reply to Munsat," *Mind* (1972). Smart's articles include "Sensations and Brain Processes," *Philosophical Review* (1959) and "Materialism," *Journal of Philosophy* (1959). Among the articles written in reply to Smart's work are K. Baier, "Smart on Sensations," *Australasian Journal of Philosophy* (1962); J. Margolis, "Brain Processes and Sensations," *Theoria* (1965); J. R. Stevenson, "Sensations and Brain Processes:

A Reply to J. J. C. Smart," *Philosophical Review* (1960); and J. Shaffer, "Could Mental Events Be Brain Processes?" *Journal of Philosophy* (1961). Shaffer's article elicited the response of R. Coburn, "Shaffer on the Identity of Mental States and Brain Processes," *Journal of Philosophy* (1963), and J. Cornman's "The Identity of Mind and Body," *Journal of Philosophy* (1962). Shaffer replied in "Mental Events and the Brain," *Journal of Philosophy* (1963). Three recent articles attempting to justify the identity theory by construing sensations as theoretical entities are D. Lewis, "An Argument for the Identity Theory," *Journal of Philosophy* (1966); T. Nagel, "Physicalism," *Philosophical Review* (1965); and R. Rorty, "Mind–Body Identity, Privacy, and Categories" (reprinted in *Philosophy of Mind*). Although also interpreting sensations as theoretical, W. Sellars finds problems for the identity theory in "The Identity Approach to the Mind-Body Problem" (reprinted in *Philosophy of Mind*).

More articles on the identity theory are C. Crittenden, "Ontology and Mind–Body Identity," *Philosophical Forum* (1970–71); S. J. Noren, "Smart's Materialism," *Australasian Journal of Philosophy* (1970), "Identity, Materialism, and the Problem of the Danglers," *Metaphilosophy* (1970), and "Smart's Identity Theory, Translation, and Incorrigibility," *Mind* (1972); S. Candlish, "Mind, Brain and Identity," *Mind* (1970); C. H. Whiteley, "The Mind-Brain Identity Hypothesis," *Philosophical Quarterly* (1970); J. Heil, "Sensations, Experiences and Brain Processes," *Philosophy* (1970); M. A. Simon, "Materialism, Mental Language, and Mind-Body Identity," *Philosophy and Phenomenological Research* (1970); J. Tannenbaum, "In Defense of the Brain Process Theory," *Philosophy and Phenomenological Research* (1971); R. Martin, "A Reason to Believe in Mind-Body Identity," *Personalist* (1972); J. J. Clarke, "Mental Structure and the Identity Theory," *Mind* (1971); F. Stoutland, "Ontological Simplicity and the Identity Hypothesis," *Philosophy and Phenomenological Research* (1971); D. Locke, "Must a Materialist Pretend He's Anaesthetized?" *Philosophical Quarterly* (1971); W. L. Rowe, "Neurophysiological Laws and Purposive Principles," *Philosophical Review* (1971); J. Carney, "The Compatibility of the Identity Theory with Dualism," *Mind* (1971); R. Abelson, "A Refutation of Mind-Body Identity," *Philosophical Studies* (1970), to which there are several replies in *Philosophical Studies* (1972); E. E. Harris, "The Neural Identity Theory and the Person," *International Philosophical Quarterly* (1966).

One way of justifying the identity theory, at least in some of its versions, would be to *reduce* talk about mental states to talk about brain states. Such reduction seems to require laws correlating mental states with brain states. Focusing on these correlation laws are J. A. Gray, "The Mind-Brain Identity Theory as a Scientific Hypothesis," *Philosophical Quarterly* (1971); C. G. Hedman, "On Correlating Brain States with Psychological States," *Australasian Journal of Philosophy* (1970), which deals with J. Fodor's arguments against mind–brain correlations contained in his book *Psychological Explanation*, listed above. Another article dealing with the same aspects of Fodor's book is M. Martin, "Neurophysiological Reduction and Psychological Explanation," *Philosophy of Social Science* (1971). Other articles on mind–brain correlations are G. J. Nathan and J. Wolfe, "The Identity Thesis as a Scientific Hypothesis," *Dialogue* (1968); J. Kim, "Psychophysical Laws and Theories of Mind," *Theoria* (1967); C. Taylor, "Mind-Body Identity, A Side Issue," *Philosophical Review* (1967); J. Teichmann, "The Contingent Identity of Minds and Brains," *Mind* (1967); R. Ziedins, "Identification of Characteristics of Mental Events with Characteristics of Brain Events," *American Philosophical Quarterly* (1971); M. Michael, "The Mind-Body Problem and Neurophysiological Reduction," *Theoria* (1971); B. Goldberg, "The Correspondence Hypothesis," *Philosophical Review* (1968). Goldberg argues that the correspondence hypothesis is "disguised nonsense"; L. Resnick has replied to this in "Thinking and Correspondence," *Philosophical Review* (1969).

D. M. Armstrong's book *A Materialist Theory of the Mind*, which argues for a version of the identity thesis, has drawn replies from T. Nagel, "Armstrong on the Mind," *Philosophical Review* (1970); N. Fleming, "Mind as the Cause of Motion," *Australasian Journal of Philosophy* (1969); C. Taylor, "Two Issues About Materialism," *Philosophical Quarterly* (1969); R. Pucetti, "A Materialist Fallacy of Mind," *Philosophy* (1970), replied to by L. Stevenson, "An Alleged Materialist Fallacy of Mind," *Philosophy* (1971). Armstrong defends materialism against one purported problem in "The Headless Woman Illusion and the Defence of Materialism," *Analysis* (1968), which is replied to in K. Ward, "The Headless Woman," *Analysis* (1969).

Several further articles on the identity theory are R. Brandt, "Doubts About the Identity Theory," in *Dimensions of Mind;* J. Kim, "On the Psycho-Physical Identity Theory," *American Philosophical Quarterly* (1966) and "Materialism and the Criteria of the Mental," *Synthese* (1971); R. Brandt and J. Kim, "The Logic of the Identity Theory," *Journal of Philosophy* (1967).

Rather than argue that the mental is *reducible* to the physical, some philosophers have argued instead for *eliminative materialism,* according to which mental states and events are construed as theoretical entities which will turn out not to be needed by the ultimate scientific framework in terms of which we will come to explain the world. R. Rorty has been a chief exponent of this view, setting it forth in such articles as "Mind-Body Identity, Privacy, and Categories," listed above, "Incorrigibility as the Mark of the Mental," *Journal of Philosophy* (1970), and

"In Defense of Eliminative Materialism," *Review of Metaphysics* (1970). This last article deals with attacks on Rorty's views contained in J. Cornman, "On the Elimination of 'Sensations' and Sensations," *Review of Metaphysics* (1968), and R. Bernstein, "The Challenge of Scientific Materialism," *International Philosophical Quarterly* (1968). Another article on materialism is M. Hocutt, "In Defense of Materialism," *Philosophy and Phenomenological Research* (1967). In addition, the April 1972 issue of *The Monist* is devoted to the topic of "Materialism Today."

N. Malcolm has attacked materialism in any of its versions in "Scientific Materialism and the Identity Theory," *Dialogue* (1964) and "The Conceivability of Mechanism," *Philosophical Review* (1968). Replies to Malcolm have come from M. Martin, "On the Conceivability of Mechanism," *Philosophy of Science* (1971); A. Goldman, "The Compatibility of Mechanism and Purpose," *Philosophical Review* (1969); E. Sosa, "Professor Malcolm on 'Scientific Materialism and the Identity Theory,'" in *The Mind-Brain Identity Theory*, listed above. Malcolm replies to Sosa in the same book.

Another position that has received considerable attention is *analytical behaviorism*. It has been defended by R. Carnap, "Psychology in Physical Language," in A. J. Ayer, ed., *Logical Positivism* (New York: The Free Press, 1959); H. Feigl, "Logical Analysis of the Psycho-physical Problem," *Philosophy of Science* (1934); C. Hempel, "The Logical Analysis of Psychology" (reprinted in *Readings in Philosophical Analysis* (New York: Appleton-Century-Crofts, Inc., 1949), edited by H. Feigl and W. Sellars); and C. A. Mace, "Some Implications of Analytical Behaviorism," *Aristotelian Society Proceedings* (1948–1949). A strong attack against analytic behaviorism has come from R. Chisholm, "A Note on Carnap's Meaning Analysis," *Philosophical Studies* (1955), "Intentionality and the Theory of Signs," *Philosophical Studies* (1952), and "Sentences about Believing" (reprinted in *Minnesota Studies in the Philosophy of Science*, vol. II). Other relevant articles are J. Cornman, "Intentionality and Intensionality," *Philosophical Quarterly* (1962); H. Heidelberger, "On Characterizing the Psychological," *Philosophy and Phenomenological Research* (1966); H. H. Price, "Some Objections to Behaviorism" (in *Dimensions of Mind*); P. Ziff, "About Behaviorism" (reprinted in *The Philosophy of Mind*).

Another problem receiving considerable attention is the *problem of other minds*. Some of the most recent articles are B. Aune, "The Problem of Other Minds," *Philosophical Review* (1961); J. L. Austin, "Other Minds," *Aristotelian Society Supplement* (1946); A. J. Ayer, "Other Minds," *Aristotelian Society Supplement* (1946), and "One's Knowledge of Other Minds," (*Theoria*, 1953); H. Castañeda, "Criteria, Analogy, and Knowledge of Other Minds," *Journal of Philosophy* (1962); H. Feigl,

"Other Minds and the Egocentric Predicament," *Journal of Philosophy* (1958); N. Malcolm, "Knowledge of Other Minds" (reprinted in *The Philosophy of Mind*); J. Margolis, "The Problems of Other Minds," *Synthese* (1963); W. W. Mellor, "Three Problems about Other Minds," *Mind* (1956); P. Olscamp, "Wittgenstein's Refutation of Skepticism," *Philosophy and Phenomenological Research* (1965); A. Pap, "Other Minds and the Principle of Verifiability," *Revue Internationale de Philosophie* (1951); H. H. Price, "Our Knowledge of Other Minds," *Aristotelian Society Proceedings* (1931–1932); J. F. Thomson, "The Argument from Analogy and Our Knowledge of Other Minds," *Mind* (1951); J. Watling, "Ayer on Other Minds," *Theoria* (1954); John Wisdom, "Other Minds," *Aristotelian Society Proceedings* (1946).

A. Plantinga deals with the *problem of other minds* in "Induction and Other Minds," *Review of Metaphysics* (1966). Responding to this article is M. A. Slote, "Induction and Other Minds," *Review of Metaphysics* (1966); Plantinga replies to Slote in "Induction and Other Minds, II," *Review of Metaphysics* (1968). Other articles on the same problem are A. Hyslop, "The Identity Theory and Other Minds," *Philosophical Forum* (1970); I. Thalberg, "Other Times, Other Places, Other Minds," *Philosophical Studies* (1969); L. J. Goldstein, "Why the Problem of Other Minds," *Philosophical Forum* (1970–1971); J. J. Benton, "The Problem of Other Minds," *Kinesis* (1969); G. W. Pilkington, "Other Minds on Evidential Necessity," *Mind* (1970), which deals with A. H. Narveson, "Evidential Necessity and Other Minds," *Mind* (1966).

Related to the problem of other minds is the *problem of the privacy of the mental* and the resultant problem of whether there can be a language about private entities. Articles on this topic have been written by A. J. Ayer, "Can There Be a Private Language?" *Aristotelian Society Supplement* (1954); J. Carney, "Private Language–The Logic of Wittgenstein's Argument," *Mind* (1960); H. Castañeda, "The Private-Language Argument" in *Knowledge and Experience* (Pittsburgh: University of Pittsburgh Press), edited by C. Rollins; J. Cook, "Wittgenstein on Privacy," *Philosophical Review* (1965); J. Cornman, "Private Languages and Private Entities," *Australasian Journal of Philosophy* (1967); C. Mundle, " 'Private Language' and Wittgenstein's Kind of Behaviorism," *Philosophical Quarterly* (1966); K. Stern, "Private Language and Skepticism," *Journal of Philosophy* (1963); M. Stocker, "Memory and the Private Language Argument," *Philosophical Quarterly* (1966); J. J. Thomson, "Private Languages," *American Philosophical Quarterly* (1964). A. Hyslop, in "The Plight of the Inner Process," *Australasian Journal of Philosophy* (1969), discusses D. Locke's treatment of the privacy of the mental in his book *Myself and Others,* listed above. Another article on this topic is S. Candlish, "Physiological Discoveries: Criteria or Symptoms," *Analysis* (1971), which discusses the views of Baier and Malcolm.

Much recent discussion has been centered on the concept of the person and the *problem of personal identity*. P. F. Strawson's article "Persons" has been much discussed in this connection by, among others, A. J. Ayer, "The Concept of a Person" [in *The Concept of a Person and Other Essays* (New York: Macmillan, 1963)]; J. Cornman, "Strawson's 'Person,'" *Theoria* (1964); S. Coval, "Persons and Criteria in Strawson," *Philosophy and Phenomenological Research* (1964); R. Freed and J. Fodor, "Pains, Puns, Persons, and Pronouns," *Analysis* (1961); G. Iseminger, "Meaning, Criteria, and P-predicates," *Analysis* (1962); D. Mannison, "On the Alleged Ambiguity of Strawson's P-Predicates," *Analysis* (1962); D. Pears, "*Individuals* by P. F. Strawson," *Philosophical Quarterly* (1961); A. Plantinga, "Things and Persons," *Review of Metaphysics* (1960–1961); C. Rollins, "Personal Predicates," *Philosophical Quarterly* (1960). Others who have discussed Strawson's views on persons are N. Burstein, "Strawson on the Concept of a Person," *Mind* (1971); D. Sievert, "Strawson on Persons," *Modern Scholasticism* (1971); R. Puccetti, "Mr. Strawson's Concept of a Person," *Australasian Journal of Philosophy* (1967); D. van de Vate, "Strawson's Concept of a Person," *Southern Journal of Philosophy* (1969); D. Bloor, "Explanation and Analysis in Strawson's Persons," *Australasian Journal of Philosophy* (1970); K. Ward, "The Ascription of Experiences," *Mind* (1970); D. F. Gustafson, "Are Strawson's Persons Immortal?" *Philosophical Studies* (1967), which drew a reply from P. Klein, "'Are Strawson's Persons Immortal'—A Reply," *Philosophical Studies* (1969).

Other articles on the concept of a person and the problem of personal identity are M. Polanyi, "On Body and Mind," *New Scholasticism* (1969); D. Odegard, "On an Argument Against Mind-Body Monism," *Philosophical Studies* (1970), which deals with J. Shaffer's discussion of this topic in his "Persons and Their Bodies," *Philosophical Review* (1966); R. Squires, "On One's Mind," *Philosophical Quarterly* (1970); D. Odegard, "Persons and Bodies," *Philosophy and Phenomenological Research* (1970); R. Puccetti, "Brain Transplantation and Personal Identity," *Analysis* (1968–1969), replied to by A. Brennan, "Persons and Their Brains," *Analysis* (1969), which was in turn responded to by Puccetti in "Mr. Brennan on Persons' Brains," *Analysis* (1970); G. H. Bird, "Minds and States of Mind," *Philosophical Quarterly* (1971); D. Murray, "Disembodied Brains," *Proceedings of the Aristotelian Society* (1969–1970); B. Smart, "Can Disembodied Persons Be Spatially Located?" *Analysis* (1971); T. Nagel, "Brain Bisection and the Unity of Consciousness," *Synthese* (1971); L. C. Feldstein, "Reflections on the Ontology of the Person," *International Philosophical Quarterly* (1969).

The question of modeling the mind in machines is discussed in J. E. Tomberlin, "About the Identity Theory," *Australasian Journal of Philosophy* (1965), which deals with H. Putnam's article "Minds and Machines," in *Dimensions of Mind*. Tomberlin's article was replied to in R. H. Kane, "Turing Machines and Mental Reports," *Australasian Journal of Philosophy* (1966). Another article dealing with Putnam is B. Gibbs, "Putnam on Brains and Behavior," *Analysis* (1969). Another dispute has arisen over J. R. Lucas, "Minds, Machines and Godel," *Philosophy* (1961). Two articles replying to Lucas are D. Cooper, "Godel's Theorem and Mechanism," *Philosophy* (1969) and D. Lewis, "Lucas Against Mechanism," *Philosophy* (1969). Lucas defends himself against these attacks in "Mechanism: A Rejoinder," *Philosophy* (1970). Other articles on this topic are T. C. Mayberry, "Consciousness and Robots," *Personalist* (1970); B. A. Farrell, "On the Design of a Conscious Device," *Mind* (1970); J. Webb, "Metamathematics and the Philosophy of Mind," *Philosophy of Science* (1968); P. T. Manicas, "Men, Machines, Materialism, and Morality," *Philosophy and Phenomenological Research* (1966); Y. Leibowitz, "Neuro-Physiology, Neuro-Psychology and Cybernetics," *Iyyun* (1968); M. A. Boden, "Intentionality and Physical Systems," *Philosophy of Science* (1970).

Dualistic interactionism in its various forms is discussed in D. C. Long, "Descartes' Argument for Mind-Body Dualism," *Philosophical Forum* (1969); P. J. White, "Materialism and the Concept of Motion in Locke's Theory of Sense-Idea Causation," *Studies in the History and Philosophy of Science* (1971); D. Radner, "Descartes' Notion of the Union of Mind and Body," *Journal of the History of Philosophy* (1971); C. Kim, "Cartesian Dualism and the Unity of a Mind," *Mind* (1971); D. Odegard, "Locke and Mind-Body Dualism," *Philosophy* (1970); J. A. Foster, "Psychophysical Causal Relations," *American Philosophical Quarterly* (1968).

Finally, some critical studies of some of the books listed above, and three other interesting articles on the mind–body problem. Among the many articles written in response to G. Ryle's influential *The Concept of Mind* are A. C. Ewing, "Professor Ryle's Attack on Dualism," *Aristotelian Society Proceedings* (1952); J. Findlay, "Linguistic Approach to Psychophysics," *Aristotelian Society Proceedings* (1949–1950); A. Garnett, "Minds as Minding," *Mind* (1952); S. Hampshire, "The Concept of Mind. By Gilbert Ryle," *Mind* (1950); M. Mandelbaum, "Professor Ryle and Psychology," *Philosophical Review* (1958); A. Pap, "Semantic Analysis and Psycho-Physical Dualism," *Mind* (1952); T. Penelhum, "The Logic of Pleasure," *Philosophy and Phenomenological Research* (1956–1957); J. J. C. Smart, "Ryle on Mechanism and Psychology," *Philosophical Quarterly* (1959); D. C. Bloor, "Is the Official Theory of Mind

Absurd," *British Journal for the Philosophy of Science* (1970); J. Harrison, "A Philosopher's Nightmare, or The Ghost Not Laid," *Proceedings of the Aristotelian Society* (1966–1967); G. B. Matthews, "Dualism and Solecism," *Philosophical Review* (1971). A study of D. Locke's *Myself and Others* is S. Shoemaker's "Critical Study: Myself and Others," *Philosophical Quarterly* (1969). R. Binkley's "Intentionality, Minds and Behavior," *Nous* (1969) is a study of the book of the same title edited by H. Castañeda, listed above. The three other interesting articles are I. I. Mitroff, "Solipsism: An Essay in Psychological Philosophy," *Philosophy of Science* (1971), in which Mitroff argues that philosophers of mind need to know psychology; P. Oppenheim and N. Brody, "An Application of Bohr's Principle of Complementarity to the Mind–Body Problem," *Journal of Philosophy* (1969); and R. Taylor, "How to Bury the Mind–Body Problem," *American Philosophical Quarterly* (1969).

THE PROBLEM OF JUSTIFYING BELIEF IN GOD

CHAPTER FIVE

One of the most widespread beliefs among mankind is the belief in a supreme being, some being to whom we ordinary beings owe our existence but which depends upon nothing else for its own existence. Such a being we call God. We have previously examined quite different beliefs—beliefs that we have free will, that every event has a cause, that humans possess an immaterial mind as well as a body. In each case, we have been trying to become as clear as possible about what is believed; and we have then examined the belief to see whether or not it is justified. These two tasks face us once again. We must first consider what is being believed when someone believes that a supreme being exists; then we must try to discover whether or not this belief can be justified.

It may be objected here that the belief in a supreme being is un-like any of the other beliefs we have examined because a supreme being is unlike any other being, so that this belief, unlike our other beliefs, is not open to scrutiny. It is true that a being we would be willing to call God would be different in many important respects from most beings that we ordinarily believe exist, but this alone does not warrant the claim that the belief in the existence of God should be exempt from the scrutiny we give more ordinary beliefs. There are many fanciful beliefs, such as beliefs in the existence of witches, wizards, fountains of youth, which are beliefs in things that differ in many important respects from those ordinary beings that we believe exist. Yet we think that all such beliefs must be scrutinized carefully so that we have grounds for either accepting or rejecting them. Thus, initially at least, the belief in the existence of a supreme being seems open to the examination we apply to any other belief, so it seems that no one is justified in such a belief unless he can pro-vide some reason for thinking that such a being exists, or, at the very least, that there is no reason for thinking that such a being does not exist. However, although we have said that this seems to be true initially, we also want to leave open the possibility that after our examination of this belief we might be able to conclude on the basis of what we have found that the belief in a supreme being is, after all, *sui generis*, or unique, so that we could perhaps be justified in holding such a belief even in the face of what seems to be contrary evidence.

EXAMINATION OF THE CONCEPT OF SUPREME BEING

The first task mentioned previously is the task of becoming as clear as we can about the nature of the belief. To do this we must become as clear as possible about the concept of God. Let us do so now. What we want to do is find those characteristics or qualities of a being which we would be convinced is God. To begin let us distin-guish between the terms 'god' and 'God.' We can talk about one god or many gods, lesser gods and false gods. That is, the term 'god' is a general term, such as 'man,' 'horse,' and 'stone,' and as such can apply to a whole range of entities. On the other hand, the term 'God' is usually used to talk about one specific being, namely, the one and only supreme being. Thus, we cannot talk about many Gods or lesser Gods, because if God exists then there is exactly one being which is supreme. In line with this we shall use 'God' to mean 'the supreme being,' and will use it interchangeably with 'the supreme being' throughout the following discussion.

The problem before us is to characterize adequately a being we would call God. We already have some idea of where to begin, because the word 'supreme' is involved in the concept we are characterizing. Our question is the following: What characteristics are we ascribing to a being in calling it supreme? We may ask, "Supreme in what regard?" Surely not supreme in evil, or merely in physical size or prowess, or even in physical beauty. We generally mean that the supreme being is supreme in those characteristics or properties that make a being more perfect than it would be if it lacked them, so that we would call a being God only if it were the most perfect being of which we could conceive. Consequently, we would claim that the supreme being is one who is supreme in its ability to perform actions and to know what occurs, and one who is certainly supreme in goodness. Thus we think of God as the being who is all-good, all-knowing, and all-powerful. That is, he is supreme in goodness, knowledge, and power. Let us then consider these three characteristics separately.

THE SUPREME BEING IS ALL-GOOD

We can understand the statement that the supreme being is all-good to mean that whatever the supreme being wills or commands or does is the right thing to do. Thus whatever God decides, does, or commands is morally right. In addition, however, he always has good motives for willing, doing, or commanding in the way he does because he is a loving God who cares about the world and its inhabitants. Thus God does not do the right things with the wrong motives, nor does he have good motives but mistakenly do the wrong things. Let us take the statement 'God is good' to mean that God has good motives and whatever he wills, does, or commands is morally right. There is, however, a problem about how to interpret this. We could interpret it to mean that if a being is the supreme being and he wills or commands or does something, then *by definition* this is the right thing to do. On the second interpretation the

statement means that if a being is the supreme being and if he wills
or commands or does something, then *as a matter of fact,* this is
the right thing to do. Which interpretation should we use? It has
been claimed that neither alternative is appealing because each is
faced with a problem. If we accept the first interpretation, then it
would be true that if the supreme being willed or commanded that
someone wantonly inflict pain on innocent babies, or inflicted such
pain himself, then inflicting pain on innocent babies would be
defined as being the right thing to do. Although we shall not consider moral problems in any detail until the next chapter, it surely
seems that if wantonly inflicting pain on innocent babies is morally
right, then nothing is morally wrong. We want to deny that this
could be morally right. Yet if a supreme being's doing or commanding it, which is surely possible, entails that it is right, we cannot
justify such a denial. If it be objected at this point that God would
not engage in or command wanton infliction of pain, we can ask,
"Why not?" The answer cannot be that he would not because he is
good and inflicting pain is wrong. For if he were to inflict pain, then,
on this view, it would follow that doing this is right. Nor can we find
another answer any more helpful. This view, therefore, seems faced
with an insoluble problem.

Let us turn to the second alternative. On this view it is possible
that what God does is wrong although as a matter of fact what he
does always turns out to be right. Thus although it is true that if
God does or commands an act then it is right, it does not follow
from this that if God were to wantonly inflict pain, then that would
be right. We can say that if God were to wantonly inflict pain, then
he would do something wrong, but that as a matter of fact, God
never would inflict pain needlessly. Thus the second interpretation
avoids the problem facing the first interpretation. However, there
seems to be one consequence of this view that some people have
found objectionable. It is claimed that if God does not prescribe the
standard of what ought to be done, then there is a moral standard
which exists independently of God so that he can be judged by
reference to it. Surely, it is argued, something has gone wrong with
a view if it entails that it is possible for us to judge the moral
worth of the supreme being. However, it is not clear why anyone
objects to a view that entails that it is logically possible to judge
God's commands and acts by a standard. If the view entailed that it
is not only logically possible but also morally permissible for a

human being to judge God, then it might well be objectionable. But the view does not entail that statement. The second interpretation, then, seems to be able to avoid the objection to it. Let us, therefore, define the sentence 'The supreme being is all-good' as 'All motives of the supreme being are good and all acts the supreme being wills, does, or commands are, as a matter of fact, the right things to do.'

THE SUPREME BEING IS OMNIPOTENT

The quickest way to define this statement is by saying that it means that the supreme being has the ability to do anything at all. But this definition is too loose, because it does not decide the issue of whether God can do something that involves a logical contradiction. Does God, for example, have the ability to make the mercury in one thermometer be 1 inch from the bottom of the thermometer at the same time that it is 2 inches from the bottom? Does he have the ability to make a lake frozen at the same time that there is no ice on it? Some have argued that if we claim that God does not have the ability to do something involving a logical contradiction, then we must conclude that he does not have the ability to do everything and thus is not omnipotent. However, there seems to be no reason why it would be limiting God's power to say that he is able to do anything that it is logically possible to do. This rules out nothing that has been claimed to be among God's acts, including creation out of nothing. It rules out only acts the descriptions of which involve a contradiction. Let us therefore try the following: 'The supreme being has the ability to do anything that it is logically possible to do' as the definition of 'The supreme being is omnipotent.'

At first glance this definition surely seems satisfactory, but we shall have to make another revision. Consider the act of sitting in a chair at a time when God is not sitting there. It is clear that you, I, and almost everyone are able to sit in a chair at a time when God is not sitting there. But is God able to do this? Is God able to sit in a chair at the same time God is not sitting there? Clearly not, and, because it is logically possible to do it (you and I do it), we must conclude by the preceding definition that God is not omnipotent.

It does not seem, however, that because God or anyone else cannot both be at one place and not be there at the same time, this is any limitation on his power. It is, therefore, not the kind of inability that should be allowed to count against his omnipotence. Let us, consequently, revise the definition as follows: 'The supreme being is omnipotent' means 'The supreme being has the ability to do anything that is logically possible that he do.' Using this definition we can avoid concluding that God is not omnipotent because of the above inability. The sentence

> The supreme being is sitting in a chair at a time when he is not sitting there

is a self-contradiction, and so it is logically impossible that God perform this act.

The definition we have settled on not only avoids the preceding problem, but it also allows us to solve an ancient puzzle. Consider a boulder so heavy that God does not have the ability to lift it. Does God have the ability to create such a rock or not? If he has this ability then there is something else God does not have the ability to do, namely, lift the rock. But either he has the ability to create the boulder or he does not. Therefore there is something God does not have the ability to do, either lift or create a certain boulder. Therefore God is not omnipotent.[1]

How might we refute this argument? The first thing to notice is that it contains two conclusions: that there is something God is unable to do and, consequently, that God is not omnipotent. We must surely accept the first, simply because there are many things God cannot do (that is, whatever involves a logical contradiction). But because God's inability to do self-contradictory things does not limit his power, we should question whether we can draw the second conclusion that his inability either to create or lift this boulder limits his power. Using the preceding definition, the question is whether or not the statement that God does these tasks is self-contradictory. If his doing at least one of them is self-contradictory, then it is fallacious to draw the conclusion that God is not

---

[1] For recent discussions of this problem see G. Mavrodes, "Some Puzzles Concerning Omnipotence," *The Philosophical Review* (1963), pp. 221–23; and H. G. Frankfurt, "The Logic of Omnipotence," *The Philosophical Review* (1964), pp. 262–63.

omnipotent. There seems to be no contradiction involved in saying that God creates a rock he is unable to lift, so let us not try to avoid this problem by agreeing that God is unable to create the rock. The question, then, is whether it is logically possible that God lift such a boulder. That is, is it logically possible that God lift a boulder that he is unable to lift? The answer is clearly that it is logically impossible for God to perform this act, and, therefore, his inability to lift it does not limit his power. We can, therefore, avoid the conclusion that God is not omnipotent by agreeing that God is unable to lift such a rock, because such an inability does not limit his power.

There is, however, one more objection to the preceding definition of 'omnipotence' which is worth considering because of its consequences for what is called "backward causation." Consider the following sentence:

> The supreme being brings it about in 1974 that Henry VIII has exactly one wife during his lifetime.

This sentence is not self-contradictory, and so, by the preceding definition, if God is omnipotent, he is able to do this. But Henry VIII died in 1547 after having six wives, and so no one, not even God, is able *now* to make Henry have only one wife in the past. No one is able to change the past. Consequently, given the preceding definition, God is not omnipotent.

In order to see the mistake in this objection it is important to distinguish between two different ways of affecting the past. The first is that someone now changes the way the past was, such as God now causing Henry VIII, who had six wives, to have had only one wife. This is surely not in the power of anyone, including God, because it implies that Henry had only one wife and also had six wives. The second way of affecting the past is to cause, without changing the past, something which previously occurred. Although this may seem quite unusual, it is surely not self-contradictory. For example, it is logically possible that God now causes Henry to have had six wives, and thus God has this ability to affect the past. But does he now have the ability to cause Henry to have had only one wife as the preceding definition allows? Given his ability to affect the past when that does not require changing it, we can see that he does have this ability, but, because Henry had six wives, God is not now exercising, nor did he or will he ever exercise this ability. This is not unusual because it is clear that there are many things God is able to do that he does not do. This is just one of them. Consequently, this final objection fails. Its plausibility arose from confusing two different ways of affecting the past, and over-looking the difference between having an ability and exercising it.

THE SUPREME BEING IS OMNISCIENT

We can begin our definition of the sentence 'The supreme being is omniscient' as we did the previous definition—that is, by saying that it means that the supreme being knows everything. But again we must be careful because not even God can be said to know a falsehood. Thus, it would be better to say that a supreme being knows all truths. There is, however, still a problem that should be considered. If God knows all truths then he knows truths about the future, that is, he knows what will happen. But, it has been claimed, if God knows that something is going to happen before it happens—for example, that I will write the word 'thus' at the beginning of the next sentence—then it follows that I must write 'thus' there. Thus, God's foreknowledge, and hence his knowledge of all truths, is incompatible with my free will. Consequently, either no one has free will or God cannot foresee all future events and he is not omniscient. Must we surrender our belief that men have free will in order to guarantee God's omniscience? We can avoid this because in the premise 'If God foresees that I do something then I must do it,' the word 'must' indicates that the consequent follows logically from the antecedent. So the premise can be restated as 'It is logically necessary that if God (or anyone else for that matter) foresees that I do something then I *will* do it.' But it does not follow from the fact that I will do something that I *must*, in the sense of being coerced or forced to do it against my will. Thus it does not follow from foreknowledge of what I will do that I will not do it of my own free will.[2]

At this point someone might try a new line of attack. If someone

---

[2] For an argument for the incompatibility of free will and foreknowledge see N. Pike, "Divine Omniscience and Voluntary Action," *The Philosophical Review* (1965), pp. 27–46.

has foreknowledge of what I do then he can correctly predict what I will do. But he can correctly predict what I will do only if what I will do is causally determined and thus predictable on the basis of causal laws. Consequently, foreknowledge of what I do is not compatible with my doing it of my own free will. The first thing that can be said here is that the conclusion follows only if free will and causal determinism are incompatible. But we have previously found reason to deny this.[3] Secondly, there is no reason to think that someone can make a correct prediction only on the basis of causal laws. We often justifiably predict that, for example, Jones will decide to forgive his wife her latest infidelity because we know what he has done in the past, not because we know the causal laws relevant to predicting what he will decide. In addition, it is not clear that foreknowledge correctly describes God's knowledge of my future. It has been claimed that for God the whole of the temporal span of the universe—past, present, and future—is like a brief moment of time for us and thus God knows what I will do in the way I know what I am doing now. No prediction is involved. Thus there are reasons for rejecting this second line of attack upon the compatibility of God's foreknowledge and our free will.

Before we move on there is one other problem concerning God's omniscience that we should consider. Let us say that at a certain time, t_n, God decides for the first time to do something (for example, create a particular universe). If at that time, t_n, God decides for the first time to create this world, then at no time before t_n did God know what his decision at t_n would be because if he did, then he would not have decided for the first time at t_n. But if God is omniscient, then there is no time at which he does not know all truths, so that if God is omniscient then at every moment before t_n, he knows what he decides for the first time at t_n to do. Thus if God decides for the first time at t_n to do something, then God is not omniscient, for there is a time before t_n at which he did not know what he would decide. There are several ways to avoid this conclusion. One is to deny there is a time at which God first decides to do something. Two different reasons have been given for this. The first reason is that no matter how far back in time you might go God has already made all his decisions. The second is to claim that, un-

---

[3] See Chapter 3, *passim.*

like us, none of God's decisions are made at some time, because God is not a member of the world of temporal objects.

There is another way to avoid this problem. This is to deny that it is impossible for anyone to know at t_n what he will do and at a later time, $t_n + 1$, to decide for the first time what he will do. Such a situation is odd, but according to this proposal, it is not logically impossible.[4] It surely seems possible, for example, that Jones knows now that he later will decide for the first time to forgive his wife her latest in a series of infidelities, although he is firmly resolved not to forgive her now. He knows this on the basis of what he has done in the past, each time resolving not to forgive her but each time finally giving in. If Jones can know beforehand what he will decide to do, then surely God can. There is no contradiction here.

We can finally rest content with the definition of 'The supreme being is omniscient.' It means that the supreme being knows all truths.

OTHER CHARACTERISTICS OF A SUPREME BEING

We have discussed three essential characteristics of a supreme being—the characteristics of supreme goodness, omnipotence, and omniscience. The question now arises of whether there are any other characteristics an entity would have if he were the supreme being. There seems to be four additional properties. Because the supreme being is all-powerful, he can be neither created nor destroyed and is therefore eternal. Furthermore, he is the creator of "heaven and earth and all things" who loves and cares about the creatures he creates. And, finally, God is holy. There is no problem about what it means to say that God is loving. In being all-good, he is not merely fair and just, but is also benevolent and merciful toward his creatures, and deeply concerned about their welfare. The only problem about what is meant by calling the supreme being the creator of everything is whether this means that he created what there is *ex nihilo* (that is, out of nothing) or whether

---

[4] For two opposing views on this point, see C. Ginet, "Can the Will Be Caused?" *The Philosophical Review* (1962), pp. 49–55; and K. Lehrer, "Decisions and Causes," *The Philosophical Review* (1963), pp 224–27.

he created what there is out of some primordial chaos. Because there is disagreement about which is the correct interpretation, let us leave the question open by defining 'The supreme being is the creator of heaven and earth and all things' as 'The supreme being caused heaven and the physical universe to exist in their present form.' Thus we have not decided by definition whether or not God's creation of things is *ex nihilo*.

There are two possible ways to interpret 'The supreme being is eternal.' The first is that as a matter of fact there is no time at which the supreme being begins to exist and no time at which he ceases to exist. The second interpretation is that 'The supreme being is eternal' means that *it is logically necessary* that there is no time at which the supreme being begins to exist and no time at which he ceases to exist. You will notice that neither interpretation begs the question of whether or not God exists because that there is no time at which he begins to exist and no time at which he ceases to exist is consistent both with his always existing and with his never existing. There is, however, an important difference between the two interpretations. On the first interpretation it is logically possible that God be created and destroyed, but on the second, it is logically impossible that anything create or destroy God. Let us characterize the two interpretations of 'The supreme being is eternal' by saying that on the first if he exists then he always exists, whereas on the second, if he exists then he necessarily exists.

Which interpretation shall we choose? Although some people have argued for the first interpretation, the following, which echoes the ontological argument that we shall consider later, will justify our choosing the second. We have said that any being we would call God must be the being supreme in perfection, so that if we can think of a being more perfect than some particular being, then we would not call the latter one God. Furthermore, if it is logically possible that something create or destroy God, then we can think of a being more powerful and therefore more perfect than God, namely, a being it is logically impossible to create or destroy. Therefore we can conclude that it is logically impossible that anything create or destroy God. We want, then, to characterize God in such a way that it is logically impossible that he be created or destroyed. However, if his eternality is merely a factual contingency, then it is logically possible that something create or destroy him. But if he is necessarily eternal, then this guarantees that it is not possible that anything create or destroy him. Therefore in order to have this guarantee let us use the second interpretation.

The last characteristic of a supreme being we have to consider is that such a being is holy. It is perhaps the hardest of all the characteristics to define. When we say that God is holy we are trying to express something of our feeling that God is worthy, even more than worthy, of our full devotion, adoration, and reverence; that God is that being whom we should worship, honor, and obey. This characteristic is important for our purposes because it can be used as a test of the adequacy of the sum total of the other characteristics we have ascribed to the supreme being. If we have provided an adequate characterization then the quality of holiness should really be redundant because the total of the other characteristics should include all and only those characteristics which would make any being having them the being whom we would find to be most worthy of our worship. In line with this, let us define 'The supreme being is holy' as 'The supreme being is that being who is most worthy of the complete devotion and reverence of mankind.'

We are now ready to move on. We have characterized the supreme being as the eternal, loving, and holy being who created all things out of his omniscience, omnipotence, and supreme goodness, and we have analyzed what we are to mean by each of these terms. The question now before us is whether or not there is any reason to think that this concept of the supreme being that we have carefully tried to analyze applies to anything. It is obvious that many people believe that such a being exists. It is also true that other people deny that there is a supreme being. Which position is correct? Which, if either, is the more reasonable? To arrive at an answer to this question let us investigate whether or not the belief in a supreme being can be justified.

CAN THE BELIEF IN THE EXISTENCE OF A SUPREME BEING BE JUSTIFIED?

Generally when we want to convince someone that something exists we show it to him whenever we can. That is, we try to get him to see it or touch it or in some way experience the entity in question. Getting someone to experience something is the surest way to convince him of its existence. If, for example, someone doubts that there is a four-legged animal which has a bill like a duck, the best way to convince him is to show him a duckbill platypus, and the next best is to have reliable witnesses tell him that they have seen such an animal. Similarly, the strongest proof for the existence of God would be one based on someone's experience of God, that is, one based on a case of someone who actually experienced God. Let us, therefore, consider whether or not there are good reasons to think that someone has experienced God, because if there are then we have excellent reason to believe that God exists.

APPEAL TO EXPERIENCE OF GOD

There have been repeated examples of people who in all sincerity claim to have experienced God. William James in his study of religious experience quotes the reports of several such people, including the following:

> I remember the night, and almost the very spot on the hilltop, where my soul opened out, as it were, into the Infinite, and there was a rushing together of the two worlds, the inner and the outer. It was deep calling unto deep—the deep that my own struggle had opened up within being answered by the unfathomable deep without, reaching beyond the stars. I stood alone with Him who had made me, and all the beauty of the world, and love, and sorrow, and even temptation. I did not seek Him, but felt the perfect unison of my spirit with His. The ordinary sense of things around me faded. For the moment nothing but an ineffable joy and exultation remained. It is impossible fully to describe the experience. It was like the effect of some great orchestra when all the separate notes have melted into one swelling harmony that leaves the listener conscious of nothing save that his soul is being wafted upwards, and almost bursting with its own emotion. The perfect stillness of the night was thrilled by a more solemn silence. The darkness held a presence that was all the more felt because it was not seen. I

could not any more have doubted that He was there than that I was. Indeed, I felt myself to be, if possible, the less real of the two.[5]

Here, clearly, is a person convinced beyond all doubt that during a mystical religious experience he had come in contact with God. From this we can construct the following quick proof of God's existence:

1. If someone experiences an entity, then the entity exists.
2. Some people have experienced God.
   Therefore
3. God exists.

Let us interpret what it is to experience an entity so that we can experience something only if it exists. On this interpretation premise (1) is true. This, however, does not also show (2) to be true, because there are many illusory experiences in which people think they experience entities but they are mistaken. Thus although the person James quotes was convinced he had experienced God, he may have been mistaken; his experience may have been illusory. Obviously, then, premise (2) is the crucial one. Have people experienced God?

People who think that premise (2) is true usually point to three different kinds of experiences to support their position—religious mystical experiences, revelations, and miracles. In these three cases, such people argue, either what is experienced is God, or what is experienced is the direct result of something God does. There is, however, an important difference between religious mystical experiences and the other two. If in a mystical experience someone experiences God, then, as in the case quoted, he does so by being transported in some way beyond the natural world into the otherworldly presence of God. In the case of revelations and miracles, on the other hand, God participates by actually intervening in the ordinary course of the natural world. For example, the ten commandments were supposedly revealed to Moses by means of inscriptions on ordinary stone tablets. Miracles, such as turning water

[5] W. James, *The Varieties of Religious Experience* (New York: Collier Books, 1961), p. 69.

into wine, supposedly were witnessed by people in this the natural world. Because of this important difference between these kinds of religious experiences we should consider their relevance to the argument from religious experience separately.

THE ARGUMENT FROM MYSTICAL EXPERIENCE

We must begin by clarifying what we mean by 'religious mystical experience.' We have a choice in such a definition. We can define a religious mystical experience either as an experience in which, among other things, a person actually does experience God or as an experience in which, among other things, a person believes that he experiences God. The difference between the two is that in the first case many experiences which people believe to be mystical experiences are not, because God is not actually experienced in them. In the second case we can grant all such experiences to be mystical but this implies nothing about whether God is experienced. Because in either case we must justify one claim, either that some experiences are mystical or that God is experienced in some mystical experiences, let us then choose the second kind of definition. This will allow us to define mystical experiences phenomenologically, without considering whether any entity is actually experienced.

In defining 'mystical experience' we can once again turn to William James. As a result of studying reports of mystical experiences such as the one quoted, James stated what he took to be the essential characteristics of such experiences. He said that mystical experiences are ineffable, transient, and noetic experiences in which the person involved is quite passive. Let us consider each of these characteristics.

1. *Ineffability.* The subjects of mystical experiences say that such an experience "defies expression, that no adequate report of the contents can be given in words. It follows from this that its quality must be directly experienced; it cannot be imparted or transferred to others."[6]
2. *Noetic Quality.* Those who have mystical experiences claim that they have gotten or received deeply significant and im-

---

[6] Ibid., p. 300.

portant insights during the experiences. Thus, to the person who experiences mystical states, they seem to be states of knowledge. They seem to be "states of insights into depths of truth unplumbed by the discursive intellect."[7] In the case of the religious mystic (that is, a person who thinks he experiences God in his mystical experiences), the insights or illuminations the subject thinks he attains are believed by him to be the result of a direct confrontation or union with the supreme being. For those whose mystical experiences are not religious, the insights are thought to be the result of a new and more heightened way of experiencing the world around us, rather than a result of contact with anything supernatural.

3. *Transiency.* As James points out, "Mystical states cannot be sustained for long. Except in rare instances half an hour, or at most an hour or two, seems to be the limit beyond which they fade into the light of common day."[8]

4. *Passivity of the Subject.* Although a person can prepare himself for and help bring about mystical experiences, "when the characteristic sort of consciousness once has set in, the mystic feels as if his own will were in abeyance, and indeed sometimes as if he were grasped and held by a superior power."[9]

All four of these qualities are exemplified in the report quoted previously. The subject claims he could not fully describe the experience; that he became aware of, was even in unison with, his maker; that the ineffable joy and exultation which accompanied the experience lasted a moment; and that he did not seek unison with his maker, but passively felt it take place. This is, then, a clear example of a religious mystical experience. Our problem is to discover whether such an experience can be used to justify premise (2), the claim that some people have experienced God. The argument in which we are interested can be put as follows:

4. Some people have had religious mystical experiences.
5. In religious mystical experiences God is experienced.

[7] Ibid.
[8] Ibid.
[9] Ibid.

Therefore
2. Some people have experienced God.

If there is good reason to accept premise (5), then we can justifiably conclude that God exists. We surely must agree that religious mystics do have strange experiences very much like the one described, so that we can accept (4). But is there good reason for us to admit as well that during these experiences the mystics actually get insight into reality, that they experience God in ways that they cannot describe to us? Might it not be true that a mystic is like a person who is hallucinating, like one who see a mirage and thinks that he is experiencing a real object? How are we to decide whether at least some religious mystics truly experience God or whether all such mystics have merely very unusual illusory experiences? We cannot check the claims of mystics in the way we often check possible cases of illusory experiences, such as mirages, because we cannot observe whether or not there is an object experienced. We can, for example, go to the location in the desert where a man claims to have seen an oasis and carefully investigate the whole area, but we cannot in any comparable manner go to the "region" in which the mystic claims to have been aware of God.

SUPPORT FOR THE ARGUMENT: GOD AS CAUSE OF INEXPLICABLE EXPERIENCES

There is one kind of obtainable evidence which would make it reasonable to accept the mystic's claim. If there are some of these very strange experiences which seem inexplicable in terms of the natural causes which are the subject matter of the natural sciences such as psychology, physiology, and biology, then we have at least some reason to think that the cause of such experiences is supernatural or divine. That is, we may have to postulate a supernatural cause to explain certain experiences. We could then justify the existence of such a being the way we justify postulating explanatory theoretical entities such as electrons, protons, and neutrons. These theoretical entities are postulated to explain certain observable phenomena. Such postulation is justified only if there is no way to explain what is observed without postulating something or other. If satisfactory explanations can be made without postulating such entities, then, as we saw in Chapter 4 about the witch-doctor's demons, we cannot justify the existence of such entities.[10] The question, then, is whether there is any reason to think that some mystical experiences cannot be explained by means of natural causes, so that there is reason to postulate a supernatural cause to explain them. If there is, then we may be able to use mystical experiences to justify premise (2). If there is not, then we shall have to conclude that whether or not the mystic experiences God, we have no grounds for claiming that he does and no way of using these experiences to justify premise (2).

OBJECTION: NO NEED TO POSTULATE SUPERNATURAL CAUSES

Many people claim that we can explain such experiences without any reference to a confrontation with anything supernatural or divine. They say that mystical experiences, like many other strange experiences, are really the result of abnormal states of mind, and like other psychological abnormalities they are the proper subject of physiology and psychology. Evidence in favor of this view comes from the fact that certain experiences which fit completely the description of mystical experiences given by James have quite natural explanations. Experiences which seem to provide indescribable insights into reality have been induced by inhalation of nitrous oxide (laughing gas), ether, and chloroform. It has also been found that certain drugs, such as mescaline and LSD, produce experiences with the phenomenological characteristics of mystical experiences. Surely, it is claimed, all these are merely abnormal experiences produced by natural causes.

Given all this evidence, it is reasonable to conclude that many mystical experiences have natural causes. We should be careful, however, about inferring from this that all mystical experiences can be given naturalistic, scientific explanations. Nevertheless, in the face of such evidence, there is little justification for holding that some mystical experiences are not scientifically explainable. We can conclude, therefore, that there is no reason to postulate that some supernatural force is the cause of religious mystical experiences. We can, as a result, also conclude that mystical experiences do not provide grounds sufficient to justify premise (2), that

[10] See pp. 299–300.

some people have experienced God. We cannot, however, draw the stronger conclusion that God is not experienced in such mystical experiences, because the mystic is not committed to the view that God is, either totally or in part, the cause of mystical experiences. He need only claim that as a result of being in a mystical state he experiences God, and this is consistent with saying that all mystical states are abnormal psychological states, and are the results of bodily causes. Consequently, however odd it may seem to some, it is possible that mystical experiences induced by gas or drugs are experiences in which some people become aware of God. The mystic, then, who becomes convinced by his experience that he experiences God, is not unreasonable, because we have not found grounds for claiming that the experience is illusory. But because there are not sufficient grounds for the rest of us to justify the claims of mystics, we must look elsewhere for an argument which justifies belief in God.

THE ARGUMENT FROM REVELATIONS AND MIRACLES

Revelations and miracles both differ from mystical experiences in that in the former, unlike the latter, God is thought to intervene in the ordinary course of the natural world. By 'God's intervention' is meant 'an occurrence in this, the natural world, which is not brought about by physical causes but is, rather, directly caused by God.' Thus, according to this definition, something is a revelation or a miracle only if it has a supernatural cause. Most people would probably agree that this is true of revelations where, for example, a vision appearing in a bush which burns but which is never consumed, is said to reveal some word of God. There has been, however, much disagreement regarding miracles. No one denies that some miracles—such as the Biblical miracles of turning water into wine, feeding a multitude from a few fish and loaves of bread, walking on water, and the vertical parting of the waters of the Red Sea—would be the direct result of supernatural causes, because in each case some law of nature would have been violated. That is, if each of these events occurred, there has been a violation of some scientific law which has been repeatedly confirmed to hold universally. Thus if we have reason to think that such events have occurred, then we have some reason to believe that God exists.

It has been claimed, however, that not all miracles involve a

violation of a natural law otherwise confirmed to hold universally.
R. F. Holland, for example, considers the case of a child who has
wandered onto a railroad track unaware of a train approaching
around a curve, so that there is no chance for the engineer to see
the child in time to stop. The mother, watching from a distance and
unable to help, sees the train approach and grind to a halt a few
feet from her child.

> The mother thanks God for the miracle; which she never ceases
> to think of as such although, as she in due course learns, there
> was nothing supernatural about the manner in which the brakes
> of the train came to be applied. The driver had fainted, for a
> reason that had nothing to do with the presence of the child
> on the line, and the brakes were applied automatically as his
> hand ceased to exert pressure on the control lever.[11]

It was an amazing coincidence that a particular natural process cul-
minated in his fainting at just the time he did.

Let us call any miracle, such as the preceding, which does not
violate any law of nature a "coincidence-miracle," and the kind
which does violate a law of nature, a "violation-miracle." Although
these two concepts of miracle differ importantly, there are three
features anything must have to be a miracle. First, whether or not
he intervenes, God is in some way involved in and responsible for
what occurs; secondly, what occurs is amazing and unusual; and,
thirdly, some disaster is avoided, or at least someone is aided, by
what occurs. In both cases the feature that is most relevant for our
purposes is that God is in some way involved in what occurs. Thus
if there is reason to think that either kind of miracle has ever occurred, then we are justified in believing that God exists. We are
interested in the following argument:

6. Some people have experienced miracles.
7. Miracles are, by definition, situations in which God participates.
   Therefore
2. Some people have experienced God.

---

[11] R. F. Holland, "The Miraculous," *American Philosophical Quarterly*
(1965), pp. 43–51.

In this argument, unlike the argument involving mystical experiences, the point that can be questioned is whether miracles ever occur, and thus whether people have ever experienced them. This is because miracles, unlike mystical experiences, occur only if God exists. Do we have any reason to think miracles have occurred? Let us consider each kind separately.

There have been many cases of amazing coincidence where horrible disasters have been averted. Do we have any reason to think that these are coincidence-miracles? We must also admit that there are many cases of incredible coincidences where horrible disaster has resulted. How should we handle these? Is there any reason, in either case, to reject the claim that these are no more than very rare and most improbable coincidences? So long as each such event is explainable, each in its own way, in terms of a coincidence of individually quite ordinary occurrences, then there is no reason to regard the coincidence as anything more than that; there is no reason to think that something supernatural is involved. Given all the many chances for coincidences, it is not at all surprising that once in a while some very surprising things occur quite naturally. Thus, there is no reason to believe that coincidence-miracles have occurred.

The more usual attempt to justify belief in God on the basis of miracles, however, is premised on the existence of violation-miracles. If there are grounds to believe that some law of nature confirmed to hold universally has been violated in such a way that some disaster has been averted, or someone aided, or some insight received, then this is surely some evidence for justifying the claim that occasionally God has intervened in the natural course of things, either to bring about a miracle or to reveal something. Are there, then, grounds for believing that there have been miraculous violations of laws of nature? The most celebrated attempt to deny such grounds is that made by David Hume.

HUME'S OBJECTION: BELIEF IN
VIOLATION-MIRACLES IS ALWAYS UNJUSTIFIED

Hume says,

> A miracle is a violation of the laws of nature; and as a firm and unalterable experience has established these laws, the

proof against a miracle, from the very nature of the fact, is as
entire as any argument from experience can possibly be imagined. . . . Nothing is esteemed a miracle, if it ever happens
in the common course of nature. It is no miracle that a man,
seemingly in good health, should die of a sudden; because such
a kind of death, though more unusual than any other, has yet
been frequently observed to happen. But it is a miracle that a
dead man should come to life; because that has never been
observed in any age or country. There must, therefore, be a
uniform experience against every miraculous event, otherwise
the event would not merit the appellation. And as a uniform
experience amounts to a proof, there is here a direct and full
proof, from the nature of the fact, against the existence of any
miracle; nor can such a proof be destroyed, or the miracle
rendered credible, but by an opposite proof, which is superior.[12]

Hume's point here is that we have grounds for believing that any
particular event is a violation-miracle or, similarly, a revelation,
only if we have reason to believe that the event violates a law which
has been confirmed to hold universally without exception. If a law
is violated which is already in doubt, then the violation would
provide further evidence that the law must be revised or replaced
by another which accounts for the event which violates the first
law. But once this is done there is no reason to think a violation-
miracle has occurred, because the event violates no acceptable law.
Consequently, to be counted a violation-miracle an event must
violate a law previously found to hold without exception. But,
claims Hume, because all the evidence relevant to such a law has
confirmed it as having no exceptions, all the evidence relevant to
the event being a violation of the law counts against the event
being a violation-miracle.

The crucial premise in Hume's argument is his claim that all the
evidence relevant to the event counts as evidence against it being a
violation of a law. It is true that all the evidence independent of the

[12] Hume, *Enquiries* (Oxford: Oxford University Press, 1955), edited by L. A.
Selby-Bigge, pp. 114–15.

event itself counts against a violation, but that does not rule out evidence provided by the event itself which might count in favor of a violation. Surely, it might be claimed, if someone personally witnesses an event which as he describes it is a clear violation of a law, then we have good reason to think that a violation has occurred. If, for example, someone claims that he witnessed a violation of a natural law, such as a dead man restored to life, then we have eye-witness evidence which, it could be argued, outweighs the independent evidence. Hume, however, has an answer to this argument. He agrees that we should weigh the two sets of conflicting evidence. The question, then, is whether it is more probable that such an eye witness is deceived about what he claims to have seen, or whether it is more probable that a dead man has been restored to life. Is it, as Hume asks it, more miraculous that what the person claims is false or more miraculous that a dead man is restored to life? He answers,

> I weigh the one miracle against the other; and according to the superiority which I discover, I pronounce my decision, and always reject the greater miracle. If the falsehood of his testimony would be more miraculous than the event which he relates, then, and not till then, can he pretend to command my belief or opinion.[13]

And because for any human the falsehood of his testimony, even when completely sincere, is less miraculous, that is, more probable than that a law of nature is violated, we should, as Hume implies, believe the person is mistaken rather than believe that the violation-miracle occurred.

Following Hume we can agree that the independent evidence outweighs the testimony of others. But what about a case in which someone himself experiences what surely seems to him to be a violation of a law of nature? This case is something like that of the mystic. It seems to both that they have experienced an event which in important ways is quite different from what has been established by uniform experience. Is it reasonable for a person

---

[13] Ibid., p. 116.

who has had a certain kind of experience which seems to violate a law of nature to believe that a violation actually has occurred? We have seen that the person who has had a mystical experience is not unreasonable in believing that he has experienced God, but we also saw that there is not sufficient reason to justify his belief. The case of miracles, however, differs from the mystic's case in an important respect. There is no evidence against the claim that the mystic experiences God because his experience may well result from perfectly natural causes. There is, however, a great deal of evidence against the claim that a violation has occurred. Thus, not only is there not sufficient reason to justify a claim that a violation-miracle occurred, but there is surely a question of whether one should trust one's own testimony in the face of the overwhelming evidence against the violation he seems to have witnessed. In short, the reasonable conclusion is that what was experienced is the result of natural causes in spite of the way it may seem. Hume's argument, therefore, seems to be sound, and its conclusion is justified, that is, there are no grounds for believing in violation-miracles or revelations. We cannot appeal to violations of laws of nature, whether violation-miracles or revelations, to justify belief in the existence of God. And because we have seen that we cannot appeal to coincidence-miracles, we must give up the attempt to justify God's existence by means of miracles and revelations.

We have been unable to justify belief in God by appealing to the experience of God. Is there any other kind of experience we might appeal to which would justify the belief? Some people have claimed that certain facts which we experience in this world can be used as a basis for justifying the belief, although they are not experiences of God. We often justify the existence of other entities in this way. For example, we justify the existence of subatomic particles, such as electrons and neutrinos, not by experiencing them, but by inferring their existence from the existence of things we do experience, such as visible traces in cloud chambers. Others have claimed, however, that because a supreme being lies outside the realm of what we can experience in this world, we cannot justify his existence by arguments that rely on what we experience. These people claim we must use what we can call, using the terminology of St. Thomas Aquinas, *a priori* proofs instead of *a posteriori* proofs. The difference between these two kinds of proof is that an *a posteriori* proof is a proof in which at least one premise is an *a posteriori* statement, and an *a priori* proof is one in which no premises are *a posteriori*, that is, all the premises are *a priori*.[14]

THREE *A POSTERIORI* ARGUMENTS

The proofs we have already examined and dismissed are a *posteriori*. The question before us now is whether there are any other *a posteriori* proofs which we might be able to use to justify belief in God. Aquinas, who thought that there are no *a priori* proofs of the existence of God thought there were several sound *a posteriori* proofs. He produced five different *a posteriori* ways to prove that God exists, the most plausible of which we shall consider now. They are the arguments from motion and from causation (which we shall examine together as the first-cause argument), the argument from contingency, and the argument from design.

THE FIRST-CAUSE ARGUMENT

The first two ways of Aquinas have basically the same structure. The main difference between the two is that in the first way, the argument from motion, Aquinas begins with the *a posteriori* truth that some things are in motion, whereas in the second he begins with the *a posteriori* truth that there is an order of efficient causes. Because Aquinas takes motion to include not merely locomotion or change of spatial position, but all kinds of change, let us say that the first-cause argument as we shall first construe it is based on the empirical fact that there are changes and causes of change. This argument, then, starts with the *a posteriori* truth that there are changes taking place now which are caused. It goes on to consider what would be the case if everything that causes a change were itself caused to change by something else, and concludes that

---

[14] For the distinction between *a priori* and *a posteriori*, see pp. 32–36.

its chain of causes would be infinitely long. That is, no matter how many items in its causal chain had been enumerated, there would always be at least one that had not been enumerated. But, so the argument goes, such a causal chain cannot go on to infinity in this way, because without a first or initiating cause of change there would be no intermediate causes of change and thus no change now, contrary to the facts. Consequently, because there is change now, there is a first or initiating cause of change, which, as Aquinas says, we call God.[15] Let us lay out this argument in some detail so that we can examine it thoroughly:

1. There are now things changing and things causing change.
2. If there are now things changing and things causing change, and something causes change only if it is caused to change by something else, then its causal chain is infinitely long. *Therefore*
3. If something causes change only if it is caused to change by something else, then its causal chain is infinitely long.
4. No causal chain can be infinitely long. *Therefore*
5. There is something that causes change but is not caused to change by anything else, that is, there is a first cause, namely, God.

FIRST INTERPRETATION: TEMPORALLY FIRST CAUSE
Before we begin to evaluate the argument we must settle the problem of interpretation. For most of us today it seems obvious that the first-cause argument is concerned with causes which temporally precede their effects and thus with a causal chain stretching back into the past. On this interpretation premise (4) asserts that a causal chain could not stretch back into the past over an infinite duration of time, because if there were no temporally prior, or first, cause of change then there could be no temporally subsequent causes of

[15] For Aquinas' statement of the first-cause argument, see St. Thomas Aquinas, *Basic Writings*, ed. A. C. Pegis (New York: Random House, 1945), Vol. I, p. 22.

change and no change now. However, there are two reasons for rejecting this interpretation. The first is that premise (4) seems to be false on this interpretation. There is no reason to think that a series of causes stretching infinitely back into the past is impossible. It is quite possible, and some people believe quite likely, that the raw material of which the universe in its present state is composed has existed in some state or other over an infinite period of time. Why could not change have been going on for an infinitely long period of time? It is only if at some time before now there were no change and now there is change, that we must postulate a temporally original cause of change. But if change has always occurred, there was no temporally first cause and therefore no creator *ex nihilo*. Such a situation can be illustrated by considering a phonograph record of a song being sung by a human voice. Let us assume that this record was recorded from another record, which was itself recorded from another record. Could this series of recordings go on to infinity? Some people might want to claim that somewhere in the past there must have been a human singer recorded. But it is surely possible that no matter how far back into the past you go you will always turn up another record. Consequently, if we are to make the argument as strong as possible, as we should always do before evaluating any argument, then we should look for a more plausible interpretation. Another reason for looking for a better interpretation is that the argument equates the first cause with God. But if by 'first' we mean 'temporally first' there is no reason to say that the first cause of change, which existed at least many thousands of years ago, still exists now. Thus, there is no reason to equate God with a temporally first cause.

SECOND INTERPRETATION: ONTOLOGICALLY ULTIMATE CAUSE

Is there a more plausible interpretation available? F. C. Copleston in his book *Aquinas* distinguishes two different ways in which one thing can be causally dependent on something else; consequently, he distinguishes two different kinds of causal orders, a temporal series of causes and an ontological hierarchy of causes. According to Copleston, for Aquinas the phrase 'first cause' does not mean first in the temporal order of causes, but rather supreme or first in the ontological order of causes.[16] This interpretation of 'first cause' as 'ontologically ultimate cause' rather than 'temporally first cause' allows us to avoid one of the problems facing the first interpretation. An ontologically ultimate cause exists now so that, unlike the temporally first cause, if we prove that there is such a cause we have no problem concerning its present existence. We might illustrate the difference between a temporal series and an ontological hierarchy of causes as follows. Consider a room with perfect reflecting mirrors on two opposite sides. In the middle of the room burns a candle which is reflected in the mirrors. We can imagine that this candle has been burning for an infinite period of time. That is, for an infinite period of time there have been light waves reflecting back and forth from one mirror to the other causing images in the two mirrors. Thus there has been causal action occurring over an infinite period of time. But, and here is where this example differs from the phonograph example, at any one moment the mirror images exist only if the candle exists at that moment. Although a recording of a voice can exist after what has caused the recording no longer exists, mirror images cannot. Thus we might say that the candle is of a different ontological order from the images. They depend for their very existence at any and every moment on the existence of the candle, but the existence of the candle in no way depends on the images for its existence. On this interpretation, then, the argument asserts that God is to things in the world what the candle is to its reflected images.

There is one problem that faces the first interpretation that we have not yet applied to Copleston's interpretation. We saw that there is no reason why an infinite temporal series of causes could not occur so that premise (4) seemed dubious. How does premise (4) fare on the second interpretation? Are there things in the world like the candle images in that for each of them they can exist at some time only if something else quite different also exists at that time? We know at least that for any human being to exist for any period of time, he is causally dependent upon what might indeed be interpreted as a hierarchy of coexistent causes. For example, his existence is dependent upon the temperature of the earth remaining

---

[16] See F. C. Copleston, *Aquinas* (Baltimore: Penguin Books, 1957), pp. 117–18.

within a certain range, which in turn is dependent upon the earth's distance from the sun, which is dependent upon the gravitational and centripetal forces affecting the earth, which are dependent upon the masses of the earth and sun, which are dependent upon the chemical constituents of the earth and sun, which are dependent upon the atomic and subatomic makeup of the earth and sun. We have, then, for each human being not only a series of antecedently preceding causes, but an order of contemporaneous causal factors. This does not seem to be what Copleston means, however, because this order of causes leads neither to infinity nor to anything we would call God. It seems to go to basic subatomic particles. What might Copleston reply here? He might claim that the basic subatomic particles are no different from anything else in the world. They also are causally dependent on something for their existence because their existence needs to be explained just like anything else in the world. In other words, he might link causes and causal orders with explanations as he did in a discussion of the topic with Bertrand Russell. He said, "Cause is a kind of sufficient reason. Only contingent beings can have a cause. God is His own sufficient reason; and He is not cause of Himself. By sufficient reason in the full sense I mean an explanation adequate for the existence of some particular being."[17] The point here is that if we are looking for the cause of something, we are looking for a sufficient reason for—that is, a complete explanation of—its existence. Perhaps, then, we should consider a first or ultimate explanation of why there are things like people, horses, stones, and even neutrinos, rather than considering first causes of change.

THIRD INTERPRETATION:
ULTIMATE EXPLANATION OF THINGS
We can state the argument as follows:

1. There are now things existing and things explaining their existence.
2. If there are now things existing and things explaining their existence and each thing that explains something else com-

[17] F. C. Copleston, from a debate on the Third Program of the British Broadcasting Corp., 1948.

pletely explains it only if it is itself explained by something
else, then its complete explanation is infinitely long.
Therefore
3. If each thing that explains something else completely explains it only if it is itself explained by something else, then
   its complete explanation is infinitely long.
4. No complete explanation can be infinitely long.
   Therefore
5. There is something that completely explains other things
   and is not explained by anything else, that is, there is something which is the ultimate explanation of things, namely,
   God.

It should be noted that on this interpretation the crucial claim in
the argument is not that there would be an infinite number of
different explanations, but that any complete explanation would be
infinitely long. The idea here is that if the explanation of one thing
requires reference to something else which itself needs to be explained, then the explanation of the first thing is not complete unless the second is completely explained.

One important consequence of this stress on the completeness of
the explanation of one thing is that it is possible to give a quite
plausible argument to support premise (4). Consider that we would
not call something an explanation unless we could completely express it, because the function of an explanation is to make what it
explains intelligible, and something is intelligible only if it can be
expressed. But a statement that is infinitely long is one that cannot
ever be fully stated or expressed. Thus, no complete explanation
can be infinitely long. Premise (4), then, no longer seems dubious.
Can we now accept the argument as sound? Not yet, because we
have not yet examined premise (2), which on this interpretation
may be the dubious one.

A PROBLEM: ARE ADEQUATE SCIENTIFIC
EXPLANATIONS COMPLETE EXPLANATIONS?

We can show premise (2) to be false if we can find an example
where one thing is explained by reference to something else in such
a way that even if we assume that each explaining thing must be

explained by something else, the original explanation is, nevertheless, both complete and finite in length. If we find such an example, then even if an infinite number of different explanations were required in order to explain completely everything there is, it would still be true that some specific explanations of individual things would be complete and finite, so that premise (2) would be false.

It seems quite easy to find many examples which can be used to show that premise (2) is false. Consider how we would explain that there is a high tide at a particular time and at a particular location of a certain ocean. We would do it in part by reference to the position of the moon relative to the location of the tide. Although the resulting explanation might seem quite complicated because it requires mathematical laws relating the relevant masses and the resulting gravitational attraction between the moon and the ocean it is clearly finite in length. Furthermore, it would seem, whether or not the position of the moon is to be explained by reference to something else, as it surely is, and even if the "chain" of separate explanations started in this way is infinitely long, that the adequacy of the original explanation of the high tide is unaffected. It is a completely adequate scientific explanation as it stands, regardless of what else needs to be explained. It surely seems, therefore, that the high tide is completely explained once a completely adequate scientific explanation is given. The explanation of the high tide is finite in length and seems to be complete even if we assume that each explaining thing must itself be explained by another. It seems, then, that premise (2) is false.

It is not hard to construct what the reply to this example would be. We said that the idea behind this interpretation is that to explain something completely, everything referred to in the explanation must also be completely explained. But this clearly cannot be achieved if an infinite number of different explanations is required. Therefore, this reply would go, the explanation of the high tides is incomplete because it does not explain the position of the moon; thus the example does not refute premise (2). The important point to notice about this reply is that someone who makes it is committed to the position that a completely adequate scientific explanation of the high tide is, nevertheless, not a complete explanation. This is exactly the point Copleston makes at another place in his debate with Russell.

Russell: But when is an explanation adequate? Suppose I am about to make a flame with a match. You may say that the adequate explanation of that is that I rub it on the box.

Copleston: Well, for practical purposes—but theoretically, that is only a partial explanation. An adequate explanation must ultimately be a total explanation to which nothing further can be added.

Russell: Then I can only say that you're looking for something which can't be got, and which one ought not to expect to get.

Copleston: To say that one has not found it is one thing; to say that one should not look for it seems to me rather dogmatic.[18]

Who is right in this debate? Russell claims that science is our means of explaining facts about the universe. Whatever science cannot explain is, according to Russell, beyond the realm of explanation. But should we accept anything as beyond explanation? Consider the widely accepted principle that is called the "principle of sufficient reason," but that we might also call the "principle of complete explanation," that is, the principle that everything that exists or occurs can be completely explained. If this principle is true, then it would seem that nothing should be beyond the realm of scientific explanation if science is the one means of explanation, as Russell claims. Two questions immediately arise here. First, is there something science cannot, in principle, explain; and second, is the principle of complete explanation true? Although there is no reason to think that science cannot come to explain each individual thing that occurs (and indeed perhaps some day even answer the question astronomers sometimes ask, "Why is there this particular universe rather than some other?"), there is another question it seems that science cannot answer. That question is, "Why is there any universe at all, rather than nothing at all?" Science may be able to explain why there is this particular universe by reference, for example, to the big-bang theory of the origin of the universe. On this theory this universe resulted from the explosion of one primordial mass that sent bits and pieces in all directions and formed the various galaxies that make up the universe. But, for example, science could

[18] Ibid.

not explain why, rather than nothing at all, there was this primordial mass waiting to explode. Here scientific explanation comes to an end, for there is nothing in terms of which the existence of the primordial mass can be scientifically explained. Thus if the principle of complete explanation is true, then it seems that there is at least one thing to be explained that science cannot explain. Copleston, then, might be able to begin a defense of premise (2) against the counterexample we have taken from scientific explanation.

Is there reason to think that the principle of complete explanation is true? Copleston might attempt to turn the principle against Russell by claiming that it is certainly a presupposition of science, for scientific progress is premised on the doctrine that everything can be explained. We might agree that the achievements of science surely argue for a kind of justification of the principle as it is used by science, but must we then go on to agree with Copleston that science cannot do the complete job? Following Russell, we could interpret the principle so that it is sufficient for scientific purposes but does not open the door to let in Copleston's nonscientific explanation. Science explains particular things and events so that the form of the principle needed for science is that there is a complete explanation of each particular event and each individual entity. Thus this version of the principle, while allowing science all it needs, in no way states that the universe as a whole must be explainable independently of the particular explanations of each of the things that make up the whole universe. If we accept this version then we can agree with Russell that a completely adequate scientific explanation is a complete explanation and the high-tide example would falsify premise (2). There would, then, be no reason to claim that God is necessary to explain the world around us, no reason to postulate God as a theoretical explanatory entity. Science does not, however, answer questions such as, "Why is there something rather than nothing?" so perhaps we should agree that some kind of nonscientific explanation is required. It is not clear which position is more reasonable; thus we have reached an impasse on this point. We can, nevertheless, draw a conclusion about our main interest in explanation. Because we have not been able to resolve the debate about explanation in Copleston's favor, we can conclude that, although premise (2) may be true, it is open to doubt and therefore cannot be used to justify the conclusion that God exists.

Thus, we should reject the third and final version of the first-cause argument. We cannot use it to justify belief in the existence of God.

THE ARGUMENT FROM CONTINGENCY

The third way of Aquinas is a most ingenious attempt to establish the existence of God. It begins with the *a posteriori* truth that there are contingent things, that is, things such that it is possible that they begin to exist and possible that they cease to exist, and concludes that there exists a necessary being, that is, a being such that it is impossible that it begin to exist or cease to exist. Such a being is said to exist necessarily and is what we call God.[19] Aquinas moves from the premise concerning the existence of contingent things to his conclusion by adding that it is impossible that contingent things always exist. Thus, he says, if everything is contingent then at some time before now nothing existed. But if at some time before now nothing at all existed, then nothing exists now, which is plainly false. Therefore there is a noncontingent, i.e., necessary, being, namely God. As stated, the crucial point in the argument is Aquinas' conclusion that if everything is contingent then at some time before now nothing existed. Copleston claims that "Aquinas is clearly supposing for the sake of the argument the hypothesis of infinite time, and his proof is designed to cover this hypothesis."[20] What Copleston seems to mean is that Aquinas was claiming that given that there has been an infinite amount of time before now during which there were contingent things, and that it is possible for all contingent things not to exist, it follows that at some time before now none of them existed. It would seem that this argument is based on two assumptions: that there was no first moment of time and that there have been contingent things at some time or other throughout an infinite duration of time. We can, how-

[19] For Aquinas' statement of the argument from contingency, see Aquinas, op. cit., pp. 22–23.
[20] Copleston, *Aquinas*, p. 120.

ever, reconstruct the argument so that it rests at most on the first assumption of infinite time. That is, we can reconstruct it so that it assumes neither that there have been things for an infinite amount of time nor that there have been things for only a finite amount of time. In other words, it assumes neither of the two different possibilities about the past existence of things. The first is that there is no time in the past before which nothing existed, that is, no matter how long ago a certain time, *t*, was, something existed at an earlier time. Notice that this is consistent with nothing existing precisely at *t*. The second possibility is that there is some time in the past before which nothing existed. Consequently, this version is to be preferred to one that assumes both infinite time and the existence of contingent things over an infinite amount of time, because there are fewer ways it can be refuted. Incidentally, this version also makes the argument consistent with a belief Aquinas surely held, namely, that God created the world *ex nihilo* at some time in the finite past. It can be stated as follows:

1. Either there have been things for an infinite amount of time or there have been things for only a finite amount of time.
2. If there have been things for an infinite amount of time, then each different sum total of existing entities that can occur has occurred at some time or other before now.
3. If the only things that exist are contingent, then one possibility is that at some time before now none of them existed.
   Therefore
4. If there have been things for an infinite amount of time and the only things that exist are contingent, then at some time before now nothing existed.   (from 2, 3)
5. If there have been things for only a finite amount of time and the only things that exist are contingent, then at some time before now nothing existed.
   Therefore
6. If the only things that exist are contingent, then at some time before now nothing existed.   (from 1, 4, 5)
7. If at some time before now nothing existed, then nothing exists now.

Therefore
8. If the only things that exist are contingent, then nothing exists now.   (from 6, 7)
9. It is false that nothing exists now.
Therefore
10. It is false that the only things that exist are contingent, that is, there is a necessary being, namely God.   (from 8, 9)

Although in premises (2) and (3) the argument considers the consequences of contingent things existing over an infinite duration of time, it also, in premise (5), considers the consequence of contingent things existing only over a finite duration of time. Premise (5) states that if things have existed for only a finite duration of time before now, then there was some first moment at which something began to exist so that at any time before that moment nothing existed. This is surely true if we grant that time is infinite whether or not things have existed for an infinite duration of time. So, given the addition of this premise and premise (1), which is an obvious truth, we can conclude (6), which contains no reference to either hypothesis about how long things have existed. Thus if premises (2) and (3) are true, then on this version of the argument from contingency we can draw a conclusion that does not depend on which hypothesis is correct. This is why it was claimed that this is a stronger argument than one based on the assumption that things have existed for an infinite time. However, the major question is whether premises (2) and (3) are true. We can surely accept (9). Premise (7), although not a necessary truth, can be restated as a more general version of the principle of the conservation of mass-energy, which states, roughly, that in a closed system no amount of energy, including that in the form of mass, can be either created or destroyed. Thus, if something new appears, this principle claims that it cannot have come from nothing, but requires a transfer of energy from something else. When premise (7) is considered in this light, it seems to be acceptable.

The crucial premises are clearly (2) and (3). Let us carefully consider both premises, beginning with premise (3), which is initially more plausible. If everything that has ever existed is contingent, then it is possible that each one ceases to exist at some time. Generally things cease existing at different times, so that usually at any one time some of them exist. But if we restrict our sample—for example, to the freshman class of a particular college—then although the members of the class will cease to exist at different times, there will come a time when all of these contingent beings have ceased to exist. If we now enlarge our sample to include all people and indeed all physical objects, we can see quite clearly that in this age of nuclear armament it is very possible that there come a time when no persons and indeed no physical objects exist. Surely, then, if only contingent things have ever existed, it is possible that at some time, which may as a matter of fact have occurred before now, every one of those things that had previously existed had ceased existing and no new one had begun to exist. Notice that this is not to claim it has happened, but only that it is possible that it has happened, which is a much weaker claim.

Premise (3) seems to be acceptable. But is it? Consider once again the principle of the conservation of mass-energy which we used as a reason for accepting premise (7). This principle states that if we take the universe to be a closed system, then no energy can be created or destroyed. But this looks familiar, because we can restate it to read that in the universe energy is such that it is impossible that some amount of it begin to exist and impossible that some amount of it cease to exist. Thus, given the truth of premise (9), once it is adapted to refer to energy, we must conclude that it is impossible that at some time before now nothing, including energy, existed. This will lead us to conclude that premise (3) is false unless we wish to claim that mass-energy exists necessarily rather than contingently, because it is something that can neither be created nor destroyed. But this is really not a viable way out, because when we characterized God as eternal, we decided that this should be interpreted so that it is logically impossible that he either begins to exist or ceases to exist. Thus a necessary being is one that is logically impossible to create or destroy. Therefore energy is contingent because it is logically possible to create or destroy it.

OBJECTION: AN EQUIVOCATION—PHYSICAL VS. LOGICAL POSSIBILITY

Something has gone wrong. On the one hand, premise (3) seems acceptable; on the other, it seems false. It surely seems possible that nothing exists, but it also seems impossible because the energy there is now could not have been created and cannot be destroyed. It seems that we have a problem about what is possible and what is not. To solve it we must examine the concept of possibility. It is important to note that there are several different kinds of possibility, two of which are relevant to our problem: logical possibility and physical possibility.

A. *Logical Possibility:* Something is logically possible if and only if it does not violate the laws of logic, that is, it does not logically imply a contradiction when it is conjoined with any analytically true sentence and the laws of logic. By this definition it is logically impossible that there is a married spinster living somewhere.

B. *Physical Possibility:* Something is physically possible if and only if (1) it is logically possible, and (2) it does not violate the physical laws of nature, that is, it is false that it logically implies a contradiction when conjoined with any true sentence (with which it is logically compatible) and with the laws of physics and logic. By this definition it is physically impossible that some cow jumped over the moon from the earth with no help.

If we re-examine premise (3) we shall find that it is acceptable when we interpret 'possible' one way, but quite dubious when we interpret it the other way. Let us consider physical possibility first. Thus (3) becomes:

3a. If the only things that have ever existed are logically contingent, then one physical possibility is that at some time before now nothing existed.

We can quickly show that (3a) is false by referring to the conservation principle. Let us assume that everything that has ever existed is some amount of energy, whether in the form of mass or some other form such as heat. Consequently, the only things that have existed are logically contingent. None are such that it is logically impossible to create or destroy them. Nevertheless, it is not physically possible that at some time before now nothing existed. Energy, although logically contingent, is physically necessary, that is, it is physically impossible to create and destroy it. Consequently, (3a) is false. It was when we construed 'possibility' as 'physical possibility' that (3) seemed false.

At this point someone might object that this way of handling (3a) rules out completely the claim that God created the world *ex nihilo*, because the law of the conservation of mass-energy, as here interpreted to apply to the universe as a whole, entails that a certain amount of energy has always existed. It is true that applying the law in this way makes creation *ex nihilo* physically impossible, but this does not rule out creation. Such a creation is surely a miracle and, like all violation-miracles, involves the physically impossible. Thus, although we would agree with Hume that violation-miracles and *a fortiori* creation *ex nihilo* are highly improbable, on the basis of what has been repeatedly established, this does not rule them out completely. That is, it does not make it logically impossible that they occur and, as we have also seen, it is only if miracles and creation *ex nihilo* were logically impossible that God would be unable to perform them.

Because (3a) using 'physical possibility' will not do, let us try 'logical possibility,' so that (3) becomes:

3b. If the only things that exist are logically contingent, then one logical possibility is that at some time before now nothing existed.

It can be quickly seen that (3b) is true. If we claim that everything is such that it is logically possible that it cease to exist, then there is no logical contradiction in also claiming that nothing exists. We contradict ourselves only if we claim that something exists necessarily, that is, it exists now and it is logically impossible that it begin or cease to exist, and also claim that at some time nothing exists. We should then use (3b) in the argument from contingency.

Premise (2) is surely the most dubious of the premises, but I think we can make it seem somewhat more plausible by using on analogy involving coins. Consider two coins which are such that for each it is possible that it comes up heads and possible that it comes up tails. What are the possibilities available? There are 2^n possibilities, where n is the number of coins involved. Thus for two coins there are four possibilities: heads, heads; heads, tails; tails, heads; and tails, tails. If we are given an infinite number of flips of these two coins we can surely conclude that at some time or other each of these possibilities will occur. Thus if premise (2) were stated as the flipping of two coins rather than the existence of objects, we could conclude that it is true. Furthermore, if we consider a million such coins, although there would be 2^{10^6} possibilities, nevertheless given an infinite series of flips of all million coins, it would still seem likely that each of the 2^{10^6} possibilities would have occurred at least once at some time or other. Indeed no matter how many coins we have, as long as the number is finite, it would seem that, given an infinite number of flips, each possibility would occur at least once. If we now apply the analogy so that we move from coins that can come up heads and can come up tails, to objects that can begin to exist and can cease existing, then we can see that given an infinite amount of time there may be some reason to claim that each possibility would occur at some time or other, and thus with premise (3) we would conclude, as in (4), that the one possibility of none of these objects existing would occur.

If, as the coin analogy implies, we might be able to accept premise (2), then the present interpretation of the argument from contingency may well be sound, because each premise is plausible and the argument is valid. One thing that should give us pause, however, is that the plausibility of premise (3) depends on which sense of 'possibility' is used. Which one have we used to make premise (2) plausible? To find out let us consider another example, this time involving a roulette wheel. Given that there are an infinite number of turns of the wheel, it would seem that the ball would stop at least one time at each number at which it is physically possible for the ball to stop, no matter how large the roulette wheel is. Would it also stop at each logically possible number? Consider a roulette wheel that is fixed so that it is physically impossible for the ball to stop at the number 1. In such a case, the ball would not stop at least once at each number at which it is logically possible to stop, because there is no logical contradiction in the claim about a roulette wheel that its ball will stop at number 1, even if one also asserts that the wheel is fixed so that it is physically impossible that it stop at the number 1. Consequently, if the universe is more like a fixed roulette wheel than like one which runs randomly, then some things that are logically possible will not occur. Although it is logically possible that some day the cow will jump over the moon with no one helping it, it is surely physically impossible, so that we can conclude that it will not happen. It is physical possibility rather than logical possibility that is important for what occurs. Furthermore, because the law of the conservation of mass-energy can be used to show that certain logically possible situations, such as the situation in which nothing at all exists, are physically impossible and thus will not occur unless miraculously, we must use 'physical possibility' in (2) if we are to make it at all plausible.

We must use 'physical possibility' in premise (2) to make it plausible, but we had to use 'logical possibility' in (3) to make it plausible. We need to use different senses of 'possibility' in these two premises for both to be plausible. The result is that we can make them both plausible only by equivocating in our use of the word 'possibility.' But this makes the argument invalid, because any argument to be valid must use all its terms univocally, with one meaning, throughout. Therefore the argument from contingency is faced with the following dilemma: if there is no equivocation on the word 'possible,' then at least one premise is false and the argument is unsound. If there is an equivocation on 'possible,' then the argument is invalid and, consequently, unsound. From this we can conclude that the argument is unsound. We cannot justify belief in God using the argument from contingency.

THE ARGUMENT FROM DESIGN

One of the most discussed arguments that has been used to justify belief in the existence of God is the argument from design, or, as it is called, the teleological argument. Although this argument is like those we have already examined in that it is an *a posteriori* argument, it differs from them in an important way. Unlike the previous arguments, which are all deductive, the argument from design is essentially an inductive argument. It is an attempt to construe the universe, or at least certain characteristics of the universe, as being like certain things humans have designed and created, so that we can inductively infer from this evidence of design that there is a designer or creator like the intelligent designer of human artifacts but, obviously, much more intelligent. At the core of the argument, then, lies an analogy between the universe and things we know to be designed and created by intelligent beings. The argument from design, then, is an analogical argument, and we should, therefore, briefly examine the form of an analogical argument. Let us assume that there is some object O_1 and that we want to find out whether it has some property P_1, but we cannot find this out in any direct way. If we compare O_1 with some other objects we know to have property P_1 and find that O_1 is like the others in several other respects but differs from them in no important respects, then we can conclude that probably O_1 has property P_1. It is important, of course, that all the available evidence be considered, because there may be differences which make it improbable that O_1 has property P_1.

ANALOGICAL ARGUMENTS

We can state the general form of an analogical argument as follows:

1. Objects $O_1, O_2, O_3, \ldots O_n$ have properties $P_2, P_3, P_4, \ldots P_n$ in common.
2. Objects $O_2, O_3, \ldots O_n$ have property P_1.
   Therefore, probably
3. Object O_1 has property P_1.

We have said that all the available evidence must be considered if a statement such as (3) is to be justified in this way, because there are certain kinds of factors which decrease the probability of the conclusion. There are also, however, factors that raise the probability, thereby strengthening the argument. Therefore, as with any inductive argument, the requirement to use all available evidence—called the requirement of total evidence—is essential. To see the importance of this requirement, consider the following example. Let us assume that O_1 is a car you wish to buy, that P_1 is the property of having a gas consumption of at least fifteen miles per gallon, and that you cannot test the car before you buy it. You can get some idea of the gas consumption of the car by comparing it with the gas consumption of other cars. The more cars you know about that get at least fifteen miles per gallon—that is, the greater the number of cars included in $O_2 \ldots O_n$ that have property P_1—the more probable it will be that car O_1 has property P_1. Furthermore, the more properties that these other cars have in common with car O_1—such as the number of cylinders, the kind of transmission, the make of the car, the age of the engine, and the like—the more probable it will be that car O_1 will also get at least fifteen miles per gallon. However, if you find that many cars that have the same number of cylinders, the same kind of transmission, the same age engine, and so on, do not get at least fifteen miles per gallon, then the probability that the car you are thinking of buying will get fifteen miles per gallon will decrease markedly. Furthermore if, given the same information in your premises, you are interested in eighteen miles per gallon instead of fifteen miles per gallon, then the probability that your car will get eighteen miles per gallon is less than the probability that it will get fifteen miles per gallon.

From this example we can extract four different kinds of factors which will affect the probability of the conclusion. These and other relevant factors must be weighed in arriving at any final statement about the probability or improbability of a conclusion. The following two factors will strengthen the argument, that is, increase the probability of the conclusion:

   i. The greater the number of objects included in $O_2 \ldots O_n$ having properties $P_1 \ldots P_n$, the more probable is the conclusion.
   ii. The greater the number of properties included in $P_2 \ldots P_n$ that the objects $O_1 \ldots O_n$ have in common, the more probable is the conclusion.

The following two factors decrease the probability of the conclusion:

   iii. The greater the number of objects that have $P_2 \ldots P_n$ but that do not have P_1, the less probable is the conclusion.
   iv. The stronger the claim made in the conclusion, relative to the premise, the less probable is the conclusion.

Let us return now to the argument from design. But let us also keep in mind these four factors that affect the probability or likelihood of the conclusions of analogical arguments so that we do not overlook them and thereby fail to meet the requirement of total evidence.[21]

---

[21] See I. Copi, *Introduction to Logic* (New York: Macmillan, 1965), Chap. 11, for a more detailed examination of analogical arguments.

TWO VERSIONS OF THE ARGUMENT FROM DESIGN

The two most celebrated versions of the argument from design are found in Hume's *Dialogues on Natural Religion* and the fifth way of Aquinas. Aquinas states his version as follows:

> We see that things which lack knowledge, such as natural bodies, act for an end, and this is evident from their acting always, or nearly always, in the same way, so as to obtain the best result. Hence it is plain that they achieve their end, not fortuitously, but designedly. Now whatever lacks knowledge cannot move towards an end, unless it be directed by some being endowed with knowledge and intelligence; as the arrow is directed by the archer. Therefore some intelligent being exists by whom all natural things are directed to their end; and this being we call God.[22]

In the *Dialogues* it is Cleanthes who proposes the argument in the following way:

> Look around the world: Contemplate the whole and every part of it: You will find it to be nothing but one great machine, subdivided into an infinite number of lesser machines, which again admit of subdivisions, to a degree beyond what human senses and faculties can trace and explain. All these various machines, and even their most minute parts, are adjusted to each other with an accuracy, which ravishes into admiration all men, who have ever contemplated them. The curious adapting of means to ends, throughout all nature, resembles exactly, though it much exceeds, the production of human contrivance; of human design, thought, wisdom, and intelligence. Since therefore the effects resemble each other, we are led to infer, by all the rules of analogy, that the causes also resemble, and that the Author of nature is somewhat similar to the mind of man, though possessed of much larger faculties, proportioned to the grandeur of the work, which He has executed. By this argument *a posteriori*, and by this argument

---

[22] Aquinas, p. 23.

alone, do we prove at once the existence of a Deity and His similarity to human mind and intelligence.[23]

What both versions have in common is the claim that in the universe and among its natural parts there is evidence of a design or purpose, and that this design or purpose requires the existence of an intelligent being who directs the universe and its parts according to his purpose. However, there are two important differences between these two versions that we should consider before we critically evaluate them. To see better what these differences are let us lay out the arguments formally. We can interpret Aquinas' version as follows:

1. The natural objects that make up the universe (that is, the nonsentient, nonmanmade objects, such as trees, rocks, mountains, planets) act to achieve some end or goal.
2. If something acts to achieve an end, then it is directed toward that end by some intelligent being.
3. No natural objects are intelligent beings.
   Therefore
4. There exists some intelligent being that directs the natural objects to achieve some end or goal.
5. This director is God.

Cleanthes' version can be stated as follows:

1. The universe is like a huge manmade machine made up of many lesser machines, except that the universe is much more complex than any manmade machine.
2. Like effects have like causes.
3. The cause of a manmade machine is an intelligent being.
   Therefore, probably
4. The cause of the universe is an intelligent being.
5. This cause is God.

One difference, immediately evident, is that whereas Cleanthes' ver-

---

[23] Hume, *Dialogues Concerning Natural Religion* (Indianapolis: Bobbs-Merrill), p. 143.

sion is plainly an inductive analogical argument, Aquinas' version appears to be a straightforward deductive argument. Where is the inductive feature we claimed is essential to the argument from design? If we scrutinize the first premise of each argument we can see the reason Aquinas' version seems to lack the analogical character of Cleanthes' version. Aquinas' first premise is surely much more dubious than that of Cleanthes, because whereas Aquinas claims that natural objects act for an end, Cleanthes claims merely that they are like things that we know to act for an end—for example, machines. What reason could there be to accept Aquinas' first premise? The obvious justification would require an analogical argument such as:

6. The natural objects that make up the universe are like things which act to achieve some end or goal.
Therefore, probably
1. The natural objects that make up the universe act to achieve some end or goal.

For the argument from Aquinas, then, the analogy with things known to be designed seems to be what justifies the first premise. And because this is the only dubious premise, premises (2) and (3) being acceptable, the analogy lies at the core of the argument. We can accept premise (2) because it surely seems that only a being with intelligence could set a goal to be achieved and set about achieving it by various means. Furthermore, because we have seen that by 'natural objects' we mean those nonsentient, nonmanmade objects which make up the universe, we can grant that premise (3) is true by definition.

The second difference between the two versions is more important. Aquinas talks only of an intelligent being who directs natural objects to some goal, whereas Cleanthes talks about the author of nature. That is, Aquinas' version proves only that there is some very intelligent director or designer who has planned the course of the universe, but Cleanthes' version proves that an extremely intelligent being created the universe in accordance with some plan or purpose. Before we examine the argument we must decide which conclusion to use. We know that Cleanthes' conclusion is stronger than Aquinas' because it claims that there is a creator and designer whereas Aquinas' conclusion merely claims there is a designer. Thus Aquinas' conclusion will be more probable than that of Cleanthes relative to the same set of premises. However, the purpose of the argument is to establish the existence of God, and what we would call God is not merely the designer, but also the creator of the universe. Consequently, if we merely establish that there is a designer or architect of the universe, there is some doubt whether we are justified in calling such a being God. Let us, then, use Cleanthes' version for the purpose of a critical evaluation.

We can put Cleanthes' argument into the form of analogical arguments that we have previously discussed by letting O_1 = the universe, $O_2 \ldots O_n$ = various kinds of machines, P_1 = the property of having an intelligent designer and creator and $P_2 \ldots P_n$ = various properties O_1 has in common with $O_2 \ldots O_n$. If we pick for an example of a machine a watch as used by another defender of the argument, William Paley, we can point out several properties in common.[24] A watch has gears which revolve in a certain orderly way on certain axes, some of which affect others so as to cause the regular ticking off of the seconds, minutes, and hours. Similarly, we can observe the moon revolving around the earth and the earth revolving on its axis, and also around the sun, in a certain orderly way so as to cause the regular rising and falling of the tides and the regular coming of day and night. The earth, moon, and sun in their various relationships to each other produce a regular temporal procession just as do the gears of a watch in their various relationships. And because a watch has property P_1 (that is, has an intelligent designer and creator), so also, most probably, does the earth and the rest of the universe. This, then, is the argument that we shall consider. However, this is not the only analogy possible. Although we have followed Cleanthes and likened the universe to a machine, there is also design to be found in human works of art. The formal relationships of shapes and colors which go together to produce the beautiful design of a painting are much like the shapes and colors which go together to produce the quiet beauty of a sunset reflected in a mountain pool, or the brilliant beauty of a New England fall, with the colors of leaves contrasting with the white of birch trunks. If we were to

[24] See W. Paley, *Evidences of the Existence and Attributes of the Deity.*

use this analogy, then God would be the supreme artist rather than the greatest inventor. We shall, however, continue to use Cleanthes' machine analogy, because there seems to be no reason to think that the art analogy is any better.

In evaluating Cleanthes' argument we can do no better than to turn to his antagonist in the *Dialogues*, Philo, for the crucial objections. Philo's chief objections are aimed at two places: at the strength of the analogy and thus at the strength of the analogical justification of (4), and at the inference from (4) to (5)—that is, from the claim supported by the analogy that there is a cause of the universe to the conclusion that this cause is God.

OBJECTION TO CLEANTHES' ANALOGY:
NONINTELLIGENT CAUSES OF DESIGN

Philo's objection to the analogical grounds of the argument is essentially an attempt to show that there is no reason to think that the universe resembles the creation of an intelligent being any more than the causal product of nonintelligent forces. In effect, Philo is trying to show that many objects have properties $P_2 \ldots P_n$ in common with the universe, but do not have property P_1, that is, do not have an intelligent designer and creator. Philo is, then, applying factor (iii) in order to decrease the probability of the conclusion to a point where it is no longer probable. Philo claims that although what order and design we find in the universe might be attributed to intelligence, there are at least three other causes of order and design which have equal claim. Consider the order and design that results from vegetable reproduction, animal reproduction, and instinct.[25] We can find intricate order, design, and beauty in a flower, bush, or tree, and all of these are brought about not by an intelligent being but come from a seed in the ground which receives water and sunlight. In none of these four factors—seed, earth, water, sunlight—is there any hint of intelligence. Furthermore, consider a beautiful Persian cat, a peacock, exotic tropic fish, or even a particular human being. The ordering of parts of such organisms, the interrelating functioning of parts, the beauty of

[25] See Hume, *Dialogues Concerning Natural Religion*, pp. 178–80.

many of them are all the causal result of the fertilization of an egg in an act of animal reproduction. Here again there is no reason to think that intelligence was at all relevant, not even in the case of humans, where intelligence is usually used to avoid fertilization. Think also of the marvelous order and design produced by instinct. The geometric precision of bee hives, the intricate pattern of ant tunnels, the functional design of birds' nests and beaver dams all seem to be effects of instinctive forces rather than the studied result of some intelligent planning. What grounds are there for picking one from among four quite different causes of order and design? It is no less reasonable to claim, and therefore no less probable, that the earth and the other parts of the universe have sprouted from some seed or matured from some egg fertilized eons ago, or some residual part of the instinctive production of some animal long since extinct, than to claim that it is the planned result of some unseen being with great intelligence. Indeed, as Philo says in countering Cleanthes' analogy with one of his own,

> Now if we survey the universe, so far as it falls under our knowledge, it bears a great resemblance to an animal or organized body, and seems actuated with a like principle of life and motion. A continual circulation of matter in it produces no disorder: A continual waste in every part is incessantly repaired: The closest sympathy is perceived throughout the entire system: and each part or member, in performing its proper office, operates both to its own preservation and to that of the whole. The world, therefore, I infer, is an animal; and the Deity is the *soul* of the world actuating it, and actuated by it.[26]

There are other ways that order and design can come about, one of the most usual being by purely physical forces. Millions of uniquely complex and lovely designs are found by examining snow flakes and crystals of certain salts. The flakes are the effects of temperature on water vapor and the crystals are the effects of a supersaturation of a salt solution. In neither case do we find intelligence. Order and design are all around us produced in many

[26] Ibid., pp. 170–71.

different ways by many different forces. This may cause us to marvel at the wonder of it all, and unable to believe that it could happen merely by chance, we sometimes are led to conclude there must be some guiding force behind it all. But if there is such a force it might be instinct, purely mechanical force, or indeed a combination of many varied kinds of forces, each producing its own kind of order and design. It will do no good to try to claim that all these other causes of order and design are the result of intelligence or that they are evidence of some more basic originating intelligent force. Although this claim might be true, we cannot assume it, because it is what the argument is attempting to prove. Furthermore, there is no reason to think that it is true. Indeed if we consider that part of the universe that we inhabit, as we must in drawing analogies from what we know, we find that each intelligent being was brought about by some particular act of animal reproduction, but that so far at least there is no reason to think that any cases of animal reproduction are the result of intelligence. Thus on the basis of the available evidence we should conclude that probably intelligence is not the originating cause of order and design; perhaps it is merely one of the resultant causes. This conclusion is bolstered by the theory of evolution, which claims that human beings, with their intelligence, have evolved over a long period from forms of life lacking intelligence and that they have done so as a result of the interplay of such nonintelligent factors as random mutation, food shortages, and the instinct for survival. If this theory is correct, then intelligence is a very recent addition to those forces that can bring about order and design.

From the preceding discussion we can conclude, with Philo, that because intelligence is only one among many things in this world that produce order and design, there is no reason to think it is any more probable that an intelligent being produced the universe than that one of the other causes of order and design produced the universe. Consequently, although we can agree with Cleanthes that the universe is in several respects like a machine which has property P_1, we have also found that it is like many things that do not have property P_1, so that the probability that the universe has property P_1 is quite low indeed. It is surely too low to conclude that from among all the kinds of causes of order and design we can pick out one which is probably the cause of the universe and that one is intelligence.

OBJECTION TO INFERRING THE CAUSE
OF THE UNIVERSE IS GOD:
LIKE EFFECTS HAVE LIKE CAUSES

We have seen that the analogy essential to the argument from design cannot support the conclusion, statement (4)—'The cause of the universe is an intelligent being.' In a sense, then, it is superfluous to go on to show that even if statement (4) is granted, the move from (4) to (5)—'This cause is God'—is unsound. However, not only is Philo's objection to this move interesting in its own right, but it stresses another important point relevant to supporting conclusions about unknown things by means of analogies with known things. Philo points out that if we conclude (4) on the basis of the similarity between the universe and some human artifact, such as a watch or ship or house, then we must conclude in accordance with the principle that like effects have like causes, that the causes of the artifacts and of the universe are equally similar. In other words, although the more similar the universe and human artifacts are, the more probable premise (4) is, it is also true that the more similar they are, the more similar are their causes. Thus if the similarity is sufficient to make (4) probable, then we must follow through with the analogy and conclude that probably the causes are much alike. But if this is so, and if we accept the inference from (4) to (5), then, as Philo points out, we would have to attribute some most ungodlike characteristics to God. Consider the following points made by Philo:

[1] Even if this world were perfect it must still remain uncertain, whether all the excellences of the work can justly be ascribed to the workman. If we survey a ship, what an exalted idea must we form of the ingenuity of the carpenter, who framed so complicated, useful and beautiful a machine? And what surprise must we entertain, when we find him a stupid mechanic, who imitated others, and copied an art, which, through a long succession of ages, after multiplied trials, mistakes, corrections, deliberations, and controversies, had been gradually improving? Many worlds might have been botched and bungled, throughout an eternity, ere this system was struck out: Much labour lost: Many fruitless trials made: And a slow but continued

improvement carried on during infinite ages in the art of world making.[27]

[2] And what shadow of an argument, continued Philo, can you produce, from your hypothesis, to prove the unity of the Deity? A great number of men join in building a house or ship, in rearing a city, in framing a commonwealth: Why may not several deities combine in contriving and framing a world? This is only so much greater similarity to human affairs.[28]

[3] But further, Cleanthes; men are mortal, and renew their species by generation; and this is common to all living creatures. Why must this circumstance, so universal, so essential, be excluded from those numerous and limited Deities?[29]

[4] And why not become a perfect anthropomorphite? Why not assert the Deity or Deities to be corporeal, and to have eyes, a nose, mouth, ears, etc.?[30]

Philo summarizes his point by saying that a person who adopts Cleanthes' analogy might perhaps be able to assert that the universe is the product of some designer, but he can go no further on the basis of the analogy.

This world, for aught he knows, is very faulty and imperfect, compared to a superior standard; and was only the first rude essay of some infant Deity, who afterwards abandoned it, ashamed of his lame performance; it is the work only of some dependent, inferior Deity; and is the object of derision to his superiors: it is the production of old age and dotage in some superannuated Deity; and ever since his death, has run on at adventures, from the first impulse and active force which it received from him. . . .[31]

[27] Ibid., p. 167.
[28] Ibid.
[29] Ibid., p. 168.
[30] Ibid.
[31] Ibid., p. 169.

In short, if the analogy with human artifacts is close enough to make it probable that an intelligent being created the universe, it is close enough to make the creator so much more like man than like God that we must reject the claim made in (5) that the creator of the universe as established in (4) is God. We cannot establish (5) by means of the argument from design.

We have found two objections to the design argument which are sufficient to eliminate it as an inductive justification of the belief that God exists. This is the last plausible *a posteriori* argument for the existence of God. The natural move at this point is to reject *a posteriori* proofs and claim that if the belief in the existence of God is to be justified it must be by some *a priori* proof, some proof that uses no premises which are justified by evidence gathered through the experiences men have in this world. Let us consider such a proof.

AN *A PRIORI* ARGUMENT

One of the simplest yet most intriguing and baffling arguments that has ever been devised is the ontological argument. From the time of St. Anselm, in the eleventh century, to the present it has been endlessly discussed. Time and time again it has been thought to be refuted and finally laid to rest, only to reappear as troublesome as ever. There have been two classical statements of the argument, one by St. Anselm and one by René Descartes. We shall consider Descartes' version first because it is the simpler argument of the two and brings out more directly one of the central points of contention.

THE ONTOLOGICAL ARGUMENT: DESCARTES' VERSION

Descartes argues that

whenever I choose to think of the First and Supreme Being, and as it were bring out the idea of him from the treasury of my mind, I must necessarily ascribe to him all perfections, even if I do not at the moment enumerate them all, or attend to each. This necessity clearly ensures that, when later on I observe that existence is a perfection, I am justified in concluding that the First and Supreme Being exists.[32]

We can lay out Descartes' argument in the following simple form:

1. All perfections are properties of the supreme being.
2. Existence is a perfection.
    Therefore
3. The supreme being has existence, that is, exists.

Although the first premise is usually granted, the second has come under repeated severe attacks. One kind of attack on premise (2) has been to argue that if existence is a perfection, then it is a property or characteristic some things have and some things do not have; and if existence is a property of things, then the word 'existence' is a predicate, because properties of things are referred to by predicates. But the word 'existence' is not a predicate, so that existence is not a perfection. The obvious reply to this objection is that existence surely is a predicate, because it can be predicated of a subject in a sentence. However, those who use this refutation of premise (2) are not denying that 'existence' is a grammatical predicate. They put their point in several different ways, but the central claim of them all is that 'existence' is not a descriptive predicate. That is, it is not a predicate that can be used to describe things; it is not a predicate that can be used to refer to some property which things might have. If it can be shown that 'existence' is not such a predicate, then there is good reason to conclude that existence is not a property and, therefore, not a perfection.

KANT'S OBJECTION: 'EXISTENCE' IS NOT A PREDICATE
The classical and perhaps strongest attempt to show that 'existence' is not a predicate is based on the objection made by Immanuel

---

[32] Descartes, *Philosophical Writings*, edited by E. Anscombe and P. T. Geach (Edinburgh: T. Nelson, 1959), pp. 104–105.

Kant nearly two centuries ago. This has been considered by many people to be the objection which once and for all refuted Descartes' version of the ontological argument. The crucial part of his objection centers on the concept of a real predicate, that is, according to Kant, a predicate "which determines a thing." In other words, a real predicate is one which can be used to help define what something is. It is, then, what we can call a defining predicate. Kant argues as follows:

> *Being* is obviously not a real predicate; that is it is not a concept of something which could be added to the concept of a thing. It is merely the positing of a thing, or of certain determinations, as existing in themselves. Logically it is merely the copula of a judgment. The proposition, 'God is omnipotent,' contains two concepts, each of which has its object—God and omnipotence. . . . If, now, we take the subject (God) with all its predicates (among which is omnipotence), and say 'God is,' or 'There is a God,' we attach no new predicate to the concept of God, but only posit the subject in itself with all its predicates, and indeed posit it as an *object* that stands in relation to my *concept*.[33]

It will be helpful to interpret this argument as being concerned with how one term can be used to change the meaning of another. This will give us some better way to interpret what Kant means by one concept being added to another concept. For example, we consider that the term 'bachelor' is defined by the two predicates 'unmarried' and 'male.' We could, however, "add" another predicate to the definition such as 'happy,' and so change the meaning of 'bachelor.' Any predicate which can help determine the meaning of a term in this way is a defining predicate. Thus a term can be a defining predicate whether or not it is ever actually used in a definition. The only requirement is that it be possible to use it in such a manner. We can now construe Kant's argument as:

1. If a term is a real (defining) predicate, then it can be added to the meaning of a term to change its meaning.

---

[33] Kant, *Critique of Pure Reason*, translated by N. K. Smith (London: Macmillan, 1958), pp. 504–505.

2. The term 'exist' cannot be added to the meaning of a term
to change its meaning.
Therefore
3. The term 'exist' is not a real predicate.

Premise (1) is surely acceptable, because if a predicate can be used
to define a term, then it can be used to redefine a term and thereby
change its meaning. Premise (2), however, is not so clearly true.
Kant defends it by claiming that whenever we assert that something
exists, although we predicate 'exist' of a term, we are saying, in
effect, that the term *with the meaning it has* applies to something
or other. Thus we do not ever change the meaning of a term when
we use it to say that something exists. When we say, for example,
that some happy bachelors exist, in no case are we trying to change
the meaning of the phrase 'happy bachelor.' We are claiming instead that the phrase as given applies to some entities. If Kant's
defense of premise (2) is sound, then it seems that he has established
that 'existence' is not a real or defining predicate.

Although this is a rather persuasive argument there are at least
two objections that can be raised against it. First, even if the argument is sound it is not clear how it shows that existence is not a
property. The most it can show is that existence is not a defining
property of anything. In other words, all it shows is that any statement which asserts that something exists is synthetic rather than
analytic, but this is not enough to show that existence is not a
property. Some people have argued that showing that no existence
statements are analytic is sufficient to refute Descartes' version of
the ontological argument. If so, then enough has been done for our
purposes. This is wrong, however. Although in many passages
Descartes can be interpreted as claiming that 'God exists' is
analytic, his argument, either as quoted or as we have recon-
structed it, does not imply that it is necessary that God exists.
Consequently, the argument does not imply that 'God exists' is
analytic. It is true that Descartes claims that God necessarily has all
perfections, but he does not claim that it is necessary that existence
is a perfection. Thus the argument is compatible with 'God exists'
being logically contingent (nonanalytic). Descartes' argument, therefore, cannot be refuted merely by showing that 'exist' is not a defining or real predicate.

There is a reply to this objection which consists in adding one premise to Kant's argument:

1*a.* If a term is a descriptive predicate, then it is a defining predicate.

This is surely plausible because if a term describes some entity by referring to a property of the entity, then it can be used to help define some term which refers to the entity. Thus if Kant's argument is sound we can infer with the help of (1*a*) that 'exist' is not a descriptive predicate and that, according to this argument, existence is not a property.

This defense of Kant's argument raises a point which leads to a serious objection. Let us grant premise (2) for the sake of the argument on the grounds that verbs are not used to refer to properties of things and therefore are not real or defining predicates. They are not used in the kinds of definitions we are considering here. But this gives us no reason to think that the adjective 'existent' cannot be used in definitions, and thus no reason to think that 'existent' is not a descriptive predicate. Indeed 'existent' seems to be a real predicate. Consider the following definitions:

Let the term 'reggad' mean 'existent dagger' and the term 'nonreggad' mean 'nonexistent dagger.'

We can use these terms quite meaningfully to say, for example, that in his disturbed state of mind Macbeth saw a nonreggad which he thought was a reggad. And because we can use 'existent' in such definitions of new terms, we can surely use it to redefine terms already in use. Therefore whether or not premise (2) of Kant's argument is true for the verb 'exist,' it is false for the adjective 'existent,' and this is enough to cast doubt on this, the most plausible attempt to show that 'existence' is not a descriptive predicate and that existence is not a property.

ANOTHER OBJECTION: EXISTENCE IS NOT A PERFECTION

We have found that the first kind of attack on the second premise of the ontological argument fails. Let us consider another. The point here is that even if 'existence' is a predicate, even if existence is a property, existence is surely not a perfection. For our purposes here it will do to say that a perfection is a property an object has which goes together with certain other properties to make a being perfect. Thus we can compare two things and decide which one is the better or more nearly perfect. We would decide the issue by considering the perfections each had and each lacked. For example, someone might describe two different men in great detail but not tell us whether or not they exist. He then asks us which description more nearly approaches the ideal or perfect man. We decide on the basis of the properties he has described. Suppose that after we have decided he says that he forgot to give us one piece of information. The man we had thought less perfect is actually alive but the other is merely a fictitious character. Should we re-evaluate our decision in the light of this new evidence? It would seem not. The one man more nearly attains perfection than the other whether or not he exists. Existence, then, is not a perfection.

There is surely some force to this argument. When we decide who is the greatest president or the greatest painter or the saintliest person we do not need to consider whether he exists now or ever. We can evaluate both fictional and real people. Existence seems to be irrelevant to perfection. Consequently, we should conclude that premise (2) of Descartes' version of the ontological argument is too dubious to support the conclusion.

THE ONTOLOGICAL ARGUMENT:
ST. ANSELM'S VERSION

Let us turn to St. Anselm's version which, as we shall see, is not so intimately reliant on the thesis that existence is a perfection. St. Anselm starts by saying that we understand the concept of supreme being.

> And whatever is understood, exists in the understanding. And assuredly that, than which nothing greater can be conceived, cannot exist in the understanding alone. For, suppose it exists

in the understanding alone: then it can be conceived to exist in reality; which is greater.

Therefore, if that, than which nothing greater can be conceived, exists in the understanding alone, the very being, than which nothing greater can be conceived, is one, than which a greater can be conceived. But, obviously this is impossible. Hence, there is no doubt that there exists a being, than which nothing greater can be conceived. . . .[34]

Although it may not be historically accurate, we can untangle some of the complexity of Anselm's argument by replacing 'can be conceived' with 'is possible' and 'does not exist in the understanding alone' with 'exists.' We can then state the core of the argument as follows:

1. If the greatest being possible does not exist, then it is possible that there exists a being greater than the greatest being possible.
2. It is not possible that there exists a being greater than the greatest being possible.
   Therefore
3. The greatest being possible exists.

It should be noted that this argument claims neither that existence is a perfection nor that statement (3) is a necessary truth. Consequently, it seems to be open to none of those objections that we have seen launched against Descartes' version. However, Gaunilo, a contemporary of Anselm, offered a different objection which we must consider.

GAUNILO'S OBJECTION:
THE GREATEST ISLAND POSSIBLE
Gaunilo asks Anselm to consider an island which is the most excellent of all islands and to consider the following argument:

And since it is more excellent not to be in the understanding

---

[34] St. Anselm, *Basic Writings* (La Salle, Ill.: Open Court, 1962), p. 8.

alone, but to exist both in the understanding and in reality, for this reason it must exist. For if it does not exist, any land which really exists will be more excellent than it; and so the island already understood by you to be more excellent will not then be more excellent.[35]

Gaunilo's point here is that Anselm's argument proves too much so that it is surely unsound. We can prove by this argument that the greatest possible object of any kind, whether it be island or scholar or athlete or dinner or whatever, exists, and this is surely mistaken. Anselm's reply was merely to say that the logic of his argument applies only to the greatest *being* possible and to no other.

REPLY TO GAUNILO: A BEING GREATER THAN THE GREATEST ISLAND POSSIBLE

Was Anselm's reply to Gaunilo justified? To see what both men were driving at, let us use variables in the premises instead of constants. However, there are two ways we can do this: we can let 'being' be what replaces the variable X or we can let 'greatest possible being' be the substituend for X. The premises will differ accordingly. Argument form A will be the following:

1a. If the greatest X possible does not exist, then it is possible that there exists an X greater than the greatest X possible.
2a. It is not possible there exists an X greater than the greatest X possible.

And argument form B will be the following:

1b. If X does not exist, then it is possible that there exists a being greater than X.
2b. It is not possible there exists a being greater than X.

We can see that we can substitute innumerable terms for X in (1a) and (2a), so that we could prove that the greatest possible object *of any kind* exists. Surely something is wrong with this argument, as Gaunilo claims. However, the second argument form, B, supports Anselm's claim that his argument works only for 'the greatest being

[35] Ibid., p. 151.

possible.' Premise (2b) is true when 'the greatest being possible' is substituted for X, but there is no reason to think it true for anything else such as 'the greatest island possible' because the statement:

> It is not possible there exists a *being* greater than the greatest island possible.

seems to be false. Many beings, especially gods, are certainly greater beings than any piece of earth. Consequently, it would seem that Anselm had something like the second argument form in mind, and thus, as he claimed, his argument is not open to Gaunilo's objections.[36]

ANOTHER OBJECTION: THE DIRTIEST BEING POSSIBLE

Can we accept this version of Anselm's argument? It has avoided all the objections we have examined, and therefore we have found no reason to reject either premise. Furthermore, premise (2) is certainly acceptable. We can, however, find some reason for rejecting premise (1) when interpreted as (1b), a reason similar to Gaunilo's. Consider argument form C:

> 1c. If X does not exist, then it is possible that there exists a being more Y than X.
> 2c. It is not possible there exists a being more Y than X.

Here we have replaced 'great' in argument form B by the variable Y. In order for (2c) to be true X would have to equal 'the most Y being possible.' But we can substitute any adjective at all for Y and thus prove not only that the most *great* of any kind of being exists, as Gaunilo tried to prove, but also that a being that is superlative *in any way at all* exists. Thus we could prove by this argument that the happiest or saddest or cleanest or dirtiest, or fattest, or thinnest, or most absurd, or most evil being possible exists. In this case the two premises would be the following:

---

[36] Although I am responsible for this chapter, Mr. Lehrer should be given credit for this way of showing how St. Anselm can avoid Gaunilo's objection. —J.W.C.

If the most (dirty, absurd, evil, and so on) being possible does not exist, then there exists a being more (dirty, absurd, evil, and so on) than the most (dirty, absurd, evil, and so on) being possible.

and:

It is not possible that there exists a being more (dirty, absurd, evil, and so on) than the most (dirty, absurd, evil, and so on) being possible.

We can even prove that the being whose description involves the most contradictions possible exists. But it is not possible that a being whose description involves even one contradiction exists. Thus many arguments of the form C are unsound. But because the argument form is valid and the relevant premises of the form $(2c)$ are true, it follows that the premises of the form $(1c)$ are false. Furthermore because $(1b)$ is $(1c)$ with one less variable this surely casts doubt on premise (1) when taken as an instance of $(1b)$. If at this point Anselm were to reply to us, similarly to the way he replied to Gaunilo, that his argument applies only to the one adjective 'great,' we could reply in turn that there seems to be no difference between the adjective 'great' and many others relevant to existence. If a defender of the ontological argument thinks that there is, then it is up to him to show it. It may be possible to do so but so far no one has. Once again we have reached a point where we are unable to justify a premise. Thus although the premise may be true, we are unable to use it in an argument to justify a conclusion. We should, then, reject the ontological argument, as we have the others, as being inadequate to justify the belief that God exists.

A PRAGMATIC JUSTIFICATION OF BELIEF IN THE EXISTENCE OF GOD

We have rejected the most plausible *a posteriori* and *a priori* proofs for the existence of God and thus have found no way to justify the belief that God exists. Unless we can find some other way to justify beliefs, we shall have to conclude that this belief is not justified. All the arguments we have examined have tried to justify the belief by giving reasons for thinking that the belief is true. However, such pragmatists as William James have tried to develop a different kind of reason for holding a belief. Some beliefs that we are unable to prove to be either true or false play such an important role in our lives that, according to James, we are justified in believing them under certain conditions. This "pragmatic" justification of certain beliefs, then, does not depend upon any evidence or reason in favor of the truth of what is believed. James, in his article "The Will to Believe," has applied this kind of justification to the belief that God exists. Let us examine what he says:

> The thesis I defend is, briefly stated, thus: *Our passional nature not only lawfully may, but must, decide an option between propositions, whenever it is a genuine option that cannot by its nature be decided on intellectual grounds; for to say, under such circumstances, "Do not decide, but leave the question open," is itself a passional decision—just like deciding yes or no—and is attended with the same risk of losing the truth.*[37]

The crucial phrase here is 'genuine option,' and James defines it to mean a choice between alternative hypotheses that is living, momentous, and forced. By a *living* option he means a choice between hypotheses at least one of which is of some interest to the person faced with the choice. Many options are not living, but are what James calls dead. The option of whether or not to believe that I have an odd number of hairs on my head is certainly of no interest to almost everyone.

We shall say that a *momentous* option is one where to decide for or against one of the hypotheses in the option is to decide for or against something which is very important. The option offered an astronaut to accept or reject the assignment to be the first man to land on the moon is a momentous option. The last characteristic necessary for a genuine option is that the opinion be forced. A *forced* option is one in which there is no way to avoid a decision.

[37] W. James, *Essays in Pragmatism* (New York: Hafner, 1960), p. 95.

A man held up at gun point, with no chance of escape, and given the choice, "Your money right now or your life," is faced with a forced option. He cannot avoid a decision by escaping, or by refusing to respond to the robber, because by refusing he would fail to hand over his money and thereby, in effect, agree to lose his life. However, the option to watch television or go to a movie is not forced because one can do neither—for example, by reading a book.[38]

THE RELIGIOUS OPTION AND THE RIGHT TO BELIEVE

Having defined James' terms we can now lay out his argument as follows:

1. If someone is faced with an option which is genuine and cannot be decided by rational inquiry, then he is justified in deciding it according to his desires.
2. If the religious option is a living option for someone, then it is a genuine option for him.
3. The religious option cannot be decided by rational inquiry.
   Therefore
4. If the religious option is a living option for someone, then he is justified in deciding it according to his desires.

James is arguing, then, that if someone has the will to believe, if he wants to believe, then he has the right to believe. Of course, if believing that God exists or that he does not exist is of no interest to someone, then James' argument does not apply to him. It applies to the person who wants to believe, the person for whom the option is live, but who withholds believing because he has no reason to think that the belief is true. Notice, incidentally, that not only the would-be believer but also the would-be atheist can justify his belief. Thus someone who wants to believe that God does *not* exist but has refrained because he cannot provide reasons for such a belief will also find James' argument helpful.

Some people have complained that James' argument provides us with "an unrestricted license for wishful thinking," but if we look closely at the argument we shall see that this is not so. James' argument applies only to genuine options which cannot be decided

[38] Ibid., pp. 88–90.

by rational inquiry. This eliminates the great majority of our options which can be decided by a rational investigation of the relevant facts. James' argument applies to a quite limited group of options. The question with which we are concerned is whether it applies to what James calls the religious option. For James, when we are faced with the religious option, the hypothesis in question is not 'God exists,' but rather something more complicated. James' religious hypothesis has two parts, the first of which I shall rephrase as 'God exists,' and the second as 'We are better off even now and surely later if we believe that God exists.' For James, then, the religious hypothesis is a conjunction of two hypotheses and the religious option is the decision of whether or not to believe the religious hypothesis.[39]

Let us consider the premises. The first seems acceptable because if someone wants to make an important decision, there is no way he can avoid making it, and there is absolutely no way to bring any evidence or reasons to bear on the decision, then surely he has the right to decide the way he wants. There is no argument that can be used to condemn such a decision as irrational. He cannot avoid the choice, because it is forced; and he cannot just shrug it off because it is important. In such a case he is justified in doing as he wants. There is nothing relevant to the decision which overrides his desires.

The problem for the second premise is to decide whether or not James' religious option is momentous and forced. If it is both, then the premise is true. James says that

> we see, first, that religion offers itself as a *momentous* option. We are supposed to gain, even now, by our belief, and to lose by our non-belief, a certain vital good. Secondly, religion is a forced option so far as that goes. We cannot escape the issue by remaining skeptical and waiting for more light, because, although we do avoid error in that way *if religion be untrue*, we lose the good, *if it be true*, just as certainly as if we positively chose to disbelieve.[40]

We can agree with James that his religious option is momentous,

---

[39] See ibid., p. 105, for James' way of stating the religious hypothesis.
[40] Ibid., pp. 105–106.

because to decide to believe the hypothesis is to decide in favor of extremely important benefits right now and also in the eternity of afterlife. However, it is not clear why James thinks that his option is forced. He seems to think that if we decide either to disbelieve or to refrain from believing his religious hypothesis, then we in effect have decided against attaining certain present benefits. But this is not so. We can reject his religious hypothesis, which is a conjunction, merely by rejecting just one of the conjuncts. Thus if we reject the second conjunct, that believing brings us benefits, but believe that God exists, then we have not rejected the benefits, because receiving them requires only that we believe that God exists. Similarly, we can refrain from believing the religious hypothesis without any risk of loss if we only refrain from believing the second conjunct. Consequently, the religious hypothesis offered by James does not result in a forced option, and thus the second premise of James' argument is false.

However, we may be able to devise another religious hypothesis which will result in a forced as well as a momentous option. The simpler hypothesis that God exists will provide the forced option of whether to believe that God exists or not to believe that God exists. If I refrain from deciding, then, of course, I have in effect decided not to believe that God exists. This, of course, is different from deciding to believe that God does not exist. The option, however, is not momentous, as we have defined it. I have not decided for or against any present benefits if I either believe or refrain from believing that God exists—especially if I believe, for example, that if there were a god, he would reward me not for my belief in him, but for how I treat my fellow men. Thus I may decide to treat others with love and respect and so decide in favor of the benefits. I may be wrong about what would bring benefits, but I face that risk no matter what I decide. The point, nevertheless, is that in deciding only about God's existence, I have not decided for or against the benefits. The following hypothesis, however, which I shall call H, avoids this problem:

H. God exists and only those who believe the teachings of God (which include H) will receive certain important benefits now and also later.

In the case of H we must believe both parts of the conjunction in order to receive the benefits, so that if we either reject or refrain from believing either part of the conjunction we have in effect decided against the benefits. Thus an option concerning *H* is forced and is certainly momentous. Let us then accept the second premise of James' argument once we interpret the religious hypothesis as *H*.

We are left with the task of evaluating the third premise. We have found no sound arguments for God's existence, whether *a priori* or *a posteriori*. It may be thought that this is sufficient to justify premise (3), but there are two other ways that it might still be refuted. First, throughout the preceding discussion we have assumed that it is either true or false that God exists, and although this seems to be a reasonable assumption, it has come under vigorous attack. It has been claimed that no religious utterances, including 'God exists,' are assertions; they are all utterances which are neither true nor false. According to this claim, religious utterances do not function to make assertions about things, but have a quite different linguistic function. Consequently, it is wrong to conclude that it is either true or false that God exists and also wrong to talk of a religious option involving the hypothesis that God exists. To talk this way is to be mistaken about language and to be misled into pseudoproblems involving pseudohypotheses.[41]

The second attack on premise (3) is quite different. It grants that it is either true or false that God exists and that there is no evidence in favor of the hypothesis that God exists. It states, however, that there surely is evidence against the hypothesis, evidence which should lead us to conclude that God does not exist. Let us consider each of these quite different attacks separately.

FIRST OBJECTION:
RELIGIOUS UTTERANCES ARE NOT ASSERTIONS
We know of many uses of language which do not involve assertions. When we ask a question or give a command or tell a joke or recite a line of poetry or do numerous other things with language, we are not asserting something true or false. If I say, "Shut the door!" or, "Please pass the salt," it would be inappropriate to reply, "That's true," or "That's false." Similarly, if I say, "Oh what a wonderful

---

[41] See A. J. Ayer, *Language, Truth and Logic* (New York: Dover, 1952), pp. 114–20 for this view of religious language.

meal!" or, "Let's go team!" I am expressing my feelings, my attitudes about certain things. What I utter is neither true nor false. It has been claimed that religious utterances are not assertions but rather function to express, for example, our feelings of awe and wonder about the strange and mysterious aspects of the world around and even within us. This characterization of religious utterances may be correct, but is there any reason to accept it? The best-known attempt to substantiate this view is that made by Anthony Flew, who begins his discussion with a parable, which he adapts from an article by John Wisdom, about a most peculiar gardener. He says,

Once upon a time two explorers came upon a clearing in the jungle. In the clearing were growing many flowers and many weeds. One explorer says, "Some gardener must tend this plot." The other disagrees, "There is no gardener." So they pitch their tent and set a watch. No gardener is ever seen. "But perhaps he is an invisible gardener." So they set up a barbed-wire fence. They electrify it. They patrol with bloodhounds. (For they remember how H. G. Wells' The Invisible Man could be both smelt and touched though he could not be seen.) But no shrieks ever suggest that some intruder has received a shock. No movement of the wire ever betrays an invisible climber. The bloodhounds never give cry. Yet still the Believer is not convinced. "But there is a gardener, invisible, intangible, insensitive to electric shocks, a gardener who comes secretly to look after the garden which he loves." At last the Skeptic despairs, "But what remains of your original assertion? Just how does what you call an invisible, intangible, eternally elusive gardener differ from an imaginary gardener or from no gardener at all?"[42]

Flew's claim is that just as the utterance of the man who believes that there is a gardener has at the end of the parable become compatible with every possible state of affairs, so can the same be said

[42] A. Flew, "Theology and Falsification," in A. Flew and A. MacIntyre, eds., New Essays in Philosophical Theology (London: SCM Press, 1958), p. 96. Wisdom's parable comes from his article "Gods" in A. Flew, ed., Logic and Language, first series (Oxford: Blackwell, 1963), pp. 187–206.

for religious utterances. He concludes from this that a religious utterance is not an assertion.

> For if the utterance is indeed an assertion, it will necessarily be equivalent to a denial of the negation of that assertion. And anything which would count against the assertion, or which would induce the speaker to withdraw it and to admit that it had been mistaken, must be part of (or the whole of) the meaning of the negation of that assertion. And to know the meaning of the negation of an assertion is, as near as makes no matter, to know the meaning of that assertion. And if there is nothing which a putative assertion denies then there is nothing which it asserts either: and so it is not really an assertion.[43]

If Flew is right here, then it is mistaken to say that 'God exists' is either true or false. Thus this utterance does not express any beliefs (either true or false) about certain facts. Rather it expresses feelings or attitudes we have toward the world, so that if Flew is right then James is wrong in thinking that we have an option involving a belief that God exists.

REPLY TO OBJECTION:
RESTS ON DUBIOUS THEORY OF MEANING

The core of Flew's argument can be put as follows:

1. If nothing counts against an utterance, then its denial has no meaning.
2. If the denial of an utterance has no meaning, then there is nothing the utterance denies.
3. If there is nothing an utterance denies, then there is nothing it asserts.
4. If there is nothing an utterance asserts, then it is not an assertion, that is, it is neither true nor false.
5. Nothing counts against 'God exists.'
   Therefore
6. 'God exists' is not an assertion.

---

[43] Flew, "Theology and Falsification," p. 98.

Premises (2), (3), and (4) may be granted, but neither (1) nor (5) are immune from attack. One attack on premise (5) is the same as the second objection to James' third premise, that is, there is some evidence against 'God exists.' We shall examine this objection later. The other attack stems from the claim that whether or not any experiences that men have in this world are relevant to 'God exists,' there is at least one kind of experience relevant to that utterance. This is the experience involved in what Hick calls "eschatological verification," or verification after bodily death.[44] The utterance 'God exists' could certainly be verified by certain experiences which some people would have if there is a life after death. Similarly, whether or not any experience in this world would falsify or count against 'God exists,' surely certain experiences after death, such as the experience of an all-powerful malicious demon, would provide an eschatological falsification of 'God exists.' Thus something counts against 'God exists.' Flew could avoid this objection, however, by revising (5) to refer only to evidence discoverable in this world, that is, empirical evidence. Premise (5) then would state that nothing empirical counts against 'God exists,' that is, 'God exists' is not empirically falsifiable. However, in order to save premise (5) in this way we must rewrite (1) as:

1a. If no empirical evidence counts against an utterance, then its denial has no meaning.

But if we realize that evidence against an utterance is evidence for its denial, and that the denial of an utterance is meaningful just in case the utterance is also, we can rephrase (1a) as:

1b. If no empirical evidence counts for an utterance, then the utterance has no meaning.

When we look at premise (1) as transformed into (1b) it becomes clear what lies behind this argument—the verifiability criterion of meaning. Premise (1b), which, in effect, asserts that if an utterance is meaningful then it is empirically verifiable, is really a statement

---

[44] See J. Hick, "Theology and Verification," in J. Hick, ed., *The Existence of God* (New York: Macmillan, 1964), pp. 252–74.

of the verifiability criterion which, as we have seen in the preceding chapter, is highly dubious.[45] Premise (1), then, is highly dubious when amended to avoid an objection to premise (5). Consequently, because this and other attempts to establish that religious utterances are not assertions have all relied upon the dubious verifiability criterion of meaning, we can reject the first attack on James' third premise. There is no reason to doubt that 'God exists' is an assertion.

SECOND OBJECTION: THERE IS EVIDENCE AGAINST THE RELIGIOUS HYPOTHESIS

But can we also reject the second attack on premise (3)? Can we accept what both James and Flew accept, namely, that no empirical evidence is relevant to the utterance 'God exists'? If we find this acceptable, then although it will not save Flew's argument, it will allow us to accept the third premise of James' argument and, thereby, James' argument. From our previous discussion we have found good reason to agree that there is no supporting evidence relevant to the utterance 'God exists,' but we have not considered whether there might be some evidence which counts against the utterance. We can, I think, pass over many facts that people have claimed are evidentially relevant to the existence of God, but there are other facts that are not so easily avoided. According to many people, the existence in this world of much evil cannot be ignored except by someone so irrational in his beliefs about God that he would not be willing to consider even the possibility that something counts as evidence against the existence of God. We must, therefore, consider the problem of evil.

EVIL AS EVIDENCE AGAINST THE EXISTENCE OF GOD

The problem of evil is one of the most troublesome problems that faces anyone who believes that there exists an all-good, all-knowing,

---

[45] The problems confronting the verifiability criterion are discussed in some detail on pp. 287–91.

and all-powerful God who created this world we live in. We can begin to see this problem in the following way. If you were all-good, all-knowing, and all-powerful, and you were going to create a universe in which there were sentient beings—beings that are happy and sad; enjoy pleasure; feel pain; express love, anger, pity, hatred—what kind of world would you create? Being all-powerful, you would have the ability to create any world that it is logically possible for you to create, and being all-knowing you would know how to create any of these logically possible worlds. Which one would you choose? Obviously you would choose the best of all the possible worlds because you would be all-good and would want to do what is best in everything you do. You would, then, create the best of all the possible worlds, that is, that world containing the least amount of evil possible. And because one of the most obvious kinds of evil is suffering, hardship, and pain, you would create a world in which the sentient beings suffered the least. Try to imagine what such a world would be like. Would it be like the one which actually does exist, this world we live in? Would you create a world such as this one if you had the power and knowhow to create any logically possible world? If your answer is "no," as it seems it must be, then you should begin to understand why the evil of suffering and pain in this world is such a problem for anyone who thinks God created this world. This does not seem to be the kind of world God would create, and certainly not the kind of world he would sustain. Given this world, then, it seems we should conclude that it is improbable that it was created or sustained by anything we would call God. Thus, given this particular world, it seems we should conclude that it is improbable that God—who if he exists, created this world—exists. Consequently, the belief that God does not exist, rather than the belief that he exists, would seem to be justified by the evidence we find in this world.

OBJECTION: MEN ARE RESPONSIBLE FOR EVIL

The problem of evil is not merely a problem for someone who wishes to justify belief in God by, for example, the argument from design. It is a problem for anyone who wishes to claim that his belief in God is not unreasonable, not contrary to what ought to be believed on the basis of the available evidence. Is there any way to solve or avoid this problem? Can we in some way justify the ways of God to man given the way things are in this world? Such a task is what has been called theodicy, which is the attempt to justify the claim that in spite of the evil we find here, this is the best of all possible worlds. In a sense the problem is to find a way to absolve God of the moral responsibility for suffering. One attempt to do this places the responsibility, and thereby the blame, for suffering on men rather than on God. On this view God created man in his own image and because of this men have free will. And because men have free will they and not God are morally responsible for all the suffering they cause. Surely the ways of man to man can be quite horrible as the road from cannibalism, to the Inquisition, to Nazi concentration camps, and to mass bombing of civilians testifies. Men often seem more adept at devising and using the instruments of torture than the means to charity.

REPLY: MORAL VS. NATURAL EVIL

Men are surely responsible for much of the suffering inflicted on other men, but nevertheless, there is much for which they do not seem to be responsible. To see this let us differentiate what has been called moral evil from natural evil. Moral evil consists of all the evil in the world which is the causal result of those morally responsible agents who exist as part of the world. Natural evil includes all the other evil that there may be. Thus although the massive suffering at Auschwitz is surely a moral evil, the also immense suffering resulting from such natural disasters as earthquakes, floods, droughts, hurricanes, and the like are not the causal result of any moral agent in the world. They are natural evils, evils for which no man is responsible. Let us, then, grant for the purposes of this discussion that much evil is moral evil and that God is not responsible for this. But this only means that the problem of evil can be redefined as the problem of natural evil, a problem no easier to solve.

OBJECTION: SATAN AS ONE CAUSE OF NATURAL EVIL

It may be objected here that although men are not morally responsible for natural evils because they do not cause them, nevertheless such evils do occur as tests, warnings, and punishment to men for the evils they do cause. Consequently, so the objection goes, although God is indeed the cause of natural evils, he is justified in causing them because of the way men act toward other men and toward God. A refinement of this objection is to include Satan as a cause of some natural evil, so that only certain natural evils are caused by God and the rest by Satan. This objection is important because it helps us delimit the problem we are discussing. We are not interested in whether the existence of the evil we find in this world is compatible with (that is, logically consistent with) the existence of God, but what effect it has on the likelihood that God exists. We can admit that it is logically possible that God created this world because it is logically possible that this world, with all its evils, is the best of all possible worlds.[46] But there are many improbable logical possibilities and the claim that God created this world seems at this point to be one of them. Thus although what the preceding objection claims *may* be true, the question is whether there is any reason to think that it is true. Natural evils indiscriminately afflict the guilty and innocent alike. Certainly the suffering of innocent babies as the result of an earthquake cannot be justified, not even as a warning to men to mend their ways. If such suffering is said to be Satan's work we can ask why Satan is allowed to continue his work. It cannot be that God is powerless to stop Satan. This Manichaean doctrine that there are two gigantic forces, one good and one evil, neither of which can overcome the other, is ruled out because God is omnipotent, and it certainly is logically possible that Satan be destroyed or at least shackled. It must be that God allows Satan his ways. But this would seem to be like someone who has the power to stop another, allowing the second one to inflict suffering at will. This does not seem to be the kind of thing that an all-good being would allow.

At this point it might be replied that Satan, like man, has free will and that God, having given this free will, does not want to interfere just as he allows so many moral evils because he does not want to interfere with man's free will. Let us grant that God does not want to interfere with the free exercise of any being's will, perhaps because this is God's unique and most precious gift to those who have

---

[46] For a defense of the consistency of the existence of both God and evil, see A. Plantinga, "The Free Will Defense," in M. Black, ed., *Philosophy in American* (London: Allen & Unwin, 1965), pp. 204–20.

it. Such an attitude seems clearly admirable; most of us want to be allowed the free exercise of our wills, and many of us think that this right belongs to all men. Nevertheless there are many situations in which we think that the only morally right thing to do is to limit someone's freedom so that he cannot do anything he wants. There are many cases in which we ought to confine someone to a mental hospital or in a prison to keep him from harming others. If, as it surely seems, there are clear cases where the only right thing is to restrict someone's free will, then surely, if Satan is the cause of natural evils, the only right thing to do is restrict Satan. Thus an all-good being would restrict Satan's actions if he could. And clearly God could, if he existed.

REPLY: NATURAL EVIL EXPLAINABLE BY NATURAL CAUSES

It seems that postulating Satan as the cause of certain natural evils will not help save the hypothesis that God exists. There is another reason why this is so. Satan as the unobservable cause of certain observable events would play the same role as such theoretical entities as electrons, protons, and neutrons in scientific theories. Such theoretical entities are postulated to explain what is observed. We have seen that such postulations are justified only if some kind of theoretical entity is necessary to explain the events. Thus we have seen that the postulation of demons by witch-doctors as the causes of certain illnesses, and of God as the cause of mystical experiences cannot be justified in this way.[47] Is the case any different with Satan as the cause of observable evils? It seems not. We have every reason to think that all natural evils have perfectly natural causes. It is, therefore, unreasonable to postulate some nonnatural cause to explain their occurrences. Again, there may be such a cause, but we cannot justify it in this way. We cannot even justify postulating the existence of Satan to save the hypothesis that God exists. We might provide such an indirect justification if there were some reason to think that God is necessary as a theoretical explanatory entity, but with the failure of the ultimate explanation argument there is no reason to think such a postulation necessary. We cannot justify the

---

[47] See pp. 298–300 for a discussion of demons as theoretical entities.

postulation of one unnecessary explanatory entity for the purpose of saving a second unnecessary explanatory entity.

OBJECTION: ALL EVILS ARE NECESSARY

There is another traditional attempt to avoid the problem of evil that we should consider. This position attempts to reconcile the evil we find in this world with the claim that this is the best of all possible worlds by claiming that the evils we find in this world are all necessary or unavoidable evils so that any other would have more evils. The claim is often based on the view that the best world for a being such as man is an orderly world in which he can predict the course of events with a degree of accuracy sufficient to guide his life safely and prosperously. Such a world must proceed in a lawlike way, and according to the present claim, this requires a world which proceeds in accordance with causal laws. In any such universe some degree of suffering and hardship is bound to result when men are faced with natural forces much too powerful for them. The claim, in brief, is that this is the best of all possible worlds, for all its evils are necessary. This world has the minimum amount of natural evil consistent with a world which proceeds in accordance with laws. As with the previous objection we can admit that it is possible that this claim is true. But we can also ask, as did Philo, whether this claim or its denial is more probable based on the evidence we can gather from this world. That is, if we could find some examples of evil in this world which surely seem to be avoidable and thus unnecessary, then the claim would seem to be improbable.

REPLY: EXAMPLES OF UNNECESSARY EVILS

Let us once again turn to Philo, who lists several examples of what he thinks are avoidable evil. Philo is willing to grant that pain can serve a valuable function in warning sentient beings of bodily ills and that it is better for man that the course of nature proceed in an orderly fashion. But he finds no reason to think that pain is necessary for the purpose of warning sentient beings, or that causal laws are necessary for the course of nature being orderly. He says,

The *first* circumstance which introduces evil, is that contrivance or economy of the animal creation, by which pains, as well as pleasures, are employed to excite all creatures to action, and make them vigilant in the great work of self-preservation. Now pleasure alone, in its various degrees, seems to human understanding sufficient for this purpose. All animals might be constantly in a state of enjoyment; but when urged by any of the necessities of nature, such as thirst, hunger, weariness; instead of pain, they might feel a diminution of pleasure, by which they might be prompted to seek that object, which is necessary to their subsistence. Men pursue pleasure as eagerly as they avoid pain; at least, they might have been so constituted. It seems, therefore, plainly possible to carry on the business of life without any pain. Why then is any animal ever rendered susceptible of such a sensation?[48]

There may be some who disagree with Philo, some who think that some degree of pain is a much better way to implement learning than a mere diminution of pleasure. Yet it seems most unreasonable to believe that any animals need to be as susceptible to very intense pain as are humans. A world like this one in all respects except that animals have a much lower susceptibility to pain would be a better world, and one which seems quite possible. Thus pain, or at least certain intensities of pain, is an unnecessary, or avoidable, evil.

Concerning the necessity of causal laws in the best of all possible worlds, and thus in an orderly world, Philo claims,

But a capacity of pain would not alone produce pain, were it not for the *second* circumstance, viz. the conducting of the world by general laws; and this seems nowise necessary to a very perfect Being. It is true; if everything were conducted by particular volitions, the course of nature would be perpetually broken, and no man could employ his reason in the conduct of life. But might not other particular volitions remedy this inconvenience? In short, might not the Deity exterminate all ill, wherever it were to be found; and produce all good, without any preparation or long progress of causes and effects?[49]

[48] Hume, *Dialogues Concerning Natural Religion*, pp. 205–206.
[49] Ibid., p. 206.

Philo's point is that an omniscient and omnipotent being could control the course of events by particular acts of his will in as orderly a fashion as if all events were parts of continuous causal chains subject to causal laws. Consequently, causal laws are not necessary for the kind of orderly universe that is most helpful to men. Therefore it seems clear that such a being could, by an orderly procession of acts, avoid and eradicate much evil found in the world.

Furthermore, even in a universe in which the course of events is governed by causal laws, there are so many factors causally relevant to most events that insofar as humans can tell, the events are mere coincidences of accidents. As Philo says,

> A Being, therefore, who knows the secret springs of the universe, might easily, by particular volitions, turn all these accidents to the good of mankind, and render the whole world happy, without discovering himself in any operation. A fleet, whose purposes were salutary to society, might always meet with a fair wind: Good princes enjoy sound health and long life: Persons born to power and authority, be framed with good tempers and virtuous dispositions. A few such events as these, regularly and wisely conducted, would change the face of the world; and yet would no more seem to disturb the course of nature or confound human conduct, than the present economy of things, where the causes are secret, and variable, and compounded.[50]

Even if most events occurred as parts of continuous causal chains, even if God only acted occasionally, he could do it in such a way that it would be unknown to humans. They would find no break in the causal order; what would appear to them to be coincidence and accident could in many cases be the work of God, who could quite easily, by indiscernible coincidence-miracles, help humans more often than they are now helped by coincidences. Once again certain features of the universe, unbroken causal chains that often result in pain and other evils, are not necessary in the best of all possible worlds.

[50] Ibid., pp. 206–207.

Perhaps the most decisive example used by Philo concerns what he calls the "inaccurate workmanship of all the springs and principles of the great machine of nature."[51] He is willing to admit that certain parts of this universe may indeed be necessary for man's welfare, but certain of the effects of these parts which cause suffering are by no means necessary.

> Thus the winds are requisite to convey the vapours along the surface of the globe, and to assist men in navigation: But how oft, rising up to tempests and hurricanes, do they become pernicious? Rains are necessary to nourish all the plants and animals of the earth: But how often are they defective? How often excessive? Heat is requisite to all life and vegetation, but is not always found in due proportion. On the mixture and secretion of the humours and juices of the body depend the health and prosperity of the animal: But the parts perform not regularly their proper function.[52]

In short, although wind currents, rain, a certain amount of heat, and such bodily fluids as blood may be necessary for human life, it seems quite unnecessary that there be hurricanes, tornadoes, floods, droughts, extreme cold or heat, or blood defects such as leukemia.

At this stage of the discussion we seem warranted in concluding that the existence of what surely seems to be unnecessary evil in this world provides inductive grounds for the belief that God does not exist, because it is probable that if he once existed he would have created a different world and that if he now exists he would control the course of nature so as to avoid many pernicious events that occur.

OBJECTION: EVIDENCE AVAILABLE TO MAN IS INSUFFICIENT

But although such a conclusion seems warranted, there is one way it still might be avoided. There are many who would reject the

[51] Ibid., p. 209.
[52] Ibid., p. 210.

claim that humans can gather evidence from what they know that will affect the probability or improbability of the existence of God. Consider the following analogy. Suppose that a young child is brought up in a primitive society in which the highest perfection is to be a great hunter with immense physical prowess. Suppose further that he is taken to a university where there is an acknowledged great mathematician. The child comes into contact with some of the effects of the mathematician's work. He sees strange white markings left all over a blackboard. He looks at pieces of paper with equally strange markings on them. Occasionally he hears people say how great this man is, but never once do they mention hunting. He also hears others say that they cannot figure out what this mathematician thinks he is doing, and still others talk about his lack of physical exercise and the fact that he continually sits at a desk. On the basis of these bits of information it would be quite natural for the child to think that this man was perhaps quite strange, but certainly not a great man. But we would not want to say that the child had an inductive justification for the claim that the cause of these effects he had seen was not a remarkable being. His information was so paltry that it was insufficient to justify any belief about the greatness of the man. Although the analogy is not perfect, it has been claimed that the information that humans have about the ways of God is like the information that the child has about the mathematician, except that it is more paltry. How then could we think that the information we have obtained in our limited way is at all close to being sufficient to justify any belief about the greatness of the cause of the universe?

If we accept this analogy between our evidence relevant to God and the boy's evidence relevant to the mathematician, then instead of concluding that it is improbable that God exists we should conclude that no argument based on the evidence available to men is capable of affecting the justification of the statement that God exists. We should also conclude that James is correct in his claim that we are justified in believing the religious hypothesis even when there is no evidence to support it. Where there is no evidence against one hypothesis of a genuine option we are justified in believing it. Thus if we can accept the analogy then, even in the face of the seemingly contrary evidence provided by the natural evil present in this world, there would be nothing irrational about believing that God exists.

REPLY: BELIEVE IN ACCORDANCE WITH
THE TOTAL EVIDENCE AVAILABLE

There is, however, an important difference between our situation relevant to God and the native boy's situation relevant to the mathematician, and this difference vitiates the relevance of the analogy to our problem. When someone is attempting to justify a belief by means of a body of evidence, he can be said to have justified the belief only if he has considered the total amount of evidence available to him. The native boy clearly could have found more evidence relevant to the greatness of the mathematician, evidence which surely could have led him to revise his belief that there was nothing great about the man. We, however, at this stage of our discussion have good reason to think we have examined, at least to some extent, practically all the available evidence, so that we, unlike the boy, can be said to meet the requirement of total evidence. Where someone meets that requirement, then, no matter how paltry his evidence is, if it tips the scale, no matter how little, in favor of one hypothesis, then the rational course is to believe in accordance with the evidence.

CONCLUSION

Thus, although the evidence provided by the existence of evil in this world may be quite paltry relative to evidence unavailable to us, it is sufficient, nevertheless, to tip the scale of total available evidence in favor of the hypothesis that God does not exist. Although God may exist, as evidence unavailable to human beings might indeed show, the conclusion that we as rational beings should draw, based on the evidence discussed in this chapter, is that God does not exist, and, because he can neither be created nor destroyed, he never did and never will exist.

EXERCISES

1. According to the characterization of God in the text, which of the following would God be able to do? Explain.

   Make hot ice.   Destroy himself.
   Cause a triangle to have four angles.   Forget.
   Make 2 plus 2 equal 5.   Inflict suffering sadistically.

2. Evaluate the following objection to the claim that God is omnipotent.

   It is possible that at time t_1 someone, namely me, lifts the stone I lift by myself at t_1. But it is not possible that at t_1 God lifts the stone I lift by myself at t_1. Therefore, I can do something God cannot do and he is not omnipotent.

3. In the Gospels it is stated that Christ told Peter, "This night, before the cock crow, thou shalt deny me thrice," and that this happened in spite of Peter's protests that it would not happen. This seems to be an example of divine omniscience. Explain whether you think Peter could have had free will given Christ's foreknowledge of what he would do.

4. Discuss the following argument.

   Mystical experiences are ineffable, therefore they cannot be accurately described. Thus, any report of them must be misleading and hence unable to provide evidence for any claim. It follows that belief in God cannot be justified by appealing to mystical experiences.

5. Is there any possible situation in which you think a scientist should admit supernatural causes? If so, describe such a situation and justify your conclusion. If not, explain why not.

6. Do you think that there is any historical evidence—scriptural or otherwise—that supports, at least to some degree, the claim that God has revealed himself to man? Justify your answer.

7. Show which premises in the first-cause argument and in the argument from contingency are *a posteriori* and which are *a priori*. Are the conclusions *a posteriori* or *a priori*? If they are *a posteriori*,

explain what empirical evidence is relevant to them. If they are *a priori* explain how an *a priori*, and thus necessary, statement can be derived from premises some of which are *a posteriori*, and thus contingent.

8. The central question at issue in the third version of the first-cause argument is whether it is senseless to ask for an explanation of why there is something rather than nothing. One reason to think that it is a legitimate question is that, because everything in the universe is contingent so also is the universe. Thus the existence of the universe, just like the existence of anything else, must be explained. Bertrand Russell's answer to this is that the error in this reasoning is the fallacy illustrated by the argument, 'Every man has a mother; therefore the human race has a mother.' Evaluate these two conflicting positions.

9. State some examples of things that are logically possible but physically impossible. Is anything logically impossible but not physically impossible? Consider, for example, the sentence 'God is omniscient and God is not omniscient.' Does this violate a law of physics? Is it physically impossible according to the definition on page 364?

10. It is often claimed that the theory of evolution has rendered the argument from design untenable. Yet Copleston, in his book *Aquinas*, says, "If Aquinas had lived in the days of the evolutionary hypothesis, he would doubtless have argued this hypothesis supports rather than invalidates the conclusion of the [design] argument." Explain how Aquinas might have used this theory to bolster the argument from design.

11. Criticize the following argument:

God is a being who can do all things that it is logically possible for him to do. But a nonexistent being can do nothing at all, much less everything logically possible. Therefore God exists.

12. Explain whether this is an *a posteriori* or an *a priori* argument.

It is clear that 'Existence is a perfection' is not an analytic statement, so that it is a contingent rather than a necessary statement. But if it is contingent, it must be *a posteriori*, and Descartes' ontological argument, which contains it as a premise, is *a posteriori* instead of *a priori*, as claimed in the text.

13. The French philosopher Pascal proposed that the way to decide whether or not to believe in God is to discover whether belief or dis-

belief is the better and bet accordingly. This is known as Pascal's wager. He tells us to consider the odds.

> If we wager that God exists and he does then we gain eternal bliss; if he does not, we have lost nothing. If we wager that God does not exist and he does, then eternal misery is our share; if he does not, we gain only a lucky true belief. The obvious wager is to bet God exists. With such a bet we have everything to gain and nothing to lose. This is far superior to a bet where we have little to gain and everything to lose.

Evaluate this attempt to justify belief in God. Compare it with James' attempt.

14. It was concluded in this chapter that reports of various kinds of religious experiences do not provide sufficient evidence to justify belief in God. Might not the existence of such reports, however, show an important difference between God and Flew's "eternally elusive gardener"? Justify your answer.

15. One kind of argument to justify the existence of God not covered in the text is that known as the moral argument. Evaluate the following brief version.

> If God did not exist, then there would be no objective moral law because moral laws must be decreed by some being, a being that is all-good. Furthermore, no objective law depends merely on a human being. But, surely, there are objective moral laws, so God exists.

Is this an *a priori* or an *a posteriori* argument? Explain.

16. It has been maintained that even the problem of moral evil is not solved by appealing to man's free will. For God could have given men free will and also intervene miraculously to thwart at least the most heinous crimes. In fact, God could intervene to thwart evil intentions in ways that would be coincidence-miracles. Thus, no laws of nature would have to be broken. Does this claim seem well founded? Explain your answer.

17. Discuss the following.

> The problem of evil is no problem at all for Christianity because any amount of earthly misery is literally nothing when compared with the infinite and eternal bliss that Christianity promises.

18. St. Augustine held that although we think that there are natural

evils, there really are none. We think this way because our own natures are insufficiently real (that is, not enough like God's) to apprehend things as they really are (that is, good). Thus if we could view an earthquake or a plague through God's eyes, we should then see that it is exactly the right thing to happen at a particular place and at a particular time. Critically evaluate this argument.

19. One theory explains the evil of the world by postulating an evil God as its creator. Is this theory faced with a "problem of good" corresponding to the problem of evil which faces the theist? Why cannot the theist point to the great amount of good in the world in order to counter the problem of evil?

20. Do you disagree with the conclusion of this chapter? If so, how would you reply to its arguments?

BIBLIOGRAPHY

HISTORICAL SOURCES

I. Original Works
The views of Plato can be found in *The Laws*, Book X, and Aristotle's in *Metaphysics* A. St. Anselm's famous statement of the ontological argument occurs in the *Proslogion* and the five ways of St. Thomas Aquinas in *Summa Theologica*, Part I. René Descartes argues for the existence of God in the third of his Meditations; his version of the ontological argument occurs in the fifth *Meditation*. Benedict Spinoza presents his justification of God, and nature as the one and only substance in *Short Treatise on God, Man, and His Well-being*, Part I, Chapter 1; and Gottfried Leibniz states his position that God is the cause of this, the best of all possible worlds, in *New Essays Concerning Human Understanding*, Appendix I, and in *Theodicy*. The classical dissection of the argument from design and statement of the problem of evil occur in *Dialogues Concerning Natural Religion* by David Hume. Hume also discusses and refutes the argument from miracles in *An Enquiry Concerning Human Understanding*, Section X, *Of Miracles*. Immanuel Kant offers his refutation of the standard arguments for the existence of God and proposes his own version of the moral argument in *Critique of Pure Reason*, B611–670, and *Critique of Practical Reason*, Book II, Chapter II. In *Three Essays on*

Religion, John Stuart Mill states his views on natural theology, the problem of evil and a limited God. Christian existentialism was given its classical statement by S. Kierkegaard in *Concluding Unscientific Postscript.*

II. Collections Containing Excerpts from Historical Works

Each of the following anthologies is devoted entirely to the philosophy of religion, and contains selections from historical works on various topics in this area. Some of these anthologies also contain contemporary articles and commentaries on the historical works they include. *A Modern Reader in the Philosophy of Religion* (New York: Appleton-Century-Crofts, Inc., 1966), edited by W. Arnett; *Classical and Contemporary Readings in the Philosophy of Religion* (Englewood Cliffs, N.J.: Prentice-Hall, Inc., 1964), edited by J. Hick; *God and Evil* (Englewood Cliffs, N.J.: Prentice-Hall, Inc., 1964), edited by N. Pike; *Philosophy of Religion* (New York: Macmillan Publishing Co., Inc., 1965), edited by J. E. Smith; *Religious Belief and Philosophical Thought* (New York: Harcourt Brace Jovanovich, Inc., 1963), edited by W. Alston; *The Existence of God* (New York: Macmillan Publishing Co., Inc., 1964), edited by J. Hick; *The Ontological Argument* (Garden City, N.Y.: Doubleday & Company, Inc., 1965), edited by A. Plantinga; *Cosmological Arguments* (Garden City, N.Y.: Doubleday & Company, Inc., 1967), edited by D. R. Burrill.

General anthologies containing sections on the philosophy of religion are *A Modern Introduction to Philosophy,* revised edition (New York: The Free Press, 1965), edited by P. Edwards and A. Pap; *Knowledge and Value* (New York: Harcourt Brace Jovanovich, Inc., 1959), edited by E. Sprague and P. Taylor; *Philosophic Problems* (New York: Macmillan Publishing Co., Inc., 1957), edited by M. Mandelbaum, F. Gramlich, and A. R. Anderson; and *Reason and Responsibility* (Belmont, Calif.: Dickenson, 1965), edited by J. Feinberg.

RECENT AND CONTEMPORARY SOURCES

I. Original Works

Among books which discuss various issues in the philosophy of religion, including some of those discussed in this chapter, are W. James, *The Varieties of Religious Experience* (New York: Longmans, Green & Company, 1902), and *The Will to Believe* (New York: Longmans, Green & Company, 1897); W. T. Stace, *Time and Eternity* (Princeton, N. J.: Princeton University Press, 1952); C. J. Ducasse, *A Philosophical Scrutiny of Religion* (New York: The Ronald Press Company, 1953); W. Kaufman, *Critique of Religion and Philosophy* (New York: Harper & Row, Publishers, Inc., 1958); G. H. Joyce, *The Principles of Natural Theology* (New York: Longmans, Green & Company, 1951); J. F. Ross,

Philosophical Theology (Indianapolis: The Bobbs-Merrill Co., Inc., 1969); A. Plantinga, *God and Other Minds* (Ithaca, N.Y.: Cornell University Press, 1967); P. R. Baelz, *Christian Theology and Metaphysics* (London: Epworth Press, 1968); P. T. Geach, *God and the Soul* (New York: Schocken Books, 1969); the books by Ross and Plantinga are especially to be recommended; both contain extremely sophisticated discussions of various proofs for the existence of God, the problem of evil, and, in Plantinga's case, the rationality of believing in God without having a proof for his existence.

Several recent books have been devoted exclusively to the problem of the nature of religious knowledge and its relation to faith and to other sorts of knowledge. Among these are G. Mavrodes, *Belief in God: A Study in the Epistemology of Religion* (New York: Random House, Inc., 1970); J. Gill, *The Possibility of Religious Knowledge* (Grand Rapids: Eerdmans, 1971); W. Blackstone, *The Problem of Religious Knowledge* (Englewood Cliffs, N.J.: Prentice-Hall, Inc., 1963); H. P. Owen, *Christian Knowledge of God* (London: Athlone Press, 1969); J. Hick, *Faith and Knowledge* (Ithaca, N.Y.: Cornell University Press, 1957); C. Martin, *Religious Belief* (Ithaca, N.Y.: Cornell University Press, 1959); P. Schmidt, *Religious Knowledge* (New York: The Free Press, 1961).

Works on the way in which God is to be conceived of include J. Collins, *God in Modern Philosophy* (Chicago: Henry Regnery Co., 1959); C. Hartshorne, *Divine Relativity* (New Haven: Yale University Press, 1948); N. Pike, *God and Timelessness* (New York: Schocken Books, 1970); H. P. Owen, *Concepts of Deity* (London: Macmillan & Company, Ltd., 1971); R. Otto, *The Idea of the Holy* (Oxford: Galaxy Books, 1968); P. Bertocci, *The Person God Is* (London: George Allen & Unwin, Ltd., 1970); F. Sontag, *Divine Perfection: Possible Ideas of God* (New York: Harper & Row, Publishers, Inc., 1962).

The problem of religious language and its meaningfulness had received much discussion since the logical positivists declared all language purporting to be about metaphysics, including religious language, to be cognitively meaningless. The classical logical positivistic view is stated in Chapter 4 of A. J. Ayer, *Language, Truth, and Logic* (New York: Dover Publications, Inc., 1952). Book-length treatment has been given to this topic in L. Dewart, *Religion, Language and Truth* (New York: Herder and Herder, 1970); J. Macquarrie, *God-Talk* (New York: Harper & Row, Publishers, Inc., 1967); B. L. Clarke, *Language and Natural Theology* (The Hague: Mouton and Co., 1966); I. Ramsey, *Religious Language* (London: SCM Press, 1957); F. Ferre, *Language, Logic and God* (London: Eyre & Spottiswoode, Ltd., 1962).

Several books devoted entirely to a discussion of the various proofs for the existence of God are J. Hick, *Arguments for the Existence of God* (London: Macmillan & Company, Ltd., 1970); C. Hartshorne, *Anselm's Discovery* (La Salle, Ill.: Open Court Publishing Company, 1965), *Man's Vision of God and the Logic of Theism* (Chicago: Willet, Clark, 1941), *The Logic of Perfection* (La Salle, Ill.: Open Court Publishing Company, 1962); A. Kenny, *The Five Ways* (London: Routledge and Kegan Paul, 1969); H. P. Owen, *The Moral Argument for Christian Theism* (London: George Allen & Unwin, Ltd., 1965); W. Matson, *The Existence of God* (Ithaca, N.Y.: Cornell University Press, 1965).

The problem of evil has also called forth several book-length treatments in recent years. Among these are E. H. Madden and P. H. Hare, *Evil and the Concept of God* (Springfield, Ill.: Charles C Thomas, Publisher, 1968); J. Hick, *Evil and the Love of God* (London: Macmillan & Company, Ltd., 1966); C. S. Lewis, *The Problem of Pain* (New York: Macmillan Publishing Co., Inc., 1962); W. Fitch, *God and Evil* (London: Pickering and Inglis, 1967); F. Sontag, *God of Evil* (New York: Harper & Row, Publishers, Inc., 1970).

Finally, several books devoted to general critiques of religion are B. Russell's *Religion and Science* (New York: Oxford University Press, 1935), and *Why I Am Not a Christian* (New York: Simon & Schuster, Inc., 1957); K. Nielsen, *Contemporary Critiques of Religion* (New York: Herder and Herder, 1971); H. R. Burkle, *Non-Existence of God* (New work: Herder and Herder, 1969).

II. Collections of Articles and Textbooks

Each of the following collections contains contemporary articles devoted to the philosophy of religion, many of which are directly relevant to the problems discussed in this chapter: *New Essays in Philosophical Theology* (New York: Macmillan Publishing Co., Inc., 1955), edited by A. Flew and A. MacIntyre; *Religious Experience and Truth* (New York: New York University Press, 1966), edited by S. Hook; *New Essays on Religious Language* (New York: Oxford University Press, 1969), edited by D. M. High; *Religious Language and the Problem of Religious Knowledge* (Bloomington: Indiana University Press, 1968), edited by R. E. Santoni; *The Philosophy of Religion* (London: Oxford University Press, 1971), and *Faith and Logic* (Boston: Beacon Press, 1957), both edited by B. Mitchell; *Faith and the Philosophers* (New York: St. Martin's Press, 1964), edited by J. Hick; *Faith and Philosophy* (Grand Rapids: Wm. B. Eerdmans Publishing Co., 1964), edited by A. Plantinga; *Rationality and Belief in God* (Englewood Cliffs, N.J.: Prentice-Hall, Inc., 1970), edited by G. Mavrodes; *The Many-Faced Argument* (New York: Macmillan Publishing Co., Inc., 1967), edited by J. Hick and A. C. McGill; *Idea of God: Philosophical Perspectives* (Springfield, Ill.: Charles C

Thomas, Publisher, 1968), edited by E. H. Madden; *Philosophy of Religion* (New York: Harper & Row, Publishers, Inc., 1970), edited by S. M. Cahn; *Talk of God* (New York: St. Martin's Press, 1969), edited by G. N. A. Vesey; *Logical Analysis and Contemporary Theism* (New York: Fordham University Press, 1972), edited by J. Donnelly; *The Encyclopedia of Philosophy* (New York: Collier-Macmillan, 1967), edited by P. Edwards, also contains many excellent articles on the philosophy of religion.

Among the textbooks on the philosophy of religion are N. Smart, *Philosophy and Religious Truth* (New York: Macmillan Publishing Co., Inc., 1969), and *The Philosophy of Religion* (New York: Random House, Inc., 1970), both of which discuss several less-discussed topics, along with the standard topics in the philosophy of religion; J. F. Ross, *Introduction to the Philosophy of Religion* (New York: Macmillan Publishing Co., Inc., 1969); J. Hick, *Philosophy of Religion* (Englewood Cliffs, N.J.: Prentice-Hall, Inc., 1963); J. K. Roth, *Problems of the Philosophy of Religion* (San Francisco: Chandler Publishing Co., 1971); S. Thompson, *A Modern Philosophy of Religion* (Chicago: Henry Regnery Co., 1955); G. MacGregor, *Introduction to Religious Philosophy* (Boston: Houghton Mifflin Company, 1959); D. Trueblood, *Philosophy of Religion* (New York: Harper & Row, Publishers, Inc., 1957); E. A. Burtt, *Types of Religious Philosophy* (New York: Harper & Row, Publishers, Inc., 1951). Some textbooks with sections on the philosophy of religion are E. Beardsley and M. Beardsley, *Philosophical Thinking* (New York: Harcourt Brace Jovanovich, Inc., 1965); J. Hospers, *An Introduction to Philosophical Analysis* (Englewood Cliffs, N.J.: Prentice-Hall, Inc., 1953), M. Scriven, *Primary Philosophy* (New York: McGraw-Hill Book Company, 1966); and R. Taylor, *Metaphysics* (Englewood Cliffs, N.J.: Prentice-Hall, Inc., 1963).

III. Articles

Several articles on *the characteristics of a supreme being* have been written, especially on the *concept of omnipotence*. Some of these are G. B. Keene, "A Simpler Solution to the Problem of Omnipotence," *Mind* (1960), to which B. Mayo replied with "Mr. Keene on Omnipotence," *Mind* (1961). Mr. Keene gave his reply to Mr. Mayo in "Capacity Limiting Statements," *Mind* (1961). G. Mavrodes proposed a solution to the problem of omnipotence in "Some Puzzles Concerning Omnipotence," *Philosophical Review* (1963), to which H. Frankfurt added a note in "The Logic of Omnipotence," *Philosophical Review* (1964); and about which C. W. Savage wrote "The Paradox of the Stone," *Philosophical Review* (1967). Another recent article on the stone paradox is "God and the Stone Paradox: Three Comments," *Sophia* (1971), by D. Londey, B.

Miller, and J. King-Farlow. Two other articles on omnipotence are P. G. Kuntz, "Omnipotence, Tradition and Revolt in Philosophical Theology," *The New Scholasticism* (1968) and N. Pike, "Omnipotence and God's Ability to Sin," *American Philosophical Quarterly* (1969).

The *concept of necessary being* has also been widely discussed, often in connection with *the argument from contingency*. Among others are P. Brown, "St. Thomas' Doctrine of Necessary Being," *Philosophy Review* (1964); R. Franklin, "Necessary Being," *Analysis* (1957); J. Hick, "God as Necessary Being," *Journal of Philosophy* (1960); P. Hutchins, "Necessary Being," *Australasian Journal of Philosophy* (1957); T. Penelhum, "Divine Necessity," *Mind* (1960); J. F. Ross, "God and Logical Necessity," *Philosophical Quarterly* (1961); J. A. Brunton, "The Logic of God's Necessary Existence," *International Philosophical Quarterly* (1970); B. R. Reichenbach, "Divine Necessity and the Cosmological Argument," *Monist* (1970).

The *concept of God's omniscience* and its relationship to man's free will has brought forth articles by N. Kretzmann, "Omniscience and Immutability," *Journal of Philosophy* (1966), to which H. Castañeda has responded in "Omniscience and Indexical Reference," *Journal of Philosophy* (1967); N. Pike, "Divine Omniscience and Voluntary Action," *Philosophical Review* (1965), to which J. Saunders replied in "Of God and Freedom," *Philosophical Review* (1966). A. N. Prior has written "The Formalities of Omniscience," *Philosophy* (1962). There have been many articles on the problem of free will and foreknowledge. An interesting approach is taken by C. Ginet in "Can the Will Be Caused?" *Philosophical Review* (1962) and replied to by, among others, K. Lehrer, "Decisions and Causes," *Philosophical Review* (1963) and A. Oldenquist, "Causes, Predictions, and Decisions," *Analysis* (1964).

Other interesting articles on the concept of God are D. Bennett, "Deity and Events," *Journal of Philosophy* (1967); J. Donceel, "Second Thoughts on the Nature of God," *Thought* (1971); S. Coval, "Worship, Superlatives, and Concept Confusion," *Mind* (1959). Replies to this last article came from M. Fisher, "S. Coval on Worship, Superlatives, and Concept Confusions," *Mind* (1960) and R. Franklin, "Worship and God," *Mind* (1960). Many other recent articles by British and American linguistic philosophers relevant to the concept of God are listed in the following paragraphs on religious language and religious belief and experience.

The argument for the existence of God most discussed in current literature is *the ontological argument*. A sampling is W. Baumer, "Anselm, Truth and Necessary Being," *Philosophy* (1962); R. Carnes, "Descartes and the Ontological Argument," *Philosophy and Phenomenological Research* (1963–1964); J. Findlay, "Can God's Existence Be Disproved?"

Mind (1948); F. Fitch, "The Perfection of Perfection," *The Monist* (1963); C. Hartshorne, "The Logic of the Ontological Argument," *Journal of Philosophy* (1961); D. Henry, "St. Anselm and Nothingness," *Philosophical Quarterly* (1965); N. Malcolm, "Anselm's Ontological Arguments," *Philosophical Review* (1960), which brought replies in *The Philosophical Review* (1961) from R. Abelson, "Not Necessarily"; R. Allen, "The Ontological Argument"; P. Henle, "Uses of the Ontological Argument"; T. Penelhum, "On the Second Ontological Argument"; A. Plantinga, "A Valid Ontological Argument?"; G. Mathews "On Conceivability in Anselm and Malcolm"; and other replies from W. Huggett, "The Nonexistence of Ontological Arguments," *Philosophical Review* (1962); J. Shaffer, "Existence, Predication and the Ontological Argument," *Mind* (1962).

More articles on the argument are G. Mathews, "Aquinas on Saying 'God Doesn't Exist,' " *The Monist* (1963); J. Nelson, "Modal Logic and the Ontological Proof," *Review of Metaphysics* (1963–1964); R. Puccetti, "The Concept of God," *Philosophical Quarterly* (1964); N. Rescher, "The Ontological Argument Revisited," *Australasian Journal of Philosophy* (1959) replied to by K. Gunderson and R. Routley, "Mr. Rescher's Reformulation of the Ontological Proof," *Australasian Journal of Philosophy* (1960); J. F. Ross, "Logically Necessary Existential Statements," *Journal of Philosophy* (1961); F. Zabeeh, "Category–Mistake," *Philosophy and Phenomenological Research* (1962–1963); D. Haight and M. Haight, "An Ontological Argument for the Devil," *Monist* (1970); W. E. Mann, "Definite Descriptions and the Ontological Argument," *Theoria* (1967); R. J. Connelly, "The Ontological Argument: Descartes' Advice to Hartshorne," *The New Scholasticism* (1969); D. R. Keyworth, "Modal Proofs and Disproofs of God," *Personalist* (1969). Both the last two articles deal with Charles Hartshorne's proofs for the existence of God. L. S. Feuer has written "God, Guilt, and Logic–The Psychological Basis of the Ontological Argument," *Inquiry* (1968), which drew a response from W. L. Sessions, "Feuer, Psychology, and the Ontological Argument," *Inquiry* (1969). Other articles are R. M. Adams, "The Logical Structure of Anselm's Arguments," *Philosophical Review* (1971); J. Kellenberger, "The Ontological Principle and God's Existence," *Philosophy* (1970); C. Harrison, "The Ontological Argument in Modal Logic," *Monist* (1970); R. A. Imlay, "Descartes' Ontological Argument," *The New Scholasticism* (1969).

Articles concerning the objection to the ontological argument that *existence is not a property* are W. Alston, "The Ontological Argument Revisited," *Philosophical Review* (1960); K. Baier, "Existence," *Aristotelian Society Proceedings* (1960–1961); R. Cartwright, "Negative Existentials," *Journal of Philosophy* (1960); C. Hartshorne, "Is the Denial of Existence Ever Contradictory?" *Journal of Philosophy* (1966); M. Kitely, "Is Existence a Predicate?" *Mind* (1964); W. Kneale, "Is Existence a Predicate?" *Aristotelian Society Supplement* (1936); G. E. Moore, "Is Existence a Predicate?" *Aristotelian Society Supplement* (1936); G. Nakhnikian and W. Salmon, " 'Exists' as a Predicate," *Philosophical Review* (1957).

The *cosmological argument* has also received significant discussion recently. Some relevant articles are R. Hepburn, "From World to God," *Mind* (1963); W. Kennick, "A New Way with the Five Ways," *Australasian Journal of Philosophy* (1960); J. Owens, "Aquinas on Infinite Regress," *Mind* (1962); W. L. Rowe, "The Cosmological Argument and the Principle of Sufficient Reason," *Man and World* (1968), "Cosmological Argument," *Nous* (1971), and "Two Criticisms of the Cosmological Argument," *Monist* (1970); R. G. Swinburne, "Whole and Part in Cosmological Arguments," *Philosophy* (1969); W. N. Clarke, "A Curious Blindspot in the Anglo-American Tradition of Anti-Theistic Argument," *Monist* (1970); F. B. Dilley, "Descartes' Cosmological Argument," *Monist* (1970); P. A. Bertocci, "The Cosmological Argument, Revisited and Revised," *Proceedings of the American Catholic Philosophical Association* (1967); B. Miller, "The Contingency Argument," *Monist* (1970).

Several articles on the *design argument* are J. Narveson, "On a New Argument from Design," *Journal of Philosophy* (1965); E. D. Klemke, "The Argument from Design," *Ratio* (1969); R. G. Swinburne, "The Argument from Design," *Philosophy* (1968). On a related topic, E. G. King has discussed Berkeley's divine language argument in "Language, Berkeley, and God," *International Journal of Philosophy and Religion* (1970).

Discussions of *Pascalian-type arguments* for the rationality of belief in God are to be found in W. N. Christensen and J. King-Farlow, "Gambling on Other Minds—Human and Divine," *Sophia* (1971); P. T. Landsberg, "Gambling on God," *Mind* (1971); M. B. Turner, "Deciding for God—The Bayesian Support of Pascal's Wager," *Philosophy and Phenomenological Research* (1968). The first of these articles has drawn responses from L. Resnick, "Evidence, Utility and God," *Analysis* (1971); and J. Rudinow, "Gambling on Other Minds and God," *Sophia* (1971).

Articles on *other arguments* for the existence of God or on the *arguments in general* are R. Holland, "The Miraculous," *American Philosophical Quarterly* (1965); J. Hutchinson, "The Uses of Natural Theology: An Essay in Redefinition," *Journal of Philosophy* (1958); J. Jack, "A Recent Attempt to Prove God's Existence," *Philosophy and Phenomenological Research* (1964–1965); G. Mathews, "Theology and Natural Theology," *Journal of Philosophy* (1964); J. F. Ross, "Did God Create the Only Possible World?" *Review of Metaphysics* (1962–1963), and "On Proofs for the Existence of God," *Monist* (1970); J. Smart, "The Existence of God," reprinted in *New Essays in Philosophical Theology;* J. E. Smith, "The Experiential Foundations of Religion," *Journal of Philosophy* (1958), and "The Present Status of Natural Theology," *Journal of Philosophy* (1958); C. Williams, "Hie autem non est procedere in infinitum: . . . (St. Thomas Aquinas)," *Mind* (1960); J. Kellenberger, "We No Longer Have Need of That Hypothesis," *Sophia* (1969); C. Hartshorne, "Six Theistic Proofs," *Monist* (1970); H. A. Durfee, "The Reformulation of the Question As to the Existence of God," *Philosophy and Phenomenological Research* (1968); M. B. Zeldin, "Principles of Reason, Degrees of Judgment, and Kant's Argument for the Existence of God," *Monist* (1970); W. Sacksteder, "Of God: That He Exists More or Less," *Personalist* (1970); and S. M. Cahn, "The Irrelevance to Religion of Philosophic Proofs for the Existence of God," *American Philosophical Quarterly* (1969).

Religious language and verification has been rather widely discussed by, among others, B. Clark, "Linguistic Analysis and the Philosophy of Religion," *The Monist* (1963); R. Coburn, "A Neglected Use of Theological Language," *Mind* (1963). J. Hick, "Theology and Verification," *Theology Today* (1960) is on the concept of eschatological verification and was replied to by D. Duff-Forbes, "Theology and Falsification Again," *Australasian Journal of Philosophy* (1961); B. Mitchell, "The Justification of Religious Belief," *Philosophical Quarterly* (1961); and K. Nielsen, "Eschatalogical Verification," *The Canadian Journal of Theology* (1963). Other articles are J. Losee, "Two Proposed Demarcations for Theological Statements," *Monist* (1963); J. Riser, "Toward the Philosophical Analysis of Religious Statements," *Monist* (1963); P. Hayner, "Analogical Predication," *Journal of Philosophy* (1958); J. F. Ross, "A New Theory of Analogy," *Proceedings of the American Catholic Philosophical Association* (1970), and "Analogy and the Resolution of Some Cognitivity Problems," *Journal of Philosophy* (1970); J. F. Harris, "The Epistemic Status of Analogical Language," *International Journal of Philosophy and Religion* (1970); M. Durrant, "God and Analogy," *Sophia* (1969); K. Nielsen, "The Significance of God-Talk," *Religious Humanism* (1969); J. Donnelly, "Moral and Religious Assertions," *International Journal of Philosophy and Religion* (1971); J. Gill, "J. L. Austin and the Religious Use of Language," *Sophia* (1969); D. Z. Phillips, "Religious Beliefs and Language Games," *Ratio* (1970); J. S. Morris, "Religion and Theological Language," *Hibbert Journal* (1967); H. E. Allison, "Faith and Falsifiability," *Review of Metaphysics* (1969); A. M. Wheeler, "Are Theological Utterances Assertions?" *Sophia* (1969); J. Ferrater-Mora, "The Language of Religious Experience," *International Journal of Philosophy and Religion* (1970); W. Swanson, "Religious Discourse and Rational Preference Rankings," *American Philosophical Quarterly* (1967). M.B. Hesse, in her "Talk of God" has reviewed the book of the same title, edited by G. N. A. Vesey, listed above. In addition to these, the 1967 volume of the *Pacific Philosophy Forum* contains many articles on religious language.

Articles on the nature of *religious belief*, knowledge, and experience, and the possible justification of religious belief in the face of less than adequate evidence, are P. Weiss, "Religious Experience," *Review of Metaphysics* (1963–1964); D. Platt, "God: From Experience to Inference: A Phenomenological Study," *International Philosophical Quarterly* (1970); J. Moulder, "Aspectual and Religious Perceptions," *Sophia* (1969); D. Z. Phillips, "Religion and Epistemology, Some Contemporary Confusions," *Australasian Journal of Philosophy* (1966); A. Dulles, "Faith, Reason, and the Logic of Discovery," *Thought* (1970). N. Malcolm's "Is It a Religious Belief That 'God Exists,'" in *Faith and the Philosophers*, edited by J. Hick, drew a reply from K. Nielsen, "On Believing That God Exists," *Southern Journal of Philosophy* (1967). J. Pashman's "Is the Genetic Fallacy a Fallacy?" *Southern Journal of Philosophy* (1970), has been responded to by L. Kleiman, "Pashman on Freud and the Genetic Fallacy," *Southern Journal of Philosophy* (1970), to which Pashman has in turn replied in "Reply to Mr. Kleiman," *Southern Journal of Philosophy* (1971). Another controversy has arisen over J. Hick's argument for the "no-evidence" defense of the rationality of theistic belief, given in his book *Philosophy of Religion*. Discussions of this type of argument occur in R. A. Oakes, "Is Probability Inapplicable-in-Principle to the God-Hypothesis?" *The New Scholasticism* (1970); D. F. Henze, "Faith, Evidence, and Coercion," *Philosophy* (1967), replied to by J. King-Farlow, "Cogency, Conviction, and Coercion," *International Philosophical Quarterly* (1968); D. R. Duff-Forbes, "Faith, Evidence, Coercion," *Australasian Journal of Philosophy* (1969), replied to by J. Hick, "Faith, Evidence, Coercion Again," *Australasian Journal of Philosophy* (1971).

Other articles on religious belief are J. King-Farlow, "Justification of Religious Beliefs," *Philosophical Quarterly* (1962); L. Pearl, "Religious and Secular Beliefs," *Mind* (1960); G. Weiler, "How Rational Is Religious Belief," *Philosophical Quarterly* (1962); D. M. Levin, "Reasons and Religious Belief," *Inquiry* (1969); J. Wisdom, "Gods," *Aristotelian Society Proceedings* (1944), and "The Modes of Thought and the Logic of God," printed in *The Existence of God*, edited by J. Hick. The two articles by Wisdom have had widespread influence among linguistic philosophers. Springing from them, and also widely discussed are the contributions to a debate on theology and falsification by A. Flew, R. M. Hare, B. Mitchell, and I. M. Crombie, reprinted as Chapter VI of *New Essays in Philosophical Theology*, which is listed above. On the same topic see also D. Z. Phillips, "Wisdom's Gods," *Philosophical Quarterly* (1969).

The *problem of evil*, especially the question of whether the existence of both God and evil is possible, is discussed in H. Aiken, "God and Evil," *Ethics* (1958); R. Ehman, "On Evil and God," *The Monist* (1963); P. Farrel, "Evil and Omnipotence," *Mind* (1958); J. Mackie, "Evil and Omnipotence," *Mind* (1955); A. Plantinga, "The Free Will Defense," in *Philosophy in America* (Ithaca, N.Y.: Cornell University Press, 1965), edited by M. Black. A debate on this article occurred in *Journal of Philosophy* (1966) between N. Pike, "Plantinga on the Free Will Defense: A Reply"; and Plantinga, "Pike and Possible Persons." Other articles are G. Schlesinger, "The Problem of Evil and the Problem of Suffering," *American Philosophical Quarterly* (1964); N. Smart, "Omnipotence, Evil, and Supermen," *Philosophy* (1961); M. Zimmerman, "A Note on the Problem of Evil," *Mind* (1961).

E. H. Madden has written extensively on the problem of evil (see the book by Madden and Hare on this topic, listed above). Among his articles are "The Many Faces of Evil," *Philosophy and Phenomenological Research* (1963–1964), "Evil and the Concept of a Limited God," *Philosophical Studies* (1967), and, with P. H. Hare, "Evil and Unlimited Power," *Review of Metaphysics* (1966), and "On the Difficulty of Evading the Problem of Evil," *Philosophy and Phenomenological Research* (1967). J. King-Farlow has replied to Madden in two articles, "Must Gods Madden Madden?" *Philosophy and Phenomenological Research* (1969), and "The Liabilities of Limited Gods," *Philosophical Studies* (1969).

More articles on the problem of evil are K. E. Yandell, "Ethics, Evils and Theism," *Sophia* (1969); G. S. Kane, "Theism and Evil," *Sophia* (1970); C. F. Keilkopf, "Emotivism as the Solution to the Problem of Evil," *Sophia* (1970); C. Dore, "An Examination of the 'Soul-Making Theodicy,'" *American Philosophical Quarterly* (1970); G. Wall, "Emphysema, Earthquakes, and the Benevolence of a Finite God," *Personalist* (1969); G. Mavrodes, "The Problem of Evil as a Rhetorical Problem," *Philosophy and Rhetoric* (1968); R. M. Chisholm, "The Defeat of Good and Evil," *Proceedings of the American Philosophical Association* (1968–1969). W. E. McMahon's "The Problem of Evil and the Possibility of a Better World," *Journal of Value Inquiry* (1969) drew a response by J. T. King, "The Meta-Ethical Dimension of the Problem of Evil," *Journal of Value Inquiry* (1971). G. Schlesinger's "The Problem of Evil and the Problem of Suffering," *American Philosophical Quarterly* (1964) was responded to by J. F. Rosenberg, "The Problem of Evil Revisited," and W. W. Shea, "God, Evil, and Professor Schlesinger," both in the *Journal of Value Inquiry* (1970).

Alvin Plantinga's book *God and Other Minds* (listed above) has received extensive comment since its publication. Some of the relevant articles are here listed: G. Mavrodes, "Some Recent Philosophical Theology," *Review of Metaphysics* (1970), discusses both Plantinga's book and J. F. Ross's *Philosophical Theology*. Other articles on Plantinga: W. L. Rowe, "God and Other Minds," *Nous* (1969); C. J. Dore, "Plantinga on the Free Will Defense," *Review of Metaphysics* (1971); B. L. Tapscott, "Plantinga, Properties and the Ontological Argument," *Philosophy and Phenomenological Research* (1971); J. E. Tomberlin, "Is Belief in God Justified?" *Journal of Philosophy* (1970), and "Plantinga's Puzzles About God and Other Minds,' *Philosophical Forum* (1969); I. Hedenius, "Disproofs of God's Existence?" *Personalist* (1971); G. E. Hughes, "Plantinga on the Rationality of God's Existence," *Philosophical Review* (1970).

THE PROBLEM
OF JUSTIFYING
AN ETHICAL STANDARD

CHAPTER
SIX

There is one kind of problem that continually confronts most people. At one time or another we are faced with deciding what we ought to do. We also often wonder whether we have done the right thing, and we accuse others, as well as ourselves, of not doing what ought to be done. In many of these cases we are making moral or ethical judgments, judging the moral worth of actions we or others have done or are thinking of doing. Think back about some of your past actions. Probably you can find some actions you think you shouldn't have done. Perhaps it was lying about your age to get served liquor in a bar, or taking a glance at the test paper next to you in an examination, or indefinitely "borrowing" a library book without signing for it. Even now you may be thinking about some course of action in the future, whether to use the fraternity files for a course paper, whether to bury yourself in your work and avoid participating in social action, or whether to ignore an oft-proclaimed principle of your own in order to avoid some physical hardship. Where there is a person who thinks about what he and others have done and are doing, rather than acting without thinking, there we find a person who is faced with making a moral judgment. And with any judgment, when we make it we like to think we made the correct judgment or at least that we are justified in the judgment we make.

How can we justify our moral judgments? When we decide what we ought to do we would like to base our decisions on sound reasons, although, as in many other areas of human endeavor, we often decide without thinking. Usually when we try to defend our moral decisions and actions we do so by reference to some moral rule or standard, such as "Thou shalt not kill" or "Lying and cheating are wrong." That is, we often justify a claim that a particular action is right or wrong by reference to some ethical rule or standard which applies to the action. It is obvious, however, that we cannot show an action to be right or wrong unless we have appealed to the correct standard. For example, the attempt to absolve a white man of the killing of a Negro by appealing to the standard that no white man ought to be convicted of a crime when the victim is a Negro, may convince some people, but it fails to justify the act morally, because the standard appealed to is incorrect. On the other hand, attempting to eliminate acts of capital punishment by appealing to the standard that no man, or group of men, has the right to take the life of another man surely has some force to it. Those who defend capital punishment usually will not attack the standard but try to show that it must be modified to account for certain exceptions. An important part of justifying a particular moral decision, then, is basing it upon the correct ethical standard.

If we can find some way to justify a standard or a group of standards, then the only other particularly moral task we have left— probably the most difficult task of all—is the task of applying the standards throughout our lives. The second task faces us all, including philosophers, who are in no better positions to achieve success than anyone else. Philosophers are particularly suited to the first task, however, because they are centrally interested in and uniquely trained for critical investigations of the arguments men propose to justify their actions and beliefs. In this chapter we shall examine the various leading theories which propose and defend particular moral standards, and we shall attempt a philosophical examination of each, with the hope that we can draw a justified conclusion about correct ethical standards.

EVALUATING ACTIONS VS. EVALUATING PEOPLE

Before we move on to consider ethical theories (that is, theories that propose ethical standards) two points should be emphasized. The first is that we are interested in a standard that can be used to prescribe and evaluate particular courses of action, that is, a standard that can be used to prescribe what we ought to do and evaluate what we have done. We are, then, not interested in a standard that is to be used to evaluate morally the people who perform actions, but rather in a standard for evaluating the *actions* people perform. We certainly use both kinds of standards, for we not only decide that what someone did was right or wrong, but we also praise or blame the person for doing it and sometimes judge him to be moral or immoral. Both kinds of standards are important, but they are different. It seems essential in morally evaluating a person for what he does that we consider his motives, his beliefs, and the particular circumstances surrounding his decision to act, but it is not clear that any of these are relevant to the evaluation of his action. For example, many people have claimed that it was wrong to drop the first atomic bomb on Hiroshima, and they have consequently blamed President Truman for ordering the bomb to be dropped. However, these are two quite separate issues. We might argue that it was morally wrong to drop the first bomb on a city because a less populated site might have been equally effective. Here we decide the issue without considering President Truman's motives, beliefs, and the pressures under which he made the decision. But in deciding whether to blame the President we must consider his motive, his beliefs about the war and whether they were reasonable, and the external and internal forces playing upon the one man who had to make the decision. It may be, then, that the action he took was wrong, but he should not be blamed for it.

Similarly, someone might do something which, contrary to what he intended, turns out to be right. In such a case the action may be right but the person blameworthy. Consequently, we should remember to distinguish between these two kinds of standards, because we are considering only standards for evaluating moral actions and because failure to distinguish the two has often led to unjust accusations of blame and unnecessary feelings of guilt. There are many actions which are wrong but which reflect no blame or guilt on the doer. Understanding rather than blame is often appropriate.

METHOD OF CRITICALLY EVALUATING
ETHICAL THEORIES

The second point concerns the means we shall use to evaluate critically the various ethical theories. In general we shall proceed as we did in Chapter 4, in which we considered various mind–body theories. That is, we shall try to elaborate each position clearly, consider the problems confronting each, and then decide which position is least troubled by serious objections. We must, then, elaborate and evaluate the most serious objections to each theory. We shall find, for example, that the standards proposed by some theories do not apply to all situations, that other standards result in unresolvable moral conflicts when applied to certain situations, and that still others prescribe morally repugnant courses of action in certain situations. This last point is very important and deserves further comment.

We shall claim that someone has some reason to reject a standard which is clearly contrary to what, in an uncritical way, he feels certain is correct. It is important to notice that it is not enough that the person is uncertain about whether what the standard prescribes is correct; he must be certain that it is incorrect. Each person, then, is to rely *in part* on his own rather intuitive sense of what is right and wrong when he evaluates, or tests, ethical standards. This is not to say, however, that it is reasonable for him to accept a standard only if what it prescribes agrees in every case with what he tends to believe is right or wrong. It is quite unlikely that any standard would be in accordance with all of a person's beliefs about right and wrong. For one reason, few people have self-consciously examined the whole spectrum of their moral opinions and decisions, and so it is likely that many people are inconsistent. They decide differently at different times, even under similar conditions, and especially when the action involves someone they love or hate. Where someone finds he has some inconsistent beliefs, then, even if he believes one of them quite strongly, he should not use it to test a standard. Consequently, a person should rely on his own intuitive opinions of what is right and what is wrong only when he feels quite certain of those opinions, and none of his other beliefs are incompatible with those opinions.

It surely can be objected, however, that it is a mistake to rely on this intuitive test of ethical standards, because people's ethical opinions, even their strongly held opinions, differ extremely widely about particular cases. For example, many Jews find to be obviously morally repugnant certain actions which many Nazis found quite acceptable. Also there clearly are equally deeply felt disagreements between many pacifists and many military rulers. It surely is mistaken, according to this objection, to rely on a method of evaluation that allows Nazis and some of the most callous military rulers to be justified in holding a standard because they do not find that it prescribes anything morally repugnant, when so many other people find it clearly abhorrent.

It must be admitted that relying, even in part, on the intuitive opinions allows for different standards to be justified for different people. We find, however, that some such relativity of justification is inevitable. The question is whether the proposed method sanctions justification of standards which are clearly mistaken. There are two reasons why it is plausible to expect that the proposed method will not have this consequence. The first is that, as briefly mentioned above, this intuitive test is but one of several tests or conditions for a satisfactory ethical principle. Many standards that will meet this test for a particular person will fail because they do not meet the other conditions. Part of what we will do, as we examine various proposed ethical standards throughout the chapter, is to try to uncover these other important conditions for a satisfactory standard. We will do this primarily by examining the reasons we found for rejecting unsatisfactory proposals. By the time we have finished, it is hoped that we will have found not only a satisfactory theory, but also the conditions and tests it has met in proving to be satisfactory.

The second reason is that we do not even expect widespread divergences among standards that meet the intuitive test. A standard is not shown to meet this test for someone if he finds he is not bothered by any of the actions it prescribed that most people find morally repugnant. He must find it meets this test in a wide variety of other cases as well. For example, many Nazis would find it morally repugnant for anyone to put loyal Nazis in gas chambers. But in certain conditions in different countries, such actions might well be prescribed by the same standard that he otherwise finds acceptable. Thus a person is not to select in a biased way the cases he uses to test a standard. He must examine a wide range of possible as well as actual cases to see if it prescribes anything he feels quite certain is mistaken. It is only once he has done this that he can justify that a standard meets this particular test. And once he has done this, a person will find that many fewer standards meet the test than he might have expected.

THEOLOGICAL ETHICS

Much of our ethical training and learning takes place in a religious context. Indeed ethics seems to be an essential part of religion. In both the Old and New Testaments and in most other religious documents, such as the Koran, there are ethical teachings. In the Old Testament the Ten Commandments are central and in the New Testament we have, among others, the teachings of the Sermon on the Mount. It is natural, then, to associate ethics and morality with religion, so that it is also natural to look to religion for the ethical standards we can use to prescribe and evaluate our actions. And if we think back about the discussion of God in the last chapter, we might derive a standard from the discussion of the goodness of the supreme being. That is, we might propose that the correct ethical standard is the following:

Whatever God wills is what ought to be done.

If this is the correct ethical standard then whenever we are deciding what ought to be done or what ought to have been done we should base our decision on what God wills.

What we must do to make this standard applicable to specific situations is to find some way to discover what God would will in the situation. There are two ways we can discover this. First, God might reveal his will to us by directly communicating with us, or he might reveal his will to someone else who relays it to the rest of us. For most of us, if God's will is revealed to us at all, it is only indirectly, with someone else as the intermediary. Consequently, if we are to apply the theological standard on the basis of God's will as indirectly revealed we must be able to justify some particular claim about what God wills, for example, the Ten Commandments. But we have already seen in the last chapter how difficult it is to provide grounds for thinking that any revelation of God's will has occurred, let alone show that any one particular claim is correct.[1]

OBJECTION: MUST JUSTIFY RELIGIOUS CLAIMS BY ETHICAL CLAIMS

Let us assume someone claims that what God wills is that men obey the Ten Commandments. We now have an ethical standard that we can apply to particular situations. But how are we to justify the claim that this is the correct criterion? We cannot do so merely by claiming that God revealed the commandments to Moses, because we must justify the claim that it was God who gave them to Moses. Consider what we would do if we read that Moses had returned with such commandments as "Make love to thy neighbor's wife," "Steal thy neighbor's goods," and "Take advantage of thy parents." We would decide that whatever was revealed to Moses, it was not the will of God, because these are immoral commandments. We do not justify that something is moral by showing that it expresses God's will, because the only available way to evaluate conflicting claims about what God wills is by finding which one is in accordance with what is moral. Thus we must use ethical claims to justify

[1] See pp. 345–50.

religious claims rather than ground ethics upon the claims of some religion.[2]

This is not to deny that religion is for many people the psychological basis of ethics. It may be, then, that religion has an important psychological relationship to ethics. Nor is this to deny that God has willed or prescribed certain moral commandments. Everything just discussed can be accepted by someone who believes that whatever God wills should be done. Furthermore, nothing said so far gives any reason to think that the Ten Commandments do not express the revealed word of God. They might. If they do, they will also express at least part of a correct ethical standard. The only claim made here is that we cannot justify that they or any other ethical standards are correct by appealing to the pronouncements of some particular religion, because we must justify that these pronouncements express the revealed word of God by showing that they are the correct moral pronouncements. Because our task here is to find and justify some ethical standard, we cannot stop with the pronouncements of some religion even if they are correct. We must find some way to show that they are correct, and this we cannot do by appealing to the religion itself.

We are in no better position if we try to ground an ethical standard on direct revelation. It may be that some day you will have a religious experience in which certain commands are issued to you. You may, as others have after similar experiences, uncritically accept these as revealing the word of God and proclaim them to all. But we are here interested not in what you might do, but in whether you would be justified in claiming that you had heard the word of God. That you have received these commands in a very strange and unique way is not enough. There are many cases of a person who has followed his "voices" and has committed ghastly crimes. In such cases we usually think that the "voices" are the result of psychological disturbances. Furthermore, it is possible that not only God, but also the devil reveals his will to men. Consequently, you

---

[2] For a clear argument against theological ethics, see Jeremy Bentham's discussion of the theological principle in *An Introduction to the Principles of Morals and Legislation* in *The Utilitarians* (Garden City, N.Y.: Doubleday, 1961). John Stuart Mill also discusses theological ethics in *Utilitarianism,* also in *The Utilitarians,* p. 423.

could justify your claim that you had heard the word of God only if you could provide reason to think that the word expressed a command of God rather than one of the devil. You cannot do this by appealing to your religious experience. Thus in the case of direct revelation as in the case of indirect revelation, justification of an ethical claim cannot be based on a religious claim.

The conclusion we have reached is that although a religion may help us psychologically to decide what to do, it cannot help us justify what we decide to do. The justification of our ethical standards and thereby our actions proceeds independently of appeals to religion. Because of this, the existence of God is irrelevant to the justification of ethical standards. Thus those who find they can no longer believe in God are not forced to the conclusion that nothing is right or wrong. There is nothing inconsistent in holding some particular ethical standard and also believing that God does not exist. As brought out earlier, and as we shall see, the critical evaluation and justification of ethical standards is carried on without reference to religion.

Nevertheless there is a widespread view that if there is no God, then nothing is moral or immoral, nothing is right or wrong. This is the view that if anything is right and anything is wrong, it is so because it has been decreed so by God. Notice that this is a different claim from the one we previously examined. The previous claim is

If something is willed by God, then it ought to be done.

but the present claim is

If something is the right thing to do (ought to be done), then it is willed (proclaimed or commanded) by God.

Although the first statement is acceptable the second is surely debatable. For one thing, there is no reason to think that all right actions are willed or commanded by God, because there is no reason to think that God issues commands covering every moral situation. It may be that if in a certain situation a particular action is right, then if God were to command some action in that situation he would command that action. But this claim does not lead to the conclusion that if there is no God, then nothing is right or wrong. Secondly, it is at least possible that we shall be able to justify some ethical standard as correct, and because, as we have seen, such a justification does not require reference to God, there is no reason to think that the correct ethical standard must issue from God. However, no matter what causes them to do it many people talk of the breakdown of morality and the destruction of ethical standards, which they often blame on the decline of religion. The result of this, they claim, is that morality is relative, so that nothing is right or wrong, and what it is right for me to do is merely what I want to do. Although it is not unusual to hear such a claim, the claim itself is quite unusual, because it embodies three distinctly different ethical positions—ethical relativism, ethical nihilism, and ethical egoism. In one way or another these positions are prominent among the views about ethics expressed today. Consequently, each deserves individual attention here.

ETHICAL RELATIVISM

Ethical relativism seems to be expressed by the frequent claim:

What's right for you is not always right for me.

And because this claim seems to be true many people become convinced of ethical relativism. But this is an ambiguous claim and those interpretations of it which are readily acceptable are not those which imply ethical relativism. One interpretation of 'What's right for you is not always right for me' is the following:

The right action for you is not always the right action for me.

This interpretation is often true because two people are often quite different, but it does not imply ethical relativism. For example, if you are a good swimmer and I cannot swim, then in the same situation where each sees a child drowning, it is right for you to swim to help the child, but right for me to run off for help. But although what each of us ought to do in this same situation differs, it is still true that both of us should do our best to help the child. There is nothing relative about this.

ACTION RELATIVISM vs. STANDARD RELATIVISM

What we must do to avoid confusion here is to distinguish between the relativism of ethical actions and the relativism of ethical standards.

> *Action Relativism:* Actions are in some situations right and in some situations wrong.
> *Standard Relativism:* Ethical standards are in some situations correct and in some situations incorrect.

We have seen a case of action relativism in the example of the drowning child, but this was not a case of standard relativism. Both you and I applied the same standard, that we ought to do our best to help the child. Thus there can be relativism of right actions without relativism of ethical standards. Consequently, as presently interpreted,

> What's right for you is not always right for me.

expresses an action relativism, but because ethical relativism concerns standard relativism and because action relativism does not imply standard relativism, this often true claim does not imply ethical relativism. What may be confusing is that there are some ethical standards which claim that certain acts are always wrong, such as "Thou shalt not kill," so it may seem that what we can call standard absolutism implies action absolutism. But there are many other cases such as "Honor thy father and mother" where no specific actions are forbidden. Thus those who rebel against action absolutism are not forced to ethical relativism, because the correct ethical standard may allow that whether a specific action is right or wrong depends upon the specific circumstances in which it is done. How we honor our parents at some time depends upon them, us, and the particular circumstances.

Another interpretation of 'What's right for you is not always right for me' is the following:

> What you think is right is not always what I think is right.

On this interpretation the claim is surely true. But all it expresses then is that you and I sometimes disagree about what we think is right and this is quite compatible with standard absolutism. Thus this interpretation does not lead to ethical relativism. In order to get to ethical relativism we need an interpretation which will make ethical *standards* relative. Another interpretation which comes closer and is often thought to lead to ethical relativism is the following:

> The standard you are justified in accepting as correct is not always the standard I am justified in accepting.

This interpretation, although once again true, does not lead to ethical relativism, because someone can be justified in accepting something as correct when it is not correct. For example, we would certainly agree that someone who believed that the velocity of objects can be indefinitely increased was justified in his belief before Einstein propounded his theory. But we would also claim that although he was justified, his belief is incorrect. Furthermore, as we have seen, it is possible that our method of evaluating ethical standards, which uses each person's strongly held moral convictions as one of several tests, will result in some relativity in the justification of ethical standards. But as with scientific hypotheses, although different people might be justified in accepting different standards, any one of them, indeed all of them, might nevertheless be mistaken. Thus although there is a relativity of justification, this does not imply a relativity of correctness. Even though which beliefs are *justified* differs as men's knowledge changes, this does not affect which are the *true* or correct beliefs. Relativity of when a man is justified in accepting a belief or standard does not help the ethical relativist, who requires a relativity of correct standards. The kind of interpretation we need for ethical relativism is one such as the following:

> The correct ethical standard for you is not always the correct ethical standard for me.

This interpretation implies ethical relativism because it implies that an ethical standard is correct relative to some situations and incorrect relative to others. However, on this interpretation, the claim is no longer obviously true. We must consider what reasons there might be for accepting it.

DEFINITION OF ETHICAL RELATIVISM
Le us first define ethical relativism as follows:

> *Ethical Relativism:* Different ethical standards are correct for different groups of people.

This definition is stated broadly to allow for various different kinds of ethical relativism. For example, one species of ethical relativism which some sociologists and anthropologists are tempted to accept is *cultural relativism,* which is the theory that whether an ethical standard is correct depends upon the culture or society of the person concerned. There is also *class relativism* which, having its roots in Marxism, makes the correct standard relative to the economic class of the person. There is also a relativism which appeals to historians, *historical relativism,* and which makes the correct standards relative to the particular times at which the person lived. None of these species of ethical relativism is any better justified than the general theory. Therefore if we find reason to reject this general theory we will be justified in rejecting each of its specific versions as well.

Let us begin the examination of ethical relativism by considering two of the main arguments used to justify it, the argument from differing ethical judgments and the argument from different ethical standards.

THE ARGUMENT FROM DIFFERING ETHICAL JUDGMENTS
One of the most widely accepted facts relevant to ethics is that there is, has been, and probably always will be widespread disagreement about what is right and what is wrong. It is not merely that the judgments of people of one culture differ greatly from the judgments of people of another culture, nor is it merely that the judgments of people at one stage of history are quite different from those of people at some earlier or later time. We find widely divergent ethical judgments within one culture and at the same time. Surely, this objection states, if over centuries and throughout the world people have continually made widely divergent and often contradictory moral judgments, then it must be that the ethical standards of people differ from place to place and time to time

relative to the situations in which the people live. Therefore, according to this argument, correct standards are relative to the situations of the people who apply the standards. That is, we must conclude that ethical relativism is true.

Let us outline this argument so that we can critically evaluate it. It can be stated as follows:

1. The ethical judgments people make differ greatly, depending on where and when they live.
2. If the ethical judgments people make differ greatly, then the ethical standards people use differ greatly.
   Therefore
3. The ethical standards people use differ greatly.
   Therefore
4. Ethical relativism is true.

There are two objections that can be raised against this argument. First, although premise (1) is acceptable, there is reason to doubt the truth of the second premise. We have already seen that action relativism does not imply standard relativism, and there is also little reason to think that a judgment relativism implies a standard relativism. Indeed, some anthropologists and sociologists who agree with (1) are not at all sure about (2). Many quite divergent judgments can be explained by pointing out that the people concerned have different beliefs about what the facts are rather than different ethical standards. For example, in one society, the people had the custom of killing their parents when they began to grow old. In Western cultures such an act is considered completely immoral. Most of us judge that killing one's parents is wrong, because we employ the standard that we should honor our parents. It certainly seems that we can conclude that the people of this society had no such standard, but this would be wrong. These people believed that each of us spends his afterlife in the physical state in which he dies. Thus to allow someone to grow old and decrepit would not be honoring him. These people did what they thought best for their parents, and thus honored them by helping them obtain immortality in an enjoyable physical state.[3] In this example, they and we seem

---

[3] This kind of example is discussed by Solomon E. Asch in *Social Psychology*

to use the same ethical standard, but because we disagree about the facts of afterlife the judgments we make differ greatly. In such a way many differences of actual judgments can be explained without postulating different ethical standards. Some anthropologists hope to find that certain ethical standards are universally believed to be correct. If this is so, it would certainly make premise (2) highly dubious.

However, even if the divergence of ethical standards is not as great as some people claim, the evidence presently available supports the claim that people often have different beliefs about which ethical standards are correct. Consequently, we can defend (3) interpreted as follows:

> 3a. The ethical standards believed to be correct by people often differ.

Thus because we can accept (3a), we can also accept (4) if the inference from (3a) to (4) is valid. However, as it stands, the inference is invalid because (3a) is a statement only about what people *believe* to be correct and (4) is a statement about what is *in fact* correct. This is the second objection to the argument from differing ethical judgments—it is invalid because the inference from (3a) to (4) is invalid. What we must do is find a premise which, with (3a), will allow us to infer (4). This takes us to the second argument for ethical relativism.

THE ARGUMENT FROM DIFFERENT
ETHICAL STANDARDS

It may seem to some that although the inference from (3a) to (4) is, strictly speaking, invalid, it resembles the inference from 'Socrates is a man' to 'Socrates is mortal'—what is missing is an obvious truth such as 'All men are mortal.' However, the dubious part of such an enthymematic argument is very often that missing premise. Let us examine the present case by constructing the argument as follows:

(Englewood Cliffs, N.J.: Prentice-Hall, 1952), Chapter 13, especially p. 377, where he is trying to show how widely different ethical practices can result from divergent factual beliefs instead of from different ethical standards.

3a. The ethical standards believed to be correct by people often differ.

5. If the ethical standards that people believe to be correct often differ, then the ethical standards which are correct often differ for these different people.

Therefore

4. The ethical standards which are correct are often different for different people, i.e., ethical relativism is true.

What we have done is add statement (5) as the missing premise to make the argument valid. Consequently, because we have seen that (3a) is acceptable, we should accept (4) if we can justify (5). Let us consider (5), which is a sentence of the form:

5a. If the x's which people believe to be correct often differ, then the x which is correct often differs for these different people.

When we consider (5a) we see that there are many sentences of that form which are plainly false. For example, many people differ in their beliefs about the world around us but this does not imply that in each case a different belief is correct. If I believe that the correct number of planets is eight and you believe that the correct number is ten, it is not that one number is correct for me and another correct for you. In this case both you and I are wrong, both of our beliefs are incorrect, because there is one and only one correct number of planets and that number is nine. In general, sentences of the form of (5a) are false. Furthermore, there is no reason to think that beliefs about ethical standards are relevantly different from those beliefs for which (5a) is false. We have, therefore, reason to conclude that (5) is false.

Because both arguments supporting ethical relativism are unsound, we have found no reason to accept it. Moreover, because it is clearly contrary to our ordinary conception of morality, there is some reason to reject it. When we claim that lying, cheating, and killing are wrong, we do not claim that these prohibitions are derived from standards which correctly apply to some of us but not to others. We think that an ethical standard is either correct or incorrect for one and for all, and because we have found no reason to deny this we can continue to accept it.

The way seems open to search for an ethical standard we can justify as the correct standard for all. Our search, however, may be frustrated in another way. What reason have we for thinking that there is any correct standard of right and wrong either for some or for all? It is true that when we make moral judgments we act on the assumption that there is such a standard, but perhaps nothing is right and nothing is wrong; perhaps there is no correct ethical standard. If this is true, it is foolish to struggle to justify that some standard is correct. We should thus examine the claim of ethical nihilism before embarking on a critical examination of particular ethical standards.

ETHICAL NIHILISM

We can define ethical nihilism quite simply as follows:

> *Ethical Nihilism:* There is nothing morally right and nothing morally wrong.

If this position is correct, then because no actions are either right or wrong, it follows that nothing we do is moral and nothing immoral, that everything is permitted and nothing either morally forbidden or obligatory. It also follows that there are no correct ethical standards, because if there were, then the actions they required would be morally obligatory, and the actions they forbad would be morally prohibited. Such a view is quite contrary to our ordinary beliefs. Most of us feel quite certain that some actions are right and some are wrong. Consequently, unless there are cogent reasons for accepting ethical nihilism, we can reject it as we did ethical relativism. Generally, the debate about ethical nihilism does not center directly on the question of whether any particular actions are morally right or wrong, because the issue can best be discussed by reference to ethical standards. If there is good reason to think that some ethical standard is correct, there is good reason to reject ethical nihilism. If there is good reason to think that no ethical standard is correct, there is some reason to doubt that any actions are right or wrong.

It is important to note here that it is possible that actions are right or wrong but that no ethical standard is correct. We might some-how "sense" that particular actions are right just as we visually sense that objects are red. As with seeing, such moral "sensing" would not depend on the existence of any standard. Nevertheless, the ethical nihilist argues his point by trying to show that there are no correct ethical standards, because this is the best way he can defend his position. He generally depends on two main arguments, one of them resembling the second argument for ethical relativism because it is taken from the disagreement about correct ethical standards, and the second derived from the lack of a justification of any ethical standards.

THE ARGUMENT FROM DIFFERENT
ETHICAL STANDARDS

Some people claim it is wrong to infer ethical relativism from the widespread and enduring divergence of beliefs about which ethical standards are correct. Such a disagreement, which has persisted for centuries everywhere, instead testifies that there really are not any correct ethical standards. Such an argument, as you can probably see, is no better than the corresponding argument for ethical relativism. We can show this by presenting the argument as follows:

1. The ethical standards which people believe to be correct differ throughout the world and time.
2. If the ethical standards which people believe to be correct differ throughout the world and time, there are no correct ethical standards.
   Therefore
3. There are no correct ethical standards.

As might be guessed, premise (2), which is like premise (5) in the corresponding argument for ethical relativism, is highly suspect. Premise (2) is of the form:

(2a). If the x's which people believe to be correct differ, then there is no correct x.

And many sentences of this form are quite clearly false. For exam-ple, there are many divergent beliefs about life on distant stars, but this does not imply that none of these beliefs is correct. Some beliefs about life on stars are correct and some are not. One often finds a wide range of different beliefs on a difficult topic, most of which are wrong, but some of which are right. We can, therefore, reject this argument for ethical nihilism as no better than the corresponding argument for ethical relativism.

THE ARGUMENT FROM THE LACK OF JUSTIFICATION

It becomes apparent when critically evaluating the various leading candidates for the correct ethical standard that none has overcome problems important enough to keep it from being justified. Thus, this argument goes, because no ethical standards are justified, all are unjustified and therefore none is the correct standard. We can state the argument as follows:

1. No ethical standards are justified.
   Therefore
2. All ethical standards are unjustified.
3. If all ethical standards are unjustified, then no ethical standards are correct.
   Therefore
4. No ethical standards are correct (and thus ethical nihilism is reasonable).

There is a certain plausibility to this argument because we can gather evidence to support (1), the immediate inference from (1) to (2) is certainly valid, and (3) appears true. That is, if no possible ethical standard can be justified to be correct so that all are unjustified, it certainly seems reasonable to conclude that none of them is correct. Thus because both premises (1) and (3) seem acceptable and the argument is valid, it seems that we should accept the conclusion. But think about it some more. We have accepted (1) on the grounds that none of the candidates has yet overcome problems, so that none has yet been justified. However, when we supported (3) we did so by talking about what is implied if no candidates can ever be justified. There is a difference between 'not yet justified' and 'cannot be justified,' for the first is compatible with a future justification but the second precludes any possiblity of justification. The argument, then, seems to involve an equivocation of the word 'unjustified,' because (2) seems to require one sense of 'unjustified' and (3) a different sense. Thus the argument is invalid as it stands. We can bring out the equivocation and make the argument valid by replacing premise (3) with two other premises, namely,

> 3a. If all ethical standards are not yet justified, then all ethical standards are unjustifiable (cannot be justified).

and

> 3b. If all ethical standards are unjustifiable (cannot be justified), then no ethical standards are correct.

When we do this it is easy to see that (3a) is false and there is also some doubt about (3b).

In general it is false to state that if we have not yet justified some of a group of alternative claims, then no such claims can be justified. No particular claim about whether there is life on distant stars can now be justified, that is, there is not enough evidence to strongly support any particular claim. But this does not imply it is not possible that someday one claim will be justified. Thus in this example, as in ethics, if no position has been justified, we need not conclude that no position can be justified. We should reject premise (3a) and with it the argument containing it.

Although rejecting (3b) as well as (3a) is not necessary for our purposes, it is worthwhile to point out that (3b) derives from the claim that there are no correct but unjustifiable assertions. That is, it derives from the position that if an utterance makes a true assertion it is at least possible to justify it. But as we saw in the last chapter it is very hard to establish such a claim. Even if the utterance 'God exists' is made compatible with every possible state of affairs, it has not been shown that the utterance is not a true assertion. Premise (3b), then, although by no means as dubious as (3a), is by no means obviously acceptable either. In any event, because (3a) is dubious we have reason to reject the argument from lack of justification.

We have found no reason to think that ethical nihilism is true, so we have no reason to think that nothing we or anyone else does is morally wrong. Furthermore, because certain actions clearly seem to be wrong and others right, we have some reason to reject ethical nihilism. Consequently, we can cast ethical nihilism aside with ethical relativism.

ETHICAL SKEPTICISM

It seems we can begin our attempt to justify some ethical standard as correct. Before we do so, however, there is one other view relevant to our interests which deserves mention, especially because it is often confused with ethical nihilism. It is the view that no ethical standards can be known to be correct, because no opinion is more reasonable than all the others and consequently, no ethical standard is justifiable as the correct one. We are, then, wasting our time trying. This is ethical skepticism, which is different from ethical nihilism in that it merely claims that no standard is known to be correct, or is justifiable as correct, rather than that no standard actually is correct. It is, then, a weaker claim than ethical nihilism. Moreover, it is by no means unreasonable. In fact, it might be claimed that we have good inductive evidence to support ethical skepticism because it seems that, as of now, none of all the ethical standards proposed throughout history has been justified. Such evidence, if correct, makes ethical skepticism more reasonable than not, and if we must accept this evidence and find no counterbalancing evidence, then it seems that the correct position for us to take is that of ethical skepticism. However, if we are to justify such a position we must examine the evidence ourselves. That is, we must critically evaluate the various candidates for a correct ethical standard. Thus although ethical skepticism may be the correct position, we cannot justify it until we have completed the task we have set before us.

ETHICAL EGOISM

Sometimes a person claims that no one has the right to tell him what to do, because he can do whatever he wants. Such a claim sounds like a statement of both ethical nihilism and egoism, and if he adds that anyone else can do what he wants also, it sounds like ethical relativism as well. But we must be careful to separate these three different claims, because taken together they are incompatible. The claim that each person can do what he wants is not a form of ethical relativism because it is a claim that applies to one and all. If the claim is that it is correct for me but not for anyone else to do what he wants, then it would be a form of relativism. But this is not what we are discussing. The claim might be an assertion of ethical nihilism if what is meant is that we are all permitted to do whatever we want because nothing is right and nothing is wrong. But this claim, in denying that there is a correct standard, is incompatible with both ethical relativism, which states that there are several correct standards, and ethical egoism, which claims there is just one, namely:

> *Ethical Egoism:* Each person ought to act to maximize his own good or well-being.

Consequently, although we have cast doubt on both ethical relativism and nihilism, nothing we have said yet casts any doubt on ethical egoism.

Strictly speaking, if someone is expressing an egoistic ethical theory when he says that he can do whatever he wants to do, it is more likely that he is asserting the species of ethical egoism known as egoistic hedonism, because he is talking about what he wants or desires. This brand of egoism often equates what is good with pleasure or happiness:

> *Egoistic Hedonism:* What each person ought to do is to act to maximize his own pleasure or happiness.

Let us interpret this statement of egoistic hedonism as the following:

> A person ought to perform an action in a situation if and only if he does it in order to maximize his own pleasure or happiness.

This will give us a standard we can use not only to decide what we ought to do, but also to decide what we have no obligation to do.

On this interpretation if I do something to maximize my pleasure then I ought to do it; if it is not something I do to maximize my pleasure then it is not true that I ought to do it (which means that it is morally permissible for me not to do it). Notice that the claim is that this interpretation provides a standard for what we are not obligated to do rather than a standard for what we are obligated not to do. This is an important difference because, for example, although we are not obligated to tie our left shoe laces before the right, this does not mean that we are obligated not to tie the left before the right. The first tells us that we have no moral obligations about the order of tying shoe laces, whereas the second states that we have a moral obligation not to tie them in a certain order, that is, we are forbidden to tie the left lace before the right. Using the standard of hedonistic egoism we find out what we ought not do, what is morally forbidden or prohibited, by finding which actions are the contradictories of those actions we ought to do. For example, if I ought to tell the truth, then I am forbidden to fail to tell the truth, that is, I ought not lie. With these distinctions in mind let us examine that most widespread species of egoism, egoistic hedonism.

EGOISTIC HEDONISM

Before we begin a critical evaluation of this theory we must be sure of what it implies and what it does not imply, because certain objections to the theory have arisen from misunderstanding it. This is one kind of hedonistic theory and thus proclaims that pleasure is the one thing good in itself. That is, it proclaims that whereas certain things may be good as means to certain other things, pleasure is the one thing good as an end, the one thing to be sought for its own sake. Other things are to be sought only if they are means to pleasure. Thus, medicine is not good as an end, but it is good as a means because it leads to pleasure by helping to cure us of diseases. Pleasure, therefore, is what has been called the *summum bonum,* or the highest good. Some people have objected to equating the *summum bonum* with pleasure, because they equate pleasure with such bodily pleasures as those provided by sex, food, and drink. But a

hedonist is not committed to such a position, because he can recognize what have been called the "higher" pleasures, such as aesthetic pleasures and the pleasures of contemplation, invention, and
artistic creation. Consequently, a hedonist can aim at these "higher"
pleasures and thus justify performing the activities which are the
means to achieving them.

An egoistic hedonist is interested in doing what maximizes his
own pleasure. Many people picture such a person as one who every
minute is seeking immediate thrills and excitement without a
thought for the future. This, however, is wrong because the amount
of pleasure someone gets from an act depends not only on the present pleasures he receives, but also on the longer-range consequences
of the act. A hedonist need not be shortsighted, because he can
realize that by abstaining from pleasures now he might maximize
the pleasure he gets throughout his life. A hedonist who refused a
rabies shot after being bitten by a rabid dog because of the present
pain of the shots would be a poor hedonist indeed, because the
future pain of the disease far outweighs the pain of the shots. A
hedonist, therefore, need not be one who lives for the moment and
seeks sensual pleasures. He can aim at the intellectual pleasures by
carefully planning his daily life, with his sights set on some future
goals. Egoistic hedonism, then, is not what it might first appear to be.
Nevertheless, it does seem to be contrary to our usual conception
of morality, because it seems to condone a kind of selfishness. Consequently, unless there are good reasons for accepting egoistic hedonism, it is a theory that we should reject.

However, most people who profess egoistic hedonism are not disturbed by the challenge to defend their position, because they base
it on a certain theory about the psychological abilities and limitations of human beings, which they think is clearly true. Although
there are several versions of this theory, many of them state that
whether a person has the ability to do a certain action in a particular
situation depends on which of his desires is strongest at that time.
And, furthermore, in any situation, a person's strongest desire is
always to increase his own pleasure or happiness as much as possible. Thus in any situation a person acts to maximize his own happiness, regardless of anything else. This theory is psychological
egoism, and can be defined as follows:

   Psychological Egoism: A human being is psychologically able to perform an action if and only if he does it in order to maximize his own pleasure or happiness.

Notice how psychological egoism differs from ethical egoistic hedonism. The first states conditions for what we have the ability to do, whereas the second states conditions for what we have a moral obligation to do. They are, then, importantly different. The first is purely a factual statement, but the second expresses an ethical standard. Nevertheless, the factual, psychological claim is thought to provide reason for accepting the ethical claim.

THE ARGUMENT FROM PSYCHOLOGICAL EGOISM

The argument from psychological egoism can be stated as follows: The only actions a person is psychologically able to perform are those in accordance with his strongest desire, or in other words, those which he does to maximize his own pleasure. But surely we are under an obligation to do something only if we are capable of doing it. That is, we ought to do something only if we can do it. Therefore, the only things we ought to do are things which we do to maximize our own pleasure. Egoistic hedonism is true.

Let us examine this argument by putting it in the following form:

1. A person has an obligation to do an action only if he is able to do it.
2. A person is able to do something only if he does it to maximize his own pleasure or happiness.
   Therefore
3. A person has an obligation to do an action only if he does it to maximize his own pleasure or happiness.
   Therefore
4. Ethical egoistic hedonism is true.

The first thing to notice about this argument is that the inference from (3) to (4) is invalid because egoistic hedonism states not only that someone has an obligation to do something *only if* he does it to maximize his own pleasure, but also that he ought to do it *if* it is something he does to maximize his own pleasure. The second part of the claim is important for our purposes because we are searching for a justifiable standard or criterion for deciding what

we ought to do, which means that we want something that is a sufficient rather than a necessary condition for moral obligation. Thus
egoistic hedonism cannot be established merely by an appeal to the
hedonistic psychological theory. However, because the inference
from (1) and (2) to (3) is valid, an egoistic hedonist can, if (1) and
(2) are true, establish that we have no obligation to do anything
unless we do it to maximize our own pleasure. That is, what this argument can establish, if sound, is that any ethical standard that requires someone to perform actions that he would not do to maximize
his own pleasure is an incorrect standard. Consequently, any correct
ethical standard would have to prescribe only actions which someone does to maximize his own pleasure, whether or not it also states
that he ought to do those actions *because* they are the actions he does
to maximize his own pleasure. The argument, then, although it does
not establish egoistic hedonism, does provide us with a way of evaluating those ethical standards which compete with egoistic hedonism. And because it seems clear that most other standards will
sometimes prescribe actions which someone would not do to maximize his own pleasure, this argument, if sound, provides a powerful
means of eliminating alternative ethical standards, perhaps to the
point where only egoistic hedonism remains unscathed. It is important, then, to examine this argument.

Premise (1), often expressed as the dictum that "ought implies
can," is a generally accepted principle. Generally we agree that no
one has an obligation to do something if it is impossible for him to
do it, for example, if he has some disability. Thus in the example
of the drowning child used earlier, I have no obligation to jump
into the water to save the child if I cannot swim. And if people
blame me for not swimming out to the child instead of running
after help, I can absolve myself of blame by telling them I could
not swim. Thus I had an obligation to swim to the child only if I
could swim. Premise (1), then, is acceptable.

OBJECTION TO PSYCHOLOGICAL EGOISM:
PEOPLE SOMETIMES ACT BENEVOLENTLY

The crucial part of the argument is obviously premise (2), the one
derived from psychological egoism. Let us examine it. It might be
claimed, however, that a philosopher has no business critically
evaluating premise (2), because it is a claim within the domain of

the empirical science of psychology. But although it is generally true that philosophers are not competent to evaluate empirical scientific claims, we shall find grounds for thinking that if, as claimed, psychological egoism is an empirical claim, then its falsity is so apparent that no special training is needed to show it false.

We are assuming that like any competing psychological theory, the theory we have called psychological egoism is an empirical scientific theory. As such it should have one feature in common with other empirical theories, that is, it should be empirically falsifiable. There should, then, be some empirically ascertainable situation which if it occurred would falsify the theory. What we seem to need to test psychological egoism is a case where someone did not act in order to maximize his own pleasure or happiness. We can use, therefore, a case where someone acted to sacrifice his own happiness for the happiness of another, or, it would seem, any case of someone acting altruistically or benevolently. But surely cases of people acting benevolently are not uncommon. We read of parents working many extra hours to help educate their children, of people donating a kidney to help a man dying for lack of one, of missionaries who risk their lives to bring help and knowledge to backward peoples. In these and many other cases we surely seem to have people acting benevolently for others instead of acting for themselves. Thus it seems we can conclude not only that psychological egoism is falsifiable, but also that it has been quite easily falsified. The argument we have used goes as follows:

5. If psychological egoism is true, then each person always acts to maximize his own happiness.
6. If each person always acts to maximize his own happiness, then no one acts benevolently.
7. Some people act benevolently.
    Therefore
8. Psychological egoism is false.

REPLY: PEOPLE ALWAYS ACT OUT OF SELF-LOVE

Defenders of psychological egoism can be expected to reply with a counterargument also based on premise (6) but with the conclusion that (7) is false, for the reason that people always act out of self-love or self-interest even when what they do helps others. The point is that, although it is true that people often do benevolent acts (that is, acts which actually help others), they do not act benevolently (that is, act *for the sake of the others* they help). People always act for their own happiness even when what they do helps others. This—one of the chief arguments to show that, in spite of the way things seem, no one acts benevolently—can be stated as follows:

6. If each person always acts out of self-love (that is, to maximize his own happiness), then he never acts benevolently (that is, for the sake of others).

9. People always act out of self-love.
   Therefore

10. No person ever acts benevolently [and (7) is false].

BUTLER'S ARGUMENT: ACTING BENEVOLENTLY AND ACTING OUT OF SELF-LOVE ARE COMPATIBLE

The previous argument has been widely discussed, but the classical refutation of it occurs in the works of Bishop Joseph Butler.[4] The brunt of Butler's attack is aimed at premise (6), the premise common to this and the previous argument. Thus if his attack is sound both arguments fail. He denies that acting out of self-love or self-interest is incompatible with acting benevolently, and argues that even if we always act out of self-love we may still sometimes act benevolently. Butler begins by noting that acting out of self-love can be described as acting to satisfy the desire for our own happiness. But such a desire is not a specific or particular desire such as the desire for a chocolate ice cream cone. It is a general desire, like the desire we hope to find in our politicians to promote the general welfare of the people. And just as someone can act to satisfy the desire for the general welfare only by doing specific acts, such as passing specific laws, so we can act to satisfy the (general) desire for our own happiness only by doing specific acts, such as buying a chocolate ice cream cone. There is, then, no one specific act which satisfies the general desire for our own happiness so that when we act we always

---

[4] See Joseph Butler, *Five Sermons* (New York: Liberal Arts Press, 1950), pp. 12–17 and pp. 49–65.

act to satisfy some specific desire whether or not we also act to satisfy the general desire for our own happiness.

We can distinguish two kinds of specific desires and thus two kinds of specific acts. First, there are *self-directed desires*—such as desires of hunger, sex, pride, and those desires relevant to our own health and knowledge. In each of these cases we satisfy a specific desire by doing something for (or against) ourselves. And although all selfish acts, e.g., taking candy from a baby, are self-directed, it does not seem that all self-directed acts, e.g., buying candy for oneself in normal circumstances, are selfish.

Second, there are *other-directed desires,* such as desires to help or harm someone else. In these cases we do something specific for or against someone else rather than for or against ourselves. When we act out of self-love we often do so by acting to satisfy specific self-directed desires, as when we eat, make love, practice tennis, take pills, and sometimes read books. Sometimes, indeed, we act selfishly when we do these things. However, we also often act out of self-love by acting to satisfy other-directed and thereby clearly unselfish desires, as when we get satisfaction from helping someone, teaching someone, or even harming him. In the first cases we are acting specifically for ourselves, but in the second we are not, because in the first we are acting to satisfy specific self-directed desires, but in the second we are acting to satisfy specific other-directed desires. Consequently, we can conclude that although acting to satisfy specific self-directed desires is inconsistent with acting benevolently, because acting benevolently is acting specifically for someone else, acting out of self-love and acting benevolently are not inconsistent, because acting to satisfy specific other-directed desires is consistent with acting to satisfy the general desire for our own happiness. We can, then, act for ourselves in general at the same time we act for (or against) others specifically. Acting benevolently is not precluded by self-love, and premise (6) is thus false.

At this point a defender of psychological egoism might go so far as to assert dogmatically that we never do act to satisfy other-directed desires—that is, he might claim that we always act specifically for or against ourselves and thus never act benevolently, although of course we sometimes do benevolent acts. But dogmatism is of no help because it does seem that people do, all too seldom perhaps, act benevolently. Therefore unless there is a sound argument to the contrary we should accept premise (7) as true. The

psychological egoist need not take such a desperate course, however, because, as we have seen the previous objection to premise
(6) destroys not only the argument against (7), but also the argument we used to prove that psychological egoism is false. We were
wrong, consequently, to think that we could use examples of acting
benevolently to refute psychological egoism.

FINAL OBJECTION: PEOPLE DO NOT ALWAYS ACT
OUT OF SELF-LOVE

Our mistake was to stress examples of acting benevolently. We
need, rather, to point out clear examples of people acting contrary
to their own happiness, because taking such examples with premise
(5):

> If psychological egoism is true, then each person
> always acts to maximize his own happiness.

we can clearly show psychological egoism to be false. Once again it
seems we have a straightforward empirical question before us, and
once again the answer seems to be that there are cases where it is
most implausible to claim that a person is satisfying a desire for his
own happiness. People sometimes seem to sacrifice their own happiness when they act out of a sense of duty to do what they think is
right. Many patriotic soldiers are convinced by intimate experiences
that war is hell, yet they volunteer for dangerous missions which
surely seem to be contrary to their own well-being and happiness.
There have also been cases of people bent on revenge who plainly
do not care what happens to them just as long as they destroy someone else. In such cases, it seems clear that we should conclude that
these people are acting to satisfy other-directed desires rather than
their desires for their own happiness. Consequently, once again it
seems that we should conclude that psychological egoism is false.

At this point the almost invariable reply is that people act out of
self-love even in those cases in which it seems evident that they do
not act out of self-love. Once this move has been made, psychological egoism becomes like two other often heard claims (that is,
people always act to satisfy their strongest desire, and people always act to reduce tension), in that even the most obvious contrary
cases are not taken to count against the claim. That is, the theory

has been made immune to empirical falsification. It is not merely claimed that there have been no actual cases which would falsify the theory, but rather that no case we could possibly conceive would falsify it. Psychological egoism is often held in this dogmatic way, but when it is, it is no longer an empirical scientific theory open to checking by observation. It has become consistent with anything we might observe and thus no longer a theory of the empirical science of psychology. Consequently, it is no longer the kind of theory that can be justified by the findings of psychology, so that science will not provide a reason for accepting it.

Should we reject this modified form of psychological egoism as we have the earlier version? Unlike the previous version, it really does not matter what we do. Recall that the previous version, if acceptable, was to be used as a test of what persons can do and thus as a means for rejecting ethical standards which prescribe actions incompatible with it. It was, then, importantly relevant to ethics. But the present version has been made compatible with any behavior we could observe, and thus it cannot be used to test the actions prescribed by standards that compete with egoistic hedonism. Psychological egoism has been weakened to such a degree that it cannot help us decide among ethical standards. Thus any ethical theorist can accept it. We can, if we like, also accept this version of psychological egoism, but if we do we can immediately ignore it because it has no relevance to ethics, or for that matter, to psychology.

We have found that the ethical egoist cannot rely on psychological egoistic hedonism to help him justify his position. If the theory is empirical it surely seems to be false, and if it is nonempirical it does not help provide reasons to choose ethical egoism instead of some other ethical theory. Consequently, the ethical egoist must find some other way to justify his theory. The only other remotely plausible argument is based on the fact that when someone asks us why we did something we often answer him by saying it was because we wanted to and that settles it. For example, if you ask me why I went to the movies instead of studying last night I might answer that I felt like going to the movies or that I did not want to study, and when I reply this way the question is answered. Now, the argument states, because such a question is a request for justification of my action, I have justified my action by answering the question. Thus, I have provided a good reason for what I did by reference to what I wanted, so that my doing what I want is justified and therefore is what I ought to do. Because this argument, which we can call the argument from good reasons, embodies two mistakes that are relevant to our current interests, we should examine the argument with some care.

THE ARGUMENT FROM GOOD REASONS
The crux of the argument can be outlined as follows:

1. If I desire to do something (do something to get pleasure), then I can justify doing it by reference to the desire (pleasure).
2. If I can justify doing something, then I have a good reason for doing it.
3. If I have a good reason for doing something, then it is what I ought to do.
   Therefore
4. If I desire to do something (do something to get pleasure), then it is what I ought to do.

This argument, like the previous argument, fails to justify ethical egoism, but for different reasons. First, it provides only a sufficient condition of obligation, whereas ethical egoism states a necessary condition as well. Admittedly, this is not a vital point, because we can design a parallel argument which would allow us to conclude that if I do not desire to do something, then it is not what I ought to do. The second reason is that ethical egoism refers to what maximizes my pleasure rather than to what merely gives me pleasure. We can fix this, however, by referring to what I most desire and what I do to maximize my pleasure. Let us assume, then, that from this argument, with the parallel negative argument, we can infer that ethical egoism is true. But is the argument sound?

OBJECTION: DESIRING TO DO SOMETHING
DOES NOT JUSTIFY DOING IT
We have based premise (1) on the fact that we quite often can answer a "Why?" question once and for all by saying that we wanted to. Thus we often can answer a request for justification by

such an answer. But we have inferred from this that we provide a justification for what we do whenever we answer in this way. There are two reasons why this is a mistaken inference. First, when I reply to a question such as, "Why did you go to the movies instead of studying?" by saying, "I wanted to," or, "I felt like it," my answer does not provide a good reason for what I did, but rather is used to refuse to give a reason or to claim that no reason is necessary. It functions more like "No reason," "I don't know," "Because," or even a shrug of the shoulders. Thus when someone answers this way he is not justifying his action, but rather is claiming that there is nothing to justify or is refusing to give a justification. Such an answer may stop the questioning but it does not justify the action. This can be illustrated by a different example. Suppose that you ask someone why he shot that old lady as she crossed the street and that he answers that he felt like it and will say no more. He might have just as well shrugged his shoulders, for in neither case would he justify what he did. In this example we are not satisfied with his answer because here, unlike the first example, a justification is called for and he has provided none. Thus although we can sometimes answer requests for justification by talking about our desires and pleasure, we have not provided a justification for our actions, because such an answer is adequate only when no justification is required. Secondly, moreover, even if we were to agree that sometimes we can justify our actions in this way, the shooting example shows that there are many times when we cannot. There are situations in which only I am affected, so that the only morally relevant factors are my own preferences. But where others are affected there are other morally relevant factors. Thus we can reject premise (1) and with it this argument for ethical egoism.

Before we move on we should also note that premise (3) is false, because this re-emphasizes an important distinction. It is true that if I have a good reason for doing something then it is permissible for me to do it, that is, it is not wrong for me to do it. But it does not follow that it is always something I ought to do. Often when we justify an action we show that it is not prohibited rather than that it is obligatory. For example, it seems that many times people can provide good reasons for not helping someone who is being attacked by a gang of knife wielders in the caverns of some large city. But although such reasons show he has no obligation to help, and therefore is morally permitted not to help, they would not show that he had an obligation not to help. Once again we must distinguish between 'no obligation to' and 'obligation not to' to emphasize that, although the person who does not help in this case should not feel immoral, neither should he feel particularly moral.

REJECTION OF EGOISTIC HEDONISM: PRESCRIBES MORALLY REPUGNANT ACTS

We have found no way to justify that species of ethical egoism we have called egoistic hedonism. Should we reject it? We have been operating on the principle that if an ethical standard prescribes certain actions we feel certain are morally wrong, and if there are no counterbalancing arguments in its favor, then we should reject it. This is the case with egoistic hedonism. Consider a sadist or someone who hates a whole race of people. The catalogue of sadistic pleasures found in *Justine* by the Marquis de Sade is enough to show that many actions which give people pleasure are morally repugnant. The pleasure some Nazis found in torturing, maiming, and killing Jews, the attitudes of thrill murderers, and the boastful and brash killings of Negroes by certain white Southerners all testify that egoistic hedonism would not only permit, but also make obligatory some of the most horrendous deeds ever committed. We should, then, reject ethical hedonistic egoism because by making each man's pleasure his guide to what is right, it prescribes the kind of selfishness which ignores the happiness and welfare of any other person.

NONHEDONISTIC ETHICAL EGOISM

We have rejected egoistic hedonism which is one form of ethical egoism, but should we also reject ethical egoism in general? To answer this we must do the things we did in evaluating egoistic hedonism, that is, find out whether there are any arguments which justify it and find out whether it prescribes any actions that we are convinced are wrong. We have defined ethical egoism as the theory that makes the following claim:

> Each person ought to act to maximize his own good or well-being.

Corresponding to the standard we used for egoistic hedonism we have the following:

> A person ought to perform an action if and only if he does it to maximize his own well-being (that is, if and only if he does it to maximize his own best interest).

We have come to this standard by substituting 'well-being' for 'pleasure.' Consequently, we can arrive at the arguments for ethical egoism by the same substitution. What we find, then, is an argument based on the theory that we always act for our own well-being or self-interest, and an argument based on the claim that we can justify our actions by reference to self-interest. We shall leave it to the reader to substantiate that the arguments in this form are no better than those in the previous form. Consequently, if the general theory of ethical egoism prescribes actions we are certain are morally wrong, we can reject it with egoistic hedonism.

OBJECTION TO ETHICAL EGOISM: PRESCRIBES MORALLY REPUGNANT ACTS

The first thing to note in examining what ethical egoism prescribes is that it does not prescribe many of the specific actions prescribed by egoistic hedonism, because what provides me maximum pleasure often is not what maximizes my well-being. This is especially noticeable if we identify our well-being and self-interest with mental and physical health and abilities. Some people have a choice between, on the one hand, a life of intense pleasures in which their health deteriorates and they do not develop their abilities, and, on the other, a restrained often arduous and regimented life in which they maintain their health and develop their abilities. It is not unlikely that the first life, even if considerably shortened by an early death—especially if it came quickly and painlessly—would contain more pleasure than the second. But the second would be more conducive to the well-being of the person. Thus these two different standards might often differ in what they prescribe, so that the examples we used against egoistic hedonism cannot be used in their present form against ethical egoism. Nevertheless examples can be devised which will provide grounds for rejecting ethical egoism. One example is the case where three people have a disease which is fatal unless they take certain pills. One of these men, unknown to anyone else, has the only three pills available, and he knows that if a person takes one he has 90 per cent chance of surviving the disease, if he takes two he has a 94 per cent chance, and if he takes all three he has a 99 per cent chance. What ought he to do? It seems clear that he ought to give each man one pill. But ethical egoism prescribes he maximize his own well-being; that in this case he ought to take all three pills himself and let the others die.

PLATO ON MORALITY AND SELF-INTEREST

Only one reply seems open to an ethical egoist at this point and that is the claim that taking all three pills is not really in the man's own best interest, but it is not clear how this can be defended. Most modern philosophers have not tried to defend it and have in general rejected ethical egoism. However, this was not true of the ancient Greek philosopher Plato. He was interested in attempts to justify actions as moral or immoral and he thought that one way to do so, and perhaps the only way, is by establishing that moral actions benefit the doer and immoral actions injure the doer. That is, he tried to show that acting morally is in the best interest of the doer and acting immorally is against his best interest, in spite of the way it often seems. If he had succeeded, then it might be claimed that we would have the best defense of morality possible, because if we could convince someone that acting morally benefits him, then he would be no less than foolish if he did not act morally.

We can see Plato's argument by reading an excerpt from the debate between Socrates, who expresses Plato's view, and Polus in the Platonic dialogue *Gorgias*. In this part of the dialogue Socrates is trying to show Polus that the worst thing that can happen to a man is that he do an unjust or immoral act and escape punishment for it. Thus the man who commits an unending procession of horrendous crimes against mankind and, escaping punishment, provides for himself a luxurious life of ease and pleasure which he seems to enjoy completely, is, according to Socrates, in a worse position than a man who committed the same crimes and is caught and punished.

Further, both men are in a worse position than a man who always acts justly and as a consequence spends his life in unending pain and burdensome toil. Thus, according to Socrates, no matter how it might seem, it is always more in your own self-interest to act justly. We can see how Socrates argues for this implausible position by joining the discussion at the following point:

Socrates: Look at the matter in this way: In respect of a man's estate, do you see any greater evil than poverty?

Polus: There is no greater evil.

S: Again, in a man's bodily frame, you would say that the evil is weakness and disease and deformity, and the like. And do you not imagine that the soul likewise has some evil of her own? And this you would call injustice and ignorance and cowardice, and the like?

P: Certainly.

S: So then, in mind, body, and estate, which are three, you have pointed out three corresponding evils—injustice, disease, poverty. And which of the evils is the most disgraceful?—Is not the most disgraceful of them injustice, and in general the evil of the soul?

P: By far the most.

S: And if the most disgraceful, then also the worst?

P: What do you mean, Socrates?

S: I mean to say that what is most disgraceful has been already admitted to be so, without exception, because it is most painful, or hurtful, or both. And now injustice and evil in the soul has been admitted by us to be most disgraceful. And most disgraceful either because most painful and causing excessive pain, or most hurtful, or both?

P: Certainly.

S: And therefore to be unjust and intemperate, and cowardly and ignorant, is more painful than to be poor and sick?

P: Nay, Socrates; the painfulness does not appear to me to follow from your premises.

S: Then since the evil of the soul is of all evils the most disgraceful, but (as you argue) is not so by reason of its painfulness, the cause must be some enormous harm and evil, of preternatural magnitude. And I take it that that which is greatest in harmfulness will be the greatest of evils?

P: Yes.

S: Then injustice and intemperance, and in general the depravity of the soul, are the greatest of evils?

P: That is evident.

S: Now, what art is there which delivers us from poverty? Does not the art of making money? And what art frees us from disease? Does not the art of medicine? And what from vice and injustice? If you are not able to answer at once, ask yourself whither we go with the sick, and to whom we take them.

P: To the physicians, Socrates.

S: And to whom do we go with persons acting unjustly or intemperately?

P: To the judges, you mean.

S: —Who are to punish them?

P: Yes.

S: And do not those who rightly punish others, punish them in accordance with a certain rule of justice?

P: Clearly.

S: Then the art of money-making frees a man from poverty; medicine from disease; and justice from intemperance and injustice?

P: That is evident.

S: Which, then, is the best of these three?

P: Justice, Socrates, far excels the two others.

S: And justice, if the best, gives the greatest pleasure or advantage or both. But is the being healed a pleasant thing, and are those who are being healed pleased?

P: I think not.

S: A useful thing, then?

P: Yes.

S: Yes, because the patient is delivered from a great evil; and it is worth his while to endure the pain, and get well?

P: Certainly.

S: And would he be the happier man in his bodily condition, who is healed, or who never was out of health?

P: Clearly he who was never out of health.

S: Yes; for happiness surely does not consist in being delivered from evils, but in never having had them. And suppose the case of two persons who have some evil in their bodies or in their souls, and that one of them is being treated and delivered from evil, and another is not being treated, but retains the evil—which of them is the more miserable?

P: Clearly he who is not being treated.

S: And was not punishment said by us to be a deliverance from the greatest of evils, which is vice? For justice chastens us, and makes us more just, and is the medicine of our vice. He, then, has the first place in the scale of happiness who has no vice in his soul; for this has been shown to be the greatest of evils. And he has the second place, who is being delivered from vice. That is to say, he who is receiving admonition and rebuke and punishment. Then he lives worst, who, being unjust, is not being delivered from injustice?

P: Certainly.[5]

We shall leave it to the reader to discover the flaws in the steps by which Polus let himself be led to Socrates' position, but it should be noted here that even if Socrates had succeeded in justifying his position he would have done so only by stripping ethical egoism of any value as a moral standard. Socrates claims that being just or moral is what is most beneficial to the soul and thereby to man, in spite of appearances to the contrary. Thus we must find out what is in our own best interest by finding out what are the right things to do. That is, we must know what is right in order to find out what is best for ourselves, because no matter what may seem to be most beneficial, it is not if it is unjust. Thus instead of self-interest providing the criterion of what is right as required by ethical egoism, we would need some independent ethical standard to determine what is right in order to discover what is really in our own best interest. Plato, by making what is right the basis of deciding what is

---

[5] Adapted with changes from *The Dialogues of Plato,* edited by B. Jowett (New York: Random House, 1937), Vol. I, pp. 537–39.

most beneficial, has made it impossible to use ethical egoism as a criterion for deciding what is right.

CONCLUSION ABOUT ETHICAL EGOISM: SHOULD BE REJECTED

Because there seems to be no better way to justify the general theory of ethical egoism than there is to justify that brand of egoism we have called egoistic hedonism, we should conclude that ethical egoism ought to be rejected. This is because there is no sound argument to support it and because it prescribes certain morally repugnant actions. These are actions which, if we look back at the relevant examples, we find have one morally relevant feature in common. In each case the action ethical egoism prescribes is morally repugnant because the standard ignores the happiness and welfare of other people affected by the prescribed action. In short, the standard of ethical egoism seems to be misguided because it ignores one ingredient of morality which seems to be essential, namely, impartiality. In deciding what ought to be done it seems that each person who is to be affected by the action should be taken into account. No one should be ignored and no one should be given privileged status. Let us turn to a theory which explicitly incorporates impartiality into its standard.

UTILITARIANISM: BENTHAM'S VERSION

Utilitarianism is not only the name of a particular ethical theory, but it is the name of the doctrine that called for social reforms to be achieved by bringing the actions of persons and also governments in line with the ethical principle of utility. This principle as an ethical and social weapon for reform received its first eloquent expression in the writings of Jeremy Bentham, who defined it as follows:

By the principle of utility is meant that principle which approves or disapproves of every action whatsoever, according to the tendency which it appears to have to augment or diminish the happiness of the party whose interest is in question; or, what is the same thing in other words, to promote or to oppose that happiness. I say of every action whatsoever; and therefore not only of every action of a private individual, but of every measure of government.[6]

As Bentham himself realized, it might be more perspicuous to call his ethical principle the greatest happiness principle rather than the principle of utility, because the principle is to be concerned with happiness, pleasure, and pain of the parties affected by actions. And as he said in a footnote added later,

The word 'utility' does not so clearly point to the ideas of *pleasure* and *pain* as the words 'happiness' and 'felicity' do: nor does it lead us to the consideration of the *number*, of the interests affected; to the *number*, as being the circumstance, which contributes, in the largest proportion, to the formation of the standard here in question; *the standard of right and wrong*, by which alone the propriety of human conduct, in every situation, can with propriety be tried.[7]

It is important, then, to note that utilitarianism, which is the theory proposing the principle of utility as the correct ethical standard, equates the utility of something with its tendency to produce happiness or pleasure. Thus the word 'utility' as we shall be using it here is not synonymous with 'usefulness,' so that when we consider the utility of something we shall not be considering what use it has or how useful it is, but its relationship to the production of happiness.

THE PRINCIPLE OF UTILITY
Let us try to state the utilitarian standard clearly. A first approximation is the following:

[6] Bentham, op. cit., pp. 17–18.
[7] Ibid., p. 291.

> An action ought to be done if and only if it maximizes the pleasure of those parties affected by the action.

This statement, however, can be made more precise by specifying what is to count as an affected party. It may seem evident to many that the reference is to persons, but Bentham realized that the state or community as a whole can be an interested and affected party. There are, for example, crimes against the state, and some heads of state have insisted that the interests of the state are distinct from those of its citizens. Thus leaders have called on citizens to sacrifice themselves for the fatherland, that is, sacrifice their own happiness, even their lives, for the state. There have been men who claim that the state is not only a distinct individual, but that it is an individual of more worth than any or even all of its citizens. It is surely important for our purposes, then, whether or not we are to count the state or community as a separate affected individual in formulating this standard. Bentham realized this and clarified what he meant by 'party.'

> The community is a fictitious *body,* composed of the individual persons who are considered as constituting as it were its *members*. The interest of the community then is, what?—The sum of the interests of the several members who compose it.[8]

According to Bentham, then, we need not consider the state as a separate affected party, so that we can change the standard to read:

> An action ought to be done if and only if it maximizes the pleasure of those people affected by the action.

This formulation is still ambiguous, however, because it might be interpreted as stating that an action is right only if the pleasure of each person affected is maximized. Not only is this not what Bentham meant, it is a standard which could rarely be met. In most situations it is not possible to maximize the happiness or pleasure of each person involved. Usually someone is going to be less than completely satisfied with what happens. What Bentham means is that

---

[8] Ibid., p. 18.

the action which ought to be done in a particular situation is that one which maximizes the sum total of pleasure produced. Thus although in many situations some of those affected will be made unhappy and made to feel pain, we might try characterizing right actions as those which minimize the number of people made to be unhappy and to feel pain. However, even this modification is not quite right because an action which causes several people to have a slight headache is better than an action in which, all else being equal, only one person suffers an almost unendurable pain. Thus we must consider not merely how many people receive pleasure or pain from the action, but also how intense each pleasure or pain is. Thus let us take the principle to consider the total amount of pleasure and pain produced where the amount is a function of intensity per person and number of people affected. We can now state the principle in the following form:

> An action ought to be done if and only if it maximizes the total amount of pleasure of those persons affected by the action.

We are not yet finished amending it. Although it may seem obvious that the feature of morality which we saw was missing from ethical egoism—that is, impartiality—is included in the preceding formulation of the utilitarian principle, there is still room for partiality. How we arrive at the total amount can be affected by many factors, including whether or not we give equal weight to each person affected. In any society where some people are considered second-class citizens then someone using the last version of the principle might weight the per cent of the total pleasure or pain contributed by each person according to his status as a full-fledged or secondary citizen. It seems clear that Negro pleasure and pain in many parts of this country are not added in on equal grounds with white pleasure and pain. There are also examples where the pleasures of kings have been taken to count for more than those of their subjects. Bentham, however, wants no such fractionalizing, so we must state the factor of impartiality explicitly. This will give us the final version of the principle of utility:

> An action ought to be done if and only if it maximizes the total amount of pleasure of those persons affected by the ac-

tion, counting each person as one and no person as more than one.

We shall use this statement in our critical evaluation of Bentham's standard, which we shall begin by examining the proofs that have been offered to support it.

ARGUMENTS FOR THE PRINCIPLE OF UTILITY

As Bentham realized, two kinds of proofs can be offered in defense of an ethical principle—one he called direct proof, the other we can call indirect proof. The first kind of proof is a deductive proof in which the conclusion is the principle itself. Thus this kind of proof argues directly for the principle. In an indirect proof the principle is supported indirectly by refuting objections to it and by showing that there are objections to the opposing alternatives. This is the way we argued in critically evaluating the various positions proposed as solutions to the mind–body problem and the way we have been approaching the various ethical theories. Obviously an indirect proof cannot provide an argument as rigorous or grounds as solid as can a direct proof. Let us then begin by seeing whether there are any direct proofs available for the principle of utility.

DIRECT PROOFS FOR THE PRINCIPLE OF UTILITY: DERIVING 'OUGHT' FROM 'IS'

Bentham thought that there were no direct proofs of his principle, "for that which is used to prove everything else, cannot itself be proved: a chain of proofs must have their commencement somewhere."[9] Bentham's point here is that he is proposing the principle of utility as the ultimate or basic ethical standard. Therefore although other ethical principles may be deducible from it, it is not deducible from any other ethical principle. Although we can deduce certain obligations from certain ethical standards and perhaps those standards from others, the process of deduction must begin with some one or more ethical principles that are not deducible from any others. These are the basic principles. For Bentham, as for most

[9] Ibid., p. 19.

ethical theorists, there is only one basic principle and this cannot be deduced from a more basic ethical principle.

It may occur to someone that although the basic ethical principle cannot be deduced from other ethical principles, this does not show that the basic principle cannot be deduced from any premises at all. Indeed why can the basic ethical principle not be deduced from some factual premises about the way things are? This has been tried. People have tried to deduce moral obligations from the nature of man, from the facts of evolution, or from facts about societies, cultures, and economic classes. In each case they have tried to deduce a normative ought-statement from a factual is-statement.

HUME'S OBJECTION: NO 'OUGHT' IS DEDUCIBLE FROM 'IS'

One of the first to cast suspicion upon deducing 'ought' from 'is' was David Hume, who said,

> In every system of morality, which I have hitherto met with, I have always remark'd, that the author proceeds for some time in the ordinary way of reasoning, and establishes the being of a God, or makes observation concerning human affairs; when of a sudden I am surpriz'd to find, that instead of the usual copulations of propositions, *is,* and *is not,* I meet with no proposition that is not connected with an *ought,* or an *ought not.* This change is imperceptible; but is, however, of the last consequence. For as this *ought,* or *ought not,* expresses some new relation or affirmation, 'tis necessary that it shou'd be observ'd and explain'd; and at the same time that a reason should be given, for what seems altogether inconceivable, how this new relation can be a deduction from others, which are entirely different from it.[10]

Hume is making the straightforward logical point here that no ought-statement, that is, one that makes only an ought-claim and therefore no factual claim, is logically deducible from a factual is-

---

[10] D. Hume, *A Treatise of Human Nature,* edited by L. A. Selby-Bigge (New York: Oxford University Press, 1960), p. 469.

statement, that is, one that makes only a factual claim and therefore no ought-claim. This is because for any two propositions, say P and Q, if Q is logically deducible from P, then an explicit self-contradiction is deducible from the conjunction of P and not Q. For example, let $P =$ 'It is raining and it is cloudy,' and $Q =$ 'It is raining.' In this case, from P and not Q we can deduce the explicit self-contradiction that it is raining and it is not raining. But in no case where we have two logically self-consistent claims, one of which is a factual claim with no 'ought' (such as 'Helping others is maximizing happiness'), and the other of which is a normative claim with no 'is' (such as 'We ought not help others'), will the conjunction of the two claims result in an explicit self-contradiction.[11]

We cannot, then, deduce that an action ought to be done from the premise that it maximizes the general happiness or the total amount of pleasure. However, we have not yet reached a conclusion about the principle of utility or any other ethical standards, because such standards include both ought-claims and is-claims. However, we can use Hume's conclusion to draw one about ethical standards. Let us assume that O is some ought-statement, F is some factual statement which consists of a conjunction of all true is-statements that make factual claims, and S is some ethical standard such that O or some other ought-statement is deducible from S, depending upon which factual statements are conjoined with S. Thus if S were the principle of utility and F includes the statement F_1, 'A is an action that maximizes the total amount of pleasure,' then we could deduce O, 'A ought to be done.' Now we have seen that no ought-statement is deducible from any purely factual statement. Consequently, O is not deducible from F alone, but, we can assume, O is deducible from S and F. From this we can conclude that S, which stands for any ethical standard, is not deducible from F alone, the conjunction of all true factual statements. Thus, no ethical standard is deducible from any or even all true factual premises.

A FURTHER OBJECTION: NATURALISTIC
(DEFINIST) FALLACY

We have seen that no ultimate ethical standard is deducible from any other ethical standard and that no ethical standard is deducible

---

[11] See Chapter 1, pp. 7–12, for a discussion of deducibility.

from purely factual premises. It would seem, then, that we could conclude that there is no direct proof possible for an ultimate ethical standard. However, such a conclusion would be premature. Although no ought-statements and no ethical standards are deducible from a set of premises all of which are factual is-statements, it might be true nevertheless that with the addition of only certain analytic premises we can deduce some ought-statement or some ethical standard. If this can be done, then, because the additional premise is logically necessary, we can conclude that it is logically necessary that if the factual premises are true, then so also is the ought-conclusion. That is, the factual premise would entail the ought-conclusion, and, after all, 'ought' could be derived from 'is.'[12]

To see how this might be applied to 'ought' and 'is,' let us consider the following argument:

1. A is an action that maximizes the total amount of happiness.
Therefore
2. A ought to be done.

This argument with a factual is-premise and an ought-conclusion is invalid. But if we add as a premise:

3. Whatever maximizes the total amount of happiness is what ought to be done.

then the argument is valid. And if (3) is an analytic statement and therefore necessarily true, then we can conclude that (1) entails (2). Consequently, someone might offer the preceding argument to show how 'ought' can be derived from 'is.' This, of course, raises the question of whether (3) is analytic, that is, a statement whose truth can be established by appealing only to logic and the meaning of its terms. Some people seem to have thought that it is, and the view has even been ascribed to Bentham in spite of the fact that he thinks the principle of utility requires an indirect proof. We should, therefore, examine the claim that (3) is analytic, because if it is, then we need proceed no further in our search for a justifiable ethical standard.

---

[12] See Chapter 1, pp. 31–32, for a discussion of analyticity and entailment.

Some might argue that (3) is analytic on the grounds that, first, it is analytic that what ought to be done is what maximizes what is good, and second, that the general happiness is, by definition, what is good. This is the way that G. E. Moore interprets Bentham when he claims that Bentham, like many others, commits what Moore calls the "naturalistic fallacy."[13] This fallacy, according to Moore, is committed by anyone who defines an ethical term such as 'good,' or 'right,' or 'wrong' by terms that are purely factual or descriptive, and therefore have no evaluative force. Thus the naturalistic fallacy is committed when someone defines ethical terms such as 'good' using only such empirical terms as 'pleasure,' 'happiness,' 'desire,' or 'interest.' However, the fallacy is not restricted to those definitions that contain only naturalistic, i.e., empirical, terms. It has been pointed out that this fallacy might better be called the definist fallacy because, as Moore says himself, it is committed whenever someone defines an evaluative term such as 'good' by any nonevaluative term.[14] Thus not only naturalistic or empirical definitions, but also metaphysical and religious definitions would involve the fallacy. Thus if Moore is right, to define 'good' as 'what God wills' is to commit the same fallacy as to define it as 'pleasure.'

Now we must ask why Moore thinks that any such definition is fallacious. His primary reason is that any such definition would make many open or debatable questions closed and trivial. For example, if someone were to define 'what is always good' as 'pleasure,' then the seemingly debatable question 'Is pleasure always good?' becomes no more than the trivial question 'Is pleasure pleasure?' It surely seems worth debating whether pleasure is always good, but no one would spend time debating whether pleasure is pleasure. Another way of seeing this is by realizing that many statements we use to commend or condemn someone for doing something would become mere trivially true analytic sentences and lose their evaluative force. For example, if I tell someone that he ought to promote the general happiness because promoting the general happiness is

[13] See G. E. Moore, *Principia Ethica* (New York: Cambridge University Press, 1960), pp. 5–21.

[14] See W. Frankena, "The Naturalistic Fallacy," in W. Sellars and J. Hospers, eds., *Readings in Ethical Theory*, second edition (New York: Appleton-Century-Crofts, 1970), pp. 54–62.

promoting what is good, I mean to support a certain kind of action by commending it. But if 'what is good' means 'the general happiness' then all I have said is that he ought to promote the general happiness because promoting the general happiness is promoting the general happiness. This latter claim is not only absurd, but it is clearly not a case of supporting something by commending it.[15] I might just have said, "because killing is killing," or "promoting misery is promoting misery." But the original claim is not absurd. Therefore the latter is not an adequate translation of the original claim, and any other translation which leaves out the evaluative, and thereby the moral, element will also be inadequate.

The consequences of this fallacy are important. We can now state that no ethical claim is derivable from factual premises, because none is entailed by any factual statement. Any such entailment would involve the naturalistic or definist fallacy. Therefore we can also conclude that no ethical standard is entailed by any factual statement. In this way we have established what has been called the autonomy of ethics. That is, no ethical statements are derivable from any nonethical statements, so that no scientific findings entail any ethical principle, no metaphysical claims entail any ethical principle, and no (nonethical) religious claims entail any ethical principle. We cannot, then, hope to find a direct proof of the principle of utility or of any other ethical principle in which the principle is to be deduced from nonethical premises. And because we have seen that no ultimate ethical principle can be deduced from ethical premises, we can conclude that Bentham was right: There is no direct proof of the principle of utility or of any other ultimate ethical principle.

BENTHAM'S INDIRECT PROOF OF
THE PRINCIPLE OF UTILITY

Bentham uses just the kind of indirect proof we are using throughout the chapter. First, he claims,

> By the natural constitution of the human frame, on most occa-

---

[15] See R. M. Hare, *The Language of Morals* (New York: Oxford University Press, 1952), Chap. 5, for a more detailed discussion of how the naturalistic fallacy results in the word 'good' losing its function of commending.

sions of their lives men in general embrace this principle, without thinking of it: if not for the ordering of their own actions, yet for the trying of their own actions, as well as those of other men.[16]

That is, according to Bentham, the principle of utility prescribes actions which in their uncritical way human beings believe to be right. Second, all principles which differ in what they prescribe from the principle of utility are confronted with objections sufficient for rejecting them. From these two premises, Bentham concludes that we are surely justified in accepting the principle of utility as the correct ethical standard.

Although by and large Bentham leaves it to the reader to investigate whether his principle is in line with our ordinary ethical beliefs, he does provide reasons for rejecting all opposing principles. He says that any principle different from his is either completely opposed to it or only sometimes opposed to it. The first opposing principle he calls the *principle of asceticism,* which, he says, "like the principle of utility, approves or disapproves of any action, according to the tendency which it appears to have to augment or diminish the happiness of the party whose interest is in question; but in an inverse manner: approving of actions in as far as they tend to diminish his happiness; disapproving of them as far as they tend to augment it."[17] As Bentham points out, if such a principle were consistently followed, the earth would be turned into a living hell in a very short time. But Bentham's main attack is to point out that humans are incapable of consistently pursuing this principle. Consequently, because, as we have already seen, 'ought' implies 'can,' we can conclude that it is false that anyone ought to use such a principle. We can agree with Bentham that we should reject this principle.

All principles of the second kind opposed to the principle of utility, the kind which only in some situations opposes what the principle of utility prescribes, Bentham lumps together as various versions of what he calls *the principle of sympathy and antipathy.* By this he means

[16] Bentham, op. cit., pp. 19–20.
[17] Ibid., p. 21.

that principle which approves or disapproves of certain actions, not on account of their tending to augment the happiness, nor yet on account of their tending to diminish the happiness of the party whose interest is in question, but merely because a man finds himself disposed to approve or disapprove of them: holding up that approbation or disapprobation as a sufficient reason for itself, and disclaiming the necessity of looking out for any extrinsic ground.[18]

Such principles, as Bentham points out, do not appeal to any standard independent of the feelings and sentiment of those who propose the principles. The appeal is in every case to what someone or other happens to approve or disapprove. Surely no justifiable ethical standard can be derived in this way. If Bentham is correct here, we should reject not only the principle completely opposed to his own, but also all those sometimes opposed. Only Bentham's principle would remain.

OBJECTION TO BENTHAM'S PROOF: DOES NOT DISPROVE ALL OPPOSING VIEWS

There are two points at which we can attack Bentham's proof: his reason for rejecting all principles that are in some situations opposed to the principle of utility, and, second, his claim that no actions prescribed by his principle are morally repugnant. First, consider how Bentham characterizes all versions of the principle of sympathy and antipathy. No such principles, he claims, are standards independent of the feelings of people. This, of course, is not enough to distinguish these principles from his own, which is concerned with the happiness of people. However, he goes on to characterize these rival theories as replacing an objective standard by a mere reliance on feelings of approval and disapproval. Thus, according to Bentham, all these theories reduce to claims that we should make moral judgments merely on the basis of how we feel at the time. We can agree with Bentham that all versions of the principle of sympathy and antipathy should be rejected, but what seems clearly false is his claim that all principles sometimes opposed to his own are versions

[18] Ibid., p. 28.

of the principle of sympathy and antipathy. Consider, for example, ethical egoism, which sometimes prescribes actions opposed to Bentham's principle of utility. It is clearly an objective standard applicable to all people at all times, and does not prescribe actions on the basis of what someone happens to find right or wrong at the moment. It is sometimes opposed to Bentham's principle, though not a version of the principle of sympathy and antipathy. Bentham's defense of his own principle fails, consequently, because he has not considered all rival principles.

Bentham might reply that principles sometimes opposed to his own also fail because they do not consider all people involved. But although this is true of egoism, it need not be true of any other rival to Bentham's principle, for they could be genuine rivals and consider all people involved so long as they did not consider only the happiness of all involved. It will not do, of course, for Bentham to reject the opposing principles on the grounds that they do not consider just the happiness of all. If he did, he would only show that they differ from his own principle, but this is not a sufficient reason for rejecting them. Therefore, this part of Bentham's indirect proof fails because he has failed to show that only the principle of utility and the previously rejected principle of asceticism are universally applicable principles which can be applied in an objective way.

THE HEDONIC CALCULUS

Although, as we have seen, Bentham has not shown that all principles different from his own can be rejected, this failure is not vital if, as Bentham thinks, his principle and his principle alone prescribes no actions that are morally repugnant to mankind. However, if we find situations in which what his principle prescribes is morally repugnant, then he is in serious difficulty. Let us, then, try to think of such a situation. To do so we must get some idea of how we are to arrive at a conclusion about what maximizes the total amount of pleasure in any one situation. The method proposed by Bentham is what has been called the hedonic calculus, because it proposes a way to calculate the total amount of pleasure by bringing in all the relevant factors. According to Bentham there are seven different relevant factors which we can break down into three different basic categories. The first kind of factor is that which includes the relevant characteristics of each pleasure and pain produced by the action being considered; the second kind includes the tendency of a particular pleasure or pain to be followed by more pleasure and pain; and the third kind consists in the method of including in the calculations all the pleasures and pains which result from the action being considered. Let us list these factors as follows:

Intrinsic Characteristics of Pleasure and Pain
1. *Intensity* of each pleasure or pain.
2. *Duration* or length of time of each pleasure or pain.
3. *Probability* that the pleasure or pain will occur after the act. This is affected by:
4. *Propinquity* or nearness in time of the pleasure or pain to the act.

Consequential Characteristics of Pleasure and Pain
5. *Fecundity* or probability that the sensation will be followed by other sensations of the *same* kind.
6. *Impurity* or probability that the sensation will be followed by other sensations of the *opposite* kind.

Summation of All Pleasures and Pains Resulting from Act
7. Extent of pleasures and pains.[19]

We can illustrate by a simple example how these factors might affect the sum total of pleasure and pain resulting from an act. Let us say that you, a person with barely enough money to eat, find a wallet containing $1,000 and cards identifying the owner as a multimillionaire. You plan to send back the wallet, but you are debating whether or not to send back the money. What should you do? To decide, you turn to the hedonic calculus. You calculate that because neither you nor the millionaire have any dependents no one must be considered but the two of you. You only have to weigh your pleasure and his pain if you keep the money against your pain and his pleasure if you send it back. We can surely assume that the intensity of pleasure you can obtain by using the money to buy food, drink, and entertainment far outweighs the intensity of the millionaire's irritation at not having the money returned. Furthermore, the duration of your pleasure will probably far exceed his irritation. We can assume that it is quite probable that you will get the pleasure

---

[19] See ibid., pp. 37–40, for Bentham's statement of the hedonic calculus.

and he will become irritated, so that factors (3) and (4) will not have much effect. We can also discount the effect of (5) and (6) in the case of the millionaire, because once his irritation is gone he will have too many more important things to think about. But if we assume that you probably will drink too much as a result of keeping the money, we can say that the pleasure is somewhat impure because of the hangover which follows it. Thus we must subtract some part of the total of your pleasure. And because such pleasures usually are not followed by additional pleasures as well as the pains of hangovers, we can conclude that your pleasure is not at all fecund. Nevertheless, it seems clear that if you keep the money your pleasure far exceeds the millionaire's displeasure, so that there is a considerable overall increase in the total amount of pleasure. But if you return the money, the little pleasure the millionaire receives hardly outweighs the unhappiness you feel when you think of the good times you are missing. Given all this, the decision is easy. You should, if you apply the principle of utility, keep the money.

We have seen a simple example of how the principle of utility is to be applied in a specific situation. The question before us is whether there are certain situations in which the principle would prescribe morally repugnant actions. Someone might claim that we already have found such a situation because we always ought to return lost items to their owner. However, there are exceptions to this rule, such as the one cited by Plato where we should not return a lethal weapon to its rightful owner who has become a homicidal maniac. Furthermore, although the example we have used may seem to some to be a case where what is prescribed by the principle of utility is wrong, what it prescribes is not a clear-cut example of a morally repugnant act. It is by no means a clear counterexample to Bentham's claim that his principle generally prescribes actions in line with what we think is right. We need a stronger case to refute Bentham's claim.

AN OBJECTION TO BENTHAM'S PRINCIPLE: SADISTIC PLEASURES

We are to use the hedonic calculus to find out what we ought to do, so that if the calculus prescribes an obviously immoral action we can reject Bentham's principle. Let us take an example from the Marquis de Sade. There is a roomful of men who get extreme pleasure from the sadistic mutilation of the girl Justine.[20] She suffers great pain, but all the men enjoy great pleasure so that the sum total of pleasure in this case is greater than if the men forego their pleasure by allowing Justine to go her way unharmed. If we apply Bentham's principle, once again it is clear what ought to be done. The men should take their sadistic pleasures and Justine should suffer. But this is surely morally repugnant. Something has gone horribly wrong with a principle which prescribes such sadistic acts. It might be objected, however, that because the mutilation Justine suffers results in prolonged pain, whereas the pleasures of the sadists are short-lived, the total amount of pain outweighs the total amount of pleasure. This objection can easily be avoided by changing the situation to one in which this particular group always kills the object of their sadism at the end of the festivities by skillfully administering a drug that kills quickly and painlessly. Here we have an example in which murder, by cutting short sadistically inflicted pain, would, on Bentham's principle, remove an objection to willful injury.

Consider another example which illustrates again how emphasis on pleasure as the *summum bonum* can justify murder. Let us replace the sadists by a cult of people who hate pain but who get immense pleasure from mutilating a warm human body. This group carefully picks a victim who has no close family or friends and whose life is not particularly pleasurable. If they can, they try to choose someone who suffers from an illness so they can eliminate pain. They kill such a person as skillfully and painlessly as the sadists; then they have their joyous rites. Such murders seem justified by Bentham's principle, but clearly they are wrong. Somehow, although the principle is, as we have seen, impartial, it still has omitted something essential to morality. We should, then, reject Bentham's principle of utility as we have rejected ethical egoism before it, because we have found no reason to accept the principle, but we have found reason to reject it.

This does not mean, however, that we have found reasons sufficient for rejecting utilitarianism, because Bentham's version is only one particular version. Another version, that proposed by John

---

[20] Marquis de Sade, *Justine,* translated by Richard Seaver and Austryn Wainhouse (New York: Grove Press, 1965).

Stuart Mill, who followed Bentham in his ideas about social reform, is an explicit attempt to meet the kind of objection we have just raised. Let us turn, therefore, to consider Mill's ethical theory.

UTILITARIANISM: MILL'S VERSION

John Stuart Mill, whose father James Mill was a contemporary follower of Bentham, had ample opportunity to become acquainted with all the various objections raised against Bentham's theory. Consequently, in his book *Utilitarianism* Mill set out to state and justify a version of the utilitarian principle. Like Bentham he attempted to refute objections to the principle and raise objections to opposing principles. Unlike Bentham he tried to construct a less indirect proof of his principle, but his proof was an obvious failure. We are primarily interested here in his defense of utilitarianism, in particular his refutation of the objection that if we treat all pleasures equally, as we must in applying the hedonic calculus, then sadistic pleasures as well as the merely bodily pleasures are to count on a par with the pleasures of contemplation, creation, discovery and other so-called mental pleasures. That is, it is better to be a pig satisfied than a human dissatisfied; better in some situations that sadists are satisfied than that they are not satisfied. Mill answers this objection as follows:

> It is quite compatible with the principle of utility to recognize the fact that some *kinds* of pleasure are more desirable and more valuable than others. It would be absurd that, while, in estimating all other things, quality is considered as well as quantity, the estimation of pleasures should be supposed to depend on quantity alone.[21]

QUALITY vs. QUANTITY OF PLEASURE

It is obvious that, contrary to what Mill says, qualitative distinctions between pleasures are inconsistent with at least one form of utili-

[21] Op. cit., p. 408.

tarianism, namely, Bentham's. The only characteristics of pleasure and pain we are to consider in the hedonic calculus are their intensity and duration. There is no factor available for distinguishing among different kinds of pleasures and different kinds of pains. Thus Mill has taken a radical departure from Bentham's theory. Just how radical his departure is can be seen by examining the criterion Mill proposes to distinguish between qualitative levels of pleasures. He says,

Of two pleasures, if there be one to which all or almost all who have experience of both give a decided preference, irrespective of a feeling of moral obligation to prefer it, that is the more desirable pleasure. If one of the two is, by those who are competently acquainted with both, placed so far above the other that they prefer it, even though knowing it to be attended with a greater amount of discontent, and would not resign it for any quantity of the other pleasure which their nature is capable of, we are justified in ascribing to the preferred enjoyment a superiority in quality, so far outweighing quantity as to render it, in comparison, of small account.[22]

Mill's criterion tells us to decide which pleasures are qualitatively superior by what amounts to a poll of those who have experienced the pleasures in question. This seems to be an eminently democratic way to decide the issue but we shall see that it is not. It is possible that the results of such a poll will show merely a wide range of disagreement or even a preference for "pig" pleasures. Mill, however, seems to dismiss this possibility immediately, for he assumes that the "verdict of the only competent judges" will be that "the pleasures derived from the higher faculties [are] preferable *in kind,* apart from the question of intensity, to those of which the animal nature, disjoined from the higher faculties, is susceptible. . . ."[23] It seems clear to Mill that the nobler pleasures, those associated with man's intellect, will win the poll over the lower bodily or "pig" pleasures. Thus, for Mill, utilitarianism can avoid the objection that it is a pig philosophy. To understand why Mill is so certain of the out-

22 Ibid., p. 409.
23 Ibid., pp. 411–12.

come of such a poll we must concentrate on the key phrase, 'only competent judges.' In using this phrase Mill implies that the man who has savored the nobler pleasures but who prefers bodily pleasures is a backslider, a man of weak will who is not competent to judge. His vote, therefore, is not to be counted.

It may be that we can find some way to justify revoking the voting rights of the skid-row inhabitants who have fallen from some previous higher estate, but it is not clear what grounds there would be. It is by no means clear, however, how we are to handle sadists, masochists, arsonists, voyeurs, and others who might prefer exotic pleasures to the "noble" ones. Perhaps we should call these people perverts and allow only normal people to decide. But even if we could decide who is normal in some way that is not question-begging, we would still find many men like D. H. Lawrence who, if they were asked to choose between intellectual pleasures and sexual pleasures, would without hesitation claim the latter should be chosen. It would be very hard to show that these men are backsliders or perverts. Furthermore, they often try to justify their choice on the grounds that, for example, without sexual pleasures men become isolated, lonely, hollow shells with no capacity to communicate with their fellow man. These men often argue that in this age of alienation and automation the one way to avoid dehumanization is through a passionate clinging together built upon the emotional base of the joys and pleasures of shared sexual acts. There are of course many others, including many philosophers, who agree with Mill, but taking a poll is hardly the way to show they are right. And what happens to the great number of people who all their lives long have little chance to experience the noble pleasures through no fault of their own? On this issue these people do not count as one and, as a result, once a hierarchy of pleasures is decided, they might not count as one when applying the utilitarian principle.

A poll does not seem the way to decide the issue, but how else can it be decided? Very often when the issue is debated the argument proceeds by referring to what the various pleasures are associated with or lead to. The qualitatively superior pleasures turn out to be those associated with what is better, for example, man's intellect or man's love of his fellow man. But once this line is taken utilitarianism has been abandoned, because the basic ethical principle is the one used to distinguish the hierarchy of things which are good and for this there is no need of a reference to pleasure. A utilitarian cannot take this line. If we are going to be utilitarians we must agree either that all pleasures or else that only certain pleasures are the only things intrinsically good. If we take the first alternative, then the objection arises that utilitarianism implies that it is better to be a pig satisfied than Socrates dissatisfied. If we try the second, then we can merely list the qualitative hierarchy of pleasures without justifying the list by reference to anything else intrinsically good. Consequently, there will be no way to decide among alternative lists and thus no basis for deciding what ought to be done in particular situations. Because neither alternative is attractive, perhaps we should abandon utilitarianism and with it the claim, which we have been considering since our examination of egoistic hedonism, that pleasure is the one thing intrinsically good.

AN OBJECTION TO UTILITARIANISM: SPECIAL DUTIES

There are additional problems facing utilitarianism. Both Mill's and Bentham's versions face two additional serious objections. The first is based on the inability of utilitarianism to account for *special duties*. There surely seem to be duties or obligations that some people have because of their particular and special status, but that other people do not have. Consequently, these duties are different from the obligations we all have, for example, to maximize happiness. People who are parents, teachers, or judges, for example, have special obligations to their children, students, and defendants, respectively, obligations which others do not have to these same people. Utilitarianism seems unable to account for these duties. When a teacher grades a paper or an examination, he does not decide the grade on the basis of what would maximize the overall happiness in this particular case. He tries to grade solely on the basis of the quality of the work done even if the resulting grade produces more pain than pleasure. If he produces more pain, is he being immoral? Many students seem to think so, but it can hardly be right to adjust a grade according to how it affects the happiness of all those concerned. We can imagine a lonely student unjustly despised by his fellow students who would be handicapped unfairly relative to more popular students. Thus teachers seem to have, because of their unique position, an obligation completely independent of the principle of utility. Special duties, therefore, present another problem for utilitarianism and for its central claim that only pleasures are intrinsically good.

We have just seen an example in which applying the principle of utility results in someone being treated unfairly. A similar problem could arise if a judge or jury were instructed to decide guilt on the basis of what maximizes the overall happiness. This would be unfair, unjust in many cases. This points to perhaps the most serious problem facing utilitarianism, the problem of fairness or justice. This seems to be a problem independent of the problem of special duties because not only judges and juries ought to be just; it is an obligation each of us seems to have regarding our fellow men. It may seem strange that fairness should be a problem for utilitarianism, because we moved to utilitarianism from ethical egoism in search of an impartial standard. It is true that utilitarianism is impartial in counting each person as one and no one more than one regarding at least quantities of pleasure and pain, but this is not the only kind of morally relevant impartiality, and surely not the only kind that can be relevant to justice.

ANOTHER OBJECTION TO UTILITARIANISM: THE PROBLEM OF JUSTICE

The problem justice raises for utilitarianism is demonstrated by a scapegoat example. Imagine a town in which the young blond daughter of a prominent family had recently been kidnapped in broad daylight, then raped, and brutally murdered. The police are completely baffled and among the citizenry, aroused by the local newspaper, there is growing contempt for the police. It is becoming harder for the police to control the youth of the town, crime is on the increase, and fear is widespread. It seems that something should be done to restore confidence in law and the police. At this point the chief of police decides to find someone who can be accused of the crimes and brought to a speedy and decisive trial. The first hobo off the next through train is apprehended, and with planted witnesses and carefully chosen jurists quickly condemned to death. The town breathes easier, the police are praised, happiness and tranquility are restored—except for one police patrolman who knew that the executed man was not guilty. But he is quickly reassured by the police chief who, not previously known for his morality, gives him a quick course in utilitarianism and then shows how the overall happiness has been maximized.

This is an example of an obvious miscarriage of justice. Such a case might occur, as can be readily shown if we describe the city as in the southern United States and both the rapist and hobo as Negro. Nevertheless no such cases should occur and certainly any ethical principle which prescribes them is clearly wrong. Thus utilitarianism, because it sacrifices justice to the overall happiness and thereby omits an essential ingredient of impartiality, should be rejected in favor of an ethical theory that takes justice as an essential part of morality. To find such a theory we shall turn to a standard that differs radically from any we have examined so far in that it does not consider the consequences of an act as relevant to deciding the rightness of the act. Such an ethical theory has been called "deontological" because it stresses that morality is essentially based upon the relationship an act has to moral laws or principles rather than its relationship to its consequences.

DEONTOLOGICAL ETHICS: KANT'S THEORY

All the ethical theories we have examined so far have had two things in common: They propose something as the *summum bonum* or highest good, and they prescribe that what ought to be done is to maximize whatever is the highest good. For example, both egoistic hedonism and Bentham's utilitarianism agree that because pleasure or happiness is the one thing good in itself, it is the *summum bonum* and we ought to bring it about wherever possible. Where they differ is in their claims about whose pleasure each person ought to maximize. For such theories what is morally important is whether or not our actions have consequences that bring about what is the highest good. Theories that emphasize the consequences of actions have been called "teleological" ethical theories.

THE HIGHEST GOOD: A GOOD WILL

The great German philosopher Immanuel Kant propounded an ethical theory that is very difficult to interpret, but it has generally been construed as a prime example of a deontological theory. We shall follow this interpretation. Kant began his search for a basic ethical principle in the same way as Bentham and Mill. He also began by attempting to find the highest good. What he concluded, however, was so different from the conclusions reached by the others that on his theory what is the highest good can be realized regardless of the consequences of an act. To see how he arrived at this conclusion we must understand the conditions he required of anything for it to be the highest good. According to Kant, the highest good must not only be good in itself, it must also be good without qualification.[24] This means that there are no situations in which the addition of what is the highest good makes the situation morally worse. Using this as his criterion Kant can eliminate all the leading candidates for the highest good for the reason that each one when added to certain situations makes them worse. He eliminates the "higher" faculties such as intelligence and judgment because if a man with evil designs also has a high degree of intelligence, the results are worse. He eliminates traits of persons such as courage, resoluteness, and perseverance because "they can become extremely bad and harmful if the will, which is to make use of these gifts of nature and which in its special constitution is called character, is not good."[25] He rejects what he calls gifts of fortune, including power, riches, honor, and the utilitarian candidate, pleasure, because they too can make certain situations worse than if they were lacking. If, for example, we were to hear that the executioners at Auschwitz got pleasure from their horrible deeds and even if we agree that pleasure is good in itself, we would not think that this pleasure made the situation better. Instead we would think it made their deeds all that much worse. After rejecting these candidates Kant proposes the one

[24] Kant discusses what is good without qualification in the first section of *The Foundations of the Metaphysics of Morals* (New York: Liberal Arts Press, 1959), pp. 9–10.

[25] Ibid., p. 9.

thing he can find that meets his criterion. He says, in a famous passage:

> Nothing in the world—indeed nothing even beyond the world— can possibly be conceived which could be called good without qualification except a *good will*.[26]

Kant claims that the one thing good without qualification is a good will, but explaining what he means by 'good will' is far from easy. For our purposes it will be enough to begin by noting that according to Kant "the good will is not good because of what it effects or accomplishes or because of its adequacy to achieve some proposed end."[27] This is because what we do as a result of willing may, through chance, bungling, or interference of others, be quite the opposite of what we decided. We know of the good-intentioned bungler and the villain who in spite of all he plans actually aids the hero. Kant says that the will "is good only because of its willing, that is, it is good of itself."[28] This means that whether a will is good does not depend on the consequences of willing but upon the manner of willing. This is brought out by the following definition we can use to express Kant's point:

S has a good will = $_{df.}$ S acts out of respect for moral laws.

This is still only a beginning because we have introduced two new terms Kant uses, both of which require explanation, 'act out of respect for' and 'moral law.' The first can be explained by distinguishing it from 'act in accordance with' in the following way:

S *acts in accordance with* principle $P = _{df.}$ S does something that is consistent with what P prescribes.
S *acts out of respect for* principle $P = _{df.}$ S does something solely for the reason that what he is doing is consistent with what P prescribes.

---

[26] Ibid.
[27] Ibid., p. 10.
[28] Ibid.

We can often act in accordance with a principle without even being aware of it or even when trying to violate it. Most of us when we drive a car act in accordance with laws regarding speed limits, sometimes because we want to, other times without any thoughts or desires about it, and sometimes even when we try to break the law if, for example, we mistakenly think the limit is lower than it is. In none of these cases do we act out of respect for the laws. We act out of respect for a law only when our decision to do something is based on and only on the reason that what we do is consistent with what the law prescribes. Thus to act out of respect for law we must decide on the basis of reason alone, that is, without reliance on our inclinations and desires, to do what is consistent with what the law prescribes. If we then act on the basis of our decision, we can be said to act out of respect for the law.

THE MORAL LAW AND THE CATEGORICAL IMPERATIVE
The expression 'moral law' is more difficult to explain. We know three things:

1. A moral law prescribes what ought to be done.
2. What ought to be done is to bring about whatever is the highest good.
3. A will that acts out of respect for moral laws is the highest good.

From this we can conclude that a moral law prescribes just one thing, namely, that we act out of respect for moral laws. There are two important consequences of this. First, there is only one moral law, for there is only one thing prescribed. Second, because the moral law merely requires that we act out of respect for itself, it is unlike any previous basic ethical principle we have examined. They all prescribe what acts we should do, but this one prescribes how we should do any act. Therefore it is not the particular actions a law prescribes that make it a moral law, that is, it is not the particular content of any law that makes it moral. And because any particular law consists only of some particular content embedded in a lawlike form, it must be this lawlikeness of a law that makes it moral. Thus if we can find a law that expresses merely this lawlike form of laws, then we will have found the one and only moral law.

What is the form of all prescriptive laws? They can be distinguished from explanatory laws, such as scientific laws, in that they can be expressed as imperatives about men's actions. Thus legal prescriptive laws are often stated in the imperative mood such as "Do not speed!" and "No smoking!" And because there is no restriction upon the moral imperative except that it expresses the form of lawfulness, there are no conditions that must be met for it to be applicable. It is then an unconditional or categorical imperative and an imperative with universal application. Thus the moral law, by requiring that we act out of respect for itself, requires that we act out of respect for universal and unconditional lawfulness. The moral law requires that whenever we decide to do something we should decide to do it solely for the reason that doing it is consistent with what universal and unconditional lawfulness requires. And, as we are interpreting Kant, universal and unconditional lawfulness requires that the principles we actually base our decisions on, what Kant calls "maxims," should have the form of universal and unconditional laws. The moral imperative, therefore, requires that we are morally permitted to act on a maxim only if our decision to act on it is consistent with our willing to make the maxim a universal and unconditional law governing the actions of everyone, including ourselves. Kant formulates the moral imperative as

> Act only according to that maxim by which you can at the same time will that it should become a universal law.[29]

THE FIRST FORMULATION OF THE CATEGORICAL IMPERATIVE

The preceding formulation of the categorical imperative is not the only formulation given by Kant, but it is the one he derives first. We shall examine his second formulation later. One thing both formulations have in common is that they prescribe principles, and

[29] Ibid., p. 39.

therefore actions based on the principles, independent of the consequences of the actions. An ethical theory that takes this as its basic
ethical principle is a deontological theory. This, like other ethical
theories, faces objections, but before we assess the objections we
must decide whether we should interpret Kant's principle as expressing both a necessary and sufficient condition of moral permis-
sion, or merely a necessary condition. As stated earlier it seems to
express merely a necessary condition because of the word 'only.'
That is, it seems equivalent to

> You are permitted to act on a principle P *only if* you can will
> P to be a universal law.

Furthermore, if we try to interpret it as a sufficient condition as well,
then immediate objections arise. If the possibility of someone willing that a principle be a universal law is a sufficient condition of the
principle being one he ought to act on, then we get morally repugnant results. For example, a masochistic sadist might have no trouble willing that the principle "Give Smith five lashes a day," be universalized to "Give everyone five lashes a day." But it should not be
concluded from this that he is permitted to act on the principle of
giving Smith five lashes a day. Therefore we should restrict the
principle to stating merely a necessary condition.

Once we restrict the categorical imperative in this way, however,
another objection arises. The restricted imperative is not helpful in
cases where we can will a principle universalized, but are not sure
of whether we ought to act on the principle. The most the imperative can tell us is that if we cannot will a principle to be universalized then we are not permitted to, that is, we ought not act on it.
Consequently, Kant's imperative, although it may be an essential
element of a basic ethical principle, cannot be the basic principle,
because it is not applicable in many situations. Indeed, it might
also be objected, it is not clear how it is applicable in any situation
because it is not clear how we can derive particular obligations
from such an abstract principle. Kant tries to rebut this second
objection by showing how to derive particular duties from his imperative. What he attempts to do is show that someone who does
a particular act on the basis of a particular immoral maxim would
become involved in some kind of inconsistency if he also willed
that the maxim become a universal law. Thus what Kant means

by 'You cannot will the maxim you act on to be a universal law' is that if you do, then you will be in some way inconsistent and thus your decision will be irrational. But making an irrational decision is contrary to acting out of respect for the moral law, because, as we have seen, we act out of respect for the moral law only if we decide on the basis of reason alone to act in accordance with it.

Let us examine two of Kant's examples to illustrate his method. One duty he derives from the first formulation is the duty not to make a deceitful promise, in order to borrow money, for example. In this case, according to Kant, the maxim would be

> When I believe myself to be in need of money, I will borrow money and promise to repay it, although I know I shall never do so.[30]

If this maxim is universalized, we would have a law that whenever anyone needs money he makes a lying promise in order to get it. If this were a law governing everyone's actions, then, according to Kant, no one would believe a promise made under such circumstances and no one would be fooled into believing the false promise. The result is an inconsistency between the intention of the liar to deceive others and his willing a universal law that eliminates the deception. We can conclude then that we ought not make a lying promise. Here is an ethical principle prohibiting specific acts so that, if Kant's derivation is sound, he has shown us how to apply his abstract principle to specific acts. No act of lying is right.

Another of Kant's examples concerns the man who decides not to help someone who needs help. In this example Kant understands the maxim to be the following:

> I shall not help another person even when he needs help.

If we were to make this into a universal law it would be a law that no one is to help any other person who needs help. But, claims Kant, all of us desire that someone help us when we are in trouble so that our desire for help would conflict with our willing this to be

---

[30] Ibid., p. 40.

a universal law governing all human actions. Thus we have an obligation to help others in a specific situation when they need help.

OBJECTION TO FIRST FORMULATION: WHICH MAXIMS TO UNIVERSALIZE?

We have seen from the preceding two examples that Kant's method of deriving specific duties from the first formulation of the categorical imperative depends upon deriving an inconsistency when certain maxims are universalized. There are two basic problems for this derivation. The first is the problem of applying the first formulation to maxims. To which is it to be applied and to which should it not be applied? The second is the problem of whether or not Kant can, as he claims, derive a clear inconsistency in applying the first formulation. To see the first problem consider a wretched, starving person who makes a promise which he knows he cannot keep to an extremely wealthy man in order to get money for much-needed food and medicine. To what maxim are we to apply the imperative? Is it to Kant's quite general maxim or a more restricted one, such as:

> Whenever I am starving and need food and medicine and the only way to get it is to make a deceitful promise, I will deceitfully promise a wealthy man who can spare the money.

It is by no means clear that this is an immoral maxim even if the man's intention in acting on it is in some way inconsistent with his willing to universalize it.

Consider also a very sly universalizer who whenever he makes a deceitful promise claims that his maxim is something like the following:

> Whenever anyone is 6 feet tall, has one blue and one brown eye, a three inch scar on his left cheek, a bullet wound in his right palm, a gold ring in his left ear, and needs money, he is to borrow money and make a deceitful promise to repay it.

What makes this universalizer sly is that the only person who fits this description is himself. Furthermore, he claims that this maxim is universal as it stands, for it is of the form:

Whenever anyone is X, he is to do Y.

which is the form of Kant's universalized maxim. Indeed, the maxim applies to *everyone* who is X. It is only a contingent fact that only he is X. Consequently, our universalizer, who uses this form with the preceding description for all his maxims, finds that nothing is forbidden and nothing is obligatory, because all his maxims are universal. Thus he can act on them and will them to be universal laws without inconsistency. The obvious reply to this is to say that some restriction must be placed on what we are allowed to substitute for 'X,' but it is not clear how to allow a phrase such as 'desperately in need of food,' but rule out the longer phrase invented by the sly universalizer.

ANOTHER OBJECTION: CANNOT DERIVE SPECIFIC DUTIES

The first is not the more serious problem, however, because it may be possible to place a satisfactory restriction upon the application of the imperative but it is not clear how to avoid the second problem. It is essential for Kant to derive some kind of inconsistency. The most plausible example he gives is the case of deceitful promising, but even here his derivation fails. There is an inconsistency only if someone decides to deceive someone and also decides to do something that stops him from deceiving the person. But the deception would not be stopped if the *only* thing that were to happen is that the actions of everyone who needed money became governed by a law requiring them to make deceitful promises. If the person a liar was trying to deceive did not know that there was such a law or did not realize that this was a situation covered by the law about needing money, then there is a very good chance that he would be deceived, especially if the deceiver were clever. Even if this practice had been occurring universally for centuries, there is, as the saying goes, "a sucker born every minute." There is, unfortunately, very often little resemblance between what people are willing to believe and the truth.

The problem is more evident in the second example, for in order to arrive at the inconsistency Kant must claim that all of us desire someone to help us when we are in trouble. If someone did not have this desire, then his universalizing the maxim not to help another would not be inconsistent with any of his desires. He would, consequently, not be obligated to help others. There are, I am sure, some people who do not have this desire—people, for example, who claim they belong to that almost mythical breed of men known as rugged individualists. Kant can at most claim that we nonrugged people would become involved in an inconsistency, but even here problems arise. First there is, as before, the problem of restricting the application of the imperative. Even if we specify in the maxim merely the way in which help is needed, such as 'needs help crossing the street,' some of us are at least rugged enough not to desire this kind of help. Second, in absolving the rugged individualist from responsibility for helping others, Kant seems to condone what we might call the rugged individualist fallacy: Because I need no help and everyone should be like me, I have no obligation to help anyone. Unfortunately, whatever we should all be, most of us are not rugged individualists. We sometimes need help and therefore there are times others should help us whether or not they need help themselves.

There are, then, serious difficulties facing Kant's first formulation of the categorical imperative, difficulties which eliminate it as being sufficient to stand alone as the basic moral imperative. However, we should not reject it entirely, because it may be an important element in a satisfactory formulation of such an imperative.

THE SECOND FORMULATION OF THE CATEGORICAL IMPERATIVE

Having rejected Kant's first formulation someone might wonder why we are going to examine his second formulation and, indeed, why we have considered Kant at all when our purpose has been to find an ethical theory that can accommodate justice. Although it is not obvious that the first formulation is related to justice, Kant, by requiring that the maxims we act on be universalized so as to be equally applicable to all, has incorporated into his imperative something essential to justice. When we get to the second formulation, however, we shall see clearly how Kant's theory overcomes the kind of difficulty justice poses for utilitarianism.

Kant, in stating his second formulation, gave expression to one of the greatest humanistic doctrines. It sums up in one short imperative the doctrine of the dignity and worth of the individual person:

Act so that you treat humanity, whether in your own person or in that of another, always as an end and never as a means only.[31]

There are two important prescriptions in this imperative. We are to treat people as ends, that is, we are to treat them as beings having intrinsic value in themselves regardless of whatever value they may have or lack as a means to some end. We are also never to treat people as things that are mere means. That is, although we can, do, and often must treat people as means, in so doing we must also treat them as ends. Thus the farmer treats his plow and hired hands as means, a manufacturer treats his machines and laborers as means, and a student treats his books and teachers as means. But although it is all right to treat the plow, the machinery, and the books merely as means, the hired hands, laborers, and teachers must also be treated as ends. This implies that no person should be a slave or racially discriminated against or used as a scapegoat. Each person is an end in himself and must be treated that way. Here, surely, is the very essence of justice.

Kant claims that this formulation is just another way to express the very same moral law expressed by the first formulation. Although it is by no means clear why Kant thought this, perhaps the following will help explain what he had in mind. We have already seen that Kant holds that the good will is the highest good, so that a good will is an end in itself and should be treated as such. But we can treat a faculty of some being as an end in itself only by treating the being itself as an end. And because only a being who can act out of respect for law, that is, only a rational being, can possess a good will, it follows that we should treat rational beings with good wills as ends. Furthermore, because we cannot know from its effects whether a will is good, we cannot be sure whether or not any particular will is good. Consequently, in order not to omit any beings with good wills, we must treat all rational beings and therefore all human beings as ends in themselves. In this way, starting

[31] Ibid., p. 47.

from the same premises as were used to arrive at the first formulation, we arrive by a slightly different route at the second formulation. In such a way Kant might have arrived at the second formulation and at the conclusion that it was equivalent to the first.

Another reason Kant might have had for thinking that the two formulations are equivalent, and thus formulations of the same law, is that he thought the same duties could be derived from each. He illustrated this by deriving the same duties from each formulation. Let us examine how he derives these two duties previously discussed. We shall see that the derivation is easier and more plausible in this case. Kant derives the duty not to make deceitful promises from the prescription not to treat people as means only by arguing that anyone who intends to make such a promise "sees immediately that he intends to use another man merely as a means."[32] In this Kant surely is right, for deceiving someone to get something for ourselves is using the other merely as a means to our own gain. The obligation we have to help others is derived from the other prescription in the second formulation, that we treat people as ends. This means that we ought to further the well-being of people because this is how we should treat an end in itself. Consequently, it is not enough that we avoid treating people merely as means; we ought to do more.

> Humanity might indeed exist if no one contributed to the happiness of others, provided he did not intentionally detract from it; but this harmony with humanity as an end in itself is only negative rather than positive if everyone does not also endeavor, so far as he can, to further the ends of others.[33]

Although Kant is far from being a utilitarian he arrives at an obligation which sounds quite utilitarian, that we ought to promote the happiness of others by treating each person as an end. Thus Kant's second formulation may provide a way to accommodate the greatest happiness principle and justice. However, in order to evaluate it we must see whether it faces other problems.

---

[32] Ibid., p. 48.
[33] Ibid., pp. 48–49.

AN OBJECTION TO KANT'S THEORY: NOT APPLICABLE IN ALL SITUATIONS

There are three objections that cast doubt on Kant's second formulation of the categorical imperative, but they can all be adapted to apply to the first formulation also; thus they are really objections to the whole of Kant's ethical theory. We have already seen the first objection as it applies to the first formulation. Neither formulation is applicable in all situations. This problem arises for the second formulation in two kinds of situations. The first situation is one in which all the possible alternatives require treating someone as a means only, such as in the example of an overcrowded lifeboat where someone must be sacrificed as a means of preserving the others. Kant's imperative provides us with no way to decide. The second situation is one in which all the alternatives allow us to treat someone as an end, but each alternative involves different people. This is the problem confronting someone who is in charge of distributing welfare funds so limited that not everyone needing help can be aided. Kant's imperative does not provide a way to decide between, for example, a family with a talented child, another with a child needing medical attention, and another with a mentally disturbed child who terrorizes the neighborhood. Although in both of these kinds of cases the decisions are most difficult, a principle which would provide a way to distinguish among the alternatives would be superior in at least one respect to Kant's imperative.

A SECOND OBJECTION: ABSOLUTE VS. *PRIMA FACIE* DUTIES

The second objection is a more serious one. According to Kant the duties we derive from the categorical imperative are absolute duties. He is therefore committed to what we previously called action absolutism, that is, that certain acts are always right or always wrong. Thus for Kant the obligation not to lie is an absolute duty, so that we ought not to lie under any conditions. This, however, leads to some results that are surely morally repugnant. Assume that you are trusted by the local Nazi commander in occupied Holland and that you are harboring an important Jewish refugee for whom the commander is searching. The commander comes to your door and, trusting you, asks if you are hiding the refugee. You know that he will go away without searching if you say you are hiding no one, and that saying nothing would amount to telling him the truth. It seems clear that you should lie in this situation, but a Kantian who remembers the absolute duty to tell the truth would say that you should admit you are hiding the refugee. Clearly such a Kantian is wrong.

It seems, therefore, that the duties derived from the categorical imperative should not be construed as absolute duties but rather as what have been called *prima facie* duties.[34] That is, Kantian duties are duties we are required to perform unless they are overruled or overridden by something else required of us. Thus the duty not to lie is not an absolute duty but merely a *prima facie* duty, because in some situations it is overridden by some other *prima facie* duty, such as helping a deserving friend in distress. And, in any particular situation, that *prima facie* duty which overrides all others is our duty proper, that is, what we ought to do in the situation.

We can state the distinction between an absolute duty and a *prima facie* duty by defining the key terms.

> A has a *prima facie* duty to do $P = {}_{df}$. There is something C_1 that requires A do P.

However, because a *prima facie* duty can be overridden and therefore might not be what we ought to do, we should also relate '*prima facie* duty' to 'override' and to 'ought.'

> A's *prima facie* duty to do P is overridden in situation $S = {}_{df}$. There is something C_1 that requires A do P, but there is something else C_2 such that C_1 and C_2 together do *not* require A do P in situation S.

This expresses what happens to the *prima facie* obligation to tell the truth in the refugee example. In this situation there is something, for example, a Kantian rule, that taken by itself requires you to tell the truth, but that, when taken with the conflicting requirement to help the refugee, does not require that you tell the truth. Furthermore, in this situation you surely seem to be required to do some-

---

[34] The concept of *prima facie* duty derives from D. Ross, *The Right and the Good* (New York: Oxford University Press, 1955), pp. 18–20.

thing instead of telling the truth. What you are required to do, what you ought to do, what we have called a duty proper, is to lie. Thus

> A ought (has a duty proper) in situation S to do $P = _{df}$. There is something C_1 that requires A do P in situation S, and there is nothing else C_2 such that C_1 and C_2 together do not require A do P in situation S.[35]

Thus any *prima facie* obligation that is not overridden in some situation is a duty proper and we ought to do it in that situation.

We can now define 'absolute duty' as a duty for which there is no situation in which someone is required to do something instead of it. It is, consequently, a duty that is never overridden.

> A has an absolute duty to do $P = _{df}$. There is something C_1 that requires A do P, and there is *no* situation in which A is required to do something instead of P.

Once we see what is necessary for a duty to be an absolute duty we can also see that there are very few, if any, duties that are absolute. There generally is some situation in which a duty is overridden, indeed, in which we are required to do something else. Most of our duties, therefore, are more properly called *prima facie* duties.

It seems that Kantian duties are more accurately described as *prima facie* duties than as absolute duties for, as we have seen, there are situations in which they are overridden. We can handle the refugee example in this way, but if we do we must conclude that Kant's theory is not adequate because it cannot accommodate the concept of overriding. The problem is further emphasized by the third and most serious objection to Kant's theory.

A THIRD OBJECTION: CANNOT RESOLVE CONFLICTS OF DUTY

The refugee example not only shows that there is a problem for Kant's theory because it seems to prescribe morally repugnant ac-

---

[35] This way of defining these distinctions is derived from R. M. Chisholm, "The Ethics of Requirement," *American Philosophical Quarterly* (1964), pp. 147–53.

tions in certain situations, but it can also illustrate the problem that conflicts of duty produce for his theory. In the refugee example the man is faced with what is clearly a conflict of duties, for he has a duty to help the refugee and a duty to tell the truth. In this case it should be easy to resolve the conflict, but Kant's theory cannot handle it. If, as Kant thinks, his theory prescribes absolute duties, then in this example the person ought to do two things he cannot possibly do together. Thus not only is he obliged to do something he cannot do, but he is also unable to justify choosing one rather than the other. If we interpret the theory to prescribe *prima facie* duties, then, although the man is not obliged to do two conflicting things, he still has no way of deciding what to do. Consequently, Kant's theory cannot handle conflicts of duty. It seems that he has so divorced morality from the consequences of our acts that in a case like the refugee example where the consequences seem most relevant, Kant's theory is unable to help us.

We have found three objections to Kant's deontological ethical theory which, taken together, constitute a sufficient reason for rejecting the theory as providing the basic ethical principle. Thus, we must continue our search. We should not, however, reject Kant's theory outright because it embodies something that seems essential to any satisfactory basic principle, the requirement to treat all people as ends, and therefore justly. It seems, consequently, that Kant's imperative should be included in any satisfactory basic standard. The question is how to include it. A recent and much-discussed answer is the theory called rule utilitarianism.

RULE UTILITARIANISM

Two of the main problems facing Kant's theory are that it cannot handle conflicts of duty and that there are situations in which it is not applicable. Two of the main problems for utilitarianism are the problem of the lower pleasures and the problem of justice. Because Kant's theory can accommodate what causes the utilitarian trouble and utilitarianism can avoid what causes Kant trouble, it seems that if the two could be encapsulated in one theory which eliminated the weaknesses of both while maintaining the strong points of each, then we might well have a satisfactory theory. Kant's theory stresses the importance of moral laws that prescribe duties. This enables it to account for justice. Utilitarianism, on the other hand, proposes a standard that can be applied to every situation. It can also be applied to laws; that is, we can evaluate a law by deciding whether or not its enforcement tends to maximize the overall happiness. Indeed it has been claimed that the way to evaluate any juridical law, newly proposed or in force, is to apply the principle of utility to it, because the purpose of government and thus of juridical laws is to maximize the general welfare.

ACTS, LAWS, JUDGES, AND LEGISLATORS

The applicability of the utilitarian principle to juridical laws has led some philosophers to propose that the correct ethical standard should be constructed on an analogy with the way the utilitarian principle applies to juridical laws. To do this we must understand and distinguish between the relationship of a judge to a law and the relationship of a legislator to a law. P. H. Nowell-Smith claims,

> The duty of the judge is to pronounce verdict and sentence in accordance with the law; and the question "What verdict and sentence ought he pronounce?" turns solely on the question "What verdict and sentence are laid down in the law for this crime?" As judge, he is not concerned with the consequences, beneficial or harmful, of what he pronounces. Similarly, the question "Was that a just sentence?" is one that cannot be settled by reference to its consequences, but solely by reference to the law.[36]

The judge, as Nowell-Smith points out, is concerned with deciding individual cases and in doing so he can rely only on the laws in effect. He cannot use the consequences, whether for good or ill, to help justify his decision. The judge, therefore, because his decisions are bound by a network of laws, functions in a somewhat deontological way. As Nowell-Smith says, however,

---

[36] P. H. Nowell-Smith, *Ethics* (Baltimore: Penguin Books, 1954), p. 236.

The duty of the legislator is quite different. It is not to decide whether a particular application of the law is just or not, but to decide what laws ought to be adopted and what penalties are to be laid down for the breach of each law. And these questions cannot be decided in the way that the judge decides what verdict and sentence to pronounce.[37]

The legislator should evaluate laws by their consequences rather than by some other set of laws, although, of course, what the consequences of a particular law are depends in part upon what other laws are already in effect. The legislator, then, because he evaluates not by means of laws but by consequences, functions in a somewhat utilitarian way. Using this analogy with legality, Nowell-Smith concludes,

> The obligation to obey a rule does not, in the opinion of most ordinary men, rest on the beneficial consequences of obeying it in a particular case in either the short or the long run, as utilitarians have almost always supposed. But the reasons for adopting a rule may well be of the kind that utilitarians suggest.[38]

In other words, Nowell-Smith is proposing an ethical theory that restricts the application of the utilitarian principle to rules of conduct rather than to particular actions. The particular actions we do and contemplate doing are to be evaluated by moral rules which are in turn justified by the utilitarian principle. Let us call moral rules that are justified by the utilitarian principle "utilitarian rules." We have, then, what has been called both a *restricted utilitarianism*, because it restricts the application of the utilitarian principle, and a *rule utilitarianism*, because it restricts the principle to rules. This theory, therefore, differs from a theory that applies the utilitarian principle to acts. Thus it differs from Bentham's and Mill's theories, which we have interpreted as versions of *act utilitarianism*. We can better understand this difference by stating a two-part principle containing the central doctrine of rule utilitarianism.

[37] Ibid., p. 237.
[38] Ibid., p. 239.

1. Someone has a *prima facie* duty to obey a *rule* of conduct if and only if having the rule in effect tends to maximize the overall happiness of those to whom it applies (that is, the rule is a *utilitarian rule*).
2. Someone has a *prima facie* duty to do an *act* if and only if the act is prescribed by a utilitarian rule.

SIX REQUIREMENTS FOR A SATISFACTORY ETHICAL STANDARD AND AN EXAMINATION OF RULE UTILITARIANISM

We have arrived at the rule utilitarian principle with the hope that it will incorporate the strengths of Kant's and Bentham's theories while eliminating their weaknesses. Let us, therefore, see how rule utilitarianism fares, but let us do so by bringing to bear upon it all the problems and objections we used to reject all the preceding theories, and what, as a result, we have found to be required for a satisfactory ethical theory. Any completely satisfactory ethical theory must provide a basic ethical principle which:

1. Is applicable in any situation requiring a moral choice. (Kant's theory and Mill's utilitarianism, which provides no justifiable way to evaluate pleasures qualitatively, fail to meet this condition.)
2. Accommodates special duties. (Act utilitarianism and ethical egoism fail here.)
3. Resolves conflicts of duty. (Kant's theory fails here.)
4. Guarantees the treatment of people as ends and thereby guarantees justice and impartiality. (Act utilitarianism and ethical egoism fail here.)
5. Provides for consideration of the consequences of actions for human happiness. (Kant's theory seems to fail here.)
6. Prescribes no acts we feel certain are wrong. (Ethical egoism and Bentham's utilitarianism fail here.)

It is clear that rule utilitarianism meets condition (5) and there is no reason to think it cannot meet conditions (1) and (6), although it is hard to evaluate with regard to (1) and (6) because little work has been done concerning specific recommendations for utilitarian rules. Nevertheless there seems to be no reason why there cannot be a utilitarian moral rule covering every situation and why any acts prescribed by these rules should be morally repugnant. At any rate, for the present let us assume that rule utilitarianism meets conditions (1), (5), and (6). It may seem that it cannot meet (2), (3), and (4), but rule utilitarians have concentrated on showing how their theory meets these conditions. They claim that the special duties of the parent, judge, and teacher can be handled because there are utilitarian rules imposing these duties, that is, rules that can be justified as tending to maximize the overall happiness of those affected. Although this has not been established it is at least plausible to think that the practices prescribed by such "special" laws have beneficial consequences for people. Therefore we can also grant that rule utilitarianism seems to meet condition (2).

Condition (3) seems to raise a serious problem, however, because, as we have seen, when there are several moral rules there will be conflicts of duty. Rule utilitarianism is faced with conflicts of duties, and as we have stated its principle, there is no way it can resolve such conflicts. The rule utilitarian's reply to this is that the principle is incomplete as stated. A provision must be added to the effect that, when there is conflict between the *prima facie* duties prescribed by utilitarian rules, then the overriding duty, the one that ought to be done, is to be decided by direct application of the utilitarian principle to the *action*. Thus when and only when someone faces a situation in which two or more conflicting *prima facie* duties are prescribed by utilitarian rules, he is to decide which action to do by the utilitarian principle. In all other situations the principle is to be applied only to rules. Thus condition (3) is met (and, incidentally, met in a way that justifies lying in the refugee example).

This brings us to the problem of justice, which causes the act utilitarian so much trouble. Is the rule utilitarian able to avoid the pitfalls of the scapegoat example? He tries to avoid it by handling justice in the same way he handles special duties. He claims that the obligation to be just follows from a rule which can be justified by application of the utilitarian principle. Thus the practice of treating people justly is prescribed by a utilitarian rule, because it is a practice having beneficial consequences for those affected. It seems, then, quite plausible to conclude that rule utilitarianism is a satisfactory ethical theory because the basic ethical principle it proposes seems to meet all the conditions we have found required of any satisfactory ethical theory.

OBJECTION TO RULE UTILITARIANISM: NO GUARANTEE OF JUSTICE

However, before we conclude we have found the theory for which we have been looking, we should consider in more detail how the rule utilitarian accommodates justice. On this theory justice is assured only as long as the general practice of being just tends to maximize the overall happiness. It is possible, therefore, that in some societies a rule requiring justice would not maximize happiness. It is possible that a law which forces people into slave labor might in certain circumstances tend to maximize the overall happiness, even counting the unhappiness of the slaves. In such a situation the guarantee of justice disappears. Thus although rule utilitarianism can accommodate justice, whereas act utilitarianism cannot, there is no guarantee that it will. The kind of justification of rules required by rule utilitarianism depends so much on the particular circumstances that we cannot be sure any particular rule will be justified.

This is not the only way justice can be thwarted on the basis of the rule utilitarian theory. By this theory the rule of justice is merely one of many rules justified by the utilitarian principle. We have seen that where there is more than one of these rules it is likely that they will sometimes conflict, and when they do we are to apply the utilitarian principle directly to the action to determine what we ought to do. It is, therefore, likely that there will be occasions when the *prima facie* obligation to be just will be overridden so that on those occasions we ought to be unjust. Consider, for example, a society in which one rule justified by the utilitarian principle is that respect for law enforcement ought to be maintained. What such a rule prescribes could quite easily conflict with the obligation to be just. In such a situation the principle of utility would be applied directly to the action and the scapegoat problem would arise again. Accordingly, even if a rule prescribing justice is justified, it may well be that in particular instances unjust treatment would be obligatory. Therefore, although rule utilitarianism seems preferable to the other theories we have examined, it still has a flaw. We should continue the search.

It seems that if we want justice guaranteed we must incorporate it in the basic ethical principle, rather than justifying it in some derivative way. The only theory we have found which does this is Kant's deontological theory. If we can somehow make Kant's principle basic and also retain the features of rule utilitarianism, we shall have found a satisfactory theory.

We have seen that Kant's second formulation has two parts, one which prescribes that we treat no person as a means only and the other that we treat all people as ends in themselves. If we can in some way give content to what it is to treat people as ends, we may be able to find the theory we want. And although we only noted it in passing, we have already seen the hint we want in Kant himself. We know that in treating someone as an end, the minimum requirement is that we bring about and maintain the conditions necessary for his continued existence. But as with anything that is an end we should also promote his well-being. According to Kant (see p. 494), we should also treat him in a utilitarian way; we ought to promote his happiness. This suggests that we should take Kant's principle, and thus justice, as basic and use the utilitarian principle to help derive certain duties consistent with Kant's principle. What is wrong with rule utilitarianism is that it makes justice derivative instead of basic. Indeed it is more reasonable to justify maximizing human happiness by some reference to the principle that humans should be treated as ends, that is, in a Kantian way, than to justify treating people justly by reference to the principle that we ought to maximize human happiness. Human happiness is morally important because human beings are important. It is not that humans are morally important because human happiness is.

A PROPOSAL FOR A SATISFACTORY STANDARD: A UTILITARIAN KANTIAN PRINCIPLE

Our job is to find some way to graft the utilitarian principle to Kant's second formulation. We know two things: First, the basic prescription is, if possible, to treat no one merely as a means, but if this is not possible in a particular situation, then we should treat as few people as possible as mere means. The overcrowded lifeboat example illustrates a situation in which someone must be sacrificed, treated as a mere means, in order to save the others. In such a situation it is obvious that as few as possible should be sacrificed. Second, we should treat as many people as ends as possible. We have interpreted this to imply that we should actively promote the well-being of those affected by the action in question. However, because promoting the well-being of as many people as possible could conflict with treating as few people as mere means as possible, and because the most basic imperative is not to treat people as mere means, the second imperative must be restricted so that it is consistent with the first.

At this point an objection can be raised. We can avoid treating a person as mere means by doing nothing at all. Consequently, in any situation we can avoid treating anyone as a mere means. If we accept the preceding imperative as basic, we should sacrifice no one in the lifeboat example, because that would be to treat as mere means as few people as possible. But that would result in needless loss of life. We must, then, find a different basic principle.

We can avoid the objection by construing the treatment of someone as mere means to include doing nothing to help him when he truly needs help, especially when his life is imperiled. Not to do anything to help someone in such a situation is to respond to him as something with no intrinsic worth. This amounts to treating him as a mere means. We can, then, take the basic imperative to be

> In any situation, (a) treat as mere means as few people as possible, and (b) treat as ends as many people as is consistent with (a).

We have claimed that promoting someone's happiness is important for treating him as an end. We should, then, incorporate into our imperative a prescription to promote the happiness of those affected by an action. However, because promoting as much happiness as possible often conflicts with the previously stated basic imperative, any prescription to promote happiness must be restricted so that following it is consistent with what our basic Kantian imperative prescribes.

Although this gives the essential skeleton of the principle, there is still the question of how we are to relate the treatment of as many people as ends as possible to the promotion of happiness. The problem is that there are several conflicting ways we could do this. We treat one person as an end by promoting his happiness. We could, then, require the action that promotes to some degree the happiness of the greatest number of people, or we could be utilitarian at this point and require that it maximize the total amount of happiness, counting, of course, each one as one and no one more than one. Let us initially choose an act utilitarian interpretation that gives us the following principle:

An action ought to be done in a situation if and only if
1. doing the action, (a) treats as mere means as few people as possible in the situation, and (b) treats as ends as many people as is consistent with (a), *and*
2. doing the action in the situation brings about as much overall happiness as is consistent with (1).

As the reader can discover for himself, this principle seems to meet all of the first five conditions that any satisfactory ethical theory must meet, except for (3), which concerns special duties. By applying the act utilitarianism principle to treatment of people as ends we have allowed the problem of the special duties of teachers to arise again. However, because this problem can be handled by rule utilitarianism, we can accommodate special duties by applying the rule utilitarian principle. Here again we have a choice to make. We can assume, as a rule utilitarian does, that there are utilitarian rules covering every situation involving a moral choice. Or we can make provisions for the existence of some situations not covered by these rules by requiring that the act utilitarian principle apply in these situations. Let us here, however, accept the rule utilitarian's assumption. What we can call "the utilitarian Kantian principle" will be

An action ought to be done in a situation if and only if
1. doing the action, (a) treats as mere means as few people as possible in the situation, and (b) treats as ends as many people as is consistent with (a), *and*
2. doing the action is prescribed by any utilitarian rule that (a)

does not violate condition (1) in the situation, and (b) is not overridden by another utilitarian rule that does not violate condition (1) in the situation.

To help understand this principle, let us see what it would prescribe in one particular lifeboat example. Let us assume that you are the captain of a ship that has just sunk, and you are in charge of the one remaining lifeboat, which has too many people crammed into it and three others, who are taking their turns in the water, hanging onto the sides of the boat. Suppose further that it is clear that a dangerous storm is quickly approaching and that the boat will capsize unless five people at minimum are cast adrift. You must decide what ought to be done. The utilitarian Kantian principle requires you to sacrifice some people, but as few as possible, in the situation in order to save the rest. In this way you would treat as few as possible as mere means, and as many as possible as ends in this situation.

Once this decision is made you are faced with the problem of finding a procedure for deciding who is to be sacrificed. One decision procedure which clearly treats no one as a mere means is to draw straws, but another one is to ask for volunteers. The basic Kantian requirement expressed in condition (1) provides no way to choose between the two procedures. Thus you must consider any relevant utilitarian rules. To see which rules apply, let us further assume that five people in the boat have publicly volunteered to be sacrificed. Consider now the following rule:

Whenever it is required that some people be sacrificed to save others, and some people have publicly volunteered to be sacrificed, then there is a *prima facie* obligation to sacrifice the volunteers.

This rule clearly applies in this situation and it does not violate what the basic Kantian condition requires. Furthermore, it is reasonable to think it is a utilitarian rule because its being in effect tends to maximize the overall happiness of those to whom it applies. Indeed, it is quite likely that if this rule were not followed when it applies, there would be great unhappiness, and strong resistance, or even mutiny, when those who did not volunteer, but know others did volunteer, are asked to take a chance on being sacrificed. And,

given the additional plausible assumption that this rule is not overridden in this situation, your obligation is to ask for volunteers,
rather than have the passengers draw straws.

The principle we have finally reached is complex. As can be seen
from the preceding example, it requires of anyone that he consider
and relate many factors in order to decide what he ought to do in
any particular situation. For many people in many situations it is
practically impossible to complete such a complex task. Each of us
should, of course, do the best he can, and where anyone has done
a reasonably good job but failed to decide correctly, no blame or
guilt should be attached to him. As brought out in the beginning of
this chapter, the standards appropriate for morally evaluating actions are different from those appropriate for morally evaluating
persons. Although we have not considered the latter kind of standard here, one thing is clear: Many actions that are quite clearly
wrong do not reflect blame or guilt upon the doer.

CONCLUSION

We have not considered whether the utilitarian Kantian principle
meets the sixth condition—that it prescribes no acts we feel certain
are wrong. This task is left to the reader. If he finds that it meets
condition (6), then he has good reason to think that it is a satisfactory ethical theory. There may be, however, a better theory that
we have not considered. There are, for example, ways we have not
examined for applying the utilitarian principle to the basic Kantian
standard. Consequently, although we have, in this book, stopped
examining ethical standards, the examination itself is not over. But
it has come a long way. Early in the chapter we found reason to reject several views: theological ethics, ethical relativism, nihilism,
and egoism, but we left open the question of whether we should accept ethical skepticism. We decided that if by the conclusion of our
examination of ethical standards, we found none satisfactory, we
would have good inductive grounds for the claim of the ethical
skeptic that there are no justifiable ethical standards. Although the
examination is not completed, we have, even at this point, some
reason to think we have found a standard that at least approximates

a justifiable one. We may be wrong, but even if we are, there are definite signs that progress has been and still is being made. We have, then, grounds for concluding that ethical skepticism is wrong. Although the task of justifying an ethical standard is most difficult and often discouraging, we have found reason to keep on trying with hope of achieving success.

EXERCISES

1. Which of the following do you think are moral judgments? Which are not? Explain your answers.

    Men have an inalienable right to life, liberty, and the pursuit of happiness.
    God punishes those who break his laws.
    Thou shalt not kill.
    Stealing is against the law.
    We should always obey the law.
    The use of narcotics is harmful to society.
    'Ought' implies 'can.'
    Nothing is right or wrong but thinking makes it so.

2. State whether or not each of the following are clear examples of ethical relativism as it is defined in the text. Explain your answers.

    Polygamy was morally permissible in Abraham's time but it is immoral today.
    What you claim is right is only your opinion and therefore it is no better than anyone else's.
    What is wrong is that which harms society, so what is wrong in one society is often right in another.
    The principle of utilitarianism may be all right for Western cultures, but it surely is wrong for Oriental cultures.
    There are no ethical standards, each of us just "sees" what is right and what is wrong.

3. Evaluate the following argument:

    Causal determinism is true, from which it follows that no one has free will, and, consequently, no one is morally responsible for what he does. But if no one is responsible for what he does, then he cannot be obligated to do anything. That is, there is nothing he ought to do; nothing is right and nothing is wrong. Therefore, ethical nihilism is correct.

4. Evaluate the following argument:

Ethical skepticism is correct because, in the last analysis, no man can do any more than follow his own conscience in ethical matters, and nothing can be justified in that way.

5. Suppose that someone named Jones had risked his life to save a drowning child. Discuss the following explanation of his actions.

Jones did not really act unselfishly, that is, he did not risk his own life for the sake of the drowning child. Rather, Jones is the sort of person who gets satisfaction and pleasure as a result of helping others, and his desire for this kind of pleasure was so great it even outweighed his desire to protect his own life. Jones, therefore, was really acting to get the future pleasure, not to save the child.

6. It has been claimed that some pleasures (for example, aesthetic pleasures) are higher than others (for example, sexual pleasures). Explain what someone might mean by such a claim. Would a psychological hedonist be consistent if he maintained some pleasures are higher than others? Would an ethical hedonist be consistent? Explain.

7. Egoistic hedonism was rejected on the grounds that there were no sound arguments in its favor and it prescribes morally repugnant acts. Suppose that an egoistic hedonist were to reply as follows:

My theory does not prescribe morally repugnant acts because such acts are clearly those that harm others and to harm another is to invite retaliation or punishment. Because it is obviously not in one's interest to bring injury to oneself, then on the basis of egoistic hedonism the correct conclusion is that we should not harm others. My theory, therefore, does not prescribe any morally repugnant acts.

Evaluate his reply.

8. Consider Socrates' argument on pp. 459–61. Is he justified in his claim that when a man is unjust, the injustice is a disease of his soul and, as for all diseases, the man would be better off if he had never been unjust at all? Consider a man who lives "happily ever after" on

the spoils of his crimes. Is there some way he is really more miserable than if he had remained in just but grinding poverty?

9. One objection to Bentham's version of utilitarianism is that it assumes a "hedonic calculus," that is, a system by which various pains and pleasures can be added and subtracted as if they were apples or oranges. Thus we are supposed to be able to add the pleasure you get from making an important discovery to the pleasure I get from drinking fine wine, and get a result that is, let us say, three times the amount that Jones gets from calling a bluff in poker minus the headache Smith has. Surely, the objection goes, the very idea of such a calculus is absurd. Consequently, Bentham's principle of utility is absurd. Evaluate this objection.

10. The following seems to be a case of deriving an 'ought' conclusion from an 'is' premise. Does it, therefore, refute Hume's claim that 'ought' cannot be derived from 'is'? Explain your answer.

   1. Old Mrs. Smith *is* in need of help.
   Therefore
   2. If I *ought* to help old ladies in need of help, then I *ought* to help old Mrs. Smith.

11. Is the following derivation of 'ought' from a factual claim valid? Explain your answer.

   1. Mike says, "I hereby promise to help Smitty escape from jail."
   2. If someone says that he promises something, then he is obliged to do what he promises.
   3. If someone is obliged to do what he promises, then he ought to do what he promises.
   Therefore
   4. Mike ought to help Smitty escape from jail.

12. Which of the following clearly commit the definist fallacy and which do not. Justify your answers.

   What is good is what is commanded by God.
   The word 'good' means 'what ought to be maximized.'
   Pleasure is, by virtue of the meaning of words, the one and only thing good in itself.
   The good is, clearly, that at which all things aim.
   To say that something is good is to say that it is an object of human interest.

13. Evaluate the following objection to utilitarianism.

According to the principle of utility we are to treat each person as one and no one as more than one. Thus, each person is to get equal consideration. But if we accept the principle of utility we cannot do this, for some people are much more sensitive to pleasures and pains than others, and so when we "add" pleasures or pains an extremely sensitive person would weigh more heavily in our calculations than normally sensitive people. Thus, if we use the principle of utility we cannot give all people equal consideration as the principle requires. The principle, therefore, is inconsistent and should not be followed.

14. Smith, a Kantian, decides to make it his rule to eat dinner at 6:00 P.M. Accordingly, he universalizes this rule, that is, conceives of it as universal law, and is horrified at the result. If everyone ate dinner at 6:00, essential services would go unmanned, patients would be left on the operating table, airliners would crash, ships would run aground, and so on. Because he could not will this state of affairs, he concludes that he must reject his rule. Yet the same objection applies to a rule prescribing dinner at any other time, and he is faced with starvation. Has Smith made a mistake in employing the first formulation of the categorical imperative? If so, spell it out carefully.

15. It has been objected that Kant's ethical theory requires people to be bloodless and inhuman. According to this objection, Kant says that if I come across an injured man lying by the roadside, it would be wrong to help him because I feel sorry for him. That would be to act out of inclination or desire; rather, I should act out of respect for the moral law, on the basis of reason alone. If Kant is right, then we should be cold, unemotional, and unsympathetic. We should be highly moral machines. Because this is surely a repugnant view of how men should act, Kant's theory should be rejected. Evaluate this objection.

16. Suppose you want to decide whether or not to cheat on an exam. Find the maxim by which you would be acting if you did so and test it by means of each version of the categorical imperative.

17. Consider the following objection to utilitarian ethical theories, and compare how an act utilitarian could reply to it with how a rule utilitarian could reply to it.

Jones is dying in great pain and has possibly a month to live with no hope of recovery. Jones has no relatives and no one who stands to gain or lose by his death. His doctor, a good utilitarian, decides upon a mercy killing. Jones, however, objects and says that he wants to live as long as possible, however great his pain might be. Nevertheless, his doctor goes ahead and ends Jones's life. This would seem to be the action that utilitarian ethical theories prescribe, but it is clearly wrong.

18. One moral issue not discussed in the text is the problem of punishment. Compare the ethical theories discussed in the text concerning the justification of capital punishment not only for crimes such as kidnapping, but also for cases of first-degree murder by a man already sentenced to imprisonment for the duration of his life for another crime. Explain which of the ethical theories you think provides the most reasonable position on capital punishment.

19. Morally evaluate acts of the following kinds by the standard stated on pp. 506–507. If you think that the situation in some cases must be given in greater detail, you may make reasonable stipulations. Does the standard prescribe anything morally repugnant in these cases? If so, should we reject the standard? Explain.

> Premarital sexual intercourse.
> Refusing to serve in a war which you consider unjust.
> Failing to report a friend whom you have seen cheating.
> Retaliating in kind to someone who has harmed you.
> Stealing from a large, impersonal institution, such as a university or bookstore.

20. In light of your answer to question 19 and the many other factors discussed in the text, do you think the ethical standard stated on pp. 506–507 is justified? Explain your answer. If you think not, do you think some other standard is justified or do you conclude that we should accept ethical skepticism? Justify your conclusions.

21. Ethical standards are used not only for moral evaluation of the actions of individuals, but also for moral evaluation of the laws of governments and societies. Is there some way to adapt the utilitarian Kantian principle to apply to laws? For example, consider and critically evaluate the following which is based on the thesis that no law should prescribe that any person or group of persons is to be treated as mere means, and so the basic prescription is that laws, and indeed systems of laws, should be fair.

> A law (system of laws) is morally just if and only if (a) what it prescribes is fair to all persons and groups to whom it applies, and (b) it is a utilitarian rule (system of rules) which is consistent with condition (a).

BIBLIOGRAPHY

HISTORICAL SOURCES

I. Original Works
The main sources for the views of Plato are in his dialogues *Gorgias, Protagoras,* and his most comprehensive work, the *Republic.* His refutation of theological ethics occurs in *Euthyphro.* There have been many commentaries on Plato's ethical views, including F. Cornford, *Before and After Socrates* (London: Cambridge University Press, 1932), Chapters II, III; and G. Grube, *Plato's Thought* (London: Methuen & Co., Ltd., 1935), Chapter VII. For Aristotle's views see *Nicomachean Ethics* and the commentary by W. D. Ross, *Aristotle* (London: Methuen & Co., Ltd., 1923), Chapter VII. The rather prudent hedonism of Epicurus is found in the few of his remaining works, such as his letter to Menoeceus and a statement of his principal doctrines, for which see *Epicurus* (Oxford: Clarendon Press, 1926), translated by C. Bailey. The views of the Roman stoic Epictetus are given in *The Enchiridion* or manual; and the otherworldly, Christian views about good and evil held by St. Augustine are found in *The Enchiridion* and *The City of God.*

Thomas Hobbes expressed his psychological egoism in *Leviathan,* Part I, and Joseph Butler offered his classic refutation of egoism in *Fifteen Sermons Upon Human Nature,* especially sermon XI. The view that morality rests ultimately not on reason but on emotions is expressed by David Hume in *An Enquiry Concerning the Principles of Morals,* and the attempt to found morality on reason is exemplified in Immanuel Kant's *Foundations of the Metaphysics of Morals* and *The Critique of Practical Reason.* N. K. Smith has discussed Hume's views in *The Philosophy of David Hume* (New York: Macmillan Publishing Co., Inc., 1941), Chapter VI, as has J. Kemp, in *Ethical Naturalism: Hobbes and Hume* (New York: St. Martin's Press, Inc., 1970). Kant's views have been discussed by, among others, L. W. Beck, *A Commentary on Kant's Critique of Practical Reason* (Chicago: University of Chicago Press, 1960); S. Körner, *Kant* (Baltimore: Penguin Books, Inc., 1955), Chapter 6; W. D. Ross, *Kant's Ethical Theory* (London: Oxford University Press, 1954); and H. J. Paton, *The Categorical Imperative: A Study in Kant's Moral Philosophy,* 6th ed. (London: Hutchinson & Co., Ltd., 1967). A reaction to the rationalism of Kant by basing all men's motives on will and morality on compassion is found in A. Schopenhauer, *On the Basis of Morality*. A reaction not only against Kant but also the whole tradition of Western morality is found in the ethics based on power of F. Nietzsche, *Beyond Good and Evil*. Utilitarian principles are expounded by Jeremy Bentham, *An Introduction to the Principles of Morals and Legislation* and J. S. Mill, *Utilitarianism;* whereas an intuitionistic utilitarianism is stated by H. Sidgwick, *The Methods of Ethics*. The views of earlier British philosophers who have written on ethics, those of the seventeenth and eighteenth century, are represented in *British Moralists*, edited by L. Selby-Bigge. Bentham's views, in particular, are discussed in D. Baumgardt, *Bentham and the Ethics of Today* (New York: Octagon Books, 1966).

II. Collections Containing Excerpts from Historical Works
Useful selections from the preceding and other works can be found in *Ethics* (New York: Holt, Rinehart & Winston, Inc., 1965), edited by O. Johnson; *Ethics* (New York: Macmillan Publishing Co., Inc., 1965), edited by M. Mothersill; *Ethical Theories*, second edition (Englewood Cliffs, N.J.: Prentice-Hall, Inc., 1955), edited by A. Melden; *Ethics and Metaethics* (New York: St. Martin's Press, Inc., 1963), edited by R. Abelson; *Problems of Ethics* (New York: Macmillan Publishing Co., Inc., 1961), edited by R. Dewey, F. Gramlich, D. Loftsgordon; *Problems of Moral Philosophy* (Belmont, Calif.: Dickenson, 1967), edited by P. Taylor; *Readings in Ethics* (New York: Appleton-Century-Crofts, Inc., 1931), edited by G. Clark and T. Smith; *Readings in Moral Philosophy* (Boston: Houghton Mifflin Company, 1965), edited by A. Oldenquist; *Readings in the Problems of Ethics* (New York: Charles Scribner's Sons, 1965), edited by R. Ekman; *Value and Obligation* (New York: Harcourt Brace Jovanovich, Inc., 1961), edited by R. Brandt; *Writers on Ethics* (New York: Van Nostrand Reinhold Company, 1962), edited by J. Katz, P. Nochlin, R. Stover; *Approaches to Ethics* (New York: McGraw-Hill Book Company, 1969), edited by W. T. Jones and others; and *Approaches to Morality* (New York: Harcourt Brace Jovanovich, Inc., 1966), edited by J. A. Mann and G. F. Kreyche.

RECENT AND CONTEMPORARY SOURCES

I. Original Works
Much of the most influential twentieth-century books on ethics can be grouped under four headings: Naturalism, the attempt to provide a factual or scientific reduction of ethics; intuitionism, the claim that there are unique nonnatural properties intuited in making ethical judgments; emotivism, the theory that ethical utterances are noncognitive because they are primarily ways of expressing certain emotions; good-reasons

theory, the view of many linguistic philosophers that there is a unique logic of ethical discourse which, while allowing ethical discourse to be reasonable and not merely the expression of emotions, is quite different from the logic of factual discourse.

The leading *naturalists* have been J. Dewey, *Human Nature and Conduct* (New York: Holt, Rinehart & Winston, Inc., 1922), and *The Theory of Valuation* (Chicago: University of Chicago Press, 1939); R. B. Perry, *General Theory of Value* (Cambridge, Mass.: Harvard University Press, 1926); W. T. Stace, *The Concept of Morals* (New York: Macmillan Publishing Co., Inc., 1937). A recent naturalistic theory is P. B. Rice, *Our Knowledge of Good and Evil* (New York: Random House, Inc., 1959). The leading *intuitionist* is G. E. Moore, *Principia Ethica* (Cambridge, Eng.: Cambridge University Press, 1903) and *Ethics* (London: Oxford University Press, 1912). Others who have approached ethics similarly are A. C. Ewing, *The Definition of Good* (New York: Macmillan Publishing Co., Inc., 1947); H. Prichard, *Moral Obligation* (Oxford: Clarendon Press, 1949); W. D. Ross, *The Right and the Good* (London: Oxford University Press, 1931) and *The Foundations of Ethics* (Oxford: Clarendon Press, 1939). Intuitionism has been discussed recently in W. D. Hudson, *Ethical Intuitionism* (New York: St. Martins Press, Inc., 1967). The *emotive theory* of ethics found early expression in C. Ogden and I. Richards, *The Meaning of Meaning* (London: Routledge and Kegan Paul, 1923); A. J. Ayer, *Language, Truth, and Logic* (New York: Dover Publications, Inc., 1952); and R. Carnap, *Philosophy and Logical Syntax* (London: Routledge and Kegan Paul, 1935). The most developed emotive theory is found in C. Stevenson, *Ethics and Language* (New Haven: Yale University Press, 1943) and in a later collection of his articles, *Facts and Values* (New Haven: Yale University Press, 1963). J. O. Urmson discusses the emotive theory in detail in *The Emotive Theory of Ethics* (London: Hutchinson & Co., Ltd., 1968). The *good-reasons approach* to ethics is found in the works of S. Toulmin, *The Place of Reason in Ethics* (London: Cambridge University Press, 1950); R. M. Hare, *The Language of Morals* (Oxford: Clarendon Press, 1950); P. H. Nowell-Smith, *Ethics* (Baltimore: Penguin Books, Inc., 1955); C. Wellman, *The Language of Ethics* (Cambridge, Mass.: Harvard University Press, 1961). A book which discusses the last three of these trends in ethics is G. C. Kerner, *The Revolution in Ethical Theory* (London: Oxford University Press, 1966). G. J. Warnock, *Contemporary Moral Philosophy* (New York: St. Martin's Press, Inc., 1967) also discusses these recent trends.

Other contemporary books which do not fit easily into the preceding groupings are H. Aiken, *Reason and Conduct* (New York: Alfred A. Knopf, Inc., 1962); K. Baier, *The Moral Point of View* (Ithaca, N.Y.: Cornell University Press, 1958); B. Blanshard, *Reason and Goodness*

(London: George Allen & Unwin, Ltd., 1961); C. D. Broad, *Five Types of Ethical Theory* (Paterson, N.J.: Littlefield, Adams and Co., 1959). A. Edel has written several books on ethics, including *Ethical Judgment* (New York: The Free Press, 1955), *Science and the Structure of Ethics* (Chicago: University of Chicago Press, 1961), and with M. Edel, *Anthropology and Ethics* (Cleveland: The Press of Case-Western Reserve, 1968). Other works are P. Edwards, *Logic of Moral Discourse* (New York: The Free Press, 1955); J. N. Findlay, *Axiological Ethics* (New York: St. Martin's Press, Inc., 1970); A. Flew, *Evolutionary Ethics* (New York: St. Martin's Press, Inc., 1968); B. Gert, *Moral Rules* (New York: Harper & Row, Publishers, Inc., 1970); G. R. Grice, *The Grounds of Moral Judgment* (New York: Cambridge University Press, 1967); E. W. Hall, *What Is Value?* (New York: Humanities Press, 1952); J. Harrison, *Our Knowledge of Right and Wrong* (New York: Humanities Press, 1971); O. Johnson, *Moral Knowledge* (The Hague: Martinus Nijhoff, 1966), and *Moral Life* (London: George Allen & Unwin, Ltd., 1969); J. Kovesi, *Moral Notions* (New York: Humanities Press, 1967); J. J. Kupperman, *Ethical Knowledge* (New York: Humanities Press, 1970); D. Lyons, *Forms and Limits of Utilitarianism* (Oxford: Clarendon Press, 1965); J. Margolis, *Values and Conduct* (New York: Oxford University Press, 1971); M. Mandelbaum, *The Phenomenology of Moral Experience* (New York: The Free Press, 1955); B. Mayo, *Ethics and the Moral Life* (New York: Alfred A. Knopf, Inc., 1961); H. M. McCloskey, *Meta-Ethics and Normative Ethics* (The Hague: Martinus Nijhoff, 1969); A. I. Melden, *Rights and Right Conduct* (Oxford: Basil Blackwell & Mott, Ltd., 1959); K. B. Miller, *Ideology and Moral Philosophy* (New York: Humanities Press, 1971); D. H. Monro, *Empiricism and Ethics* (New York: Cambridge University Press, 1967); S. Moser, *Absolutism and Relativism in Ethics* (Springfield, Ill.: Charles C Thomas, Publisher, 1966); T. Nagel, *The Possibility of Altruism* (Oxford: Clarendon Press, 1970); J. Narveson, *Morality and Utility* (Baltimore: Johns Hopkins Press, 1967); A. N. Prior, *Logic and the Basis of Ethics* (Oxford: Clarendon Press, 1949); P. Roubiczek, *Ethical Value in an Age of Science* (New York: Cambridge University Press, 1969); M. Singer, *Generalization in Ethics* (New York: Alfred A. Knopf, Inc., 1961); R. Taylor, *Good and Evil: A New Direction* (New York: Macmillan Publishing Co., Inc., 1970); H. B. Veatch, *For an Ontology of Morals: A Critique of Contemporary Ethical Theory* (Evanston, Ill.: Northwestern University Press, 1971); G. H. von Wright, *The Varieties of Goodness* (London: Routledge and Kegan Paul, 1963); and S. Zink, *The Concepts of Ethics* (New York: St. Martin's Press, Inc., 1962).

Several works that seek to relate topics in the philosophy of mind with ethics are F. D'Arcy, *Human Acts: An Essay in Their Moral Evalu-*

ation (Oxford: Clarendon Press, 1963); J. N. Findlay, *Values and Intentions* (New York: Humanities Press, 1961); and G. H. von Wright, *Norm and Action* (London: Routledge and Kegan Paul, 1963). Important work in *deontic logic* has been done by von Wright in *Essay in Deontic Logic and the General Theory of Action* (Amsterdam: North-Holland Publishing Co., 1969). Finally, two other books which might be of interest to the student are H. E. Barnes, *Existentialist Ethics* (New York: Alfred A. Knopf, Inc., 1967); and W. D. Hudson, *Modern Moral Philosophy* (Garden City, N.Y.: Doubleday & Company, Inc., 1970).

II. Collections of Articles and Textbooks
Contemporary articles are collected in *Moral Rules and Particular Circumstances* (Englewood Cliffs, N.J.: Prentice-Hall, Inc., 1970), edited by B. A. Brody; *Morality and Moral Reasoning* (New York: Barnes & Noble, Inc., 1971), edited by J. Casey; *Morality and the Language of Conduct* (Detroit: Wayne State University Press, 1963), edited by H. Castañeda and G. Nakhnikian; *Determinism, Free Will and Moral Responsibility* (Englewood Cliffs, N.J.: Prentice-Hall, Inc., 1970), edited by G. Dworkin; *Ethics* (New York: Harper & Row, Publishers, Inc., 1968), edited by G. Dworkin and J. J. Thomson; *Moral Concepts* (New York: Oxford University Press, 1969), edited by J. Feinberg; *Theories of Ethics* (London: Oxford University Press, 1967), edited by P. Foot; *Deontic Logic: Introductory and Systematic Readings* (Dordrecht: Reidel, 1971), edited by R. Hilpinen; *The Is-Ought Question* (New York: St. Martin's Press, Inc., 1969), edited by W. D. Hudson; *Ethics and Social Justice* (Albany: State University of New York Press, 1970), edited by H. Keifer and M. Munitz; *Contemporary Ethical Theory* (New York: Random House, Inc., 1966), edited by J. Margolis; *Ethical Theories: A Book of Readings* (Englewood Cliffs, N.J.: Prentice-Hall, Inc., 1967), edited by A. I. Melden; *Readings in Contemporary Ethical Theory* (Englewood Cliffs, N.J.: Prentice-Hall, Inc., 1970), edited by K. Pahel and M. Schiller; *Moral Problems: A Collection of Philosophical Essays* (New York: Harper & Row, Publishers, Inc., 1971), edited by J. Rachels; *Readings in Ethical Theory* (New York: Appleton-Century-Crofts, Inc., 1952), edited by W. Sellars and J. Hospers; and *The Moral Judgment: Readings in Contemporary Meta-Ethics* (Englewood Cliffs, N.J.: Prentice-Hall, Inc., 1963), edited by P. Taylor.

Some of the many textbooks on ethics are W. A. Banner, *Ethics: An Introduction to Moral Philosophy* (New York: Charles Scribner's Sons, 1968); R. N. Beck and J. B. Orr, *Ethical Choice* (New York: The Free Press, 1970); L. Binkley, *Contemporary Ethical Theories* (New York: Citadel Press, 1961); R. Brandt, *Ethical Theories* (Englewood Cliffs, N.J.: Prentice-Hall, Inc., 1959); A. C. Ewing, *Ethics* (New York: Colliers

Books, 1962); W. Frankena, *Ethics* (Englewood Cliffs, N.J.: Prentice-Hall, Inc., 1963); R. T. Garner and B. Rosen, *Moral Philosophy* (New York: Macmillan Publishing Co., Inc., 1967); T. M. Garrett, *Problems and Perspectives in Ethics* (New York: Sheed & Ward, 1968); T. Hill, *Contemporary Ethical Theories* (New York: Macmillan Publishing Co., Inc., 1960); J. Hospers, *Human Conduct* (New York: Harcourt Brace Jovanovich, Inc., 1961); W. Lillie, *An Introduction to Ethics* (New York: Barnes & Noble, Inc., 1948); J. D. Mabbott, *An Introduction to Ethics* (New York: Doubleday Anchor, 1969); I. P. McGreal, *Problems of Ethics* (San Francisco: Chandler Publishing Co., 1970); J. A. Oesterle, *Ethics: The Introduction to Moral Science* (Englewood Cliffs, N.J.: Prentice-Hall, Inc., 1957); S. Pepper, *Ethics* (New York: Appleton-Century-Crofts, Inc., 1960); V. C. Punzo, *Reflective Naturalism: An Introduction to Moral Philosophy* (New York: Macmillan Publishing Co., Inc., 1969); P. W. Taylor, *Problems of Moral Philosophy* (Encino, Cal.: Dickenson Publishing Co., 1972); and J. Wilson, *Reason and Morals* (New York: Cambridge University Press, 1961).

III. Contemporary Articles

What follows is a selection of contemporary articles listed by topics, generally in the order in which they appear in the chapter. *Theological ethics* has been discussed recently by T. C. Mayberry in several articles, including "God and Moral Authority," *Monist* (1970), "Laws, Morals, and God's Commands," *Journal of Value Inquiry* (1970), and "Standards and Criteria: Can God Be the Standard of the Good?" *Mind* (1972). Other articles on this topic are W. W. Bartley, "The Reduction of Morality to Religion," *Journal of Philosophy* (1970); M. H. Kerr, "Moral and Legal Judgment Independent of Revelation," *Philosophy East and West* (1968); and P. Brown, "Religious Morality," *Mind* (1963). The last article drew replies from A. Flew, "The 'Religious Morality' of Mr. Patterson Brown," *Mind* (1965), and K. Campbell, "Patterson Brown on God and Evil," *Mind* (1965); Brown replied in "Religious Morality: A Reply to Flew and Campbell," *Mind* (1968).

Ethical relativism and skepticism has been discussed in R. Benedict, "Anthropology and the Abnormal," *Journal of General Psychology* (1934); K. Duncker, "Ethical Relativity?" *Mind* (1939); A. Garnett, "Relativity and Absolutism in Ethics," *Ethics* (1943–1944); M. Ginsburg, "The Function of Reason in Morals," *Philosophy and Phenomenological Research* (1938–1939); J. Jarvis, "In Defense of Moral Absolutes," *Journal of Philosophy* (1958); C. Kluckhohn, "Ethical Relativity," *Journal of Philosophy* (1955); L. G. Miller, "Moral Skepticism," *Philosophy and Phenomenological Research* (1961–1962); S. Moser, "Some Remarks about Relativism and Pseudo-relativism in Ethics," *Inquiry* (1962); C.

Stevenson, "Relativism and Non-relativism," *Proceedings and Addresses of the Amverican Philosophical Assoc.* (1961–1962)); W. Swabey, "Westermarkian Relativity," *Ethics* (1941–1942); P. Taylor, "Social Science and Ethical Relativism," *Journal of Philosophy* (1958); C. Waddington, "Naturalism in Ethics and Biology," *Philosophy* (1962); C. Wellman, "Ethical Implications of Cultural Relativity," *Journal of Philosophy* (1963). In addition there has been a symposium, "Is Anthropology Relevant to Ethics?" *Aristotelian Society Supplement* (1946), with articles by L. Russell, J. Mabbott and A. Macbeath, and the September, 1962, issue of *The Monist* was on the topic of anthropology and ethics. It contains articles by M. Edel and A. Edel, P. Krausser, T. McClintock, A. Garnett, P. Taylor, J. Ladd, A. Louch, and D. Bidney.

More recent writers on *ethical relativism* include G. W. Roberts, "Some Refutations of Private Subjectivism in Ethics," *Journal of Value Inquiry* (1971); T. McClintock, "The Definition of Ethical Relativism," *Personalist* (1969), "The Basic Varieties of Ethical Skepticism," *Metaphilosophy* (1971), and "Skepticism About Basic Moral Principles," *Metaphilosophy* (1971); K. Nielsen, "Anthropology and Ethics," *Journal of Value Inquiry* (1971); P. H. Nowell-Smith, "Cultural Relativism," *Philosophy of the Social Sciences* (1971); B. S. Crittenden, "Sociology of Knowledge and Ethical Relativism," *Studies in Philosophy and Education* (1966); and V. A. Howard, "Do Anthropologists Become Moral Relativists by Mistake?" *Inquiry* (1968). Several articles are collected in *Ethical Relativism* (Belmont, Calif.: Wadsworth Publishing Co., 1973), edited by J. Ladd.

Articles on the topics of *psychological and ethical egoism* include R. Blake, "Why Not Hedonism? a Protest," *Ethics* (1926–1927); C. D. Broad, "Bishop Butler's Conception of Human Nature," and "Remarks on Psychological Hedonism" both in *Five Types of Ethical Theory;* R. Jackson, "Bishop Butler's Refutation of Psychological Hedonism," *Philosophy* (1945); J. Laird, "Other People's Pleasure and One's Own," *Philosophy* (1941); H. McCloskey, "Toward an Objective Ethic," *Ethics* (1962–1963); J. Margolis, "Egoism and the Confirmation of Metamoral Theories," *American Philosophical Quarterly* (1970); J. Kalin, "Baier's Refutation of Ethical Egoism," *Philosophical Studies* (1971); T. McClintock, "The Egoist's Psychological Argument," *American Philosophical Quarterly* (1971); H. S. Silverstein, "Universalizability and Egoism," *Australasian Journal of Philosophy* (1968); W. Glasgow, "The Contradiction in Ethical Egoism," *Philosophical Studies* (1968); E. Skorpen, "Ethical Egoism's Brief and Mistaken History," *Personalist* (1969); J. L. Lahey, "Ethical Egoism: Can It Be Refuted?" *Dialogue* (Phi Sigma Tau) (1971); E. Mack, "How to Derive Ethical Egoism," *Personalist* (1971). A debate between N. Branden and D. Emmons on egoism has occurred in the pages of *Personalist:* Emmons wrote "Refuting the Egoist" (1969) and "Rational Egoism: Random Observations" (1971); and Branden wrote "Rational Egoism" and "Rational Egoism: A Reply to Professor Emmons," both in 1970.

Act utilitarianism and rule or restricted utilitarianism have been widely discussed in contemporary articles. Among the many are J. Cargile, "Utilitarianism and the Desert-Island Problem," *Analysis* (1964–1965); B. Diggs, "Rules and Utilitarianism," *American Philosophical Quarterly* (1964); G. Ezorsky, "Utilitarianism and Rules," *Australasian Journal of Philosophy* (1965); D. Gauthier, "Rule Utilitarianism and Randomization," *Analysis* (1964–1965); J. Harrison, "Utilitarianism, Universalisation, and Our Duty to be Just," *Aristotelian Society Proceedings* (1953); R. Harrod, "Utilitarianism Revised," *Mind* (1936); C. Landesman, "A Note on Act Utilitarianism," *Philosophical Review* (1964); J. Mabbot, "Interpretation of Mill's 'Utilitarianism,'" *Philosophical Quarterly* (1956); J. Margolis, "Rule-Utilitarianism," *Australasian Journal of Philosophy* (1965); H. McCloskey, "A Note on Utilitarian Punishment," *Mind* (1963), "An Examination of Restricted Utilitarianism," *Philosophical Review* (1957), and "Mill's Liberalism," *Philosophical Quarterly* (1963); S. Moser, "A Comment on Mill's Argument for Utilitarianism," *Inquiry* (1963), and "Utilitarian Theories of Punishment," *Philosophical Studies* (1957); J. Narveson, "The Desert-Island Problem," *Analysis* (1962–1963), and "Utilitarianism and Formalism," *Australasian Journal of Philosophy* (1965); J. Smart, "Extreme and Restricted Utilitarianism," *Philosophical Quarterly* (1956); J. Rawls, "Two Concepts of Rules," *Philosophical Review* (1955), and "Justice as Fairness" *Philosophical Review* (1958); J. Urmson, "The Interpretation of the Moral Philosophy of J. S. Mill," *Philosophical Quarterly* (1953). There was also a symposium, "Negative Utilitarianism," *Aristotelian Society Supplement* (1963) with articles by H. Acton and J. Watkins. Many of these articles have been collected in *Contemporary Utilitarianism* (Garden City, N.Y.: Doubleday & Company, Inc., 1968), edited by M. Bayles; *Mill's Utilitarianism* (Indianapolis: The Bobbs-Merrill Co., Inc., 1971), edited by S. Gorovitz; and *Mill's Utilitarianism* (Belmont, Calif.: Wadsworth Publishing Co., Inc., 1969), edited by J. Smith and E. Sosa.

Rawls' article "Justice as Fairness" has drawn considerable comment, including L. Pollock, "A Dilemma for Rawls?" *Philosophical Studies* (1971); R. P. Wolff, "A Refutation of Rawls' Theorem on Justice," *Journal of Philosophy* (1966); B. Barry, "On Social Justice," *Oxford Review* (1967); J. O'Connor, "Wolff, Rawls, and the Principles of Justice," *Philosophical Studies* (1968); D. W. Brock, "Contractualism, Utilitarianism and Social Inequalities," *Social Theory and Practice* (1971); and R. L. Cunningham, "Justice: Efficiency or Fairness?" *Personalist* (1971).

Utilitarianism has recently been studied extensively through the use of formal techniques. Among others who have written in this vein are H. Castañeda, "Ought, Value, and Utilitarianism," *American Philosophical Quarterly* (1969); J. H. Sobel, "Value, Alternatives, and Utilitarianism," *Nous* (1971), "Utilitarianisms: Simple and General," *Inquiry* (1970), and "Rule-Utilitarianism," *Australasian Journal of Philosophy* (1968); P. C. Fishburn, "Utility Theory with Inexact Preferences and Degrees of Preference," *Synthese* (1970); D. Goldstick, "Assessing Utilities," *Mind* (1971); L. Bergstroem, "Utilitarianism and Alternative Actions," *Nous* (1971); D. Braybrook, "The Choice Between Utilitarianisms," *American Philosophical Quarterly* (1967); R. C. Jeffrey, "On Interpersonal Utility Theory," *Journal of Philosophy* (1971); and L. Aqvist, "Improved Formulations of Act-Utilitarianism," *Nous* (1969).

Other recent writers on utilitarianism have been M. Mandelbaum, "On Interpreting Mill's Utilitarianism," *Journal of the History of Philosophy* (1968); D. Mitchell, "Mill's Theory of Value," *Theoria* (1970); J. Narveson, "Utilitarianism and Moral Norms," *Journal of Value Inquiry* (1970), and "Utilitarianism and New Generations," *Mind* (1967). This last article drew a response from H. Vetter, "The Production of Children as a Problem of Utilitarian Ethics," *Inquiry* (1969); and "Utilitarianism and New Generations," *Mind* (1970). Other articles are K. L. Curzie, "Analysis of the Utilitarian Maxim: 'The Greatest Good for the Greatest Number,' " *Dialogue* (Phi Sigma Tau) (1970); M. Stocker, "Mill on Desire and Desirability," *Journal of the History of Philosophy* (1969); B. Lang and G. Stahl, "Mill's 'Howlers' and the Logic of Naturalism," *Philosophy and Phenomenological Research* (1969); N. Cooper, "Mill's 'Proof' of the Principle of Utility," *Mind* (1969), replied to in N. Griffin, "Cooper's Reconstruction of Mill's 'Proof,' " *Mind* (1972); R. B. Brandt, "A Utilitarian Theory of Excuses,' *Philosophical Review* (1969); D. Lyons, "On Sanctioning Excuses," *Journal of Philosophy* (1969); R. T. Garner, "Some Remarks on Act Utilitarianism," *Mind* (1969); G. C. Kerner, "The Immorality of Utilitarianism and the Escapism of Rule-Utilitarianism," *Philosophical Quarterly* (1971); J. M. Baker, "Utilitarianism and Secondary Principles," *Philosophical Quarterly* (1971); R. I. Sikora, "Unforeseeable Consequences," *Analysis* (1969); R. Sartorius, "Utilitarianism and Obligation," *Journal of Philosophy* (1969); R. F. Bales, "Act-Utilitarianism: Account of Right-Making Characteristics or Decision-Making Procedure?" *American Philosophical Quarterly* (1971); L. Stern, "Deserved Punishment, Deserved Harm, Deserved Blame," *Philosophy* (1970); B. Brody, "The Equivalence of Act and Rule Utilitarianism," *Philosophical Studies* (1967); J. Margolis, "Mill's Utilitarianism Again," *Australasian Journal of Philosophy* (1967); J. Feinberg, "The Forms and Limits of Utilitarianism," *Philosophical Review*

(1967), a review of D. Lyons' book of the same title; P. Nowell-Smith, "Utilitarianism and Treating Others as Ends," *Nous* (1967); H. J. Mc-Closkey, "Utilitarian and Retributive Punishment," *Journal of Philosophy* (1967); D. Macrae, "Utilitarian Ethics and Social Change," *Ethics* (1968); S. K. Wertz, "Composition and Mill's Utilitarian Principle," *Personalist* (1971); L. W. Sumner, "Cooperation, Fairness and Utility," *Journal of Value Inquiry* (1971); R. G. Henson, "Utilitarianism and the Wrongness of Killing," *Philosophical Review* (1971); C. I. Smith, "Bentham's Second Rule," *Journal of the History of Ideas* (1970); G. W. Barnes, "Utilitarianisms," *Ethics* (1971).

Recently there has been a revival of interest in a *Kantian approach to ethics*, especially regarding the importance of *universalizability* for moral principles. Some of the articles on these topics are C. Caton, "In What Sense and Why Ought-Judgments Are Universalizable," *Philosophical Quarterly* (1963); J. Cargile, "The Universalizability of Lying," *Australasian Journal of Philosophy* (1965); N. Dorman, "The Refutation of the Generalization Argument," *Ethics* (1963–1964); D. Emmet, "Universalizability and Moral Judgments," *Philosophical Quarterly* (1963); A. Ewing, "What Would Happen if Everybody Acted Like Me," *Philosophy* (1953); G. Field, "A Criticism of Kant," from *Moral Theory* (London: Methuen & Co., Ltd., 1921), and "Kant's First Moral Principle," *Mind* (1932); A. Garnett, "A New Look at the Categorical Imperative," *Ethics* (1963–1964); J. Hems, "What Is Wrong with Obligation," *Philosophy and Phenomenological Research* (1961–1962); R. Holmes, "Generalization," *Journal of Philosophy* (1963), and "Descriptivism, Supervenience, and Universalizability," *Journal of Philosophy* (1966); J. Margolis, " 'Lying is Wrong' and 'Lying Is Not Always Wrong,' " *Philosophy and Phenomenological Research* (1962–1963); D. Mitchell, "Are Moral Principles Really Necessary?" *Australasian Journal of Philosophy* (1963); R. Montague, "Universalizability," *Analysis* (1964–1965); M. Mothersill, "C. I. Lewis: Hedonistic Ethics on a Kantian Model," *Philosophical Studies* (1954); G. Nakhnikian, "Generalization in Ethics," *Review of Metaphysics* (1963–1964); A. Ryan, "Universalizability," *Analysis* (1964–1965); M. Singer, "Generalization in Ethics," *Mind* (1955), and "The Golden Rule," *Philosophy* (1963); J. Sobel, "Generalization Arguments," *Theoria* (1964); A. Stout, "But Suppose Everyone Did the Same," *Australasian Journal of Philosophy* (1954); P. Winch, "Universalizability of Moral Judgments," *Monist* (1965).

More recently, on the same topic, there are M. S. Gram, "Kant and Universalizability Once More and Again," *Kantstudien* (1967); J. G. Murphy, "Kant's Concept of a Right Action," *Monist* (1967); R. P. Blum, "The True Function of the Generalization Argument," *Inquiry* (1970); J. E. Atwell, "Are Kant's First Two Moral Principles Equivalent?" *Jour-*

nal of the History of Philosophy (1969); R. E. Laymon and P. K. Machamer, "Personal Decisions and Universalizability," Mind (1970); S. B. Thomas, "The Status of the Generalization Principle," American Philosophical Quarterly (1968), and "Jesus and Kant: A Problem in Reconciling Two Different Points of View," Mind (1970); W. Schwarz, "Kant's Refutation of Charitable Lies," Ethics (1970); D. Locke, "The Trivializability of Universalizability," Philosophical Review (1968); A. Gewirth, "The Non-Trivializability of Universalizability," Australasian Journal of Philosophy (1969); W. G. Lycan, "Hare, Singer and Gewirth on Universalizability," Philosophical Quarterly (1969); H. J. White, "An Analysis of Hare's Application of the Thesis of Universalizability in His Moral Arguments," Australasian Journal of Philosophy (1969); and R. Glass, "The Contradictions in Kant's Examples," Philosophical Studies (1971).

Of great recent interest is the problem of the naturalistic fallacy and the attempt to derive 'ought' from 'is.' The naturalistic fallacy has been discussed by G. Field, "The Place of Definition in Ethics," Aristotelian Society Proceedings (1931–1932); W. Frankena, "The Naturalistic Fallacy," Mind (1939); S. Hampshire, "Fallacies in Moral Philosophy," Mind (1949); N. Kretzmann, "Desire as Proof of Desirability," Philosophical Quarterly (1958); G. E. Moore, "The Indefinability of Good," (from Principia Ethica); A. Stroll, "Mill's Fallacy," Dialogue (1964); R. G. Durrant, "Identity of Property and the Definition of Good," Australasian Journal of Philosophy (1970); A. C. Genova, "Institutional Facts and Brute Values," Ethics (1970); W. H. Bruening, "Moore and 'Is-Ought,'" Ethics (1971); E. H. Duncan, "Has Anyone Committed the Naturalistic Fallacy?" Southern Journal of Philosophy (1970); B. H. Baumrin, "Is There a Naturalistic Fallacy?" American Philosophical Quarterly (1968); D. P. Gauthier, "Moore's Naturalistic Fallacy," American Philosophical Quarterly (1967); G. O. Allen, "From the 'Naturalistic Fallacy' to the Ideal Observer Theory," Philosophy and Phenomenological Research (1970); N. R. Luebke, "Frankena on the Naturalistic Fallacy," Journal of Thought (1970).

Two recent articles, J. Searle, "How to Derive 'Ought' from 'Is,'" and M. Black, "The Gap Between 'Is' and 'Should'" both in the Philosophical Review (1964) attempted to close the gap between 'is' and 'ought.' They have resulted in many replies, among which are M. Cohen, "'Is' and 'Should': An Unbridged Gap," Philosophical Review (1965); A. Flew, "On Not Deriving Ought from Is," Analysis (1964–1965); W. Hudson, "The 'Is-Ought' Controversy," Analysis (1964–1965); E. Jobe, "On Deriving 'Ought' from 'Is,'" Analysis (1964–1965); G. Mavrodes "'Is' and 'Ought,'" Analysis (1964–1965); J. McClellan and B. Komesar, "On Deriving 'Ought' from 'Is,'" Analysis (1964–1965); R. Montague, "'Is' to 'Ought,'" Analysis (1965–1966); D. Phillips, "The Possibility of Moral

Advice," *Analysis* (1964–1965); P. Shaw, "Ought and Can," *Analysis* (1964–1965); J. and J. Thomson, "How Not to Derive 'Ought' from 'Is,'" *Philosophical Review* (1964); R. Croel, "The 'Is-Ought' Controversy," *Kinesis* (1969); B. T. Wilkins, "The 'Is'-'Ought' Controversy," *Ethics* (1970); E. Roma, "'Ought'-'Is' and the Demand for Explanatory Completeness," *Journal of Value Inquiry* (1970); D. Mitchell, "Must We Talk About Is and Ought?" *Mind* (1968); W. K. Frankena, "Ought and Is Once More," *Man and World* (1969); C. F. Kielkopf, "Ought Does Not Imply Can," *Theoria* (1967); R. V. Hannaford, "You Ought to Derive 'Ought' From 'Is,'" *Ethics* (1972); J. R. Cameron, "'Ought' and Institutional Obligation," *Philosophy* (1971); F. E. Brouwer, "A Difficulty with 'Ought Implies Can,'" *Southern Journal of Philosophy* (1969); M. H. Linger, "John R. Searle's Derivation of 'Ought' From 'Is,'" *Dialogue* (Phi Sigma Tau) (1972). Some philosophers feel that only in the context of a complete *deontic logic* can the is-ought problem be properly discussed and resolved; some workers in this area are H. Castañeda, "Imperatives, Oughts and Moral Oughts," *Australasian Journal of Philosophy* (1966); A. R. Anderson, "Some Nasty Problems in the Formal Logic of Ethics," *Nous* (1967); A. Sloman, "How to Derive Better from Is," *American Philosophical Quarterly* (1969); and K. B. Tranoy, "Deontic Logic and Deontically Perfect Worlds," *Theoria* (1970). Some of these articles have been collected in *The Is-Ought Question* (New York: St. Martin's Press, Inc., 1969), edited by W. D. Hudson.

There has not been much recent work done on the concept of *prima facie duties*, but R. Chisholm, "The Ethics of Requirement," *American Philosophical Quarterly* (1964) has defined this concept and other related ones. Other recent articles on this topic are B. Baumrin, "Prima Facie Duties," and R. Shope, "Prima Facie Duty," both in *Journal of Philosophy* (1965); P. Jones, "Doubts About Prima Facie Duties," *Philosophy* (1970). In "A Theory of Morality," *Philosophy and Phenomenological Research* (1957) H. Castañeda uses formal techniques in an attempt to clarify many ethical concepts, including that of *prima facie* duty.

There are many articles not directly on the topics of the chapter, but which deal with ethical problems and are therefore of general interest and relevance. Several which consider the question, "Why should I be moral?" are K. Nielsen, "Why Should I Be Moral?" *Methodos* (1963); P. Wadia, "Why Should I Be Moral?" *Australasian Journal of Philosophy* (1964); L. Caroline, "Why Be Moral?" *Southwestern Journal of Philosophy* (1970); D. A. L. Thomas, "Why Should I Be Moral?" *Philosophy* (1970); D. Mitchell, "Why Should I Be Moral?" *Ratio* (1970); A. Gewirth, "Must One Play the Moral Language Game?" *American Philosophical Quarterly* (1970).

A fairly large literature has grown up around the question of the *meanings and uses of moral terms.* Central issues here are whether moral terms merely express emotions and have, therefore, merely emotive meaning, or whether they are cognitively meaningful as well; whether moral terms are purely prescriptive, or descriptive as well; whether the applicability of moral terms is verifiable or not. R. M. Hare, whose name appears several times in titles of the following articles, is the primary exponent of prescriptivism; C. L. Stevenson is an emotivist. Some articles on these topics are W. Kneale, "Objectivity in Morals," *Philosophy* (1950); M. T. Thornton, "Hare's View of Morality," *Mind* (1971); L. Pollock, "Formal Moral Arguments," *Personalist* (1972); G. B. Wall, "Perspectives on the Objectivity of Moral Judgments," *Journal of Thought* (1971); A. Oldenquist, "Universalizability and the Advantages of Nondescriptivism," *Journal of Philosophy* (1968), replied to in D. Greenlee, "Oldenquist on Moral Judgments and Moral Principles," *Journal of Value Inquiry* (1969); R. W. Newell, "Ethics and Description," *Philosophy* (1968); H. D. Ruf, "On Being Morally Justified," *Journal of Value Inquiry* (1969); H. Meynell, "The Objectivity of Value Judgments," *Philosophical Quarterly* (1971); D. Haight, "Naturalism, Prescriptivism, and Their Reconciliation," *Journal of Value Inquiry* (1971); E. F. Walter, "Empiricism and Ethical Reasoning," *American Philosophical Quarterly* (1970); H. S. Silverstein, "Prescriptivism and Akrasia," *Philosophical Studies* (1970); H. Castañeda, "Ethics and Logic, Stevensonian Emotivism Revisited," *Journal of Philosophy* (1967); M. E. Lean, "Aren't Moral Judgments 'Factual'?" *Personalist* (1970); E. F. Walter, "Empiricism and Ethical Reasoning," *American Philosophical Quarterly* (1970); L. W. Sumner, "Hare's Arguments Against Ethical Naturalism," *Journal of Philosophy* (1967); C. Wellman, "Emotivism and Ethical Objectivity," *American Philosophical Quarterly* (1968); and C. Humphrey, "The Testability of Value Claims," *Journal of Value Inquiry* (1969).

Other articles, which do not fit neatly into any of the preceding classifications: W. Blackstone, "Can Science Justify an Ethical Code?" *Inquiry* (1960); S. M. Brown, "Inalienable Rights," *Philosophical Review* (1955); M. Bunge, "Ethics as a Science," *Philosophy and Phenomenological Research* (1961–1962); R. Ehman, "Moral Judgment and Ultimate Ends," *Philosophy and Phenomenological Research* (1964–1965); H. L. A. Hart, "Are There Any Natural Rights," *Philosophical Review* (1955); H. Gompertz, "When Does the End Justify the Means?" *Ethics* (1943–1944); H. Lewis, "Obedience to Conscience," *Mind* (1945); J. Meiland, "Duty and Interest," *Analysis* (1962–1963); H. Ofstad, "The Ethics of Resistance to Tyranny," *Inquiry* (1961); J. Rawls, "The Sense of Justice," *Philosophical Review* (1963); W. Spratt, "Psychology and the Moral Problems of Our Time," *Philosophy* (1948); J. Stolnitz, "Notes on Ethical Indeterminacy," *Journal of Philosophy* (1958); P. Taylor, "Moral Virtue and

Responsibility for Character," *Analysis* (1964–1965); S. Toulmin, "Knowledge of Right and Wrong," *Aristotelian Society Proceedings* (1950–1951); G. Williams, "Normative Naturalistic Ethics," *Journal of Philosophy* (1950); V. J. Bourke, "Recent Trends in Ethics," *The New Scholasticism* (1970); J. G. Gill, "An Abstract Definition of the Good," *Ethics* (1970); R. C. Solomon, "Normative and Meta-Ethics," *Philosophy and Phenomenological Research* (1970); A. Gewirth, "Metaethics and Moral Neutrality," *Ethics* (1968); W. P. Alston, "Moral Attitudes and Moral Judgment," *Nous* (1968); T. D. Perry, "Moral Autonomy and Reasonableness," *Journal of Philosophy* (1968); P. Kurtz, "Has Ethical Naturalism Been Refuted?" *Journal of Value Inquiry* (1970); L. Foster, "Inductive and Ethical Validity," *American Philosophical Quarterly* (1971); H. Khatchadourian, "Intrinsic and Instrumental Good: An Untenable Dichotomy," *Journal of Value Inquiry* (1970); K. Ward, "Moral Seriousness," *Philosophy* (1970); G. C. Kerner, "Passions and the Cognitive Foundation of Ethics," *Philosophy and Phenomenological Research* (1970); A. Quinton, "The Bounds of Morality," *Metaphilosophy* (1970); W. H. Walsh, "Social and Personal Factors in Morality," *Idealistic Studies* (1971); A. Ralls, "Rational Morality for Empirical Man," *Philosophy* (1969); J. A. Shaffer, "The Philosophy of Mind and Some Ethical Implications," *Philosophic Exchange* (1971); H. Terrell, "Are Moral Considerations Always Overriding?" *Australasian Journal of Philosophy* (1969); J. Margolis, "Human Acts and Moral Judgments," *Ethics* (1969); G. R. Fischer, "Search for Ethics," *Ethics* (1971). R. L. Holmes, "Some Conceptions of Analysis in Recent Ethical Theory," *Metaphilosophy* (1971); J. Feinberg, "The Nature and Value of Rights," *Journal of Value Inquiry* (1970); C. Dyke, "The Vices of Altruism," *Ethics* (1971); W. Sellars, "On Knowing the Better and Doing the Worse," *International Philosophical Quarterly* (1970).

Finally, note that since the first edition of this book was published, there has been some discussion of the *utilitarian–Kantian principle* proposed at the end of this chapter. See M. Martin and H. Ruf, "A Utilitarian Kantian Principle," *Philosophical Studies* (1970), in which a counterexample to the principle is offered, and H. S. Silverstein, "A Defense of Cornman's Utilitarian Kantian Principle," *Philosophical Studies* (1972). This debate is carried further by Martin and Ruf in "Silverstein's Defense of Cornman," and Silverstein in "Reply to Martin and Ruf," both in *Philosophical Studies* (1972).

SUBJECT INDEX

A

A posteriori proofs, first-cause argument, 351–59; argument from contingency, 360–67; argument from design, 367–79

A posteriori statement, characterized, 33; not all conclusively verifiable, 33f.; some both verifiable and falsifiable and some neither, 35–37

A priori statement, characterized, 32f.

Absolute duty, defined, 497

Absolutism, *See* standard absolutism *and* action absolutism.

Acting, from strongest desire, 166f.; from duty, 166f.

Action absolutism, 433; and Kant's categorical imperative, 495f.

Action relativism, defined and discussed, 433ff.

Actions, and determinism, 154ff., 208–10; free, 163ff.; deliberation and free, 164–166, caused by volitions, 205; and volitions,

AUTHOR INDEX

The letter b *following a page number indicates a bibliography entry.*

A

Aaron, R .I., 146b
Abbott, W. R., 149b
Abelson, Raziel, 234b, 315, 320b, 417b, 515b
Ackermann, R. J., 53b
Acton, H., 521b
Adams R. M., 417b
Adler, M. J., 233b
Agassi, Joseph, 150b
Aiken, H., 421b, 516b
Allen, G. O., 524b
Allen, R., 417b

Allison, H. E., 419b
Alston, W. P., 412b, 417b, 527b
Ammerman, Robert R., 147b
Anderson, A. R., 146b, 232b, 316b, 318b, 412b, 525b
Annis, David, 149b
Anscombe, G. E. M., 145b, 318b, 380*n.*
Anselm, St., 379, 284–88, 411b, 416b, 417b
Aquinas, St. Thomas, 315b, 350–53, 360f, 370–73, 409, 411b, 417b, 418b
Aqvist, L., 522b

Radford, Colin, 149b
Radner, D., 325b
Ralls, A., 527b
Ramsey, I., 413b
Ranken, Nani L., 234b
Rankin, K. W., 233b
Rawls, John, 521b, 526b
Reeves, J. W., 316b
Reichenbach, B. R., 416b
Reichenbach, Hans, 147b
Reid, Thomas, 163, 178–79, 231b
Rescher, Nicholas, 54b, 149b,
    150b, 417b
Resnick, L., 321b, 418b
Rice, P. B., 516b
Richards, I., 516b
Riser, J., 419b
Roberts, G. W., 520b
Robinson, Richard, 149b
Rollins, 323b, 324b
Roma, E., 525b
Rorty, Richard, 150b, 298–300,
    320b, 321–22b
Rosen, Bernard, 149b, 519b
Rosenberg, J. F., 421b
Rosenkrantz, Peter, 55b
Rosenthal, D. M., 318b
Ross, D., 496n.
Ross, G. R. T., 87n.
Ross, J. F., 412–13b, 413b, 415b,
    416b, 417b, 418–19b, 419b,
    422b
Ross, Jacob Joshua, 146b
Ross, W. D., 514b, 516b
Roth, J. K., 415b
Roth, Michael D., 147b
Roubiczek, P., 517b
Routley, R., 417b
Rowe, W. L., 320b, 418b, 422b
Rudinow, J., 418b
Ruf, H. D., 526b, 527b
Russell, Bertrand, 58–59, 145b,
    316b, 355, 357–59, 409, 414b
Russell, L., 520b

Ryan, A., 523b
Ryle, Gilbert, 145b, 232b, 309n.,
    317–18b, 325b

S

Sacksteder, W., 419b
Salmon, Wesley, 40n., 53b, 55b,
    418b
Santayana, 270
Santoni, R. E., 414b
Sartorius, R., 522b
Sartre, Jean-Paul, 211, 233b
Saunders, John Turk, 148b, 416b
Savage, C. W., 415b
Savage, Leonard J., 55b
Sayre, K., 317b, 319b
Scarrow, David S., 235b
Scheer, R. K., 150b
Scheffler, Israel, 290n.
Schiller, M., 518b
Schilpp, Paul Arthur, 54b
Schlesinger, George, 55b, 421b
Schmidt, P., 413b
Schopenhauer, A., 231b, 514–15b
Schrodinger, E., 316b
Schwarz, W., 524b
Scriven, M., 319b, 415b
Searle, John R., 524b, 525b
Selby-Bigge, L. A., 467n., 515b
Sellars, Wilfrid, 54b, 55b, 59,
    145b, 146b, 232b, 287n., 320b,
    470n., 518, 527b
Sessions, W. L., 417b
Shaffer, Jerome, A., 319b, 320b,
    324b, 417b, 527b
Shaw, P., 525b
Shea, W. W., 421b
Sher, J., 318b
Shoemaker, S., 326b
Shope, R., 525b
Sidgwick, Henry, 515b
Sievert, D., 324b
Sikora, R. I., 522b